The Editor

MICHAEL PATRICK GILLESPIE is Louise Edna Goeden Professor of English at Marquette University. He is the author of *Oscar Wilde and the Poetics of Ambiguity*, *The Aesthetics of Chaos: Nonlinear Thinking and Contemporary Literary Criticism*, *Inverted Volumes Improperly Arranged: James Joyce and His Trieste Library*, *Reading the Book Himself: Narrative Strategies in the Works of James Joyce*, and *Reading William Kennedy*, among others. His edited works include the Norton Critical Edition of *The Importance of Being Earnest*, *James Joyce and the Fabrication of an Irish Identity*, and *Joyce through the Ages: A Non-Linear View*.

A NORTON CRITICAL EDITION

Oscar Wilde

THE PICTURE OF DORIAN GRAY

AUTHORITATIVE TEXTS

BACKGROUNDS

REVIEWS AND REACTIONS

CRITICISM

SECOND EDITION

Edited by

MICHAEL PATRICK GILLESPIE
MARQUETTE UNIVERSITY

First Edition edited by

DONALD L. LAWLER
EAST CAROLINA UNIVERSITY

W • W • NORTON & COMPANY • *New York* • *London*

W. W. Norton & Company has been independent since its founding in 1923, when William Warder Norton and Mary D. Herter Norton first published lectures delivered at the People's Institute, the adult education division of New York City's Cooper Union. The Nortons soon expanded their program beyond the Institute, publishing books by celebrated academics from America and abroad. By midcentury, the two major pillars of Norton's publishing program—trade books and college texts—were firmly established. In the 1950s, the Norton family transferred control of the company to its employees, and today—with a staff of four hundred and a comparable number of trade, college, and professional titles published each year—W. W. Norton & Company stands as the largest and oldest publishing house owned wholly by its employees.

The text of this book is composed in
Fairfield Medium, with the display
set in Bernhard Modern.
Manufacturing by the Maple-Vail Book Group.
Composition by Binghamton Valley Composition.
Book design by Antonina Krass.
Production manager: Benjamin Reynolds.

Library of Congress Cataloging-in-Publication Data

Wilde, Oscar, 1854–1900.
The picture of Dorian Gray : authoritative text, backgrounds
and contexts, criticism / Oscar Wilde ;
edited by Michael Patrick Gillespie.
p. cm. — (A Norton critical edition)

ISBN 13: 978-0-393-92754-2 (pbk.)
ISBN 10: 0-393-92754-7 (pbk.)

1. Wilde, Oscar, 1854–1900. Picture of Dorian Gray.
2. Appearance (Philosophy)—Fiction. 3. Conduct of life—Fiction.
4. Portraits—Fiction. I. Gillespie, Michael Patrick.
II. Title.
PR5819.A2G56 2006
823'.8—dc22
2006046642

W. W. Norton & Company, Inc., 500 Fifth Avenue, New York, N.Y. 10110
www.wwnorton.com

W. W. Norton & Company Ltd., Castle House, 75/76 Wells Street,
London W1T 3QT

Dedicated to the Memory of Vincent J. Gillespie
1953–2005
Son, brother, husband, father, friend

Contents

Criticism   391

Preface

In a letter composed on 12 February 1894 and sent to Ralph Payne, who had written to praise *The Picture of Dorian Gray*, Oscar Wilde neatly summarizes his relations to the central characters and gently mocks simplistic reactions to them through a series of concise analogies. "I am so glad you like that strange coloured book of mine: it contains much of me in it. Basil Hallward is what I think I am: Lord Henry what the world thinks me: Dorian what I would like to be—in other ages perhaps" (*The Letters of Oscar Wilde*, 352). While the passage from his letter catches the tone of Wilde's insouciant wit and sly self-deprecation, it also neatly suggests a number of elements central to an understanding of the novel.

Even allowing for his irrepressible flamboyance, Wilde certainly came very close to the mark in relating how diverse perceptions of his own nature inform conceptions of the characters in his novel. For all its originality, *The Picture of Dorian Gray* takes up themes of aesthetics, sensuality, and personal independence that Wilde had explored in lectures and in writings for over a decade before the book appeared. The novel, however, enjoys the distinction of allowing for extended discussions of all of those themes and of providing a relatively safe venue for elaborating upon a broad range of indulgences at which previous expressions could only hint.

Though Edward Carson, who prosecuted Wilde for immoral acts in 1895, sought to make the book a manifesto of Wilde's hedonistic life style, I think it more accurate to see it as a rigorous examination of the limitations of the aesthetic views that had come to shape his art. *The Picture of Dorian Gray* articulates, without offering a clear resolution, the conflict that arises as a result of the struggle within an individual's nature between the impulse toward self-gratification and the sense of guilt that is a consequence of acting upon that inclination.

Nonetheless, one can understand, if not sympathize with, Carson's inclination to collapse fact and fiction. All of Wilde's writing has an intensely personal tone to it, and the issues of art, imagination, and sensuality outlined in the novel were at the time unsettled in Wilde's own life. *The Picture of Dorian Gray* merely provides greater space than heretofore available for a wide-ranging exposition of his interests and concerns. Though the consequent aesthetic and ethical issues that arise in the narrative may seem daunting, one can come to a solid understanding of the novel by keeping in mind a few fundamental concepts.

The Trinitarian description that he favors in his February 12 letter neatly captures the way Wilde's life informed both the composition and perception of the work. The tension between the probity of Basil Hallward, the immorality of Lord Henry, and the unabashed self-indulgence of Dorian combine to echo the author's conflicting feelings during this period, evident in any biographical account of him. At the same time, the similarities can prove to be a trap for hasty readers who seek to interpret the work by simply imposing Wilde and their impressions of him on the central characters of the novel. In fact, *The Picture of Dorian Gray* presents a complex view of the conflicted inter-relation between fantasy and fact that characterized Wilde's world and his writings, and it presents contemporary readers with the challenge of forming understandings without mistaking Wilde for his characters.

Of course, Wilde did much to encourage this blurring of distinctions. From the time of his permanent move to London in 1879, flamboyance had characterized his approach to the world. With a single-minded determination, Wilde made himself a public personality well before he had gained prominence as a writer. Indeed, for much of the 1880s his determined advocacy of "art for art's sake" seemed as much self-parody as sincere assertion of belief.

When *The Picture of Dorian Gray* appeared, however, its narrative went beyond the flummery often characterizing his public performances. Its discourse demanded that points of view Wilde had previously thrown out casually at dinner parties or alluded to obliquely in public lectures now be given full and sustained scrutiny. Further, its sustained tone of intellectual rigor—evident in Lord Henry Wotton's explanation of New Hedonism—insisted that equally serious attention be paid to Wilde as its author.

Taking Oscar Wilde seriously was a new proposition for late-Victorian London. He had already gained notoriety as a journalist, critic, and short story writer, but *The Picture of Dorian Gray* offered readers the first substantial piece of evidence of Wilde's far-ranging creative ability. Although much of the dialogue features the same style of repartee that made Wilde such a desirable dinner guest and many of the descriptions have the same fascination with excess that punctuated his poems and public lectures, the content of the novel lays out serious consideration of ethical issues relating to the movement from the nineteenth century's fixation upon society to the twentieth century's celebration of the individual. Critics may debate whether *The Picture of Dorian Gray* stands as the first English Modernist novel, but few will disagree that it touches on the same issues—the role that one should allow social institutions in shaping an individual's character—that writers like James Joyce, D. H. Lawrence, and Virginia Woolf would minutely explore in the next quarter century.

Wilde could make these great thematic strides because he relied on stylistic forms he had been practicing to perfection for a decade. The narrative of his novel builds on the strengths of his earlier work—a fascination for detail, a love of paradox, and a deft sense of humor. This allows its content to go well beyond the scope of any previous writing. Both in novella and novel form, the story of Dorian Gray explores with great sensitivity the relation of art to morality, the impact of hedonism, and the inescapability of spiritual questions. Wilde pursues these topics without turning the book into a polemic because his formal writing skills give him the ability to engage ideas without seeming to assume a didactic mode.

The duality exercised in the form and content stands as the key to the novel's lasting success. In publishing *The Picture of Dorian Gray* Wilde showed himself capable of much more than a flippant response to the world. His representations of the major characters show a keen sensitivity to human appetites, human needs, and most of all human weaknesses. At the same time, Wilde refuses to recapitulate the standard pieties or received wisdoms of his Victorian contemporaries. Instead, *The Picture of Dorian Gray* shows an author determined to explore the contradictory elements of human nature without falling back on conventional pieties.

Not surprisingly, the boldness of his ideas created a great deal of consternation among a number of readers and reviewers who saw the first version of Dorian Gray's story in novella form in *Lippincott's Magazine* in June of 1890. As the excerpts from contemporaneous reviews reprinted in this edition attest, the apparent open advocacy of a lifestyle based solely upon gratification, the New Hedonism expounded by Lord Henry, was more than many could bear. Despite the death of Dorian at the end of the tale, the self-indulgence in which he had partaken over the course of the narrative maddened some readers. (One is reminded of the observation that Puritans disapproved of bear baiting not because of the suffering endured by the animal but because of the enjoyment experienced by the audience.)

The events leading to the composition of *The Picture of Dorian Gray* gave little indication of the impact it would produce. In the fall of 1889, J. Marshall Stoddart, the American editor of *Lippincott's Magazine*, traveled to England. Stoddart previously had met Wilde in 1882 while the latter was touring America, and at a dinner party in London Stoddart persuaded Wilde and Arthur Conan Doyle to contribute novella length works to the magazine. (Doyle subsequently sent Stoddart his second Sherlock Holmes adventure, "The Sign of Four.") Wilde initially proposed that *Lippincott's* use a story that he had already written, "The Fisherman and His Soul," but Stoddart rejected the idea. Wilde wrote to Stoddart on 17 December 1889 that he had "invented a new story which is better than 'The Fisherman and His Soul' and I am quite ready to set to work at once on it" (*The Letters of Oscar Wilde*, 251).

Wilde sent the initial version of the work to Stoddart early in 1890. As the manuscript, held by the Clark Library, attests, Stoddart did not hesitate to excise portions that he felt would be too graphic for his readers' sensibilities. (A full discussion of the first manuscript appears in the Donald L. Lawler essay in this collection.) Stoddart apparently had a good idea of the taste of American readers. The novella appeared in the July 1890 issue of *Lippincott's*. The issue in which it appeared quickly sold out, and American critics praised the work as a modern morality tale. That was not the case in England, however, where a number of reviewers excoriated the work. A lively debate, lasting into the fall, took place in the columns of various newspapers between Wilde and his supporters on one hand and hostile reviewers on the other.

Although Wilde steadfastly defended his work, the criticism did in fact have an impact on his revisions when he rewrote it as a full-length novel. In its expanded form, published by Ward, Lock & Company in 1891, *The Picture of Dorian Gray* retains its essential narrative elements. However, Wilde made modifications that present some of his more daring ideas in a less direct fashion and he included a Preface that addresses through aphoristic statements the charges of immorality leveled against the novella. Individual readers can judge the effect of these changes. (To facilitate comparison, the original *Lippincott's* version immediately follows the expanded text of *The Picture of Dorian Gray* in this edition.) However, one cannot dispute that the novel, as we now have it, has exercised a powerful impact upon its readers for well over a century.

In organizing this edition, I have tried to provide s sampling of the aesthetic world that informed Wilde's creative efforts. Selections from Walter Pater and Joris Karl Huysmans provide glimpses of the writings that shaped Wilde's views, and portions of two of his essays offer clear articulations of his adaptation and application. Likewise, an extensive selection of responses to the novella's appearance shows not only the public perception of the work but also Wilde's sense of what his writing aimed at.

The criticism gathered here reflects the range of approaches that offer effective methods for understanding Wilde's novel. The section begins with my essay highlighting interpretive alternatives presented by the narrative. Simon Joyce explores the impact of sexuality on our readings, while Donald L. Lawler traces the evolution of the work's composition. Sheldon W. Liebman presents an insightful view of the development of character in the novel, while Maureen O'Connor and Ellie Ragland-Sullivan present very different approaches to the way the identity of the author informs our sense of his writing. And John Paul Riquelme explains how elements of the Gothic exert a powerful impact on the novel. While these selections cannot exhaust possibilities for reading, they do underscore the variety of approaches that can produce a satisfying understanding of the novel.

Many people have contributed to this project, and I realize that to a great extent whatever success it enjoys relates directly to their efforts. No two people have done more to shape this volume than my editors at Norton, Carol Bemis and Brian Baker. Their enthusiasm, energy, and trust have been invaluable. Their sound judgments have saved me from numerous false steps, and their warm support has made working on this edition a pleasure. There may still be shortcomings here that even they could not find, but the value of this book comes to a large degree from their careful scrutiny. I also wish to thank the staff at the Clark Library, John Espy, A. Nicholas Fargnoli, Paula Gillespie, Merlin Holland, Neil Hultgren, Tim Machan, Michael McKinney, Joan Navarre, John Paul Riquelme, Albert Rivero, David Rose, Sara Schepis, and Joan Sommers and the Inter-Library Loan staff at Marquette University.

A Note on the Texts

The Picture of Dorian Gray first appeared as a novella of over fifty thousand words. It was published in the July 1890 issue of *Lippincott's Monthly*. The revised and expanded novel length version was printed by Ward, Lock and Company in April 1891 and sold for six shillings. This was the same company that bound the British edition of *Lippincott's* magazine. A new printing was called for in October 1895, by which time the publisher had become Ward, Lock and Bowden. The novel was not reprinted again until 1901, the year following Wilde's death, by Charles Carrington, a slightly disreputable English publisher of pornographic literature in Paris, who, following Wilde's bankruptcy in 1895, had acquired the rights in expectation that profit was to be made from the scandal surrounding the novel, which figured prominently in Wilde's famous trials. Robert Ross, as executor of the Wilde estate, eventually reacquired the rights to the novel. Since that time, the novel has never been out of print.

In the March 1891 edition of Frank Harris's *Fortnightly Review* Wilde published "A Preface to 'Dorian Gray.' " It consisted of twenty-three aphorisms, written by Wilde in response to the criticisms made of the *Lippincott's Dorian Gray* (see Reviews and Reactions, pp. 352–66). By the time Ward, Lock and Company brought out the novel-length version in April, Wilde had added a new aphorism to the Preface ("No artist is ever morbid. The artist can express everything") and had divided the original ninth aphorism (beginning "The nineteenth century dislike of Realism . . .") to make a final total of twenty-five aphorisms.

As in the first Norton publication of *The Picture of Dorian Gray*, this edition reprints the texts of the original 1890 *Lippincott's* novella and the revised and expanded version into the novel published by Ward, Lock and Company in 1891. These were the only two versions prepared for and seen through publication by the author. The revised version of 1891, representing Wilde's final intentions, appears ahead of the *Lippincott's* text of 1890. Obvious typographical errors have been silently emended. With that exception, this edition reproduces the settings, including Wilde's punctuation, of the 1891 edition.

The Texts of
THE PICTURE OF
DORIAN GRAY

The Preface[1]

The artist is the creator of beautiful things.

To reveal art and conceal the artist is art's aim.

The critic is he who can translate into another manner or a new material his impression of beautiful things.

The highest as the lowest form of criticism is a mode of autobiography.

Those who find ugly meanings in beautiful things are corrupt without being charming. This is a fault.

Those who find beautiful meanings in beautiful things are the cultivated. For these there is hope.

They are the elect to whom beautiful things mean only Beauty.

There is no such thing as a moral or an immoral book. Books are well written, or badly written. That is all.

The nineteenth century dislike of Realism is the rage of Caliban seeing his own face in a glass.

The nineteenth century dislike of Romanticism is the rage of Caliban not seeing his own face in a glass.

The moral life of man forms part of the subject-matter of the artist, but the morality of art consists in the perfect use of an imperfect medium.

No artist desires to prove anything. Even things that are true can be proved.

No artist has ethical sympathies. An ethical sympathy in an artist is an unpardonable mannerism of style.

No artist is ever morbid. The artist can express everything.

Thought and language are to the artist instruments of an art.

Vice and virtue are to the artist materials for an art.

From the point of view of form, the type of all the arts is the art of the musician. From the point of view of feeling, the actor's craft is the type.

All art is at once surface and symbol.

Those who go beneath the surface do so at their peril.

Those who read the symbol do so at their peril.

---

1. Wilde's preface to *Dorian Gray* appeared in Frank Harris's *Fortnightly Review* several months before the second edition of the novel. It seems to have three aims. The first is to take weapons out of the hands of the critics who had attacked the *Lippincott's* edition of *Dorian Gray* by anticipating some of the charges likely to be made against it. The second intent is to respond to some of the criticism made of the magazine edition. In so doing, Wilde was to repeat rather sententiously the major points of his aesthetic creed at the time (and to anticipate the main line of his defense of *Dorian Gray* at the trials). The third intention is expressed in the tone and manner of the epigrams, which anticipate those Wilde published in 1894 under the title "Phrases and Philosophies for the Use of the Young" in *The Chameleon*, an Oxford undergraduate journal. The paradoxes are not so plentiful in the former as in the latter, and the manner is less insolent, but the intent is to be provocative. It was this adopted manner that revealed Wilde could be every bit as pompous as those he ridiculed and that earned him the title "sovereign of insufferables" from Ambrose Bierce.

It is the spectator, and not life, that art really mirrors.

Diversity of opinion about a work of art shows that the work is new, complex, and vital.

When critics disagree the artist is in accord with himself.

We can forgive a man for making a useful thing as long as he does not admire it. The only excuse for making a useless thing is that one admires it intensely.

All art is quite useless.

OSCAR WILDE

The Picture of Dorian Gray
(1891)

Chapter I

The studio[1] was filled with the rich odour of roses, and when the light summer wind stirred amidst the trees of the garden there came through the open door the heavy scent of the lilac, or the more delicate perfume of the pink-flowering thorn.

From the corner of the divan of Persian saddle-bags on which he was lying, smoking, as was his custom, innumerable cigarettes, Lord Henry Wotton could just catch the gleam of the honey-sweet and honey-coloured blossoms of a laburnum,[2] whose tremulous branches seemed hardly able to bear the burden of a beauty so flame-like as theirs; and now and then the fantastic shadows of birds in flight flitted across the long tussore-silk[3] curtains that were stretched in front of the huge window, producing a kind of momentary Japanese effect, and making him think of those pallid jade-faced painters of Tokio[4] who, through the medium of an art that is necessarily immobile, seek to convey the sense of swiftness and motion. The sullen murmur of the bees shouldering their way through the long unmown grass, or circling with monotonous insistence round the dusty gilt horns of the straggling woodbine,[5] seemed to make the stillness more oppressive. The dim roar of London was like the bourdon[6] note of a distant organ.

1. The exotic decor is a reproduction of Charles Ricketts's studio in London, where Wilde was a frequent visitor. Ricketts (1866–1931) may have been the original for Basil Hallward. He designed the title page and binding for *Dorian Gray* and for many other Wilde volumes.
2. A small tree or shrub bearing clusters of yellow flowers.
3. A coarse brown silk from India.
4. In Wilde's "Decay of Lying," Vivian's prescription for anyone desiring a true Japanese effect is not to go to Tokyo but to "stay at home and steep yourself in the work of certain Japanese artists, and then when you have absorbed the spirit of their style, and caught their imaginative manner of vision, you will go some afternoon and sit in the park . . . and if you cannot see an absolutely Japanese effect there, you will not see it anywhere."
5. A name for various plants of a climbing habit; in early use (later only dial.), convolvulus and ivy; now chiefly (*U.S.*) the Virginia Creeper *Ampelopsis quinquefolia*, and the West Indian *Ipomœa tuberosa* (Spanish Woodbine). 2. *esp.* The common honeysuckle, *Lonicera Periclymenum*, a climbing shrub with pale yellow fragrant flowers; also extended to other species, as the N. American *L. grata*. OED
6. A low, reverberating sound, as the bass stop of an organ.

In the centre of the room, clamped to an upright easel, stood the full-length portrait of a young man of extraordinary personal beauty, and in front of it, some little distance away, was sitting the artist himself, Basil Hallward, whose sudden disappearance some years ago caused, at the time, such public excitement, and gave rise to so many strange conjectures.

As the painter looked at the gracious and comely form he had so skilfully mirrored in his art, a smile of pleasure passed across his face, and seemed about to linger there. But he suddenly started up, and, closing his eyes, placed his fingers upon the lids, as though he sought to imprison within his brain some curious dream from which he feared he might awake.

"It is your best work, Basil, the best thing you have ever done," said Lord Henry, languidly. "You must certainly send it next year to the Grosvenor.[7] The Academy[8] is too large and too vulgar. Whenever I have gone there, there have been either so many people that I have not been able to see the pictures, which was dreadful, or so many pictures that I have not been able to see the people, which was worse. The Grosvenor is really the only place."

"I don't think I shall send it anywhere," he answered, tossing his head back in that odd way that used to make his friends laugh at him at Oxford. "No: I won't send it anywhere."

Lord Henry elevated his eyebrows, and looked at him in amazement through the thin blue wreaths of smoke that curled up in such fanciful whorls from his heavy opium-tainted cigarette.[9] "Not send it anywhere? My dear fellow, why? Have you any reason? What odd chaps you painters are! You do anything in the world to gain a reputation. As soon as you have one, you seem to want to throw it away. It is silly of you, for there is only one thing in the world worse than being talked about, and that is not being talked about. A portrait like

---

7. A Bond Street art gallery established by the painter Sir Coutts Lindsay in May 1877 as an alternative to the galleries of the Royal Academy. It came to be known as the "Temple of the Aesthetic" and was parodied by Gilbert and Sullivan in *Patience* as the "greenery-yallery, Grosvenor Gallery" because of its dominant color keys. Wilde had done reviews of exhibits there in the late 1870s and early 1880s and shared Lord Henry's opinion of its worth. The painting on the cover of this edition shows Wilde at a private viewing of one such exhibit.

8. The Royal Academy of Arts (an honorary society of painters, architects, and sculptors founded in 1768) represented the art establishment of the day.

9. Wilde gave many of his own habits and much of his own background to the three main characters, each of whom represents, alternately, idealized, true-to-life, and extreme views of their creator. Thus, Wilde attended Oxford as did Basil and smoked Egyptian, opium-tainted cigarettes as did Henry. However, there is little doubt that Wilde drew his characters from others as well. Basil combines qualities of Ricketts and his friend Charles H. Shannon (1863–1937), who shared lodgings with him in Chelsea. Shannon designed the bindings for Wilde's plays. He and Ricketts edited the *Dial* from 1889 to 1897. Lord Henry may have a touch of Whistler in him and much of Wilde, but critical consensus makes Lord Ronald Sutherland-Gower (1845–1916) the leading candidate as the inspiration for Lord Henry. Gower knew Wilde at Oxford, and the two were intimates in the 1870s and 1880s.

this would set you far above all the young men in England, and make the old men quite jealous, if old men are ever capable of any emotion."

"I know you will laugh at me," he replied, "but I really can't exhibit it. I have put too much of myself into it."

Lord Henry stretched himself out on the divan and laughed.

"Yes, I knew you would; but it is quite true, all the same."

"Too much of yourself in it! Upon my word, Basil, I didn't know you were so vain; and I really can't see any resemblance between you, with your rugged strong face and your coal-black hair, and this young Adonis,[1] who looks as if he was made out of ivory and rose-leaves. Why, my dear Basil, he is a Narcissus,[2] and you—well, of course you have an intellectual expression, and all that. But beauty, real beauty, ends where an intellectual expression begins. Intellect is in itself a mode of exaggeration, and destroys the harmony of any face. The moment one sits down to think, one becomes all nose, or all forehead, or something horrid. Look at the successful men in any of the learned professions.[3] How perfectly hideous they are! Except, of course, in the Church.[4] But then in the Church they don't think. A bishop keeps on saying at the age of eighty what he was told to say when he was a boy of eighteen, and as a natural consequence he always looks absolutely delightful. Your mysterious young friend, whose name you have never told me, but whose picture really fascinates me, never thinks. I feel quite sure of that. He is some brainless, beautiful creature, who should be always here in winter when we have no flowers to look at, and always here in summer when we want something to chill our intelligence. Don't flatter yourself, Basil: you are not in the least like him."

"You don't understand me, Harry," answered the artist. "Of course I am not like him. I know that perfectly well. Indeed, I should be sorry to look like him. You shrug your shoulders? I am telling you the truth. There is a fatality about all physical and intellectual distinction, the sort of fatality that seems to dog through history the faltering steps of kings. It is better not to be different from one's fellows. The ugly and the stupid have the best of it in this world. They can sit at their ease and gape at the play. If they know nothing of victory, they are at least spared the knowledge of defeat. They live

---

1. In Greek mythology, a youth of extraordinary good looks, beloved of Aphrodite, killed by a wild boar.
2. In mythology, the youth who spurned the love of the nymph Echo, causing her death. His punishment was to fall in love with his own reflected image and pine away till death, at which moment he was transformed into the flower.
3. Any profession wherein one must attend study and/or university in order to pursue the desired occupation.
4. An abbreviated reference to The Church of England. During the Reformation it repudiated the supremacy of the Pope, and asserted that of the Sovereign over all persons and in all causes, ecclesiastical as well as temporal, in his dominions.

as we all should live, undisturbed, indifferent, and without disquiet. They neither bring ruin upon others, nor ever receive it from alien hands. Your rank and wealth, Harry; my brains, such as they are— my art, whatever it may be worth; Dorian Gray's good looks—we shall all suffer for what the gods have given us, suffer terribly."

"Dorian Gray? Is that his name?" asked Lord Henry, walking across the studio towards Basil Hallward.

"Yes, that is his name. I didn't intend to tell it to you."

"But why not?"

"Oh, I can't explain. When I like people immensely I never tell their names to any one. It is like surrendering a part of them. I have grown to love secrecy. It seems to be the one thing that can make modern life mysterious or marvellous to us. The commonest thing is delightful if one only hides it. When I leave town now I never tell my people where I am going. If I did, I would lose all my pleasure. It is a silly habit, I dare say, but somehow it seems to bring a great deal of romance into one's life. I suppose you think me awfully foolish about it?"

"Not at all," answered Lord Henry, "not at all, my dear Basil. You seem to forget that I am married, and the one charm of marriage is that it makes a life of deception absolutely necessary for both parties. I never know where my wife is, and my wife never knows what I am doing. When we meet—we do meet occasionally, when we dine out together, or go down to the Duke's—we tell each other the most absurd stories with the most serious faces. My wife is very good at it—much better, in fact, than I am. She never gets confused over her dates, and I always do. But when she does find me out, she makes no row at all. I sometimes wish she would; but she merely laughs at me."

"I hate the way you talk about your married life, Harry," said Basil Hallward, strolling towards the door that led into the garden. "I believe that you are really a very good husband, but that you are thoroughly ashamed of your own virtues. You are an extraordinary fellow. You never say a moral thing, and you never do a wrong thing.[5] Your cynicism is simply a pose."

"Being natural is simply a pose, and the most irritating pose I know," cried Lord Henry, laughing; and the two young men went out into the garden together, and ensconced themselves on a long bamboo seat that stood in the shade of a tall laurel bush. The sunlight slipped over the polished leaves. In the grass, white daisies were tremulous.

After a pause, Lord Henry pulled out his watch. "I am afraid I

---

5. This may be an echo of John Wilmot's (earl of Rochester) epitaph for Charles II: "Here lies a Great and Mighty King / Whose Promise none rely'd on; / He never said a Foolish Thing? / Nor ever did a Wise One" (*Dorian Gray*, Murray 239).

must be going, Basil," he murmured, "and before I go, I insist on your answering a question I put to you some time ago."

"What is that?" said the painter, keeping his eyes fixed on the ground.

"You know quite well."

"I do not, Harry."

"Well, I will tell you what it is. I want you to explain to me why you won't exhibit Dorian Gray's picture. I want the real reason."

"I told you the real reason."

"No, you did not. You said it was because there was too much of yourself in it. Now, that is childish."

"Harry," said Basil Hallward, looking him straight in the face, "every portrait that is painted with feeling is a portrait of the artist, not of the sitter. The sitter is merely the accident, the occasion. It is not he who is revealed by the painter; it is rather the painter who, on the coloured canvas, reveals himself. The reason I will not exhibit this picture is that I am afraid that I have shown in it the secret of my own soul."

Lord Henry laughed. "And what is that?" he asked.

"I will tell you," said Hallward; but an expression of perplexity came over his face.

"I am all expectation, Basil," continued his companion, glancing at him.

"Oh, there is really very little to tell, Harry," answered the painter; "and I am afraid you will hardly understand it. Perhaps you will hardly believe it."

Lord Henry smiled, and, leaning down, plucked a pink-petalled daisy from the grass, and examined it. "I am quite sure I shall understand it," he replied, gazing intently at the little golden white-feathered disk, "and as for believing things, I can believe anything, provided that it is quite incredible."

The wind shook some blossoms from the trees, and the heavy lilac-blooms, with their clustering stars, moved to and fro in the languid air. A grasshopper began to chirrup by the wall, and like a blue thread a long thin dragon-fly floated past on its brown gauze wings. Lord Henry felt as if he could hear Basil Hallward's heart beating, and wondered what was coming.

"The story is simply this," said the painter after some time. "Two months ago I went to a crush[6] at Lady Brandon's. You know we poor artists have to show ourselves in society from time to time, just to remind the public that we are not savages. With an evening coat and a white tie, as you told me once, anybody, even a stock-broker, can gain a reputation for being civilized. Well, after I had been in the

---

6. A crowded social gathering.

room about ten minutes, talking to huge overdressed dowagers and tedious Academicians, I suddenly became conscious that some one was looking at me. I turned half-way round, and saw Dorian Gray for the first time. When our eyes met, I felt that I was growing pale. A curious sensation of terror came over me. I knew that I had come face to face with some one whose mere personality was so fascinating that, if I allowed it to do so, it would absorb my whole nature, my whole soul, my very art itself. I did not want any external influence in my life. You know yourself, Harry, how independent I am by nature. I have always been my own master; had at least always been so, till I met Dorian Gray. Then—but I don't know how to explain it to you. Something seemed to tell me that I was on the verge of a terrible crisis in my life. I had a strange feeling that Fate had in store for me exquisite joys and exquisite sorrows. I grew afraid, and turned to quit the room. It was not conscience that made me do so: it was a sort of cowardice. I take no credit to myself for trying to escape."

"Conscience and cowardice are really the same things, Basil. Conscience is the trade-name of the firm.[7] That is all."

"I don't believe that, Harry, and I don't believe you do either. However, whatever was my motive—and it may have been pride, for I used to be very proud—I certainly struggled to the door. There, of course, I stumbled against Lady Brandon. 'You are not going to run away so soon, Mr. Hallward?' she screamed out. You know her curiously shrill voice?"[8]

"Yes; she is a peacock in everything but beauty," said Lord Henry, pulling the daisy to bits with his long, nervous fingers.

"I could not get rid of her. She brought me up to Royalties, and people with Stars and Garters,[9] and elderly ladies with gigantic tiaras and parrot noses. She spoke of me as her dearest friend. I had only met her once before, but she took it into her head to lionize me. I believe some picture of mine had made a great success at the time, at least had been chattered about in the penny newspapers, which is the nineteenth-century standard of immortality. Suddenly I found myself face to face with the young man whose personality had so strangely stirred me. We were quite close, almost touching. Our eyes met again. It was reckless of me, but I asked Lady Brandon to introduce me to him. Perhaps it was not so reckless, after all. It was simply

7. An epigram revised from its earlier form in Wilde's 1883 play, *The Duchess of Padua*, act 1: "Conscience is but the name which cowardice / Fleeing from battle scrawls upon its shield" (*Complete Works* 569).
8. Some critics haves asserted that the cameo of Lady Brandon is based in part on Wilde's mother, Lady Jane Wilde, a writer and supporter of Irish revolution in her youth. She was known for her salons in Dublin and later, in reduced circumstances, in London. However, Wilde's devotion to her makes it doubtful that he would present such a satirical critique here and in the dialogue that follows.
9. The Order of the Garter was the highest of all English knightly orders. Stars and "orders and ribbons" (below) refer to insignia of English orders of knighthood.

inevitable. We would have spoken to each other without any introduction. I am sure of that. Dorian told me so afterwards. He, too, felt
that we were destined to know each other."

"And how did Lady Brandon describe this wonderful young man?"
asked his companion. "I know she goes in for giving a rapid *précis*[1] of
all her guests. I remember her bringing me up to a truculent and red-
faced old gentleman covered all over with orders and ribbons, and
hissing into my ear, in a tragic whisper which must have been perfectly audible to everybody in the room, the most astounding details.
I simply fled. I like to find out people for myself. But Lady Brandon
treats her guests exactly as an auctioneer treats his goods. She either
explains them entirely away, or tells one everything about them
except what one wants to know."

"Poor Lady Brandon! You are hard on her, Harry!" said Hallward,
listlessly.

"My dear fellow, she tried to found a *salon*,[2] and only succeeded in
opening a restaurant. How could I admire her?[3] But tell me, what did
she say about Mr. Dorian Gray?"

"Oh, something like, 'Charming boy—poor dear mother and I
absolutely inseparable. Quite forget what he does—afraid he—
doesn't do anything—oh, yes, plays the piano—or is it the violin, dear
Mr. Gray?' Neither of us could help laughing, and we became friends
at once."

"Laughter is not at all a bad beginning for a friendship, and it is far
the best ending for one," said the young lord, plucking another daisy.

Hallward shook his head. "You don't understand what friendship is,
Harry," he murmured—"or what enmity is, for that matter. You like
every one; that is to say, you are indifferent to every one."

"How horribly unjust of you!" cried Lord Henry, tilting his hat
back, and looking up at the little clouds that, like ravelled skeins of
glossy white silk, were drifting across the hollowed turquoise of the
summer sky. "Yes; horribly unjust of you. I make a great difference
between people. I choose my friends for their good looks, my
acquaintances for their good characters, and my enemies for their
good intellects. A man cannot be too careful in the choice of his enemies. I have not got one who is a fool. They are all men of some intellectual power, and consequently they all appreciate me. Is that very
vain of me? I think it is rather vain."

1. A summary.
2. The reception-room of a Parisian lady of fashion; hence, a reunion of notabilities at the
house of such a lady; also, a similar gathering in other capitals. OED
3. A quip Wilde had once directed at Marc-André Raffalovich (1865–1934), thereby inciting
the latter's enmity.

"I should think it was, Harry. But according to your category I must be merely an acquaintance."

"My dear old Basil, you are much more than an acquaintance."

"And much less than a friend. A sort of brother, I suppose?"

"Oh, brothers! I don't care for brothers. My elder brother won't die, and my younger brothers seem never to do anything else."

"Harry!" exclaimed Hallward, frowning.

"My dear fellow, I am not quite serious. But I can't help detesting my relations. I suppose it comes from the fact that none of us can stand other people having the same faults as ourselves. I quite sympathize with the rage of the English democracy against what they call the vices of the upper orders. The masses feel that drunkenness, stupidity, and immorality should be their own special property, and that if any one of us makes an ass of himself he is poaching on their preserves. When poor Southwark got into the Divorce Court,[4] their indignation was quite magnificent. And yet I don't suppose that ten per cent of the proletariat[5] live correctly."

"I don't agree with a single word that you have said, and, what is more, Harry, I feel sure you don't either."

Lord Henry stroked his pointed brown beard, and tapped the toe of his patent-leather boot with a tasselled ebony cane. "How English you are Basil! That is the second time you have made that observation. If one puts forward an idea to a true Englishman—always a rash thing to do—he never dreams of considering whether the idea is right or wrong. The only thing he considers of any importance is whether one believes it oneself. Now, the value of an idea has nothing whatsoever to do with the sincerity of the man who expresses it. Indeed, the probabilities are that the more insincere the man is, the more purely intellectual will the idea be, as in that case it will not be coloured by either his wants, his desires, or his prejudices. However, I don't propose to discuss politics, sociology, or metaphysics with you. I like persons better than principles, and I like persons with no principles better than anything else in the world.[6] Tell me more about Mr. Dorian Gray. How often do you see him?"

"Every day. I couldn't be happy if I didn't see him every day. He is absolutely necessary to me."

---

4. The Court for Divorce and Matrimonial Causes, established in 1857, took over the jurisdiction for hearing such cases from the church courts. At that time, men could obtain divorce by proving a wife committed adultery, but women could obtain one only after proving cruelty or desertion, in addition to their husband's adultery. In 1923 women were allowed to use the same grounds for divorce as men. In 1969, 'irretrievable breakdown' became the test for divorce.
5. That class of the community which is dependent on daily labour for subsistence, and has no reserve or capital; the indigent wage-earners; sometimes extended to include all wage-earners; working men, the laboring classes.
6. "and I like . . . world" added in this edition. See notes to the *Lippincott's* edition.

"How extraordinary! I thought you would never care for anything but your art."

"He is all my art to me now," said the painter, gravely. "I sometimes think, Harry, that there are only two eras of any importance in the world's history. The first is the appearance of a new medium for art, and the second is the appearance of a new personality for art also. What the invention of oil-painting was to the Venetians, the face of Antinous[7] was to late Greek sculpture, and the face of Dorian Gray will some day be to me. It is not merely that I paint from him, draw from him, sketch from him. Of course, I have done all that. But he is much more to me than a model or a sitter. I won't tell you that I am dissatisfied with what I have done of him, or that his beauty is such that Art cannot express it. There is nothing that Art cannot express, and I know that the work I have done, since I met Dorian Gray, is good work, is the best work of my life. But in some curious way—I wonder will you understand me?—his personality has suggested to me an entirely new manner in art, an entirely new mode of style. I see things differently, I think of them differently. I can now recreate life in a way that was hidden from me before. 'A dream of form in days of thought':[8]—who is it who says that? I forget; but it is what Dorian Gray has been to me. The merely visible presence of this lad—for he seems to me little more than a lad, though he is really over twenty—his merely visible presence—ah! I wonder can you realize all that that means? Unconsciously he defines for me the lines of a fresh school, a school that is to have in it all the passion of the romantic spirit, all the perfection of the spirit that is Greek.[9] The harmony of soul and body—how much that is! We in our madness have separated the two, and have invented a realism that is vulgar, an ideality that is void. Harry! if you only knew what Dorian Gray is to me! You remember that landscape of mine, for which Agnew[1] offered me such a huge price, but which I would not part with? It is one of the best things I have ever done. And why is it so? Because, while I was painting it, Dorian Gray sat beside me. Some subtle influence passed from him to me, and for the first time in my life I saw in the plain woodland the wonder I had always looked for, and always missed."

"Basil, this is extraordinary! I must see Dorian Gray."

Hallward got up from the seat, and walked up and down the garden. After some time he came back. "Harry," he said, "Dorian Gray

---

7. A companion of the Roman emperor Hadrian, and an ideal of manly grace and beauty. He is the first of a series of male homosexual pinups out of history alluded to in the text.
8. "A dream of form in days of thought" is from "To a Greek Girl" by Austin Dobson.
9. Basil's aestheticism is an ideal combination of the teaching of John Ruskin ("all the passion of the romantic spirit") and Walter Pater ("all the perfection of the spirit that is Greek"). Both taught Wilde at Oxford in the 1870s.
1. Thomas Agnew & Sons are to this day art dealers in London's Old Bond Street.

is to me simply a motive in art. You might see nothing in him. I see everything in him. He is never more present in my work than when no image of him is there. He is a suggestion, as I have said, of a new manner. I find him in the curves of certain lines, in the loveliness and subtleties of certain colours. That is all."

"Then why won't you exhibit his portrait?" asked Lord Henry.

"Because, without intending it, I have put into it some expression of all this curious artistic idolatry, of which, of course, I have never cared to speak to him. He knows nothing about it. He shall never know anything about it. But the world might guess it; and I will not bare my soul to their shallow, prying eyes. My heart shall never be put under their microscope.[2] There is too much of myself in the thing, Harry—too much of myself!"

"Poets are not so scrupulous as you are. They know how useful passion is for publication. Nowadays a broken heart will run to many editions."

"I hate them for it," cried Hallward. "An artist should create beautiful things, but should put nothing of his own life into them. We live in an age when men treat art as if it were meant to be a form of autobiography. We have lost the abstract sense of beauty. Some day I will show the world what it is; and for that reason the world shall never see my portrait of Dorian Gray."

"I think you are wrong, Basil, but I won't argue with you. It is only the intellectually lost who ever argue. Tell me, is Dorian Gray very fond of you?"

The painter considered for a few moments. "He likes me," he answered after a pause; "I know he likes me. Of course I flatter him dreadfully. I find a strange pleasure in saying things to him that I know I shall be sorry for having said. As a rule, he is charming to me, and we sit in the studio and talk of a thousand things. Now and then, however, he is horribly thoughtless, and seems to take a real delight in giving me pain. Then I feel, Harry, that I have given away my whole soul to some one who treats it as if it were a flower to put in his coat, a bit of decoration to charm his vanity, an ornament for a summer's day."

"Days in summer, Basil, are apt to linger," murmured Lord Henry. "Perhaps you will tire sooner than he will. It is a sad thing to think of, but there is no doubt that Genius lasts longer than Beauty. That accounts for the fact that we all take such pains to over-educate ourselves. In the wild struggle for existence, we want to have something that endures, and so we fill our minds with rubbish and facts,

---

2. An echo of Swinburne's satirical rebuttal to his critics, titled "Under the Microscope" (1872), in which he also defended Dante Gabriel Rossetti and other Pre-Raphaelites from charges of excessive sensuality and immorality.

in the silly hope of keeping our place. The thoroughly well-informed man—that is the modern ideal. And the mind of the thoroughly well-informed man is a dreadful thing. It is like a bric-à-brac shop, all monsters and dust, with everything priced above its proper value. I think you will tire first, all the same. Some day you will look at your friend, and he will seem to you to be a little out of drawing, or you won't like his tone of colour, or something. You will bitterly reproach him in your own heart, and seriously think that he has behaved very badly to you. The next time he calls, you will be perfectly cold and indifferent. It will be a great pity, for it will alter you. What you have told me is quite a romance, a romance of art one might call it, and the worst of having a romance of any kind is that it leaves one so unromantic."

"Harry, don't talk like that. As long as I live, the personality of Dorian Gray will dominate me. You can't feel what I feel. You change too often."

"Ah, my dear Basil, that is exactly why I can feel it. Those who are faithful know only the trivial side of love: it is the faithless who know love's tragedies." And Lord Henry struck a light on a dainty silver case, and began to smoke a cigarette with a self-conscious and satisfied air, as if he had summed up the world in a phrase.[3] There was a rustle of chirruping sparrows in the green lacquer leaves of the ivy, and the blue cloud-shadows chased themselves across the grass like swallows. How pleasant it was in the garden! And how delightful other people's emotions were!—much more delightful than their ideas, it seemed to him. One's own soul, and the passions of one's friends—those were the fascinating things in life. He pictured to himself with silent amusement the tedious luncheon that he had missed by staying so long with Basil Hallward. Had he gone to his aunt's, he would have been sure to have met Lord Goodbody there, and the whole conversation would have been about the feeding of the poor, and the necessity for model lodging-houses. Each class would have preached the importance of those virtues, for whose exercise there was no necessity in their own lives. The rich would have spoken on the value of thrift, and the idle grown eloquent over the dignity of labour. It was charming to have escaped all that! As he thought of his aunt, an idea seemed to strike him. He turned to Hallward, and said, "My dear fellow, I have just remembered."

"Remembered what, Harry?"

"Where I heard the name of Dorian Gray."

"Where was it?" asked Hallward, with a slight frown.

"Don't look so angry, Basil. It was at my aunt, Lady Agatha's. She told me she had discovered a wonderful young man, who was going

---

3. A statement Wilde was later to apply to himself in *De Profundis* (*Letters* 466).

to help her in the East End,[4] and that his name was Dorian Gray. I
am bound to state that she never told me he was good-looking.
Women have no appreciation of good looks; at least, good women
have not. She said that he was very earnest, and had a beautiful
nature. I at once pictured to myself a creature with spectacles and
lank hair, horribly freckled, and tramping about on huge feet. I wish
I had known it was your friend."

"I am very glad you didn't, Harry."

"Why?"

"I don't want you to meet him."

"You don't want me to meet him?"

"No."

"Mr. Dorian Gray is in the studio, sir," said the butler, coming into
the garden.

"You must introduce me now," cried Lord Henry, laughing.

The painter turned to his servant, who stood blinking in the sunlight. "Ask Mr. Gray to wait, Parker: I shall be in in a few moments."
The man bowed, and went up the walk.

Then he looked at Lord Henry. "Dorian Gray is my dearest friend,"
he said. "He has a simple and a beautiful nature. Your aunt was quite
right in what she said of him. Don't spoil him. Don't try to influence
him. Your influence would be bad. The world is wide, and has many
marvellous people in it. Don't take away from me the one person who
gives to my art whatever charm it possesses: my life as an artist
depends on him. Mind, Harry, I trust you." He spoke very slowly, and
the words seemed wrung out of him almost against his will.

"What nonsense you talk!" said Lord Henry, smiling, and, taking
Hallward by the arm, he almost led him into the house.

Chapter II

As they entered they saw Dorian Gray.[1] He was seated at the piano,
with his back to them, turning over the pages of a volume of Schumann's "Forest Scenes."[2] "You must lend me these, Basil," he cried.
"I want to learn them. They are perfectly charming."

"That entirely depends on how you sit to-day, Dorian."

---

4. A notorious slum section of London containing the dock district. It was the scene of many
   charitable enterprises and was often mentioned in connection with the work of the Christian Socialists and the Salvation Army.
1. John Espey proposes an etymology for "Dorian" from "Doric," with the implied association
   to "Greek or masculine love" (38). See John Espey, "Resources for Wilde Studies at the
   Clark Library," *Oscar Wilde, Two Approaches: Papers Read at a Clark Library Seminar, April
   17, 1976*, ed. Richard Ellmann and John Espey (Los Angeles: William Andrew Clark
   Memorial Library, 1977).
2. Pastoral piano music by Robert Schumann (1810–56), whose melodic, romantic, and
   intricate compositions were highly esteemed by aesthetes.

"Oh, I am tired of sitting, and I don't want a life-sized portrait of myself," answered the lad, swinging round on the music-stool in a wilful, petulant manner. When he caught sight of Lord Henry, a faint blush coloured his cheeks for a moment, and he started up. "I beg your pardon, Basil, but I didn't know you had any one with you."

"This is Lord Henry Wotton, Dorian, an old Oxford friend of mine. I have just been telling him what a capital sitter you were, and now you have spoiled everything."

"You have not spoiled my pleasure in meeting you, Mr. Gray," said Lord Henry, stepping forward and extending his hand. "My aunt has often spoken to me about you. You are one of her favourites, and, I am afraid, one of her victims also."

"I am in Lady Agatha's black books at present," answered Dorian, with a funny look of penitence. "I promised to go to a club in Whitechapel[3] with her last Tuesday, and I really forgot all about it. We were to have played a duet together—three duets, I believe. I don't know what she will say to me. I am far too frightened to call."

"Oh, I will make your peace with my aunt. She is quite devoted to you. And I don't think it really matters about your not being there. The audience probably thought it was a duet. When Aunt Agatha sits down to the piano she makes quite enough noise for two people."

"That is very horrid to her, and not very nice to me," answered Dorian, laughing.

Lord Henry looked at him. Yes, he was certainly wonderfully handsome, with his finely-curved scarlet lips, his frank blue eyes, his crisp gold hair. There was something in his face that made one trust him at once. All the candour of youth was there, as well as all youth's passionate purity. One felt that he had kept himself unspotted from the world.[4] No wonder Basil Hallward worshipped him.

"You are too charming to go in for philanthropy, Mr. Gray—far too charming." And Lord Henry flung himself down on the divan, and opened his cigarette-case.

The painter had been busy mixing his colours and getting his brushes ready. He was looking worried, and when he heard Lord Henry's last remark he glanced at him, hesitated for a moment, and

---

3. A district of London bordering on the East End, where service and volunteer clubs served the poor. Whitechapel contained the Jewish ghetto, especially Polish and European Jews, and Chinatown. It was described at the time as "grubby but not unprosperous." General Booth began the Salvation Army in Whitechapel in 1865.

4. "unspotted from the world" is a direct quote from the New Testament, James 1.27, in the King James version of the Bible, the form with which Wilde would have been most familiar. This idealized male image exactly corresponds to the forged painting in "The Picture of Mr. W. H." and to the appearance of many of Wilde's friends and intimates, most notably R. H. Sherard, a friend and future biographer; John Gray, the poet; and Lord Alfred Douglas. The last correspondence reflects perhaps Wilde's conception of male beauty rather than a specific model since he did not meet Lord Alfred until two months after the novel-length version of *The Picture of Dorian Gray* appeared in print.

18   THE PICTURE OF DORIAN GRAY (1891)

then said, "Harry, I want to finish this picture to-day. Would you think it awfully rude of me if I asked you to go away?"

Lord Henry smiled, and looked at Dorian Gray. "Am I to go, Mr. Gray?" he asked.

"Oh, please don't, Lord Henry. I see that Basil is in one of his sulky moods; and I can't bear him when he sulks. Besides, I want you to tell me why I should not go in for philanthropy."

"I don't know that I shall tell you that, Mr. Gray. It is so tedious a subject that one would have to talk seriously about it. But I certainly shall not run away, now that you have asked me to stop. You don't really mind, Basil, do you? You have often told me that you liked your sitters to have some one to chat to."

Hallward bit his lip. "If Dorian wishes it, of course you must stay. Dorian's whims are laws to everybody, except himself."

Lord Henry took up his hat and gloves. "You are very pressing, Basil, but I am afraid I must go. I have promised to meet a man at the Orleans.[5] Good-bye, Mr. Gray. Come and see me some afternoon in Curzon Street.[6] I am nearly always at home at five o'clock. Write to me when you are coming. I should be sorry to miss you."

"Basil," cried Dorian Gray, "if Lord Henry Wotton goes I shall go too. You never open your lips while you are painting, and it is horribly dull standing on a platform and trying to look pleasant. Ask him to stay. I insist upon it."

"Stay, Harry, to oblige Dorian, and to oblige me," said Hallward, gazing intently at his picture. "It is quite true, I never talk when I am working, and never listen either, and it must be dreadfully tedious for my unfortunate sitters. I beg you to stay."

"But what about my man at the Orleans?"

The painter laughed. "I don't think there will be any difficulty about that. Sit down again, Harry. And now, Dorian, get up on the platform, and don't move about too much, or pay any attention to what Lord Henry says. He has a very bad influence over all his friends, with the single exception of myself."

Dorian Gray stepped up on the dais, with the air of a young Greek martyr, and made a little *moue*[7] of discontent to Lord Henry, to whom he had rather taken a fancy. He was so unlike Basil. They made a delightful contrast. And he had such a beautiful voice. After a few moments he said to him, "Have you really a very bad influence, Lord Henry? As bad as Basil says?"

5. A London club on King Street decorated with sporting scenes. The marquess of Queensberry, Wilde's nemesis, was a member.
6. In Mayfair, east of Hyde Park, south of Berkeley Square, and north of Green Park. All the London Streets mentioned in *Dorian Gray* may be found on a surveyor's map of London. Basil, Lord Henry, and Dorian all live in or near Mayfair, which remains a fashionable district of London.
7. A pouting grimace.

"There is no such thing as a good influence, Mr. Gray. All influence is immoral—immoral from the scientific point of view."[8]

"Why?"

"Because to influence a person is to give him one's own soul. He does not think his natural thoughts, or burn with his natural passions. His virtues are not real to him. His sins, if there are such things as sins, are borrowed. He becomes an echo of some one else's music, an actor of a part that has not been written for him. The aim of life is self-development. To realize one's nature perfectly—that is what each of us is here for. People are afraid of themselves, nowadays. They have forgotten the highest of all duties, the duty that one owes to one's self. Of course they are charitable. They feed the hungry, and clothe the beggar. But their own souls starve, and are naked. Courage has gone out of our race. Perhaps we never really had it. The terror of society, which is the basis of morals, the terror of God, which is the secret of religion—these are the two things that govern us. And yet—"

"Just turn your head a little more to the right, Dorian, like a good boy," said the painter, deep in his work, and conscious only that a look had come into the lad's face that he had never seen there before.

"And yet," continued Lord Henry, in his low, musical voice, and with that graceful wave of the hand that was always so characteristic of him, and that he had even in his Eton[9] days, "I believe that if one man were to live out his life fully and completely, were to give form to every feeling, expression to every thought, reality to every dream— I believe that the world would gain such a fresh impulse of joy that we would forget all the maladies of mediaevalism, and return to the Hellenic ideal[1]—to something finer, richer, than the Hellenic ideal, it may be. But the bravest man amongst us is afraid of himself. The mutilation of the savage has its tragic survival in the self-denial that mars our lives. We are punished for our refusals. Every impulse that we strive to strangle broods in the mind, and poisons us. The body sins once, and has done with its sin, for action is a mode of purification. Nothing remains then but the recollection of a pleasure, or the luxury of a regret. The only way to get rid of a temptation is to yield

---

8. This scientific view combines Darwinism, especially Darwin's theories about child development, and the psychology of William James and the new psychoanalytic schools in Germany and Austria, all of which are bound together in this novel, in Wilde's speculative thinking at the time, and in the Decadent Movement.

9. The most prestigious public school in England. English public schools are equivalent to U.S. private schools.

1. In this *raisonneur* speech, Henry outlines a philosophy remarkably similar to that expressed by Wilde as his own in *De Profundis*. Some of it, at least, is based upon Wilde's interpretation of Pater, especially two chapters from *The Renaissance* in this volume. The tradition in art that Pater called the "Hellenic Ideal" reached from Classical antiquity to the present. It was the ideal of beauty of form combined with sensuous appeal of both subject and treatment. Henry's version of the ideal is Wilde's variation, emphasizing Aestheticism and hedonism.

to it. Resist it, and your soul grows sick with longing for the things it has forbidden to itself, with desire for what its monstrous laws have made monstrous and unlawful. It has been said that the great events of the world take place in the brain. It is in the brain, and the brain only, that the great sins of the world take place also. You, Mr. Gray, you yourself, with your rose-red youth and your rose-white boyhood, you have had passions that have made you afraid, thoughts that have filled you with terror, day-dreams and sleeping dreams whose mere memory might stain your cheek with shame—"

"Stop!" faltered Dorian Gray, "stop! you bewilder me. I don't know what to say. There is some answer to you, but I cannot find it. Don't speak. Let me think. Or, rather, let me try not to think."

For nearly ten minutes he stood there, motionless, with parted lips, and eyes strangely bright. He was dimly conscious that entirely fresh influences were at work within him. Yet they seemed to him to have come really from himself. The few words that Basil's friend had said to him—words spoken by chance, no doubt, and with wilful paradox in them—had touched some secret chord that had never been touched before, but that he felt was now vibrating and throbbing to curious pulses.

Music had stirred him like that. Music had troubled him many times. But music was not articulate. It was not a new world, but rather another chaos, that it created in us. Words! Mere words! How terrible they were! How clear, and vivid, and cruel! One could not escape from them. And yet what a subtle magic there was in them! They seemed to be able to give a plastic form to formless things, and to have a music of their own as sweet as that of viol or of lute. Mere words! Was there anything so real as words?[2]

Yes; there had been things in his boyhood that he had not understood. He understood them now. Life suddenly became fiery-coloured to him. It seemed to him that he had been walking in fire. Why had he not known it?

With his subtle smile, Lord Henry watched him. He knew the precise psychological moment when to say nothing. He felt intensely interested. He was amazed at the sudden impression that his words had produced, and, remembering a book that he had read when he was sixteen, a book which had revealed to him much that he had not known before, he wondered whether Dorian Gray was passing through a similar experience.[3] He had merely shot an arrow into the air. Had it hit the mark? How fascinating the lad was!

2. Another Pater echo, this time from *Gaston de Latour*. Lord Henry's remark on p. xx, "Nothing can cure the soul but the senses, just as nothing can cure the senses but the soul," recalls a doctrine expounded by Pater in *Marius the Epicurean* (1885) and earlier by William Blake.
3. Wilde often spoke of such an influence in his own life but never revealed the book in question.

Hallward painted away with that marvellous bold touch of his, that had the true refinement and perfect delicacy that in art, at any rate comes only from strength. He was unconscious of the silence.

"Basil, I am tired of standing," cried Dorian Gray, suddenly. "I must go out and sit in the garden. The air is stifling here."

"My dear fellow, I am so sorry. When I am painting, I can't think of anything else. But you never sat better. You were perfectly still. And I have caught the effect I wanted—the half-parted lips, and the bright look in the eyes. I don't know what Harry has been saying to you, but he has certainly made you have the most wonderful expression. I suppose he has been paying you compliments. You mustn't believe a word that he says."

"He has certainly not been paying me compliments. Perhaps that is the reason that I don't believe anything he has told me."

"You know you believe it all," said Lord Henry, looking at him with his dreamy, languorous eyes. "I will go out to the garden with you. It is horribly hot in the studio. Basil, let us have something iced to drink, something with strawberries in it."

"Certainly, Harry. Just touch the bell, and when Parker comes I will tell him what you want. I have got to work up this background, so I will join you later on. Don't keep Dorian too long. I have never been in better form for painting than I am to-day. This is going to be my masterpiece. It is my masterpiece as it stands."

Lord Henry went out to the garden, and found Dorian Gray burying his face in the great cool lilac-blossoms, feverishly drinking in their perfume as if it had been wine. He came close to him, and put his hand upon his shoulder. "You are quite right to do that," he murmured. "Nothing can cure the soul but the senses, just as nothing can cure the senses but the soul."

The lad started and drew back. He was bare-headed, and the leaves had tossed his rebellious curls and tangled all their gilded threads. There was a look of fear in his eyes, such as people have when they are suddenly awakened. His finely-chiselled nostrils quivered, and some hidden nerve shook the scarlet of his lips and left them trembling.

"Yes," continued Lord Henry, "that is one of the great secrets of life—to cure the soul by means of the senses, and the senses by means of the soul. You are a wonderful creation. You know more than you think you know, just as you know less than you want to know."

Dorian Gray frowned and turned his head away. He could not help liking the tall, graceful young man who was standing by him. His romantic olive-coloured face and worn expression interested him. There was something in his low, languid voice that was absolutely fascinating. His cool, white, flower-like hands, even, had a curious charm. They moved, as he spoke, like music, and seemed to have a language of their own. But he felt afraid of him, and ashamed of being afraid. Why had it been left for a stranger to reveal him to himself? He had known Basil Hallward for months, but the friendship between them had never altered him. Suddenly there had come some one across his life who seemed to have disclosed to him life's mystery. And, yet, what was there to be afraid of? He was not a schoolboy or a girl. It was absurd to be frightened.

"Let us go and sit in the shade," said Lord Henry. "Parker has brought out the drinks, and if you stay any longer in this glare you will be quite spoiled, and Basil will never paint you again. You really must not allow yourself to become sunburnt. It would be unbecoming."[4]

"What can it matter?" cried Dorian Gray, laughing, as he sat down on the seat at the end of the garden.

"It should matter everything to you, Mr. Gray."

"Why?"

"Because you have the most marvellous youth, and youth is the one thing worth having."

"I don't feel that, Lord Henry."

"No, you don't feel it now. Some day, when you are old and wrinkled and ugly, when thought has seared your forehead with its lines, and passion branded your lips with its hideous fires, you will feel it, you will feel it terribly. Now, wherever you go, you charm the world. Will it always be so? . . . You have a wonderfully beautiful face, Mr. Gray. Don't frown. You have. And Beauty is a form of Genius—is higher, indeed, than Genius, as it needs no explanation. It is of the great facts of the world, like sunlight, or spring-time, or the reflection in dark waters of that silver shell we call the moon. It cannot be questioned. It has its divine right of sovereignty. It makes princes of those who have it. You smile? Ah! when you have lost it you won't smile. . . . People say sometimes that Beauty is only superficial. That may be so. But at least it is not so superficial as Thought is. To me, Beauty is the wonder of wonders. It is only shallow people who do not judge by appearances. The true mystery of the world is the visible, not the invisible. . . . Yes, Mr. Gray, the gods have been good to you. But what the gods give they quickly take away. You have only a few years in which to live really, perfectly, and fully. When your youth goes, your beauty will go with it, and then you will suddenly discover that there are no triumphs left for you, or have to content yourself with those mean triumphs that the memory of your past will make more bitter than defeats. Every month as it wanes brings you

---

4. Paul Fussell chronicles the twentieth-century change in English attitudes toward tanning in his book *Abroad: British Literary Traveling between the Wars*. New York: Oxford University Press, 1980.

nearer to something dreadful. Time is jealous of you, and wars against your lilies and your roses. You will become sallow, and hollow-cheeked, and dull-eyed. You will suffer horribly. . . . Ah! realize your youth while you have it. Don't squander the gold of your days, listening to the tedious, trying to improve the hopeless failure, or giving away your life to the ignorant, the common, and the vulgar. These are the sickly aims, the false ideals, of our age. Live! Live the wonderful life that is in you! Let nothing be lost upon you. Be always searching for new sensations. Be afraid of nothing. . . . A new Hedonism[5]—that is what our century wants. You might be its visible symbol. With your personality there is nothing you could not do. The world belongs to you for a season. . . . The moment I met you I saw that you were quite unconscious of what you really are, of what you really might be. There was so much in you that charmed me that I felt I must tell you something about yourself. I thought how tragic it would be if you were wasted. For there is such a little time that your youth will last—such a little time. The common hill-flowers wither, but they blossom again. The laburnum will be as yellow next June as it is now. In a month there will be purple stars on the clematis, and year after year the green night of its leaves will hold its purple stars. But we never get back our youth. The pulse of joy that beats in us at twenty, becomes sluggish. Our limbs fail, our senses rot. We degenerate into hideous puppets, haunted by the memory of the passions of which we were too much afraid, and the exquisite temptations that we had not the courage to yield to. Youth! Youth! There is absolutely nothing in the world but youth!"[6]

Dorian Gray listened, open-eyed and wondering. The spray of lilac fell from his hand upon the gravel. A furry bee came and buzzed round it for a moment. Then it began to scramble all over the oval stellated globe of the tiny blossoms. He watched it with that strange interest in trivial things that we try to develop when things of high import make us afraid, or when we are stirred by some new emotion for which we cannot find expression, or when some thought that terrifies us lays sudden siege to the brain and calls on us to yield. After a time the bee flew away. He saw it creeping into the stained trumpet of a Tyrian convolvulus.[7] The flower seemed to quiver, and then swayed gently to and fro.

5. One can trace old hedonism back to the teaching of Aristippus, foregrounding pleasure as the chief end of human action. Lord Henry's new hedonism offers an aesthetic refinement, privileging the acquisition of new sensations. The philosophy as practiced by Dorian Gray might have been described better as a new antinomianism. Dorian sees himself absolved by the portrait from the effects of a life of self-indulgence.

6. Henry's speech reflects Wilde's own synthesis of Pater, Arnold (worship of youth and fear of declining powers), Whistler (superiority of art to nature), Blake, and assorted French geniuses from Gautier to Huysmans.

7. The convolvulus, or bindweed, is native to Mediterranean limestone hills, and its presence in Basil's garden underscores the Edenic overtones of the scene.

Suddenly the painter appeared at the door of the studio, and made staccato signs for them to come in. They turned to each other, and smiled.

"I am waiting," he cried. "Do come in. The light is quite perfect, and you can bring your drinks."

They rose up, and sauntered down the walk together. Two green-and-white butterflies fluttered past them, and in the pear-tree at the corner of the garden a thrush began to sing.

"You are glad you have met me, Mr. Gray," said Lord Henry, looking at him.

"Yes, I am glad now. I wonder shall I always be glad?"

"Always! That is a dreadful word. It makes me shudder when I hear it. Women are so fond of using it. They spoil every romance by trying to make it last for ever. It is a meaningless word, too. The only difference between a caprice and a life-long passion is that the caprice lasts a little longer."

As they entered the studio, Dorian Gray put his hand upon Lord Henry's arm. "In that case, let our friendship be a caprice," he murmured, flushing at his own boldness, then stepped up on the platform and resumed his pose.

Lord Henry flung himself into a large wicker arm-chair, and watched him. The sweep and dash of the brush on the canvas made the only sound that broke the stillness, except when, now and then, Hallward stepped back to look at his work from a distance. In the slanting beams that streamed through the open doorway the dust danced and was golden. The heavy scent of the roses seemed to brood over everything.

After about a quarter of an hour Hallward stopped painting, looked for a long time at Dorian Gray, and then for a long time at the picture, biting the end of one of his huge brushes, and frowning. "It is quite finished," he cried at last, and stooping down he wrote his name in long vermilion letters[8] on the left-hand corner of the canvas.

Lord Henry came over and examined the picture. It was certainly a wonderful work of art, and a wonderful likeness as well.

"My dear fellow, I congratulate you most warmly," he said. "It is the finest portrait of modern times. Mr. Gray, come over and look at yourself."

The lad started, as if awakened from some dream. "Is it really finished?" he murmured, stepping down from the platform.

"Quite finished," said the painter. "And you have sat splendidly today. I am awfully obliged to you."

---

8. James McNeill Whistler (1834–1903), the American artist and friend of Wilde, would often sign his paintings in vermilion.

"That is entirely due to me," broke in Lord Henry. "Isn't it, Mr. Gray?"

Dorian made no answer, but passed listlessly in front of his picture and turned towards it. When he saw it he drew back, and his cheeks flushed for a moment with pleasure. A look of joy came into his eyes, as if he had recognized himself for the first time. He stood there motionless and in wonder, dimly conscious that Hallward was speaking to him, but not catching the meaning of his words. The sense of his own beauty came on him like a revelation. He had never felt it before. Basil Hallward's compliments had seemed to him to be merely the charming exaggerations of friendship. He had listened to them, laughed at them, forgotten them. They had not influenced his nature. Then had come Lord Henry Wotton with his strange panegyric on youth, his terrible warning of its brevity. That had stirred him at the time, and now, as he stood gazing at the shadow of his own loveliness, the full reality of the description flashed across him. Yes, there would be a day when his face would be wrinkled and wizen, his eyes dim and colourless, the grace of his figure broken and deformed. The scarlet would pass away from his lips, and the gold steal from his hair. The life that was to make his soul would mar his body. He would become dreadful, hideous, and uncouth.

As he thought of it, a sharp pang of pain struck through him like a knife, and made each delicate fibre of his nature quiver. His eyes deepened into amethyst, and across them came a mist of tears. He felt as if a hand of ice had been laid upon his heart.

"Don't you like it?" cried Hallward at last, stung a little by the lad's silence, not understanding what it meant.

"Of course he likes it," said Lord Henry. "Who wouldn't like it? It is one of the greatest things in modern art. I will give you anything you like to ask for it. I must have it."

"It is not my property, Harry."

"Whose property is it?"

"Dorian's, of course," answered the painter.

"He is a very lucky fellow."

"How sad it is!" murmured Dorian Gray, with his eyes still fixed upon his own portrait. "How sad it is! I shall grow old, and horrible, and dreadful. But this picture will remain always young. It will never be older than this particular day of June. . . . If it were only the other way! If it were I who was to be always young, and the picture that was to grow old! For that—for that—I would give everything! Yes, there is nothing in the whole world I would not give! I would give my soul for that!"

"You would hardly care for such an arrangement, Basil," cried Lord Henry, laughing. "It would be rather hard lines on your work."

"I should object very strongly, Harry," said Hallward.

Dorian Gray turned and looked at him. "I believe you would, Basil. You like your art better than your friends. I am no more to you than a green bronze figure. Hardly as much, I dare say."

The painter stared in amazement. It was so unlike Dorian to speak like that. What had happened? He seemed quite angry. His face was flushed and his cheeks burning.

"Yes," he continued, "I am less to you than your ivory Hermes or your silver Faun.[9] You will like them always. How long will you like me? Till I have my first wrinkle, I suppose. I know, now, that when one loses one's good looks, whatever they may be, one loses everything. Your picture has taught me that. Lord Henry Wotton is perfectly right. Youth is the only thing worth having. When I find that I am growing old, I shall kill myself."

Hallward turned pale, and caught his hand. "Dorian! Dorian!" he cried, "don't talk like that. I have never had such a friend as you, and I shall never have such another. You are not jealous of material things, are you?—you who are finer than any of them!"

"I am jealous of everything whose beauty does not die. I am jealous of the portrait you have painted of me. Why should it keep what I must lose? Every moment that passes takes something from me, and gives something to it. Oh, if it were only the other way! If the picture could change, and I could be always what I am now! Why did you paint it? It will mock me some day—mock me horribly!" The hot tears welled into his eyes; he tore his hand away, and, flinging himself on the divan, he buried his face in the cushions, as though he was praying.

"This is your doing, Harry," said the painter, bitterly.

Lord Henry shrugged his shoulders. "It is the real Dorian Gray—that is all."

"It is not."

"If it is not, what have I to do with it?"

"You should have gone away when I asked you," he muttered.

"I stayed when you asked me," was Lord Henry's answer.

"Harry, I can't quarrel with my two best friends at once, but between you both you have made me hate the finest piece of work I have ever done, and I will destroy it. What is it but canvas and colour? I will not let it come across our three lives and mar them."

Dorian Gray lifted his golden head from the pillow, and with pallid face and tear-stained eyes looked at him, as he walked over to the deal painting-table that was set beneath the high curtained window.

9. Hermes is the son of Zeus, wing-footed messenger of the gods, and inventor of the lyre. Mercury is his Latin name. A faun was a rural demigod of lustful disposition, portrayed as half-human with goat's legs. Fauns were deities of farmers and shepherds.

What was he doing there? His fingers were straying about among the litter of tin tubes and dry brushes, seeking for something. Yes, it was for the long palette-knife, with its thin blade of lithe steel. He had found it at last. He was going to rip up the canvas.

With a stifled sob the lad leaped from the couch, and, rushing over to Hallward, tore the knife out of his hand, and flung it to the end of the studio. "Don't, Basil, don't!" he cried. "It would be murder!"

"I am glad you appreciate my work at last, Dorian," said the painter, coldly, when he had recovered from his surprise. "I never thought you would."

"Appreciate it? I am in love with it, Basil. It is part of myself. I feel that."

"Well, as soon as you are dry, you shall be varnished, and framed, and sent home. Then you can do what you like with yourself." And he walked across the room and rang the bell for tea. "You will have tea, of course, Dorian? And so will you, Harry? Or do you object to such simple pleasures?"

"I adore simple pleasures," said Lord Henry. "They are the last refuge of the complex. But I don't like scenes, except on the stage. What absurd fellows you are, both of you! I wonder who it was defined man as a rational animal.[1] It was the most premature definition ever given. Man is many things, but he is not rational. I am glad he is not, after all: though I wish you chaps would not squabble over the picture. You had much better let me have it, Basil. This silly boy doesn't really want it, and I really do."

"If you let any one have it but me, Basil, I shall never forgive you!" cried Dorian Gray; "and I don't allow people to call me a silly boy."

"You know the picture is yours, Dorian. I gave it to you before it existed."

"And you know you have been a little silly, Mr. Gray, and that you don't really object to being reminded that you are extremely young."

"I should have objected very strongly this morning, Lord Henry."

"Ah! this morning! You have lived since then."

There came a knock at the door, and the butler entered with a laden tea-tray and set it down upon a small Japanese table. There was a rattle of cups and saucers and the hissing of a fluted Georgian urn. Two globe-shaped china dishes were brought in by a page. Dorian Gray went over and poured out the tea. The two men sauntered languidly to the table, and examined what was under the covers.

---

1. This definition of man, which predates Plato, was best known in the Latin formula *ratio animalis*. Although discredited in nearly every age, it has perversely survived to the present on the strength of tradition and style. Lord Henry's critique echoes that of Swift in *Gulliver's Travels*.

"Let us go to the theatre to-night," said Lord Henry. "There is sure to be something on, somewhere. I have promised to dine at White's,[2] but it is only with an old friend, so I can send him a wire to say that I am ill, or that I am prevented from coming in consequence of a subsequent engagement. I think that would be a rather nice excuse: it would have all the surprise of candour."

"It is such a bore putting on one's dress-clothes," muttered Hallward. "And, when one has them on, they are so horrid."

"Yes," answered Lord Henry, dreamily, "the costume of the nineteenth century is detestable. It is so sombre, so depressing. Sin is the only real colour-element left in modern life."

"You really must not say things like that before Dorian, Harry."

"Before which Dorian? The one who is pouring out tea for us, or the one in the picture?"

"Before either."

"I should like to come to the theatre with you, Lord Henry," said the lad.

"Then you shall come; and you will come too, Basil, won't you?"

"I can't, really. I would sooner not. I have a lot of work to do."

"Well, then, you and I will go alone, Mr. Gray."

"I should like that awfully."

The painter bit his lip and walked over, cup in hand, to the picture. "I shall stay with the real Dorian," he said, sadly.

"Is it the real Dorian?" cried the original of the portrait, strolling across to him. "Am I really like that?"

"Yes; you are just like that."

"How wonderful, Basil!"

"At least you are like it in appearance. But it will never alter," sighed Hallward. "That is something."

"What a fuss people make about fidelity!" exclaimed Lord Henry. "Why, even in love it is purely a question for physiology. It has nothing to do with our own will. Young men want to be faithful, and are not; old men want to be faithless, and cannot: that is all one can say."[3]

"Don't go to the theatre to-night, Dorian," said Hallward. "Stop and dine with me."

"I can't, Basil."

"Why?"

---

2. On St. James's Street, one of the older, established London clubs, known as a sporting and gambling club for the gentry. The then Prince of Wales, later King Edward VII, was a member.
3. Lord Henry underlines his view of the irreconcilable conflict of the will allied with conscience against the appetites and instincts perceived as forces of necessity. At least that is the way it appeared manifested in Darwinism and its corollaries to contemporary observers like Wilde.

"Because I have promised Lord Henry Wotton to go with him."

"He won't like you the better for keeping your promises. He always breaks his own. I beg you not to go."

Dorian Gray laughed and shook his head.

"I entreat you."

The lad hesitated, and looked over at Lord Henry, who was watching them from the tea-table with an amused smile.

"I must go, Basil," he answered.

"Very well," said Hallward; and he went over and laid down his cup on the tray. "It is rather late, and, as you have to dress, you had better lose no time. Good-bye, Harry. Good-bye, Dorian. Come and see me soon. Come to-morrow."

"Certainly."

"You won't forget?"

"No, of course not," cried Dorian.

"And . . . Harry!"

"Yes, Basil?"

"Remember what I asked you, when we were in the garden this morning."

"I have forgotten it."

"I trust you."

"I wish I could trust myself," said Lord Henry, laughing. "Come, Mr. Gray, my hansom[4] is outside, and I can drop you at your own place. Good-bye, Basil. It has been a most interesting afternoon."

As the door closed behind them, the painter flung himself down on a sofa, and a look of pain came into his face.

Chapter III[1]

At half-past twelve next day Lord Henry Wotton strolled from Curzon Street[2] over to the Albany[3] to call on his uncle, Lord Fermor, a genial if somewhat rough-mannered old bachelor, whom the outside world called selfish because it derived no particular benefit from him, but who was considered generous by Society as he fed the people who amused him. His father had been our ambassador at Madrid

---

4. A hired horse-drawn cab.
1. This marks the first of five new chapters added in the revised edition.
2. A fashionable area of central London, just to the east of Hyde Park and to the north of Green Park.
3. The building, once the former Piccadilly residence of the Duke of York, second son of George III, was converted into elegant private apartments in 1802 and is still regarded as one of the most exclusive addresses in London. Among its distinguished residents have been Lord Byron, Thomas Babington Macaulay, and Matthew G. ("Monk") Lewis. Ernest Worthing of *The Importance of Being Earnest* has his London residence there in apartment B.4.

when Isabella was young, and Prim[4] unthought of, but had retired from the Diplomatic Service in a capricious moment of annoyance on not being offered the Embassy at Paris, a post to which he considered that he was fully entitled by reason of his birth, his indolence, the good English of his dispatches, and his inordinate passion for pleasure. The son, who had been his father's secretary, had resigned along with his chief, somewhat foolishly as was thought at the time, and on succeeding some months later to the title, had set himself to the serious study of the great aristocratic art of doing absolutely nothing. He had two large town houses, but preferred to live in chambers[5] as it was less trouble, and took most of his meals at his club. He paid some attention to the management of his collieries in the Midland counties,[6] excusing himself for this taint of industry on the ground that the one advantage of having coal was that it enabled a gentleman to afford the decency of burning wood on his own hearth.[7] In politics he was a Tory, except when the Tories were in office, during which period he roundly abused them for being a pack of Radicals.[8] He was a hero to his valet,[9] who bullied him, and a terror to most of his relations, whom he bullied in turn. Only England could have produced him, and he always said that the country was going to the dogs. His principles were out of date, but there was a good deal to be said for his prejudices.

When Lord Henry entered the room, he found his uncle sitting in a rough shooting coat, smoking a cheroot[1] and grumbling over *The Times*.[2] "Well, Harry," said the old gentleman, "what brings you out so early? I thought you dandies never got up till two, and were not visible till five."

4. Isabella and Prim were two figures in nineteenth-century Spanish politics. Isabella II (1830–1904) reigned from 1843 to 1868. Both her accession to the throne and her abdication were engineered by soldier-statesman, Juan Prim (1814–70), whose career included military honors, titles, imprisonment, exile in England, and finally assassination.
5. I.e., Lord Fermor lived in rented rooms and leased his two townhouses.
6. The Midland counties are noted for mining and heavy industry, with Birmingham as the industrial hub. Midlands was also renowned hunt country and the site, in Nottinghamshire, of Sherwood Forest.
7. An oblique allusion to the view that a gentleman did not acquire money through trade or commerce.
8. Tories were more commonly referred to as conservatives in the later nineteenth century. They were led by Benjamin Disraeli and generally supported the policies of the Crown and the growth of the Empire. Radicals were associated with the Liberal party, led by William Gladstone, and favored social reform policies. But "Radicals" also referred to the "Philosophical Radicals" of an earlier generation, whose economic and social theories descended from Adam Smith, Jeremy Bentham, and Thomas Malthus.
9. A variation on the eighteenth-century phrase "Il n'ya point de héros pour son valet de chambre." No man is a hero to his valet, from a 13 August 1728 letter from Mme. A. M. Bignot de Cornuel to Mlle Assé.
1. A cigar originally made in Southern India or Manilla. This sort being truncated at both ends, the name was extended to all cigars with the two extremities cut off square, as distinguished from the ordinary cigar, which has one end pointed.
2. *The London Times*, the most popular and well-respected newspaper at the time.

"Pure family affection, I assure you, Uncle George. I want to get something out of you."

"Money, I suppose," said Lord Fermor, making a wry face. "Well, sit down and tell me all about it. Young people, nowadays, imagine that money is everything."

"Yes," murmured Lord Henry, settling his button-hole[3] in his coat; "and when they grow older they know it. But I don't want money. It is only people who pay their bills who want that, Uncle George, and I never pay mine. Credit is the capital of a younger son, and one lives charmingly upon it. Besides, I always deal with Dartmoor's tradesmen,[4] and consequently they never bother me. What I want is information: not useful information, of course; useless information."

"Well, I can tell you anything that is in an English Blue-book,[5] Harry, although those fellows nowadays write a lot of nonsense. When I was in the Diplomatic,[6] things were much better. But I hear they let them in now by examination. What can you expect? Examinations, sir, are pure humbug from beginning to end. If a man is a gentleman, he knows quite enough, and if he is not a gentleman, whatever he knows is bad for him."

"Mr. Dorian Gray does not belong to Blue-books, Uncle George," said Lord Henry, languidly.

"Mr. Dorian Gray? Who is he?" asked Lord Fermor, knitting his bushy white eyebrows.

"That is what I have come to learn, Uncle George. Or rather, I know who he is. He is the last Lord Kelso's[7] grandson. His mother was a Devereux, Lady Margaret Devereux. I want you to tell me about his mother. What was she like? Whom did she marry? You have known nearly everybody in your time, so you might have known her. I am very much interested in Mr. Gray at present. I have only just met him."

"Kelso's grandson!" echoed the old gentleman—"Kelso's grandson! . . . Of course. . . . I knew his mother intimately. I believe I was at her christening. She was an extraordinarily beautiful girl, Margaret

---

3. A flower worn through the lapel buttonhole: hence the popular name. Throughout the manuscript, Wilde alternates the spelling between buttonhole and button-hole.
4. Dartmoor is an area of in the southwest of England and consequently quite far from London, so Lord Henry is joking that tradesmen have too far to travel to pursue their bills with him.
5. Parliamentary reports: the most memorable treated social abuses in the nineteenth century.
6. The British Diplomatic Service. Prior to 1856 (when examinations were instituted), the main criteria for admission to the BDS was genealogy rather than merit.
7. Kelso is a place in Scotland and the family seat of Sir George Brisbane Scott-Douglas, whom Wilde visited and considered "a type of old fashioned propriety" (*Letters* 273n). Wilde habitually named his characters after places and his fictitious places after friends and acquaintances. Lord Henry's name comes from Wotton-under-Edge in Gloucestershire, near the home of More Adey, Wilde's friend.

Devereux, and made all the men frantic by running away with a penniless young fellow, a mere nobody, sir, a subaltern in a foot regiment, or something of that kind. Certainly. I remember the whole thing as if it happened yesterday. The poor chap was killed in a duel at Spa a few months after the marriage. There was an ugly story about it. They said Kelso got some rascally adventurer, some Belgian brute, to insult his son-in-law in public, paid him, sir, to do it, paid him, and that the fellow spitted his man as if he had been a pigeon. The thing was hushed up, but, egad, Kelso ate his chop alone at the club for some time afterwards. He brought his daughter back with him, I was told, and she never spoke to him again. Oh, yes; it was a bad business. The girl died too, died within a year. So she left a son, did she? I had forgotten that. What sort of boy is he? If he is like his mother he must be a good-looking chap."

"He is very good-looking," assented Lord Henry.

"I hope he will fall into proper hands," continued the old man. "He should have a pot of money waiting for him if Kelso did the right thing by him. His mother had money too. All the Selby property came to her, through her grandfather. Her grandfather hated Kelso, thought him a mean dog. He was, too. Came to Madrid once when I was there. Egad, I was ashamed of him. The Queen used to ask me about the English noble who was always quarrelling with the cabmen about their fares. They made quite a story of it. I didn't dare show my face at Court for a month. I hope he treated his grandson better than he did the jarvies."[8]

"I don't know," answered Lord Henry. "I fancy that the boy will be well off. He is not of age yet. He has Selby, I know. He told me so. And . . . his mother was very beautiful?"

"Margaret Devereux was one of the loveliest creatures I ever saw, Harry. What on earth induced her to behave as she did, I never could understand. She could have married anybody she chose. Carlington was mad after her. She was romantic, though. All the women of that family were. The men were a poor lot, but, egad! the women were wonderful. Carlington went on his knees to her. Told me so himself. She laughed at him, and there wasn't a girl in London at the time who wasn't after him. And by the way, Harry, talking about silly marriages, what is this humbug your father tells me about Dartmoor wanting to marry an American? Ain't English girls good enough for him?"

"It is rather fashionable to marry Americans just now, Uncle George."

"I'll back English women against the world, Harry," said Lord Fermor, striking the table with his fist.

8. Cabdrivers.

"The betting is on the Americans."

"They don't last, I am told," muttered his uncle.

"A long engagement exhausts them, but they are capital at a stee-plechase.[9] They take things flying. I don't think Dartmoor has a chance."

"Who are her people?" grumbled the old gentleman. "Has she got any?"

Lord Henry shook his head. "American girls are as clever at con-cealing their parents, as English women are at concealing their past," he said, rising to go.

"They are pork-packers, I suppose?"

"I hope so, Uncle George, for Dartmoor's sake. I am told that pork-packing is the most lucrative profession in America, after politics."[1]

"Is she pretty?"

"She behaves as if she was beautiful. Most American women do. It is the secret of their charm."[2]

"Why can't these American women stay in their own country? They are always telling us that it is the Paradise for women."

"It is. That is the reason why, like Eve, they are so excessively anx-ious to get out of it," said Lord Henry. "Good-bye, Uncle George. I shall be late for lunch, if I stop any longer. Thanks for giving me the information I wanted. I always like to know everything about my new friends, and nothing about my old ones."

"Where are you lunching, Harry?"

"At Aunt Agatha's. I have asked myself and Mr. Gray. He is her lat-est *protégé*."

"Humph! tell your Aunt Agatha, Harry, not to bother me any more with her charity appeals. I am sick of them. Why, the good woman thinks that I have nothing to do but to write cheques for her silly fads."

"All right, Uncle George, I'll tell her, but it won't have any effect. Philanthropic people lose all sense of humanity. It is their distin-guishing characteristic."

The old gentleman growled approvingly, and rang the bell for his servant. Lord Henry passed up the low arcade into Burlington Street, and turned his steps in the direction of Berkeley Square.[3]

So that was the story of Dorian Gray's parentage. Crudely as it had

9. An obstacle (horse) race run over a measured course. Henry uses the reference to play off his uncle's metaphor.

1. Wilde had visited America in 1882–83 and again the following year. He knew enough about America to understand the punning connection between "pork-packing" (with the same connotations as "pork barrel") and politics suggested here, but the reference is primarily aimed at nouveau riche Americans who had made their money through commerce.

2. Wilde canceled the following in MS for this added chapter: "'Clever?' / 'So clever that if Dartmoor doesn't propose to her before the end of the week, she is quite certain to pro-pose to him.' / 'He hasn't got a chance, then?' / 'I don't think so.'"

3. Regarded as the finest square in London.

been told to him, it had yet stirred him by its suggestion of a strange, almost modern romance. A beautiful woman risking everything for a mad passion. A few wild weeks of happiness cut short by a hideous, treacherous crime. Months of voiceless agony, and then a child born in pain. The mother snatched away by death, the boy left to solitude and the tyranny of an old and loveless man. Yes; it was an interesting background. It posed the lad, made him more perfect as it were. Behind every exquisite thing that existed, there was something tragic. Worlds had to be in travail, that the meanest flower might blow.[4] . . . And how charming he had been at dinner the night before, as with startled eyes and lips parted in frightened pleasure he had sat opposite to him at the club, the red candleshades staining to a richer rose the wakening wonder of his face. Talking to him was like playing upon an exquisite violin. He answered to every touch and thrill of the bow. . . . There was something terribly enthralling in the exercise of influence. No other activity was like it. To project one's soul into some gracious form, and let it tarry there for a moment; to hear one's own intellectual views echoed back to one with all the added music of passion and youth; to convey one's temperament into another as though it were a subtle fluid or a strange perfume: there was a real joy in that—perhaps the most satisfying joy left to us in an age so limited and vulgar as our own, an age grossly carnal in its pleasures, and grossly common in its aims. . . . He was a marvellous type, too, this lad, whom by so curious a chance he had met in Basil's studio, or could be fashioned into a marvellous type, at any rate. Grace was his, and the white purity of boyhood, and beauty such as old Greek marbles kept for us. There was nothing that one could not do with him. He could be made a Titan[5] or a toy. What a pity it was that such beauty was destined to fade! . . . And Basil? From a psychological point of view, how interesting he was! The new manner in art, the fresh mode of looking at life, suggested so strangely by the merely visible presence of one who was unconscious of it all; the silent spirit that dwelt in dim woodland, and walked unseen in open field, suddenly showing herself, Dryad-like[6] and not afraid, because in his soul who sought for her there had been wakened that wonderful vision to which alone are wonderful things revealed; the mere shapes and patterns of things becoming, as it were, refined, and gaining a kind of symbolical value, as though they were themselves patterns of some other and more perfect form whose shadow they made real: how

---

4. The phrase evokes the famous line from Wordsworth's "Ode: Intimations of Immortality from Recollections of Early Childhood": "the meanest flower that blows can give / Thoughts that do often lie too deep for tears."
5. One of the twelve giant gods and goddesses of Greek mythology, children of Uranus and Gaea, and, after them, the earliest of the gods.
6. Dryads were nymphs of woods and trees in Greek mythology.

strange it all was! He remembered something like it in history. Was it not Plato, that artist in thought, who had first analyzed it? Was it not Buonarrotti[7] who had carved it in the coloured marbles of a sonnet-sequence? But in our own century it was strange. . . . Yes; he would try to be to Dorian Gray what, without knowing it, the lad was to the painter who had fashioned the wonderful portrait. He would seek to dominate him—had already, indeed, half done so. He would make that wonderful spirit his own. There was something fascinating in this son of Love and Death.

Suddenly he stopped, and glanced up at the houses. He found that he had passed his aunt's some distance, and, smiling to himself, turned back.[8] When he entered the somewhat sombre hall, the butler told him that they had gone in to lunch. He gave one of the footmen his hat and stick, and passed into the dining-room.

"Late as usual, Harry," cried his aunt, shaking her head at him.

He invented a facile excuse, and having taken the vacant seat next to her, looked round to see who was there. Dorian bowed to him shyly from the end of the table, a flush of pleasure stealing into his cheek. Opposite was the Duchess of Harley, a lady of admirable good-nature and good temper, much liked by every one who knew her, and of those ample architectural proportions that in women who are not Duchesses are described by contemporary historians as stoutness. Next to her sat, on her right, Sir Thomas Burdon, a Radical member of Parliament, who followed his leader in public life, and in private life followed the best cooks, dining with the Tories, and thinking with the Liberals, in accordance with a wise and well-known rule. The post on her left was occupied by Mr. Erskine of Treadley, an old gentleman of considerable charm and culture, who had fallen, however, into bad habits of silence, having, as he explained once to Lady Agatha, said everything that he had to say before he was thirty. His own neighbour was Mrs. Vandeleur, one of his aunt's oldest friends, a perfect saint amongst women, but so dreadfully dowdy that she reminded one of a badly bound hymn-book. Fortunately for him she had on the other side Lord Faudel, a most intelligent middle-aged mediocrity, as bald[9] as a Ministerial statement in the House of Commons, with whom she was conversing in that intensely earnest manner which is the one unpardonable error, as he remarked once himself, that all really good people fall into, and from which none of them ever quite escape.

"We are talking about poor Dartmoor, Lord Henry," cried the

7. Originally appeared as Buonarotti, a typo for Michelangelo Buonarrotti (1475–1564), the Italian Renaissance master, who was a painter, sculptor, and poet.
8. Wilde canceled the MS reading: "and wondering if he, like Basil, was going to be always wrapped in dream."
9. The pun on blunt and unadorned leaves the reader to decide if the description is of Lord Faudel's appearance or demeanor.

Duchess, nodding pleasantly to him across the table. "Do you think he will really marry this fascinating young person?"

"I believe she has made up her mind to propose to him, Duchess."

"How dreadful!" exclaimed Lady Agatha. "Really, some one should interfere."

"I am told, on excellent authority, that her father keeps an American dry-goods store," said Sir Thomas Burdon, looking supercilious.

"My uncle has already suggested pork-packing Sir Thomas."

"Dry-goods! What are American dry-goods?"[1] asked the Duchess, raising her large hands in wonder, and accentuating the verb.

"American novels," answered Lord Henry, helping himself to some quail.

The Duchess looked puzzled.

"Don't mind him, my dear," whispered Lady Agatha. "He never means anything that he says."

"When America was discovered," said the Radical member, and he began to give some wearisome facts. Like all people who try to exhaust a subject, he exhausted his listeners. The Duchess sighed, and exercised her privilege of interruption. "I wish to goodness it never had been discovered at all!" she exclaimed. "Really, our girls have no chance nowadays. It is most unfair."

"Perhaps, after all, America never has been discovered," said Mr. Erskine; "I myself would say that it had merely been detected."

"Oh! but I have seen specimens of the inhabitants," answered the Duchess, vaguely. "I must confess that most of them are extremely pretty. And they dress well, too. They get all their dresses in Paris. I wish I could afford to do the same."

"They say that when good Americans die they go to Paris," chuckled Sir Thomas, who had a large wardrobe of Humour's cast-off clothes.

"Really! And where do bad Americans go to when they die?" inquired the Duchess.

"They go to America," murmured Lord Henry.

Sir Thomas frowned. "I am afraid that your nephew is prejudiced against that great country," he said to Lady Agatha. "I have travelled all over it, in cars provided by the directors, who, in such matters, are extremely civil. I assure you that it is an education to visit it."

"But must we really see Chicago in order to be educated?" asked Mr. Erskine, plaintively. "I don't feel up to the journey."

Sir Thomas waved his hand. "Mr. Erskine of Treadley has the world on his shelves. We practical men like to see things, not to read about them. The Americans are an extremely interesting people. They are

---

1. American dry goods are textiles, clothes, notions, and the like. British dry goods, meaning groceries not liquid, would refer chiefly to produce, especially grains.

absolutely reasonable. I think that is their distinguishing characteristic. Yes, Mr. Erskine, an absolutely reasonable people. I assure you
there is no nonsense about the Americans."

"How dreadful!" cried Lord Henry. "I can stand brute force, but
brute reason is quite unbearable. There is something unfair about its
use. It is hitting below the intellect."

"I do not understand you," said Sir Thomas, growing rather red.

"I do, Lord Henry," murmured Mr. Erskine, with a smile.

"Paradoxes are all very well in their way . . ." rejoined the Baronet.

"Was that a paradox?" asked Mr. Erskine. "I did not think so. Perhaps it was. Well, the way of paradoxes is the way of truth. To test
Reality we must see it on the tight-rope. When the Verities become
acrobats we can judge them."[2]

"Dear me!" said Lady Agatha, "how you men argue! I am sure I
never can make out what you are talking about. Oh! Harry, I am quite
vexed with you. Why do you try to persuade our nice Mr. Dorian Gray
to give up the East End? I assure you he would be quite invaluable.
They would love his playing."

"I want him to play to me," cried Lord Henry, smiling, and he
looked down the table and caught a bright answering glance.

"But they are so unhappy in Whitechapel,"[3] continued Lady
Agatha.

"I can sympathize with everything, except suffering," said Lord
Henry, shrugging his shoulders. "I cannot sympathize with that. It is
too ugly, too horrible, too distressing. There is something terribly
morbid in the modern sympathy with pain. One should sympathize
with the colour, the beauty, the joy of life. The less said about life's
sores the better."

"Still, the East End is a very important problem," remarked Sir
Thomas, with a grave shake of the head.

"Quite so," answered the young lord. "It is the problem of slavery,
and we try to solve it by amusing the slaves."

The politician looked at him keenly. "What change do you propose,
then?" he asked.

Lord Henry laughed. "I don't desire to change anything in England
except the weather," he answered. "I am quite content with philo-
sophic contemplation. But, as the nineteenth century has gone bankrupt through an over-expenditure of sympathy, I would suggest that
we should appeal to Science to put us straight. The advantage of the
emotions is that they lead us astray, and the advantage of Science is
that it is not emotional."

2. Wilde added "Paradoxes are all . . . judge them" to the margin of the MS.
3. An economically depressed area of London, now notorious for the Jack the Ripper murders.

"But we have such grave responsibilities," ventured Mrs. Vandeleur, timidly.

"Terribly grave," echoed Lady Agatha.

Lord Henry looked over at Mr. Erskine. "Humanity takes itself too seriously. It is the world's original sin. If the caveman had known how to laugh, History would have been different."

"You are really very comforting," warbled the Duchess. "I have always felt rather guilty when I came to see your dear aunt, for I take no interest at all in the East End. For the future I shall be able to look her in the face without a blush."

"A blush is very becoming, Duchess," remarked Lord Henry.

"Only when one is young," she answered. "When an old woman like myself blushes, it is a very bad sign. Ah! Lord Henry, I wish you would tell me how to become young again."

He thought for a moment. "Can you remember any great error that you committed in your early days, Duchess?" he asked, looking at her across the table.

"A great many, I fear," she cried.

"Then commit them over again," he said, gravely. "To get back one's youth, one has merely to repeat one's follies."

"A delightful theory!" she exclaimed. "I must put it into practice."

"A dangerous theory!" came from Sir Thomas's tight lips. Lady Agatha shook her head, but could not help being amused. Mr. Erskine listened.

"Yes," he continued, "that is one of the great secrets of life. Nowadays most people die of a sort of creeping common sense, and discover when it is too late that the only things one never regrets are one's mistakes."

A laugh ran round the table.

He played with the idea, and grew wilful; tossed it into the air and transformed it; let it escape and recaptured it; made it iridescent with fancy, and winged it with paradox. The praise of folly,[4] as he went on, soared into a philosophy, and Philosophy herself became young, and catching the mad music of Pleasure, wearing, one might fancy, her wine-stained robe and wreath of ivy, danced like a Bacchante over the hills of life, and mocked the slow Silenus for being sober.[5] Facts fled before her like frightened forest things. Her white feet trod the huge press at which wise Omar sits,[6] till the seething grape-juice rose

4. The allusion is to Erasmus's *In Praise of Folly*. This scene has been noted especially by Wilde's biographers as illustrative of Wilde's best table-talk manner.
5. A leader of the satyrs and a notoriously drunken follower of Bacchus in mythology. Bacchante, above, refer to Maenads, female worshipers of Bacchus whose orgiastic rites were performed in the wild.
6. The Persian poet-astronomer whose work was immortalized in English by Edward FitzGerald's rendering of *The Rubaiyat of Omar Khayyam*, a poem much admired by the

round her bare limbs in waves of purple bubbles, or crawled in red foam over the vat's black, dripping, sloping sides. It was an extraordinary improvisation. He felt that the eyes of Dorian Gray were fixed on him, and the consciousness that amongst his audience there was one whose temperament he wished to fascinate, seemed to give his wit keenness, and to lend colour to his imagination. He was brilliant, fantastic, irresponsible. He charmed his listeners out of themselves, and they followed his pipe laughing. Dorian Gray never took his gaze off him, but sat like one under a spell, smiles chasing each other over his lips, and wonder growing grave in his darkening eyes.

At last, liveried in the costume of the age, Reality entered the room in the shape of a servant to tell the Duchess that her carriage was waiting. She wrung her hands in mock despair. "How annoying!" she cried. "I must go. I have to call for my husband at the club, to take him to some absurd meeting at Willis's Rooms,[7] where he is going to be in the chair. If I am late he is sure to be furious, and I couldn't have a scene in this bonnet. It is far too fragile. A harsh word would ruin it. No, I must go, dear Agatha. Good-bye, Lord Henry, you are quite delightful, and dreadfully demoralizing. I am sure I don't know what to say about your views. You must come and dine with us some night. Tuesday? Are you disengaged Tuesday?"

"For you I would throw over anybody, Duchess," said Lord Henry, with a bow.

"Ah! that is very nice, and very wrong of you," she cried; "so mind you come;" and she swept out of the room, followed by Lady Agatha and the other ladies.

When Lord Henry had sat down again,[8] Mr. Erskine moved round, and taking a chair close to him, placed his hand upon his arm.

"You talk books away," he said; "why don't you write one?"

"I am too fond of reading books to care to write them, Mr. Erskine. I should like to write a novel certainly, a novel that would be as lovely as a Persian carpet and as unreal. But there is no literary public in England for anything except newspapers, primers, and encyclopædias. Of all people in the world the English have the least sense of the beauty of literature."

"I fear you are right," answered Mr. Erskine. "I myself used to have literary ambitions, but I gave them up long ago. And now, my dear

---

Decadents. Omar drank wine to forget the pangs of both mortality and his loss of faith in God.

7. Formerly Almack's Assembly Rooms, a club in King Street frequented by Wilde. It was in the eighteenth century one of the most fashionable clubs for ladies and gentlemen.

8. Wilde canceled the following in manuscript (MS): "he poured himself a glass of green Chartreuse and asked the butler for a light."

young friend, if you will allow me to call you so, may I ask if you really meant all that you said to us at lunch?"

"I quite forget what I said," smiled Lord Henry. "Was it all very bad?"

"Very bad indeed. In fact I consider you extremely dangerous, and if anything happens to our good Duchess we shall all look on you as being primarily responsible. But I should like to talk to you about life. The generation into which I was born was tedious. Some day, when you are tired of London, come down to Treadley, and expound to me your philosophy of pleasure over some admirable Burgundy I am fortunate enough to possess."

"I shall be charmed. A visit to Treadley would be a great privilege. It has a perfect host, and a perfect library."

"You will complete it," answered the old gentleman, with a courteous bow. "And now I must bid good-bye to your excellent aunt. I am due at the Athenæum.⁹ It is the hour when we sleep there."

"All of you, Mr. Erskine?"

"Forty of us, in forty arm-chairs. We are practising for an English Academy of Letters."

Lord Henry laughed, and rose. "I am going to the Park," he cried.

As he was passing out of the door Dorian Gray touched him on the arm. "Let me come with you," he murmured.

"But I thought you had promised Basil Hallward to go and see him," answered Lord Henry.

"I would sooner come with you; yes, I feel I must come with you. Do let me. And you will promise to talk to me all the time? No one talks so wonderfully as you do."

"Ah! I have talked quite enough for to-day," said Lord Henry, smiling. "All I want now is to look at life. You may come and look at it with me, if you care to."

Chapter IV¹

One afternoon, a month later, Dorian Gray was reclining in a luxurious arm-chair, in the little library² of Lord Henry's house in Mayfair.³ It was, in its way, a very charming room, with its high panelled wainscoting of olive-stained oak, its cream-coloured frieze and ceiling of raised plaster-work, and its brickdust felt carpet strewn with

9. The leading literary club of London, located in Pall Mall.
1. The former chapter 3 in the *Lippincott's Magazine* edition.
2. Lord Henry's library bears a striking resemblance in several details to Wilde's library in his Tite Street, Chelsea, home.
3. The well-to-do area bounded by Park-lane, Picadilly, Bond-street, and Brook-street.

silk long-fringed Persian rugs. On a tiny satin-wood table stood a statuette by Clodion,[4] and beside it lay a copy of "Les Cent Nouvelles,"[5]
bound for Margaret of Valois by Clovis Eve,[6] and powdered with the
gilt daisies that Queen had selected for her device. Some large blue
china jars and parrot-tulips were ranged on the mantelshelf, and
through the small leaded panes of the window streamed the apricot-
coloured light of a summer day in London.

Lord Henry had not yet come in. He was always late on principle,
his principle being that punctuality is the thief of time. So the lad was
looking rather sulky, as with listless fingers he turned over the pages
of an elaborately-illustrated edition of "Manon Lescaut"[7] that he had
found in one of the bookcases. The formal monotonous ticking of the
Louis Quatorze clock[8] annoyed him. Once or twice he thought of
going away.

At last he heard a step outside, and the door opened. "How late you
are, Harry!" he murmured.

"I am afraid it is not Harry, Mr. Gray," answered a shrill voice.

He glanced quickly round, and rose to his feet. "I beg your pardon.
I thought—"

"You thought it was my husband. It is only his wife. You must let
me introduce myself. I know you quite well by your photographs. I
think my husband has got seventeen of them."

"Not seventeen, Lady Henry?"

"Well, eighteen, then. And I saw you with him the other night at
the Opera." She laughed nervously as she spoke, and watched him
with her vague forget-me-not eyes. She was a curious woman, whose
dresses always looked as if they had been designed in a rage and put
on in a tempest. She was usually in love with somebody, and, as her
passion was never returned, she had kept all her illusions. She tried
to look picturesque, but only succeeded in being untidy. Her name
was Victoria, and she had a perfect mania for going to church.

"That was at 'Lohengrin,'[9] Lady Henry, I think?"

"Yes; it was at dear 'Lohengrin.' I like Wagner's music better than

---

4. Claude Michel Clodion (1738–1814) was specially noted for his antique subjects.
5. A collection of bawdy French tales (1462), perennially a favorite of illustrators and collectors and prized for its spirit of pleasant indecency.
6. Margaret of Valois (1553–1615), married to Henry of Navarre, was as notorious for her
   dissolute behavior as she was renowned for her beauty. Clovis Eve (1584–1635) was a
   French bookbinder and illustrator for the royal court, remembered as the designer of the
   "fanfare" style of bindery decoration admired by the Aesthetes.
7. Novel (1731) by Abbé de Prevost, the theme of which is the struggle between romantic love
   and self-indulgence. It was considered scandalous by the Victorians, who judged nearly all
   French novels too graphic.
8. A clock designed in the baroque manner of the period of Louis XIV of France
   (1638–1715).
9. Lohengrin, the Richard Wagner (1813–83) opera, was first performed in 1850. It was
   based on one of the Grail cycle stories, that of Lohengrin, Knight of the Swan.

anybody's. It is so loud that one can talk the whole time without other people hearing what one says. That is a great advantage: don't you think so, Mr. Gray?"

The same nervous staccato laugh broke from her thin lips, and her fingers began to play with a long tortoise-shell paper-knife.

Dorian smiled, and shook his head: "I am afraid I don't think so, Lady Henry. I never talk during music—at least, during good music. If one hears bad music, it is one's duty to drown it in conversation."

"Ah! that is one of Harry's views, isn't it, Mr. Gray? I always hear Harry's views from his friends. It is the only way I get to know of them. But you must not think I don't like good music. I adore it, but I am afraid of it. It makes me too romantic. I have simply worshipped pianists—two at a time, sometimes, Harry tells me. I don't know what it is about them. Perhaps it is that they are foreigners. They all are, ain't they? Even those that are born in England become foreigners after a time, don't they? It is so clever of them, and such a compliment to art. Makes it quite cosmopolitan, doesn't it? You have never been to any of my parties, have you, Mr. Gray? You must come. I can't afford orchids, but I share no expense in foreigners. They make one's rooms look so picturesque. But here is Harry!—Harry, I came in to look for you, to ask you something—I forget what it was—and I found Mr. Gray here. We have had such a pleasant chat about music. We have quite the same ideas. No; I think our ideas are quite different. But he has been most pleasant. I am so glad I've seen him."

"I am charmed, my love, quite charmed," said Lord Henry, elevating his dark crescent-shaped eyebrows and looking at them both with an amused smile. "So sorry I am late, Dorian. I went to look after a piece of old brocade in Wardour Street,[1] and had to bargain for hours for it. Nowadays people know the price of everything, and the value of nothing."[2]

"I am afraid I must be going," exclaimed Lady Henry, breaking an awkward silence with her silly sudden laugh. "I have promised to drive with the Duchess. Good-bye, Mr. Gray. Good-bye, Harry. You are dining out, I suppose? So am I. Perhaps I shall see you at Lady Thornbury's."

"I dare say, my dear," said Lord Henry, shutting the door behind her, as, looking like a bird of paradise that had been out all night in the rain, she flitted out of the room, leaving a faint odour of frangipani.[3] Then he lit a cigarette, and flung himself down on the sofa.

"Never marry a woman with straw-coloured hair, Dorian," he said, after a few puffs.

1. Famous for antique shops.
2. This epigram originally appeared in *Lady Windermere's Fan* near the end of act 3 as Lord Darlington's definition to Cecil Graham of a cynic.
3. A perfume derived from the Plumeria flower.

"Why, Harry?"

"Because they are so sentimental."

"But I like sentimental people."

"Never marry at all, Dorian. Men marry because they are tired; women, because they are curious: both are disappointed."

"I don't think I am likely to marry, Harry. I am too much in love. That is one of your aphorisms. I am putting it into practice, as I do everything that you say."

"Who are you in love with?" asked Lord Henry, after a pause.

"With an actress," said Dorian Gray, blushing.

Lord Henry shrugged his shoulders. "That is a rather common-place *début*."

"You would not say so if you saw her, Harry."

"Who is she?"

"Her name is Sibyl Vane."

"Never heard of her."

"No one has. People will some day, however. She is a genius."

"My dear boy, no woman is a genius. Women are a decorative sex. They never have anything to say, but they say it charmingly. Women represent the triumph of matter over mind, just as men represent the triumph of mind over morals."

"Harry, how can you?"

"My dear Dorian, it is quite true. I am analysing women at present, so I ought to know. The subject is not so abstruse as I thought it was. I find that, ultimately, there are only two kinds of women, the plain and the coloured. The plain women are very useful. If you want to gain a reputation for respectability, you have merely to take them down to supper. The other women are very charming. They commit one mistake, however. They paint in order to try and look young. Our grand-mothers painted in order to try and talk brilliantly. *Rouge and esprit*[4] used to go together. That is all over now. As long as a woman can look ten years younger than her own daughter, she is perfectly satisfied. As for conversation, there are only five women in London worth talking to, and two of these can't be admitted into decent society. However, tell me about your genius. How long have you known her?"

"Ah! Harry, your views terrify me."

"Never mind that. How long have you known her?"

"About three weeks."

"And where did you come across her?"

"I will tell you, Harry; but you mustn't be unsympathetic about it. After all, it never would have happened if I had not met you. You

---

4. A combination of beauty and wit (literally, makeup and liveliness of mind). Compare this to Max Beerbohm's argument in "A Defense of Cosmetics," in *The Yellow Book* 1 (April 1894): 65–82.

filled me with a wild desire to know everything about life. For days after I met you, something seemed to throb in my veins. As I lounged in the park, or strolled down Piccadilly, I used to look at every one who passed me and wonder, with a mad curiosity, what sort of lives they led. Some of them fascinated me. Others filled me with terror. There was an exquisite poison in the air. I had a passion for sensa-tions. . . . Well, one evening about seven o'clock, I determined to go out in search of some adventure. I felt that this grey, monstrous Lon-don of ours, with its myriads of people, its sordid sinners, and its splendid sins, as you once phrased it, must have something in store for me. I fancied a thousand things. The mere danger gave me a sense of delight. I remembered what you had said to me on that wonderful evening when we first dined together, about the search for beauty being the real secret of life. I don't know what I expected, but I went out and wandered eastward, soon losing my way in a labyrinth of grimy streets and black, grassless squares. About half-past eight I passed by an absurd little theatre, with great flaring gas-jets and gaudy play-bills. A hideous Jew, in the most amazing waistcoat I ever beheld in my life, was standing at the entrance, smoking a vile cigar. He had greasy ringlets, and an enormous diamond blazed in the cen-tre of a soiled shirt. 'Have a box, my Lord?' he said, when he saw me, and he took off his hat with an air of gorgeous servility. There was something about him, Harry, that amused me. He was such a mon-ster. You will laugh at me, I know, but I really went in and paid a whole guinea for the stage-box. To the present day I can't make out why I did so; and yet if I hadn't—my dear Harry, if I hadn't, I should have missed the greatest romance of my life. I see you are laughing. It is horrid of you!"

"I am not laughing, Dorian; at least I am not laughing at you. But you should not say the greatest romance of your life. You should say the first romance of your life. You will always be loved, and you will always be in love with love. A *grande passion* is the privilege of people who have nothing to do. That is the one use of the idle classes of a country. Don't be afraid. There are exquisite things in store for you. This is merely the beginning."

"Do you think my nature so shallow?" cried Dorian Gray angrily.

"No; I think your nature so deep."

"How do you mean?"

"My dear boy, the people who love only once in their lives are really the shallow people. What they call their loyalty, and their fidelity, I call either the lethargy of custom or their lack of imagina-tion. Faithfulness is to the emotional life what consistency is to the life of the intellect—simply a confession of failure. Faithfulness! I must analyse it some day. The passion for property is in it. There are many things that we would throw away if we were not afraid that others might pick them up. But I don't want to interrupt you. Go on with your story."

"Well, I found myself seated in a horrid little private box, with a vulgar drop-scene[5] staring me in the face. I looked out from behind the curtain, and surveyed the house. It was a tawdry affair, all Cupids and cornucopias, like a third-rate wedding-cake. The gallery and pit were fairly full, but the two rows of dingy stalls were quite empty, and there was hardly a person in what I suppose they called the dress-circle.[6] Women went about with oranges and ginger-beer, and there was a terrible consumption of nuts going on."

"It must have been just like the palmy days of the British Drama."

"Just like, I should fancy, and very depressing. I began to wonder what on earth I should do, when I caught sight of the play-bill. What do you think the play was, Harry?"

"I should think 'The Idiot Boy, or Dumb but Innocent.'[7] Our fathers used to like that sort of piece, I believe. The longer I live, Dorian, the more keenly I feel that whatever was good enough for our fathers is not good enough for us. In art, as in politics, *les grandpéres ont toujours tort.*"[8]

"This play was good enough for us, Harry. It was 'Romeo and Juliet.' I must admit that I was rather annoyed at the idea of seeing Shakespeare done in such a wretched hole of a place. Still, I felt interested, in a sort of way. At any rate, I determined to wait for the first act. There was a dreadful orchestra, presided over by a young Hebrew who sat at a cracked piano, that nearly drove me away, but at last the drop-scene was drawn up, and the play began. Romeo was a stout elderly gentleman, with corked eyebrows, a husky tragedy voice, and a figure like a beer-barrel. Mercutio was almost as bad. He was played by the low-comedian, who had introduced gags of his own and was on most friendly terms with the pit. They were both as grotesque as the scenery, and that looked as if it had come out of a country-booth. But Juliet! Harry, imagine a girl, hardly seventeen years of age, with a little flower-like face, a small Greek head with plaited coils of dark-brown hair, eyes that were violet wells of passion, lips that were like the petals of a rose. She was the loveliest

---

5. A stage curtain on which a scene or design has been painted. At the time, scenes were usually stylized landscapes or gardens.
6. Gallery seats are the cheapest in the theater, usually furthest from the stage. The pit is located in the ground floor, behind the stalls. The stalls are ground floor seats at the front of the theater. The dress circle is a circular row of seats in a theater, usually the gallery next above the floor. The spectators seated there were originally expected to be in dress-clothes.
7. The title is Wilde's parody of a type of rustic melodrama that still appealed to lower-class audiences in the 1890s but that had reached the peak of its appeal in the mid-nineteenth century, inspired, perhaps, by the novels of Walter Scott and the philosopher-rustics of William Wordsworth. There was a play, *The Idiot of the Mill*, which may have inspired the mocking title (*Dorian Gray*, Murray 241).
8. "Grandfathers are always wrong": a most un-Victorian sentiment.

thing I had ever seen in my life.[9] You said to me once that pathos left you unmoved, but that beauty, mere beauty, could fill your eyes with tears. I tell you, Harry, I could hardly see this girl for the mist of tears that came across me. And her voice—I never heard such a voice. It was very low at first, with deep mellow notes, that seemed to fall singly upon one's ear. Then it became a little louder, and sounded like a flute or a distant hautbois.[1] In the garden-scene it had all the tremulous ecstasy that one hears just before dawn when nightingales are singing. There were moments, later on, when it had the wild passion of violins. You know how a voice can stir one. Your voice and the voice of Sibyl Vane are two things that I shall never forget. When I close my eyes, I hear them, and each of them says something different. I don't know which to follow. Why should I not love her? Harry, I do love her. She is everything to me in life. Night after night I go to see her play. One evening she is Rosalind,[2] and the next evening she is Imogen.[3] I have seen her die in the gloom of an Italian tomb, sucking the poison from her lover's lips.[4] I have watched her wandering through the forest of Arden, disguised as a pretty boy in hose and doublet and dainty cap. She has been mad, and has come into the presence of a guilty king, and given him rue to wear, and bitter herbs to taste of. She has been innocent, and the black hands of jealousy have crushed her reed-like throat. I have seen her in every age and in every costume. Ordinary women never appeal to one's imagination. They are limited to their century. No glamour ever transfigures them. One knows their minds as easily as one knows their bonnets. One can always find them. There is no mystery in any of them. They ride in the Park in the morning, and chatter at tea-parties in the afternoon. They have their stereotyped smile, and their fashionable manner. They are quite obvious. But an actress! How different an actress is! Harry! why didn't you tell me that the only thing worth loving is an actress?"

"Because I have loved so many of them, Dorian."

"Oh, yes, horrid people with dyed hair and painted faces."

"Don't run down dyed hair and painted faces. There is an extraordinary charm in them, sometimes," said Lord Henry.

"I wish now I had not told you about Sibyl Vane."

---

9. In a letter to Lillie Langtry, famous beauty and actress (December 1883), Wilde announced his intention to marry "a beautiful girl called Constance Lloyd, a grave, slight, violet-eyed little Artemis, with great coils of heavy brown hair which make her flower-like head droop like a blossom. . . ." (*Letters* 154).
1. An oboe.
2. The heroine of Shakespeare's *As You Like It*.
3. The daughter of Cymbeline in Shakespeare's play of the same name.
4. Thus Juliet dies, but in *Hamlet* 3.1.155–56, Ophelia complains, "And I, of ladies most deject and wretched / That suck'd the honey of his music vows."

"You could not have helped telling me, Dorian. All through your life you will tell me everything you do."

"Yes, Harry, I believe that is true. I cannot help telling you things. You have a curious influence over me. If I ever did a crime, I would come and confess it to you. You would understand me."

"People like you—the wilful sunbeams of life—don't commit crimes, Dorian. But I am much obliged for the compliment, all the same. And now tell me—reach me the matches, like a good boy: thanks—what are your actual relations with Sibyl Vane?"

Dorian Gray leaped to his feet, with flushed cheeks and burning eyes. "Harry! Sibyl Vane is sacred!"

"It is only the sacred things that are worth touching, Dorian," said Lord Henry, with a strange touch of pathos in his voice. "But why should you be annoyed? I suppose she will belong to you some day.[5] When one is in love, one always begins by deceiving one's self, and one always ends by deceiving others. That is what the world calls a romance. You know her, at any rate, I suppose?"

"Of course I know her. On the first night I was at the theatre, the horrid old Jew came round to the box after the performance was over, and offered to take me behind the scenes and introduce me to her. I was furious with him, and told him that Juliet had been dead for hundreds of years, and that her body was lying in a marble tomb in Verona. I think, from his blank look of amazement, that he was under the impression that I had taken too much champagne, or something."

"I am not surprised."

"Then he asked me if I wrote for any of the newspapers. I told him I never even read them. He seemed terribly disappointed at that, and confided to me that all the dramatic critics were in a conspiracy against him, and that they were every one of them to be bought."

"I should not wonder if he was quite right there. But, on the other hand, judging from their appearance, most of them cannot be at all expensive."

"Well, he seemed to think they were beyond his means," laughed Dorian. "By this time, however, the lights were being put out in the theatre, and I had to go. He wanted me to try some cigars that he strongly recommended. I declined. The next night, of course, I arrived at the place again. When he saw me he made me a low bow, and assured me that I was a munificent patron of art. He was a most offensive brute, though he had an extraordinary passion for Shakespeare.

---

5. One of J. M. Stoddart's substitutions made in the magazine edition and retained here. The Clark typescript (TS) originally read "She will be your mistress someday."

He told me once, with an air of pride, that his five bankruptcies were entirely due to 'The Bard,' as he insisted on calling him. He seemed to think it a distinction."

"It was a distinction, my dear Dorian—a great distinction. Most people become bankrupt through having invested too heavily in the prose of life. To have ruined one's self over poetry is an honour. But when did you first speak to Miss Sibyl Vane?"

"The third night. She had been playing Rosalind. I could not help going round. I had thrown her some flowers, and she had looked at me; at least I fancied that she had. The old Jew was persistent. He seemed determined to take me behind, so I consented. It was curious my not wanting to know her, wasn't it?"

"No; I don't think so."

"My dear Harry, why?"

"I will tell you some other time. Now I want to know about the girl."

"Sibyl? Oh, she was so shy, and so gentle. There is something of a child about her. Her eyes opened wide in exquisite wonder when I told her what I thought of her performance, and she seemed quite unconscious of her power. I think we were both rather nervous. The old Jew stood grinning at the doorway of the dusty greenroom,[6] making elaborate speeches about us both, while we stood looking at each other like children. He would insist on calling me 'My Lord,' so I had to assure Sibyl that I was not anything of the kind. She said quite simply to me, 'You look more like a prince. I must call you Prince Charming.'"

"Upon my word, Dorian, Miss Sibyl knows how to pay compliments."

"You don't understand her, Harry. She regarded me merely as a person in a play. She knows nothing of life. She lives with her mother, a faded tired woman who played Lady Capulet[7] in a sort of magenta dressing-wrapper on the first night, and looks as if she had seen better days."

"I know that look. It depresses me," murmured Lord Henry, examining his rings.

"The Jew wanted to tell me her history, but I said it did not interest me."

"You were quite right. There is always something infinitely mean about other people's tragedies."

"Sibyl is the only thing I care about. What is it to me where she came from? From her little head to her little feet, she is absolutely

---

6. A reception room and lounge for performers in a theater.
7. Juliet's mother in *Romeo and Juliet*.

and entirely divine. Every night of my life I go to see her act, and every night she is more marvellous."

"That is the reason, I suppose, that you never dine with me now. I thought you must have some curious romance on hand. You have; but it is not quite what I expected."

"My dear Harry, we either lunch or sup together every day, and I have been to the Opera with you several times," said Dorian, opening his blue eyes in wonder.

"You always come dreadfully late."

"Well, I can't help going to see Sibyl play," he cried, "even if it is only for a single act. I get hungry for her presence; and when I think of the wonderful soul that is hidden away in that little ivory body, I am filled with awe."

"You can dine with me to-night, Dorian, can't you?"

He shook his head. "To-night she is Imogen," he answered, "and to-morrow night she will be Juliet."

"When is she Sibyl Vane?"

"Never."

"I congratulate you."

"How horrid you are! She is all the great heroines of the world in one. She is more than an individual. You laugh, but I tell you she has genius. I love her, and I must make her love me. You, who know all the secrets of life, tell me how to charm Sibyl Vane to love me! I want to make Romeo jealous. I want the dead lovers of the world to hear our laughter, and grow sad. I want a breath of our passion to stir their dust into consciousness, to wake their ashes into pain. My God, Harry, how I worship her!" He was walking up and down the room as he spoke. Hectic spots of red burned on his cheeks. He was terribly excited.

Lord Henry watched him with a subtle sense of pleasure. How different he was now from the shy, frightened boy he had met in Basil Hallward's studio! His nature had developed like a flower, had borne blossoms of scarlet flame. Out of its secret hiding-place had crept his Soul, and Desire had come to meet it on the way.

"And what do you propose to do?" said Lord Henry, at last.

"I want you and Basil to come with me some night and see her act. I have not the slightest fear of the result. You are certain to acknowledge her genius. Then we must get her out of the Jew's hands. She is bound to him for three years—at least for two years and eight months—from the present time. I shall have to pay him something, of course. When all that is settled, I shall take a West End theatre and bring her out properly. She will make the world as mad as she has made me."

"That would be impossible, my dear boy."

"Yes, she will. She has not merely art, consummate art-instinct, in her, but she has personality also; and you have often told me that it is personalities, not principles, that move the age."

"Well, what night shall we go?"

"Let me see. To-day is Tuesday. Let us fix to-morrow. She plays Juliet to-morrow."

"All right. The Bristol[8] at eight o'clock; and I will get Basil."

"Not eight, Harry, please. Half-past six. We must be there before the curtain rises. You must see her in the first act, where she meets Romeo."

"Half-past six! What an hour! It will be like having a meat-tea,[9] or reading an English novel. It must be seven. No gentleman dines before seven. Shall you see Basil between this and then? Or shall I write to him?"

"Dear Basil! I have not laid eyes on him for a week. It is rather horrid of me, as he has sent me my portrait in the most wonderful frame, specially designed by himself, and, though I am a little jealous of the picture for being a whole month younger than I am, I must admit that I delight in it. Perhaps you had better write to him. I don't want to see him alone. He says things that annoy me. He gives me good advice."

Lord Henry smiled. "People are very fond of giving away what they need most themselves. It is what I call the depth of generosity."

"Oh, Basil is the best of fellows, but he seems to me to be just a bit of a Philistine. Since I have known you, Harry, I have discovered that."

"Basil, my dear boy, puts everything that is charming in him into his work. The consequence is that he has nothing left for life but his prejudices, his principles, and his common sense. The only artists I have ever known, who are personally delightful, are bad artists. Good artists exist simply in what they make, and consequently are perfectly uninteresting in what they are. A great poet, a really great poet, is the most unpoetical of all creatures. But inferior poets are absolutely fascinating. The worse their rhymes are, the more picturesque they look. The mere fact of having published a book of second-rate sonnets makes a man quite irresistible. He lives the poetry that he cannot write. The others write the poetry that they dare not realize."

"I wonder is that really so, Harry?" said Dorian Gray, putting some perfume on his handkerchief out of a large, gold-topped bottle that stood on the table. "It must be, if you say it. And now I am off. Imogen is waiting for me. Don't forget about to-morrow. Good-bye."

As he left the room, Lord Henry's heavy eyelids drooped, and he

8. A luxury hotel near the Ritz in Piccadilly.
9. A tea at which meat is served, also called "high tea."

began to think. Certainly few people had ever interested him so much as Dorian Gray, and yet the lad's mad adoration of some one else caused him not the slightest pang of annoyance or jealousy. He was pleased by it. It made him a more interesting study. He had been always enthralled by the methods of natural science, but the ordinary subject-matter of that science had seemed to him trivial and of no import. And so he had begun by vivisecting himself, as he had ended by vivisecting others. Human life—that appeared to him the one thing worth investigating. Compared to it there was nothing else of any value. It was true that as one watched life in its curious crucible of pain and pleasure, one could not wear over one's face a mask of glass, nor keep the sulphurous fumes from troubling the brain and making the imagination turbid with monstrous fancies and mis-shapen dreams. There were poisons so subtle that to know their prop-erties one had to sicken of them. There were maladies so strange that one had to pass through them if one sought to understand their nature. And, yet, what a great reward one received! How wonderful the whole world became to one! To note the curious hard logic of pas-sion, and the emotional coloured life of the intellect—to observe where they met, and where they separated, at what point they were in unison, and at what point they were at discord—there was a delight in that! What matter what the cost was? One could never pay too high a price for any sensation.

He was conscious—and the thought brought a gleam of pleasure into his brown agate eyes—that it was through certain words of his, musical words said with musical utterance, that Dorian Gray's soul had turned to this white girl[1] and bowed in worship before her. To a large extent the lad was his own creation. He had made him prema-ture. That was something. Ordinary people waited till life disclosed to them its secrets, but to the few, to the elect, the mysteries of life were revealed before the veil was drawn away. Sometimes this was the effect of art, and chiefly of the art of literature, which dealt immedi-ately with the passions and the intellect. But now and then a com-plex personality took the place and assumed the office of art, was indeed, in its way, a real work of art, Life having its elaborate mas-terpieces, just as poetry has, or sculpture, or paintings.

Yes, the lad was premature. He was gathering his harvest while it was yet spring. The pulse and passion of youth were in him, but he was becoming self-conscious. It was delightful to watch him. With his beautiful face, and his beautiful soul, he was a thing to wonder at. It was no matter how it all ended, or was destined to end. He was like one of those gracious figures in a pageant or a play, whose joys

---

1. A reference to Whistler's picture of that name, on which Swinburne based his poem "Before the Mirror," in *Poems and Ballads* (1866).

seem to be remote from one, but whose sorrows stir one's sense of beauty, and whose wounds are like red roses.

Soul and body, body and soul—how mysterious they were! There was animalism[2] in the soul, and the body had its moments of spirituality. The senses could refine, and the intellect could degrade. Who could say where the fleshly impulse ceased, or the psychical impulse began? How shallow were the arbitrary definitions of ordinary psychologists! And yet how difficult to decide between the claims of the various schools! Was the soul a shadow seated in the house of sin? Or was the body really in the soul, as Giordano Bruno[3] thought? The separation of spirit from matter was a mystery, and the union of spirit with matter was a mystery also.

He began to wonder whether we could ever make psychology so absolute a science that each little spring of life would be revealed to us. As it was, we always misunderstood ourselves, and rarely understood others. Experience was of no ethical value. It was merely the name men gave to their mistakes. Moralists had, as a rule, regarded it as a mode of warning, had claimed for it a certain ethical efficacy in the formation of character, had praised it as something that taught us what to follow and showed us what to avoid. But there was no motive power in experience. It was as little of an active cause as conscience itself. All that it really demonstrated was that our future would be the same as our past, and that the sin we had done once, and with loathing, we would do many times, and with joy.

It was clear to him that the experimental method was the only method by which one could arrive at any scientific analysis of the passions; and certainly Dorian Gray was a subject made to his hand, and seemed to promise rich and fruitful results. His sudden mad love for Sibyl Vane was a psychological phenomenon of no small interest. There was no doubt that curiosity had much to do with it, curiosity and the desire for new experiences; yet it was not a simple but rather a very complex passion. What there was in it of the purely sensuous instinct of boyhood had been transformed by the workings of the imagination, changed into something that seemed to the lad himself to be remote from sense, and was for that very reason all the more dangerous. It was the passions about whose origin we deceived ourselves that tyrannized most strongly over us. Our weakest motives were those of whose nature we were conscious. It often happened

2. Animal activity, physical exercise and enjoyment but it can be taken as mere animal enjoyment, sensuality.
3. Proponent of the new astronomy of Copernicus and an advocate of freedom of thought. Bruno (1584–1600) was put to death by the Inquisition, largely as the result of his attacks on orthodox Aristotelianism. Pater wrote an essay on Bruno, which appeared in *The Fortnightly Review* (August 1889); Wilde would have known it. Bruno has been a cultural hero of writers and intellectuals since the mid-nineteenth century.

that when we thought we were experimenting on others we were really experimenting on ourselves.

While Lord Henry sat dreaming on these things, a knock came to the door, and his valet entered, and reminded him it was time to dress for dinner. He got up and looked out into the street. The sunset had smitten into scarlet gold the upper windows of the houses opposite. The panes glowed like plates of heated metal. The sky above was like a faded rose. He thought of his friend's young fiery-coloured life, and wondered how it was all going to end.

When he arrived home, about half-past twelve o'clock, he saw a telegram lying on the hall table. He opened it, and found it was from Dorian Gray. It was to tell him that he was engaged to be married to Sibyl Vane.

Chapter V[1]

"Mother, mother, I am so happy!" whispered the girl, burying her face in the lap of the faded, tired-looking woman who with back turned to the shrill intrusive light, was sitting in the one arm-chair that their dingy sitting-room contained. "I am so happy!" she repeated, "and you must be happy too!"

Mrs. Vane winced, and put her thin bismuth-whitened hands[2] on her daughter's head. "Happy!" she echoed, "I am only happy, Sibyl, when I see you act. You must not think of anything but your acting. Mr. Isaacs has been very good to us, and we owe him money."

The girl looked up and pouted. "Money, mother?" she cried, "what does money matter? Love is more than money."

"Mr. Isaacs has advanced us fifty pounds to pay off our debts, and to get a proper outfit for James. You must not forget that, Sibyl. Fifty pounds is a very large sum.[3] Mr. Isaacs has been most considerate."

"He is not a gentleman, mother, and I hate the way he talks to me," said the girl, rising to her feet, and going over to the window.

"I don't know how we could manage without him," answered the elder woman, querulously.

Sibyl Vane tossed her head and laughed. "We don't want him any more, mother. Prince Charming[4] rules life for us now." Then she paused. A rose shook in her blood, and shadowed her cheeks. Quick

---

1. The second of the new chapters written for the revised edition.
2. Bismuth, a whitening agent in paints and cosmetics, is still used in the theater, especially by mimes and clowns.
3. In 2004, £50 from 1891 was worth around £3,500 or about $6,000 using the retail price index as the benchmark.
4. Dorian's performance as Sibyl's Prince Charming is a cruel reversal of the fairy tale prince; Sibyl's fate is similarly reversed.

breath parted the petals of her lips. They trembled. Some southern wind of passion swept over her, and stirred the dainty folds of her dress. "I love him," she said simply.

"Foolish child! foolish child!" was the parrot-phrase flung in answer. The waving of crooked, false-jewelled fingers gave grotesqueness to the words.

The girl laughed again. The joy of a caged bird was in her voice. Her eyes caught the melody, and echoed it in radiance: then closed for a moment, as though to hide their secret. When they opened, the mist of a dream had passed across them.

Thin-lipped wisdom spoke at her from the worn chair, hinted at prudence, quoted from that book of cowardice whose author apes the name of common sense. She did not listen. She was free in her prison of passion.[5] Her prince, Prince Charming, was with her. She had called on Memory to remake him. She had sent her soul to search for him, and it had brought him back. His kiss burned again upon her mouth. Her eyelids were warm with his breath.

Then Wisdom altered its method and spoke of espial and discovery. This young man might be rich. If so, marriage should be thought of. Against the shell of her ear broke the waves of worldly cunning. The arrows of craft shot by her. She saw the thin lips moving, and smiled.

Suddenly she felt the need to speak. The wordy silence troubled her. "Mother, mother," she cried, "why does he love me so much? I know why I love him. I love him because he is like what Love himself should be. But what does he see in me? I am not worthy of him. And yet—why, I cannot tell—though I feel so much beneath him, I don't feel humble. I feel proud, terribly proud. Mother, did you love my father as I love Prince Charming?"

The elder woman grew pale beneath the coarse powder that daubed her cheeks, and her dry lips twitched with a spasm of pain. Sybil rushed to her, flung her arms round her neck, and kissed her. "Forgive me, mother. I know it pains you to talk about our father. But it only pains you because you loved him so much. Don't look so sad. I am as happy to-day as you were twenty years ago. Ah! let me be happy for ever!"

"My child, you are far too young to think of falling in love. Besides, what do you know of this young man? You don't even know his name. The whole thing is most inconvenient, and really, when James is going away to Australia,[6] and I have so much to think of, I must say

---

5. An allusion to the theme of Richard Lovelace's "To Althea from Prison," with another reversal of roles of lover / beloved.
6. Although Australia had been designated as a British penal colony since 1788, by the late 1800s, it had become a prime destination of fortune hunters and low-income Britons. Gold had been discovered there in 1823, thus inciting a gold rush, and one could easily procure a free passage to the Colonies.

that you should have shown more consideration. However, as I said before, if he is rich . . ."

"Ah! mother, mother, let me be happy!"

Mrs. Vane glanced at her, and with one of those false theatrical gestures that so often become a mode of second nature to a stage-player, clasped her in her arms. At this moment the door opened, and a young lad with rough brown hair came into the room. He was thick-set of figure, and his hands and feet were large, and somewhat clumsy in movement. He was not so finely bred as his sister.[7] One would hardly have guessed the close relationship that existed between them. Mrs. Vane fixed her eyes on him, and intensified her smile. She mentally elevated her son to the dignity of an audience. She felt sure that the *tableau*[8] was interesting.

"You might keep some of your kisses for me, Sibyl, I think," said the lad, with a good-natured grumble.

"Ah! but you don't like being kissed, Jim," she cried. "You are a dreadful old bear." And she ran across the room and hugged him.

James Vane looked into his sister's face with tenderness. "I want you to come out with me for a walk, Sibyl. I don't suppose I shall ever see this horrid London again. I am sure I don't want to."

"My son, don't say such dreadful things," murmured Mrs. Vane, taking up a tawdry theatrical dress, with a sigh, and beginning to patch it. She felt a little disappointed that he had not joined the group. It would have increased the theatrical picturesqueness of the situation.

"Why not, mother? I mean it."

"You pain me, my son. I trust you will return from Australia in a position of affluence. I believe there is no society of any kind in the Colonies, nothing that I would call society; so when you have made your fortune you must come back and assert yourself in London."

"Society!" muttered the lad. "I don't want to know anything about that. I should like to make some money to take you and Sibyl off the stage. I hate it."

"Oh, Jim!" said Sibyl, laughing, "how unkind of you! But are you really going for a walk with me? That will be nice! I was afraid you were going to say good-bye to some of your friends—to Tom Hardy, who gave you that hideous pipe, or Ned Langton, who makes fun of you for smoking it. It is very sweet of you to let me have your last afternoon. Where shall we go? Let us go to the Park."[9]

---

7. The physical appearance of James Vane appears to owe a good deal to the appearance of Willie, Oscar Wilde's older brother.
8. A striking theatrical arrangement of persons in a frozen dramatic pose, very popular with theatergoers of the times.
9. Hyde Park.

"I am too shabby," he answered, frowning. "Only swell[1] people go to the Park."

"Nonsense, Jim," she whispered, stroking the sleeve of his coat.

He hesitated for a moment. "Very well," he said at last, "but don't be too long dressing." She danced out of the door. One could hear her singing as she ran upstairs. Her little feet pattered overhead.

He walked up and down the room two or three times. Then he turned to the still figure in the chair. "Mother, are my things ready?" he asked.

"Quite ready, James," she answered, keeping her eyes on her work. For some months past she had felt ill at ease when she was alone with this rough, stern son of hers. Her shallow secret nature was troubled when their eyes met. She used to wonder if he suspected anything. The silence, for he made no other observation, became intolerable to her. She began to complain. Women defend themselves by attacking, just as they attack by sudden and strange surrenders. "I hope you will be contented, James, with your sea-faring life," she said. "You must remember that it is your own choice. You might have entered a solicitor's[2] office. Solicitors are a very respectable class, and in the country often dine with the best families."

"I hate offices, and I hate clerks," he replied. "But you are quite right. I have chosen my own life. All I say is, watch over Sibyl. Don't let her come to any harm. Mother, you must watch over her."

"James, you really talk very strangely. Of course I watch over Sibyl."

"I hear a gentleman comes every night to the theatre, and goes behind to talk to her. Is that right? What about that?"

"You are speaking about things you don't understand, James. In the profession we are accustomed to receive a great deal of most gratifying attention. I myself used to receive many bouquets at one time. That was when acting was really understood. As for Sibyl, I do not know at present whether her attachment is serious or not. But there is no doubt that the young man in question is a perfect gentleman. He is always most polite to me. Besides, he has the appearance of being rich, and the flowers he sends are lovely."

"You don't know his name, though," said the lad harshly.

"No," answered his mother, with a placid expression in her face. "He has not yet revealed his real name. I think it is quite romantic of him. He is probably a member of the aristocracy."

James Vane bit his lip. "Watch over Sibyl, mother," he cried, "watch over her."

---

1. Fashionable and wealthy.
2. In the English court system, this refers to one properly qualified and formally admitted to practice as a law-agent in any court. Solicitors commonly instruct barristers, who then argue cases.

"My son, you distress me very much. Sibyl is always under my special care. Of course, if this gentleman is wealthy, there is no reason
why she should not contract an alliance with him. I trust he is one of
the aristocracy. He has all the appearance of it, I must say. It might
be a most brilliant marriage for Sibyl. They would make a charming
couple. His good looks are really quite remarkable; everybody notices
them."

The lad muttered something to himself, and drummed on the
window-pane with his coarse fingers. He had just turned round to say
something, when the door opened, and Sibyl ran in.

"How serious you both are!" she cried. "What is the matter?"

"Nothing," he answered. "I suppose one must be serious sometimes. Good-bye, mother; I will have my dinner at five o'clock. Everything is packed, except my shirts, so you need not trouble."

"Good-bye, my son," she answered, with a bow of strained stateli-
ness.

She was extremely annoyed at the tone he had adopted with her,
and there was something in his look that had made her feel afraid.

"Kiss me, mother," said the girl. Her flower-like lips touched the
withered cheek, and warmed its frost.

"My child! my child!" cried Mrs. Vane, looking up to the ceiling in
search of an imaginary gallery.

"Come, Sibyl," said her brother, impatiently. He hated his mother's
affectations.

They went out into the flickering wind-blown sunlight, and strolled
down the dreary Euston Road.[3] The passers-by glanced in wonder at
the sullen, heavy youth, who, in coarse, ill-fitting clothes, was in the
company of such a graceful, refined-looking girl. He was like a common gardener walking with a rose.

Jim frowned from time to time when he caught the inquisitive
glance of some stranger. He had that dislike of being stared at which
comes on geniuses late in life, and never leaves the commonplace.
Sibyl, however, was quite unconscious of the effect she was producing. Her love was trembling in laughter on her lips. She was thinking
of Prince Charming, and, that she might think of him all the more,
she did not talk of him, but prattled on about the ship in which Jim
was going to sail, about the gold he was certain to find, about the
wonderful heiress whose life he was to save from the wicked, red-
shirted bushrangers.[4] For he was not to remain a sailor, or a super-
cargo, or whatever he was going to be. Oh, no! A sailor's existence

3. Three great rail terminals in Euston Road helped turn the district into the site of flop-
   houses, pawnshops, second-hand dealers, brothels, and cheap theaters. The giant Doric
   granite portal of Euston Road was symbolic of the commercial gateway to the city.
4. The slang designation for an escaped convict who took refuge in the Australian "bush" who
   subsisted by robbery.

was dreadful. Fancy being cooped up in a horrid ship, with the hoarse, hump-backed waves trying to get in, and a black wind blowing the masts down, and tearing the sails into long screaming ribands! He was to leave the vessel at Melbourne, bid a polite good-bye to the captain, and go off at once to the gold-fields. Before a week was over he was to come across a large nugget of pure gold, the largest nugget that had ever been discovered, and bring it down to the coast in a waggon guarded by six mounted policemen. The bushrangers were to attack them three times, and be defeated with immense slaughter. Or, no. He was not to go to the gold-fields at all. They were horrid places, where men got intoxicated, and shot each other in bar-rooms, and used bad language. He was to be a nice sheep-farmer, and one evening, as he was riding home, he was to see the beautiful heiress being carried off by a robber on a black horse, and give chase, and rescue her. Of course she would fall in love with him, and he with her, and they would get married, and come home, and live in an immense house in London. Yes, there were delightful things in store for him. But he must be very good, and not lose his temper, or spend his money foolishly. She was only a year older than he was, but she knew so much more of life. He must be sure, also, to write to her by every mail, and to say his prayers each night before he went to sleep. God was very good, and would watch over him. She would pray for him too, and in a few years he would come back quite rich and happy.

The lad listened sulkily to her, and made no answer. He was heart-sick at leaving home.

Yet it was not this alone that made him gloomy and morose. Inexperienced though he was, he had still a strong sense of the danger of Sibyl's position. This young dandy who was making love to her could mean her no good. He was a gentleman, and he hated him for that, hated him through some curious race-instinct for which he could not account, and which for that reason was all the more dominant within him. He was conscious also of the shallowness and vanity of his mother's nature, and in that saw infinite peril for Sibyl and Sibyl's happiness. Children begin by loving their parents; as they grow older they judge them; sometimes they forgive them.

His mother! He had something on his mind to ask of her, something that he had brooded on for many months of silence. A chance phrase that he had heard at the theatre, a whispered sneer that had reached his ears one night as he waited at the stage-door, had set loose a train of horrible thoughts. He remembered it as if it had been the lash of a hunting-crop across his face. His brows knit together into a wedge-like furrow, and with a twitch of pain he bit his under-lip.

"You are not listening to a word I am saying, Jim," cried Sibyl, "and

I am making the most delightful plans for your future. Do say something."

"What do you want me to say?"

"Oh! that you will be a good boy, and not forget us," she answered, smiling at him.

He shrugged his shoulders. "You are more likely to forget me, than I am to forget you, Sibyl."

She flushed. "What do you mean, Jim?" she asked.

"You have a new friend, I hear. Who is he? Why have you not told me about him? He means you no good."

"Stop, Jim!" she exclaimed. "You must not say anything against him. I love him."

"Why, you don't even know his name," answered the lad. "Who is he? I have a right to know."

"He is called Prince Charming. Don't you like the name. Oh! you silly boy! you should never forget it. If you only saw him, you would think him the most wonderful person in the world. Some day you will meet him: when you come back from Australia. You will like him so much. Everybody likes him, and I . . . love him. I wish you could come to the theatre to-night. He is going to be there, and I am to play Juliet. Oh! how I shall play it! Fancy, Jim, to be in love and play Juliet! To have him sitting there! To play for his delight! I am afraid I may frighten the company, frighten or enthrall them. To be in love is to surpass one's self. Poor dreadful Mr. Isaacs will be shouting 'genius' to his loafers at the bar. He has preached me as a dogma; to-night he will announce me as a revelation. I feel it. And it is all his, his only, Prince Charming, my wonderful lover, my god of graces. But I am poor beside him. Poor? What does that matter? When poverty creeps in at the door, love flies in through the window. Our proverbs want re-writing. They were made in winter, and it is summer now; springtime for me, I think, a very dance of blossoms in blue skies."

"He is a gentleman," said the lad, sullenly.

"A Prince!" she cried, musically. "What more do you want?"

"He wants to enslave you."

"I shudder at the thought of being free."

"I want you to beware of him."

"To see him is to worship him, to know him is to trust him."

"Sibyl, you are mad about him."

She laughed, and took his arm. "You dear old Jim, you talk as if you were a hundred. Some day you will be in love yourself. Then you will know what it is. Don't look so sulky. Surely you should be glad to think that, though you are going away, you leave me happier than I have ever been before. Life has been hard for us both, terribly hard and difficult. But it will be different now. You are going to a new

world, and I have found one. Here are two chairs; let us sit down and
see the smart people go by."

They took their seats amidst a crowd of watchers. The tulip-beds
across the road flamed like throbbing rings of fire. A white dust,
tremulous cloud of orris-root[5] it seemed, hung in the panting air. The
brightly-coloured parasols danced and dipped like monstrous butterflies.

She made her brother talk of himself, his hopes, his prospects. He
spoke slowly and with effort. They passed words to each other as
players at a game pass counters. Sibyl felt oppressed. She could not
communicate her joy. A faint smile curving that sullen mouth was all
the echo she could win. After some time she became silent. Suddenly
she caught a glimpse of golden hair and laughing lips, and in an open
carriage with two ladies Dorian Gray drove past.

She started to her feet. "There he is!" she cried.

"Who?" said Jim Vane.

"Prince Charming," she answered, looking after the victoria.[6]

He jumped up, and seized her roughly by the arm. "Show him to
me. Which is he? Point him out. I must see him!" he exclaimed; but
at that moment the Duke of Berwick's four-in-hand[7] came between,
and when it had left the space clear, the carriage had swept out of the
Park.

"He is gone," murmured Sibyl, sadly. "I wish you had seen him."

"I wish I had, for as sure as there is a God in heaven, if he ever does
you any wrong, I shall kill him."

She looked at him in horror. He repeated his words. They cut the
air like a dagger. The people round began to gape. A lady standing
close to her tittered.

"Come away, Jim; come away," she whispered. He followed her
doggedly, as she passed through the crowd. He felt glad at what he
had said.

When they reached the Achilles Statue[8] she turned round. There
was pity in her eyes that became laughter on her lips. She shook her
head at him. "You are foolish, Jim, utterly foolish; a bad-tempered
boy, that is all. How can you say such horrible things? You don't know
what you are talking about. You are simply jealous and unkind. Ah! I
wish you would fall in love. Love makes people good, and what you
said was wicked."

"I am sixteen," he answered, "and I know what I am about. Mother

---

5. Used as a perfume, it has the scent of violets.
6. A light, low, four-wheeled carriage having a collapsible hood, with seats (usually) for two
persons and an elevated seat in front for the driver.
7. A vehicle with four horses driven by one person.
8. A giant nude bronze statue by Sir Richard Westmacott, a copy of the original in Cavallo,
Italy, erected by the ladies of England in 1822 to commemorate the Duke of Wellington's
victories. James and Sibyl are now near the southeast corner of Hyde Park.

is no help to you. She doesn't understand how to look after you. I wish now that I was not going to Australia at all. I have a great mind to chuck the whole thing up. I would, if my articles[9] hadn't been signed."

"Oh, don't be so serious, Jim. You are like one of the heroes of those silly melodramas mother used to be so fond of acting in. I am not going to quarrel with you. I have seen him, and oh! to see him is perfect happiness. We won't quarrel. I know you would never harm any one I love, would you?"

"Not as long as you love him, I suppose," was the sullen answer.

"I shall love him for ever!" she cried.

"And he?"

"For ever, too!"

"He had better."

She shrank from him. Then she laughed and put her hand on his arm. He was merely a boy.

At the Marble Arch[1] they hailed an omnibus,[2] which left them close to their shabby home in the Euston Road. It was after five o'clock, and Sibyl had to lie down for a couple of hours before acting. Jim insisted that she should do so. He said that he would sooner part with her when their mother was not present. She would be sure to make a scene, and he detested scenes of every kind.

In Sybil's own room they parted. There was jealousy in the lad's heart, and a fierce murderous hatred of the stranger who, as it seemed to him, had come between them. Yet, when her arms were flung round his neck, and her fingers strayed through his hair, he softened, and kissed her with real affection. There were tears in his eyes as he went downstairs.

His mother was waiting for him below. She grumbled at his unpunctuality, as he entered. He made no answer, but sat down to his meagre meal. The flies buzzed round the table, and crawled over the stained cloth. Through the rumble of omnibuses, and the clatter of street-cabs, he could hear the droning voice devouring each minute that was left to him.

After some time, he thrust away his plate, and put his head in his hands. He felt that he had a right to know. It should have been told to him before, if it was as he suspected. Leaden with fear, his mother watched him. Words dropped mechanically from her lips. A tattered lace handkerchief twitched in her fingers. When the clock struck six, he got up, and went to the door. Then he turned back, and looked

9. An employment contract to serve on shipboard.
1. A triumphal single arch modeled after that of Titus at Rome and located at the northeast entrance to Hyde Park.
2. A large public horse-drawn vehicle carrying passengers by road, running on a fixed route and typically requiring the payment of a fare.

at her. Their eyes met. In hers he saw a wild appeal for mercy. It enraged him.

"Mother, I have something to ask you," he said. Her eyes wandered vaguely about the room. She made no answer. "Tell me the truth. I have a right to know. Were you married to my father?"

She heaved a deep sigh. It was a sigh of relief. The terrible moment, the moment that night and day, for weeks and months, she had dreaded, had come at last, and yet she felt no terror. Indeed in some measure it was a disappointment to her. The vulgar directness of the question called for a direct answer. The situation had not been gradually led up to. It was crude. It reminded her of a bad rehearsal.

"No," she answered, wondering at the harsh simplicity of life.

"My father was a scoundrel then!" cried the lad, clenching his fists.

She shook her head. "I knew he was not free. We loved each other very much. If he had lived, he would have made provision for us. Don't speak against him, my son. He was your father, and a gentleman. Indeed he was highly connected."

An oath broke from his lips. "I don't care for myself," he exclaimed, "but don't let Sibyl. . . . It is a gentleman, isn't it, who is in love with her, or says he is? Highly connected, too, I suppose."

For a moment a hideous sense of humiliation came over the woman. Her head drooped. She wiped her eyes with shaking hands. "Sibyl has a mother," she murmured; "I had none."

The lad was touched. He went towards her, and stooping down he kissed her. "I am sorry if I have pained you by asking about my father," he said, "but I could not help it. I must go now. Good-bye. Don't forget that you will have only one child now to look after, and believe me that if this man wrongs my sister, I will find out who he is, track him down, and kill him like a dog. I swear it."

The exaggerated folly of the threat, the passionate gesture that accompanied it, the mad melodramatic words, made life seem more vivid to her. She was familiar with the atmosphere. She breathed more freely, and for the first time for many months she really admired her son. She would have liked to have continued the scene on the same emotional scale, but he cut her short. Trunks had to be carried down, and mufflers[3] looked for. The lodging-house drudge bustled in and out. There was the bargaining with the cabman. The moment was lost in vulgar details. It was with a renewed feeling of disappointment that she waved the tattered lace handkerchief from the window, as her son drove away. She was conscious that a great opportunity had been wasted. She consoled herself by telling Sibyl how desolate she felt her life would be, now that she had only one child to look after. She remembered the phrase. It had pleased her.

---

3. A wrap or scarf (frequently of wool or silk) worn around the neck for warmth.

Of the threat she said nothing. It was vividly and dramatically expressed. She felt that they would all laugh at it some day.

Chapter VI[1]

I suppose you have heard the news, Basil?" said Lord Henry that evening, as Hallward was shown into a little private room at the Bristol where dinner had been laid for three.

"No, Harry," answered the artist, giving his hat and coat to the bowing waiter. "What is it? Nothing about politics, I hope? They don't interest me. There is hardly a single person in the House of Commons[2] worth painting; though many of them would be the better for a little whitewashing."

"Dorian Gray is engaged to be married," said Lord Henry, watching him as he spoke.

Hallward started, and then frowned. "Dorian engaged to be married!" he cried. "Impossible!"

"It is perfectly true."

"To whom?"

"To some little actress or other."

"I can't believe it. Dorian is far too sensible."

"Dorian is far too wise not to do foolish things now and then, my dear Basil."

"Marriage is hardly a thing that one can do now and then, Harry."

"Except in America," rejoined Lord Henry, languidly. "But I didn't say he was married. I said he was engaged to be married. There is a great difference. I have a distinct remembrance of being married, but I have no recollection at all of being engaged. I am inclined to think that I never was engaged."

"But think of Dorian's birth, and position, and wealth. It would be absurd for him to marry so much beneath him."[3]

"If you want to make him marry this girl tell him that, Basil. He is sure to do it, then. Whenever a man does a thoroughly stupid thing, it is always from the noblest motives."

"I hope the girl is good, Harry. I don't want to see Dorian tied to some vile creature, who might degrade his nature and ruin his intellect."

"Oh, she is better than good—she is beautiful," murmured Lord Henry, sipping a glass of vermouth and orange-bitters. "Dorian says she is beautiful; and he is not often wrong about things of that kind.

1. Chapter 4 in the *Lippincott's Magazine* edition.
2. The lower house of the Parliament of Great Britain. Unlike the House of Lords, the upper house, it is made up of elected representatives.
3. Basil is speaking in terms of social class rather than moral character.

Your portrait of him has quickened his appreciation of the personal appearance of other people. It has had that excellent effect, amongst others. We are to see her to-night, if that boy doesn't forget his appointment."

"Are you serious?"

"Quite serious, Basil. I should be miserable if I thought I should ever be more serious than I am at the present moment."

"But do you approve of it, Harry?" asked the painter, walking up and down the room, and biting his lip. "You can't approve of it, possibly. It is some silly infatuation."

"I never approve, or disapprove, of anything now. It is an absurd attitude to take towards life. We are not sent into the world to air our moral prejudices. I never take any notice of what common people say, and I never interfere with what charming people do. If a personality fascinates me, whatever mode of expression that personality selects is absolutely delightful to me. Dorian Gray falls in love with a beautiful girl who acts Juliet, and proposes to marry her. Why not? If he wedded Messalina[4] he would be none the less interesting. You know I am not a champion of marriage. The real drawback to marriage is that it makes one unselfish. And unselfish people are colourless. They lack individuality. Still, there are certain temperaments that marriage makes more complex. They retain their egotism, and add to it many other egos. They are forced to have more than one life. They become more highly organized, and to be highly organized is, I should fancy, the object of man's existence. Besides, every experience is of value, and, whatever one may say against marriage, it is certainly an experience. I hope that Dorian Gray will make this girl his wife, passionately adore her for six months, and then suddenly become fascinated by some one else. He would be a wonderful study."

"You don't mean a single word of all that, Harry; you know you don't. If Dorian Gray's life were spoiled, no one would be sorrier than yourself. You are much better than you pretend to be."

Lord Henry laughed. "The reason we all like to think so well of others is that we are all afraid for ourselves. The basis of optimism is sheer terror. We think that we are generous because we credit our neighbour with the possession of those virtues that are likely to be a benefit to us. We praise the banker that we may overdraw our account, and find good qualities in the highwayman in the hope that he may spare our pockets. I mean everything that I have said. I have the greatest contempt for optimism. As for a spoiled life, no life is spoiled but one whose growth is arrested. If you want to mar a nature, you have merely to reform it. As for marriage, of course that

4. Empress of Rome, wife of Claudius, put to death in A.D. 48 for gross indecency and treason.

would be silly, but there are other and more interesting bonds between men and women. I will certainly encourage them. They have the charm of being fashionable. But here is Dorian himself. He will tell you more than I can."

"My dear Harry, my dear Basil, you must both congratulate me!" said the lad, throwing off his evening cape with its satin-lined wings, and shaking each of his friends by the hand in turn. "I have never been so happy. Of course it is sudden: all really delightful things are. And yet it seems to me to be the one thing I have been looking for all my life." He was flushed with excitement and pleasure, and looked extraordinarily handsome.

"I hope you will always be very happy, Dorian," said Hallward, "but I don't quite forgive you for not having let me know of your engagement. You let Harry know."

"And I don't forgive you for being late for dinner," broke in Lord Henry, putting his hand on the lad's shoulder, and smiling as he spoke. "Come, let us sit down and try what the new *chef* here is like, and then you will tell us how it all came about."

"There is really not much to tell," cried Dorian, as they took their seats at the small round table. "What happened was simply this. After I left you yesterday evening, Harry, I dressed, had some dinner at that little Italian restaurant in Rupert Street, you introduced me to, and went down at eight o'clock to the theatre. Sibyl was playing Rosalind. Of course, the scenery was dreadful, and the Orlando absurd. But Sibyl! You should have seen her! When she came on in her boy's clothes she was perfectly wonderful. She wore a moss-coloured velvet jerkin[5] with cinnamon sleeves, slim brown cross-gartered hose, a dainty little green cap with a hawk's feather caught in a jewel, and a hooded cloak lined with dull red. She had never seemed to me more exquisite. She had all the delicate grace of that Tanagra figurine that you have in your studio,[6] Basil. Her hair clustered round her face like dark leaves round a pale rose. As for her acting—well, you shall see her to-night. She is simply a born artist. I sat in the dingy box absolutely enthralled. I forgot that I was in London and in the nineteenth century. I was away with my love in a forest that no man had ever seen. After the performance was over I went behind, and spoke to her. As we were sitting together, suddenly there came into her eyes a look that I had never seen there before. My lips moved towards hers. We kissed each other. I can't describe to you what I felt at that moment. It seemed to me that all

5. A vest. Rosalind is disguised as a boy, Ganymede, for much of *As You Like It.* Many of the Shakespeare allusions are to plays in which disguises conceal the true sex of the character: in most instances, young women are disguised as young men. The charade is further complicated because boys played all the female roles in Shakespeare's theater.
6. Wilde admired Tanagra statuettes on his early trips to Greece and kept one in the library of his Tite Street house. They were molded out of red clay.

my life had been narrowed to one perfect point of rose-coloured joy. She trembled all over, and shook like a white narcissus. Then she flung herself on her knees and kissed my hands. I feel that I should not tell you all this, but I can't help it. Of course our engagement is a dead secret. She has not even told her own mother. I don't know what my guardians will say. Lord Radley is sure to be furious. I don't care. I shall be of age in less than a year, and then I can do what I like. I have been right, Basil, haven't I, to take my love out of poetry, and to find my wife in Shakespeare's plays? Lips that Shakespeare taught to speak have whispered their secret in my ear. I have had the arms of Rosalind around me, and kissed Juliet on the mouth."

"Yes, Dorian, I suppose you were right," said Hallward, slowly.

"Have you seen her to-day?" asked Lord Henry.

Dorian Gray shook his head. "I left her in the forest of Arden, I shall find her in an orchard in Verona."[7]

Lord Henry sipped his champagne in a meditative manner. "At what particular point did you mention the word marriage, Dorian? And what did she say in answer? Perhaps you forgot all about it."

"My dear Harry, I did not treat it as a business transaction, and I did not make any formal proposal. I told her that I loved her, and she said she was not worthy to be my wife. Not worthy! Why, the whole world is nothing to me compared with her."

"Women are wonderfully practical," murmured Lord Henry,— "much more practical than we are. In situations of that kind we often forget to say anything about marriage, and they always remind us."

Hallward laid his hand upon his arm. "Don't, Harry. You have annoyed Dorian. He is not like other men. He would never bring misery upon any one. His nature is too fine for that."

Lord Henry looked across the table. "Dorian is never annoyed with me," he answered. "I asked the question for the best reason possible, for the only reason, indeed, that excuses one for asking any question— simple curiosity. I have a theory that it is always the women who propose to us, and not we who propose to the women. Except, of course, in middle-class life. But then the middle classes are not modern."

Dorian Gray laughed, and tossed his head. "You are quite incorrigible, Harry; but I don't mind. It is impossible to be angry with you. When you see Sibyl Vane you will feel that the man who could wrong her would be a beast, a beast without a heart. I cannot understand how any one can wish to shame the thing he loves. I love Sibyl Vane. I want to place her on a pedestal of gold, and to see the world worship the woman who is mine. What is marriage? An irrevocable vow. You

7. That is, Sibyl performed in *As You Like It* the previous night and will act in *Romeo and Juliet* tonight.

mock at it for that. Ah! don't mock. It is an irrevocable vow that I want to take. Her trust makes me faithful, her belief makes me good. When I am with her, I regret all that you have taught me. I become different from what you have known me to be. I am changed, and the mere touch of Sibyl Vane's hand makes me forget you and all your wrong, fascinating, poisonous, delightful theories."

"And those are . . . ?" asked Lord Henry, helping himself to some salad.

"Oh, your theories about life, your theories about love, your theories about pleasure. All your theories, in fact, Harry."

"Pleasure is the only thing worth having a theory about," he answered, in his slow, melodious voice. "But I am afraid I cannot claim my theory as my own. It belongs to Nature, not to me. Pleasure is Nature's test, her sign of approval. When we are happy we are always good, but when we are good we are not always happy."

"Ah! but what do you mean by good?" cried Basil Hallward.

"Yes," echoed Dorian, leaning back in his chair, and looking at Lord Henry over the heavy clusters of purple-lipped irises that stood in the centre of the table, "what do you mean by good, Harry?"

"To be good is to be in harmony with one's self," he replied, touching the thin stem of his glass with his pale, fine-pointed fingers. "Discord is to be forced to be in harmony with others. One's own life—that is the important thing. As for the lives of one's neighbours, if one wishes to be a prig[8] or a Puritan, one can flaunt one's moral views about them, but they are not one's concern. Besides, Individualism has really the higher aim. Modern morality consists in accepting the standard of one's age. I consider that for any man of culture to accept the standard of his age is a form of the grossest immorality."

"But, surely, if one lives merely for one's self, Harry, one pays a terrible price for doing so?" suggested the painter.

"Yes, we are overcharged for everything nowadays. I should fancy that the real tragedy of the poor is that they can afford nothing but self-denial. Beautiful sins, like beautiful things, are the privilege of the rich."

"One has to pay in other ways but money."

"What sort of ways, Basil?"

"Oh! I should fancy in remorse, in suffering, in . . . well, in the consciousness of degradation."

Lord Henry shrugged his shoulders. "My dear fellow, mediæval art is charming, but mediæval emotions are out of date. One can use them in fiction, of course. But then the only things that one can use in fiction are the things that one has ceased to use in fact. Believe

---

8. Someone who cultivates or affects a propriety of culture, learning, or morals that offends or bores others; a conceited or self-important and didactic person.

me, no civilized man ever regrets a pleasure, and no uncivilized man ever knows what a pleasure is."

"I know what pleasure is," cried Dorian Gray. "It is to adore some one."

"That is certainly better than being adored," he answered, toying with some fruits. "Being adored is a nuisance. Women treat us just as Humanity treats its gods. They worship us, and are always bothering us to do something for them."

"I should have said that whatever they ask for they had first given to us," murmured the lad, gravely. "They create Love in our natures. They have a right to demand it back."

"That is quite true, Dorian," cried Hallward.

"Nothing is ever quite true," said Lord Henry.

"This is," interrupted Dorian. "You must admit, Harry, that women give to men the very gold of their lives."

"Possibly," he sighed, "but they invariably want it back in such very small change. That is the worry. Women, as some witty Frenchman once put it, inspire us with the desire to do masterpieces, and always prevent us from carrying them out."

"Harry, you are dreadful! I don't know why I like you so much."

"You will always like me, Dorian," he replied. "Will you have some coffee, you fellows?—Waiter, bring coffee, and *fine-champagne*,[9] and some cigarettes. No: don't mind the cigarettes; I have some. Basil, I can't allow you to smoke cigars. You must have a cigarette. A cigarette is the perfect type of a perfect pleasure. It is exquisite, and it leaves one unsatisfied. What more can one want? Yes, Dorian, you will always be fond of me. I represent to you all the sins you have never had the courage to commit."

"What nonsense you talk, Harry!" cried the lad, taking a light from a fire-breathing silver dragon that the waiter had placed on the table. "Let us go down to the theatre. When Sibyl comes on the stage you will have a new ideal of life. She will represent something to you that you have never known."

"I have known everything," said Lord Henry, with a tired look in his eyes, "but I am always ready for a new emotion. I am afraid, however, that, for me at any rate, there is no such thing. Still, your wonderful girl may thrill me. I love acting. It is so much more real than life. Let us go. Dorian, you will come with me. I am so sorry, Basil, but there is only room for two in the brougham.[1] You must follow us in a hansom."

They got up and put on their coats, sipping their coffee standing. The painter was silent and preoccupied. There was a gloom over him.

---

9. A brandy liqueur rather than a type of champagne.
1. A closed, boxlike carriage with a driver's seat outside in front, synonymous with luxurious appointments.

He could not bear this marriage, and yet it seemed to him to be better than many other things that might have happened. After a few
minutes, they all passed downstairs. He drove off by himself, as had
been arranged, and watched the flashing lights of the little brougham
in front of him. A strange sense of loss came over him. He felt that
Dorian Gray would never again be to him all that he had been in the
past. Life had come between them. . . . His eyes darkened, and the
crowded, flaring streets became blurred to his eyes. When the cab
drew up at the theatre, it seemed to him that he had grown years
older.

Chapter VII[1]

For some reason or other, the house was crowded that night, and the
fat Jew manager who met them at the door was beaming from ear to
ear with an oily, tremulous smile. He escorted them to their box with
a sort of pompous humility, waving his fat jewelled hands, and talking at the top of his voice. Dorian Gray loathed him more than ever.
He felt as if he had come to look for Miranda and had been met by
Caliban.[2] Lord Henry, upon the other hand, rather liked him. At least
he declared he did, and insisted on shaking him by the hand, and
assuring him that he was proud to meet a man who had discovered a
real genius and gone bankrupt over a poet. Hallward amused himself
with watching the faces in the pit. The heat was terribly oppressive,
and the huge sunlight[3] flamed like a monstrous dahlia with petals of
yellow fire. The youths in the gallery had taken off their coats and
waistcoats and hung them over the side. They talked to each other
across the theatre, and shared their oranges with the tawdry girls who
sat beside them. Some women were laughing in the pit. Their voices
were horribly shrill and discordant. The sound of the popping of
corks came from the bar.

"What a place to find one's divinity in!" said Lord Henry.

"Yes!" answered Dorian Gray. "It was here I found her, and she is
divine beyond all living things. When she acts you will forget everything. These common, rough people, with their coarse faces and brutal gestures, become quite different when she is on the stage. They
sit silently and watch her. They weep and laugh as she wills them to
do. She makes them as responsive as a violin. She spiritualizes them,
and one feels that they are of the same flesh and blood as one's self."

---

1. This was chapter 5 in the *Lippincott's* edition.
2. Miranda is the daughter of Prospero, and Caliban is their reluctant savage servant in *The
   Tempest*.
3. A skylight.

"The same flesh and blood as one's self! Oh, I hope not!"[4] exclaimed Lord Henry, who was scanning the occupants of the gallery through his opera-glass.

"Don't pay any attention to him, Dorian," said the painter. "I understand what you mean, and I believe in this girl. Any one you love must be marvellous, and any girl who has the effect you describe must be fine and noble. To spiritualize one's age—that is something worth doing.[5] If this girl can give a soul to those who have lived without one, if she can create the sense of beauty in people whose lives have been sordid and ugly, if she can strip them of their selfishness and lend them tears for sorrows that are not their own, she is worthy of all your adoration, worthy of the adoration of the world. This marriage is quite right. I did not think so at first, but I admit it now. The gods made Sibyl Vane for you. Without her you would have been incomplete."

"Thanks, Basil," answered Dorian Gray, pressing his hand. "I knew that you would understand me. Harry is so cynical, he terrifies me. But here is the orchestra. It is quite dreadful, but it only lasts for about five minutes. Then the curtain rises, and you will see the girl to whom I am going to give all my life, to whom I have given everything that is good in me."

A quarter of an hour afterwards, amidst an extraordinary turmoil of applause, Sibyl Vane stepped on to the stage. Yes, she was certainly lovely to look at—one of the loveliest creatures, Lord Henry thought, that he had ever seen. There was something of the fawn in her shy grace and startled eyes. A faint blush, like the shadow of a rose in a mirror of silver, came to her cheeks as she glanced at the crowded, enthusiastic house. She stepped back a few paces, and her lips seemed to tremble. Basil Hallward leaped to his feet and began to applaud. Motionless, and as one in a dream, sat Dorian Gray, gazing at her. Lord Henry peered through his glasses, murmuring, "Charming! charming!"

The scene was the hall of Capulet's house, and Romeo in his pilgrim's dress had entered with Mercutio and his other friends. The band, such as it was, struck up a few bars of music, and the dance began. Through the crowd of ungainly, shabbily-dressed actors, Sibyl Vane moved like a creature from a finer world. Her body swayed, while she danced, as a plant sways in the water. The curves of her throat were the curves of a white lily. Her hands seemed to be made of cool ivory.

4. Lord Henry's repetition of Basil's phrase was an added touch in the second edition and recalls one of Wilde's epigrams in "The Decay of Lying": "In point of fact what is interesting about people in good society . . . is the mask that each of them wears, not the reality that lies behind the mask. It is a humiliating confession, but we are all of us made out of the same stuff."
5. An allusion to an important theme in *Marius the Epicurean* by Walter Pater.

Yet she was curiously listless. She showed no sign of joy when her eyes rested on Romeo. The few words she had to speak—

> *Good pilgrim, you do wrong your hand too much,*
> *Which mannerly devotion shows in this;*
> *For saints have hands that pilgrims' hands do touch,*
> *And palm to palm is holy palmers' kiss—*[6]

with the brief dialogue that follows, were spoken in a thoroughly artificial manner. The voice was exquisite, but from the point of view of tone it was absolutely false. It was wrong in colour. It took away all the life from the verse. It made the passion unreal.

Dorian Gray grew pale as he watched her. He was puzzled and anxious. Neither of his friends dared to say anything to him. She seemed to them to be absolutely incompetent. They were horribly disappointed.

Yet they felt that the true test of any Juliet is the balcony scene of the second act. They waited for that. If she failed there, there was nothing in her.

She looked charming as she came out in the moonlight. That could not be denied. But the staginess of her acting was unbearable, and grew worse as she went on. Her gestures became absurdly artificial. She over-emphasized everything that she had to say. The beautiful passage—

> *Thou knowest the mask of night is on my face,*
> *Else would a maiden blush bepaint my cheek*
> *For that which thou hast heard me speak to-night—*[7]

was declaimed with the painful precision of a school-girl who has been taught to recite by some second-rate professor of elocution. When she leaned over the balcony and came to those wonderful lines—

> *Although I joy in thee,*
> *I have no joy of this contract to-night:*
> *It is too rash, too unadvised, too sudden;*
> *Too like the lightning, which doth cease to be*
> *Ere one can say, "It lightens." Sweet, good-night!*
> *This bud of love by summer's ripening breath*
> *May prove a beauteous flower when next we meet—*[8]

she spoke the words as though they conveyed no meaning to her. It was not nervousness. Indeed, so far from being nervous, she was

6. *Romeo and Juliet* 1.5.97–100.
7. *Romeo and Juliet* 2.2.85–87.
8. *Romeo and Juliet* 2.2.116–22.

absolutely self-contained. It was simply bad art. She was a complete failure.

Even the common, uneducated audience of the pit and gallery lost their interest in the play. They got restless, and began to talk loudly and to whistle. The Jew manager, who was standing at the back of the dress-circle, stamped and swore with rage. The only person unmoved was the girl herself.

When the second act was over there came a storm of hisses, and Lord Henry got up from his chair and put on his coat. "She is quite beautiful, Dorian," he said, "but she can't act. Let us go."

"I am going to see the play through," answered the lad, in a hard, bitter voice. "I am awfully sorry that I have made you waste an evening, Harry. I apologize to you both."

"My dear Dorian, I should think Miss Vane was ill," interrupted Hallward. "We will come some other night."

"I wish she were ill," he rejoined. "But she seems to me to be simply callous and cold. She has entirely altered. Last night she was a great artist. This evening she is merely a commonplace, mediocre actress."

"Don't talk like that about any one you love, Dorian. Love is a more wonderful thing than Art."

"They are both simply forms of imitation," remarked Lord Henry. "But do let us go. Dorian, you must not stay here any longer. It is not good for one's morals to see bad acting. Besides, I don't suppose you will want your wife to act. So what does it matter if she plays Juliet like a wooden doll? She is very lovely, and if she knows as little about life as she does about acting, she will be a delightful experience. There are only two kinds of people who are really fascinating—people who know absolutely everything, and people who know absolutely nothing. Good heavens, my dear boy, don't look so tragic! The secret of remaining young is never to have an emotion that is unbecoming. Come to the club with Basil and myself. We will smoke cigarettes and drink to the beauty of Sibyl Vane. She is beautiful. What more can you want?"

"Go away, Harry," cried the lad. "I want to be alone. Basil, you must go. Ah! can't you see that my heart is breaking?" The hot tears came to his eyes. His lips trembled, and, rushing to the back of the box, he leaned up against the wall, hiding his face in his hands.

"Let us go, Basil," said Lord Henry with a strange tenderness in his voice; and the two young men passed out together.

A few moments afterwards the footlights flared up, and the curtain rose on the third act. Dorian Gray went back to his seat. He looked pale, and proud, and indifferent. The play dragged on, and seemed interminable. Half of the audience went out, tramping in heavy boots, and laughing. The whole thing was a *fiasco*. The last act was played to almost empty benches. The curtain went down on a titter, and some groans.

As soon as it was over, Dorian Gray rushed behind the scenes into the greenroom. The girl was standing there alone, with a look of triumph on her face. Her eyes were lit with an exquisite fire. There was a radiance about her. Her parted lips were smiling over some secret of their own.

When he entered, she looked at him, and an expression of infinite joy came over her. "How badly I acted to-night, Dorian!" she cried.

"Horribly!" he answered, gazing at her in amazement—"horribly! It was dreadful. Are you ill? You have no idea what it was. You have no idea what I suffered."

The girl smiled. "Dorian," she answered, lingering over his name with long-drawn music in her voice, as though it were sweeter than honey to the red petals of her mouth—"Dorian, you should have understood. But you understand now, don't you?"

"Understand what?" he asked, angrily.

"Why I was so bad to-night. Why I shall always be bad. Why I shall never act well again."

He shrugged his shoulders. "You are ill, I suppose. When you are ill you shouldn't act. You make yourself ridiculous. My friends were bored. I was bored."

She seemed not to listen to him. She was transfigured with joy. An ecstasy of happiness dominated her.

"Dorian, Dorian," she cried, "before I knew you, acting was the one reality of my life. It was only in the theatre that I lived. I thought that it was all true. I was Rosalind one night, and Portia the other. The joy of Beatrice was my joy, and the sorrows of Cordelia were mine also.[9] I believed in everything. The common people who acted with me seemed to me to be godlike. The painted scenes were my world. I knew nothing but shadows, and I thought them real. You came—oh, my beautiful love!—and you freed my soul from prison. You taught me what reality really is. To-night, for the first time in my life, I saw through the hollowness, the sham, the silliness of the empty pageant in which I had always played. To-night, for the first time, I became conscious that the Romeo was hideous, and old, and painted, that the moonlight in the orchard was false, that the scenery was vulgar, and that the words I had to speak were unreal, were not my words, were not what I wanted to say. You had brought me something higher, something of which all art is but a reflection. You had made me

---

9. Portia is the heroine of *The Merchant of Venice*, Beatrice of *Much Ado about Nothing*, and Cordelia of *King Lear*. Taken together, they would represent a good test of an actress's range.

understand what love really is. My love! my love! Prince Charming! Prince of life! I have grown sick of shadows.[1] You are more to me than all art can ever be. What have I to do with the puppets of a play? When I came on to-night, I could not understand how it was that everything had gone from me. I thought that I was going to be wonderful. I found that I could do nothing. Suddenly it dawned on my soul what it all meant. The knowledge was exquisite to me. I heard them hissing, and I smiled. What could they know of love such as ours? Take me away, Dorian—take me away with you, where we can be quite alone. I hate the stage. I might mimic a passion that I do not feel, but I cannot mimic one that burns me like fire. Oh, Dorian, Dorian, you understand now what it signifies? Even if I could do it, it would be profanation for me to play at being in love. You have made me see that."

He flung himself down on the sofa, and turned away his face. "You have killed my love," he muttered.

She looked at him in wonder, and laughed. He made no answer. She came across to him, and with her little fingers stroked his hair. She knelt down and pressed his hands to her lips. He drew them away, and a shudder ran through him.

Then he leaped up, and went to the door. "Yes," he cried, "you have killed my love. You used to stir my imagination. Now you don't even stir my curiosity. You simply produce no effect. I loved you because you were marvellous, because you had genius and intellect, because you realized the dreams of great poets and gave shape and substance to the shadows of art. You have thrown it all away. You are shallow and stupid. My God! how mad I was to love you! What a fool I have been! You are nothing to me now. I will never see you again. I will never think of you. I will never mention your name. You don't know what you were to me, once. Why, once . . . Oh, I can't bear to think of it! I wish I had never laid eyes upon you! You have spoiled the romance of my life. How little you can know of love, if you say it mars your art! Without your art you are nothing. I would have made you famous, splendid, magnificent. The world would have worshipped you, and you would have borne my name. What are you now? A third-rate actress with a pretty face."

The girl grew white, and trembled. She clenched her hands together, and her voice seemed to catch in her throat. "You are not serious, Dorian?" she murmured. "You are acting."

"Acting! I leave that to you. You do it so well," he answered bitterly.

She rose from her knees, and, with a piteous expression of pain in her face, came across the room to him. She put her hand upon his

1. A direct allusion to Tennyson's "The Lady of Shalott."

arm, and looked into his eyes. He thrust her back. "Don't touch me!" he cried.

A low moan broke from her, and she flung herself at his feet, and lay there like a trampled flower. "Dorian, Dorian, don't leave me!" she whispered. "I am so sorry I didn't act well. I was thinking of you all the time. But I will try—indeed, I will try. It came so suddenly across me, my love for you. I think I should never have known it if you had not kissed me—if we had not kissed each other. Kiss me again, my love. Don't go away from me. I couldn't bear it. Oh! don't go away from me. My brother . . . No; never mind. He didn't mean it. He was in jest. . . . But you, oh! can't you forgive me for to-night? I will work so hard, and try to improve. Don't be cruel to me because I love you better than anything in the world. After all, it is only once that I have not pleased you. But you are quite right, Dorian. I should have shown myself more of an artist. It was foolish of me; and yet I couldn't help it. Oh, don't leave me, don't leave me." A fit of passionate sobbing choked her. She crouched on the floor like a wounded thing, and Dorian Gray, with his beautiful eyes, looked down at her, and his chiselled lips curled in exquisite disdain. There is always something ridiculous about the emotions of people whom one has ceased to love. Sibyl Vane seemed to him to be absurdly melodramatic. Her tears and sobs annoyed him.

"I am going," he said at last, in his calm, clear voice. "I don't wish to be unkind, but I can't see you again. You have disappointed me."

She wept silently, and made no answer, but crept nearer. Her little hands stretched blindly out, and appeared to be seeking for him. He turned on his heel, and left the room. In a few moments he was out of the theatre.

Where he went to he hardly knew. He remembered wandering through dimly-lit streets, past gaunt black-shadowed archways and evil-looking houses. Women with hoarse voices and harsh laughter had called after him. Drunkards had reeled by cursing, and chattering to themselves like monstrous apes. He had seen grotesque children huddled upon door-steps, and heard shrieks and oaths from gloomy courts.

As the dawn was just breaking he found himself close to Covent Garden.[2] The darkness lifted, and, flushed with faint fires, the sky hollowed itself into a perfect pearl. Huge carts filled with nodding lilies rumbled slowly down the polished empty street. The air was heavy with the perfume of the flowers, and their beauty seemed to

2. The site of the famous theater is near Trafalgar Square, an area rich in literary and the-atrical history; it was also the location of open-air markets. Wilde wrote a remarkably sim-ilar scene in "Lord Arthur Savile's Crime." Professor Henry Higgins first meets Liza Doolittle selling flowers in the market in Shaw's *Pygmalion*.

bring him an anodyne for his pain. He followed into the market, and watched the men unloading their waggons. A white-smocked carter[3] offered him some cherries. He thanked him, wondered why he refused to accept any money for them, and began to eat them list-lessly. They had been plucked at midnight, and the coldness of the moon had entered into them. A long line of boys carrying crates of striped tulips, and of yellow and red roses, defiled in front of him, threading their way through the huge jade-green piles of vegetables. Under the portico, with its grey sun-bleached pillars, loitered a troop of draggled bareheaded girls, waiting for the auction to be over. Others crowded round the swinging doors of the coffee-house in the Piazza. The heavy cart-horses slipped and stamped upon the rough stones, shaking their bells and trappings. Some of the drivers were lying asleep on a pile of sacks. Iris-necked, and pink-footed, the pigeons ran about picking up seeds.

After a little while, he hailed a hansom, and drove home. For a few moments he loitered upon the doorstep, looking round at the silent Square[4] with its blank close-shuttered windows, and its staring blinds. The sky was pure opal now, and the roofs of the houses glistened like silver against it. From some chimney opposite a thin wreath of smoke was rising. It curled, a violet riband, through the nacre-coloured air.[5]

In the huge gilt Venetian lantern, spoil of some Doge's barge,[6] that hung from the ceiling of the great oak-panelled hall of entrance, lights were still burning from three flickering jets: thin blue petals of flame they seemed, rimmed with white fire. He turned them out, and, having thrown his hat and cape on the table, passed through the library towards the door of his bedroom, a large octagonal chamber on the ground floor that, in his new-born feeling for luxury, he had just had decorated for himself, and hung with some curious Renaissance tapestries that had been discovered stored in a disused attic at Selby Royal.[7] As he was turning the handle of the door, his eye fell upon the portrait Basil Hallward had painted of him. He started back as if in surprise. Then he went on into his own room, looking somewhat puzzled. After he had taken the buttonhole out of his coat, he seemed to hesitate. Finally he came back, went over to the picture, and examined it. In the dim arrested light that struggled through the cream-coloured silk blinds, the face appeared to him to be a little changed. The expression looked different. One would have

3. One who drives a cart.
4. Grosvenor Square, where Dorian had his London residence, is located in the heart of Mayfair. Wilde once lived nearby on Charles Street prior to his marriage.
5. Nacre is mother-of-pearl.
6. The elected chief magistrate of the Venetian Republic.
7. Dorian's country estate.

said that there was a touch of cruelty in the mouth. It was certainly strange.

He turned round, and, walking to the window, drew up the blind. The bright dawn flooded the room, and swept the fantastic shadows into dusky corners, where they lay shuddering. But the strange expression that he had noticed in the face of the portrait seemed to linger there, to be more intensified even. The quivering, ardent sunlight showed him the lines of cruelty round the mouth as clearly as if he had been looking into a mirror after he had done some dreadful thing.

He winced, and, taking up from the table an oval glass framed in ivory Cupids, one of Lord Henry's many presents to him, glanced hurriedly into its polished depths. No line like that warped his red lips. What did it mean?

He rubbed his eyes, and came close to the picture, and examined it again. There were no signs of any change when he looked into the actual painting, and yet there was no doubt that the whole expression had altered. It was not a mere fancy of his own. The thing was horribly apparent.

He threw himself into a chair, and began to think. Suddenly there flashed across his mind what he had said in Basil Hallward's studio the day the picture had been finished. Yes, he remembered it perfectly. He had uttered a mad wish that he himself might remain young, and the portrait grow old; that his own beauty might be untarnished, and the face on the canvas bear the burden of his passions and his sins; that the painted image might be seared with the lines of suffering and thought, and that he might keep all the delicate bloom and loveliness of his then just conscious boyhood. Surely his wish had not been fulfilled? Such things were impossible. It seemed monstrous even to think of them. And, yet, there was the picture before him, with the touch of cruelty in the mouth.

Cruelty! Had he been cruel? It was the girl's fault, not his. He had dreamed of her as a great artist, had given his love to her because he had thought her great. Then she had disappointed him. She had been shallow and unworthy. And, yet, a feeling of infinite regret came over him, as he thought of her lying at his feet sobbing like a little child. He remembered with what callousness he had watched her. Why had he been made like that? Why had such a soul been given to him? But he had suffered also. During the three terrible hours that the play had lasted, he had lived centuries of pain, æon upon æon of torture. His life was well worth hers. She had marred him for a moment, if he had wounded her for an age. Besides, women were better suited to bear sorrow than men. They lived on their emotions. They only thought of their emotions. When they took lovers, it was merely to have some one with whom they could have scenes. Lord Henry had told him that, and Lord Henry knew what women were. Why should he trouble about Sibyl Vane? She was nothing to him now.

But the picture? What was he to say of that? It held the secret of his life, and told his story. It had taught him to love his own beauty. Would it teach him to loathe his own soul? Would he ever look at it again?

No; it was merely an illusion wrought on the troubled senses. The horrible night that he had passed had left phantoms behind it. Suddenly there had fallen upon his brain that tiny scarlet speck that makes men mad. The picture had not changed. It was folly to think so.

Yet it was watching him, with its beautiful marred face and its cruel smile. Its bright hair gleamed in the early sunlight. Its blue eyes met his own. A sense of infinite pity, not for himself, but for the painted image of himself, came over him. It had altered already, and would alter more. Its gold would wither into grey. Its red and white roses would die. For every sin that he committed, a stain would fleck and wreck its fairness. But he would not sin. The picture, changed or unchanged, would be to him the visible emblem of conscience. He would resist temptation. He would not see Lord Henry any more— would not, at any rate, listen to those subtle poisonous theories that in Basil Hallward's garden had first stirred within him the passion for impossible things. He would go back to Sibyl Vane, make her amends, marry her, try to love her again. Yes, it was his duty to do so. She must have suffered more than he had. Poor child! He had been selfish and cruel to her. The fascination that she had exercised over him would return. They would be happy together. His life with her would be beautiful and pure.

He got up from his chair, and drew a large screen right in front of the portrait, shuddering as he glanced at it. "How horrible!" he murmured to himself, and he walked across to the window and opened it. When he stepped out on to the grass, he drew a deep breath. The fresh morning air seemed to drive away all his sombre passions. He thought only of Sibyl. A faint echo of his love came back to him. He repeated her name over and over again. The birds that were singing in the dew-drenched garden seemed to be telling the flowers about her.

Chapter VIII[1]

It was long past noon when he awoke. His valet had crept several times on tiptoe into the room to see if he was stirring, and had wondered what made his young master sleep so late. Finally his bell sounded, and Victor came in softly with a cup of tea, and a pile of letters, on a small tray of old Sevres china,[2] and drew back the olive-satin curtains, with their shimmering blue lining, that hung in front of the three tall windows.

"Monsieur has well slept this morning," he said, smiling.

"What o'clock is it, Victor?" asked Dorian Gray, drowsily.

"One hour and a quarter, Monsieur."

How late it was! He sat up, and, having sipped some tea, turned over his letters. One of them was from Lord Henry, and had been brought by hand that morning. He hesitated for a moment, and then put it aside. The others he opened listlessly. They contained the usual collection of cards, invitations to dinner, tickets for private views, programmes of charity concerts, and the like, that are showered on fashionable young men every morning during the season. There was a rather heavy bill, for a chased silver Louis-Quinze[3] toilet-set, that he had not yet had the courage to send on to his guardians, who were extremely old-fashioned people and did not realize that we live in an age when unnecessary things are our only necessities; and there were several very courteously worded communications from Jermyn Street[4] money-lenders offering to advance any sum of money at a moment's notice and at the most reasonable rates of interest.

After about ten minutes he got up, and, throwing on an elaborate dressing-gown of silk-embroidered cashmere wool, passed into the onyx-paved bathroom. The cool water refreshed him after his long sleep. He seemed to have forgotten all that he had gone through. A dim sense of having taken part in some strange tragedy came to him once or twice, but there was the unreality of a dream about it.

As soon as he was dressed, he went into the library and sat down to a light French breakfast,[5] that had been laid out for him on a small round table close to the open window. It was an exquisite day. The warm air seemed laden with spices. A bee flew in, and buzzed round the blue-dragon bowl that, filled with sulphur-yellow roses, stood before him. He felt perfectly happy.

---

1. Originally chapter 6 in the *Lippincott's Magazine* version.
2. An elegant French porcelain made in Sèvres, a Paris suburb, since the eighteenth century.
3. Describes the rococo style popular in mid-eighteenth-century France during the reign of Louis XV, denoting elegance, fantasy, and luxury. "Chased" refers to a piece ornamented with embossed work or engraved in relief.
4. Located in the city of Westminster in London, rather near to Piccadilly Circus.
5. Probably coffee and pastry or toast.

Suddenly his eye fell on the screen that he had placed in front of the portrait, and he started.

"Too cold for Monsieur?" asked his valet, putting an omelette on the table. "I shut the window?"

Dorian shook his head. "I am not cold," he murmured.

Was it all true? Had the portrait really changed? Or had it been simply his own imagination that had made him see a look of evil where there had been a look of joy? Surely a painted canvas could not alter? The thing was absurd. It would serve as a tale to tell Basil some day. It would make him smile.

And, yet, how vivid was his recollection of the whole thing! First in the dim twilight, and then in the bright dawn, he had seen the touch of cruelty round the warped lips. He almost dreaded his valet leaving the room. He knew that when he was alone he would have to examine the portrait. He was afraid of certainty. When the coffee and cigarettes had been brought and the man turned to go, he felt a wild desire to tell him to remain. As the door was closing behind him he called him back. The man stood waiting for his orders. Dorian looked at him for a moment. "I am not at home to any one, Victor," he said, with a sigh. The man bowed and retired.

Then he rose from the table, lit a cigarette, and flung himself down on a luxuriously-cushioned couch that stood facing the screen. The screen was an old one, of gilt Spanish leather, stamped and wrought with a rather florid Louis-Quatorze[6] pattern. He scanned it curiously, wondering if ever before it had concealed the secret of a man's life.

Should he move it aside, after all? Why not let it stay there? What was the use of knowing.? If the thing was true, it was terrible. If it was not true, why trouble about it? But what if, by some fate or deadlier chance, eyes other than his spied behind, and saw the horrible change? What should he do if Basil Hallward came and asked to look at his own picture? Basil would be sure to do that. No; the thing had to be examined, and at once. Anything would be better than this dreadful state of doubt.

He got up, and locked both doors. At least he would be alone when he looked upon the mask of his shame. Then he drew the screen aside, and saw himself face to face. It was perfectly true. The portrait had altered.

As he often remembered afterwards, and always with no small wonder, he found himself at first gazing at the portrait with a feeling of almost scientific interest. That such a change should have taken place was incredible to him. And yet it was a fact. Was there some

6. The china decoration is named for Louis XIV of France (1638–1715), called "The Sun King," who reigned seventy-two years. The pattern referenced was a border registered under that name by Spode, England's oldest pottery company, in December of 1844.

subtle affinity between the chemical atoms, that shaped themselves into form and colour on the canvas, and the soul that was within him? Could it be that what that soul thought, they realized?—that what it dreamed, they made true? Or was there some other, more terrible reason? He shuddered, and felt afraid, and, going back to the couch, lay there, gazing at the picture in sickened horror.

One thing, however, he felt that it had done for him. It had made him conscious how unjust, how cruel, he had been to Sibyl Vane. It was not too late to make reparation for that. She could still be his wife. His unreal and selfish love would yield to some higher influence, would be transformed into some nobler passion, and the portrait that Basil Hallward had painted of him would be a guide to him through life, would be to him what holiness is to some, and conscience to others, and the fear of God to us all. There were opiates for remorse, drugs that could lull the moral sense to sleep. But here was a visible symbol of the degradation of sin. Here was an ever-present sign of the ruin men brought upon their souls.

Three o'clock struck, and four, and the half-hour rang its double chime, but Dorian Gray did not stir. He was trying to gather up the scarlet threads of life, and to weave them into a pattern; to find his way through the sanguine labyrinth of passion through which he was wandering. He did not know what to do, or what to think. Finally, he went over to the table and wrote a passionate letter to the girl he had loved, imploring her forgiveness, and accusing himself of madness. He covered page after page with wild words of sorrow, and wilder words of pain. There is a luxury in self-reproach. When we blame ourselves we feel that no one else has a right to blame us. It is the confession, not the priest, that gives us absolution. When Dorian had finished the letter, he felt that he had been forgiven.

Suddenly there came a knock to the door, and he heard Lord Henry's voice outside. "My dear boy, I must see you. Let me in at once. I can't bear your shutting yourself up like this."

He made no answer at first, but remained quite still. The knocking still continued, and grew louder. Yes, it was better to let Lord Henry in, and to explain to him the new life he was going to lead, to quarrel with him if it became necessary to quarrel, to part if parting was inevitable. He jumped up, drew the screen hastily across the picture, and unlocked the door.

"I am so sorry for it all, Dorian," said Lord Henry, as he entered. "But you must not think too much about it."

"Do you mean about Sibyl Vane?" asked the lad.

"Yes, of course," answered Lord Henry, sinking into a chair, and slowly pulling off his yellow gloves. "It is dreadful, from one point of view, but it was not your fault. Tell me, did you go behind and see her, after the play was over?"

"Yes."

"I felt sure you had. Did you make a scene with her?"

"I was brutal, Harry—perfectly brutal. But it is all right now. I am not sorry for anything that has happened. It has taught me to know myself better."

"Ah, Dorian, I am so glad you take it in that way! I was afraid I would find you plunged in remorse, and tearing that nice curly hair of yours."

"I have got through all that," said Dorian, shaking his head, and smiling. "I am perfectly happy now. I know what conscience is, to begin with. It is not what you told me it was. It is the divinest thing in us. Don't sneer at it, Harry, any more—at least not before me. I want to be good. I can't bear the idea of my soul being hideous."

"A very charming artistic basis for ethics, Dorian! I congratulate you on it. But how are you going to begin?"

"By marrying Sibyl Vane."

"Marrying Sibyl Vane!" cried Lord Henry, standing up, and looking at him in perplexed amazement. "But, my dear Dorian—"

"Yes, Harry, I know what you are going to say. Something dreadful about marriage. Don't say it. Don't ever say things of that kind to me again. Two days ago I asked Sibyl to marry me. I am not going to break my word to her. She is to be my wife."

"Your wife! Dorian! . . . Didn't you get my letter? I wrote to you this morning, and sent the note down, by my own man."

"Your letter? Oh, yes, I remember. I have not read it yet, Harry. I was afraid there might be something in it that I wouldn't like. You cut life to pieces with your epigrams."

"You know nothing then?"

"What do you mean?"

Lord Henry walked across the room, and, sitting down by Dorian Gray, took both his hands in his own, and held them tightly. "Dorian," he said, "my letter—don't be frightened—was to tell you that Sibyl Vane is dead."

A cry of pain broke from the lad's lips, and he leaped to his feet, tearing his hands away from Lord Henry's grasp. "Dead! Sibyl dead! It is not true! It is a horrible lie! How dare you say it?"

"It is quite true, Dorian," said Lord Henry, gravely. "It is in all the morning papers. I wrote down to you to ask you not to see any one till I came. There will have to be an inquest, of course, and you must not be mixed up in it. Things like that make a man fashionable in Paris. But in London people are so prejudiced. Here, one should never make one's *début* with a scandal. One should reserve that to give an interest to one's old age. I suppose they don't know your name at the theatre? If they don't, it is all right. Did any one see you going round to her room? That is an important point."

Dorian did not answer for a few moments. He was dazed with horror. Finally he stammered, in a stifled voice, "Harry, did you say an inquest? What did you mean by that? Did Sibyl—? Oh, Harry, I can't bear it! But be quick. Tell me everything at once."

"I have no doubt it was not an accident, Dorian, though it must be put in that way to the public. It seems that as she was leaving the theatre with her mother, about half-past twelve or so, she said she had forgotten something upstairs. They waited some time for her, but she did not come down again. They ultimately found her lying dead on the floor of her dressing-room. She had swallowed something by mistake, some dreadful thing they use at theatres. I don't know what it was, but it had either prussic acid or white lead in it. I should fancy it was prussic acid, as she seems to have died instantaneously."

"Harry, Harry, it is terrible!" cried the lad.

"Yes; it is very tragic, of course, but you must not get yourself mixed up in it. I see by *The Standard*[7] that she was seventeen. I should have thought she was almost younger than that. She looked such a child, and seemed to know so little about acting. Dorian, you mustn't let this thing get on your nerves. You must come and dine with me, and afterwards we will look in at the Opera. It is a Patti[8] night, and everybody will be there. You can come to my sister's box. She has got some smart women with her."

"So I have murdered Sibyl Vane," said Dorian Gray, half to himself—"murdered her as surely as if I had cut her little throat with a knife. Yet the roses are not less lovely for all that. The birds sing just as happily in my garden. And to-night I am to dine with you, and then go on to the Opera, and sup somewhere, I suppose, afterwards. How extraordinarily dramatic life is! If I had read all this in a book, Harry, I think I would have wept over it. Somehow, now that it has happened actually, and to me, it seems far too wonderful for tears. Here is the first passionate love-letter I have ever written in my life. Strange, that my first passionate love-letter should have been addressed to a dead girl. Can they feel, I wonder, those white silent people we call the dead? Sibyl! Can she feel, or know, or listen? Oh, Harry, how I loved her once! It seems years ago to me now. She was everything to me. Then came that dreadful night—was it really only last night?—when she played so badly, and my heart almost broke. She explained it all to me. It was terribly pathetic. But I was not moved a bit. I thought her shallow. Suddenly something happened that made me afraid. I can't tell you what it was, but it was terrible. I said I would go back to her. I felt I had done wrong. And now she is dead. My God! my

7. A politically conservative London morning newspaper.
8. Adelina Patti (1843–1919) was one of the most popular operatic sopranos of the period. Her performances were legendary.

God! Harry, what shall I do? You don't know the danger I am in, and there is nothing to keep me straight. She would have done that for me. She had no right to kill herself. It was selfish of her."

"My dear Dorian," answered Lord Henry, taking a cigarette from his case, and producing a gold-latten[9] matchbox, "the only way a woman can ever reform a man is by boring him so completely that he loses all possible interest in life. If you had married this girl you would have been wretched. Of course you would have treated her kindly. One can always be kind to people about whom one cares nothing. But she would have soon found out that you were absolutely indifferent to her. And when a woman finds that out about her husband, she either becomes dreadfully dowdy, or wears very smart bonnets that some other woman's husband has to pay for. I say nothing about the social mistake, which would have been abject, which, of course, I would not have allowed, but I assure you that in any case the whole thing would have been an absolute failure."

"I suppose it would," muttered the lad, walking up and down the room, and looking horribly pale. "But I thought it was my duty. It is not my fault that this terrible tragedy has prevented my doing what was right. I remember your saying once that there is a fatality about good resolutions—that they are always made too late. Mine certainly were."

"Good resolutions are useless attempts to interfere with scientific laws. Their origin is pure vanity. Their result is absolutely *nil*. They give us, now and then, some of those luxurious sterile emotions that have a certain charm for the weak. That is all that can be said for them. They are simply cheques that men draw on a bank where they have no account."

"Harry," cried Dorian Gray, coming over and sitting down beside him, "why is it that I cannot feel this tragedy as much as I want to? I don't think I am heartless. Do you?"

"You have done too many foolish things during the last fortnight to be entitled to give yourself that name, Dorian," answered Lord Henry, with his sweet, melancholy smile.

The lad frowned. "I don't like that explanation, Harry," he rejoined, "but I am glad you don't think I am heartless. I am nothing of the kind. I know I am not. And yet I must admit that this thing that has happened does not affect me as it should. It seems to me to be simply like a wonderful ending to a wonderful play. It has all the terrible beauty of a Greek tragedy, a tragedy in which I took a great part, but by which I have not been wounded."

"It is an interesting question," said Lord Henry, who found an exquisite pleasure in playing on the lad's unconscious egotism—"an

9. Gold-plated or -foiled.

extremely interesting question. I fancy that the true explanation is this. It often happens that the real tragedies of life occur in such an inartistic manner that they hurt us by their crude violence, their absolute incoherence, their absurd want of meaning, their entire lack of style. They affect us just as vulgarity affects us. They give us an impression of sheer brute force, and we revolt against that. Sometimes, however, a tragedy that possesses artistic elements of beauty crosses our lives. If these elements of beauty are real, the whole thing simply appeals to our sense of dramatic effect. Suddenly we find that we are no longer the actors, but the spectators of the play. Or rather we are both. We watch ourselves, and the mere wonder of the spectacle enthralls us. In the present case, what is it that has really happened? Some one has killed herself for love of you. I wish that I had ever had such an experience. It would have made me in love with love for the rest of my life. The people who have adored me—there have not been very many, but there have been some—have always insisted on living on, long after I had ceased to care for them, or they to care for me. They have become stout and tedious, and when I meet them they go in at once for reminiscences. That awful memory of woman! What a fearful thing it is! And what an utter intellectual stagnation it reveals! One should absorb the colour of life, but one should never remember its details. Details are always vulgar."

"I must sow poppies[1] in my garden," sighed Dorian.

"There is no necessity," rejoined his companion. "Life has always poppies in her hands. Of course, now and then things linger. I once wore nothing but violets all through one season, as a form of artistic mourning for a romance that would not die. Ultimately, however, it did die. I forget what killed it. I think it was her proposing to sacrifice the whole world for me. That is always a dreadful moment. It fills one with the terror of eternity. Well—would you believe it?—a week ago, at Lady Hampshire's, I found myself seated at dinner next the lady in question, and she insisted on going over the whole thing again, and digging up the past, and raking up the future. I had buried my romance in a bed of asphodel.[2] She dragged it out again, and assured me that I had spoiled her life. I am bound to state that she ate an enormous dinner, so I did not feel any anxiety. But what a lack of taste she showed! The one charm of the past is that it is the past. But women never know when the curtain has fallen. They always want a sixth act, and as soon as the interest of the play is entirely over they propose to continue it. If they were allowed their own way, every comedy would

1. Poppies symbolize forgetfulness and drugged sleep. Wilde changed this from "poppy" in *Lippincott's*. Flower symbolism, a familiar language to Victorians, is known today almost exclusively by florists.
2. Asphodel symbolizes death and the underworld.

have a tragic ending, and every tragedy would culminate in a farce. They are charmingly artificial, but they have no sense of art. You are more fortunate than I am. I assure you, Dorian, that not one of the women I have known would have done for me what Sibyl Vane did for you. Ordinary women always console themselves. Some of them do it by going in for sentimental colours. Never trust a woman who wears mauve, whatever her age may be, or a woman over thirty-five who is fond of pink ribbons. It always means that they have a history. Others find a great consolation in suddenly discovering the good qualities of their husbands. They flaunt their conjugal felicity in one's face, as if it were the most fascinating of sins. Religion consoles some. Its mysteries have all the charm of a flirtation, a woman once told me; and I can quite understand it. Besides, nothing makes one so vain as being told that one is a sinner. Conscience makes egotists of us all.[3] Yes; there is really no end to the consolations that women find in modern life. Indeed, I have not mentioned the most important one."

"What is that, Harry?" said the lad, listlessly.

"Oh, the obvious consolation. Taking some one else's admirer when one loses one's own. In good society that always whitewashes a woman. But really, Dorian, how different Sibyl Vane must have been from all the women one meets! There is something to me quite beautiful about her death. I am glad I am living in a century when such wonders happen. They make one believe in the reality of the things we all play with, such as romance, passion, and love."

"I was terribly cruel to her. You forget that."

"I am afraid that women appreciate cruelty, downright cruelty, more than anything else. They have wonderfully primitive instincts. We have emancipated them, but they remain slaves looking for their masters, all the same. They love being dominated. I am sure you were splendid. I have never seen you really and absolutely angry, but I can fancy how delightful you looked. And, after all, you said something to me the day before yesterday that seemed to me at the time to be merely fanciful, but that I see now was absolutely true, and it holds the key to everything."

"What was that, Harry?"

"You said to me that Sibyl Vane represented to you all the heroines of romance—that she was Desdemona one night, and Ophelia the other; that if she died as Juliet, she came to life as Imogen."

"She will never come to life again now," muttered the lad, burying his face in his hands.

"No, she will never come to life. She has played her last part. But you must think of that lonely death in the tawdry dressing-room

---

3. This is a variation of Hamlet's lament, "Thus conscience doth make cowards of us all." *Hamlet* 3.1.84.

simply as a strange lurid fragment from some Jacobean tragedy, as a wonderful scene from Webster, or Ford, or Cyril Tourneur.[4] The girl never really lived, and so she has never really died. To you at least she was always a dream, a phantom that flitted through Shakespeare's plays and left them lovelier for its presence, a reed through which Shakespeare's music sounded richer and more full of joy. The moment she touched actual life, she marred it, and it marred her, and so she passed away. Mourn for Ophelia, if you like. Put ashes on your head because Cordelia was strangled. Cry out against Heaven because the daughter of Brabantio died.[5] But don't waste your tears over Sibyl Vane. She was less real than they are."

There was a silence. The evening darkened in the room. Noise-lessly, and with silver feet, the shadows crept in from the garden. The colours faded wearily out of things.

After some time Dorian Gray looked up. "You have explained me to myself, Harry," he murmured, with something of a sigh of relief. "I felt all that you have said, but somehow I was afraid of it, and I could not express it to myself. How well you know me! But we will not talk again of what has happened. It has been a marvellous experience. That is all. I wonder if life has still in store for me anything as marvellous."

"Life has everything in store for you, Dorian. There is nothing that you, with your extraordinary good looks, will not be able to do."

"But suppose, Harry, I became haggard, and old, and wrinkled? What then?"

"Ah, then," said Lord Henry, rising to go—"then, my dear Dorian, you would have to fight for your victories. As it is, they are brought to you. No, you must keep your good looks. We live in an age that reads too much to be wise, and that thinks too much to be beautiful. We cannot spare you. And now you had better dress, and drive down to the club. We are rather late, as it is."

"I think I shall join you at the Opera, Harry. I feel too tired to eat anything. What is the number of your sister's box?"

"Twenty-seven, I believe. It is on the grand tier. You will see her name on the door. But I am sorry you won't come and dine."

"I don't feel up to it," said Dorian, listlessly. "But I am awfully obliged to you for all that you have said to me. You are certainly my best friend. No one has ever understood me as you have."

"We are only at the beginning of our friendship, Dorian," answered Lord Henry, shaking him by the hand. "Good-bye. I shall see you before nine-thirty, I hope. Remember, Patti is singing."

---

4. Webster, Ford, and Tourneur were English playwrights whose works dramatized passion and violence. They flourished during the Jacobean period (during the reign of James I of England in the early seventeenth century).
5. Lord Henry refers to the death of Desdemona in Shakespeare's *Othello*.

As he closed the door behind him, Dorian Gray touched the bell, and in a few minutes Victor appeared with the lamps and drew the blinds down. He waited impatiently for him to go. The man seemed to take an interminable time over everything.

As soon as he had left, he rushed to the screen and drew it back. No; there was no further change in the picture. It had received the news of Sibyl Vane's death before he had known of it himself. It was conscious of the events of life as they occurred. The vicious cruelty that marred the fine lines of the mouth had, no doubt, appeared at the very moment that the girl had drunk the poison, whatever it was. Or was it indifferent to results? Did it merely take cognizance of what passed within the soul? He wondered, and hoped that some day he would see the change taking place before his very eyes, shuddering as he hoped it.

Poor Sibyl! what a romance it had all been! She had often mimicked death on the stage. Then Death himself had touched her, and taken her with him. How had she played that dreadful last scene? Had she cursed him, as she died? No; she had died for love of him, and love would always be a sacrament to him now. She had atoned for everything, by the sacrifice she had made of her life. He would not think any more of what she had made him go through, on that horrible night at the theatre. When he thought of her, it would be as a wonderful tragic figure sent on to the world's stage to show the supreme reality of Love. A wonderful tragic figure? Tears came to his eyes as he remembered her childlike look and winsome fanciful ways and shy tremulous grace. He brushed them away hastily, and looked again at the picture.

He felt that the time had really come for making his choice. Or had his choice already been made? Yes, life had decided that for him— life, and his own infinite curiosity about life. Eternal youth, infinite passion, pleasures subtle and secret, wild joys and wilder sins—he was to have all these things. The portrait was to bear the burden of his shame: that was all.

A feeling of pain crept over him as he thought of the desecration that was in store for the fair face on the canvas. Once, in boyish mockery of Narcissus,[6] he had kissed, or feigned to kiss, those painted lips that now smiled so cruelly at him. Morning after morning he had sat before the portrait wondering at its beauty, almost enamoured of it, as it seemed to him at times. Was it to alter now with every mood to which he yielded? Was it to become a monstrous and loathsome thing, to be hidden away in a locked room, to be shut out

---

6. In Greek mythology, a beautiful youth who fell in love with his own reflection in water and pined to death. Hence, a person characterized by extreme self-admiration or vanity.

from the sunlight that had so often touched to brighter gold the waving wonder of its hair? The pity of it! the pity of it![7]

For a moment he thought of praying that the horrible sympathy that existed between him and the picture might cease. It had changed in answer to a prayer; perhaps in answer to a prayer it might remain unchanged. And, yet, who, that knew anything about Life, would surrender the chance of remaining always young, however fantastic that chance might be, or with what fateful consequences it might be fraught? Besides, was it really under his control? Had it indeed been prayer that had produced the substitution? Might there not be some curious scientific reason for it all? If thought could exercise its influence upon a living organism, might not thought exercise an influence upon dead and inorganic things? Nay, without thought or conscious desire, might not things external to ourselves vibrate in unison with our moods and passions, atom calling to atom in secret love or strange affinity? But the reason was of no importance. He would never again tempt by a prayer any terrible power. If the picture was to alter, it was to alter. That was all. Why inquire too closely into it?

For there would be a real pleasure in watching it. He would be able to follow his mind into its secret places. This portrait would be to him the most magical of mirrors. As it had revealed to him his own body, so it would reveal to him his own soul. And when winter came upon it, he would still be standing where spring trembles on the verge of summer. When the blood crept from its face, and left behind a pallid mask of chalk with leaden eyes, he would keep the glamour of boyhood. Not one blossom of his loveliness would ever fade. Not one pulse of his life would ever weaken. Like the gods of the Greeks, he would be strong, and fleet, and joyous. What did it matter what happened to the coloured image on the canvas? He would be safe. That was everything.

He drew the screen back into its former place in front of the picture, smiling as he did so, and passed into his bedroom, where his valet was already waiting for him. An hour later he was at the Opera, and Lord Henry was leaning over his chair.

---

7. Key words of Othello's remark to Iago in *Othello* 4.1.195–96.

Chapter IX[1]

As he was sitting at breakfast next morning, Basil Hallward was shown into the room.

"I am so glad I have found you, Dorian," he said gravely. "I called last night, and they told me you were at the Opera. Of course I knew that was impossible. But I wish you had left word where you had really gone to. I passed a dreadful evening, half afraid that one tragedy might be followed by another. I think you might have telegraphed for me when you heard of it first. I read of it quite by chance in a late edition of *The Globe*,[2] that I picked up at the club. I came here at once, and was miserable at not finding you. I can't tell you how heart-broken I am about the whole thing. I know what you must suffer. But where were you? Did you go down and see the girl's mother? For a moment I thought of following you there. They gave the address in the paper. Somewhere in the Euston Road, isn't it? But I was afraid of intruding upon a sorrow that I could not lighten. Poor woman! What a state she must be in! And her only child, too! What did she say about it all?"

"My dear Basil, how do I know?" murmured Dorian Gray, sipping some pale-yellow wine from a delicate gold-beaded bubble of Venetian glass, and looking dreadfully bored. "I was at the Opera. You should have come on there. I met Lady Gwendolen, Harry's sister, for the first time. We were in her box. She is perfectly charming; and Patti sang divinely. Don't talk about horrid subjects. If one doesn't talk about a thing, it has never happened. It is simply expression, as Harry says, that gives reality to things. I may mention that she was not the woman's only child. There is a son, a charming fellow, I believe. But he is not on the stage. He is a sailor, or something. And now, tell me about yourself and what you are painting."

"You went to the Opera?" said Hallward, speaking very slowly, and with a strained touch of pain in his voice. "You went to the Opera while Sibyl Vane was lying dead in some sordid lodging? You can talk to me of other women being charming, and of Patti singing divinely, before the girl you loved has even the quiet of a grave to sleep in? Why, man, there are horrors in store for that little white body of hers!"

"Stop, Basil! I won't hear it!" cried Dorian leaping to his feet. "You must not tell me about things. What is done is done. What is past is past."

"You call yesterday the past?"

"What has the actual lapse of time got to do with it? It is only shal-

1. Originally chapter 7 in the *Lippincott's Magazine* version.
2. An evening newspaper, also read by Sherlock Holmes.

low people who require years to get rid of an emotion. A man who is master of himself can end a sorrow as easily as he can invent a pleasure. I don't want to be at the mercy of my emotions. I want to use them, to enjoy them, and to dominate them."

"Dorian, this is horrible! Something has changed you completely. You look exactly the same wonderful boy who, day after day, used to come down to my studio to sit for his picture. But you were simple, natural, and affectionate then. You were the most unspoiled creature in the whole world. Now, I don't know what has come over you. You talk as if you had no heart, no pity in you. It is all Harry's influence. I see that."

The lad flushed up, and, going to the window, looked out for a few moments on the green, flickering, sun-lashed garden. "I owe a great deal to Harry, Basil," he said, at last—"more than I owe to you. You only taught me to be vain."

"Well, I am punished for that, Dorian—or shall be some day."

"I don't know what you mean, Basil," he exclaimed, turning round. "I don't know what you want. What do you want?"

"I want the Dorian Gray I used to paint," said the artist, sadly.

"Basil," said the lad, going over to him, and putting his hand on his shoulder, "you have come too late. Yesterday when I heard that Sibyl Vane had killed herself—"

"Killed herself! Good heavens! is there no doubt about that?" cied Hallward, looking up at him with an expression of horror.

"My dear Basil! Surely you don't think it was a vulgar accident? Of course she killed herself."

The elder man buried his face in his hands. "How fearful," he muttered, and a shudder ran through him.

"No," said Dorian Gray, "there is nothing fearful about it. It is one of the great romantic tragedies of the age. As a rule, people who act lead the most commonplace lives. They are good husbands, or faithful wives, or something tedious. You know what I mean—middle-class virtue, and all that kind of thing. How different Sibyl was! She lived her finest tragedy. She was always a heroine. The last night she played—the night you saw her—she acted badly because she had known the reality of love. When she knew its unreality, she died, as Juliet might have died. She passed again into the sphere of art. There is something of the martyr about her. Her death has all the pathetic uselessness of martyrdom, all its wasted beauty. But, as I was saying, you must not think I have not suffered. If you had come in yesterday at a particular moment—about half-past five, perhaps, or a quarter to six—you would have found me in tears. Even Harry, who was here, who brought me the news, in fact, had no idea what I was going through. I suffered immensely. Then it passed away. I cannot repeat an emotion. No one can, except sentimentalists. And you are awfully unjust, Basil. You come down here to console me. That is charming of you. You find me consoled, and you are furious. How like a sympathetic person! You remind me of a story Harry told me about a certain philanthropist who spent twenty years of his life in trying to get some grievance redressed, or some unjust law altered—I forget exactly what it was. Finally he succeeded, and nothing could exceed his disappointment. He had absolutely nothing to do, almost died of *ennui*,[3] and became a confirmed misanthrope. And besides, my dear old Basil, if you really want to console me, teach me rather to forget what has happened, or to see it from a proper artistic point of view. Was it not Gautier who used to write about *la consolation des arts*?[4] I remember picking up a little vellum-covered book in your studio one day and chancing on that delightful phrase. Well, I am not like that young man you told me of when we were down at Marlow[5] together, the young man who used to say that yellow satin could console one for all the miseries of life. I love beautiful things that one can touch and handle. Old brocades, green bronzes, lacquer-work, carved ivories, exquisite surroundings, luxury pomp, there is much to be got from all these. But the artistic temperament that they create, or at any rate reveal, is still more to me. To become the spectator of one's own life, as Harry says, is to escape the suffering of life. I know you are surprised at my talking to you like this. You have not realized how I have developed. I was a schoolboy when you knew me. I am a man now. I have new passions, new thoughts, new ideas. I am different, but you must not like me less. I am changed, but you must always be my friend. Of course I am very fond of Harry. But I know that you are better than he is. You are not stronger—you are too much afraid of life—but you are better. And how happy we used to be together! Don't leave me, Basil, and don't quarrel with me. I am what I am. There is nothing more to be said."

The painter felt strangely moved. The lad was infinitely dear to him, and his personality had been the great turning-point in his art. He could not bear the idea of reproaching him any more. After all, his indifference was probably merely a mood that would pass away. There was so much in him that was good, so much in him that was noble.

"Well, Dorian," he said at length, with a sad smile, "I won't speak to you again about this horrible thing, after to-day. I only trust your name won't be mentioned in connection with it. The inquest is to take place this afternoon. Have they summoned you?"

Dorian shook his head, and a look of annoyance passed over his face at the mention of the word "inquest." There was something so

3. Weariness of spirit.
4. Théophile Gautier (1811–72), French poet and novelist, one of the founders of Aestheticism in Europe and creator of the legend "art for art's sake."
5. A historic town on the River Thames about thirty miles west of London.

crude and vulgar about everything of the kind. "They don't know my name," he answered.

"But surely she did?"

"Only my Christian name,[6] and that I am quite sure she never mentioned to any one. She told me once that they were all rather curious to learn who I was, and that she invariably told them my name was Prince Charming. It was pretty of her. You must do me a drawing of Sibyl, Basil. I should like to have something more of her than the memory of a few kisses and some broken pathetic words."

"I will try and do something, Dorian, if it would please you. But you must come and sit to me yourself again. I can't get on without you."

"I can never sit to you again, Basil. It is impossible!" he exclaimed, starting back.

The painter stared at him. "My dear boy, what nonsense!" he cried. "Do you mean to say you don't like what I did of you? Where is it? Why have you pulled the screen in front of it? Let me look at it. It is the best thing I have ever done. Do take the screen away, Dorian. It is simply disgraceful of your servant hiding my work like that. I felt the room looked different as I came in."

"My servant has nothing to do with it, Basil. You don't imagine I let him arrange my room for me? He settles my flowers for me sometimes—that is all. No; I did it myself. The light was too strong on the portrait."

"Too strong! Surely not, my dear fellow? It is an admirable place for it. Let me see it." And Hallward walked towards the corner of the room.

A cry of terror broke from Dorian Gray's lips, and he rushed between the painter and the screen. "Basil," he said, looking very pale, "you must not look at it. I don't wish you to."

"Not look at my own work! you are not serious. Why shouldn't I look at it?" exclaimed Hallward, laughing.

"If you try to look at it, Basil, on my word of honour I will never speak to you again as long as I live. I am quite serious. I don't offer any explanation, and you are not to ask for any. But, remember, if you touch this screen, everything is over between us."

Hallward was thunderstruck. He looked at Dorian Gray in absolute amazement. He had never seen him like this before. The lad was actually pallid with rage. His hands were clenched, and the pupils of his eyes were like disks of blue fire. He was trembling all over.

"Dorian!"

"Don't speak!"

"But what is the matter? Of course I won't look at it if you don't

6. One's first, or given, name.

want me to," he said, rather coldly, turning on his heel, and going over towards the window. "But, really, it seems rather absurd that I shouldn't see my own work, especially as I am going to exhibit it in Paris in the autumn. I shall probably have to give it another coat of varnish before that, so I must see it some day, and why not to-day?"

"To exhibit it! You want to exhibit it?" exclaimed Dorian Gray, a strange sense of terror creeping over him. Was the world going to be shown his secret? Were people to gape at the mystery of his life? That was impossible. Something—he did not know what—had to be done at once.

"Yes; I don't suppose you will object to that. Georges Petit is going to collect all my best pictures for a special exhibition in the Rue de Sèze,[7] which will open the first week in October. The portrait will only be away a month. I should think you could easily spare it for that time. In fact, you are sure to be out of town. And if you keep it always behind a screen, you can't care much about it."

Dorian Gray passed his hand over his forehead. There were beads of perspiration there. He felt that he was on the brink of a horrible danger. "You told me a month ago that you would never exhibit it," he cried. "Why have you changed your mind? You people who go in for being consistent have just as many moods as others have. The only difference is that your moods are rather meaningless. You can't have forgotten that you assured me most solemnly that nothing in the world would induce you to send it to any exhibition. You told Harry exactly the same thing." He stopped suddenly, and a gleam of light came into his eyes. He remembered that Lord Henry had said to him once, half seriously and half in jest, "If you want to have a strange quarter of an hour, get Basil to tell you why he won't exhibit your picture. He told me why he wouldn't, and it was a revelation to me." Yes, perhaps Basil, too, had his secret. He would ask him and try.

"Basil," he said, coming over quite close, and looking him straight in the face, "we have each of us a secret. Let me know yours, and I shall tell you mine. What was your reason for refusing to exhibit my picture?"

The painter shuddered in spite of himself. "Dorian, if I told you, you might like me less than you do, and you would certainly laugh at me. I could not bear your doing either of those two things. If you wish me never to look at your picture again, I am content. I have always you to look at. If you wish the best work I have ever done to be hidden from the world, I am satisfied. Your friendship is dearer to me than any fame or reputation."

"No, Basil, you must tell me," insisted Dorian Gray. "I think I have

---

7. Petit founded a popular gallery there in 1882, famous for its association with the French Impressionist painters.

a right to know." His feeling of terror had passed away, and curiosity had taken its place. He was determined to find out Basil Hallward's mystery.

"Let us sit down, Dorian," said the painter, looking troubled. "Let us sit down. And just answer me one question. Have you noticed in the picture something curious?—something that probably at first did not strike you, but that revealed itself to you suddenly?"

"Basil!" cried the lad, clutching the arms of his chair with trembling hands, and gazing at him with wild startled eyes.

"I see you did. Don't speak. Wait till you hear what I have to say. Dorian, from the moment I met you, your personality had the most extraordinary influence over me. I was dominated, soul, brain, and power by you. You became to me the visible incarnation of that unseen ideal whose memory haunts us artists like an exquisite dream. I worshipped you. I grew jealous of every one to whom you spoke. I wanted to have you all to myself. I was only happy when I was with you. When you were away from me you were still present in my art. . . . Of course I never let you know anything about this. It would have been impossible. You would not have understood it. I hardly understood it myself. I only knew that I had seen perfection face to face, and that the world had become wonderful to my eyes—too wonderful, perhaps, for in such mad worships there is peril, the peril of losing them, no less than the peril of keeping them. . . . Weeks and weeks went on, and I grew more and more absorbed in you. Then came a new development. I had drawn you as Paris in dainty armour, and as Adonis with huntsman's cloak and polished boar-spear. Crowned with heavy lotus-blossoms you had sat on the prow of Adrian's barge,[8] gazing across the green turbid Nile. You had leant over the still pool of some Greek woodland, and seen in the water's silent silver the marvel of your own face. And it had all been what art should be, unconscious, ideal, and remote. One day, a fatal day I sometimes think, I determined to paint a wonderful portrait of you as you actually are, not in the costume of dead ages, but in your own dress and in your own time. Whether it was the Realism[9] of the method, or the mere wonder of your own personality, thus directly presented to me without mist or veil, I cannot tell. But I know that as I worked at it, every flake and film of colour seemed to me to reveal my secret. I grew afraid that others would know of my idolatry. I felt,

8. Antinoüs, beloved male companion of the emperor Hadrian (here Adrian) of Rome, drowned in the Nile in A.D. 130, presumably off one of the emperor's ornately decorated barges.
9. Close resemblance to what is real; fidelity of representation, rendering the precise details of the real thing or scene. In reference to art and literature, sometimes used as a term of commendation, when precision and vividness of detail are regarded as a merit, and sometimes unfavourably contrasted with idealized description or representation. It has often been used with implication that the details are of an unpleasant or sordid character.

Dorian, that I had told too much, that I had put too much of myself into it. Then it was that I resolved never to allow the picture to be exhibited. You were a little annoyed; but then you did not realize all that it meant to me. Harry, to whom I talked about it, laughed at me. But I did not mind that. When the picture was finished, and I sat alone with it, I felt that I was right. . . . Well, after a few days the thing left my studio, and as soon as I had got rid of the intolerable fascination of its presence it seemed to me that I had been foolish in imagining that I had seen anything in it, more than that you were extremely good-looking and that I could paint. Even now I cannot help feeling that it is a mistake to think that the passion one feels in creation is ever really shown in the work one creates. Art is always more abstract than we fancy. Form and colour tell us of form and colour—that is all. It often seems to me that art conceals the artist far more completely than it ever reveals him. And so when I got this offer from Paris I determined to make your portrait the principal thing in my exhibition. It never occurred to me that you would refuse. I see now that you were right. The picture cannot be shown. You must not be angry with me, Dorian, for what I have told you. As I said to Harry, once, you are made to be worshipped."

Dorian Gray drew a long breath. The colour came back to his cheeks, and a smile played about his lips. The peril was over. He was safe for the time. Yet he could not help feeling infinite pity for the painter who had just made this strange confession to him, and wondered if he himself would ever be so dominated by the personality of a friend. Lord Henry had the charm of being very dangerous. But that was all. He was too clever and too cynical to be really fond of. Would there ever be some one who would fill him with a strange idolatry? Was that one of the things that life had in store?

"It is extraordinary to me, Dorian," said Hallward, "that you should have seen this in the portrait. Did you really see it?"

"I saw something in it," he answered, "something that seemed to me very curious."

"Well, you don't mind my looking at the thing now?"

Dorian shook his head. "You must not ask me that, Basil. I could not possibly let you stand in front of that picture."

"You will some day, surely?"

"Never."

"Well, perhaps you are right. And now good-bye, Dorian. You have been the one person in my life who has really influenced my art. Whatever I have done that is good, I owe to you. Ah! you don't know what it cost me to tell you all that I have told you."

"My dear Basil," said Dorian, "what have you told me? Simply that you felt that you admired me too much. That is not even a compliment."

"It was not intended as a compliment. It was a confession. Now that I have made it, something seems to have gone out of me. Perhaps one should never put one's worship into words."

"It was a very disappointing confession."

"Why, what did you expect, Dorian? You didn't see anything else in the picture, did you? There was nothing else to see?"

"No; there was nothing else to see. Why do you ask? But you mustn't talk about worship. It is foolish. You and I are friends, Basil, and we must always remain so."

"You have got Harry," said the painter, sadly.

"Oh, Harry!" cried the lad, with a ripple of laughter. "Harry spends his days in saying what is incredible, and his evenings in doing what is improbable. Just the sort of life I would like to lead. But still I don't think I would go to Harry if I were in trouble. I would sooner go to you, Basil."

"You will sit to me again?"

"Impossible!"

"You spoil my life as an artist by refusing, Dorian. No man comes across two ideal things. Few come across one."

"I can't explain it to you, Basil, but I must never sit to you again. There is something fatal about a portrait. It has a life of its own. I will come and have tea with you. That will be just as pleasant."

"Pleasanter for you, I am afraid," murmured Hallward, regretfully. "And now good-bye. I am sorry you won't let me look at the picture once again. But that can't be helped. I quite understand what you feel about it."

As he left the room, Dorian Gray smiled to himself. Poor Basil! How little he knew of the true reason! And how strange it was that, instead of having been forced to reveal his own secret, he had succeeded, almost by chance, in wresting a secret from his friend! How much that strange confession explained to him! The painter's absurd fits of jealousy, his wild devotion, his extravagant panegyrics, his curious reticences—he understood them all now, and he felt sorry. There seemed to him to be something tragic in a friendship so coloured by romance.

He sighed, and touched the bell. The portrait must be hidden away at all costs. He could not run such a risk of discovery again. It had been mad of him to have allowed the thing to remain, even for an hour, in a room to which any of his friends had access.

Chapter X[1]

When his servant entered, he looked at him steadfastly, and wondered if he had thought of peering behind the screen. The man was quite impassive, and waited for his orders. Dorian lit a cigarette, and walked over to the glass and glanced into it. He could see the reflection of Victor's face perfectly. It was like a placid mask of servility. There was nothing to be afraid of, there. Yet he thought it best to be on his guard.

Speaking very slowly, he told him to tell the housekeeper that he wanted to see her, and then to go to the frame-maker and ask him to send two of his men round at once. It seemed to him that as the man left the room his eyes wandered in the direction of the screen. Or was that merely his own fancy?

After a few moments, in her black silk dress, with old-fashioned thread mittens on her wrinkled hands, Mrs. Leaf[2] bustled into the library. He asked her for the key of the schoolroom.

"The old schoolroom, Mr. Dorian?" she exclaimed. "Why, it is full of dust. I must get it arranged, and put straight before you go into it. It is not fit for you to see, sir. It is not, indeed."

"I don't want it put straight, Leaf. I only want the key."

"Well, sir, you'll be covered with cobwebs if you go into it. Why, it hasn't been opened for nearly five years, not since his lordship died."

He winced at the mention of his grandfather. He had hateful memories of him. "That does not matter," he answered. "I simply want to see the place—that is all. Give me the key."

"And here is the key, sir," said the old lady, going over the contents of her bunch with tremulously uncertain hands. "Here is the key. I'll have it off the bunch in a moment. But you don't think of living up there, sir, and you so comfortable here?"

"No, no," he cried, petulantly. "Thank you, Leaf. That will do."

She lingered for a few moments, and was garrulous over some detail of the household. He sighed, and told her to manage things as she thought best. She left the room, wreathed in smiles.

As the door closed, Dorian put the key in his pocket, and looked round the room. His eye fell on a large purple satin coverlet heavily embroidered with gold, a splendid piece of late seventeenth-century Venetian work that his grandfather had found in a convent near Bologna. Yes, that would serve to wrap the dreadful thing in. It had perhaps served often as a pall for the dead. Now it was to hide some-

---

1. Originally chapter 8 in the *Lippincott's Magazine* version.
2. Wilde revised this and the following page heavily from the first edition, greatly reducing the importance of "poor old Leaf" from the rich vignette of the original to a faded remnant.

thing that had a corruption of its own, worse than the corruption of death itself—something that would breed horrors and yet would never die. What the worm was to the corpse, his sins would be to the painted image on the canvas. They would mar its beauty, and eat away its grace. They would defile it, and make it shameful. And yet the thing would still live on. It would be always alive.

He shuddered, and for a moment he regretted that he had not told Basil the true reason why he had wished to hide the picture away. Basil would have helped him to resist Lord Henry's influence, and the still more poisonous influences that came from his own temperament. The love that he bore him—for it was really love—had nothing in it that was not noble and intellectual. It was not that mere physical admiration of beauty that is born of the senses, and that dies when the senses tire. It was such love as Michel Angelo had known, and Montaigne, and Winckelmann, and Shakespeare himself.[3] Yes, Basil could have saved him. But it was too late now. The past could always be annihilated. Regret, denial, or forgetfulness could do that. But the future was inevitable. There were passions in him that would find their terrible outlet, dreams that would make the shadow of their evil real.

He took up from the couch the great purple-and-gold texture that covered it, and, holding it in his hands, passed behind the screen. Was the face on the canvas viler than before? It seemed to him that it was unchanged; and yet his loathing of it was intensified. Gold hair, blue eyes, and rose-red lips—they all were there. It was simply the expression that had altered. That was horrible in its cruelty. Compared to what he saw in it of censure or rebuke, how shallow Basil's reproaches about Sibyl Vane had been!—how shallow, and of what little account! His own soul was looking out at him from the canvas and calling him to judgement. A look of pain came across him, and he flung the rich pall over the picture. As he did so, a knock came to the door. He passed out as his servant entered.

"The persons are here, Monsieur."

He felt that the man must be got rid of at once. He must not be allowed to know where the picture was being taken to. There was something sly about him, and he had thoughtful, treacherous eyes. Sitting down at the writing-table, he scribbled a note to Lord Henry, asking him to send him round something to read, and reminding him that they were to meet at eight-fifteen that evening.

3. The passage has both aesthetic and erotic implications. Montaigne and Winckelmann were two of Wilde's cultural heroes. Michel Montaigne (1533–92), French essayist, and Johann Winckelmann (1717–68), German archeologist and art historian, were believed to be homosexuals, as were Michelangelo and Shakespeare. Wilde wrote in nearly identical terms in "The Portrait of Mr. W. H." and gave an eloquent defense of "the love that dare not speak its name" at his second trial.

"Wait for an answer," he said, handing it to him, "and show the men in here."

In two or three minutes there was another knock, and Mr. Hubbard[4] himself, the celebrated frame-maker of South Audley Street,[5] came in with a somewhat rough-looking young assistant. Mr. Hubbard was a florid, red-whiskered little man, whose admiration for art was considerably tempered by the inveterate impecuniosity of most of the artists who dealt with him. As a rule, he never left his shop. He waited for people to come to him. But he always made an exception in favour of Dorian Gray. There was something about Dorian that charmed everybody. It was a pleasure even to see him.

"What can I do for you, Mr. Gray?" he said, rubbing his fat freckled hands. "I thought I would do myself the honour of coming round in person. I have just got a beauty of a frame, sir. Picked it up at a sale. Old Florentine. Came from Fonthill,[6] I believe. Admirably suited for a religious subject, Mr. Gray."

"I am so sorry you have given yourself the trouble of coming round, Mr. Hubbard. I shall certainly drop in and look at the frame—though I don't go in much at present for religious art—but to-day I only want a picture carried to the top of the house for me. It is rather heavy, so I thought I would ask you to lend me a couple of your men."

"No trouble at all, Mr. Gray. I am delighted to be of any service to you. Which is the work of art, sir?"

"This," replied Dorian, moving the screen back. "Can you move it, covering and all, just as it is? I don't want it to get scratched going upstairs."

"There will be no difficulty, sir," said the genial frame-maker, beginning, with the aid of his assistant, to unhook the picture from the long brass chains by which it was suspended. "And, now, where shall we carry it to, Mr. Gray?"

"I will show you the way, Mr. Hubbard, if you will kindly follow me. Or perhaps you had better go in front. I am afraid it is right at the top of the house. We will go up by the front staircase, as it is wider."

---

4. Hubbard was "Mr. Ashton" in the magazine edition. In *In Good Company* (London: Lane, 1917) 212–13, Coulson Kernahan, the Ward, Lock and Company editor with whom Wilde worked in preparing the revised edition, gives the following account of a hoax Wilde played on him over the name change. He reports receiving a telegram from Wilde in Paris: "Terrible blunder in book, coming back specially. Stop all proofs! Wilde." Wilde arrived at the office apparently distracted: " 'Ashton is a gentleman's name,' he spoke brokenly and wrung his hands as if in anguish, 'and I've given it—God forgive me—to a tradesman! It must be changed to Hubbard. Hubbard positively smells of the tradesman.' "
5. A street in Mayfair near Hyde Park.
6. William Beckford, author of *Vathek,* a Gothic novel much admired by Byron, built a suitably Gothic mansion in Fonthill Wood in Wiltshire. The frame would have come from the auction of Fonthill furnishings at Christie's Auction House in 1822.

He held the door open for them, and they passed out into the hall and began the ascent. The elaborate character of the frame had made the picture extremely bulky, and now and then, in spite of the obsequious protests of Mr. Hubbard, who had the true tradesman's spirited dislike of seeing a gentleman doing anything useful, Dorian put his hand to it so as to help them.

"Something of a load to carry, sir," gasped the little man, when they reached the top landing. And he wiped his shiny forehead.

"I am afraid it is rather heavy," murmured Dorian, as he unlocked the door that opened into the room that was to keep for him the curious secret of his life and hide his soul from the eyes of men.

He had not entered the place for more than four years—not, indeed, since he had used it first as a play-room when he was a child, and then as a study when he grew somewhat older. It was a large, well-proportioned room, which had been specially built by the last Lord Kelso for the use of the little grandson whom, for his strange likeness to his mother, and also for other reasons, he had always hated and desired to keep at a distance. It appeared to Dorian to have but little changed. There was the huge Italian *cassone*,[7] with its fantastically-painted panels and its tarnished gilt mouldings, in which he had so often hidden himself as a boy. There the satinwood bookcase filled with his dog-eared schoolbooks. On the wall behind it was hanging the same ragged Flemish tapestry where a faded king and queen were playing chess in a garden, while a company of hawkers rode by, carrying hooded birds on their gauntleted wrists. How well he remembered it all! Every moment of his lonely childhood came back to him as he looked round. He recalled the stainless purity of his boyish life, and it seemed horrible to him that it was here the fatal portrait was to be hidden away. How little he had thought, in those dead days, of all that was in store for him!

But there was no other place in the house so secure from prying eyes as this. He had the key, and no one else could enter it. Beneath its purple pall, the face painted on the canvas could grow bestial, sodden, and unclean. What did it matter? No one could see it. He himself would not see it. Why should he watch the hideous corruption of his soul? He kept his youth—that was enough. And, besides, might not his nature grow finer, after all? There was no reason that the future should be so full of shame. Some love might come across his life, and purify him, and shield him from those sins that seemed to be already stirring in spirit and in flesh—those curious unpictured sins whose very mystery lent them their subtlety and their charm. Perhaps, some day, the cruel look would have passed away from the

---

7. A large, ornamented Italian chest of the Renaissance.

scarlet sensitive mouth, and he might show to the world Basil Hallward's masterpiece.

No; that was impossible. Hour by hour, and week by week, the
thing upon the canvas was growing old. It might escape the hideousness of sin, but the hideousness of age was in store for it. The cheeks
would become hollow or flaccid. Yellow crow's feet would creep
round the fading eyes and make them horrible. The hair would lose
its brightness, the mouth would gape or droop, would be foolish or
gross, as the mouths of old men are. There would be the wrinkled
throat, the cold, blue-veined hands, the twisted body, that he remembered in the grandfather who had been so stern to him in his boyhood. The picture had to be concealed. There was no help for it.

"Bring it in, Mr. Hubbard, please," he said, wearily, turning round.
"I am sorry I kept you so long. I was thinking of something else."

"Always glad to have a rest, Mr. Gray," answered the frame-maker,
who was still gasping for breath. "Where shall we put it, sir?"

"Oh, anywhere. Here: this will do. I don't want to have it hung up.
Just lean it against the wall. Thanks."

"Might one look at the work of art, sir?"

Dorian started. "It would not interest you, Mr. Hubbard," he said,
keeping his eye on the man. He felt ready to leap upon him and fling
him to the ground if he dared to lift the gorgeous hanging that concealed the secret of his life. "I shan't trouble you any more now. I am
much obliged for your kindness in coming round."

"Not at all, not at all, Mr. Gray. Ever ready to do anything for you,
sir." And Mr. Hubbard tramped downstairs, followed by the assistant,
who glanced back at Dorian with a look of shy wonder in his rough
uncomely face. He had never seen any one so marvellous.

When the sound of their footsteps had died away, Dorian locked
the door, and put the key in his pocket. He felt safe now. No one
would ever look upon the horrible thing. No eye but his would ever
see his shame.

On reaching the library he found that it was just after five o'clock,
and that the tea had been already brought up. On a little table of dark
perfumed wood thickly incrusted with nacre, a present from Lady
Radley, his guardian's wife, a pretty professional invalid, who had
spent the preceding winter in Cairo, was lying a note from Lord
Henry, and beside it was a book bound in yellow paper,[8] the cover
slightly torn and the edges soiled. A copy of the third edition of *The*

---

8. Dorian's yellow book is one of the most famous puzzles in literature. The case for identifying it as J. K. Huysmans's *A Rebours* is weakened by the evidence of TS cancellations by
Stoddart of the details of "The Secret of Raoul by Catulle Sarrazin." Details of the book
make it clear that it was largely imaginary, as Wilde reported in *Letters* (313), although
partly suggested by Huysmans's novel. The imaginary "Catulle Sarrazin" seems to have
been taken from the names of two contemporary French men of letters known to Wilde:
Sarrazin, a critic, and Catulle Mendes, a poet.

St. James's Gazette[9] had been placed on the tea-tray. It was evident that Victor had returned. He wondered if he had met the men in the hall as they were leaving the house, and had wormed out of them what they had been doing. He would be sure to miss the picture—had no doubt missed it already, while he had been laying the tea-things. The screen had not been set back, and a blank space was visible on the wall. Perhaps some night he might find him creeping upstairs and trying to force the door of the room. It was a horrible thing to have a spy in one's house. He had heard of rich men who had been blackmailed all their lives by some servant who had read a letter, or overheard a conversation, or picked up a card with an address, or found beneath a pillow a withered flower or a shred of crumpled lace.

He sighed, and, having poured himself out some tea, opened Lord Henry's note. It was simply to say that he sent him round the evening paper, and a book that might interest him, and that he would be at the club at eight-fifteen. He opened *The St. James's* languidly, and looked through it. A red pencil-mark on the fifth page caught his eye. It drew attention to the following paragraph:

> "INQUEST ON AN ACTRESS.—An inquest was held this morning at the Bell Tavern, Hoxton Road, by Mr. Danby, the District Coroner, on the body of Sibyl Vane, a young actress recently engaged at the Royal Theatre, Holborn. A verdict of death by misadventure was returned. Considerable sympathy was expressed for the mother of the deceased, who was greatly affected during the giving of her own evidence, and that of Dr. Birrell, who had made the post-mortem examination of the deceased."

He frowned, and, tearing the paper in two went across the room and flung the pieces away. How ugly it all was! And how horribly real ugliness made things! He felt a little annoyed with Lord Henry for having sent him the report. And it was certainly stupid of him to have marked it with red pencil. Victor might have read it. The man knew more than enough English for that.

Perhaps he had read it, and had begun to suspect something. And, yet, what did it matter? What had Dorian Gray to do with Sibyl Vane's death? There was nothing to fear. Dorian Gray had not killed her.

His eye fell on the yellow book that Lord Henry had sent him. What was it, he wondered. He went towards the little pearl-coloured octagonal stand, that had always looked to him like the work of some

---

9. *The St. James's Gazette* was one of the London papers read by people in Wilde's set. He wrote occasional reviews and debated the art and morality issue in its columns after the appearance of the *Lippincott's* edition.

strange Egyptian bees that wrought in silver, and taking up the volume, flung himself into an arm-chair, and began to turn over the
leaves. After a few minutes he became absorbed. It was the strangest
book that he had ever read. It seemed to him that in exquisite raiment, and to the delicate sound of flutes, the sins of the world were
passing in dumb show before him. Things that he had dimly dreamed
of were suddenly made real to him. Things of which he had never
dreamed were gradually revealed.

It was a novel without a plot, and with only one character, being,
indeed, simply a psychological study of a certain young Parisian, who
spent his life trying to realize in the nineteenth century all the passions and modes of thought that belonged to every century except his
own, and to sum up, as it were, in himself the various moods through
which the world-spirit had ever passed, loving for their mere artificiality those renunciations that men have unwisely called virtue, as
much as those natural rebellions that wise men still call sin. The style
in which it was written was that curious jewelled style, vivid and
obscure at once, full of *argot*[1] and of archaisms, of technical expressions and of elaborate paraphrases, that characterizes the work of
some of the finest artists of the French school of Symbolistes.[2] There
were in it metaphors as monstrous as orchids, and as subtle in colour.
The life of the senses was described in the terms of mystical philosophy. One hardly knew at times whether one was reading the spiritual ecstasies of some mediæval saint or the morbid confessions of a
modern sinner. It was a poisonous book. The heavy odour of incense
seemed to cling about its pages and to trouble the brain. The mere
cadence of the sentences, the subtle monotony of their music, so full
as it was of complex refrains and movements elaborately repeated,
produced in the mind of the lad, as he passed from chapter to chapter, a form of reverie, a malady of dreaming, that made him unconscious of the falling day and creeping shadows.

Cloudless, and pierced by one solitary star, a copper-green sky
gleamed through the windows. He read on by its wan light till he
could read no more. Then, after his valet had reminded him several
times of the lateness of the hour, he got up, and, going into the next
room, placed the book on the little Florentine table that always stood
at his bedside, and began to dress for dinner.

It was almost nine o'clock before he reached the club, where he

---

1. The idiom or slang of a particular group or class, especially associated with lowlifes.
2. Wilde changed this from *Lippincott's* "Decadents." The Symbolistes were mainly French
   poets like Baudelaire, Rimbaud, Mallarmé, Verlaine, and Villiers d l'Isle Adam; they also
   included writers like Huysmans and Pierre Loüys, who combined strong romanticism with
   contempt for realism and middle-class values. In art, the movement led to an emphasis on
   elusive and subtle states of mind and feeling, conveyed by symbols as the language expressing realities hidden behind appearances. Arthur Symons helped to popularize the movement in England with *The Symbolist Movement in Literature* (1899).

found Lord Henry sitting alone, in the morning-room, looking very much bored.

"I am so sorry, Harry," he cried, "but really it is entirely your fault. That book you sent me so fascinated me that I forgot how the time was going."

"Yes: I thought you would like it," replied his host, rising from his chair.

"I didn't say I liked it, Harry. I said it fascinated me. There is a great difference."

"Ah, you have discovered that?" murmured Lord Henry. And they passed into the dining-room.

Chapter XI[1]

For years, Dorian Gray could not free himself from the influence of this book. Or perhaps it would be more accurate to say that he never sought to free himself from it. He procured from Paris no less than nine large-paper copies of the first edition, and had them bound in different colours, so that they might suit his various moods and the changing fancies of a nature over which he seemed, at times, to have almost entirely lost control. The hero, the wonderful young Parisian, in whom the romantic and the scientific temperaments were so strangely blended,[2] became to him a kind of prefiguring type of himself. And, indeed, the whole book seemed to him to contain the story of his own life, written before he had lived it.[3]

In one point he was more fortunate than the novel's fantastic hero. He never knew—never, indeed, had any cause to know—that somewhat grotesque dread of mirrors, and polished metal surfaces, and still water, which came upon the young Parisian so early in his life, and was occasioned by the sudden decay of a beauty that had once, apparently, been so remarkable. It was with an almost cruel joy—and perhaps in nearly every joy, as certainly in every pleasure, cruelty has its place—that he used to read the latter part of the book, with its really tragic, if somewhat overemphasized, account of the sorrow and despair of one who had himself lost what in others, and the world, he had most dearly valued.

---

1. Originally chapter 9 in the *Lippincott's Magazine* version.
2. An allusion to the chapter on Leonardo in Walter Pater's *The Renaissance* (see pp. 311–26).
3. A prophetic phrase for Wilde. After completing the *Lippincott's* edition, he was to meet two young men, either of whom might have posed for Dorian: John Gray and Lord Alfred Douglas. The Wilde-Douglas affair proved ruinous for both men, sending Wilde to prison, bankruptcy, exile, and eventually death. Douglas never fully emerged from the social stigma he courted in the affair; later in life, he wrote a series of attacks on Wilde, retractions, and apologies.

For the wonderful beauty that had so fascinated Basil Hallward, and many others besides him, seemed never to leave him. Even those who had heard the most evil things against him, and from time to time strange rumours about his mode of life crept through London and became the chatter of the clubs, could not believe anything to his dishonour when they saw him. He had always the look of one who had kept himself unspotted from the world. Men who talked grossly became silent when Dorian Gray entered the room. There was something in the purity of his face that rebuked them. His mere presence seemed to recall to them the memory of the innocence that they had tarnished. They wondered how one so charming and graceful as he was could have escaped the stain of an age that was at once sordid and sensual.

Often, on returning home from one of those mysterious and prolonged absences that gave rise to such strange conjecture among those who were his friends, or thought that they were so, he himself would creep upstairs to the locked room, open the door with the key that never left him now, and stand, with a mirror, in front of the portrait that Basil Hallward had painted of him, looking now at the evil and aging face on the canvas, and now at the fair young face that laughed back at him from the polished glass. The very sharpness of the contrast used to quicken his sense of pleasure. He grew more and more enamoured of his own beauty, more and more interested in the corruption of his own soul. He would examine with minute care, and sometimes with a monstrous and terrible delight, the hideous lines that seared the wrinkling forehead or crawled around the heavy sensual mouth, wondering sometimes which were the more horrible, the signs of sin or the signs of age. He would place his white hands beside the coarse bloated hands of the picture, and smile. He mocked the misshapen body and the failing limbs.

There were moments, indeed, at night, when, lying sleepless in his own delicately-scented chamber, or in the sordid room of the little ill-famed tavern near the Docks,[4] which, under an assumed name, and in disguise, it was his habit to frequent, he would think of the ruin he had brought upon his soul, with a pity that was all the more poignant because it was purely selfish. But moments such as these were rare. That curiosity about life which Lord Henry had first stirred in him, as they sat together in the garden of their friend, seemed to increase with gratification. The more he knew, the more he desired to know. He had mad hungers that grew more ravenous as he fed them.

Yet he was not really reckless, at any rate in his relations to society.

---

4. This is an area of London of some notoriety where a man of Dorian's reputation should not be seen for it can bring immediate censure or even alienation from his social circle.

Once or twice every month during the winter, and on each Wednesday evening[5] while the season lasted, he would throw open to the world his beautiful house and have the most celebrated musicians of the day to charm his guests with the wonders of their art. His little dinners, in the settling of which Lord Henry always assisted him, were noted as much for the careful selection and placing of those invited, as for the exquisite taste shown in the decoration of the table, with its subtle symphonic arrangements of exotic flowers, and embroidered cloths, and antique plate of gold and silver. Indeed, there were many, especially among the very young men, who saw, or fancied that they saw, in Dorian Gray the true realization of a type of which they had often dreamed in Eton or Oxford days, a type that was to combine something of the real culture of the scholar with all the grace and distinction and perfect manner of a citizen of the world. To them he seemed to be of the company of those whom Dante describes as having sought to "make themselves perfect by the worship of beauty." Like Gautier, he was one for whom "the visible world existed."[6]

And, certainly, to him Life itself was the first, the greatest, of the arts, and for it all the other arts seemed to be but a preparation. Fashion, by which what is really fantastic becomes for a moment universal, and Dandyism,[7] which, in its own way, is an attempt to assert the absolute modernity of beauty, had, of course, their fascination for him. His mode of dressing, and the particular styles that from time to time he affected, had their marked influence on the young exquisites of the Mayfair balls and Pall Mall club[8] windows, who copied him in everything that he did, and tried to reproduce the accidental charm of his graceful, though to him only half-serious, fopperies.

For, while he was but too ready to accept the position that was almost immediately offered to him on his coming of age, and found, indeed, a subtle pleasure in the thought that he might really become to the London of his own day what to imperial Neronian Rome the author of the "Satyricon"[9] once had been, yet in his inmost heart he desired to be something more than a mere *arbiter*

---

5. Wilde's at-home day was Wednesday—that is, an evening when he would entertain those who would care to call. The London social season ran from May through July.
6. The phrase is from Gautier's poem "Preface to 'Albertus'" (1832).
7. A philosophy of elegant manners and dress after the fashion of Beau Brummell (1778–1840). Dandyism takes a critical if witty view of contemporary mores and, more seriously, of the human condition. Its artificiality was intended as a protest against cant and self-righteousness.
8. One of the most famous and prestigious addresses in London, the street was celebrated for its private clubs.
9. Petronius, author of the *Satyricon*, which both satirized and was an instance of the decadence of Nero's Rome, was himself an intimate of the emperor. His title, "arbiter elegantiarum," was partly descriptive of his role as director of revels for the emperor and partly a pun on his name and fashion: Gaius Petronius Arbiter.

elegantiarum, to be consulted on the wearing of a jewel, or the knotting of a necktie, or the conduct of a cane. He sought to elaborate some new scheme of life that would have its reasoned philosophy and its ordered principles, and find in the spiritualizing of the senses its highest realization.

The worship of the senses has often, and with much justice, been decried, men feeling a natural instinct of terror about passions and sensations that seem stronger than themselves, and that they are conscious of sharing with the less highly organized forms of existence. But it appeared to Dorian Gray that the true nature of the senses had never been understood, and that they had remained savage and animal merely because the world had sought to starve them into submission or to kill them by pain, instead of aiming at making them elements of a new spirituality, of which a fine instinct for beauty was to be the dominant characteristic. As he looked back upon man moving through History, he was haunted by a feeling of loss. So much had been surrendered! and to such little purpose! There had been mad wilful rejections, monstrous forms of self-torture and self-denial, whose origin was fear, and whose result was a degradation infinitely more terrible than that fancied degradation from which, in their ignorance, they had sought to escape, Nature, in her wonderful irony, driving out the anchorite to feed with the wild animals of the desert and giving to the hermit the beasts of the field as his companions.

Yes: there was to be, as Lord Henry had prophesied, a new Hedonism[1] that was to recreate life, and to save it from that harsh, uncomely puritanism that is having, in our own day, its curious revival. It was to have its service of the intellect, certainly; yet, it was never to accept any theory or system that would involve the sacrifice of any mode of passionate experience. Its aim, indeed, was to be experience itself, and not the fruits of experience, sweet or bitter as they might be. Of the asceticism that deadens the senses, as of the vulgar profligacy that dulls them, it was to know nothing. But it was to teach man to concentrate himself upon the moments of a life that is itself but a moment.

There are few of us who have not sometimes wakened before dawn, either after one of those dreamless nights that make us almost enamoured of death, or one of those nights of horror and misshapen joy, when through the chambers of the brain sweep phantoms more terrible than reality itself, and instinct with that vivid life that lurks

---

1. If what came before was the new Dandyism of the nineteenth-century aesthete, what follows here is Wilde's variation on the philosophy put forward by Pater in the Conclusion to *The Renaissance* (see pp. 326–29) and as the "New Cyrenaicism" in his *Marius the Epicurean* 2.9.

in all grotesques, and that lends to Gothic art[2] its enduring vitality, this art being, one might fancy, especially the art of those whose minds have been troubled with the malady of reverie. Gradually white fingers creep through the curtains, and they appear to tremble. In black fantastic shapes, dumb shadows crawl into the corners of the room, and crouch there. Outside, there is the stirring of birds among the leaves, or the sound of men going forth to their work, or the sigh and sob of the wind coming down from the hills, and wandering round the silent house, as though it feared to wake the sleepers, and yet must needs call forth sleep from her purple cave. Veil after veil of thin dusky gauze is lifted, and by degrees the forms and colours of things are restored to them, and we watch the dawn remaking the world in its antique pattern. The wan mirrors get back their mimic life. The flameless tapers stand where we had left them, and beside them lies the half-cut book that we had been studying, or the wired flower that we had worn at the ball, or the letter that we had been afraid to read, or that we had read too often. Nothing seems to us changed. Out of the unreal shadows of the night comes back the real life that we had known. We have to resume it where we had left off, and there steals over us a terrible sense of the necessity for the continuance of energy in the same wearisome round of stereotyped habits, or a wild longing, it may be, that our eyelids might open some morning upon a world that had been refashioned anew in the darkness for our pleasure, a world in which things would have fresh shapes and colours, and be changed, or have other secrets, a world in which the past would have little or no place, or survive, at any rate, in no conscious form of obligation or regret, the remembrance even of joy having its bitterness, and the memories of pleasure their pain.

It was the creation of such worlds as these that seemed to Dorian Gray to be the true object, or amongst the true objects, of life; and in his search for sensations that would be at once new and delightful, and possess that element of strangeness that is so essential to romance, he would often adopt certain modes of thought that he knew to be really alien to his nature, abandon himself to their subtle influences, and then, having, as it were, caught their colour and satisfied his intellectual curiosity, leave them with that curious indifference that is not incompatible with a real ardour of temperament, and that indeed, according to certain modern psychologists, is often a condition of it.[3]

2. A style of architecture prevalent in Western Europe from the twelfth to the sixteenth century, of which the chief characteristic is the pointed arch. Applied also to buildings, architectural details, and ornamentation.
3. The reference is possibly to Wilhelm Wundt (1832–1920), Herbert Spencer (1820–1903),

It was rumoured of him once that he was about to join the Roman Catholic communion;[4] and certainly the Roman ritual had always a great attraction for him. The daily sacrifice, more awful really than all the sacrifices of the antique world, stirred him as much by its superb rejection of the evidence of the senses as by the primitive simplicity of its elements and the eternal pathos of the human tragedy that it sought to symbolize. He loved to kneel down on the cold marble pavement, and watch the priest, in his stiff flowered dalmatic, slowly and with white hands moving aside the veil of the tabernacle, or raising aloft the jewelled lantern-shaped monstrance[5] with that pallid wafer that at times, one would fain think, is indeed the "*panis cælestis*," the bread of angels, or, robed in the garments of the Passion of Christ, breaking the Host into the chalice, and smiting his breast for his sins. The fuming censers, that the grave boys, in their lace and scarlet, tossed into the air like great gilt flowers, had their subtle fascination for him. As he passed out, he used to look with wonder at the black confessionals, and long to sit in the dim shadow of one of them and listen to men and women whispering through the worn grating the true story of their lives.

But he never fell into the error of arresting his intellectual development by any formal acceptance of creed or system, or of mistaking, for a house in which to live, an inn that is but suitable for the sojourn of a night, or for a few hours of a night in which there are no stars and the moon is in travail. Mysticism,[6] with its marvellous power of making common things strange to us, and the subtle antinomianism[7] that always seems to accompany it, moved him for a season; and for a season he inclined to the materialistic doctrines of the *Darwinismus* movement in Germany,[8] and found a curious pleasure

and William James (1842–1910), German, English, and American psychologists, whose influence on the new science was definitive (although less well-known than Freud's) and whose ideas are reflected in many of the meditations of Henry, Dorian, and the narrator on the relations among psychology, physiology, and morals.

4. After flirting with conversion for nearly forty years, Wilde was received into the Catholic church on his deathbed. Many Decadents were similarly attracted to Catholicism.

5. An ornately decorated metal display stand for the consecrated host used in Roman Catholic liturgy for benedictions, processionals, and adoration vigils. An apparent confusion between consecration of the host during Mass and benediction led Wilde to substitute a vestment appropriate to the former (dalmatic) for one proper to the later (cope). A dalmatic is an outer garment, usually embroidered, having wide sleeves, worn at Mass by a deacon, abbot, bishop, or cardinal.

6. The belief in the possibility of union with or absorption into God by means of contemplation and self-surrender, also the belief in or devotion to the spiritual apprehension of truths inaccessible to the intellect.

7. Antinomianism is an unorthodox belief of certain Christians that they are freed from the restraints of moral law by virtue of grace. By extension, it is used to refer to those who rejected moral law and church teaching.

8. The application of Darwin's theories was especially strong in Germany, where the implications of biology, comparative anatomy, anthropology, psychology, and social theory were enthusiastically explored. Wilde thought Darwin and Renan the most influential men of the times. Ernst Renan (1823–92) was a French social philosopher and Orientalist, most

in tracing the thoughts and passions of men to some pearly cell in the brain, or some white nerve in the body, delighting in the conception of the absolute dependence of the spirit on certain physical conditions, morbid or healthy, normal or diseased. Yet, as has been said of him before, no theory of life seemed to him to be of any importance compared with life itself. He felt keenly conscious of how barren all intellectual speculation is when separated from action and experiment. He knew that the senses, no less than the soul, have their spiritual mysteries to reveal.

And so he would now study perfumes,[9] and the secrets of their manufacture, distilling heavily-scented oils, and burning odorous gums from the East. He saw that there was no mood of the mind that had not its counterpart in the sensuous life, and set himself to discover their true relations, wondering what there was in frankincense that made one mystical, and in ambergris that stirred one's passions, and in violets that woke the memory of dead romances, and in musk that troubled the brain, and in champak that stained the imagination; and seeking often to elaborate a real psychology of perfumes, and to estimate the several influences of sweet-smelling roots, and scented pollen-laden flowers, of aromatic balms, and of dark and fragrant woods, of spikenard that sickens, of hovenia that makes men mad, and of aloes that are said to be able to expel melancholy from the soul.

At another time he devoted himself entirely to music, and in a long latticed room, with a vermilion-and-gold ceiling and walls of olive-green lacquer, he used to give curious concerts in which mad gypsies tore wild music from little zithers, or grave yellow-shawled Tunisians plucked at the strained strings of monstrous lutes, while grinning negroes beat monotonously upon copper drums, and, crouching upon scarlet mats, slim turbaned Indians blew through long pipes of reed or brass, and charmed, or feigned to charm, great hooded snakes and horrible horned adders. The harsh intervals and shrill discords of barbaric music stirred him at times when Schubert's grace, and Chopin's beautiful sorrows, and the mighty harmonies of Beethoven himself, fell unheeded on his ear. He collected together from all parts of the world the strangest instruments that could be found, either in the tombs of dead nations or among the few savage tribes that have survived contact with Western civilizations, and loved to touch and try them. He had the mysterious *juruparis* of the Rio Negro Indians,[1] that women are not allowed to look at, and that even

---

noted for his application of scientific, historical methodology to Jewish and Christian traditional belief.
9. Des Esseintes, the hero of *A Rebours*, makes an even more detailed and intense study of perfumes, their psychological effects and the associations they produce.
1. Wilde took details of the bizarre musical instruments from Carl Engel's handbook *Musical*

youths may not see till they have been subjected to fasting and
scourging, and the earthen jars of the Peruvians that have the shrill
cries of birds, and flutes of human bones such as Alfonso de Ovalle[2]
heard in Chile, and the sonorous green jaspers that are found near
Cuzco and give forth a note of singular sweetness. He had painted
gourds filled with pebbles that rattled when they were shaken; the
long *clarin* of the Mexicans, into which the performer does not blow,
but through which he inhales the air; the harsh *ture* of the Amazon
tribes, that is sounded by the sentinels who sit all day long in high
trees, and can be heard, it is said, at a distance of three leagues; the
teponaztli, that has two vibrating tongues of wood, and is beaten
with sticks that are smeared with an elastic gum obtained from the
milky juice of plants; the *yotl*-bells of the Aztecs, that are hung in
clusters like grapes; and a huge cylindrical drum, covered with the
skins of great serpents, like the one that Bernal Diaz saw when he
went with Cortes into the Mexican temple, and of whose doleful
sound he has left us so vivid a description. The fantastic character
of these instruments fascinated him, and he felt a curious delight in
the thought that art, like Nature, has her monsters, things of bestial
shape and with hideous voices. Yet, after some time, he wearied of
them, and would sit in his box at the Opera, either alone or with
Lord Henry, listening in rapt pleasure to "Tannhäuser," and seeing
in the prelude to that great work of art a presentation of the tragedy
of his own soul.[3]

On one occasion he took up the study of jewels,[4] and appeared at
a costume ball as Anne de Joyeuse, Admiral of France,[5] in a dress

Instruments, one of the series of South Kensington Museum Art Handbooks he consulted
in writing this chapter. Many descriptions are taken directly out of Engel's text.
2. Alfonso de Ovalle (1601–51) was a Chilean Jesuit historian whose *Historica relacion del
reino de Chile* (1646) is a classic account of colonial Chile.
3. The legend of this historical figure tells the tale of a poet who sought forgiveness after having enjoyed the fleshpots of Venusberg for a year. When Tannhäuser journeys to Rome, he
is told by the Pope that forgiveness will be granted only when the Pope's staff blossoms.
The miracle occurs on the third day after Tannhäuser's departure, too late to save the
knight, who had returned to Venusberg in despair. In the Richard Wagner opera (1844),
Tannhäuser is forgiven at the end. Gilbert alludes to Tannhäuser in "The Critic as Artist,"
and the story also inspired Swinburne's "Laus Veneris." Wilde seems to have been affected
by the struggle of sacred with profane love in the legend, a frequent theme in his own
poetry and stories, and the idea of divine forgiveness through miraculous signs. Dorian is
later to search his portrait in vain for such a sign.
4. Des Esseintes's study of jewels was more elaborate in *A Rebours*. Many of the more exotic
stones mentioned here were used as a covering on the shell of a giant
tortoise, contributing to the creature's premature demise. Huysmans is interested in his
hero's use of jewels to create new sensations and new aesthetic effects in his life. Wilde
emphasizes equally the anecdotes connected to the jewels to add an occult, decadent flavor to the story. He culled his information on stones from A. H. Church's *Precious Stones*
(1882), another of the South Kensington Museum Art Handbooks. Many of the stories
come, sometimes verbatim, out of William Jones's *History and Mystery of Precious* Stones
(1880), as cited in *Dorian Gray*, Murray 246.
5. One of the favorites of Henry III (1551–89), named a duke and admiral by the king. Both
were homosexuals and appeared in public dressed as women.

covered with five hundred and sixty pearls. This taste enthralled him
for years, and, indeed, may be said never to have left him. He would
often spend a whole day settling and resettling in their cases the various stones that be had collected, such as the olive-green chrysoberyl
that turns red by lamplight, the cymophane with its wirelike line of
silver, the pistachio-coloured peridot, rose-pink and wine-yellow
topazes, carbuncles of fiery scarlet with tremulous four-rayed stars,
flame-red cinnamon-stones, orange and violet spinels, and amethysts
with their alternate layers of ruby and sapphire. He loved the red gold
of the sunstone, and the moonstone's pearly whiteness, and the broken rainbow of the milky opal. He procured from Amsterdam three
emeralds of extraordinary size and richness of colour, and had a
turquoise *de la vieille roche*[6] that was the envy of all the connoisseurs.

He discovered wonderful stories, also, about jewels. In Alphonso's
"Clericalis Disciplina" a serpent was mentioned with eyes of real
jacinth, and in the romantic history of Alexander,[7] the Conqueror of
Emathia was said to have found in the vale of Jordan snakes "with
collars of real emeralds growing on their backs." There was a gem in
the brain of the dragon, Philostratus[8] told us, and "by the exhibition
of golden letters and a scarlet robe" the monster could be thrown into
a magical sleep, and slain. According to the great alchemist, Pierre
de Boniface, the diamond rendered a man invisible, and the agate of
India made him eloquent. The cornelian appeased anger, and the
hyacinth provoked sleep, and the amethyst drove away the fumes of
wine. The garnet cast out demons, and the hydropicus deprived the
moon of her colour. The selenite waxed and waned with the moon,
and the meloceus, that discovers thieves, could be affected only by
the blood of kids. Leonardus Camillus had seen a white stone taken
from the brain of a newly killed toad, that was a certain antidote
against poison. The bezoar, that was found in the heart of the Arabian
deer, was a charm that could cure the plague. In the nests of Arabian
birds was the aspilates, that, according to Democritus,[9] kept the
wearer from any danger by fire.

The King of Ceilan[1] rode through his city with a large ruby in his
hand, as the ceremony of his coronation. The gates of the palace of
John the Priest[2] were "made of sardius, with the horn of the horned

6. "From an old stone."
7. Alexander the Great (356–323 B.C.), one of the earliest Western prototypes of the idealized monarch who combined the leadership and courage of the victorious warrior with the
   temperance and wisdom of the scholar.
8. A Greek Sophist and biographer (A.D. 170–245). The story comes from *Heroicus,* a fabulous account of the heroes of the Trojan War.
9. Greek philosopher of Athens (460–370 B.C.).
1. Ceilan, was Ceylon, now Sri Lanka.
2. Better known as Prester John, the legendary twelfth-century priest who ruled a utopian
   Christian realm in Asia or Africa.

snake inwrought, so that no man might bring poison within." Over
the gable were "two golden apples, in which were two carbuncles,"
so that the gold might shine by day, and the carbuncles by night. In
Lodge's strange romance "A Margarite of America"[3] it was stated that
in the chamber of the queen one could behold "all the chaste ladies
of the world, inchased out of silver, looking through fair mirrours of
chrysolites, carbuncles, sapphires, and greene emeraults." Marco
Polo[4] had seen the inhabitants of Zipangu place rose-coloured pearls
in the mouths of the dead. A sea-monster had been enamoured of the
pearl that the diver brought to King Perozes, and had slain the thief,
and mourned for seven moons over its loss. When the Huns lured the
king into the great pit, he flung it away—Procopius[5] tells the story—
nor was it ever found again, though the Emperor Anastasius offered
five hundred-weight of gold pieces for it. The King of Malabar had
shown to a certain Venetian a rosary of three hundred and four
pearls, one for every god that he worshipped.

When the Duke de Valentinois, son of Alexander VI, visited Louis
XII of France,[6] his horse was loaded with gold leaves, according to
Brantôme, and his cap had double rows of rubies that threw out a
great light. Charles of England had ridden in stirrups hung with four
hundred and twenty-one diamonds. Richard II had a coat, valued at
thirty thousand marks, which was covered with balas rubies. Hall
described Henry VIII, on his way to the Tower previous to his coronation, as wearing "a jacket of raised gold, the placard embroidered
with diamonds and other rich stones, and a great bauderike about his
neck of large balasses." The favourites of James I wore ear-rings of
emeralds set in gold filigrane. Edward II gave to Piers Gaveston a suit
of red-gold armour studded with jacinths, a collar of gold roses set
with turquoise-stones, and a skull-cap parsemé[7] with pearls. Henry II
wore jewelled gloves reaching to the elbow, and had a hawk-glove
sewn with twelve rubies and fifty-two great orients. The ducal hat of
Charles the Rash, the last Duke of Burgundy of his race, was hung
with pear-shaped pearls, and studded with sapphires.

How exquisite life had once been! How gorgeous in its pomp and
decoration! Even to read of the luxury of the dead was wonderful.

---

3. Thomas Lodge's euphuistic romance (1569) was based on his second voyage to South
   America.
4. Marco Polo (1254–1324), the famous Venetian trader and world traveler. His book of travels introduced the West to the culture and wonders of the Orient.
5. Sixth-century Byzantine church historian, who recorded the wars of King Perozes
   (457–84) and his death at the hands of the Ephthalites. Malabar, on the west coast of
   India, was ruled by Hindu kings but seventeenth-century Portuguese missionaries brought
   to Malabar a strong Christian influence.
6. In addition to sharing a theatrical sort of hedonism, those mentioned in this paragraph
   were considered notorious homosexuals.
7. Spangled.

Then he turned his attention to embroideries,[8] and to the tapestries that performed the office of frescoes in the chill rooms of the northern nations of Europe. As he investigated the subject—and he always had an extraordinary faculty of becoming absolutely absorbed for the moment in whatever he took up—he was almost saddened by the reflection of the ruin that Time brought on beautiful and wonderful things. He, at any rate, had escaped that. Summer followed summer, and the yellow jonquils bloomed and died many times, and nights of horror repeated the story of their shame, but he was unchanged. No winter marred his face or stained his flower-like bloom. How different it was with material things! Where had they passed to? Where was the great crocus-coloured robe, on which the gods fought against the giants, that had been worked by brown girls for the pleasure of Athena?[9] Where, the huge velarium that Nero had stretched across the Colosseum at Rome, that Titan sail of purple on which was represented the starry sky, and Apollo driving a chariot drawn by white gilt-reined steeds? He longed to see the curious table-napkins wrought for the Priest of the Sun, on which were displayed all the dainties and viands that could be wanted for a feast; the mortuary cloth of King Chilperic,[1] with its three hundred golden bees; the fantastic robes that excited the indignation of the Bishop of Pontus, and were figured with "lions, panthers, bears, dogs, forests, rocks, hunters—all, in fact, that a painter can copy from nature;" and the coat that Charles of Orleans[2] once wore, on the sleeves of which were embroidered the verses of a song beginning "*Madame, je suis tout joyeux,*" the musical accompaniment of the words being wrought in gold thread, and each note, of square shape in those days, formed with four pearls. He read of the room that was prepared at the palace at Rheims for the use of Queen Joan of Burgundy, and was decorated with "thirteen hundred and twenty-one parrots, made in broidery, and blazoned with the king's arms, and five hundred and sixty-one butterflies, whose wings were similarly ornamented with the arms of the queen, the whole worked in gold." Catherine de Médicis[3] had a

---

8. Wilde copied some of the passages in this section on embroideries from a review he once did as editor of *Woman's World* of Ernest Lefébure's *Embroidery and Lace: Their Manufacture and History from the Remotest Antiquity to the Present* (1888). The review appeared in the November 1888 issue of *Woman's World,* and Wilde referred to the work as a "fascinating book." Wilde also borrowed selectively from the text of Lefebure's work.
9. Pallas Athena was the Greek goddess of war, peace, and wisdom. Her Roman equivalent was Minerva.
1. Sixth-century Frankish king.
2. Charles d'Orleans, French poet, duke of Orleans, and father of Louis XII, spent a third of his life as a royal captive in England after Agincourt. Finally ransomed by his future wife, Mary of Cleves, he spent the last third of his life at Blois, where he kept court for the most celebrated French writers of the time, including Villon, Chastelain, and de la Marche.
3. Daughter of Lorenzo the Magnificent, became queen of France through marriage, bore nine children, was celebrated for her love of luxury, and was notorious for her plots and assassinations while regent.

mourning-bed[4] made for her of black velvet powdered with crescents and suns. Its curtains were of damask, with leafy wreaths and garlands, figured upon a gold and silver ground, and fringed along the edges with broideries of pearls, and it stood in a room hung with rows of the queen's devices in cut black velvet upon cloth of silver. Louis XIV had gold embroidered caryatides[5] fifteen feet high in his apartment. The state bed of Sobieski, King of Poland,[6] was made of Smyrna gold brocade embroidered in turquoises with verses from the Koran. Its supports were of silver gilt, beautifully chased, and profusely set with enamelled and jewelled medallions. It had been taken from the Turkish camp before Vienna, and the standard of Mohammed had stood beneath the tremulous gilt of its canopy.

And so, for a whole year, he sought to accumulate the most exquisite specimens that he could find of textile and embroidered work, getting the dainty Delhi muslins, finely wrought with gold-thread palmates and stitched over with iridescent beetles' wings; the Dacca gauzes, that from their transparency are known in the East as "woven air," and "running water," and "evening dew"; strange figured cloths from Java; elaborate yellow Chinese hangings; books bound in tawny satins or fair blue silks, and wrought with *fleurs de lys*,[7] birds, and images; veils of *lacis* worked in Hungary point; Sicilian brocades, and stiff Spanish velvets; Georgian work with its gilt coins, and Japanese *Foukousas*[8] with their green-toned golds and their marvelously-plumaged birds.

He had a special passion, also, for ecclesiastical vestments, as indeed he had for everything connected with the service of the Church. In the long cedar chests that lined the west gallery of his house he had stored away many rare and beautiful specimens of what is really the raiment of the Bride of Christ,[9] who must wear purple and jewels and fine linen that she may hide the pallid macerated body that is worn by the suffering that she seeks for, and wounded by self-inflicted pain. He possessed a gorgeous cope of crimson silk and gold-thread damask, figured with a repeating pattern of golden pomegranates set in six-petalled formal blossoms, beyond which on either side was the pine-apple device wrought in seed-pearls. The orphreys were divided into panels representing scenes from the life

4. A widow's four-poster bed entirely draped in black with neither white sheets nor pillow cases. The rest of the bedroom would have been draped in the same way.
5. Columns sculptured in the form of female figures.
6. Sobieski ruled Poland as John III (1674–96). His greatest achievement was the heroic Polish rescue of Vienna in 1683.
7. Symbol of the French aristocracy, it is a device of heraldry rather than a real flower, resembling banded petals of an iris.
8. Foukousas (or fukusa) were embroidered or brocaded silk square gift covers, not considered part of the gift itself and hence a separate art form.
9. Roman Catholic nun.

of the Virgin, and the coronation of the Virgin was figured in coloured silks upon the hood. This was Italian work of the fifteenth century. Another cope was of green velvet, embroidered with heart-shaped groups of acanthus-leaves, from which spread long-stemmed white blossoms, the details of which were picked out with silver thread and coloured crystals. The morse bore a seraph's head in gold-thread raised work. The orphreys were woven in a diaper of red and gold silk, and were starred with medallions of many saints and martyrs, among whom was St. Sebastian.[1] He had chasubles, also, of amber-coloured silk, and blue silk and gold brocade, and yellow silk damask and cloth of gold, figured with representations of the Passion and Crucifixion of Christ, and embroidered with lions and peacocks and other emblems; dalmatics of white satin and pink silk damask, decorated with tulips and dolphins and *fleurs de lys*; altar frontals of crimson velvet and blue linen; and many corporals, chalice-veils, and sudaria.[2] In the mystic offices to which such things were put, there was something that quickened his imagination.

For these treasures, and everything that he collected in his lovely house, were to be to him means of forgetfulness, modes by which he could escape, for a season, from the fear that seemed to him at times to be almost too great to be borne. Upon the walls of the lonely locked room where he had spent so much of his boyhood, he had hung with his own hands the terrible portrait whose changing features showed him the real degradation of his life, and in front of it had draped the purple-and-gold pall as a curtain. For weeks he would not go there, would forget the hideous painted thing, and get back his light heart, his wonderful joyousness, his passionate absorption in mere existence. Then, suddenly, some night he would creep out of the house, go down to dreadful places near Blue Gate Fields,[3] and stay there, day after day, until he was driven away. On his return he would sit in front of the picture, sometimes loathing it and himself, but filled, at other times, with that pride of individualism that is half the fascination of sin, and smiling, with secret

1. Third-century Roman martyr, a favorite of the emperor Diocletian, who nevertheless ordered him killed by archers for his Christian faith.
2. Ecclesiastical vestments of the Catholic church, one of Dorian's interests, were also an interest of Des Esseintes of *A Rebours*. The Victoria and Albert Museum contained a fine collection, which Wilde knew. Accounts in the paragraphs below may have been taken from Reverend Daniel Rock's *Textile Fabrics* (London, 1876). Chasubles are long, sleeveless vestments, colored and usually decorated, worn outside the alb during Mass. Altar frontals were decorated altar cloths hanging down in front of the altar. A corporal is a linen cloth on which bread and wine are placed during the consecration. Chalice veils are decorated square cloth coverings for chalices used during Mass. Sudaria are handkerchiefs or napkins used to dry perspiration. A cope, above, is a decorated hood or hooded cape worn over the chasuble.
3. In the East End near Limehouse and the London Dock, between Commercial Road and New Road.

pleasure, at the misshapen shadow that had to bear the burden that should have been his own.

After a few years he could not endure to be long out of England, and gave up the villa that he had shared at Trouville[4] with Lord Henry, as well as the little white walled-in house at Algiers where they had more than once spent the winter. He hated to be separated from the picture that was such a part of his life, and was also afraid that during his absence some one might gain access to the room, in spite of the elaborate bars that he had caused to be placed upon the door.

He was quite conscious that this would tell them nothing. It was true that the portrait still preserved, under all the foulness and ugliness of the face, its marked likeness to himself; but what could they learn from that? He would laugh at any one who tried to taunt him. He had not painted it. What was it to him how vile and full of shame it looked? Even if he told them, would they believe it?

Yet he was afraid. Sometimes when he was down at his great house in Nottinghamshire, entertaining the fashionable young men of his own rank who were his chief companions, and astounding the county by the wanton luxury and gorgeous splendour of his mode of life, he would suddenly leave his guests and rush back to town to see that the door had not been tampered with, and that the picture was still there. What if it should be stolen? The mere thought made him cold with horror. Surely the world would know his secret then. Perhaps the world already suspected it.

For, while he fascinated many, there were not a few who distrusted him.[5] He was very nearly blackballed at a West End club of which his birth and social position fully entitled him to become a member, and it was said that on one occasion, when he was brought by a friend into the smoking-room of the Churchill, the Duke of Berwick and another gentleman got up in a marked manner and went out. Curious stories became current about him after he had passed his twenty-fifth year. It was rumoured that he had been seen brawling with foreign sailors in a low den in the distant parts of Whitechapel, and that he consorted with thieves and coiners and knew the mysteries of their trade. His extraordinary absences became notorious, and, when he used to reappear again in society, men would whisper to each other in corners, or pass him with a sneer, or look at him with cold searching eyes, as though they were determined to discover his secret.

---

4. A beach resort on the English Channel in France. It was a favorite vacation spa for Wilde, as was Algiers, where foreign homosexuals lived openly.
5. Dorian has changed clubs since the *Lippincott's* edition, which had him at the Carlton, a famous conservative political club located in Pall Mall. There was nothing to prevent Dorian from belonging to more than one club, however. Wilde was in fact barred from membership in the Savile Club shortly before writing *Dorian Gray*.

Of such insolences and attempted slights he, of course, took no notice, and in the opinion of most people his frank debonnair manner, his charming boyish smile, and the infinite grace of that wonderful youth that seemed never to leave him, were in themselves a sufficient answer to the calumnies, for so they termed them, that were circulated about him. It was remarked, however, that some of those who had been most intimate with him appeared, after a time, to shun him. Women who had wildly adored him, and for his sake had braved all social censure and set convention at defiance, were seen to grow pallid with shame or horror if Dorian Gray entered the room.

Yet these whispered scandals only increased in the eyes of many, his strange and dangerous charm. His great wealth was a certain element of security. Society, civilized society at least, is never very ready to believe anything to the detriment of those who are both rich and fascinating. It feels instinctively that manners are of more importance than morals,[6] and, in its opinion, the highest respectability is of much less value than the possession of a good *chef*. And, after all, it is a very poor consolation to be told that the man who has given one a bad dinner, or poor wine, is irreproachable in his private life. Even the cardinal virtues cannot atone for half-cold *entrées*,[7] as Lord Henry remarked once, in a discussion on the subject; and there is possibly a good deal to be said for his view. For the canons of good society are, or should be, the same as the canons of art. Form is absolutely essential to it. It should have the dignity of a ceremony, as well as its unreality, and should combine the insincere character of a romantic play with the wit and beauty that make such plays delightful to us. Is insincerity such a terrible thing? I think not.[8] It is merely a method by which we can multiply our personalities.

Such, at any rate, was Dorian Gray's opinion. He used to wonder at the shallow psychology of those who conceive the Ego in man as a thing simple, permanent, reliable, and of one essence. To him, man was a being with myriad lives and myriad sensations, a complex multiform creature that bore within itself strange legacies of thought and passion, and whose very flesh was tainted with the monstrous maladies of the dead. He loved to stroll through the gaunt cold picture-gallery of his country house and look at the various portraits of those whose blood flowed in his veins. Here was Philip Herbert,[9] described by Francis Osborne, in his "Memoires on the Reigns of Queen Elizabeth and King James," as one who was "caressed by the Court for

---

6. A favorite epigram, which appears also in "The Critic as Artist" and once again in *Lady Windermere's Fan*.
7. Principal courses at meals.
8. This is the one occasion when the narrative shifts from third to first person.
9. A favorite of King James I of England. The incident is described in Osborne's *Miscellaneous Works* 2 (London, 1722) 133, (*Dorian Gray*, Murray 246).

his handsome face, which kept him not long company." Was it young Herbert's life that he sometimes led? Had some strange poisonous germ crept from body to body till it had reached his own? Was it some dim sense of that ruined grace that had made him so suddenly, and almost without cause, give utterance, in Basil Hallward's studio, to the mad prayer that had so changed his life? Here, in gold-embroidered red doublet, jewelled surcoat, and gilt-edged ruff and wrist-bands, stood Sir Anthony Sherard,[1] with his silver-and-black armour piled at his feet. What had this man's legacy been? Had the lover of Giovanna of Naples bequeathed him some inheritance of sin and shame? Were his own actions merely the dreams that the dead man had not dared to realize? Here, from the fading canvas, smiled Lady Elizabeth Devereux, in her gauze hood, pearl stomacher, and pink slashed sleeves. A flower was in her right hand, and her left clasped an enamelled collar of white and damask roses. On a table by her side lay a mandolin and an apple. There were large green rosettes upon her little pointed shoes. He knew her life, and the strange stories that were told about her lovers. Had he something of her temperament in him? These oval heavy-lidded eyes seemed to look curiously at him. What of George Willoughby,[2] with his powdered hair and fantastic patches? How evil he looked! The face was saturnine and swarthy, and the sensual lips seemed to be twisted with disdain. Delicate lace ruffles fell over the lean yellow hands that were so overladen with rings. He had been a macaroni[3] of the eighteenth century, and the friend, in his youth, of Lord Ferrars.[4] What of the second Lord Beckenham,[5] the companion of the Prince Regent in his wildest days, and one of the witnesses at the secret marriage with Mrs. Fitzherbert?[6] How proud and handsome he was, with his chestnut curls and insolent pose! What passions had he bequeathed? The world had looked upon him as infamous. He had led the orgies at Carlton House.[7] The star of the Garter glittered upon his breast.

1. One of Wilde's practical jokes. He borrowed the name from a friend and later biographer, the naïve R. H. Sherard, who was, in temperament, not at all like the fictitious lover of Giovanna of Naples. In the magazine edition, he was described as the "companion of the Prince Regent in his wildest days." When Sherard objected because he had a living relative by that name, Wilde moved him into Dorian's ancestral gallery of rogues. Elizabeth Devereux is fictitious, but her portrait seems inspired by allegorical Flemish portraits of the sixteenth century. The flower, collar, mandolin, and fruit all symbolize her domestic attributes.
2. Wilde may have taken the name from a baritone of the era who sang for a time with the D'Oyly Carte Opera Company.
3. Named after Italian dandies of the eighteenth century, remembered in the lyric of "Yankee Doodle."
4. An actual peerage that became extinct sometime before 1790.
5. A fictitious aristocrat named after the town of Beckenham.
6. The regent was George, prince of Wales, later George IV, who married Mrs. FitzHerbert in 1785. The marriage thereafter was ruled invalid, although their relationship continued long after George married Caroline of Brunswick.
7. The residence of the Prince of Wales, later George IV, from the time he attained his majority in 1783.

Beside him hung the portrait of his wife, a pallid, thin-lipped woman
in black. Her blood, also, stirred within him. How curious it all
seemed! And his mother with her Lady Hamilton face,[8] and her moist
wine-dashed lips—he knew what he had got from her. He had got
from her his beauty, and his passion for the beauty of others. She
laughed at him in her loose Bacchante dress. There were vine leaves
in her hair. The purple spilled from the cup she was holding. The
carnations of the painting had withered, but the eyes were still wonderful in their depth and brilliancy of colour. They seemed to follow
him wherever he went.

  Yet one had ancestors in literature, as well as in one's own race,
nearer perhaps in type and temperament, many of them, and certainly with an influence of which one was more absolutely conscious.
There were times when it appeared to Dorian Gray that the whole of
history was merely the record of his own life, not as he had lived it in
act and circumstance, but as his imagination had created it for him,
as it had been in his brain and in his passions. He felt that he had
known them all, those strange terrible figures that had passed across
the stage of the world and made sin so marvellous and evil so full of
subtlety. It seemed to him that in some mysterious way their lives had
been his own.

  The hero of the wonderful novel that had so influenced his life had
himself known this curious fancy. In the seventh chapter he tells how,
crowned with laurel, lest lightning might strike him, he had sat, as
Tiberius,[9] in a garden at Capri, reading the shameful books of Elephantis,[1] while dwarfs and peacocks strutted round him and the flute-
player mocked the swinger of the censer; and, as Caligula,[2] had
caroused with the green-shirted jockeys in their stables, and supped in
an ivory manger with a jewel-frontleted horse; and, as Domitian, had
wandered through a corridor lined with marble mirrors, looking round
with haggard eyes for the reflection of the dagger that was to end his
days, and sick with that ennui, that terrible *tædium vitæ*, that comes
on those to whom life denies nothing; and had peered through a clear
emerald at the red shambles of the Circus,[3] and then, in a litter of pearl

  8. Lady Emma Hamilton (1765–1815), wife of Sir William Hamilton, British envoy at
     Naples, was a village girl from Cheshire and one of the great beauties of the day. Her like-
     ness was painted by Gainsborough (1727–88), by Richard Cosway (1742–1821), and by
     George Romney (1734–1802) in a series of works. She is remembered for her beautiful
     features, her Moll Flanders-to-Roxanna rise to fame, and her long love affair with Admi-
     ral Nelson.
  9. Second Roman emperor (A.D. 14–37), who succeeded Augustus Caesar. Wilde took the
     details of the Roman emperors from Tiberius to Nero from Suetonius's *Lives of the Cae-
     sars*. The following paragraph borrows heavily from John Addington Symonds, *Renaissance
     in Italy*, 7 vols. (1875–86). See *Dorian Gray*, Murray 246–47.
  1. A Greek authoress of amatory works mentioned by Suetonius and Martial.
  2. Caligula (A.D. 12–41) and Domitian (A.D. 56–95), despotic Roman emperors who were
     assassinated.
  3. Of the major circuses of Rome (Maximus, Flaminius, Neronis, and Maxentius), this

and purple drawn by silver-shod mules, been carried through the Street of Pomegranates to a House of Gold, and heard men cry on Nero Cæsar[4] as he passed by; and, as Elagabalus,[5] had painted his face with colours, and plied the distaff among the women, and brought the Moon from Carthage, and given her in mystic marriage to the Sun.

Over and over again Dorian used to read this fantastic chapter, and the two chapters immediately following, in which, as in some curious tapestries or cunningly wrought enamels, were pictured the awful and beautiful forms of those whom Vice and Blood and Weariness had made monstrous or mad: Filippo, Duke of Milan, who slew his wife, and painted her lips with a scarlet poison that her lover might suck death from the dead thing he fondled; Pietro Barbi, the Venetian, known as Paul the Second, who sought in his vanity to assume the title of Formosus,[6] and whose tiara, valued at two hundred thousand florins, was bought at the price of a terrible sin;[7] Gian Maria Visconti,[8] who used hounds to chase living men, and whose murdered body was covered with roses by a harlot who had loved him; the Borgia on his white horse,[9] with Fratricide riding beside him, and his mantle stained with the blood of Perotto; Pietro Riario,[1] the young Cardinal Archbishop of Florence, child and minion of Sixtus IV,[2] whose beauty was equalled only by his debauchery, and who received Leonora of Aragon[3] in a pavilion of white and crimson silk, filled with nymphs and centaurs, and gilded a boy that he might serve at the

---

probably refers to Circus Neronis, built by Caligula in the gardens of Agrippina. A circus was an elliptical race course.

4. Roman emperor (A.D. 54–68.), last of the Caesar family, notorious for beginning Roman persecution of Christians and for dissolute living.

5. Also called Heliogabalus (A.D. 205–22) because of his office as boy-priest of the Syrian sun god, he became Roman emperor in 218 and set a new standard for profligate living. He was put to death by the Praetorian guard. He reigned under the name Marcus Aurelius Antoninus, but he should not be confused with the earlier, stoic philosopher-emperor of the same name (A.D. 121–80).

6. Formosus (the Latin word for beautiful or well-shaped) was pope from 891–896 during very turbulent political times. I can find no evidence of Paul II's wish to take the name Formosus.

7. Pietro Barbo (1417–1464) reigned as Pope Paul II from 1464 to1471. He patronized the arts, helped beautify Rome, and collected antiquities. In the line above, the phrase "that her lover . . . he fondled" had been removed from the TS by Stoddart before *Lippincott's* publication. Its reappearance here can be explained best if we assume that Wilde had either the MS with him or, more likely, the revised TS when he was preparing the expanded edition. Wilde performed several restorations of this kind in the expanded edition.

8. Giovanni Maria Visconti (1389–1412) a member of the family that ruled Milan from the 13th century to 1447. He was a dissolute and cruel ruler who ultimately was assassinated, with the duchy passing to his brother.

9. Cesare Borgia, (1476–1507), soldier-politician, was the prototype for Machiavelli's *The Prince*.

1. Pietro Rario (1445–74) was a sexually profligate nephew of Pope Sixtus. He was elevated to cardinal by his uncle.

2. Francesso Della Rovere (1414–84) reigned as Pope Sixtus IV (1471–84).

3. Leonora of Aragon (1450–93) Duchess of Ferrara, Reggio, and Modena and aunt of Isabella of Aragon.

feast as Ganymede or Hylas;[4] Ezzelin,[5] whose melancholy could be
cured only by the spectacle of death, and who had a passion for red
blood, as other men have for red wine—the son of the Fiend, as was
reported, and one who had cheated his father at dice when gambling
with him for his own soul; Giambattista Cibo, who in mockery took
the name of Innocent, and into whose torpid veins the blood of three
lads was infused by a Jewish doctor; Sigismondo Malatesta,[6] the lover
of Isotta, and the lord of Rimini, whose effigy was burned at Rome
as the enemy of God and man, who strangled Polyssena with a napkin, and gave poison to Ginevra d'Este[7] in a cup of emerald, and in
honour of a shameful passion built a pagan church for Christian worship; Charles VI,[8] who had so wildly adored his brother's wife that a
leper had warned him of the insanity that was coming on him, and
who, when his brain had sickened and grown strange, could only be
soothed by Saracen cards painted with the images of Love and Death
and Madness; and, in his trimmed jerkin and jewelled cap and
acanthus-like curls, Grifonetto Baglioni,[9] who slew Astorre with his
bride, and Simonetto with his page, and whose comeliness was such
that, as he lay dying in the yellow piazza of Perugia,[1] those who had
hated him could not choose but weep, and Atalanta, who had cursed
him, blessed him.

There was a horrible fascination in them all. He saw them at
night, and they troubled his imagination in the day. The Renaissance
knew of strange manners of poisoning—poisoning by a helmet and
a lighted torch, by an embroidered glove and a jewelled fan, by a
gilded pomander and by an amber chain. Dorian Gray had been poisoned by a book. There were moments when he looked on evil simply as a mode through which he could realize his conception of the
beautiful.

4. In Greek mythology, Ganymede was a beautiful young boy with whom Zeus fell in love. He
   became Zeus's cupbearer until a jealous Hera, Zeus' wife, forced Zeus to set him among
   the stars as Aquarius, the water bearer. Hylas was one of the Argonauts. Because of his
   great beauty, he was ravished by nymphs in Mysia and never seen again.
5. An Italian Ghibelline leader (1194–1259), remembered as a tyrant and for the prominent
   place assigned to him in hell by Dante. Cibo was pope from 1484 to 1492.
6. Malatesta (1416–68) was a despotic Italian Renaissance prince.
7. Ginevra d'Este (1419–40), first wife of Sigismondo Malatesta, who had her poisoned in
   1440.
8. Charles VI, known as "Charles the Mad," reigned from 1380 to 1422.
9. The Baglioni family were famous for their bloody family feuds.
1. A city in Umbria, north of Rome.

Chapter XII[1]

It was on the ninth of November, the eve of his own thirty-eighth birthday,[2] as he often remembered afterwards.

He was walking home about eleven o'clock from Lord Henry's, where he had been dining, and was wrapped in heavy furs, as the night was cold and foggy. At the corner of Grosvenor Square and South Audley Street a man passed him in the mist, walking very fast, and with the collar of his grey ulster[3] turned up. He had a bag in his hand. Dorian recognized him. It was Basil Hallward. A strange sense of fear, for which he could not account, came over him. He made no sign of recognition, and went on quickly, in the direction of his own house.

But Hallward had seen him. Dorian heard him first stopping on the pavement and then hurrying after him. In a few moments his hand was on his arm.

"Dorian! What an extraordinary piece of luck! I have been waiting for you in your library ever since nine o'clock. Finally I took pity on your tired servant, and told him to go to bed, as he let me out. I am off to Paris by the midnight train, and I particularly wanted to see you before I left. I thought it was you, or rather your fur coat, as you passed me. But I wasn't quite sure. Didn't you recognize me?"

"In this fog, my dear Basil? Why, I can't even recognize Grosvenor Square. I believe my house is somewhere about here, but I don't feel at all certain about it. I am sorry you are going away, as I have not seen you for ages. But I suppose you will be back soon?"

"No: I am going to be out of England for six months. I intend to take a studio in Paris, and shut myself up till I have finished a great picture I have in my head. However, it wasn't about myself I wanted to talk. Here we are at your door. Let me come in for a moment. I have something to say to you."

"I shall be charmed. But won't you miss your train?" said Dorian Gray, languidly, as he passed up the steps and opened the door with his latch-key.

The lamp-light struggled out through the fog, and Hallward looked at his watch. "I have heaps of time," he answered. "The train doesn't go till twelve-fifteen, and it is only just eleven. In fact, I was on my way to the club to look for you, when I met you. You see, I shan't have any delay about luggage, as I have sent on my heavy things. All I have

---

1. Formerly chapter 10 in the *Lippincott's Magazine* version.
2. Changed from November seventh in the *Lippincott's* edition. The significance is explored by Richard Ellmann in "The Critic as Artist as Wilde," *Encounter* 29 (July 1967): 33. The change does not alter Dorian's birth sign; he remains a Scorpio of the textbook variety.
3. A loose, long overcoat made of heavy, rugged fabric and often belted.

with me is in this bag, and I can easily get to Victoria[4] in twenty minutes."

Dorian looked at him and smiled. "What a way for a fashionable painter to travel! A Gladstone bag,[5] and an ulster! Come in, or the fog will get into the house. And mind you don't talk about anything serious. Nothing is serious nowadays. At least nothing should be."

Hallward shook his head, as he entered, and followed Dorian into the library. There was a bright wood fire blazing in the large open hearth. The lamps were lit, and an open Dutch silver spirit-case stood, with some siphons of soda-water and large cut-glass tumblers, on a little marqueterie[6] table.

"You see your servant made me quite at home, Dorian. He gave me everything I wanted, including your best gold-tipped cigarettes. He is a most hospitable creature. I like him much better than the Frenchman you used to have. What has become of the Frenchman, by the bye?"

Dorian shrugged his shoulders. "I believe he married Lady Radley's maid, and has established her in Paris as an English dressmaker. *Anglomanie*[7] is very fashionable over there now, I hear. It seems silly of the French, doesn't it? But—do you know?—he was not at all a bad servant. I never liked him, but I had nothing to complain about. One often imagines things that are quite absurd. He was really very devoted to me, and seemed quite sorry when he went away. Have another brandy-and-soda? Or would you like hock-and-seltzer? I always take hock-and-seltzer myself.[8] There is sure to be some in the next room."

"Thanks, I won't have anything more," said the painter, taking his cap and coat off, and throwing them on the bag that he had placed in the corner. "And now, my dear fellow, I want to speak to you seriously. Don't frown like that. You make it so much more difficult for me."

"What is it all about?" cried Dorian in his petulant way, flinging himself down on the sofa. "I hope it is not about myself. I am tired of myself to-night. I should like to be somebody else."

"It is about yourself," answered Hallward, in his grave, deep voice, "and I must say it to you. I shall only keep you half an hour."

---

4. Victoria Station. Located in central London it was the rail terminus for boat-trains to France.
5. A Gladstone bag was a hinged suitcase opening flat into two equal parts.
6. A decorative inlay design, usually of wood and ivory.
7. The love of things English.
8. Wilde's favorite drink. "Hock" is a generic term used by the British to mean a white Rhine wine (from the German *Hochheimer Wein*). Selzer was a mineral water, naturally carbonated, from the spas of Selters, a village in Prussia. The name has since become generic for carbonated mineral water, originally with a rather salty tang.

Dorian sighed, and lit a cigarette. "Half an hour!" he murmured.

"It is not much to ask of you, Dorian, and it is entirely for your own sake that I am speaking. I think it right that you should know that the most dreadful things are being said against you in London."

"I don't wish to know anything about them. I love scandals about other people, but scandals about myself don't interest me. They have not got the charm of novelty."

"They must interest you, Dorian. Every gentleman is interested in his good name. You don't want people to talk of you as something vile and degraded. Of course you have your position, and your wealth, and all that kind of thing. But position and wealth are not everything. Mind you, I don't believe these rumours at all. At least, I can't believe them when I see you. Sin is a thing that writes itself across a man's face. It cannot be concealed. People talk sometimes of secret vices. There are no such things. If a wretched man has a vice, it shows itself in the lines of his mouth, the droop of his eyelids, the moulding of his hands even. Somebody—I won't mention his name, but you know him—came to me last year to have his portrait done. I had never seen him before, and had never heard anything about him at the time, though I have heard a good deal since. He offered an extrava-gant price. I refused him. There was something in the shape of his fingers that I hated. I know now that I was quite right in what I fan-cied about him. His life is dreadful. But you, Dorian, with your pure, bright, innocent face, and your marvellous untroubled youth—I can't believe anything against you. And yet I see you very seldom, and you never come down to the studio now, and when I am away from you, and I hear all these hideous things that people are whispering about you, I don't know what to say. Why is it, Dorian, that a man like the Duke of Berwick leaves the room of a club when you enter it? Why is it that so many gentlemen in London will neither go to your house or invite you to theirs? You used to be a friend of Lord Staveley. I met him at dinner last week. Your name happened to come up in conver-sation, in connection with the miniatures you have lent to the exhi-bition at the Dudley.[9] Staveley curled his lip, and said that you might have the most artistic tastes, but that you were a man whom no pure-minded girl should be allowed to know, and whom no chaste woman should sit in the same room with. I reminded him that I was a friend of yours, and asked him what he meant. He told me. He told me right out before everybody. It was horrible! Why is your friendship so fatal to young men? There was that wretched boy in the Guards who com-mitted suicide. You were his great friend. There was Sir Henry

9. A gallery named in honor of the Lord Dudley bequest, which collection of art was placed on public display in the Egyptian Hall, Piccadilly. The Egyptian Hall, still standing when *Dorian Gray* was written, was an exhibition hall whose exterior Egyptian design contrasted grotesquely with adjoining Georgian town buildings.

Ashton, who had to leave England, with a tarnished name. You and he were inseparable. What about Adrian Singleton, and his dreadful end? What about Lord Kent's only son, and his career? I met his father yesterday in St. James's Street. He seemed broken with shame and sorrow. What about the young Duke of Perth? What sort of life has he got now? What gentleman would associate with him?"

"Stop, Basil. You are talking about things of which you know nothing," said Dorian Gray, biting his lip, and with a note of infinite contempt in his voice. "You ask me why Berwick leaves a room when I enter it. It is because I know everything about his life, not because he knows anything about mine. With such blood as he has in his veins, how could his record be clean? You ask me about Henry Ashton and young Perth. Did I teach the one his vices, and the other his debauchery? If Kent's silly son takes his wife from the streets, what is that to me? If Adrian Singleton writes his friend's name across a bill, am I his keeper? I know how people chatter in England. The middle classes air their moral prejudices over their gross dinner-tables, and whisper about what they call the profligacies of their betters in order to try and pretend that they are in smart society, and on intimate terms with the people they slander. In this country, it is enough for a man to have distinction and brains for every common tongue to wag against him. And what sort of lives do these people, who pose as being moral, lead themselves? My dear fellow, you forget that we are in the native land of the hypocrite."

"Dorian," cried Hallward, "that is not the question. England is bad enough I know, and English society is all wrong. That is the reason why I want you to be fine. You have not been fine. One has a right to judge of a man by the effect he has over his friends. Yours seem to lose all sense of honour, of goodness, of purity. You have filled them with a madness for pleasure. They have gone down into the depths. You led them there. Yes: you led them there, and yet you can smile, as you are smiling now. And there is worse behind. I know you and Harry are inseparable. Surely for that reason, if for none other, you should not have made his sister's name a by-word."

"Take care, Basil. You go too far."

"I must speak, and you must listen. You shall listen. When you met Lady Gwendolen, not a breath of scandal had ever touched her. Is there a single decent woman in London now who would drive with her in the park? Why, even her children are not allowed to live with her. Then there are other stories—stories that you have been seen creeping at dawn out of dreadful houses and slinking in disguise into the foulest dens in London. Are they true? Can they be true? When I first heard them, I laughed. I hear them now, and they make me shudder. What about your country house, and the life that is led there? Dorian, you don't know what is said about you. I won't tell you

that I don't want to preach to you. I remember Harry saying once that
every man who turned himself into an amateur curate[1] for the
moment always began by saying that, and then proceeded to break his
word. I do want to preach to you. I want you to lead such a life as will
make the world respect you. I want you to have a clean name and a
fair record. I want you to get rid of the dreadful people you associate
with. Don't shrug your shoulders like that. Don't be so indifferent.
You have a wonderful influence. Let it be for good, not for evil. They
say that you corrupt every one with whom you become intimate, and
that it is quite sufficient for you to enter a house, for shame of some
kind to follow after. I don't know whether it is so or not. How should
I know? But it is said of you. I am told things that it seems impossible to doubt. Lord Gloucester was one of my greatest friends at
Oxford. He showed me a letter that his wife had written to him when
she was dying alone in her villa at Mentone.[2] Your name was implicated in the most terrible confession I ever read. I told him that it was
absurd—that I knew you thoroughly, and that you were incapable of
anything of the kind. Know you? I wonder do I know you? Before I
could answer that, I should have to see your soul."

"To see my soul!" muttered Dorian Gray, starting up from the sofa
and turning almost white from fear.

"Yes," answered Hallward, gravely, and with deep-toned sorrow in
his voice—"to see your soul. But only God can do that."

A bitter laugh of mockery broke from the lips of the younger man.
"You shall see it yourself, to-night!" he cried, seizing a lamp from the
table. "Come: it is your own handiwork. Why shouldn't you look at
it? You can tell the world all about it afterwards, if you choose.
Nobody would believe you. If they did believe you, they would like
me all the better for it. I know the age better than you do, though
you will prate about it so tediously. Come, I tell you. You have chattered enough about corruption. Now you shall look on it face to
face."

There was the madness of pride in every word he uttered. He
stamped his foot upon the ground in his boyish insolent manner.
He felt a terrible joy at the thought that some one else was to share
his secret, and that the man who had painted the portrait that was the
origin of all his shame was to be burdened for the rest of his life with
the hideous memory of what he had done.

"Yes," he continued, coming closer to him, and looking steadfastly
into his stern eyes, "I shall show you my soul. You shall see the thing
that you fancy only God can see."

---

1. A clergyman who has the spiritual charge of a parish (or parochial district); the parson of
   a parish.
2. A popular French resort on the Riviera.

Hallward started back. "This is blasphemy, Dorian!" he cried. "You must not say things like that. They are horrible, and they don't mean anything."

"You think so?" He laughed again.

"I know so. As for what I said to you to-night, I said it for your good. You know I have been always a stanch friend to you."

"Don't touch me. Finish what you have to say."

A twisted flash of pain shot across the painter's face. He paused for a moment, and a wild feeling of pity came over him. After all, what right had he to pry into the life of Dorian Gray? If he had done a tithe of what was rumoured about him, how much he must have suffered! Then he straightened himself up, and walked over to the fireplace, and stood there, looking at the burning logs with their frost-like ashes and their throbbing cores of flame.

"I am waiting, Basil," said the young man, in a hard, clear voice.

He turned round. "What I have to say is this," he cried. "You must give me some answer to these horrible charges that are made against you. If you tell me that they are absolutely untrue from beginning to end, I shall believe you. Deny them, Dorian, deny them! Can't you see what I am going through? My God! don't tell me that you are bad, and corrupt, and shameful."

Dorian Gray smiled. There was a curl of contempt in his lips. "Come upstairs, Basil," he said quietly. "I keep a diary of my life from day to day, and it never leaves the room in which it is written. I shall show it to you if you come with me."

"I shall come with you, Dorian, if you wish it. I see I have missed my train. That makes no matter. I can go to-morrow. But don't ask me to read anything to-night. All I want is a plain answer to my question."

"That shall be given to you upstairs. I could not give it here. You will not have to read long."

Chapter XIII[1]

He passed out of the room, and began the ascent, Basil Hallward following close behind. They walked softly, as men do instinctively at night. The lamp cast fantastic shadows on the wall and staircase. A rising wind made some of the windows rattle.

When they reached the top landing, Dorian set the lamp down on the floor, and taking out the key turned it in the lock. "You insist on knowing, Basil?" he asked, in a low voice.

"Yes."

1. Originally chapter 11 in the *Lippincott's Magazine* version.

"I am delighted," he answered, smiling. Then he added, somewhat harshly, "You are the one man in the world who is entitled to know everything about me. You have had more to do with my life than you think": and, taking up the lamp, he opened the door and went in. A cold current of air passed them, and the light shot up for a moment in a flame of murky orange. He shuddered. "Shut the door behind you," he whispered, as he placed the lamp on the table.

Hallward glanced round him, with a puzzled expression. The room looked as if it had not been lived in for years. A faded Flemish tapestry, a curtained picture, an old Italian cassone,[2] and an almost empty bookcase—that was all that it seemed to contain, besides a chair and a table. As Dorian Gray was lighting a half-burned candle that was standing on the mantelshelf, he saw that the whole place was covered with dust, and that the carpet was in holes. A mouse ran scuffling behind the wainscoting. There was a damp odour of mildew.

"So you think that it is only God who sees the soul, Basil? Draw that curtain back, and you will see mine."

The voice that spoke was cold and cruel. "You are mad, Dorian, or playing a part," muttered Hallward, frowning.

"You won't? Then I must do it myself," said the young man; and he tore the curtain from its rod, and flung it on the ground.

An exclamation of horror broke from the painter's lips as he saw in the dim light the hideous face on the canvas grinning at him. There was something in its expression that filled him with disgust and loathing. Good heavens! it was Dorian Gray's own face that he was looking at! The horror, whatever it was, had not yet entirely spoiled that marvellous beauty. There was still some gold in the thinning hair and some scarlet on the sensual mouth. The sodden eyes had kept something of the loveliness of their blue, the noble curves had not yet completely passed away from chiselled nostrils and from plastic throat. Yes, it was Dorian himself. But who had done it? He seemed to recognize his own brush-work, and the frame was his own design. The idea was monstrous, yet he felt afraid. He seized the lighted candle, and held it to the picture. In the left-hand corner was his own name, traced in long letters of bright vermilion.

It was some foul parody, some infamous, ignoble satire. He had never done that. Still, it was his own picture. He knew it, and he felt as if his blood had changed in a moment from fire to sluggish ice. His own picture! What did it mean? Why had it altered? He turned, and looked at Dorian Gray with the eyes of a sick man. His mouth twitched, and his parched tongue seemed unable to articulate. He passed his hand across his forehead. It was dank with clammy sweat.

2. A large, ornamented chest of the Italian Renaissance.

The young man was leaning against the mantel-shelf, wa[tching] him with that strange expression that one sees on the faces of [those] who are absorbed in a play when some great artist is acting. There was neither real sorrow in it nor real joy. There was simply the passion of the spectator, with perhaps a flicker of triumph in his eyes. He had taken the flower out of his coat, and was smelling it, or pretending to do so.

"What does this mean?" cried Hallward, at last. His own voice sounded shrill and curious in his ears.

"Years ago, when I was a boy," said Dorian Gray, crushing the flower in his hand, "you met me, flattered me, and taught me to be vain of my good looks. One day you introduced me to a friend of yours, who explained to me the wonder of youth, and you finished a portrait of me that revealed to me the wonder of beauty. In a mad moment, that, even now, I don't know whether I regret or not, I made a wish, perhaps you would call it a prayer . . ."

"I remember it! Oh, how well I remember it! No! the thing is impossible. The room is damp. Mildew has got into the canvas. The paints I used had some wretched mineral poison in them. I tell you the thing is impossible."

"Ah, what is impossible?" murmured the young man, going over to the window, and leaning his forehead against the cold, mist-stained glass.

"You told me you had destroyed it."

"I was wrong. It has destroyed me."

"I don't believe it is my picture."

"Can't you see your ideal in it?" said Dorian, bitterly.

"My ideal, as you call it . . ."

"As you called it."

"There was nothing evil in it, nothing shameful. You were to me such an ideal as I shall never meet again. This is the face of a satyr."

"It is the face of my soul."

"Christ! what a thing I must have worshipped! It has the eyes of a devil."

"Each of us has Heaven and Hell in him,[3] Basil," cried Dorian, with a wild gesture of despair.

Hallward turned again to the portrait, and gazed at it. "My God! if it is true," he exclaimed, "and this is what you have done with your life, why, you must be worse even than those who talk against you fancy you to be!" He held the light up again to the canvas, and examined it. The surface seemed to be quite undisturbed, and as he had left it. It was from within, apparently, that the foulness and horror had

3. Milton, *Paradise Lost* 1.254–55.

come. Through some strange quickening of inner life the leprosies of sin were slowly eating the thing away. The rotting of a corpse in a watery grave was not so fearful.

His hand shook, and the candle fell from its socket on the floor, and lay there sputtering. He placed his foot on it and put it out. Then he flung himself into the ricketty chair that was standing by the table and buried his face in his hands.

"Good God, Dorian, what a lesson! what an awful lesson!" There was no answer, but he could hear the young man sobbing at the window. "Pray, Dorian, pray," he murmured. "What is it that one was taught to say in one's boyhood? 'Lead us not into temptation. Forgive us our sins. Wash away our iniquities.'[4] Let us say that together. The prayer of your pride has been answered. The prayer of your repentance will be answered also. I worshipped you too much. I am punished for it. You worshipped yourself too much. We are both punished."

Dorian Gray turned slowly around, and looked at him with tear-dimmed eyes. "It is too late, Basil," he faltered.

"It is never too late, Dorian. Let us kneel down and try if we cannot remember a prayer. Isn't there a verse somewhere, 'Though your sins be as scarlet, yet I will make them as white as snow'?"[5]

"Those words mean nothing to me now."

"Hush! don't say that. You have done enough evil in your life. My God! don't you see that accursed thing leering at us?"

Dorian Gray glanced at the picture, and suddenly an uncontrollable feeling of hatred for Basil Hallward came over him, as though it had been suggested to him by the image on the canvas, whispered into his ear by those grinning lips. The mad passions of a hunted animal stirred within him, and he loathed the man who was seated at the table, more than in his whole life he had ever loathed anything. He glanced wildly around. Something glimmered on the top of the painted chest that faced him. His eye fell on it. He knew what it was. It was a knife that he had brought up, some days before, to cut a piece of cord, and had forgotten to take away with him. He moved slowly towards it, passing Hallward as he did so. As soon as he got behind him, he seized it, and turned round. Hallward stirred in his chair as if he was going to rise. He rushed at him, and dug the knife into the great vein that is behind the ear, crushing the man's head down on the table, and stabbing again and again.

There was a stifled groan, and the horrible sound of some one choking with blood. Three times the outstretched arms shot up convulsively, waving grotesque stiff-fingered hands in the air. He stabbed him twice more, but the man did not move. Something began to

4. Basil combines elements of the Lord's Prayer and the *Lavabo* prayer of the Mass (washing of the priest's hands prior to the act of consecration).
5. Isaiah 1.18.

trickle on the floor. He waited for a moment, still pressing the head down. Then he threw the knife on the table, and listened.

He could hear nothing, but the drip, drip on the threadbare carpet. He opened the door and went out on the landing. The house was absolutely quiet. No one was about. For a few seconds he stood bending over the balustrade, and peering down into the black seething well of darkness. Then he took out the key and returned to the room, locking himself in as he did so.

The thing was still seated in the chair, straining over the table with bowed head, and humped back, and long fantastic arms. Had it not been for the red jagged tear in the neck, and the clotted black pool that was slowly widening on the table, one would have said that the man was simply asleep.

How quickly it had all been done! He felt strangely calm, and, walking over to the window, opened it, and stepped out on the balcony. The wind had blown the fog away, and the sky was like a monstrous peacock's tail, starred with myriads of golden eyes. He looked down, and saw the policeman going his rounds and flashing the long beam of his lantern on the doors of the silent houses. The crimson spot of a prowling hansom gleamed at the corner, and then vanished. A woman in a fluttering shawl was creeping slowly by the railings, staggering as she went. Now and then she stopped, and peered back. Once, she began to sing in a hoarse voice. The policeman strolled over and said something to her. She stumbled away, laughing. A bitter blast swept across the Square. The gas-lamps flickered, and became blue, and the leafless trees shook their black iron branches to and fro. He shivered, and went back, closing the window behind him.

Having reached the door, he turned the key, and opened it. He did not even glance at the murdered man. He felt that the secret of the whole thing was not to realize the situation. The friend who had painted the fatal portrait to which all his misery had been due, had gone out of his life. That was enough.

Then he remembered the lamp. It was a rather curious one of Moorish workmanship, made of dull silver inlaid with arabesques of burnished steel, and studded with coarse turquoises. Perhaps it might be missed by his servant, and questions would be asked. He hesitated for a moment, then he turned back and took it from the table. He could not help seeing the dead thing. How still it was! How horribly white the long hands looked! It was like a dreadful wax image.

Having locked the door behind him, he crept quietly downstairs. The woodwork creaked, and seemed to cry out as if in pain. He stopped several times, and waited. No: everything was still. It was merely the sound of his own footsteps.

When he reached the library, he saw the bag and coat in the corner. They must be hidden away somewhere. He unlocked a secret press that was in the wainscoting, a press in which he kept his own curious disguises, and put them into it. He could easily burn them afterwards. Then he pulled out his watch. It was twenty minutes to two.

He sat down, and began to think. Every year—every month, almost—men were strangled in England for what he had done. There had been a madness of murder in the air. Some red star had come too close to the earth. . . . And yet what evidence was there against him? Basil Hallward had left the house at eleven. No one had seen him come in again. Most of the servants were at Selby Royal. His valet had gone to bed. . . . Paris! Yes. It was to Paris that Basil had gone, and by the midnight train, as he had intended. With his curious reserved habits, it would be months before any suspicions would be aroused. Months! Everything could be destroyed long before then.

A sudden thought struck him. He put on his fur coat and hat, and went out into the hall. There he paused, hearing the slow heavy tread of the policeman on the pavement outside, and seeing the flash of the bull's-eye[6] reflected in the window. He waited, and held his breath.

After a few moments he drew back the latch, and slipped out, shutting the door very gently behind him. Then he began ringing the bell. In about five minutes his valet appeared, half dressed, and looking very drowsy.

"I am sorry to have had to wake you up, Francis," he said, stepping in; "but I had forgotten my latch-key. What time is it?"

"Ten minutes past two, sir," answered the man, looking at the clock and blinking.

"Ten minutes past two? How horribly late! You must wake me at nine to-morrow. I have some work to do."

"All right, sir."

"Did any one call this evening?"

"Mr. Hallward, sir. He stayed here till eleven, and then he went away to catch his train."

"Oh! I am sorry I didn't see him. Did he leave any message?"

"No, sir, except that he would write to you from Paris, if he did not find you at the club."

"That will do, Francis. Don't forget to call me at nine to-morrow."

"No, sir."

The man shambled down the passage in his slippers.

Dorian Gray threw his hat and coat upon the table, and passed into the library. For a quarter of an hour he walked up and down the room

---

6. Generic term for a lantern with a thick, ridged lens to magnify the light. This was probably a kerosene lamp.

biting his lip, and thinking. Then he took down the Blue Book[7] from one of the shelves, and began to turn over the leaves. "Alan Campbell, 152, Hertford Street, Mayfair."[8] Yes; that was the man he wanted.

Chapter XIV[1]

At nine o'clock the next morning his servant came in with a cup of chocolate on a tray and opened the shutters. Dorian was sleeping quite peacefully, lying on his right side, with one hand underneath his cheek. He looked like a boy who had been tired out with play, or study.

The man had to touch him twice on the shoulder before he woke, and as he opened his eyes a faint smile passed across his lips, as though he had been lost in some delightful dream. Yet he had not dreamed at all. His night had been untroubled by any images of pleasure or of pain. But youth smiles without any reason. It is one of its chiefest charms.

He turned round, and, leaning upon his elbow, began to sip his chocolate. The mellow November sun came streaming into the room. The sky was bright, and there was a genial warmth in the air. It was almost like a morning in May.

Gradually the events of the preceding night crept with silent blood-stained feet into his brain, and reconstructed themselves there with terrible distinctness. He winced at the memory of all that he had suffered, and for a moment the same curious feeling of loathing for Basil Hallward, that had made him kill him as he sat in the chair, came back to him, and he grew cold with passion. The dead man was still sitting there, too, and in the sunlight now. How horrible that was! Such hideous things were for the darkness, not for the day.

He felt that if he brooded on what he had gone through he would sicken or grow mad. There were sins whose fascination was more in the memory than in the doing of them, strange triumphs that gratified the pride more than the passions, and gave to the intellect a quickened sense of joy, greater than any joy they brought, or could ever bring, to the senses. But this was not one of them. It was a thing to be driven out of the mind, to be drugged with poppies, to be strangled lest it might strangle one itself.

When the half-hour struck, he passed his hand across his forehead, and then got up hastily, and dressed himself with even more

7. A social directory.
8. About half a mile south of Dorian's residence in Grosvenor Square.
1. Originally chapter 12 in the *Lippincott's Magazine* version.

than his usual care, giving a good deal of attention to the choice of his necktie and scarf-pin, and changing his rings more than once. He spent a long time also over breakfast, tasting the various dishes, talking to his valet about some new liveries that he was thinking of getting made for the servants at Selby, and going through his correspondence. At some of the letters he smiled. Three of them bored him. One he read several times over, and then tore up with a slight look of annoyance in his face. "That awful thing, a woman's memory!" as Lord Henry had once said.

After he had drunk his cup of black coffee, he wiped his lips slowly with a napkin, motioned to his servant to wait, and going over to the table sat down and wrote two letters. One he put in his pocket, the other he handed to the valet.

"Take this round to 152, Hertford Street, Francis, and if Mr. Campbell is out of town, get his address."

As soon as he was alone, he lit a cigarette, and began sketching upon a piece of paper, drawing first flowers, and bits of architecture, and then human faces. Suddenly he remarked that every face that he drew seemed to have a fantastic likeness to Basil Hallward. He frowned, and, getting up, went over to the bookcase and took out a volume at hazard. He was determined that he would not think about what had happened until it became absolutely necessary that he should do so.

When he had stretched himself on the sofa, he looked at the title-page of the book. It was Gautier's "Émaux et Camées," Charpentier's Japanese-paper edition,[2] with the Jacquemart etching. The binding was of citron-green leather, with a design of gilt trellis-work and dotted pomegranates. It had been given to him by Adrian Singleton. As he turned over the pages his eye fell on the poem about the hand of Lacenaire, the cold yellow hand "du supplice encore mal lavée," with its downy red hairs and its "doigts de faune."[3] He glanced at his own

2. Wilde owned a copy of the 1881 Charpentier edition of Émaux et Camées (Enamels and Cameos). The first edition was printed in Paris in 1852 and contained eighteen poems. The sixth edition, the last prepared by Gautier (1872), contained forty-seven poems.
3. The poem is the second of two titled "Etudes de Mains." Lacenaire was a notorious murderer executed by guillotine; his preserved hand was the subject of Gautier's morbid meditation on the consciousness of evil. The lines Wilde quotes are from stanzas two and three:

> Curiosité dépravée!
> J'ai touché, malgré mes dégoûts,
> Du supplice encor mal lavée,
> Cette chair froide au duvet roux.
> Momifée et toute jaune
> Comme la main d'un pharoon,
> Elle allonge ses doigts de faune
> Crispés par la tentation.

[Depraved curiosity! I have touched, despite my revulsion, out of pain an evil reborn in that cold flesh with the reddish down. Mummified and completely yellowed as the hand of

white taper fingers, shuddering slightly in spite of himself, and passed
on, till he came to those lovely stanzas upon Venice:—

> "*Sur une gamme chromatique,*
>   *Le sein de perles ruisselant,*
> *La Vénus de l'Adriatique*
>   *Sort de l'eau son corps rose et blanc.*
>
> *Les dômes, sur l'azur des ondes*
>   *Suivant la phrase au pur contour,*
> *S'enflent comme des gorges rondes*
>   *Que soulève un soupir d'amour.*
>
> *L'esquif aborde et me dépose,*
>   *Jetant son amarre au pilier,*
> *Devant une façade rose,*
>   *Sur le marbre d'un escalier.*"[4]

How exquisite they were! As one read them, one seemed to be
floating down the green water-ways of the pink and pearl city, seated
in a black gondola with silver prow and trailing curtains. The mere
lines looked to him like those straight lines of turquoise-blue that follow one as one pushes out to the Lido.[5] The sudden flashes of colour
reminded him of the gleam of the opal-and-iris-throated birds that
flutter round the tall honey-combed Campanile, or stalk, with such
stately grace, through the dim, dust-stained arcades. Leaning back
with half-closed eyes, he kept saying over and over to himself:—

> *Devant une façade rose,*
>   *Sur le marbre d'un escalier.*

The whole of Venice was in those two lines. He remembered the
autumn that he had passed there, and a wonderful love that had
stirred him to mad, delightful follies. There was romance in every
place. But Venice, like Oxford, had kept the background for romance,

---

a pharaoh, the length of its faun-colored fingers shriveled by temptation.] Dorian's own
hand in the painting drips blood, and he achieves a perverse yet detached fascination as
he compares his emotion at seeing his own hand with that generated by the voice of the
poet contemplating the hand of the murderer Lacenaire. It must have been something very
like the emotion with which Wilde contemplated himself as a sinner and criminal. Wilde's
interest in murder as an art form is expressed in his essay in *Intentions*, "Pen, Pencil and
Poison" (1889).

4. The three stanzas on this page are from Gautier's "Variations sur le Carnival de Venise,"
part 2, titled "Sur les Lagunes." They translate: As though in a chromatic scale, her pearly
breast streaming, the Venus of the Adriatic emerges from the waters, her body red and
white. The cathedral domes above the blue waters, following the perfectly contoured line,
swell as the rounded throat that heaves a sigh of love. As the gondola arrived, I cast the
rope around a piling and landed in front of a rose-colored façade upon a marble staircase.

5. Lido is a resort isle near Venice. Campanile, below, is a bell tower, probably the great bell
tower of Saint Mark's Church, although Venice boasts many bell towers.

and, to the true romantic, background was everything, or almost everything. Basil had been with him part of the time, and had gone wild over Tintoret.[6] Poor Basil! what a horrible way for a man to die!

He sighed, and took up the volume again, and tried to forget. He read of the swallows that fly in and out of the little café at Smyrna[7] where the Hadjis[8] sit counting their amber beads and the turbaned merchants smoke their long tasselled pipes and talk gravely to each other; he read of the Obelisk in the Place de la Concorde[9] that weeps tears of granite in its lonely sunless exile, and longs to be back by the hot, lotus-covered Nile, where there are Sphinxes, and rose-red ibises,[1] and white vultures with gilded claws, and crocodiles, with small beryl eyes that crawl over the green steaming mud; he began to brood over those verses which, drawing music from kiss-stained marble, tell of that curious statue that Gautier compares to a contralto voice, the *"monstre charmant"*[2] that couches in the porphyry-room of the Louvre. But after a time the book fell from his hand. He grew nervous, and a horrible fit of terror came over him. What if Alan Campbell should be out of England? Days would elapse before he could come back. Perhaps he might refuse to come. What could he do then? Every moment was of vital importance.

They had been great friends once, five years before—almost inseparable, indeed. Then the intimacy had come suddenly to an end. When they met in society now, it was only Dorian Gray who smiled: Alan Campbell never did.

He was an extremely clever young man, though he had no real appreciation of the visible arts, and whatever little sense of the

---

6. Jacopo Robusti, called Tintoretto (1518–94), was a master Venetian painter greatly admired by Ruskin. The associations between Basil and Ruskin here are specific and unmistakable. Ruskin was a graduate of Oxford and later taught there. For him, Venice was the great city of Gothic architecture and later baroque painting. *The Stones of Venice* was Ruskin's masterpiece, blending art and social criticism to trace the rise and fall of Venice as recorded in its architecture.

7. Smyrna is now called Izmir in Turkey on the Gulf of Izmir. Dorian read of swallows in Gautier's poem "Ce Que Disent les Hirondelles" (What the swallows told) from *Émaux et Camées*. Beginning "He read . . . each other" is a loose prose translation of stanzas 6 and 7 of that poem.

8. Muslims who have made the Mecca pilgrimage. The beads are prayer beads.

9. The reference is to Gautier's "Nostalgies d'Obelisques," and from this point to "steaming mud," Wilde gives an effective prose summary of "L'Obelisque de Paris," first of the two parts of the poem. In the preceeding pages since Dorian took up Gautier's volume of poems, Wilde has been demonstrating an Aesthetic reading of selected poems by Gautier as they reflect and intensify Dorian's pathology of mind and mood. The obelisk is a single block of red granite about seventy-five feet tall. It was placed before the great temple of Luxor by Ramses II in the thirteenth century B.C. It now stands in the center of the huge square in Paris, a gift of the viceroy of Egypt to King Louis Philippe in 1831.

1. A genus of large grallatorial birds of the family *Ibididæ*, allied to the stork and heron, comprising numerous species with long legs and long slender decurved bill, inhabiting lakes and swamps in warm climates; a bird of this genus, esp. (and originally) the Sacred Ibis of Egypt (*Ibis religiosa*), with white and black plumage, an object of veneration among the ancient Egyptians. OED

2. The "sweet monster" of indeterminate sex is hermaphroditic. The Louvre, in Paris, is the most famous art museum in the world.

beauty of poetry he possessed he had gained entirely from Dorian. His dominant intellectual passion was for science. At Cambridge he had spent a great deal of his time working in the Laboratory, and had taken a good class in the Natural Science Tripos of his year.[3] Indeed, he was still devoted to the study of chemistry, and had a laboratory of his own, in which he used to shut himself up all day long, greatly to the annoyance of his mother, who had set her heart on his standing for Parliament and had a vague idea that a chemist[4] was a person who made up prescriptions. He was an excellent musician, however, as well, and played both the violin and the piano better than most amateurs. In fact, it was music that had first brought him and Dorian Gray together—music and that indefinable attraction that Dorian seemed to be able to exercise whenever he wished, and indeed exercised often without being conscious of it. They had met at Lady Berkshire's the night that Rubinstein[5] played there, and after that used to be always seen together at the Opera, and wherever good music was going on. For eighteen months their intimacy lasted. Campbell was always either at Selby Royal or in Grosvenor Square. To him, as to many others, Dorian Gray was the type of everything that is wonderful and fascinating in life. Whether or not a quarrel had taken place between them no one ever knew. But suddenly people remarked that they scarcely spoke when they met, and that Campbell seemed always to go away early from any party at which Dorian Gray was present. He had changed, too—was strangely melancholy at times, appeared almost to dislike hearing music, and would never himself play, giving as his excuse, when he was called upon, that he was so absorbed in science that he had no time left in which to practise. And this was certainly true. Every day he seemed to become more interested in biology, and his name appeared once or twice in some of the scientific reviews, in connection with certain curious experiments.

This was the man Dorian Gray was waiting for. Every second he kept glancing at the clock. As the minutes went by he became horribly agitated. At last he got up, and began to pace up and down the room, looking like a beautiful caged thing. He took long stealthy strides. His hands were curiously cold.

The suspense became unbearable. Time seemed to him to be crawling with feet of lead, while he by monstrous winds was being swept towards the jagged edge of some black cleft of precipice. He

3. The Tripos is an examination at Cambridge for the honors B.A. degree. Of the two great English universities, Cambridge has traditionally excelled in the sciences, Oxford in languages and the humanities.
4. The popular English name for a pharmacist.
5. Anton Rubenstein (1830–94), composer and piano virtuoso, whose music and style of playing were heavily romantic.

knew what was waiting for him there; saw it indeed, and, shuddering, crushed with dank hands his burning lids as though he would
have robbed the very brain of sight, and driven the eyeballs back into
their cave. It was useless. The brain had its own food on which it bat-
tened, and the imagination, made grotesque by terror, twisted and
distorted as a living thing by pain, danced like some foul puppet on a
stand, and grinned through moving masks. Then, suddenly, Time
stopped for him. Yes: that blind, slow-breathing thing crawled no
more, and horrible thoughts, Time being dead, raced nimbly on in
front, and dragged a hideous future from its grave, and showed it to
him. He stared at it. Its very horror made him stone.

At last the door opened, and his servant entered. He turned glazed
eyes upon him.

"Mr. Campbell, sir," said the man.

A sigh of relief broke from his parched lips, and the colour came
back to his cheeks.

"Ask him to come in at once, Francis." He felt that he was himself
again. His mood of cowardice had passed away.

The man bowed, and retired. In a few moments Alan Campbell[6]
walked in, looking very stern and rather pale, his pallor being intensified by his coal-black hair and dark eyebrows.

"Alan! this is kind of you. I thank you for coming."

"I had intended never to enter your house again, Gray. But you said
it was a matter of life and death." His voice was hard and cold. He
spoke with slow deliberation. There was a look of contempt in the
steady searching gaze that he turned on Dorian. He kept his hands
in the pockets of his Astrakhan[7] coat, and seemed not to have noticed
the gesture with which he had been greeted.

"Yes: it is a matter of life and death, Alan, and to more than one
person. Sit down."

Campbell took a chair by the table, and Dorian sat opposite to him.
The two men's eyes met. In Dorian's there was infinite pity. He knew
that what he was going to do was dreadful.

After a strained moment of silence, he leaned across and said, very
quietly, but watching the effect of each word upon the face of him he
had sent for, "Alan, in a locked room at the top of this house, a room
to which nobody but myself has access, a dead man is seated at a
table. He has been dead ten hours now. Don't stir, and don't look at
me like that. Who the man is, why he died, how he died, are matters
that do not concern you. What you have to do is this—"

"Stop, Gray. I don't want to know anything further. Whether what

---

6. The model for Alan Campbell was identified by Hesketh Pearson, in *Oscar Wilde* (New
York: Harper, 1946), pp. 318–19, as Sir Peter Chalmers Mitchell, whom, over lunch at the
Café Royal, Wilde once asked to describe how to get rid of a body.
7. A kind of cloth used chiefly as an edging or trimming for garments.

you have told me is true or not true, doesn't concern me. I entirely decline to be mixed up in your life. Keep your horrible secrets to yourself. They don't interest me any more."

"Alan, they will have to interest you. This one will have to interest you. I am awfully sorry for you, Alan. But I can't help myself. You are the one man who is able to save me. I am forced to bring you into the matter. I have no option. Alan, you are scientific. You know about chemistry, and things of that kind. You have made experiments. What you have got to do is to destroy the thing that is upstairs—to destroy it so that not a vestige of it will be left. Nobody saw this person come into the house. Indeed, at the present moment he is supposed to be in Paris. He will not be missed for months. When he is missed, there must be no trace of him found here. You, Alan, you must change him, and everything that belongs to him, into a handful of ashes that I may scatter in the air."

"You are mad, Dorian."

"Ah! I was waiting for you to call me Dorian."

"You are mad, I tell you—mad to imagine that I would raise a finger to help you, mad to make this monstrous confession. I will have nothing to do with this matter, whatever it is. Do you think I am going to peril my reputation for you? What is it to me what devil's work you are up to?"

"It was suicide, Alan."

"I am glad of that. But who drove him to it? You, I should fancy."

"Do you still refuse to do this for me?"

"Of course I refuse. I will have absolutely nothing to do with it. I don't care what shame comes on you. You deserve it all. I should not be sorry to see you disgraced, publicly disgraced. How dare you ask me, of all men in the world, to mix myself up in this horror? I should have thought you knew more about people's characters. Your friend Lord Henry Wotton can't have taught you much about psychology, whatever else he has taught you. Nothing will induce me to stir a step to help you. You have come to the wrong man. Go to some of your friends. Don't come to me."

"Alan, it was murder. I killed him. You don't know what he had made me suffer. Whatever my life is, he had more to do with the making or the marring of it than poor Harry has had. He may not have intended it, the result was the same."

"Murder! Good God, Dorian, is that what you have come to? I shall not inform upon you. It is not my business. Besides, without my stirring in the matter, you are certain to be arrested. Nobody ever commits a crime without doing something stupid. But I will have nothing to do with it."

"You must have something to do with it. Wait, wait a moment; listen to me. Only listen, Alan. All I ask of you is to perform a certain scientific experiment. You go to hospitals and dead-houses, and the horrors that you do there don't affect you. If in some hideous dissecting-room or fetid laboratory you found this man lying on a leaden table with red gutters scooped out in it for the blood to flow through, you would simply look upon him as an admirable subject. You would not turn a hair. You would not believe that you were doing anything wrong. On the contrary, you would probably feel that you were benefiting the human race, or increasing the sum of knowledge in the world, or gratifying intellectual curiosity, or something of that kind. What I want you to do is merely what you have often done before. Indeed, to destroy a body must be far less horrible than what you are accustomed to work at. And, remember, it is the only piece of evidence against me. If it is discovered, I am lost; and it is sure to be discovered unless you help me."

"I have no desire to help you. You forget that. I am simply indifferent to the whole thing. It has nothing to do with me."

"Alan, I entreat you. Think of the position I am in. Just before you came I almost fainted with terror. You may know terror yourself some day. No! don't think of that. Look at the matter purely from the scientific point of view. You don't inquire where the dead things on which you experiment come from. Don't inquire now. I have told you too much as it is. But I beg of you to do this. We were friends once, Alan."

"Don't speak about those days, Dorian: they are dead."

"The dead linger sometimes. The man upstairs will not go away. He is sitting at the table with bowed head and outstretched arms. Alan! Alan! If you don't come to my assistance I am ruined. Why, they will hang me, Alan! Don't you understand? They will hang me for what I have done."

"There is no good in prolonging this scene. I absolutely refuse to do anything in the matter. It is insane of you to ask me."

"You refuse?"

"Yes."

"I entreat you, Alan."

"It is useless."

The same look of pity came into Dorian Gray's eyes. Then he stretched out his hand, took a piece of paper, and wrote something on it. He read it over twice, folded it carefully, and pushed it across the table. Having done this, he got up, and went over to the window.

Campbell looked at him in surprise, and then took up the paper, and opened it. As he read it, his face became ghastly pale, and he fell back in his chair. A horrible sense of sickness came over him. He felt as if his heart was beating itself to death in some empty hollow.

After two or three minutes of terrible silence, Dorian turned round, and came and stood behind him, putting his hand upon his shoulder.

"I am so sorry for you, Alan," he murmured, "but you leave me no alternative. I have a letter written already. Here it is. You see the address. If you don't help me, I must send it. If you don't help me, I will send it. You know what the result will be. But you are going to help me. It is impossible for you to refuse now. I tried to spare you. You will do me the justice to admit that. You were stern, harsh, offensive. You treated me as no man has ever dared to treat me—no living man, at any rate. I bore it all. Now it is for me to dictate terms."

Campbell buried his face in his hands, and a shudder passed through him.

"Yes, it is my turn to dictate terms, Alan. You know what they are. The thing is quite simple. Come, don't work yourself into this fever. The thing has to be done. Face it, and do it."

A groan broke from Campbell's lips, and he shivered all over. The ticking of the clock on the mantelpiece seemed to him to be dividing Time into separate atoms of agony, each of which was too terrible to be borne. He felt as if an iron ring was being slowly tightened round his forehead, as if the disgrace with which he was threatened had already come upon him. The hand upon his shoulder weighed like a hand of lead. It was intolerable. It seemed to crush him.

"Come, Alan, you must decide at once."

"I cannot do it," he said, mechanically, as though words could alter things.

"You must. You have no choice. Don't delay."

He hesitated a moment. "Is there a fire in the room upstairs?"

"Yes, there is a gas-fire with asbestos."

"I shall have to go home and get some things from the laboratory."

"No, Alan, you must not leave the house. Write out on a sheet of note-paper what you want, and my servant will take a cab and bring the things back to you."

Campbell scrawled a few lines, blotted them, and addressed an envelope to his assistant. Dorian took the note up and read it carefully. Then he rang the bell, and gave it to his valet, with orders to return as soon as possible, and to bring the things with him.

As the hall door shut, Campbell started nervously, and, having got up from the chair, went over to the chimney-piece. He was shivering with a kind of ague. For nearly twenty minutes, neither of the men spoke. A fly buzzed noisily about the room, and the ticking of the clock was like the beat of a hammer.

As the chime struck one, Campbell turned round, and, looking at Dorian Gray, saw that his eyes were filled with tears. There was something in the purity and refinement of that sad face that seemed to enrage him. "You are infamous, absolutely infamous!" he muttered.

"Hush, Alan: you have saved my life," said Dorian.

"Your life? Good heavens! what a life that is! You have gone from corruption to corruption, and now you have culminated in crime. In doing what I am going to do, what you force me to do, it is not of your life that I am thinking."

"Ah, Alan," murmured Dorian, with a sigh, "I wish you had a thousandth part of the pity for me that I have for you." He turned away as he spoke, and stood looking out at the garden. Campbell made no answer.

After about ten minutes a knock came to the door, and the servant entered, carrying a large mahogany chest of chemicals, with a long coil of steel and platinum wire and two rather curiously-shaped iron clamps.

"Shall I leave the things here, sir?" he asked Campbell.

"Yes," said Dorian. "And I am afraid, Francis, that I have another errand for you. What is the name of the man at Richmond who supplies Selby with orchids?"

"Harden, sir."

"Yes—Harden. You must go down to Richmond at once, see Harden personally, and tell him to send twice as many orchids as I ordered, and to have as few white ones as possible. In fact, I don't want any white ones. It is a lovely day, Francis, and Richmond is a very pretty place, otherwise I wouldn't bother you about it."

"No trouble, sir. At what time shall I be back?"

Dorian looked at Campbell. "How long will your experiment take, Alan?" he said, in a calm, indifferent voice. The presence of a third person in the room seemed to give him extraordinary courage.

Campbell frowned, and bit his lip. "It will take about five hours," he answered.

"It will be time enough, then, if you are back at half-past seven, Francis. Or stay: just leave my things out for dressing. You can have the evening to yourself. I am not dining at home, so I shall not want you."

"Thank you, sir," said the man, leaving the room.

"Now, Alan, there is not a moment to be lost. How heavy this chest is! I'll take it for you. You bring the other things." He spoke rapidly, and in an authoritative manner. Campbell felt dominated by him. They left the room together.

When they reached the top landing, Dorian took out the key and turned it in the lock. Then he stopped, and a troubled look came into his eyes. He shuddered. "I don't think I can go in, Alan," he murmured.

"It is nothing to me. I don't require you," said Campbell, coldly.

Dorian half opened the door. As he did so, he saw the face of his portrait leering in the sunlight. On the floor in front of it the torn curtain was lying. He remembered that the night before he had forgotten, for the first time in his life, to hide the fatal canvas, and was about to rush forward, when he drew back with a shudder.

What was that loathsome red dew that gleamed, wet and glistening, on one of the hands, as though the canvas had sweated blood? How horrible it was!—more horrible, it seemed to him for the moment, than the silent thing that he knew was stretched across the table, the thing whose grotesque misshapen shadow on the spotted carpet showed him that it had not stirred, but was still there, as he had left it.

He heaved a deep breath, opened the door a little wider, and with half-closed eyes and averted head walked quickly in, determined that he would not look even once upon the dead man. Then, stooping down, and taking up the gold-and-purple hanging, he flung it right over the picture.

There he stopped, feeling afraid to turn round, and his eyes fixed themselves on the intricacies of the pattern before him. He heard Campbell bringing in the heavy chest, and the irons, and the other things that he had required for his dreadful work. He began to wonder if he and Basil Hallward had ever met, and, if so, what they had thought of each other.

"Leave me now," said a stern voice behind him.

He turned and hurried out, just conscious that the dead man had been thrust back into the chair, and that Campbell was gazing into a glistening yellow face. As he was going downstairs he heard the key being turned in the lock.

It was long after seven when Campbell came back into the library. He was pale, but absolutely calm. "I have done what you asked me to do," he muttered, "And now, good-bye. Let us never see each other again."

"You have saved me from ruin, Alan. I cannot forget that," said Dorian, simply.

As soon as Campbell had left, he went upstairs. There was a horrible smell of nitric acid in the room. But the thing that had been sitting at the table was gone.

Chapter XV[1]

That evening, at eight-thirty, exquisitely dressed, and wearing a large buttonhole of Parma violets, Dorian Gray was ushered into Lady Narborough's drawing-room by bowing servants. His forehead was throbbing with maddened nerves, and he felt wildly excited, but his

1. Wilde wrote this and the next three chapters for this edition.

manner as he bent over his hostess's hand was as easy and graceful
as ever. Perhaps one never seems so much at one's ease as when one
has to play a part. Certainly no one looking at Dorian Gray that night
could have believed that he had passed through a tragedy as horrible
as any tragedy of our age. Those finely-shaped fingers could never
have clutched a knife for sin, nor those smiling lips have cried out on
God and goodness. He himself could not help wondering at the calm
of his demeanour, and for a moment felt keenly the terrible pleasure
of a double life.

It was a small party, got up rather in a hurry by Lady Narborough,[2]
who was a very clever woman, with what Lord Henry used to describe
as the remains of really remarkable ugliness. She had proved an
excellent wife to one of our most tedious ambassadors, and having
buried her husband properly in a marble mausoleum, which she had
herself designed, and married off her daughters to some rich, rather
elderly men, she devoted herself now to the pleasures of French fiction, French cookery, and French *esprit*[3] when she could get it.

Dorian was one of her especial favourites, and she always told him
that she was extremely glad she had not met him in early life. "I know,
my dear, I should have fallen madly in love with you," she used to say,
"and thrown my bonnet right over the mills for your sake. It is most
fortunate that you were not thought of at the time. As it was, our bonnets were so unbecoming, and the mills were so occupied in trying to
raise the wind, that I never had even a flirtation with anybody. However, that was all Narborough's fault. He was dreadfully short-
sighted, and there is no pleasure in taking in a husband who never
sees anything."

Her guests this evening were rather tedious. The fact was, as she
explained to Dorian, behind a very shabby fan, one of her married
daughters had come up quite suddenly to stay with her, and, to make
matters worse, had actually brought her husband with her. "I think it
is most unkind of her, my dear," she whispered. "Of course I go and
stay with them every summer after I come from Homburg,[4] but then
an old woman like me must have fresh air sometimes, and besides, I
really wake them up. You don't know what an existence they lead
down there. It is pure unadulterated country life. They get up early,
because they have so much to do, and go to bed early because they
have so little to think about. There has not been a scandal in the
neighbourhood since the time of Queen Elizabeth, and consequently

---

2. Walter Pater singles out these scenes of comic satire as especially effective counterpoints
   to the mounting disorder of Dorian's emotions. Frank Harris also praised the social comedy in *The Picture of Dorian Gray*, saying that none could thereafter deny Wilde a place
   among the leading comic geniuses in English. It was Harris (81) who asserted that with
   The Picture of Dorian Gray, Wilde had finally justified himself as an artist.
3. Wit: in this case, witty conversation.
4. A resort near Frankfurt, famous for its mineral springs.

they all fall asleep after dinner. You shan't sit next either of them. You shall sit by me, and amuse me."

Dorian murmured a graceful compliment, and looked round the room. Yes: it was certainly a tedious party. Two of the people he had never seen before, and the others consisted of Ernest Harrowden, one of those middle-aged mediocrities so common in London clubs who have no enemies, but are thoroughly disliked by their friends; Lady Ruxton, an overdressed woman of forty-seven, with a hooked nose, who was always trying to get herself compromised, but was so peculiarly plain that to her great disappointment no one would ever believe anything against her; Mrs. Erlynne,[5] a pushing nobody, with a delightful lisp, and Venetian-red hair; Lady Alice Chapman, his hostess's daughter, a dowdy dull girl, with one of those characteristic British faces, that, once seen, are never remembered; and her husband, a red-cheeked, white-whiskered creature who, like so many of his class, was under the impression that inordinate joviality can atone for an entire lack of ideas.

He was rather sorry he had come, till Lady Narborough, looking at the great ormolu gilt clock[6] that sprawled in gaudy curves on the mauve-draped mantelshelf, exclaimed: "How horrid of Henry Wotton to be so late! I sent round to him this morning on chance, and he promised faithfully not to disappoint me."

It was some consolation that Harry was to be there, and when the door opened and he heard his slow musical voice lending charm to some insincere apology, he ceased to feel bored.

But at dinner he could not eat anything. Plate after plate went away untasted. Lady Narborough kept scolding him for what she called "an insult to poor Adolphe, who invented the *menu* specially for you," and now and then Lord Henry looked across at him, wondering at his silence and abstracted manner. From time to time the butler filled his glass with champagne. He drank eagerly, and his thirst seemed to increase.

"Dorian," said Lord Henry, at last, as the *chaud-froid*[7] was being handed round, "what is the matter with you to-night? You are quite out of sorts."

"I believe he is in love," cried Lady Narborough, "and that he is afraid to tell me for fear I should be jealous. He is quite right. I certainly should."

"Dear Lady Narborough," murmured Dorian, smiling, "I have not

---

5. The 1891 edition various refers to Lady Ruxton and Lady Roxton. I have regularized the name to Ruxton. Mrs. Erlynne reappears as the déclassé woman with a past in Wilde's 1892 play, *Lady Windermere's Fan*. She bears a striking resemblance in more than just appearance to a middle-aged Lillie Langtry.
6. Ormolu gilt was an alloy of copper and tin or zinc resembling gold and popular during the late Victorian period for decorating furniture, jewelry, and the like.
7. A white or brown jellied sauce used as an aspic with cold meats.

been in love for a whole week—not, in fact, since Madame de Ferrol left town."

"How you men can fall in love with that woman!" exclaimed the old lady. "I really cannot understand it."

"It is simply because she remembers you when you were a little girl, Lady Narborough," said Lord Henry. "She is the one link between us and your short frocks."

"She does not remember my short frocks at all, Lord Henry. But I remember her very well at Vienna thirty years ago, and how *décol-letée*[8] she was then."

"She is still *décolletée*," he answered, taking an olive in his long fingers; "and when she is in a very smart gown she looks like an *édition de luxe*[9] of a bad French novel. She is really wonderful, and full of surprises. Her capacity for family affection is extraordinary. When her third husband died, her hair turned quite gold from grief."[1]

"How can you, Harry!" cried Dorian.

"It is a most romantic explanation," laughed the hostess. "But her third husband, Lord Henry! You don't mean to say Ferrol is the fourth?"

"Certainly, Lady Narborough."

"I don't believe a word of it."

"Well, ask Mr. Gray. He is one of her most intimate friends."

"Is it true, Mr. Gray?"

"She assures me so, Lady Narborough," said Dorian. "I asked her whether, like Marguerite de Navarre,[2] she had their hearts embalmed and hung at her girdle. She told me she didn't, because none of them had had any hearts at all."

"Four husbands! Upon my word that is *trop de zèle*."[3]

"*Trop d'audace*,[4] I tell her," said Dorian.

"Oh! she is audacious enough for anything, my dear. And what is Ferrol like? I don't know him."

"The husbands of very beautiful women belong to the criminal classes," said Lord Henry, sipping his wine.

Lady Narborough hit him with her fan. "Lord Henry, I am not at all surprised that the world says that you are extremely wicked."

"But what world says that?" asked Lord Henry, elevating his eye-

8. A low-cut or plunging neckline designed to produce a tantalizing partial exposure of the female bosom. In this context, the speakers use it as a commentary on the behavior of Madame de Ferrol.
9. A sumptuously, even extravagantly, produced book with every care given to paper, illustrations, binding, and other physical attributes.
1. Algernon Moncrieff makes the same observation about Lady Harbury in Act I of *The Importance of Being Earnest*.
2. The same person as Margaret of Valois.
3. "Too much ardor."
4. "too much impudence."

brows. "It can only be the next world. This world and I are on excellent terms."

"Everybody I know says you are very wicked," cried the old lady, shaking her head.

Lord Henry looked serious for some moments. "It is perfectly monstrous," he said, at last, "the way people go about nowadays saying things against one behind one's back that are absolutely and entirely true."

"Isn't he incorrigible?" cried Dorian, leaning forward in his chair.

"I hope so," said his hostess, laughing. "But really if you all worship Madame de Ferrol in this ridiculous way, I shall have to marry again so as to be in the fashion."

"You will never marry again, Lady Narborough," broke in Lord Henry. "You were far too happy. When a woman marries again it is because she detested her first husband. When a man marries again, it is because he adored his first wife. Women try their luck; men risk theirs."

"Narborough wasn't perfect," cried the old lady.

"If he had been, you would not have loved him, my dear lady," was the rejoinder. "Women love us for our defects. If we have enough of them they will forgive us everything, even our intellects. You will never ask me to dinner again, after saying this, I am afraid, Lady Narborough; but it is quite true."

"Of course it is true, Lord Henry. If we women did not love you for your defects, where would you all be? Not one of you would ever be married. You would be a set of unfortunate bachelors. Not, however, that that would alter you much. Nowadays all the married men live like bachelors, and all the bachelors like married men."

"*Fin de siècle*,"[5] murmured Lord Henry.

"*Fin du globe*,"[6] answered his hostess.

"I wish it were *fin du globe*," said Dorian, with a sigh. "Life is a great disappointment."

"Ah, my dear," cried Lady Narborough, putting on her gloves, "don't tell me that you have exhausted Life. When a man says that one knows that Life has exhausted him. Lord Henry is very wicked, and I sometimes wish that I had been; but you are made to be good—you look so good. I must find you a nice wife. Lord Henry, don't you think that Mr. Gray should get married?"

"I am always telling him so, Lady Narborough," said Lord Henry, with a bow.

5. "End of the century" referred more to a state of mind and style of life than to the 1890s. The French phrase became synonymous with that sense of exhausted energy, lost values, and discontent with the commonplace that was the sad side of the Gay Nineties.
6. "end of the world."

"Well, we must look out for a suitable match for him. I shall go through Debrett[7] carefully to-night, and draw out a list of all the eligible young ladies."

"With their ages, Lady Narborough?" asked Dorian.

"Of course, with their ages, slightly edited. But nothing must be done in a hurry. I want it to be what *The Morning Post* calls a suitable alliance, and I want you both to be happy."

"What nonsense people talk about happy marriages!" exclaimed Lord Henry. "A man can be happy with any woman, as long as he does not love her."

"Ah! what a cynic you are!" cried the old lady, pushing back her chair, and nodding to Lady Ruxton. "You must come and dine with me soon again. You are really an admirable tonic, much better than what Sir Andrew prescribes for me. You must tell me what people you would like to meet, though. I want it to be a delightful gathering."

"I like men who have a future, and women who have a past," he answered. "Or do you think that would make it a petticoat party?"

"I fear so," she said, laughing, as she stood up. "A thousand pardons, my dear Lady Ruxton," she added, "I didn't see you hadn't finished your cigarette."

"Never mind, Lady Narborough. I smoke a great deal too much. I am going to limit myself, for the future."

"Pray don't, Lady Ruxton,"[8] said Lord Henry. "Moderation is a fatal thing. Enough is as bad as a meal. More than enough is as good as a feast."

Lady Ruxton[9] glanced at him curiously. "You must come and explain that to me some afternoon, Lord Henry. It sounds a fascinating theory," she murmured, as she swept out of the room.

"Now, mind you don't stay too long over your politics and scandal," cried Lady Narborough from the door. "If you do, we are sure to squabble upstairs."

The men laughed, and Mr. Chapman got up solemnly from the foot of the table and came up to the top. Dorian Gray changed his seat, and went and sat by Lord Henry. Mr. Chapman began to talk in a loud voice about the situation in the House of Commons. He guffawed at his adversaries. The word *doctrinaire*[1]—word full of terror to the British mind—reappeared from time to time between his explosions. An alliterative prefix served as an ornament of oratory.

---

7. *Debrett's Peerage* was the standard reference to British and Irish aristocracy.
8. Here misprinted as "Ruxton" in the 1891 edition.
9. Here misprinted as "Ruxton" in the 1891 edition.
1. Someone obstinately devoted to a theory without regard to its appropriateness or its applicability; originally, one of the French constitutionalist party after the downfall of Napoleon.

He hoisted the Union Jack[2] on the pinnacles of Thought. The inherited stupidity of the race—sound English common sense he jovially termed it—was shown to be the proper bulwark for Society.

A smile curved Lord Henry's lips, and he turned round and looked at Dorian.

"Are you better, my dear fellow?" he asked. "You seemed rather out of sorts at dinner."

"I am quite well, Harry. I am tired. That is all."

"You were charming last night. The little Duchess is quite devoted to you. She tells me she is going down to Selby."

"She has promised to come on the twentieth."

"Is Monmouth to be there too?"

"Oh, yes, Harry."

"He bores me dreadfully, almost as much as he bores her. She is very clever, too clever for a woman. She lacks the indefinable charm of weakness. It is the feet of clay that make the gold of the image precious. Her feet are very pretty, but they are not feet of clay. White porcelain feet, if you like. They have been through the fire, and what fire does not destroy, it hardens. She has had experiences."

"How long has she been married?" asked Dorian.

"An eternity, she tells me. I believe, according to the peerage, it is ten years, but ten years with Monmouth must have been like eternity, with time thrown in. Who else is coming?"

"Oh, the Willoughbys, Lord Rugby and his wife, our hostess, Geoffrey Clouston, the usual set. I have asked Lord Grotrian."

"I like him," said Lord Henry. "A great many people don't, but I find him charming. He atones for being occasionally somewhat overdressed, by being always absolutely over-educated.[3] He is a very modern type."

"I don't know if he will be able to come, Harry. He may have to go to Monte Carlo with his father."

"Ah! what a nuisance people's people are! Try and make him come. By the way, Dorian, you ran off very early last night. You left before eleven. What did you do afterwards? Did you go straight home?"

Dorian glanced at him hurriedly, and frowned. "No, Harry," he said at last, "I did not get home till nearly three."

"Did you go to the club?"

"Yes," he answered. Then he bit his lip. "No, I don't mean that. I didn't go to the club. I walked about. I forget what I did. . . . How inquisitive you are, Harry! You always want to know what one has

---

2. The national flag of England, Scotland, and Ireland, consisting of the three crosses of each nation overlaid: the red cross of St. George, and the white crosses of St. Andrew (Scotland) and St. Patrick (Ireland) on a blue field.
3. Algernon Moncrieff uses a variation on this line in Act II of *The Importance of Being Earnest*.

been doing. I always want to forget what I have been doing. I came in at half-past two, if you wish to know the exact time. I had left my latch-key at home, and my servant had to let me in. If you want any corroborative evidence on the subject you can ask him."

Lord Henry shrugged his shoulders. "My dear fellow, as if I cared! Let us go up to the drawing-room. No sherry, thank you, Mr. Chapman. Something has happened to you, Dorian. Tell me what it is. You are not yourself to-night."

"Don't mind me, Harry. I am irritable, and out of temper. I shall come round and see you to-morrow, or next day. Make my excuses to Lady Narborough. I shan't go upstairs. I shall go home. I must go home."

"All right, Dorian. I dare say I shall see you to-morrow at tea-time. The Duchess is coming."

"I will try to be there, Harry," he said, leaving the room. As he drove back to his own house he was conscious that the sense of terror he thought he had strangled had come back to him. Lord Henry's casual questioning had made him lose his nerves for the moment, and he wanted his nerve still. Things that were dangerous had to be destroyed. He winced. He hated the idea of even touching them.

Yet it had to be done. He realized that, and when he had locked the door of his library, he opened the secret press into which he had thrust Basil Hallward's coat and bag. A huge fire was blazing. He piled another log on it. The smell of the singeing clothes and burning leather was horrible. It took him three-quarters of an hour to consume everything. At the end he felt faint and sick, and having lit some Algerian pastilles[4] in a pierced copper brazier, he bathed his hands and forehead with a cool musk-scented vinegar.

Suddenly he started. His eyes grew strangely bright, and he gnawed nervously at his under-lip. Between two of the windows stood a large Florentine cabinet, made out of ebony, and inlaid with ivory and blue lapis.[5] He watched it as though it were a thing that could fascinate and make afraid, as though it held something that he longed for and yet almost loathed. His breath quickened. A mad craving came over him. He lit a cigarette and then threw it away. His eyelids drooped till the long fringed lashes almost touched his cheek. But he still watched the cabinet. At last he got up from the sofa on which he had been lying, went over to it, and, having unlocked it, touched some hidden spring. A triangular drawer passed slowly out. His fingers moved instinctively towards it, dipped in, and closed on something. It was a small Chinese box of black and gold-dust lacquer, elaborately wrought, the sides patterned with curved waves, and the silken cords

4. Aromatic tablets burned as incense.
5. An opaque gemstone of varying shades of blue, similar in other respects to jade.

hung with round crystals and tasselled in plaited metal threads. He opened it. Inside was a green paste[6] waxy in lustre, the odour curiously heavy and persistent.

He hesitated for some moments, with a strangely immobile smile upon his face. Then shivering, though the atmosphere of the room was terribly hot, he drew himself up, and glanced at the clock. It was twenty minutes to twelve. He put the box back, shutting the cabinet doors as he did so, and went into his bedroom.

As midnight was striking bronze blows upon the dusky air, Dorian Gray, dressed commonly, and with a muffler wrapped round his throat, crept quietly out of his house. In Bond Street he found a hansom with a good horse. He hailed it, and in a low voice gave the driver an address.[7]

The man shook his head. "It is too far for me," he muttered.

"Here is a sovereign for you," said Dorian. "You shall have another if you drive fast."

"All right, sir," answered the man, "you will be there in an hour," and after his fare had got in he turned his horse round, and drove rapidly towards the river.

Chapter XVI

A cold rain began to fall, and the blurred street-lamps looked ghastly in the dripping mist. The public-houses were just closing, and dim men and women were clustering in broken groups round their doors. From some of the bars came the sound of horrible laughter. In others, drunkards brawled and screamed.

Lying back in the hansom, with his hat pulled over his forehead, Dorian Gray watched with listless eyes the sordid shame of the great city, and now and then he repeated to himself the words that Lord Henry had said to him on the first day they had met, "To cure the soul by means of the senses, and the senses by means of the soul." Yes, that was the secret. He had often tried it, and would try it again now. There were opium-dens, where one could buy oblivion, dens of horror where the memory of old sins could be destroyed by the madness of sins that were new.

The moon hung low in the sky like a yellow skull. From time to time a huge misshapen cloud stretched a long arm across and hid it. The gas-lamps grew fewer, and the streets more narrow and gloomy. Once the man lost his way, and had to drive back half a mile. A steam

---

6. Opium in a form to be smoked, usually in a porcelain pipe.
7. The address presumably was in London's Chinatown, near the docks, where opium dens prospered.

rose from the horse as it splashed up the puddles. The side-windows of the hansom were clogged with a grey-flannel mist.

"To cure the soul by means of the senses, and the senses by means of the soul!" How the words rang in his ears! His soul, certainly, was sick to death. Was it true that the senses could cure it? Innocent blood had been spilt. What could atone for that? Ah! for that there was no atonement; but though forgiveness was impossible, forget-fulness was possible still, and he was determined to forget to stamp the thing out, to crush it as one would crush the adder that had stung one. Indeed, what right had Basil to have spoken to him as he had done? Who had made him a judge over others? He had said things that were dreadful, horrible, not to be endured.

On and on plodded the hansom, going slower, it seemed to him, at each step. He thrust up the trap,[1] and called to the man to drive faster. The hideous hunger for opium began to gnaw at him. His throat burned, and his delicate hands twitched nervously together. He struck at the horse madly with his stick. The driver laughed, and whipped up. He laughed in answer, and the man was silent.

The way seemed interminable, and the streets like the black web of some sprawling spider. The monotony became unbearable, and, as the mist thickened, he felt afraid.

Then they passed by lonely brickfields. The fog was lighter here, and he could see the strange bottle-shaped kilns with their orange fan-like tongues of fire. A dog barked as they went by, and far away in the darkness some wandering sea-gull screamed. The horse stumbled in a rut, then swerved aside, and broke into a gallop.

After some time they left the clay road, and rattled again over rough-paven streets. Most of the windows were dark, but now and then fantastic shadows were silhouetted against some lamp-lit blind. He watched them curiously. They moved like monstrous marionettes, and made gestures like live things.[2] He hated them. A dull rage was in his heart. As they turned a corner a woman yelled something at them from an open door, and two men ran after the hansom for about a hundred yards. The driver beat at them with his whip.

It is said that passion makes one think in a circle. Certainly with hideous iteration the bitten lips of Dorian Gray shaped and reshaped those subtle words that dealt with soul and sense, till he had found in them the full expression, as it were, of his mood, and justified, by intellectual approval, passions that without such justification would still have dominated his temper. From cell to cell of his brain crept the one thought; and the wild desire to live, most terrible of all man's

1. A small door in the carriage which opens to allow communication with the driver
2. From "Most of the windows . . . things," Wilde paraphrases a scene in his poem "The Har-lot's House" (1885), lines 22–24. This is another instance of Wilde's habit of mediating a mood, emotion, or reflection through art.

appetites, quickened into force each trembling nerve and fibre. Ugliness that had once been hateful to him because it made things real, became dear to him now for that very reason. Ugliness was the one reality. The coarse brawl, the loathsome den, the crude violence of disordered life, the very vileness of thief and outcast, were more vivid, in their intense actuality of impression, than all the gracious shapes of Art, the dreamy shadows of Song. They were what he needed for forgetfulness. In three days he would be free.

Suddenly the man drew up with a jerk at the top of a dark lane. Over the low roofs and jagged chimney-stacks of the houses rose the black masts of ships. Wreaths of white mist clung like ghostly sails to the yards.

"Somewhere about here, sir, ain't it?" he asked huskily through the trap.

Dorian started, and peered round. "This will do," he answered, and, having got out hastily, and given the driver the extra fare he had promised him, he walked quickly in the direction of the quay.[3] Here and there a lantern gleamed at the stern of some huge merchantman. The light shook and splintered in the puddles. A red glare came from an outward-bound steamer that was coaling. The slimy pavement looked like a wet mackintosh.

He hurried on towards the left, glancing back now and then to see if he was being followed. In about seven or eight minutes he reached a small shabby house, that was wedged in between two gaunt factories. In one of the top-windows stood a lamp. He stopped, and gave a peculiar knock.

After a little time he heard steps in the passage, and the chain being unhooked. The door opened quietly, and he went in without saying a word to the squat misshapen figure that flattened itself into the shadow as he passed. At the end of the hall hung a tattered green curtain that swayed and shook in the gusty wind which had followed him in from the street. He dragged it aside, and entered a long, low room which looked as if it had once been a third-rate dancing-saloon. Shrill flaring gas-jets, dulled and distorted in the fly-blown mirrors that faced them, were ranged round the walls. Greasy reflectors of ribbed tin backed them, making quivering disks of light. The floor was covered with ochre-coloured[4] sawdust, trampled here and there into mud, and stained with dark rings of spilt liquor. Some Malays were crouching by a little charcoal stove playing with bone counters, and showing their white teeth as they chattered. In one corner with his head buried in his arms, a sailor sprawled over a table, and by the tawdrily-painted bar that ran across one complete side stood two

---

3. An artificial bank or landing-place, built of stone or other solid material, lying along or projecting into a navigable water for convenience of loading and unloading ships.
4. Of an orange-yellow color produced by certain oxides of iron.

haggard women mocking an old man who was brushing the sleeves of his coat with an expression of disgust. "He thinks he's got red ants on him," laughed one of them, as Dorian passed by. The man looked at her in terror, and began to whimper.

At the end of the room there was a little staircase, leading to a darkened chamber. As Dorian hurried up its three rickety steps, the heavy odour of opium[5] met him. He heaved a deep breath, and his nostrils quivered with pleasure. When he entered, a young man with smooth yellow hair, who was bending over a lamp lighting a long thin pipe, looked up at him, and nodded in a hesitating manner.

"You here, Adrian?" muttered Dorian.

"Where else should I be?" he answered, listlessly. "None of the chaps will speak to me now."

"I thought you had left England."

"Darlington is not going to do anything. My brother paid the bill at last. George doesn't speak to me either. . . . I don't care," he added, with a sigh. "As long as one has this stuff, one doesn't want friends. I think I have had too many friends."

Dorian winced, and looked round at the grotesque things that lay in such fantastic postures on the ragged mattresses. The twisted limbs, the gaping mouths, the staring lustreless eyes, fascinated him. He knew in what strange heavens they were suffering, and what dull hells were teaching them the secret of some new joy. They were better off than he was. He was prisoned in thought. Memory, like a horrible malady, was eating his soul away. From time to time he seemed to see the eyes of Basil Hallward looking at him. Yet he felt he could not stay. The presence of Adrian Singleton troubled him. He wanted to be where no one would know who he was. He wanted to escape from himself.

"I am going on to the other place," he said, after a pause.

"On the wharf?"

"Yes."

"That mad-cat is sure to be there. They won't have her in this place now."

Dorian shrugged his shoulders. "I am sick of women who love one. Women who hate one are much more interesting. Besides, the stuff is better."

"Much the same."

"I like it better. Come and have something to drink. I must have something."

5. Opium, originally introduced in Britain for medicinal purposes, had by the late eighteenth century become a recreational drug. Prior to the 1868 Pharmacy Act which restricted its sale to pharmacists, anyone could legally trade in opium products: As a result by the middle of the nineteenth century hundreds of opium-based products were available to the general public.

"I don't want anything," murmured the young man.

"Never mind."

Adrian Singleton rose up wearily, and followed Dorian to the bar. A half-caste,[6] in a ragged turban and a shabby ulster, grinned a hideous greeting as he thrust a bottle of brandy and two tumblers in front of them. The women sidled up, and began to chatter. Dorian turned his back on them, and said something in a low voice to Adrian Singleton.

A crooked smile, like a Malay crease, writhed across the face of one of the women. "We are very proud to-night," she sneered.

"For God's sake don't talk to me," cried Dorian, stamping his foot on the ground. "What do you want? Money? Here it is. Don't ever talk to me again."

Two red sparks flashed for a moment in the woman's sodden eyes, then flickered out, and left them dull and glazed. She tossed her head, and raked the coins off the counter with greedy fingers. Her companion watched her enviously.

"It's no use," sighed Adrian Singleton. "I don't care to go back. What does it matter? I am quite happy here."

"You will write to me if you want anything, won't you?" said Dorian, after a pause.

"Perhaps."

"Good night, then."

"Good night," answered the young man, passing up the steps and wiping his parched mouth with a handkerchief.

Dorian walked to the door with a look of pain in his face. As he drew the curtain aside a hideous laugh broke from the painted lips of the woman who had taken his money. "There goes the devil's bargain!" she hiccoughed, in a hoarse voice.

"Curse you!" he answered, "don't call me that."

She snapped her fingers. "Prince Charming is what you like to be called, ain't it?" she yelled after him.

The drowsy sailor leaped to his feet as she spoke, and looked wildly round. The sound of the shutting of the hall door fell on his ear. He rushed out as if in pursuit.

Dorian Gray hurried along the quay through the drizzling rain. His meeting with Adrian Singleton had strangely moved him, and he wondered if the ruin of that young life was really to be laid at his door, as Basil Hallward had said to him with such infamy of insult. He bit his lip, and for a few seconds his eyes grew sad. Yet, after all, what did it matter to him? One's days were too brief to take the burden of another's errors on one's shoulders. Each man lived his own

6. One of a mixed race, a half-breed; *esp.*, in India, one born to or descended from a European father and native mother.

life, and paid his own price for living it. The only pity was one had to pay so often for a single fault. One had to pay over and over again, indeed. In her dealings with man Destiny never closed her accounts.

There are moments, psychologists tell us, when the passion for sin, or for what the world calls sin, so dominates a nature, that every fibre of the body, as every cell of the brain, seems to be instinct with fearful impulses. Men and women at such moments lose the freedom of their will. They move to their terrible end as automatons move. Choice is taken from them, and conscience is either killed, or, if it lives at all, lives but to give rebellion its fascination, and disobedience its charm. For all sins, as theologians weary not of reminding us, are sins of disobedience. When that high spirit, that morning-star of evil, fell from heaven, it was as a rebel that he fell.

Callous, concentrated on evil, with stained mind, and soul hungry for rebellion, Dorian Gray hastened on, quickening his step as he went, but as he darted aside into a dim archway, that had served him often as a short cut to the ill-famed place where he was going, he felt himself suddenly seized from behind, and before be had time to defend himself he was thrust back against the wall, with a brutal hand round his throat.

He struggled madly for life, and by a terrible effort wrenched the tightening fingers away. In a second he heard the click of a revolver, and saw the gleam of a polished barrel pointing straight at his head, and the dusky form of a short thick-set man facing him.

"What do you want?" he gasped.

"Keep quiet," said the man. "If you stir, I shoot you."

"You are mad. What have I done to you?"

"You wrecked the life of Sibyl Vane," was the answer, "and Sibyl Vane was my sister. She killed herself. I know it. Her death is at your door. I swore I would kill you in return. For years I have sought you. I had no clue, no trace. The two people who could have described you were dead. I knew nothing of you but the pet name she used to call you. I heard it to-night by chance. Make your peace with God, for to-night you are going to die."

Dorian Gray grew sick with fear. "I never knew her," he stammered. "I never heard of her. You are mad."

"You had better confess your sin, for as sure as I am James Vane, you are going to die." There was a horrible moment. Dorian did not know what to say or do. "Down on your knees!" growled the man. "I give you one minute to make your peace—no more. I go on board to-night for India, and I must do my job first. One minute. That's all."

Dorian's arms fell to his side. Paralysed with terror, he did not know what to do. Suddenly a wild hope flashed across his brain.

"Stop," he cried. "How long ago is it since your sister died? Quick, tell me!"

"Eighteen years," said the man. "Why do you ask me? What do years matter?"

"Eighteen years," laughed Dorian Gray, with a touch of triumph in his voice. "Eighteen years! Set me under the lamp and look at my face!"

James Vane hesitated for a moment, not understanding what was meant. Then he seized Dorian Gray and dragged him from the archway.

Dim and wavering as was the windblown light, yet it served to show him the hideous error, as it seemed, into which he had fallen, for the face of the man he had sought to kill had all the bloom of boyhood, all the unstained purity of youth. He seemed little more than a lad of twenty summers, hardly older, if older indeed at all, than his sister had been when they had parted so many years ago. It was obvious that this was not the man who had destroyed her life.

He loosened his hold and reeled back. "My God! my God!" he cried, "and I would have murdered you!"

Dorian Gray drew a long breath. "You have been on the brink of committing a terrible crime, my man," he said, looking at him sternly. "Let this be a warning to you not to take vengeance into your own hands."

"Forgive me, sir," muttered James Vane. "I was deceived. A chance word I heard in that damned den set me on the wrong track."

"You had better go home, and put that pistol away, or you may get into trouble," said Dorian, turning on his heel, and going slowly down the street.

James Vane stood on the pavement in horror. He was trembling from head to foot. After a little while a black shadow that had been creeping along the dripping wall, moved out into the light and came close to him with stealthy footsteps. He felt a hand laid on his arm and looked round with a start. It was one of the women who had been drinking at the bar.

"Why didn't you kill him?" she hissed out, putting haggard face quite close to his. "I knew you were following him when you rushed out from Daly's.[7] You fool! You should have killed him. He has lots of money, and he's as bad as bad."

"He is not the man I am looking for," he answered, "and I want no man's money. I want a man's life. The man whose life I want must be nearly forty now. This one is little more than a boy. Thank God, I have not got his blood upon my hands."

---

7. A theater on Cranbourn Street off Leicester Square established by the American playwright Augustin Daly in 1879, long since razed.

The woman gave a bitter laugh. "Little more than a boy!" she sneered. "Why, man, it's nigh on eighteen years since Prince Charming made me what I am."

"You lie!" cried James Vane.

She raised her hand up to heaven. "Before God I am telling the truth," she cried.

"Before God?"

"Strike me dumb if it ain't so. He is the worst one that comes here. They say he has sold himself to the devil for a pretty face. It's nigh on eighteen years since I met him. He hasn't changed much since then. I have though," she added, with a sickly leer.

"You swear this?"

"I swear it," came in hoarse echo from her flat mouth. "But don't give me away to him," she whined; "I am afraid of him. Let me have some money for my night's lodging."

He broke from her with an oath, and rushed to the corner of the street, but Dorian Gray had disappeared. When he looked back, the woman had vanished also.

Chapter XVII

A week later Dorian Gray was sitting in the conservatory at Selby Royal talking to the pretty Duchess of Monmouth, who with her husband, a jaded-looking man of sixty, was amongst his guests. It was tea-time, and the mellow light of the huge lace-covered lamp that stood on the table lit up the delicate china and hammered silver of the service at which the Duchess was presiding. Her white hands were moving daintily among the cups, and her full red lips were smiling at something that Dorian had whispered to her. Lord Henry was lying back in a silk-draped wicker chair looking at them. On a peach-coloured divan sat Lady Narborough pretending to listen to the Duke's description of the last Brazilian beetle that he had added to his collection. Three young men in elaborate smoking-suits were handing tea-cakes to some of the women. The house-party consisted of twelve people, and there were more expected to arrive on the next day.

"What are you two talking about?" said Lord Henry, strolling over to the table, and putting his cup down. "I hope Dorian has told you about my plan for rechristening everything, Gladys. It is a delightful idea."

"But I don't want to be rechristened, Harry," rejoined the Duchess, looking up at him with her wonderful eyes. "I am quite satisfied with my own name, and I am sure Mr. Gray should be satisfied with his."

"My dear Gladys, I would not alter either name for the world. They are both perfect. I was thinking chiefly of flowers. Yesterday I cut an orchid, for my buttonhole. It was a marvellous spotted thing, as effective as the seven deadly sins.[1] In a thoughtless moment I asked one of the gardeners what it was called. He told me it was a fine specimen of *Robinsoniana*, or something dreadful of that kind. It is a sad truth, but we have lost the faculty of giving lovely names to things. Names are everything. I never quarrel with actions. My one quarrel is with words. That is the reason I hate vulgar realism in literature. The man who could call a spade a spade should be compelled to use one. It is the only thing he is fit for."

"Then what should we call you, Harry?" she asked.

"His name is Prince Paradox," said Dorian.

"I recognize him in a flash," exclaimed the Duchess.

"I won't hear of it," laughed Lord Henry, sinking into a chair. "From a label there is no escape! I refuse the title."

"Royalties may not abdicate," fell as a warning from pretty lips.

"You wish me to defend my throne, then?"

"Yes.

"I give the truths of to-morrow."

"I prefer the mistakes of to-day," she answered.

"You disarm me, Gladys," he cried, catching the wilfulness of her mood.

"Of your shield, Harry, not of your spear."

"I never tilt against Beauty," he said, with a wave of his hand.

"That is your error, Harry, believe me. You value beauty far too much."

"How can you say that? I admit that I think that it is better to be beautiful than to be good.[2] But on the other hand no one is more ready than I am to acknowledge that it is better to be good than to be ugly."

"Ugliness is one of the seven deadly sins, then?" cried the Duchess. "What becomes of your simile about the orchid?"

"Ugliness is one of the seven deadly virtues, Gladys. You, as a good Tory, must not underrate them. Beer, the Bible, and the seven deadly virtues have made our England what she is."

"You don't like your country, then?" she asked.

"I live in it."

"That you may censure it the better."

"Would you have me take the verdict of Europe on it?" he enquired.

"What do they say of us?"

---

1. The seven deadly sins are Pride, Envy, Wrath/Anger, Sloth, Avarice/Greed, Gluttony, and Lust
2. An echo of the phrase in "The Critic as Artist": "aesthetics are higher than ethics."

"That Tartuffe[3] has emigrated to England and opened a shop."

"Is that yours, Harry?"

"I give it to you."

"I could not use it. It is too true."

"You need not be afraid. Our countrymen never recognize a description."

"They are practical."

"They are more cunning than practical. When they make up their ledger, they balance stupidity by wealth, and vice by hypocrisy."

"Still, we have done great things."

"Great things have been thrust on us, Gladys."[4]

"We have carried their burden."

"Only as far as the Stock Exchange."

She shook her head. "I believe in the race," she cried.

"It represents the survival of the pushing."[5]

"It has development."

"Decay fascinates me more."

"What of Art?" she asked.

"It is a malady."

"Love?"

"An illusion."

"Religion?"

"The fashionable substitute for Belief."

"You are a sceptic."

"Never! Scepticism is the beginning of Faith."

"What are you?"

"To define is to limit."

"Give me a clue."

"Threads snap. You would lose your way in the labyrinth."

"You bewilder me. Let us talk of some one else."

"Our host is a delightful topic. Years ago he was christened Prince Charming."

"Ah! don't remind me of that," cried Dorian Gray.

"Our host is rather horrid this evening," answered the Duchess, colouring. "I believe he thinks that Monmouth married me on purely scientific principles as the best specimen he could find of a modern butterfly."

"Well, I hope he won't stick pins into you, Duchess," laughed Dorian.

3. The scheming religious hypocrite who is the leading character in Molière's comedy of the same name.
4. *Twelfth Night* 2.5.144–46.
5. Parody of Herbert Spencer's maxim "survival of the fittest," often applied by the Victorians to economic and social life and referred to as the doctrine of Social Darwinism.

"Oh! my maid does that already, Mr. Gray, when she is annoyed with me."

"And what does she get annoyed with you about, Duchess?"

"For the most trivial things, Mr. Gray, I assure you. Usually because I come in at ten minutes to nine and tell her that I must be dressed by half-past eight."

"How unreasonable of her! You should give her warning."

"I daren't, Mr. Gray. Why, she invents hats for me. You remember the one I wore at Lady Hilstone's garden-party? You don't, but it is nice of you to pretend that you do. Well, she made it out of nothing. All good hats are made out of nothing."

"Like all good reputations, Gladys," interrupted Lord Henry. "Every effect that one produces gives one an enemy. To be popular one must be a mediocrity."

"Not with women," said the Duchess, shaking her head; "and women rule the world. I assure you we can't bear mediocrities. We women, as some one says, love with our ears, just as you men love with your eyes, if you ever love at all."

"It seems to me that we never do anything else," murmured Dorian.

"Ah! then, you never really love, Mr. Gray," answered the Duchess, with mock sadness.

"My dear Gladys!" cried Lord Henry. "How can you say that? Romance lives by repetition, and repetition converts an appetite into an art. Besides, each time that one loves is the only time one has ever loved. Difference of object does not alter singleness of passion. It merely intensifies it. We can have in life but one great experience at best, and the secret of life is to reproduce that experience as often as possible."

"Even when one has been wounded by it, Harry?" asked the Duchess, after a pause.

"Especially when one has been wounded by it," answered Lord Henry.

The Duchess turned and looked at Dorian Gray with a curious expression in her eyes. "What do you say to that, Mr. Gray?" she enquired.

Dorian hesitated for a moment. Then he threw his head back and laughed. "I always agree with Harry, Duchess."

"Even when he is wrong?"

"Harry is never wrong, Duchess."

"And does his philosophy make you happy?"

"I have never searched for happiness. Who wants happiness? I have searched for pleasure."

"And found it, Mr. Gray?"

"Often. Too often."

The Duchess sighed. "I am searching for peace," she said, "and if I don't go and dress, I shall have none this evening."

"Let me get you some orchids, Duchess," cried Dorian, starting to his feet, and walking down the conservatory.

"You are flirting disgracefully with him," said Lord Henry to his cousin. "You had better take care. He is very fascinating."

"If he were not, there would be no battle."

"Greek meets Greek, then?"

"I am on the side of the Trojans. They fought for a woman."

"They were defeated."

"There are worse things than capture," she answered.

"You gallop with a loose rein."

"Pace gives life," was the *riposte*.[6]

"I shall write it in my diary to-night."

"What?"

"That a burnt child loves the fire."

"I am not even singed. My wings are untouched."

"You use them for everything, except flight."

"Courage has passed from men to women. It is a new experience for us."

"You have a rival."

"Who?"

He laughed. "Lady Narborough," he whispered. "She perfectly adores him."

"You fill me with apprehension. The appeal to Antiquity is fatal to us who are romanticists."

"Romanticists! You have all the methods of science."

"Men have educated us."

"But not explained you."

"Describe us as a sex," was her challenge.

"Sphinxes without secrets."

She looked at him, smiling. "How long Mr. Gray is!" she said. "Let us go and help him. I have not yet told him the colour of my frock."

"Ah! you must suit your frock to his flowers, Gladys."

"That would be a premature surrender."

"Romantic Art begins with its climax."

"I must keep an opportunity for retreat."

"In the Parthian[7] manner?"

"They found safety in the desert. I could not do that."

"Women are not always allowed a choice," he answered, but hardly

---

6. Retort. Originally, the word referred to a return thrust in fencing. The fencing here is verbal.

7. Parthians were credited with having perfected retreat as a strategy of attack by luring the enemy close enough to fire their arrows as they moved away.

had he finished the sentence before from the far end of the conservatory came a stifled groan, followed by the dull sound of a heavy fall. Everybody started up. The Duchess stood motionless in horror. And with fear in his eyes Lord Henry rushed through the flapping palms, to find Dorian Gray lying face downwards on the tiled floor in a death-like swoon.

He was carried at once into the blue drawing-room, and laid upon one of the sofas. After a short time he came to himself, and looked round with a dazed expression.

"What has happened?" he asked. "Oh! I remember. Am I safe here, Harry?" He began to tremble.

"My dear Dorian," answered Lord Henry, "you merely fainted. That was all. You must have overtired yourself. You had better not come down to dinner. I will take your place."

"No, I will come down," he said, struggling to his feet. "I would rather come down. I must not be alone."

He went to his room and dressed. There was a wild recklessness of gaiety in his manner as he sat at table, but now and then a thrill of terror ran through him when he remembered that, pressed against the window of the conservatory, like a white handkerchief, he had seen the face of James Vane watching him.

Chapter XVIII[1]

The next day he did not leave the house, and, indeed, spent most of the time in his own room, sick with a wild terror of dying, and yet indifferent to life itself. The consciousness of being hunted, snared, tracked down, had begun to dominate him. If the tapestry did but tremble in the wind, he shook. The dead leaves that were blown against the leaded panes seemed to him like his own wasted resolutions and wild regrets. When he closed his eyes, he saw again the sailor's face peering through the mist-stained glass, and horror seemed once more to lay its hand upon his heart.

But perhaps it had been only his fancy that had called vengeance out of the night, and set the hideous shapes of punishment before him. Actual life was chaos, but there was something terribly logical in the imagination. It was the imagination that set remorse to dog the feet of sin. It was the imagination that made each crime bear its misshapen brood. In the common world of fact the wicked were not punished, nor the good rewarded. Success was given to the strong, failure thrust upon the weak. That was all. Besides, had any stranger been prowling round the house he would have been seen

___
1. Last of the new chapters added to this edition by Wilde.

by the servants or the keepers. Had any footmarks been found on the flower-beds, the gardeners would have reported it. Yes: it had been merely fancy. Sibyl Vane's brother had not come back to kill him. He had sailed away in his ship to founder in some winter sea. From him, at any rate, he was safe. Why, the man did not know who he was, could not know who he was. The mask of youth had saved him.

And yet if it had been merely an illusion, how terrible it was to think that conscience could raise such fearful phantoms, and give them visible form, and make them move before one! What sort of life would his be if, day and night, shadows of his crime were to peer at him from silent corners, to mock him from secret places, to whisper in his ear as he sat at the feast, to wake him with icy fingers as he lay asleep! As the thought crept through his brain, he grew pale with terror, and the air seemed to him to have become suddenly colder. Oh! in what a wild hour of madness he had killed his friend! How ghastly the mere memory of the scene! He saw it all again. Each hideous detail came back to him with added horror. Out of the black cave of Time, terrible and swathed in scarlet, rose the image of his sin. When Lord Henry came in at six o'clock, he found him crying as one whose heart will break.

It was not till the third day that he ventured to go out. There was something in the clear, pine-scented air of that winter morning that seemed to bring him back his joyousness and his ardour for life. But it was not merely the physical conditions of environment that had caused the change. His own nature had revolted against the excess of anguish that had sought to maim and mar the perfection of its calm. With subtle and finely-wrought temperaments it is always so. Their strong passions must either bruise or bend. They either slay the man, or themselves die. Shallow sorrows and shallow loves live on. The loves and sorrows that are great are destroyed by their own plenitude. Besides, he had convinced himself that he had been the victim of a terror-stricken imagination, and looked back now on his fears with something of pity and not a little of contempt.

After breakfast he walked with the Duchess for an hour in the garden, and then drove across the park to join the shooting-party. The crisp frost lay like salt upon the grass. The sky was an inverted cup of blue metal. A thin film of ice bordered the flat reed-grown lake.

At the corner of the pine-wood he caught sight of Sir Geoffrey Clouston, the Duchess's brother, jerking two spent cartridges out of his gun. He jumped from the cart, and having told the groom to take the mare home, made his way towards his guest through the withered bracken and rough undergrowth.

"Have you had good sport, Geoffrey?" he asked.

"Not very good, Dorian. I think most of the birds have gone to the open. I dare say it will be better after lunch, when we get to new ground."

Dorian strolled along by his side. The keen aromatic air, the brown and red lights that glimmered in the wood, the hoarse cries of the beaters[2] ringing out from time to time, and the sharp snaps of the guns that followed, fascinated him, and filled him with a sense of delightful freedom. He was dominated by the carelessness of happiness, by the high indifference of joy.

Suddenly from a lumpy tussock of old grass, some twenty yards in front of them, with black-tipped ears erect, and long hinder limbs throwing it forward, started a hare. It bolted for a thicket of alders. Sir Geoffrey put his gun to his shoulder, but there was something in the animal's grace of movement that strangely charmed Dorian Gray, and he cried out at once, "Don't shoot it, Geoffrey. Let it live."

"What nonsense, Dorian!" laughed his companion, and as the hare bounded into the thicket he fired. There were two cries heard, the cry of a hare in pain, which is dreadful, the cry of a man in agony, which is worse.

"Good heavens! I have hit a beater!" exclaimed Sir Geoffrey. "What an ass the man was to get in front of the guns! Stop shooting there!" he called out at the top of his voice. "A man is hurt."

The head-keeper came running up with a stick in his hand.

"Where, sir? Where is he?" he shouted. At the same time the firing ceased along the line.

"Here," answered Sir Geoffrey, angrily, hurrying towards the thicket. "Why on earth don't you keep your men back? Spoiled my shooting for the day."

Dorian watched them as they plunged into the alder-clump, brushing the lithe, swinging branches aside. In a few moments they emerged, dragging a body after them into the sunlight. He turned away in horror. It seemed to him that misfortune followed wherever he went. He heard Sir Geoffrey ask if the man was really dead, and the affirmative answer of the keeper. The wood seemed to him to have become suddenly alive with faces. There was the trampling of myriad feet, and the low buzz of voices. A great copper-breasted pheasant came beating through the boughs overhead.

After a few moments, that were to him, in his perturbed state, like endless hours of pain, he felt a hand laid on his shoulder. He started, and looked round.

"Dorian," said Lord Henry, "I had better tell them that the shooting is stopped for to-day. It would not look well to go on."

"I wish it were stopped for ever, Harry," he answered, bitterly. "The whole thing is hideous and cruel. Is the man . . . ?"

2. A man employed in rousing and driving game.

He could not finish the sentence.

"I am afraid so," rejoined Lord Henry. "He got the whole charge of shot in his chest. He must have died almost instantaneously. Come; let us go home."

They walked side by side in the direction of the avenue for nearly fifty yards without speaking. Then Dorian looked at Lord Henry, and said, with a heavy sigh, "It is a bad omen, Harry, a very bad omen."

"What is?" asked Lord Henry. "Oh! this accident, I suppose. My dear fellow, it can't be helped. It was the man's own fault. Why did he get in front of the guns? Besides, it is nothing to us. It is rather awkward for Geoffrey, of course. It does not do to pepper beaters. It makes people think that one is a wild shot. And Geoffrey is not; he shoots very straight. But there is no use talking about the matter."

Dorian shook his head. "It is a bad omen, Harry. I feel as if something horrible were going to happen to some of us. To myself, perhaps," he added, passing his hand over his eyes, with a gesture of pain.

The elder man laughed. "The only horrible thing in the world is *ennui*, Dorian. That is the one sin for which there is no forgiveness. But we are not likely to suffer from it, unless these fellows keep chattering about this thing at dinner. I must tell them that the subject is to be tabooed. As for omens, there is no such thing as an omen. Destiny does not send us heralds. She is too wise or too cruel for that. Besides, what on earth could happen to you, Dorian? You have everything in the world that a man can want. There is no one who would not be delighted to change places with you."

"There is no one with whom I would not change places, Harry. Don't laugh like that. I am telling you the truth. The wretched peasant who has just died is better off than I am. I have no terror of Death. It is the coming of death that terrifies me. Its monstrous wings seem to wheel in the leaden air around me. Good heavens! don't you see a man moving behind the trees there, watching me, waiting for me?"

Lord Henry looked in the direction in which the trembling gloved hand was pointing. "Yes," he said, smiling, "I see the gardener waiting for you. I suppose he wants to ask you what flowers you wish to have on the table to-night. How absurdly nervous you are, my dear fellow! You must come and see my doctor, when we get back to town."

Dorian heaved a sigh of relief as he saw the gardener approaching. The man touched his hat, glanced for a moment at Lord Henry in a hesitating manner, and then produced a letter, which he handed to his master. "Her Grace told me to wait for an answer," he murmured.

Dorian put the letter into his pocket. "Tell her Grace that I am coming in," he said, coldly. The man turned round, and went rapidly in the direction of the house.

"How fond women are of doing dangerous things!" laughed Lord Henry. "It is one of the qualities in them that I admire most. A woman will flirt with anybody in the world as long as other people are looking on."

"How fond you are of saying dangerous things, Harry! In the present instance you are quite astray. I like the Duchess very much, but I don't love her."

"And the Duchess loves you very much, but she likes you less, so you are excellently matched."

"You are talking scandal, Harry, and there is never any basis for scandal."

"The basis of every scandal is an immoral certainty," said Lord Henry, lighting a cigarette.

"You would sacrifice anybody, Harry, for the sake of an epigram."

"The world goes to the altar of its own accord," was the answer.

"I wish I could love," cried Dorian Gray, with a deep note of pathos in his voice. "But I seem to have lost the passion, and forgotten the desire. I am too much concentrated on myself. My own personality has become a burden to me. I want to escape, to go away, to forget. It was silly of me to come down here at all. I think I shall send a wire to Harvey to have the yacht got ready. On a yacht one is safe."

"Safe from what, Dorian? You are in some trouble. Why not tell me what it is? You know I would help you."

"I can't tell you, Harry," he answered, sadly. "And I dare say it is only a fancy of mine. This unfortunate accident has upset me. I have a horrible presentiment that something of the kind may happen to me."

"What nonsense!"

"I hope it is, but I can't help feeling it. Ah! here is the Duchess, looking like Artemis[3] in a tailor-made gown. You see we have come back, Duchess."

"I have heard all about it, Mr. Gray," she answered. "Poor Geoffrey is terribly upset. And it seems that you asked him not to shoot the hare. How curious!"

"Yes, it was very curious. I don't know what made me say it. Some whim, I suppose. It looked the loveliest of little live things. But I am sorry they told you about the man. It is a hideous subject."

"It is an annoying subject," broke in Lord Henry. "It has no psychological value at all. Now if Geoffrey had done the thing on purpose, how interesting he would be! I should like to know some one who had committed a real murder."

---

3. In Roman mythology, goddess of fertility and twin of Apollo. Artemis frequently appeared dressed in animal hides.

"How horrid of you, Harry!" cried the Duchess. "Isn't it, Mr. Gray? Harry, Mr. Gray is ill again. He is going to faint."

Dorian drew himself up with an effort, and smiled. "It is nothing, Duchess," he murmured; "my nerves are dreadfully out of order. That is all. I am afraid I walked too far this morning. I didn't hear what Harry said. Was it very bad? You must tell me some other time. I think I must go and lie down. You will excuse me, won't you?"

They had reached the great flight of steps that led from the conservatory on to the terrace. As the glass door closed behind Dorian, Lord Henry turned and looked at the Duchess with his slumberous eyes. "Are you very much in love with him?" he asked.

She did not answer for some time, but stood gazing at the landscape. "I wish I knew," she said at last.

He shook his head. "Knowledge would be fatal. It is the uncertainty that charms one. A mist makes things wonderful."

"One may lose one's way."

"All ways end at the same point, my dear Gladys."

"What is that?"

"Disillusion."

"It was my *début* in life," she sighed.

"It came to you crowned."

"I am tired of strawberry leaves."[4]

"They become you."

"Only in public."

"You would miss them," said Lord Henry.

"I will not part with a petal."

"Monmouth has ears."

"Old age is dull of hearing."

"Has he never been jealous?"

"I wish he had been."

He glanced about as if in search of something. "What are you looking for?" she enquired.

"The button from your foil,"[5] he answered. "You have dropped it."

She laughed. "I have still the mask."

"It makes your eyes lovelier," was his reply.

She laughed again. Her teeth showed like white seeds in a scarlet fruit.

Upstairs, in his own room, Dorian Gray was lying on a sofa, with terror in every tingling fibre of his body. Life had suddenly become too hideous a burden for him to bear. The dreadful death of the unlucky beater, shot in the thicket like a wild animal, had seemed to

---

4. Since strawberry-leaf images are worked into the design of the coronet, the reference here is to Gladys's title as duchess.
5. The tip on a fencing foil was used to prevent injury during a fencing match. Dueling without the button would be a blood match.

him to pre-figure death for himself also. He had nearly swooned at
what Lord Henry had said in a chance mood of cynical jesting.

At five o'clock he rang his bell for his servant, and gave him orders
to pack his things for the night-express to town, and to have the
brougham at the door by eight-thirty. He was determined not to sleep
another night at Selby Royal. It was an ill-omened place. Death
walked there in the sunlight. The grass of the forest had been spotted with blood.

Then he wrote a note to Lord Henry, telling him that he was going
up to town to consult his doctor, and asking him to entertain his
guests in his absence. As he was putting it into the envelope, a knock
came to the door, and his valet informed him that the head-keeper
wished to see him. He frowned, and bit his lip. "Send him in," he
muttered, after some moments' hesitation.

As soon as the man entered Dorian pulled his cheque-book out of
a drawer, and spread it out before him.

"I suppose you have come about the unfortunate accident of this
morning, Thornton?" he said, taking up a pen.

"Yes, sir," answered the gamekeeper.

"Was the poor fellow married? Had he any people dependent on
him?" asked Dorian, looking bored. "If so, I should not like them to
be left in want, and will send them any sum of money you may think
necessary."

"We don't know who he is, sir. That is what I took the liberty of
coming to you about."

"Don't know who he is?" said Dorian, listlessly. "What do you
mean? Wasn't he one of your men?"

"No, sir. Never saw him before. Seems like a sailor, sir."

The pen dropped from Dorian Gray's hand, and he felt as if his
heart had suddenly stopped beating. "A sailor?" he cried out. "Did
you say a sailor?"

"Yes, sir. He looks as if he had been a sort of sailor; tattooed on both
arms, and that kind of thing."

"Was there anything found on him?" said Dorian, leaning forward
and looking at the man with startled eyes. "Anything that would tell
his name?"

"Some money, sir—not much, and a six-shooter.[6] There was no
name of any kind. A decent-looking man, sir, but rough-like. A sort of
sailor we think."

Dorian started to his feet. A terrible hope fluttered past him. He
clutched at it madly. "Where is the body?" he exclaimed. "Quick! I
must see it at once."

"It is in an empty stable in the Home Farm, sir. The folk don't like

6. A revolver capable of firing six shots without reloading; a six-chambered revolver.

to have that sort of thing in their houses. They say a corpse brings bad luck."

"The Home Farm! Go there at once and meet me. Tell one of the grooms to bring my horse round. No. Never mind. I'll go to the stables myself. It will save time."

In less than a quarter of an hour Dorian Gray was galloping down the long avenue as hard as he could go. The trees seemed to sweep past him in spectral procession, and wild shadows to fling themselves across his path. Once the mare swerved at a white gate-post and nearly threw him. He lashed her across the neck with his crop. She cleft the dusky air like an arrow. The stones flew from her hoofs.

At last he reached the Home Farm. Two men were loitering in the yard. He leapt from the saddle and threw the reins to one of them. In the farthest stable a light was glimmering. Something seemed to tell him that the body was there, and he hurried to the door, and put his hand upon the latch.

There he paused for a moment, feeling that he was on the brink of a discovery that would either make or mar his life. Then he thrust the door open, and entered.

On a heap of sacking in the far corner was lying the dead body of a man dressed in a coarse shirt and a pair of blue trousers. A spotted handkerchief had been placed over the face. A coarse candle, stuck in a bottle, sputtered beside it.

Dorian Gray shuddered. He felt that his could not be the hand to take the handkerchief away, and called out to one of the farm-servants to come to him.

"Take that thing off the face. I wish to see it," he said, clutching at the doorpost for support.

When the farm-servant had done so, he stepped forward. A cry of joy broke from his lips. The man who had been shot in the thicket was James Vane.

He stood there for some minutes looking at the dead body. As he rode home, his eyes were full of tears, for he knew he was safe.

Chapter XIX[1]

"There is no use your telling me that you are going to be good," cried Lord Henry, dipping his white fingers into a red copper bowl filled with rose-water. "You are quite perfect. Pray, don't change."

Dorian Gray shook his head. "No, Harry, I have done too many

---

1. Wilde divided the last chapter of the *Lippincott's* edition (13), made some additions and other changes, and turned it into the two last chapters of this edition.

dreadful things in my life. I am not going to do any more. I began my
good actions yesterday."

"Where were you yesterday?"

"In the country, Harry. I was staying at a little inn by myself."

"My dear boy," said Lord Henry, smiling, "anybody can be good in
the country. There are no temptations there. That is the reason why
people who live out of town are so absolutely uncivilized. Civilization
is not by any means an easy thing to attain to. There are only two
ways by which man can reach it. One is by being cultured, the other
by being corrupt. Country people have no opportunity of being either,
so they stagnate."

"Culture and corruption," echoed Dorian. "I have known something of both. It seems terrible to me now that they should ever be
found together. For I have a new ideal, Harry. I am going to alter. I
think I have altered."

"You have not yet told me what your good action was. Or did you
say you had done more than one?" asked his companion, as he spilt
into his plate a little crimson pyramid of seeded strawberries, and
through a perforated shell-shaped spoon snowed white sugar upon
them.

"I can tell you, Harry. It is not a story I could tell to any one else. I
spared somebody. It sounds vain, but you understand what I mean.
She was quite beautiful, and wonderfully like Sibyl Vane. I think it
was that which first attracted me to her. You remember Sibyl, don't
you? How long ago that seems! Well, Hetty was not one of our own
class, of course. She was simply a girl in a village. But I really loved
her. I am quite sure that I loved her. All during this wonderful May
that we have been having, I used to run down and see her two or
three times a week. Yesterday she met me in a little orchard. The
apple-blossoms kept tumbling down on her hair, and she was laughing. We were to have gone away together this morning at dawn. Suddenly I determined to leave her as flower-like as I had found her."

"I should think the novelty of the emotion must have given you a
thrill of real pleasure, Dorian," interrupted Lord Henry. "But I can
finish your idyll for you. You gave her good advice, and broke her
heart. That was the beginning of your reformation."

"Harry, you are horrible! You mustn't say these dreadful things.
Hetty's heart is not broken. Of course she cried, and all that. But
there is no disgrace upon her. She can live, like Perdita,[2] in her garden of mint and marigold."

"And weep over a faithless Florizel,"[3] said Lord Henry, laughing, as

2. Daughter of Leontes and Hermione in Shakespeare's *A Winter's Tale,* Perdita was aban-
    doned by her parents.
3. In *A Winter's Tale,* the son of King Polixenes who falls in love with Perdita, a supposed

he leaned back in his chair. "My dear Dorian, you have the most curiously boyish moods. Do you think this girl will ever be really contented now with any one of her own rank? I suppose she will be married some day to a rough carter or a grinning ploughman. Well, the fact of having met you, and loved you, will teach her to despise her husband, and she will be wretched. From a moral point of view, I cannot say that I think much of your great renunciation. Even as a beginning, it is poor. Besides, how do you know that Hetty isn't floating at the present moment in some star-lit mill-pond, with lovely water-lilies round her, like Ophelia?"[4]

"I can't bear this, Harry! You mock at everything, and then suggest the most serious tragedies. I am sorry I told you now. I don't care what you say to me. I know I was right in acting as I did. Poor Hetty! As I rode past the farm this morning, I saw her white face at the window, like a spray of jasmine. Don't let us talk about it any more, and don't try to persuade me that the first good action I have done for years, the first little bit of self-sacrifice I have ever known, is really a sort of sin. I want to be better. I am going to be better. Tell me something about yourself. What is going on in town? I have not been to the club for days."

"The people are still discussing poor Basil's disappearance."

"I should have thought they had got tired of that by this time," said Dorian, pouring himself out some wine, and frowning slightly.

"My dear boy, they have only been talking about it for six weeks, and the British public are really not equal to the mental strain of having more than one topic every three months. They have been very fortunate lately, however. They have had my own divorce-case, and Alan Campbell's suicide. Now they have got the mysterious disappearance of an artist. Scotland Yard[5] still insists that the man in the grey ulster[6] who left for Paris by the midnight train on the ninth of November was poor Basil, and the French police declare that Basil never arrived in Paris at all. I suppose in about a fortnight we shall be told that he has been seen in San Francisco. It is an odd thing, but every one who disappears is said to be seen at San Francisco. It must be a delightful city, and possess all the attractions of the next world."[7]

"What do you think has happened to Basil?" asked Dorian, holding up his Burgundy against the light, and wondering how it was that he could discuss the matter so calmly.

---

shepherdess. Florizel, however, remains faithful, and after several misadventures, the impediments are removed and the lovers marry.

4. Doomed beloved of Shakespeare's *Hamlet*; drowned in a pond.
5. Home of London's Metropolitan police department.
6. Loose long overcoat of heavy fabric; usually belted.
7. Wilde visited San Francisco in 1883 during his American lecture tour. The reference to the attractions of the other world is likely an ironic reference to Hades or the underworld.

"I have not the slightest idea. If Basil chooses to hide himself, it is no business of mine. If he is dead, I don't want to think about him. Death is the only thing that ever terrifies me. I hate it."

"Why?" said the younger man, wearily.

"Because," said Lord Henry, passing beneath his nostrils the gilt trellis of an open vinaigrette box,"[8] one can survive everything nowadays except that. Death and vulgarity are the only two facts in the nineteenth century that one cannot explain away. Let us have our coffee in the music-room, Dorian. You must play Chopin[9] to me. The man with whom my wife ran away played Chopin exquisitely. Poor Victoria! I was very fond of her. The house is rather lonely without her. Of course married life is merely a habit, a bad habit. But then one regrets the loss even of one's worst habits. Perhaps one regrets them the most. They are such an essential part of one's personality."

Dorian said nothing, but rose from the table, and, passing into the next room, sat down to the piano and let his fingers stray across the white and black ivory of the keys. After the coffee had been brought in, he stopped, and, looking over at Lord Henry, said, "Harry, did it ever occur to you that Basil was murdered?"

Lord Henry yawned. "Basil was very popular, and always wore a Waterbury watch.[1] Why should he have been murdered? He was not clever enough to have enemies. Of course he had a wonderful genius for painting. But a man can paint like Velasquez[2] and yet be as dull as possible. Basil was really rather dull. He only interested me once, and that was when he told me, years ago, that he had a wild adoration for you, and that you were the dominant motive of his art."

"I was very fond of Basil," said Dorian, with a note of sadness in his voice. "But don't people say that he was murdered?"

"Oh, some of the papers do. It does not seem to me to be at all probable. I know there are dreadful places in Paris, but Basil was not the sort of man to have gone to them. He had no curiosity. It was his chief defect."

"What would you say, Harry, if I told you that I had murdered Basil?" said the younger man. He watched him intently after he had spoken.

"I would say, my dear fellow, that you were posing for a character that doesn't suit you. All crime is vulgar, just as all vulgarity is crime. It is not in you, Dorian, to commit a murder. I am sorry if I hurt your vanity by saying so, but I assure you it is true. Crime belongs exclusively

---

8. Aromatic salts.
9. Frederic Chopin (1810–49) was one of Wilde's favorite piano composers, referred to frequently in his writing from the early poetry to *De Profundis*.
1. An inexpensive pocket watch, hence of little interest to a thief.
2. Diego Rodríguez de Silva y Velásquez (1599–1660), the great Spanish painter much admired by Wilde.

to the lower orders. I don't blame them in the smallest degree. I should fancy that crime was to them what art is to us, simply a method of procuring extraordinary sensations."

"A method of procuring sensations? Do you think, then, that a man who has once committed a murder could possibly do the same crime again? Don't tell me that."

"Oh! anything becomes a pleasure if one does it too often," cried Lord Henry, laughing. "That is one of the most important secrets of life. I should fancy, however, that murder is always a mistake. One should never do anything that one cannot talk about after dinner. But let us pass from poor Basil. I wish I could believe that he had come to such a really romantic end as you suggest; but I can't. I dare say he fell into the Seine off an omnibus, and that the conductor hushed up the scandal. Yes: I should fancy that was his end. I see him lying now on his back under those dull-green waters with the heavy barges floating over him, and long weeds catching in his hair. Do you know, I don't think he would have done much more good work. During the last ten years his painting had gone off very much."

Dorian heaved a sigh, and Lord Henry strolled across the room and began to stroke the head of a curious Java parrot, a large grey-plumaged bird, with pink crest and tail, that was balancing itself upon a bamboo perch. As his pointed fingers touched it, it dropped the white scurf of crinkled lids over black glass-like eyes, and began to sway backwards and forwards.

"Yes," he continued, turning round, and taking his handkerchief out of his pocket; "his painting had quite gone off. It seemed to me to have lost something. It had lost an ideal. When you and he ceased to be great friends, he ceased to be a great artist. What was it separated you? I suppose he bored you. If so, he never forgave you. It's a habit bores have. By the way, what has become of that wonderful portrait he did of you? I don't think I have ever seen it since he finished it. Oh! I remember your telling me years ago that you had sent it down to Selby, and that it had got mislaid or stolen on the way. You never got it back? What a pity! It was really a masterpiece. I remember I wanted to buy it. I wish I had now. It belonged to Basil's best period. Since then, his work was that curious mixture of bad painting and good intentions that always entitles a man to be called a representative British artist. Did you advertise for it? You should."

"I forget," said Dorian. "I suppose I did. But I never really liked it. I am sorry I sat for it. The memory of the thing is hateful to me. Why do you talk of it? It used to remind me of those curious lines in some play—'Hamlet,' I think—how do they run?—

> *'"Like the painting of a sorrow,*
> *A face without a heart.'*[3]

Yes: that is what it was like."

Lord Henry laughed. "If a man treats life artistically, his brain is his heart," he answered, sinking into an arm-chair.

Dorian Gray shook his head, and struck some soft chords on the piano. "'Like the painting of a sorrow,'" he repeated, "'a face without a heart.'"

The elder man lay back and looked at him with half-closed eyes. "By the way, Dorian," he said, after a pause, "'what does it profit a man if he gain the whole world and lose—how does the quotation run?—his own soul'?"[4]

The music jarred and Dorian Gray started, and stared at his friend. "Why do you ask me that, Harry?"

"My dear fellow," said Lord Henry, elevating his eyebrows in surprise, "I asked you because I thought you might be able to give me an answer. That is all. I was going through the Park last Sunday, and close by the Marble Arch there stood a little crowd of shabby-looking people listening to some vulgar street-preacher. As I passed by, I heard the man yelling out that question to his audience. It struck me as being rather dramatic. London is very rich in curious effects of that kind. A wet Sunday, an uncouth Christian in a mackintosh,[5] a ring of sickly white faces under a broken roof of dripping umbrellas, and a wonderful phrase flung into the air by shrill, hysterical lips—it was really very good in its way, quite a suggestion. I thought of telling the prophet that Art had a soul, but that man had not. I am afraid, however, he would not have understood me."

"Don't, Harry. The soul is a terrible reality. It can be bought, and sold, and bartered away. It can be poisoned, or made perfect. There is a soul in each one of us. I know it."

"Do you feel quite sure of that, Dorian?"

"Quite sure."

"Ah! then it must be an illusion. The things one feels absolutely certain about are never true. That is the fatality of Faith, and the lesson of Romance. How grave you are! Don't be so serious. What have you or I to do with the superstitions of our age? No: we have given up our belief in the soul. Play me something. Play me a nocturne,[6] Dorian, and, as you play, tell me, in a low voice, how you have kept

---

3. *Hamlet* 4.7.108–9. The lines spoken by King Claudius are part of a question: "Laertes, was your father dear to you? / Or are you like the painting of a sorrow, / A face without a heart?"
4. Mark 8.36.
5. Originally: a full-length coat or cloak made of waterproof rubberized material. Subsequently: a rainproof coat made of this or some other material.
6. A composition suggestive of night, usually of a quiet, meditative character. OED

your youth. You must have some secret. I am only ten years older than
you are, and I am wrinkled, and worn, and yellow. You are really wonderful, Dorian. You have never looked more charming than you do to-
night. You remind me of the day I saw you first. You were rather
cheeky, very shy, and absolutely extraordinary. You have changed, of
course, but not in appearance. I wish you would tell me your secret.
To get back my youth I would do anything in the world, except take
exercise, get up early, or be respectable. Youth! There is nothing like
it. It's absurd to talk of the ignorance of youth. The only people to
whose opinions I listen now with any respect are people much
younger than myself. They seem in front of me. Life has revealed to
them her latest wonder. As for the aged, I always contradict the aged.
I do it on principle. If you ask them their opinion on something that
happened yesterday, they solemnly give you the opinions current in
1820, when people wore high stocks,[7] believed in everything, and
knew absolutely nothing. How lovely that thing you are playing is! I
wonder did Chopin write it at Majorca,[8] with the sea weeping round
the villa, and the salt spray dashing against the panes? It is marvel-
lously romantic. What a blessing it is that there is one art left to us
that is not imitative! Don't stop. I want music to-night. It seems to me
that you are the young Apollo, and that I am Marsyas[9] listening to
you. I have sorrows, Dorian, of my own, that even you know nothing
of. The tragedy of old age is not that one is old, but that one is young.
I am amazed sometimes at my own sincerity. Ah, Dorian, how happy
you are! What an exquisite life you have had! You have drunk deeply
of everything. You have crushed the grapes against your palate. Nothing has been hidden from you. And it has all been to you no more
than the sound of music. It has not marred you.[1] You are still the
same."

"I am not the same, Harry."

"Yes: you are the same. I wonder what the rest of your life will be.
Don't spoil it by renunciations. At present you are a perfect type.
Don't make yourself incomplete. You are quite flawless now. You need
not shake your head: you know you are. Besides, Dorian, don't
deceive yourself. Life is not governed by will or intention. Life is a
question of nerves, and fibres, and slowly built-up cells in which

7. Neckcloths, worn in the reign of George IV (1820–30).
8. Chopin lived there with George Sand (Amandine Dupin) during their romance and wrote
   some of his finest and most tempestuous music during that time.
9. Marsyas was a minor diety who challenged Apollo to a musical contest of skill. His punishment for presumption was to be flayed alive by the god. Marsyas was adopted by the Decadents as a sort of aesthetic Prometheus, symbolizing their own rebellious artistic
   practice.
1. An echo of Pater, who compares the world's thought and experiences to "the sound of lyres
   and flutes" that lives only in the expression of Mona Lisa's face and hands (see p. 324).
   In this as in so many other instances, Lord Henry reveals how little he understands his
   protégé.

thought hides itself and passion has its dreams.[2] You may fancy yourself safe, and think yourself strong. But a chance tone of colour in a
room or a morning sky, a particular perfume that you had once loved
and that brings subtle memories with it, a line from a forgotten poem
that you had come across again, a cadence from a piece of music that
you had ceased to play—I tell you, Dorian, that it is on things like
these that our lives depend. Browning writes about that somewhere;[3]
but our own senses will imagine them for us. There are moments
when the odour of *lilas blanc* passes suddenly across me, and I have
to live the strangest month of my life over again. I wish I could
change places with you, Dorian. The world has cried out against us
both, but it has always worshipped you. It always will worship you.
You are the type of what the age is searching for, and what it is afraid
it has found. I am so glad that you have never done anything, never
carved a statue, or painted a picture, or produced anything outside of
yourself! Life has been your art. You have set yourself to music. Your
days are your sonnets."

Dorian rose up from the piano, and passed his hand through his
hair. "Yes, life has been exquisite," he murmured, "but I am not going
to have the same life, Harry. And you must not say these extravagant
things to me. You don't know everything about me. I think that if you
did, even you would turn from me. You laugh. Don't laugh."

"Why have you stopped playing, Dorian? Go back and give me the
nocturne over again: Look at that great honey-coloured moon that
hangs in the dusky air. She is waiting for you to charm her, and if you
play she will come closer to the earth. You won't? Let us go to the
club, then. It has been a charming evening, and we must end it
charmingly. There is some one at White's who wants immensely to
know you—young Lord Poole, Bournemouth's eldest son. He has
already copied your neckties, and has begged me to introduce him to
you. He is quite delightful, and rather reminds me of you."

"I hope not," said Dorian, with a sad look in his eyes. "But I am
tired to-night, Harry. I shan't go to the club. It is nearly eleven, and I
want to go to bed early."

"Do stay. You have never played so well as to-night. There was
something in your touch that was wonderful. It had more expression
than I had ever heard from it before."

"It is because I am going to be good," he answered, smiling. "I am
a little changed already."

"You cannot change to me, Dorian," said Lord Henry. "You and I
will always be friends."

2. Lord Henry's speech on art and life echoes Pater's "Leonardo Da Vinci" from *The Renaissance* (see pp. 311–326).
3. A recurrent theme in Browning's poetry, appearing in "A Toccata of Galuppi's" and more
obliquely in "Bishop Blougram's Apology," lines 183–86.

"Yet you poisoned me with a book once. I should not forgive that. Harry, promise me that you will never lend that book to any one. It does harm."

"My dear boy, you are really beginning to moralize. You will soon be going about like the converted, and the revivalist, warning people against all the sins of which you have grown tired. You are much too delightful to do that. Besides, it is no use. You and I are what we are, and will be what we will be. As for being poisoned by a book, there is no such thing as that. Art has no influence upon action. It annihilates the desire to act. It is superbly sterile. The books that the world calls immoral are books that show the world its own shame. That is all.[4] But we won't discuss literature. Come round to-morrow. I am going to ride at eleven. We might go together, and I will take you to lunch afterwards with Lady Branksome. She is a charming woman, and wants to consult you about some tapestries she is thinking of buying. Mind you come. Or shall we lunch with our little Duchess? She says she never sees you now. Perhaps you are tired of Gladys? I thought you would be. Her clever tongue gets on one's nerves. Well, in any case, be here at eleven."

"Must I really come, Harry?"

"Certainly. The Park is quite lovely now. I don't think there have been such lilacs since the year I met you."

"Very well. I shall be here at eleven," said Dorian. "Good-night, Harry." As he reached the door he hesitated for a moment, as if he had something more to say. Then he sighed and went out.

Chapter XX

It was a lovely night, so warm that he threw his coat over his arm, and did not even put his silk scarf round his throat. As he strolled home, smoking his cigarette, two young men in evening dress passed him. He heard one of them whisper to the other, "That is Dorian Gray." He remembered how pleased he used to be when he was pointed out, or stared at, or talked about. He was tired of hearing his own name now. Half the charm of the little village where he had been so often lately was that no one knew who he was. He had often told the girl whom he had lured to love him that he was poor, and she had believed him. He had told her once that he was wicked, and she had laughed at him, and answered that wicked people were always very old and very ugly. What a laugh she had!—just like a thrush singing. And how pretty she had been in her cotton dresses

---

4. Wilde took a similar line at his first trial in defending *Dorian Gray* against charges of its alleged pernicious influence.

and her large hats! She knew nothing, but she had everything that he had lost.

When he reached home, he found his servant waiting up for him. He sent him to bed, and threw himself down on the sofa in the library, and began to think over some of the things that Lord Henry had said to him.

Was it really true that one could never change? He felt a wild longing for the unstained purity of his boyhood—his rose-white boyhood, as Lord Henry had once called it. He knew that he had tarnished himself, filled his mind with corruption and given horror to his fancy; that he had been an evil influence to others, and had experienced a terrible joy in being so; and that of the lives that had crossed his own it had been the fairest and the most full of promise that he had brought to shame. But was it all irretrievable? Was there no hope for him?

Ah! in what a monstrous moment of pride and passion he had prayed that the portrait should bear the burden of his days, and he keep the unsullied splendour of eternal youth! All his failure had been due to that. Better for him that each sin of his life had brought its sure, swift penalty along with it. There was purification in punishment. Not "Forgive us our sins" but "Smite us for our iniquities" should be the prayer of man to a most just God.

The curiously-carved mirror that Lord Henry had given to him, so many years ago now, was standing on the table, and the white-limbed Cupids laughed round it as of old. He took it up, as he had done on that night of horror, when he had first noted the change in the fatal picture, and with wild tear-dimmed eyes looked into its polished shield. Once, some one who had terribly loved him, had written to him a mad letter, ending with these idolatrous words: "The world is changed because you are made of ivory and gold. The curves of your lips rewrite history." The phrases came back to his memory, and he repeated them over and over to himself. Then he loathed his own beauty, and flinging the mirror on the floor crushed it into silver splinters beneath his heel. It was his beauty that had ruined him, his beauty and the youth that he had prayed for. But for those two things, his life might have been free from stain. His beauty had been to him but a mask, his youth but a mockery. What was youth at best? A green, an unripe time, a time of shallow moods, and sickly thoughts. Why had he worn its livery? Youth had spoiled him.

It was better not to think of the past. Nothing could alter that. It was of himself, and of his own future, that he had to think. James Vane was hidden in a nameless grave in Selby churchyard. Alan Campbell had shot himself one night in his laboratory, but had not revealed the secret that he had been forced to know. The excitement, such as it was, over Basil Hallward's disappearance would soon pass away. It was already waning. He was perfectly safe there. Nor, indeed, was it the death of Basil Hallward that weighed most upon his mind. It was the living death of his own soul that troubled him. Basil had painted the portrait that had marred his life. He could not forgive him that. It was the portrait that had done everything. Basil had said things to him that were unbearable, and that he had yet borne with patience. The murder had been simply the madness of a moment. As for Alan Campbell, his suicide had been his own act. He had chosen to do it. It was nothing to him.

A new life! That was what he wanted. That was what he was waiting for. Surely he had begun it already. He had spared one innocent thing, at any rate. He would never again tempt innocence. He would be good.

As he thought of Hetty Merton, he began to wonder if the portrait in the locked room had changed. Surely it was not still so horrible as it had been? Perhaps if his life became pure, he would be able to expel every sign of evil passion from the face. Perhaps the signs of evil had already gone away. He would go and look.

He took the lamp from the table and crept upstairs. As he unbarred the door, a smile of joy flitted across his strangely young-looking face and lingered for a moment about his lips. Yes, he would be good, and the hideous thing that he had hidden away would no longer be a terror to him. He felt as if the load had been lifted from him already.

He went in quietly, locking the door behind him, as was his custom, and dragged the purple hanging from the portrait. A cry of pain and indignation broke from him. He could see no change, save that in the eyes there was a look of cunning, and in the mouth the curved wrinkle of the hypocrite. The thing was still loathsome—more loathsome, if possible, than before—and the scarlet dew that spotted the hand seemed brighter, and more like blood newly spilt. Then he trembled. Had it been merely vanity that had made him do his one good deed? Or the desire for a new sensation, as Lord Henry had hinted, with his mocking laugh? Or that passion to act a part that sometimes makes us do things finer than we are ourselves? Or, perhaps, all these? And why was the red stain larger than it had been? It seemed to have crept like a horrible disease over the wrinkled fingers. There was blood on the painted feet, as though the thing had dripped—blood even on the hand that had not held the knife. Confess? Did it mean that he was to confess? To give himself up, and be put to death? He laughed. He felt that the idea was monstrous. Besides, even if he did confess, who would believe him? There was no trace of the murdered man anywhere. Everything belonging to him had been destroyed. He himself had burned what had been below-stairs. The world would simply say that he was mad.

They would shut him up if he persisted in his story. . . . Yet it was his duty to confess, to suffer public shame, and to make public atonement. There was a God who called upon men to tell their sins to earth as well as to heaven. Nothing that he could do would cleanse him till he had told his own sin. His sin? He shrugged his shoulders. The death of Basil Hallward seemed very little to him. He was thinking of Hetty Merton. For it was an unjust mirror, this mirror of his soul that he was looking at. Vanity? Curiosity? Hypocrisy? Had there been nothing more in his renunciation than that? There had been something more. At least he thought so. But who could tell? . . . No. There had been nothing more. Through vanity he had spared her. In hypocrisy he had worn the mask of goodness. For curiosity's sake he had tried the denial of self. He recognized that now.[1]

But this murder—was it to dog him all his life? Was he always to be burdened by his past? Was he really to confess? Never. There was only one bit of evidence left against him. The picture itself—that was evidence. He would destroy it. Why had he kept it so long? Once it had given him pleasure to watch it changing and growing old. Of late he had felt no such pleasure. It had kept him awake at night. When he had been away, he had been filled with terror lest other eyes should look upon it. It had brought melancholy across his passions. Its mere memory had marred many moments of joy. It had been like conscience to him. Yes, it had been conscience. He would destroy it.

He looked round, and saw the knife that had stabbed Basil Hallward. He had cleaned it many times, till there was no stain left upon it. It was bright, and glistened. As it had killed the painter, so it would kill the painter's work, and all that that meant. It would kill the past, and when that was dead he would be free. It would kill this monstrous soul-life, and without its hideous warnings, he would be at peace.[2] He seized the thing, and stabbed the picture with it.

There was a cry heard, and a crash. The cry was so horrible in its agony that the frightened servants woke, and crept out of their rooms. Two gentlemen, who were passing in the Square below, stopped, and looked up at the great house. They walked on till they met a policeman, and brought him back. The man rang the bell several times, but there was no answer. Except for a light in one of the top windows, the house was all dark. After a time, he went away, and stood in an adjoining portico and watched.

"Whose house is that, constable?" asked the elder of the two gentlemen.

---

1. Wilde added the lines beginning "No. There had been nothing more . . ." to the end of the paragraph in this edition.
2. Wilde added this sentence to this edition.

"Mr. Dorian Gray's, sir," answered the policeman.

They looked at each other, as they walked away, and sneered. One of them was Sir Henry Ashton's uncle.

Inside, in the servants' part of the house, the half-clad domestics were talking in low whispers to each other. Old Mrs. Leaf was crying, and wringing her hands. Francis was as pale as death.

After about a quarter of an hour, he got the coachman and one of the footmen and crept upstairs. They knocked, but there was no reply. They called out. Everything was still. Finally, after vainly trying to force the door, they got on the roof, and dropped down on to the balcony. The windows yielded easily: their bolts were old.

When they entered, they found hanging upon the wall a splendid portrait of their master as they had last seen him, in all the wonder of his exquisite youth and beauty. Lying on the floor was a dead man, in evening dress, with a knife in his heart. He was withered, wrinkled, and loathsome of visage. It was not till they had examined the rings that they recognized who it was.

The Picture of Dorian Gray
(1890)

Chapter I

The studio was filled with the rich odor of roses, and when the light summer wind stirred amidst the trees of the garden there came through the open door the heavy scent of the lilac, or the more delicate perfume of the pink-flowering thorn.

From the corner of the divan of Persian saddle-bags on which he was lying, smoking, as usual,[1] innumerable cigarettes, Lord Henry Wotton could just catch the gleam of the honey-sweet and honey-colored blossoms of the laburnum, whose tremulous branches seemed hardly able to bear the burden of a beauty so flame-like as theirs; and now and then the fantastic shadows of birds in flight flitted across the long tussore-silk curtains that were stretched in front of the huge window, producing a kind of momentary Japanese effect, and making him think of those pallid jade-faced painters who, in an art that is necessarily immobile,[2] seek to convey the sense of swiftness and motion. The sullen murmur of the bees shouldering their way through the long unmown grass, or circling with monotonous insistence round the black-crocketed spires of the early June hollyhocks,[3] seemed to make the stillness more oppressive, and the dim roar of London was like the bourdon note of a distant organ.

In the centre of the room, clamped to an upright easel, stood the full-length portrait of a young man of extraordinary personal beauty, and in front of it, some little distance away, was sitting the artist himself, Basil Hallward, whose sudden disappearance some years ago caused, at the time, such public excitement, and gave rise to so many strange conjectures.

As he looked at the gracious and comely form he had so skilfully mirrored in his art, a smile of pleasure passed across his face, and seemed about to linger there. But he suddenly started up, and, closing

1. Changed to "as was his custom" in 1891.
2. Several refinements are made in this description in 1891.
3. "black-crocketed . . . hollyhocks" changed to "dusty gilt horns of the straggling woodbine" in 1891.

his eyes, placed his fingers upon the lids, as though he sought to imprison within his brain some curious dream from which he feared he might awake.

"It is your best work, Basil, the best thing you have ever done," said Lord Henry, languidly. "You must certainly send it next year to the Grosvenor. The Academy is too large and too vulgar. The Grosvenor is the only place."[4]

"I don't think I will[5] send it anywhere," he answered, tossing his head back in that odd way that used to make his friends laugh at him at Oxford. "No: I won't send it anywhere."[6]

Lord Henry elevated his eyebrows, and looked at him in amazement through the thin blue wreaths of smoke that curled up in such fanciful whorls from his heavy opium-tainted cigarette. "Not send it anywhere? My dear fellow, why? Have you any reason? What odd chaps you painters are! You do anything in the world to gain a reputation. As soon as you have one, you seem to want to throw it away. It is silly of you, for there is only one thing in the world worse than being talked about, and that is not being talked about. A portrait like this would set you far above all the young men in England, and make the old men quite jealous, if old men are ever capable of any emotion."

"I know you will laugh at me," he replied, "but I really can't exhibit it. I have put too much of myself into it."

Lord Henry stretched his long legs out on the divan and shook with laughter.[7]

"Yes, I knew you would laugh; but it is quite true, all the same."

"Too much of yourself in it! Upon my word, Basil, I didn't know you were so vain; and I really can't see any resemblance between you, with your rugged strong face and your coal-black hair, and this young Adonis, who looks as if he was made of ivory and rose-leaves. Why, my dear Basil, he is a Narcissus and you—well, of course you have an intellectual expression, and all that. But beauty, real beauty, ends where an intellectual expression begins. Intellect is in itself an exaggeration,[8] and destroys the harmony of any face. The moment one sits down to think, one becomes all nose, or all forehead, or something horrid. Look at the successful men in any of the learned professions. How perfectly hideous they are! Except, of course, in the Church. But then in the Church they don't think. A bishop keeps on saying at the age of eighty what he was told to say when he was a boy

4. This last sentence omitted in 1891.
5. Wilde wrote Coulson Kernahan, editor of the revised edition for Ward, Lock and Company, asking that he "look after my 'wills' and 'shalls' in proof," explaining that his "usage was Celtic not English" (*Letters* 289).
6. TS has "and yet, you are quite right about it. It is my best work."
7. This sentence slightly altered in 1891.
8. Changed to "a mode of exaggeration" in 1891.

of eighteen, and consequently[9] he always looks absolutely delightful. Your mysterious young friend, whose name you have never told me, but whose picture really fascinates me, never thinks. I feel quite sure of that. He is a brainless, beautiful thing, who should be always here in winter when we have no flowers to look at, and always here in summer when we want something to chill our intelligence. Don't flatter yourself, Basil: you are not in the least like him."

"You don't understand me, Harry. Of course I am not like him. I know that perfectly well. Indeed, I should be sorry to look like him. You shrug your shoulders? I am telling you the truth. There is a fatality about all physical and intellectual distinction, the sort of fatality that seems to dog through history the faltering steps of kings.[1] It is better not to be different from one's fellows. The ugly and the stupid have the best of it in this world. They can sit quietly and gape at the play. If they know nothing of victory, they are at least spared the knowledge of defeat. They live as we all should live, undisturbed, indifferent, and without disquiet. They neither bring ruin upon others nor ever receive it from alien hands. Your rank and wealth, Harry; my brains, such as they are,—my fame,[2] whatever it may be worth; Dorian Gray's good looks,—we will all suffer for what the gods have given us, suffer terribly."

"Dorian Gray? is that his name?" said Lord Henry, walking across the studio towards Basil Hallward.

"Yes; that is his name. I didn't intend to tell it to you."

"But why not?"

"Oh, I can't explain. When I like people immensely I never tell their names to any one. It seems like surrendering a part of them. You know how I love secrecy. It is the only thing that can make modern life wonderful or mysterious to us.[3] The commonest thing is delightful if one only hides it. When I leave town I never tell my people where I am going. If I did, I would lose all my pleasure. It is a silly habit, I dare say, but somehow it seems to bring a great deal of romance into one's life. I suppose you think me awfully foolish about it?"

"Not at all," answered Lord Henry, laying his hand upon his shoulder;[4] "not at all, my dear Basil. You seem to forget that I am married, and the one charm of marriage is that it makes a life of deception necessary for both parties. I never know where my wife is, and my wife never knows what I am doing. When we meet,—we do meet occasionally, when

---

9. Changed to "as a natural consequence" in 1891.
1. MS has "to dog the steps of kings."
2. Changed to "art" in 1891.
3. Wilde made four stylistic changes in the first four lines of this paragraph in 1891.
4. "laying . . . shoulder" deleted in 1891. This is the first of many such deletions or rewrites eliminating descriptions of physical contact suggestive of homoerotic behavior.

we dine out together, or go down to the duke's,—we tell each other the most absurd stories with the most serious faces. My wife is very good at it,—much better, in fact, than I am. She never gets confused over her dates, and I always do. But when she does find me out, she makes no row at all. I sometimes wish she would; but she merely laughs at me."

"I hate the way you talk about your married life, Harry," said Basil Hallward, shaking his hand off,[5] and strolling towards the door that led into the garden. "I believe that you are really a very good husband, but that you are thoroughly ashamed of your own virtues. You are an extraordinary fellow. You never say a moral thing, and you never do a wrong thing. Your cynicism is simply a pose."

"Being natural is simply a pose, and the most irritating pose I know," cried Lord Henry, laughing; and the two young men went out into the garden together, and for a time they did not speak.[6]

After a long pause Lord Henry pulled out his watch. "I am afraid I must be going, Basil," he murmured, "and before I go I insist on your answering a question I put to you some time ago."

"What is that?" asked Basil Hallward, keeping his eyes fixed on the ground.

"You know quite well."

"I do not, Harry."

"Well, I will tell you what it is."

"Please don't."[7]

"I must. I want you to explain to me why you won't exhibit Dorian Gray's picture. I want the real reason."

"I told you the real reason."

"No, you did not. You said it was because there was too much of yourself in it. Now, that is childish."

"Harry," said Basil Hallward, looking him straight in the face,[8] "every portrait that is painted with feeling[9] is a portrait of the artist, not of the sitter. The sitter is merely the accident, the occasion. It is not he who is revealed by the painter; it is rather the painter who, on the colored canvas, reveals himself. The reason I will not exhibit this picture is that I am afraid that I have shown with it the secret of my own soul."

Lord Harry laughed. "And what is that?" he asked.

"I will tell you," said Hallward; and an expression of perplexity came over his face.

---

5. "shaking . . . off" deleted in 1891.
6. Wilde changed the last phrase in 1891.
7. This sentence and Henry's "I must" deleted in 1891.
8. Wilde canceled the phrase "taking hold of his hand" in MS.
9. Wilde changed the original "passion" to "feeling" in MS.

"I am all expectation, Basil," murmured his companion, looking at him.

"Oh, there is really very little to tell, Harry," answered the young painter; "and I am afraid you will hardly understand it. Perhaps you will hardly believe it."

Lord Henry smiled, and, leaning down, plucked a pink-petalled daisy from the grass, and examined it. "I am quite sure I shall understand it," he replied, gazing intently at the little golden white-feathered disk,[1] "and I can believe anything, provided that it is incredible."

The wind shook some blossoms from the trees, and the heavy lilac-blooms, with their clustering stars, moved to and fro in the languid air. A grasshopper began to chirrup in the grass, and a long thin dragon-fly floated by on its brown gauze wings.[2] Lord Henry felt as if he could hear Basil Hallward's heart beating, and he wondered what was coming.

"Well, this is incredible," repeated Hallward, rather bitterly,— "incredible to me at times. I don't know what it means.[3] The story is simply this. Two months ago I went to a crush at Lady Brandon's. You know we poor painters have to show ourselves in society from time to time, just to remind the public that we are not savages. With an evening coat and a white tie, as you told me once, anybody, even a stock-broker, can gain a reputation for being civilized. Well, after I had been in the room about ten minutes, talking to huge overdressed dowagers and tedious Academicians, I suddenly became conscious that some one was looking at me. I turned half-way round, and saw Dorian Gray for the first time. When our eyes met, I felt that I was growing pale. A curious instinct of terror came over me. I knew that I had come face to face with some one whose mere personality was so fascinating that, if I allowed it to do so, it would absorb my whole nature, my whole soul, my very art itself. I did not want any external influence in my life. You know yourself, Harry, how independent I am by nature. My father destined me for the army. I insisted on going to Oxford. Then he made me enter my name at the Middle Temple. Before I had eaten half a dozen dinners I gave up the Bar, and announced my intention of becoming a painter.[4] I have always been my own master; had at least always been so, till I met Dorian Gray. Then—But I don't know how to explain it to you. Something seemed

---

1. Wilde deleted "that had charmed all the poets from Chaucer to Tennyson" in MS and modified the style of the epigram following in 1891. The epigram appeared written in TS.
2. Several stylistic changes made here in 1891.
3. Opening lines of this paragraph deleted in 1891.
4. "My father [p. 10] . . . painter" deleted in 1891. The Middle Temple is one of four legal societies of London through which one prepared for the practice of law before the English bar.

to tell me that I was on the verge of a terrible crisis in my life. I had a strange feeling that Fate had in store for me exquisite joys and exquisite sorrows. I knew that if I spoke to Dorian I would become absolutely devoted to him, and that I ought not to speak to him.[5] I grew afraid, and turned to quit the room. It was not conscience that made me do so: it was cowardice. I take no credit to myself for trying to escape."

"Conscience and cowardice are really the same things, Basil. Conscience is the trade-name of the firm. That is all."

"I don't believe that, Harry. However, whatever was my motive,— and it may have been pride, for I used to be very proud,—I certainly struggled to the door. There, of course, I stumbled against Lady Brandon. 'You are not going to run away so soon, Mr. Hallward?' she screamed out. You know her shrill horrid voice?"

"Yes; she is a peacock in everything but beauty," said Lord Henry, pulling the daisy to bits with his long, nervous fingers.

"I could not get rid of her. She brought me up to Royalties, and people with Stars and Garters, and elderly ladies with gigantic tiaras and hooked noses. She spoke of me as her dearest friend. I had only met her once before, but she took it into her head to lionize me. I believe some picture of mine had made a great success at the time, at least had been chattered about in the penny newspapers, which is the nineteenth-century standard of immortality. Suddenly I found myself face to face with the young man whose personality[6] had so strangely stirred me. We were quite close, almost touching. Our eyes met again. It was mad of me, but I asked Lady Brandon to introduce me to him. Perhaps it was not so mad, after all. It was simply inevitable. We would have spoken to each other without any introduction. I am sure of that. Dorian told me so afterwards. He, too, felt that we were destined to know each other."

"And how did Lady Brandon describe this wonderful young man? I know she goes in for giving a rapid *précis* of all her guests. I remember her bringing me up to a most truculent and red-faced old gentleman covered all over with orders and ribbons, and hissing into my ear, in a tragic whisper which must have been perfectly audible to everybody in the room, something like 'Sir Humpty Dumpty—you know— Afghan frontier—Russian intrigues: very successful man—wife killed by an elephant—quite inconsolable—wants to marry a beautiful American widow—everybody does nowadays—hates Mr. Gladstone— but very much interested in beetles: ask him what he thinks of Schouvaloff.'[7] I simply fled. I like to find out people for myself. But poor

---

5. "I knew . . . to him," changed in MS from "I would never leave him till either he or I were dead" and omitted from the 1891 text.
6. Changed in MS from "beauty had so stirred me."
7. "Something like . . . Schouvaloff" removed from 1891 text. Lady Brandon's rapid précis is

Lady Brandon treats her guests exactly as an auctioneer treats his goods. She either explains them entirely away, or tells one everything about them except what one wants to know. But what did she say about Mr. Dorian Gray?"

"Oh, she murmured, 'Charming boy—poor dear mother and I quite inseparable—engaged to be married to the same man—I mean married on the same day—how very silly of me! Quite forget what he does—afraid he—doesn't do anything—oh, yes, plays the piano—or is it the violin, dear Mr. Gray?' We could neither of us help laughing, and we became friends at once."

"Laughter is not a bad beginning for a friendship, and it is the best ending for one," said Lord Henry, plucking another daisy.

Hallward buried his face in his hands.[8] "You don't understand what friendship is, Harry," he murmured,—"or what enmity is, for that matter. You like every one; that is to say, you are indifferent to every one."

"How horribly unjust of you!" cried Lord Henry, tilting his hat back, and looking up at the little clouds that were drifting across the hollowed turquoise of the summer sky, like ravelled skeins of glossy white silk. "Yes; horribly unjust of you. I make a great difference between people. I choose my friends for their good looks, my acquaintances for their characters, and my enemies for their brains.[9] A man can't be too careful in the choice of his enemies. I have not got one who is a fool. They are all men of some intellectual power, and consequently they all appreciate me. Is that very vain of me? I think it is rather vain."

"I should think it was, Harry. But according to your category I must be merely an acquaintance."

"My dear old Basil, you are much more than an acquaintance."

"And much less than a friend. A sort of brother, I suppose?"

"Oh, brothers! I don't care for brothers. My elder brother won't die, and my younger brothers seem never to do anything else."

"Harry!"

"My dear fellow, I am not quite serious. But I can't help detesting my relations. I suppose it comes from the fact that we can't stand other people having the same faults as ourselves. I quite sympathize with the rage of the English democracy against what they call the vices of the upper classes. They feel that drunkenness, stupidity, and

cited by Sherard, Harris, and others as a parody of the speech of Lady Wilde, Oscar's mother. She was noted for her salons when the family lived in Dublin and later, more modestly, in London. William Gladstone (1809–98), English statesman and four-time prime minister, was known as a social and political reformer. Count Peter Schouvaloff (1827–89), Russian envoy to London from 1873 to 1879, helped preserve amicable relations with England during the Russo-Turkish War (1877–78).
8. Wilde made several stylistic changes in the preceding eight lines in the 1891 text.
9. Another epigram Wilde touched up a little in 1891.

immorality should be their own special property, and that if any one of us makes an ass of himself he is poaching on their preserves. When poor Southwark got into the Divorce Court, their indignation was quite magnificent. And yet I don't suppose that ten per cent of the lower orders live correctly."[1]

"I don't agree with a single word that you have said, and, what is more, Harry, I don't believe you do either."

Lord Henry stroked his pointed brown beard, and tapped the toe of his patent-leather boot with a tasselled malacca cane. "How English you are, Basil! If one puts forward an idea to a real Englishman,— always a rash thing to do,—he never dreams of considering whether the idea is right or wrong.[2] The only thing he considers of any importance is whether one believes it one's self. Now, the value of an idea has nothing whatsoever to do with the sincerity of the man who expresses it. Indeed, the probabilities are that the more insincere the man is, the more purely intellectual will the idea be, as in that case it will not be colored by either his wants, his desires, or his prejudices. However, I don't propose to discuss politics, sociology, or metaphysics with you. I like persons better than principles. Tell me more about Dorian Gray. How often do you see him?"

"Every day. I couldn't be happy if I didn't see him every day. Of course sometimes it is only for a few minutes. But a few minutes with somebody one worships mean a great deal."

"But you don't really worship him?"

"I do."

"How extraordinary! I thought you would never care for anything but your painting,—your art, I should say. Art sounds better, doesn't it?"[3]

"He is all my art to me now. I sometimes think, Harry, that there are only two eras of any importance in the history of the world. The first is the appearance of a new medium for art, and the second is the appearance of a new personality for art also. What the invention of oil-painting was to the Venetians, the face of Antinoüs was to late Greek sculpture, and the face of Dorian Gray will some day be to me. It is not merely that I paint from him, draw from him, model from him. Of course I have done all that. He has stood as Paris in dainty armor, and as Adonis with huntsman's cloak and polished boar-spear.

---

1. J. M. Stoddart, *Lippincott's* editor, changed TS reading "live with their wives," removing an expression inadmissible to the American public. Wilde let these and similar changes stand even though they are clearly inferior to his original.
2. Wilde altered details here and in the preceding two paragraphs in 1891. Lord Henry originally owned a "straw colored moustache" and a "Henry Deux" beard, but lost them both in MS. Both were features of the appearance of Lord Ronald Sutherland-Gower, a candidate for the original of Lord Henry.
3. Wilde revised the dialogue above in 1891, leaving out "worship" and muting the homoerotic overtones.

Crowned with heavy lotus-blossoms, he has sat on the prow of Adrian's barge, looking into the green, turbid Nile. He has leaned over the still pool of some Greek woodland, and seen in the water's silent silver the wonder of his own beauty.[4] But he is much more to me than that. I won't tell you that I am dissatisfied with what I have done of him, or that his beauty is such that art cannot express it. There is nothing that art cannot express, and I know that the work I have done since I met Dorian Gray is good work, is the best work of my life. But in some curious way—I wonder will you understand me?—his personality has suggested to me an entirely new manner in art, an entirely new mode of style. I see things differently, I think of them differently. I can now re-create life in a way that was hidden from me before. 'A dream of form in days of thought,'—who is it who says that? I forget; but it is what Dorian Gray has been to me. The merely visible presence of this lad,[5]—for he seems to me little more than a lad, though he is really over twenty,—his merely visible presence,—ah! I wonder can you realize all that that means? Unconsciously he defines for me the lines of a fresh school, a school that is to have in itself all the passion of the romantic spirit, all the perfection of the spirit that is Greek. The harmony of soul and body,—how much that is! We in our madness have separated the two, and have invented a realism that is bestial, an ideality that is void. Harry! Harry! if you only knew what Dorian Gray is to me! You remember that landscape of mine, for which Agnew offered me such a huge price, but which I would not part with? It is one of the best things I have ever done. And why is it so? Because, while I was painting it, Dorian Gray sat beside me."[6]

"Basil, this is quite wonderful! I must see Dorian Gray."[7]

Hallward got up from the seat, and walked up and down the garden.[8] After some time he came back. "You don't understand, Harry," he said. "Dorian Gray is merely to me a motive in art. He is never more present in my work than when no image of him is there. He is simply a suggestion, as I have said, of a new manner. I see him in the

---

4. "He stood . . . beauty" was moved by Wilde to another context in 1891.
5. "Lad" substituted for "boy" here and in several other places in MS. Wilde removed "Though twenty summers have shown him roses less scarlet than his lips" in MS.
6. Wilde made several changes in this paragraph in 1891. In MS, Wilde deleted "and as he leaned across to look at it, his lips just touched my hand. The world becomes young to me when I hold his hand. . . ." In 1891, Wilde added another sentence here emphasizing Dorian's influence on Basil's art.
7. Henry's response in MS is too heavily blotted to read fully, but he protests Basil's being in Dorian's power: "to make yourself the slave of your slave. It is worse than wicked, it is silly. I hate Dorian Gray!" In one stroke, Wilde rid himself of some silly dialogue and removed a clue, perhaps, to the nature of the relationship between Dorian and Basil as a form of homoerotic bondage so fashionable among the English that the French referred to it as *le vice anglais*.
8. Wilde canceled the following at this point in MS: "A curious smile crossed his face. He seemed like a man in a dream."

curves of certain lines, in the loveliness and the subtleties of certain colors. That is all."

"Then why won't you exhibit his portrait?"

"Because I have put into it all the extraordinary romance of which, of course, I have never dared to speak to him. He knows nothing about it. He will never know anything about it. But the world might guess it; and I will not bare my soul to their shallow, prying eyes. My heart shall never be put under their microscope. There is too much of myself in the thing, Harry,—too much of myself!"[9]

"Poets are not so scrupulous as you are. They know how useful passion is for publication. Nowadays a broken heart will run to many editions."

"I hate them for it. An artist should create beautiful things, but should put nothing of his own life into them. We live in an age when men treat art as if it were meant to be a form of autobiography. We have lost the abstract sense of beauty. If I live, I will show the world what it is; and for that reason the world shall never see my portrait of Dorian Gray."

"I think you are wrong, Basil, but I won't argue with you. It is only the intellectually lost who ever argue. Tell me, is Dorian Gray very fond of you?"

Hallward considered for a few moments. "He likes me," he answered, after a pause; "I know he likes me. Of course I flatter him dreadfully. I find a strange pleasure in saying things to him that I know I shall be sorry for having said. I give myself away.[1] As a rule, he is charming to me, and we walk home together from the club arm in arm, or sit in the studio and talk of a thousand things. Now and then, however, he is horribly thoughtless, and seems to take a real delight in giving me pain. Then I feel, Harry, that I have given away my whole soul to some one[2] who treats it as if it were a flower to put in his coat, a bit of decoration to charm his vanity, an ornament for a summer's day."

"Days in summer, Basil, are apt to linger. Perhaps you will tire sooner than he will. It is a sad thing to think of, but there is no doubt that Genius lasts longer than Beauty. That accounts for the fact that we all take such pains to over-educate ourselves. In the wild struggle

9. Wilde altered this and the preceding paragraphs in every revision. He removed from MS (after "the world might guess it") "where there is merely love, they would see something evil. Where there is spiritual passion, they would suggest something vile."
1. Wilde dropped this sentence from the 1891 text together with the phrase "walk home together from the club arm in arm" from the next sentence.
2. The following lines were canceled at this point in MS: "who seems to take a real delight in giving me pain. I seem quite adjusted to it. I can imagine myself doing it. But not to him, not to him. Once or twice we have been away together. Then I have had him all to myself. I am horribly jealous of him, of course. I never let him talk to me of the people he knows. I like to isolate him from the rest of life and to think that he absolutely belongs to me. He does not, I know. But it gives me pleasure to think he does."

for existence, we want to have something that endures, and so we fill our minds with rubbish and facts, in the silly hope of keeping our place. The thoroughly well informed man,—that is the modern ideal. And the mind of the thoroughly well informed man is a dreadful thing. It is like a bric-à-brac shop, all monsters and dust, and everything priced above its proper value. I think you will tire first, all the same. Some day you will look at Gray, and he will seem to you to be a little out of drawing, or you won't like his tone of color, or something. You will bitterly reproach him in your own heart, and seriously think that he has behaved very badly to you. The next time he calls, you will be perfectly cold and indifferent. It will be a great pity, for it will alter you. The worst of having a romance is that it leaves one so unromantic."[3]

"Harry, don't talk like that.[4] As long as I live, the personality of Dorian Gray will dominate me. You can't feel what I feel. You change too often."

"Ah, my dear Basil, that is exactly why I can feel it. Those who are faithful know only the pleasures of love: it is the faithless who know love's tragedies." And Lord Henry struck a light on a dainty silver case, and began to smoke a cigarette with a self-conscious and self-satisfied air, as if he had summed up life in a phrase. There was a rustle of chirruping sparrows in the ivy, and the blue cloud-shadows chased themselves across the grass like swallows. How pleasant it was in the garden! And how delightful other people's emotions were!—much more delightful than their ideas, it seemed to him. One's own soul, and the passions of one's friends,—those were the fascinating things in life. He thought with pleasure of the tedious luncheon that he had missed by staying so long with Basil Hallward. Had he gone to his aunt's, he would have been sure to meet Lord Goodbody there, and the whole conversation would have been about the housing of the poor, and the necessity for model lodging-houses.[5] It was charming to have escaped all that! As he thought of his aunt, an idea seemed to strike him. He turned to Hallward, and said, "My dear fellow, I have just remembered."

"Remembered what, Harry?"

"Where I heard the name of Dorian Gray."

"Where was it?" asked Hallward, with a slight frown.

3. In 1891, Wilde added the mitigating phrase "of any kind" after "having a romance."
4. The following lines were canceled in MS: "I am not afraid of things, but I am afraid of words. I cannot understand how it is that no prophecy has ever been fulfilled. None has I know. And yet it seems to me that to say a thing is to bring it to pass. Whatever has found expression becomes true, and what has not found expression can never happen. As for genius lasting longer than beauty, it is only the transitory that stirs me. What is permanent is monstrous and produces no effect. Our senses become dulled by what is always with us." These lines have a strong flavor of Pater about them.
5. Wilde made several alterations here in 1891, including the addition of the aphorism beginning "each class . . ." (see p. 15).

"Don't look so angry, Basil. It was at my aunt's, Lady Agatha's. She told me she had discovered a wonderful young man, who was going to help her in the East End, and that his name was Dorian Gray. I am bound to state that she never told me he was good-looking. Women have no appreciation of good looks. At least, good women have not. She said that he was very earnest, and had a beautiful nature. I at once pictured to myself a creature with spectacles and lank hair, horridly freckled, and tramping about on huge feet. I wish I had known it was your friend."

"I am very glad you didn't, Harry."

"Why?"

"I don't want you to meet him."

"Mr. Dorian Gray is in the studio, sir," said the butler, coming into the garden.

"You must introduce me now," cried Lord Henry, laughing.

Basil Hallward turned to the servant, who stood blinking in the sunlight. "Ask Mr. Gray to wait, Parker: I will be in in a few moments." The man bowed, and went up the walk.

Then he looked at Lord Henry. "Dorian Gray is my dearest friend," he said. "He has a simple and a beautiful nature. Your aunt was quite right in what she said of him. Don't spoil him for me. Don't try to influence him. Your influence would be bad. The world is wide, and has many marvellous people in it. Don't take away from me the one person that makes life absolutely lovely to me, and that gives to my art whatever wonder or charm it possesses.[6] Mind, Harry, I trust you." He spoke very slowly, and the words seemed wrung out of him almost against his will.

"What nonsense you talk!" said Lord Henry, smiling, and, taking Hallward by the arm, he almost led him into the house.[7]

Chapter II

As they entered they saw Dorian Gray. He was seated at the piano, with his back to them, turning over the pages of a volume of Schumann's "Forest Scenes." "You must lend me these, Basil," he cried. "I want to learn them. They are perfectly charming."

"That entirely depends on how you sit to-day, Dorian."

"Oh, I am tired of sitting, and I don't want a life-sized portrait of myself," answered the lad, swinging round on the music-stool, in a wilful, petulant manner. When he caught sight of Lord Henry, a faint

6. "that makes . . . me" and "or wonder" in the next line were dropped in 1891; following "possess," Wilde added "my life as an artist depends on him."

7. The original conclusion of the chapter, canceled in MS, read: "'I don't suppose I shall care for him, and I am quite sure he won't care for me,' replied Lord Henry, smiling. . . .'"

blush colored his cheeks for a moment, and he started up. "I beg your pardon, Basil, but I didn't know you had any one with you."

"This is Lord Henry Wotton, Dorian, an old Oxford friend of mine. I have just been telling him what a capital sitter you were, and now you have spoiled everything."

"You have not spoiled my pleasure in meeting you, Mr. Gray," said Lord Henry, stepping forward and shaking him by the hand. "My aunt has often spoken to me about you. You are one of her favorites, and, I am afraid, one of her victims also."

"I am in Lady Agatha's black books at present," answered Dorian, with a funny look of penitence. "I promised to go to her club in Whitechapel with her last Tuesday, and I really forgot all about it. We were to have played a duet together,—three duets, I believe. I don't know what she will say to me. I am far too frightened to call."

"Oh, I will make your peace with my aunt. She is quite devoted to you. And I don't think it really matters about your not being there. The audience probably thought it was a duet. When Aunt Agatha sits down to the piano she makes quite enough noise for two people."

"That is very horrid to her, and not very nice to me," answered Dorian, laughing.

Lord Henry looked at him. Yes, he was certainly wonderfully handsome, with his finely-curved scarlet lips, his frank blue eyes, his crisp gold hair. There was something in his face that made one trust him at once. All the candor of youth was there, as well as all youth's passionate purity. One felt that he had kept himself unspotted from the world. No wonder Basil Hallward worshipped him. He was made to be worshipped.[1]

"You are too charming to go in for philanthropy, Mr. Gray,—far too charming." And Lord Henry flung himself down on the divan, and opened his cigarette-case.

Hallward had been busy mixing his colors and getting his brushes ready. He was looking worried, and when he heard Lord Henry's last remark he glanced at him, hesitated for a moment, and then said, "Harry, I want to finish this picture to-day. Would you think it awfully rude of me if I asked you to go away?"

Lord Henry smiled, and looked at Dorian Gray. "Am I to go, Mr. Gray?" he asked.

"Oh, please don't, Lord Henry. I see that Basil is in one of his sulky moods; and I can't bear him when he sulks. Besides, I want you to tell me why I should not go in for philanthropy."

"I don't know that I shall tell you that, Mr. Gray.[2] But I certainly will not run away, now that you have asked me to stop. You don't

---

1. This last sentence was removed in 1891.
2. Wilde added an epigram here in 1891.

really mind, Basil, do you? You have often told me that you liked your sitters to have some one to chat to."

Hallward bit his lip. "If Dorian wishes it, of course you must stay. Dorian's whims are laws to everybody, except himself."

Lord Henry took up his hat and gloves. "You are very pressing, Basil, but I am afraid I must go. I have promised to meet a man at the Orleans.—Good-by, Mr. Gray. Come and see me some afternoon in Curzon Street. I am nearly always at home at five o'clock. Write to me when you are coming. I should be sorry to miss you."

"Basil," cried Dorian Gray, "if Lord Henry goes I shall go too. You never open your lips while you are painting, and it is horribly dull standing on a platform and trying to look pleasant. Ask him to stay. I insist upon it."

"Stay, Harry, to oblige Dorian, and to oblige me," said Hallward, gazing intently at his picture. "It is quite true, I never talk when I am working, and never listen either, and it must be dreadfully tedious for my unfortunate sitters. I beg you to stay."

"But what about my man at the Orleans?"

Hallward laughed. "I don't think there will be any difficulty about that. Sit down again, Harry.—And now, Dorian, get up on the platform, and don't move about too much, or pay any attention to what Lord Henry says. He has a very bad influence over all his friends, with the exception of myself."

Dorian stepped up on the dais, with the air of a young Greek martyr, and made a little *moue* of discontent to Lord Henry, to whom he had rather taken a fancy. He was so unlike Hallward. They made a delightful contrast. And he had such a beautiful voice.[3] After a few moments he said to him, "Have you really a very bad influence, Lord Henry? As bad as Basil says?"

"There is no such thing as a good influence, Mr. Gray. All influence is immoral,—immoral from the scientific point of view."

"Why?"

"Because to influence a person is to give him one's own soul. He does not think his natural thoughts, or burn with his natural passions. His virtues are not real to him. His sins, if there are such things as sins, are borrowed. He becomes an echo of some one else's music, an actor of a part that has not been written for him. The aim of life is self-development. To realize one's nature perfectly,—that is what each of us is here for. People are afraid of themselves, nowadays. They have forgotten the highest of all duties, the duty that one owes to one's self. Of course they are charitable. They feed the hungry, and clothe the beggar. But their own souls starve, and are naked. Courage has gone out of our race. Perhaps we never really had it. The terror

3. Wilde added "to whom . . . voice" in TS.

of society, which is the basis of morals, the terror of God, which is the secret of religion,—these are the two things that govern us. And yet—"

"Just turn your head a little more to the right, Dorian, like a good boy," said Hallward, deep in his work, and conscious only that a look had come into the lad's face that he had never seen there before.

"And yet," continued Lord Henry, in his low, musical voice, and with that graceful wave of the hand that was always so characteristic of him, and that he had even in his Eton days, "I believe that if one man were to live his life out fully and completely, were to give form to every feeling, expression to every thought, reality to every dream,— I believe that the world would gain such a fresh impulse of joy that we would forget all the maladies of mediævalism, and return to the Hellenic ideal,—to something finer, richer, than the Hellenic ideal, it may be. But the bravest man among us is afraid of himself. The mutilation of the savage has its tragic survival in the self-denial that mars our lives. We are punished for our refusals. Every impulse that we strive to strangle broods in the mind, and poisons us. The body sins once, and has done with its sin, for action is a mode of purifica-tion. Nothing remains then but the recollection of a pleasure, or the luxury of a regret. The only way to get rid of a temptation is to yield to it. Resist it, and your soul grows sick with longing for the things it has forbidden to itself, with desire for what its monstrous laws have made monstrous and unlawful. It has been said that the great events of the world take place in the brain. It is in the brain, and the brain only, that the great sins of the world take place also. You, Mr. Gray, you yourself, with your rose-red youth and your rose-white boyhood, you have had passions that have made you afraid, thoughts that have filled you with terror, day-dreams and sleeping dreams whose mere memory might stain your cheek with shame—"

"Stop!" murmured Dorian Gray, "stop! you bewilder me. I don't know what to say. There is some answer to you, but I cannot find it. Don't speak, Let me think, or, rather, let me try not to think."[4]

For nearly ten minutes he stood there motionless, with parted lips, and eyes strangely bright. He was dimly conscious that entirely fresh impulses[5] were at work within him, and they seemed to him to have come really from himself. The few words that Basil's friend had said to him—words spoken by chance, no doubt, and with wilful paradox in them—had yet touched some secret chord, that had never been touched before, but that he felt was now vibrating and throbbing to curious pulses.

4. Wilde added this and the following five paragraphs to TS on an inserted page and in a long marginal note ending with ". . . of the silence."
5. Wilde changed this word to "influences" in 1891.

Music had stirred him like that. Music had troubled him many times. But music was not articulate. It was not a new world, but rather a new chaos, that it created in us. Words! Mere words! How terrible they were! How clear, and vivid, and cruel! One could not escape from them. And yet what a subtle magic there was in them! They seemed to be able to give a plastic form to formless things, and to have a music of their own as sweet as that of viol or of lute. Mere words! Was there anything so real as words?

Yes; there had been things in his boyhood that he had not understood. He understood them now. Life suddenly became fiery-colored to him. It seemed to him that he had been walking in fire. Why had he not known it?

Lord Henry watched him, with his sad smile. He knew the precise psychological moment when to say nothing. He felt intensely interested. He was amazed at the sudden impression that his words had produced, and, remembering a book that he had read when he was sixteen, which had revealed to him much that he had not known before, he wondered whether Dorian Gray was passing through the same experience. He had merely shot an arrow into the air. Had it hit the mark? How fascinating the lad was!

Hallward painted away with that marvellous bold touch of his, that had the true refinement and perfect delicacy that come only from strength. He was unconscious of the silence.

"Basil, I am tired of standing," cried Dorian Gray, suddenly. "I must go out and sit in the garden. The air is stifling here."

"My dear fellow, I am so sorry. When I am painting, I can't think of anything else. But you never sat better. You were perfectly still. And I have caught the effect I wanted,—the half-parted lips, and the bright look in the eyes. I don't know what Harry has been saying to you, but he has certainly made you have the most wonderful expression. I suppose he has been paying you compliments. You mustn't believe a word that he says."

"He has certainly not been paying me compliments. Perhaps that is the reason I don't think I believe anything he has told me."

"You know you believe it all," said Lord Henry, looking at him with his dreamy, heavy-lidded eyes. "I will go out to the garden with you. It is horridly hot in the studio.—Basil, let us have something iced to drink, something with strawberries in it."

"Certainly, Harry. Just touch the bell, and when Parker comes I will tell him what you want. I have got to work up this background, so I will join you later on. Don't keep Dorian too long. I have never been in better form for painting than I am to-day. This is going to be my masterpiece. It is my masterpiece as it stands."

Lord Henry went out to the garden, and found Dorian Gray burying

his face in the great cool lilac-blossoms, feverishly drinking in their perfume as if it had been wine. He came close to him, and put his hand
upon his shoulder. "You are quite right to do that," he murmured.
"Nothing can cure the soul but the senses, just as nothing can cure the
senses but the soul."

The lad started and drew back. He was bareheaded, and the leaves
had tossed his rebellious curls and tangled all their gilded threads.
There was a look of fear in his eyes, such as people have when they
are suddenly awakened. His finely-chiselled nostrils quivered, and
some hidden nerve shook the scarlet of his lips and left them trembling.

"Yes," continued Lord Henry, "that is one of the great secrets of
life,—to cure the soul by means of the senses, and the senses by
means of the soul. You are a wonderful creature. You know more
than you think you know, just as you know less than you want to
know."

Dorian Gray frowned and turned his head away. he could not help
liking the tall, graceful young man who was standing by him. His
romantic olive-colored face and worn expression interested him.
There was something in his low, languid voice that was absolutely fascinating. His cool, white, flower-like hands, even, had a curious
charm. They moved, as he spoke, like music, and seemed to have a
language of their own. But he felt afraid of him, and ashamed of
being afraid. Why had it been left for a stranger to reveal him to himself? He had known Basil Hallward for months, but the friendship
between then had never altered him. Suddenly there had come some
one across his life who seemed to have disclosed to him life's mystery.
And, yet, what was there to be afraid of? He was not a school-boy, or
a girl. It was absurd to be frightened.

"Let us go and sit in the shade," said Lord Henry. "Parker has
brought out the drinks, and if you stay any longer in this glare you will
be quite spoiled, and Basil will never paint you again. You really must
not let yourself become sunburnt. It would be very unbecoming to
you."

"What does it matter?" cried Dorian, laughing, as he sat down on
the seat at the end of the garden.

"It should matter everything to you, Mr. Gray."

"Why?"

"Because you have now the most marvellous youth, and youth is
the one thing worth having."

"I don't feel that, Lord Henry."

"No, you don't feel it now. Some day, when you are old and
wrinkled and ugly, when thought has seared your forehead with its
lines, and passion branded your lips with its hideous fires, you will

feel it, you will feel it terribly.[6] Now, wherever you go, you charm the world. Will it always be so?

"You have a wonderfully beautiful face, Mr. Gray. Don't frown. You have. And Beauty is a form of Genius,—is higher, indeed, than Genius, as it needs no explanation. It is one of the great facts of the world, like sunlight, or spring-time, or the reflection in dark waters of that silver shell we call the moon.[7] It cannot be questioned. It has its divine right of sovereignty. It makes princes of those who have it. You smile? Ah! when you have lost it you won't smile.

"People say sometimes that Beauty is only superficial. That may be so. But at least it is not so superficial as Thought. To me, Beauty is the wonder of wonders. It is only shallow people who do not judge by appearances. The true mystery of the world is the visible, not the invisible.

"Yes, Mr. Gray, the gods have been good to you. But what the gods give they quickly take away. You have only a few years in which really to live. When your youth goes, your beauty will go with it, and then you will suddenly discover that there are no triumphs left for you, or have to content yourself with those mean triumphs that the memory of your past will make more bitter than defeats. Every month as it wanes brings you nearer to something dreadful. Time is jealous of you, and wars against your lilies and your roses. You will become sallow, and hollow-cheeked, and dull-eyed. You will suffer horribly.

"Realize your youth while you have it. Don't squander the gold of your days, listening to the tedious, trying to improve the hopeless failure, or giving away your life to the ignorant, the common, and the vulgar, which are the aims, the false ideals, of our age. Live! Live the wonderful life that is in you! Let nothing be lost upon you. Be always searching for new sensations. Be afraid of nothing.

"A new hedonism,—that is what our century wants. You might be its visible symbol. With your personality there is nothing you could not do. The world belongs to you for a season.

"The moment I met you I saw that you were quite unconscious of what you really are, what you really might be. There was so much about you that charmed me that I felt I must tell you something about yourself. I thought how tragic it would be if you were wasted. For there is such a little time that your youth will last,—such a little time.

"The common hill-flowers wither, but they blossom again. The laburnum will be as golden next June as it is now. In a month there will be purple stars on the clematis, and year after year the green

---

6. Wilde canceled these lines here in TS: "If you set yourself to know life, you will look evil; if you are afraid of life you will look common."
7. The lines "Beauty is a form of genius . . . the moon" were originally spoken by Basil in the previous chapter. Wilde relocated them here in MS and transferred them to Henry.

night of its leaves will have its purple stars. But we never get back our youth. The pulse of joy that beats in us at twenty, becomes sluggish. Our limbs fail, our senses rot. We degenerate into hideous puppets, haunted by the memory of the passions of which we were too much afraid, and the exquisite temptations that we did not dare to yield to. Youth! Youth! There is absolutely nothing in the world but youth!"

Dorian Gray listened, open-eyed and wondering. The spray of lilac fell from his hand upon the gravel. A furry bee came and buzzed round it for a moment. Then it began to scramble all over the fretted purple of the tiny blossoms. He watched it with that strange interest in trivial things that we try to develop when things of high import make us afraid, or when we are stirred by some new emotion, for which we cannot find expression, or when some thought that terrifies us lays sudden siege to the brain and calls on us to yield.[8] After a time it flew away. He saw it creeping into the stained trumpet of a Tyrian convolvulus. The flower seemed to quiver, and then swayed gently to and fro.

Suddenly Hallward appeared at the door of the studio, and made frantic signs for them to come in. They turned to each other, and smiled.

"'I am waiting," cried Hallward. "Do come in. The light is quite perfect, and you can bring your drinks."

They rose up, and sauntered down the walk together. Two green-and-white butterflies fluttered past them, and in the pear-tree at the end of the garden a thrush began to sing.

"You are glad you have met me, Mr. Gray," said Lord Henry, looking at him.

"Yes, I am glad now. I wonder shall I always be glad?"

"Always! That is a dreadful word. It makes me shudder when I hear it. Women are so fond of using it. They spoil every romance by trying to make it last forever.[9] It is a meaningless word, too. The only difference between a caprice and a life-long passion is that the caprice lasts a little longer."

As they entered the studio, Dorian Gray put his hand upon Lord Henry's arm. "In that case, let our friendship be a caprice," he murmured, flushing at his own boldness, then stepped upon the platform and resumed his pose.

Lord Henry flung himself into a large wicker arm-chair, and watched him. The sweep and dash of the brush on the canvas made the only sound that broke the stillness, except when Hallward stepped back now and then to look at his work from a distance. In the

8. Wilde added "or when we are stirred . . . to yield" in the margin of TS.
9. Wilde canceled the following at this point in MS: "Like priests, they terrify one at the prospect of certain eternity, attempt to terrify one, I should say."

slanting beams that streamed through the open door-way the dust
danced and was golden. The heavy scent of the roses seemed to brood
over everything.

After about a quarter of an hour, Hallward stopped painting,
looked for a long time at Dorian Gray, and then for a long time at the
picture, biting the end of one of his huge brushes, and smiling. "It is
quite finished," he cried, at last, and stooping down he wrote his
name in thin vermilion letters on the left-hand corner of the canvas.

Lord Henry came over and examined the picture. It was certainly
a wonderful work of art, and a wonderful likeness as well.[1]

"My dear fellow, I congratulate you most warmly," he said.—"Mr.
Gray, come and look at yourself."

The lad started, as if awakened from some dream. "Is it really finished?" he murmured, stepping down from the platform.

"Quite finished," said Hallward. "And you have sat splendidly to-
day. I am awfully obliged to you."

"That is entirely due to me," broke in Lord Henry. "Isn't it, Mr.
Gray?"

Dorian made no answer, but passed listlessly in front of his picture
and turned towards it. When he saw it he drew back, and his cheeks
flushed for a moment with pleasure. A look of joy came into his eyes,
as if he had recognized himself for the first time. He stood there
motionless, and in wonder, dimly conscious that Hallward was speaking to him, but not catching the meaning of his words. The sense of
his own beauty came on him like a revelation. He had never felt it
before. Basil Hallward's compliments had seemed to him to be
merely the charming exaggerations of friendship. He had listened to
them, laughed at them, forgotten them. They had not influenced his
nature. Then had come Lord Henry, with his strange panegyric on
youth, his terrible warning of its brevity. That had stirred him at the
time, and now, as he stood gazing at the shadow of his own loveliness,
the full reality of the description flashed across him. Yes, there would
be a day when his face would be wrinkled and wizen, his eyes dim and
colorless, the grace of his figure broken and deformed. The scarlet
would pass away from his lips, and the gold steal from his hair. The
life that was to make his soul would mar his body. He would become
ignoble,[2] hideous, and uncouth.

---

1. Wilde canceled here the following passage in MS: "Most modern portrait painting comes
under the head of elegant fiction or if it aims at realism, gives one something between a
caricature and a photograph. But this was different. It had all the mystery of life, and all
the mystery of beauty. Within the world, as men know it, there is a finer world that only
artists know of—artists or those to whom the temperament of the artist has been given.
Creation within creation—that is what Basil Hallward named it, that is what he had
attained to."
2. Wilde changed this to "dreadful" in 1891.

As he thought of it, a sharp pang of pain struck like a knife across him, and made each delicate fibre of his nature quiver. His eyes deepened into amethyst, and a mist of tears came across them. He felt as if a hand of ice had been laid upon his heart.

"Don't you like it?" cried Hallward at last, stung a little by the lad's silence, and not understanding what it meant.

"Of course he likes it," said Lord Henry. "Who wouldn't like it? It is one of the greatest things in modern art. I will give you anything you like to ask for it. I must have it."

"It is not my property, Harry."

"Whose property is it?"

"Dorian's, of course."

"He is a very lucky fellow."

"How sad it is!" murmured Dorian Gray, with his eyes still fixed upon his own portrait. "How sad it is! I shall grow old, and horrid, and dreadful. But this picture will remain always young. It will never be older than this particular day of June. . . . If it was only the other way! If it was I who were to be always young, and the picture that were to grow old! For this—for this—I would give everything! Yes, there is nothing in the whole world I would not give!"[3]

"You would hardly care for that arrangement, Basil," cried Lord Henry, laughing. "It would be rather hard lines on you."

"I should object very strongly, Harry."

Dorian Gray turned and looked at him. "I believe you would, Basil. You like your art better than your friends. I am no more to you than a green bronze figure. Hardly as much, I dare say."

Hallward stared in amazement. It was so unlike Dorian to speak like that. What had happened? He seemed almost angry. His face was flushed and his cheeks burning.

"Yes," he continued, "I am less to you than your ivory Hermes[4] or your silver Faun. You will like them always. How long will you like me? Till I have my first wrinkle, I suppose. I know, now, that when one loses one's good looks, whatever they may be, one loses everything. Your picture has taught me that. Lord Henry is perfectly right. Youth is the only thing worth having. When I find that I am growing old, I will kill myself."[5]

Hallward turned pale, and caught his hand. "Dorian! Dorian!" he cried, "don't talk like that. I have never had such a friend as you, and

3. Wilde altered this passage each time he revised his text. In MS, he canceled after "dreadful" the following: "Life will send its lines across my face. Passion will crease it and thought twist it from its form." In TS, Wilde added "Yes, there is nothing . . . give!" He added to it again in 1891: "I would give my soul for that."
4. Originally "Sylvanus" in MS, but changed there. Sylvanus was a Latin divinity, a variation of Pan, god of woods, fields, and grottoes, who looked young despite his antiquity.
5. Wilde added this sentence in TS.

I shall never have such another. You are not jealous of material things, are you?"

"I am jealous of everything whose beauty does not die. I am jealous of the portrait you have painted of me. Why should it keep what I must lose? Every moment that passes takes something from me, and gives something to it. Oh, if it was only the other way! If the picture could change, and I could be always what I am now! Why did you paint it? It will mock me some day,—mock me horribly!"[6] The hot tears welled into his eyes; he tore his hand away, and, flinging himself on the divan, he buried his face in the cushions, as if he was praying.

"This is your doing, Harry," said Hallward, bitterly.

"My doing?"

"Yes, yours, and you know it."[7]

Lord Henry shrugged his shoulders. "It is the real Dorian Gray,—that is all," he answered.

"It is not."

"If it is not, what have I to do with it?"[8]

"You should have gone away when I asked you."

"I stayed when you asked me."

"Harry, I can't quarrel with my two best friends at once, but between you both you have made me hate the finest piece of work I have ever done, and I will destroy it. What is it but canvas and color? I will not let it come across our three lives and mar them."

Dorian Gray lifted his golden head from the pillow, and looked at him with pallid face and tear-stained eyes, as he walked over to the deal painting-table that was set beneath the large curtained window. What was he doing there? His fingers were straying about among the litter of tin tubes and dry brushes, seeking for something. Yes, it was the long palette-knife, with its thin blade of lithe steel. He had found it at last. He was going to rip up the canvas.

With a stifled sob he leaped from the couch, and, rushing over to Hallward, tore the knife out of his hand, and flung it to the end of the studio. "Don't Basil, don't!" he cried. "It would be murder!"

"I am glad you appreciate my work at last, Dorian," said Hallward, coldly, when he had recovered from his surprise. "I never thought you would."

"Appreciate it? I am in love with it, Basil. It is part of myself, I feel that."

"Well, as soon as you are dry, you shall be varnished, and framed, and sent home. Then you can do what you like with yourself." And he walked across the room and rang the bell for tea. "You will have

6. "Oh, if it was only . . . horribly!" was added by Wilde in TS.
7. Wilde dropped Henry's question and Basil's answer in 1891.
8. Wilde wrote this into TS after removing *"comme vous voulez, mon cher."*

tea, of course, Dorian? And so will you, Harry? Tea is the only simple pleasure left to us."

"I don't like simple pleasures," said Lord Henry. "And I don't like scenes, except on the stage. What absurd fellows you are, both of you! I wonder who it was defined man as a rational animal. It was the most premature definition ever given. Man is many things, but he is not rational. I am glad he is not, after all: though I wish you chaps would not squabble over the picture. You had much better let me have it, Basil. This silly boy doesn't really want it, and I do."

"If you let any one have it but me, Basil, I will never forgive you!" cried Dorian Gray. "And I don't allow people to call me a silly boy."

"You know the picture is yours, Dorian. I gave it to you before it existed."

"And you know you have been a little silly, Mr. Gray, and that you don't really mind being called a boy."

"I should have minded very much this morning, Lord Henry."

"Ah! this morning! You have lived since then."[9]

There came a knock to the door, and the butler entered with the tea-tray and set it down upon a small Japanese table. There was a rattle of cups and saucers and the hissing of a fluted Georgian urn. Two globe-shaped china dishes were brought in by a page. Dorian Gray went over and poured the tea out. The two men sauntered languidly to the table, and examined what was under the covers.

"Let us go to the theatre to-night," said Lord Henry. "There is sure to be something on, somewhere. I have promised to dine at White's, but it is only with an old friend, so I can send him a wire and say that I am ill, or that I am prevented from coming in consequence of a subsequent engagement. I think that would be a rather nice excuse: it would have the surprise of candor."

"It is such a bore putting on one's dress-clothes," muttered Hallward. "And, when one has them on, they are so horrid."

"Yes," answered Lord Henry, dreamily, "the costume of our day is detestable. It is so sombre, so depressing. Sin is the only color-element left in modern life."

"You really must not say things like that before Dorian, Harry."

"Before which Dorian? The one who is pouring out tea for us, or the one in the picture?"

"Before either."

"I should like to come to the theatre with you, Lord Henry," said the lad.

"Then you shall come; and you will come too, Basil, won't you?"

"I can't really. I would sooner not. I have a lot of work to do."

"Well, then, you and I will go alone, Mr. Gray."

9. Wilde wrote the preceding three sentences into TS.

"I should like that awfully."

Basil Hallward bit his lip and walked over, cup in hand, to the picture. "I will stay with the real Dorian," he said, sadly.

"Is it the real Dorian?" cried the original of the portrait, running across to him. "Am I really like that?"

"Yes; you are just like that."

"How wonderful, Basil!"[1]

"At least you are like it in appearance. But it will never alter," said Hallward. "That is something."

"What a fuss people make about fidelity!" murmured Lord Henry. "And, after all, it is purely a question for physiology. It has nothing to do with our own will. It is either an unfortunate accident, or an unpleasant result of temperament.[2] Young men want to be faithful, and are not; old men want to be faithless, and cannot: that is all one can say."

"Don't go to the theatre to-night, Dorian," said Hallward. "Stop and dine with me."

"I can't, really."

"Why?"

"Because I have promised Lord Henry to go with him."

"He won't like you better for keeping your promises. He always breaks his own. I beg you not to go."

Dorian Gray laughed and shook his head.

"I entreat you."

The lad hesitated, and looked over at Lord Henry, who was watching them from the tea-table with an amused smile.

"I must go, Basil," he answered.

"Very well," said Hallward; and he walked over and laid his cup down on the tray. "It is rather late, and, as you have to dress, you had better lose no time. Good-by, Harry; good-by, Dorian. Come and see me soon. Come to-morrow."

"Certainly."

"You won't forget?"

"No, of course not."

"And . . . Harry!"

"Yes, Basil?"

"Remember what I asked you, when in the garden this morning."

"I have forgotten it."

"I trust you."

"I wish I could trust myself," said Lord Henry, laughing.—"Come, Mr. Gray, my hansom is outside, and I can drop you at your own place.—Good-by, Basil. It has been a most interesting afternoon."

---

1. Wilde added this and the preceding two sentences to TS.
2. Wilde dropped this sentence in 1891 and made some alterations to the sentence preceding it.

As the door closed behind them, Hallward flung himself down on a sofa, and a look of pain came into his face.

Chapter III[1]

One afternoon, a month later, Dorian Gray was reclining in a luxurious arm-chair, in the little library of Lord Henry's house in Curzon Street. It was, in its way, a very charming room, with its high panelled wainscoting of olive-stained oak, its cream-colored frieze and ceiling of raised plaster-work, and its brick-dust felt carpet strewn with long-fringed silk Persian rugs. On a tiny satinwood table stood a statuette by Clodion, and beside it lay a copy of "Les Cent Nouvelles," bound for Margaret of Valois by Clovis Eve, and powdered with the gilt daisies that the queen had selected for her device. Some large blue china jars, filled with parrot-tulips, were ranged on the mantel-shelf, and through the small leaded panes of the window streamed the apricot-colored light of a summer's day in London.

Lord Henry had not come in yet. He was always late on principle, his principle being that punctuality is the thief of time. So the lad was looking rather sulky, as with listless fingers he turned over the pages of an elaborately-illustrated edition of "Manon Lescaut" that he had found in one of the bookcases. The formal monotonous ticking of the Louis Quatorze clock annoyed him. Once or twice he thought of going away.

At last he heard a light step outside, and the door opened. "How late you are, Harry!" he murmured.

"I am afraid it is not Harry, Mr. Gray," said a woman's voice.

He glanced quickly round, and rose to his feet. "I beg your pardon. I thought—"

"You thought it was my husband. It is only his wife. You must let me introduce myself. I know you quite well by your photographs. I think my husband has got twenty-seven of them."

"Not twenty-seven, Lady Henry?"

"Well, twenty-six, then.[2] And I saw you with him the other night at the Opera." She laughed nervously, as she spoke, and watched him with her vague forget-me-not eyes. She was a curious woman, whose dresses always looked as if they had been designed in a rage and put on in a tempest. She was always in love with somebody, and, as her passion was never returned, she had kept all her illusions. She tried to look picturesque, but only succeeded in being

---

1. The first of the new chapters added in 1891 was inserted before the original chapter 3 here.
2. Wilde changed the number of photographs for humorous effect in 1891.

untidy. Her name was Victoria, and she had a perfect mania for going to church.

"That was at 'Lohengrin,' Lady Henry, I think?"

"Yes; it was at dear 'Lohengrin.' I like Wagner's music better than any other music. It is so loud that one can talk the whole time, without people hearing what one says. That is a great advantage: don't you think so, Mr. Gray?"

The same nervous staccato laugh broke from her thin lips, and her fingers began to play with a long paper-knife.

Dorian smiled, and shook his head: "I am afraid I don't think so, Lady Henry. I never talk during music,—at least during good music. If one hears bad music, it is one's duty to drown it by conversation."

"Ah! that is one of Harry's views, isn't it, Mr. Gray? But you must not think I don't like good music. I adore it, but I am afraid of it. It makes me too romantic. I have simply worshipped pianists,—two at a time, sometimes. I don't know what it is about them. Perhaps it is that they are foreigners. They all are, aren't they? Even those that are born in England become foreigners after a time, don't they? It is so clever of them, and such a compliment to art. Makes it quite cosmopolitan, doesn't it? You have never been to any of my parties, have you, Mr. Gray? You must come. I can't afford orchids, but I spare no expense in foreigners. They make one's rooms look so picturesque. But here is Harry!—Harry, I came in to look for you, to ask you something,—I forget what it was,—and I found Mr. Gray here. We have had such a pleasant chat about music. We have quite the same views. No; I think our views are quite different. But he has been most pleasant. I am so glad I've seen him."

"I am charmed, my love, quite charmed," said Lord Henry, elevating his dark crescent-shaped eyebrows and looking at them both with an amused smile.—"So sorry I am late, Dorian. I went to look after a piece of old brocade in Wardour Street, and had to bargain for hours for it. Nowadays people know the price of everything, and the value of nothing."[3]

"I am afraid I must be going," exclaimed Lady Henry, after an awkward silence, with her silly sudden laugh. "I have promised to drive with the duchess.—Good-by, Mr. Gray.—Good-by, Harry. You are dining out, I suppose? So am I. Perhaps I shall see you at Lady Thornbury's."

"I dare say, my dear," said Lord Henry, shutting the door behind her, as she flitted out of the room, looking like a bird-of-paradise that had been out in the rain, and leaving a faint odor of patchouli[4] behind

3. This well-known epigram was added in TS. It reappeared in *Lady Windermere's Fan* and for an encore in *The Importance of Being Earnest*. Wilde did not believe in running dead horses, only live ones.
4. Wilde changed the perfume to frangipanni in 1891. Patchouli was a scent identified with London prostitutes.

her. Then he shook hand with Dorian Gray, lit a cigarette, and flung himself down on the sofa.

"Never marry a woman with straw-colored hair, Dorian," he said, after a few puffs.

"Why, Harry?"

"Because they are so sentimental."

"But I like sentimental people."

"Never marry at all, Dorian. Men marry because they are tired; women, because they are curious: both are disappointed."

"I don't think I am likely to marry, Harry. I am too much in love. That is one of your aphorisms. I am putting it into practice, as I do everything you say."[5]

"Whom are you in love with?" said Lord Henry, looking at him with a curious smile.

"With an actress," said Dorian Gray, blushing.

Lord Henry shrugged his shoulders. "That is a rather common-place *début,*" he murmured.

"You would not say so if you saw her, Harry."

"Who is she?"

"Her name is Sibyl[6] Vane."

"Never heard of her."

"No one has. People will some day, however, She is a genius."

"My dear boy, no woman is a genius: women are a decorative sex. They never have anything to say, but they say it charmingly. They represent the triumph of matter over mind, just as we men represent the triumph of mind over morals. There are only two kinds of women, the plain and the colored. The plain women are very useful. If you want to gain a reputation for respectability, you have merely to take them down to supper. The other women are very charming. They commit one mistake, however. They paint in order to try to look young. Our grandmothers painted in order to try to talk brilliantly. *Rouge* and *esprit* used to go together. That has all gone out now. As long as a woman can look ten years younger than her own daughter, she is perfectly satisfied. As for conversation, there are only five women in London worth talking to, and two of these can't be admitted into decent society. However, tell me about your genius. How long have you known her?"

"About three weeks. Not so much. About two weeks and two days."

"How did you come across her?"

"I will tell you, Harry; but you mustn't be unsympathetic about it. After all, it never would have happened if I had not met you. You filled me with a wild desire to know everything about life. For days

---

5. This sentence was added in TS.
6. Stoddart changed the spelling from Wilde's "Sybil" here and throughout the text of this edition, and it remained "Sibyl" in the 1891 text.

after I met you, something seemed to throb in my veins. As I lounged in the Park, or strolled down Piccadilly, I used to look at every one who passed me, and wonder with a mad curiosity what sort of lives they led. Some of them fascinated me. Others filled me with terror. There was an exquisite poison in the air. I had a passion for sensations.

"One evening about seven o'clock I determined to go out in search of some adventure. I felt that this gray, monstrous London of ours, with its myriads of people, its splendid sinners, and its sordid sins, as you once said, must have something in store for me. I fancied a thousand things. The mere danger gave me a sense of delight. I remembered what you had said to me on that wonderful night when we first dined together, about the search for beauty being the poisonous secret of life. I don't know what I expected, but I went out, and wandered eastward, soon losing my way in a labyrinth of grimy streets and black, grassless squares. About half-past eight I passed by a little third-rate theatre, with great flaring gas-jets and gaudy play-bills. A hideous Jew,[7] in the most amazing waistcoat I ever beheld in my life, was standing at the entrance, smoking a vile cigar. He had greasy ringlets, and an enormous diamond blazed in the centre of a soiled shirt. ' 'Ave a box, my lord?' he said, when he saw me, and he took off his hat with an act of gorgeous servility. There was something about him, Harry, that amused me. He was such a monster. You will laugh at me, I know, but I really went in and paid a whole guinea for the stage-box. To the present day I can't make out why I did so; and yet if I hadn't!—my dear Harry, if I hadn't, I would have missed the greatest romance of my life. I see you are laughing. It is horrid of you!"

"I am not laughing, Dorian; at least I am not laughing at you. But you should not say the greatest romance of your life. You should say the first romance of your life. You will always be loved, and you will always be in love with love.[8] There are exquisite things in store for you. This is merely the beginning."

"Do you think my nature so shallow?" cried Dorian Gray, angrily.

" 'No; I think your nature so deep."

"How do you mean?"

"My dear boy, people who only love once in their lives are really shallow people. What they call their loyalty, and their fidelity, I call either the lethargy of custom or the lack of imagination. Faithlessness is to the emotional life what consistency is to the intellectual life,—

7. An example of modern censorship of *Dorian Gray* may be found in some recent paperback editions (Dell and Signet) in which "Jew" is silently changed to "man" here and to other equally neutral nouns throughout.
8. Wilde added three more sentences here in 1891.

simply a confession of failure.[9] But I don't want to interrupt you. Go on with your story."

"Well, I found myself seated in a horrid little private box, with a vulgar drop-scene staring me in the face. I looked out behind the curtain, and surveyed the house. It was a tawdry affair, all Cupids and cornucopias, like a third-rate wedding-cake. The gallery and pit were fairly full, but the two rows of dingy stalls were quite empty, and there was hardly a person in what I suppose they called the dress-circle. Women went about with oranges and ginger-beer, and there was a terrible consumption of nuts going on."

"It must have been just like the palmy days of the British Drama."

"Just like, I should fancy, and very horrid. I began to wonder what on earth I should do, when I caught sight of the play-bill. What do you think the play was, Harry?"

"I should think 'The Idiot Boy, or Dumb but Innocent.' Our fathers used to like that sort of piece, I believe. The longer I live, Dorian, the more keenly I feel that whatever was good enough for our fathers is not good enough for us. In art, as in politics, *les grandpères ont toujours tort.*"

"This play was good enough for us, Harry. It was 'Romeo and Juliet.' I must admit I was rather annoyed at the idea of seeing Shakespeare done in such a wretched hole of a place. Still, I felt interested, in a sort of way. At any rate, I determined to wait for the first act. There was a dreadful orchestra, presided over by a young Jew who sat at a cracked piano, that nearly drove me away, but at last the drop-scene was drawn up, and the play began. Romeo was a stout elderly gentleman, with corked eyebrows, a husky tragedy voice, and a figure like a beer-barrel. Mercutio was almost as bad. He was played by the low-comedian, who had introduced gags of his own and was on most familiar terms with the pit. They were as grotesque as the scenery, and that looked as if it had come out of a pantomime of fifty years ago. But Juliet! Harry, imagine a girl, hardly seventeen years of age, with a little flower-like face, a small Greek head with plaited coils of dark-brown hair, eyes that were violet wells of passion, lips that were like the petals of a rose. She was the loveliest thing I had ever seen in my life. You said to me once that pathos left you unmoved, but that beauty, mere beauty, could fill your eyes with tears. I tell you, Harry, I could hardly see this girl for the mist of tears that came across me. And her voice,—I never heard such a voice. It was very low at first, with deep mellow notes, that seemed to fall singly upon one's ear. Then it became a little louder, and sounded like a flute or a distant hautbois. In the garden-scene it had

9. Wilde added this epigram in TS and followed it up with four additional sentences in 1891.

all the tremulous ecstasy that one hears just before dawn when nightingales are singing. There were moments, later on, when it had the wild passion of violins. You know how a voice can stir one. Your voice and the voice of Sibyl Vane are two things that I shall never forget. When I close my eyes, I hear them, and each of them says something different. I don't know which to follow. Why should I not love her? Harry, I do love her. She is everything to me in life. Night after night I go to see her play. One evening she is Rosalind, and the next evening she is Imogen. I have seen her die in the gloom of an Italian tomb, sucking the poison from her lover's lips. I have watched her wandering through the forest of Arden, disguised as a pretty boy in hose and doublet and dainty cap. She has been mad, and has come into the presence of a guilty king, and given him rue to wear, and bitter herbs to taste of. She has been innocent, and the black hands of jealousy have crushed her reed-like throat. I have seen her in every age and in every costume. Ordinary women never appeal to one's imagination. They are limited to their century. No glamour ever transfigures them. One knows their minds as easily as one knows their bonnets. One can always find them. There is no mystery in one of them. They ride in the Park in the morning, and chatter at tea-parties in the afternoon. They have their stereotyped smile, and their fashionable manner. They are quite obvious. But an actress! How different an actress is! Why didn't you tell me that the only thing worth loving is an actress?"

"Because I have loved so many of them, Dorian."

"Oh, yes, horrid people with dyed hair and painted faces."

"Don't run down dyed hair and painted faces. There is an extraordinary charm in them, sometimes."

"I wish now I had not told you about Sibyl Vane."

"You could not have helped telling me, Dorian. All through your life you will tell me everything you do."

"Yes, Harry, I believe that is true. I cannot help telling you things. You have a curious influence over me. If I ever did a crime, I would come and confide it to you. You would understand me."

"People like you—the wilful sunbeams of life—don't commit crimes, Dorian. But I am much obliged for the compliment, all the same. And now tell me,—reach me the matches, like a good boy: thanks,—tell me, what are your relations with Sibyl Vane?"[1]

Dorian Gray leaped to his feet, with flushed cheeks and burning eyes.[2] "Harry, Sibyl Vane is sacred!"

---

1. This is another of the series of bowdlerizations by Stoddart. This line was written by Wilde: "is Sybil Vane your mistress?" Stoddart simply rewrote it in its present form, and although Wilde made an addition in 1891, he did not restore the original reading.
2. Stoddart changed TS: "How dare you suggest such a thing, Harry? It is horrible."

"It is only the sacred things that are worth touching, Dorian," said Lord Henry, with a strange touch of pathos in his voice. "But why should you be annoyed? I suppose she will be yours[3] some day. When one is in love, one always begins by deceiving one's self, and one always ends by deceiving others. That is what the world calls romance. You know her, at any rate, I suppose?"

"Of course I know her. On the first night I was at the theatre, the horrid old Jew came round to the box after the performance was over, and offered to bring me behind the scenes and introduce me to her. I was furious with him, and told him that Juliet had been dead for hundreds of years, and that her body was lying in a marble tomb in Verona. I think, from his blank look of amazement, that he thought I had taken too much champagne, or something."

"I am not surprised."

"I was not surprised either. Then he asked me if I wrote for any of the newspapers. I told him I never even read them. He seemed terribly disappointed at that, and confided to me that all the dramatic critics were in a conspiracy against him, and that they were all to be bought."

"I believe he was quite right there. But, on the other hand, most of them are not at all expensive."[4]

"Well, he seemed to think they were beyond his means. By this time the lights were being put out in the theatre, and I had to go. He wanted me to try some cigars which he strongly recommended. I declined. The next night, of course, I arrived at the theatre again. When he saw me he made me a low bow, and assured me that I was a patron of art. He was a most offensive brute, though he had an extraordinary passion for Shakespeare. He told me once, with an air of pride, that his three bankruptcies were entirely due to the poet, whom he insisted on calling 'The Bard.'[5] He seemed to think it a distinction."

"It was a distinction, my dear Dorian,—a great distinction. But when did you first speak to Miss Sibyl Vane?"

"The third night. She had been playing Rosalind. I could not help going round. I had thrown her some flowers and she had looked at me; at least I fancied that she had. The old Jew was persistent. He seemed determined to bring me behind, so I consented. It was curious my not wanting to know her, wasn't it?"

"No; I don't think so."

"My dear Harry, why?"

3. Stoddart changed this from TS: "your mistress." Wilde altered the Stoddart emendation in 1891, making it a little stronger.
4. Wilde altered this passage slightly in 1891.
5. Wilde substituted this phrase in TS for "Shakespeare." In 1891, the number of bankruptcies was increased to five.

"I will tell you some other time. Now I want to know about the girl."

"Sibyl? Oh, she was so shy, and so gentle. There is something of a child about her. Her eyes opened wide in exquisite wonder when I told her what I thought of her performance, and she seemed quite unconscious of her power. I think we were both rather nervous. The old Jew stood grinning at the door-way of the dusty greenroom, making elaborate speeches about us both, while we stood looking at each other like children. He would insist on calling me 'My Lord,' so I had to assure Sibyl that I was not anything of the kind. She said quite simply to me, 'You look more like a prince.'"

"Upon my word, Dorian, Miss Sibyl knows how to pay compliments."

"You don't understand her, Harry. She regarded me merely as a person in a play. She knows nothing of life. She lives with her mother, a faded tired woman who played Lady Capulet in a sort of magenta dressing-wrapper on the first night, and looks as if she had seen better days."

"I know that look. It always depresses me."

"The Jew wanted to tell me her history, but I said it did not interest me."

"You were quite right. There is always something infinitely mean about other people's tragedies."

"Sibyl is the only thing I care about. What is it to me where she came from? From her little head to her little feet, she is absolutely and entirely divine. I go to see her act every night of my life, and every night she is more marvellous."

"That is the reason, I suppose, that you will never dine with me now. I thought you must have some curious romance on hand. You have; but it is not quite what I expected."

"My dear Harry, we either lunch or sup together every day, and I have been to the Opera with you several times."

"You always come dreadfully late."

"Well, I can't help going to see Sibyl play, even if it is only for an act. I get hungry for her presence; and when I think of the wonderful soul that is hidden away in that little ivory body, I am filled with awe."

"You can dine with me to-night, Dorian, can't you?"

He shook his head. "To night she is Imogen," he answered, "and to-morrow night she will be Juliet."

"When is she Sibyl Vane?"

"Never."

"I congratulate you."

"How horrid you are! She is all the great heroines of the world in one. She is more than an individual. You laugh, but I tell you she has genius. I love her, and I must make her love me. You, who know all the secrets of life, tell me how to charm Sibyl Vane to love me! I want to make Romeo jealous. I want the dead lovers of the world to hear our laughter, and grow sad. I want a breath of our passion to stir their dust into consciousness, to wake their ashes into pain. My God, Harry, how I worship her!" He was walking up and down the room as he spoke. Hectic spots of red burned on his cheeks. He was terribly excited.

Lord Henry watched him with a subtle sense of pleasure. How different he was now from the shy, frightened boy he had met in Basil Hallward's studio! His nature had developed like a flower, had borne blossoms of scarlet flame. Out of its secret hiding-place had crept his Soul, and Desire had come to meet it on the way.

"And what do you propose to do?" said Lord Henry, at last.

"I want you and Basil to come with me some night and see her act. I have not the slightest fear of the result. You won't be able to refuse to recognize her genius. Then we must get her out of the Jew's hands. She is bound to him for three years—at least for two years and eight months—from the present time. I will have to pay him something, of course. When all that is settled, I will take a West-End theatre and bring her out properly. She will make the world as mad as she has made me."

"Impossible, my dear boy."

"Yes, she will. She has not merely art, consummate art-instinct, in her, but she has personality also; and you have often told me that it is personalities, not principles, that move the age."

"Well, what night shall we go?"

"Let me see. To-day is Tuesday. Let us fix to-morrow. She plays Juliet to-morrow."

"All right. The Bristol at eight o'clock; and I will get Basil."

"Not eight, Harry, please. Half-past six. We must be there before the curtain rises. You must see her in the first act, where she meets Romeo."

"Half-past six! What an hour! It will be like having a meat-tea. However, just as you wish. Shall you see Basil between this and then? Or shall I write to him?"

"Dear Basil! I have not laid eyes on him for a week. It is rather horrid of me, as he has sent me my portrait in the most wonderful frame, designed by himself, and, though I am a little jealous of it for being a whole month younger than I am, I must admit that I delight in it. Perhaps you had better write to him. I don't want to see him alone. He says things that annoy me."

Lord Henry smiled. "He gives you good advice, I suppose. People are very fond of giving away what they need most themselves."

"You don't mean to say that Basil has got any passion or any romance in him?"

"I don't know whether he has any passion, but he certainly has romance," said Lord Henry, with an amused look in his eyes. "Has he never let you know that?"

"Never. I must ask him about it. I am rather surprised to hear it.[6] He is the best of fellows, but he seems to me to be just a bit of a Philistine. Since I have known you, Harry, I have discovered that."

"Basil, my dear boy, puts everything that is charming in him into his work. The consequence is that he has nothing left for life but his prejudices, his principles, and his common sense. The only artists I have ever known who are personally delightful are bad artists. Good artists give everything to their art, and consequently are perfectly uninteresting in themselves.[7] A great poet, a really great poet, is the most unpoetical of all creatures. But inferior poets are absolutely fascinating. The worse their rhymes are, the more picturesque they look. The mere fact of having published a book of second-rate sonnets makes a man quite irresistible. He lives the poetry that he cannot write. The others write the poetry that they dare not realize."

"I wonder is that really so, Harry?" said Dorian Gray, putting some perfume on his handkerchief out of a large, gold-topped bottle that stood on the table. "It must be, if you say so. And now I must be off. Imogen is waiting for me. Don't forget about to-morrow. Good-by."

As he left the room, Lord Henry's heavy eyelids drooped, and he began to think. Certainly few people had ever interested him so much as Dorian Gray, and yet the lad's mad adoration of some one else caused him not the slightest pang of annoyance or jealousy. He was pleased by it. It made him a more interesting study. He had been always enthralled by the methods of science, but the ordinary subject-matter of science had seemed to him trivial and of no import. And so he had begun by vivisecting himself, as he had ended by vivisecting others. Human life,—that appeared to him the one thing worth investigating. There was nothing else of any value compared to it. It was true that as one watched life in its curious crucible of pain and pleasure, one could not wear over one's face a mask of glass, or keep the sulphurous fumes from troubling the brain and making the imagination turbid with monstrous fancies and misshapen dreams. There were poisons so subtle that to know their properties one had to sicken of them. There were maladies so strange that one had to

6. Wilde altered the preceding lines after "You don't mean to say . . ." in TS and again in 1891. Originally, Dorian asked whether "Basil has got a passion for somebody?" Lord Henry answered, "Yes, he has. Has he never told you?" This dialogue was canceled, and Wilde wrote the changes in the margin.
7. Wilde rewrote this sentence in 1891.

pass through them if one sought to understand their nature. And, yet, what a great reward one received! How wonderful the whole world became to one! To note the curious hard logic of passion, and the emotional colored life of the intellect,—to observe where they met, and where they separated, at what point they became, and at what point they were at discord,—there was a delight in that! What matter what the cost was? One could never pay too high a price for any sensation.

He was conscious—and the thought brought a gleam of pleasure into his brown agate eyes—that it was through certain words of his, musical words said with musical utterance, that Dorian Gray's soul had turned to this white girl and bowed in worship before her. To a large extent, the lad was his own creation. He had made him premature. That was something. Ordinary people waited till life disclosed to them its secrets, but to the few, to the elect, the mysteries of life were revealed before the veil was drawn away. Sometimes this was the effect of art, and chiefly of the art of literature, which dealt immediately with the passions and the intellect. But now and then a complex personality took the place and assumed the office of art, was indeed, in its way, a real work of art, Life having its elaborate masterpieces, just as poetry has, or sculpture, or painting.

Yes, the lad was premature. He was gathering his harvest while it was yet spring. The pulse and passion of youth were in him, but he was becoming self-conscious. It was delightful to watch him. With his beautiful face, and his beautiful soul, he was a thing to wonder at. It was no matter how it all ended, or was destined to end. He was like one of those gracious figures in a pageant or a play, whose joys seem to be remote from one, but whose sorrows stir one's sense of beauty, and whose wounds are like red roses.

Soul and body, body and soul—how mysterious they were![8] There was animalism in the soul, and the body had its moments of spirituality. The senses could refine, and the intellect could degrade. Who could say where the fleshly impulse ceased, or the psychical impulse began? How shallow were the arbitrary definitions of ordinary psychologists! And yet how difficult to decide between the claims of the various schools! Was the soul a shadow seated in the house of sin? Or was the body really in the soul, as Giordano Bruno thought? The separation of spirit from matter was a mystery, and the union of spirit with matter was a mystery also.

He began to wonder whether we should ever make psychology so absolute a science that each little spring of life would be revealed to us. As it was, we always misunderstood ourselves, and rarely

8. This sentence was a marginal addition in MS.

understood others. Experience was of no ethical value. It was merely the name we gave to our mistakes. Men had, as a rule, regarded it as a mode of warning, had claimed for it a certain moral efficacy in the formation of character, had praised it as something that taught us what to follow and showed us what to avoid. But there was no motive power in experience. It was as little of an active cause as conscience itself. All that it really demonstrated was that our future would be the same as our past, and that the sin we had done once, and with loathing, we would do many times, and with joy.

It was clear to him that the experimental method was the only method by which one could arrive at any scientific analysis of the passions; and certainly Dorian Gray was a subject made to his hand, and seemed to promise rich and fruitful results. His sudden mad love for Sibyl Vane was a psychological phenomenon of no small interest. There was no doubt that curiosity had much to do with it, curiosity and the desire for new experiences; yet it was not a simple but rather a very complex passion. What there was in it of the purely sensuous instinct of boyhood had been transformed by the workings of the imagination, changed into something that seemed to the boy himself to be remote from sense, and was for that very reason all the more dangerous. It was the passions about whose origin we deceived ourselves that tyrannized most strongly over us. Our weakest motives were those of whose nature we were conscious. It often happened that when we thought we were experimenting on others we were really experimenting on ourselves.

While Lord Henry sat dreaming on these things, a knock came to the door, and his valet entered, and reminded him it was time to dress for dinner. He got up and looked out into the street. The sunset had smitten into scarlet gold the upper windows of the houses opposite. The panes glowed like plates of heated metal. The sky above was like a faded rose. He thought of Dorian Gray's young fiery-colored life, and wondered how it was all going to end.

When he arrived home, about half-past twelve o'clock, he saw a telegram lying on the hall-table. He opened it and found it was from Dorian. It was to tell him that he was engaged to be married to Sibyl Vane.

Chapter IV[1]

"I suppose you have heard the news, Basil?" said Lord Henry on the following evening, as Hallward was shown into a little private room at the Bristol where dinner had been laid for three.

"No, Harry," answered Hallward, giving his hat and coat to the bowing waiter. "What is it? Nothing about politics, I hope? They don't interest me. There is hardly a single person in the House of Commons worth painting; though many of them would be the better for a little whitewashing."

"Dorian Gray is engaged to be married," said Lord Henry, watching him as he spoke.

Hallward turned perfectly pale, and a curious look flashed for a moment into his eyes, and then passed away, leaving them dull.[2] "Dorian engaged to be married!" he cried. "Impossible!"

"It is perfectly true."

"To whom?"

"To some little actress or other."

"I can't believe it. Dorian is far too sensible."

"Dorian is far too wise not to do foolish things now and then, my dear Basil."

"Marriage is hardly a thing that one can do now and then, Harry," said Hallward, smiling.

"Except in America.[3] But I didn't say he was married. I said he was engaged to be married. There is a great difference. I have a distinct remembrance of being married, but I have no recollection at all of being engaged.[4] I am inclined to think that I never was engaged."

"But think of Dorian's birth, and position, and wealth. It would be absurd for him to marry so much beneath him."

"If you want him to marry this girl, tell him that, Basil. He is sure to do it then.[5] Whenever a man does a thoroughly stupid thing, it is always from the noblest motives."

"I hope the girl is good, Harry. I don't want to see Dorian tied to some vile creature, who might degrade his nature and ruin his intellect."

"Oh, she is more than good—she is beautiful," murmured Lord Henry, sipping a glass of vermouth and orange-bitters. "Dorian says she is beautiful; and he is not often wrong about things of that kind. Your portrait of him has quickened his appreciation of the personal

1. Wilde added another chapter (6) here in 1891.
2. Wilde changed these lines in 1891, muting Basil's reaction.
3. Wilde added this in TS.
4. "I have a distinct . . . being engaged" was added in TS.
5. "But think of Dorian's birth . . . do it then" was added in MS margin, and the following sentence was added in TS.

appearance of other people. It has had that excellent effect, among others. We are to see her to-night, if that boy doesn't forget his appointment."[6]

"But do you approve of it, Harry?" asked Hallward, walking up and down the room, and biting his lip. "You can't approve of it, really. It is some silly infatuation."

"I never approve, or disapprove, of anything now. It is an absurd attitude to take towards life. We are not sent into the world to air our moral prejudices. I never take any notice of what common people say, and I never interfere with what charming people do. If a personality fascinates me, whatever the personality chooses to do is absolutely delightful to me. Dorian Gray falls in love with a beautiful girl who acts Shakespeare, and proposes to marry her. Why not? If he wedded Messalina he would be none the less interesting. You know I am not a champion of marriage. The real drawback to marriage is that it makes one unselfish. And unselfish people are colorless. They lack individuality. Still, there are certain temperaments that marriage makes more complex. They retain their egotism, and add to it many other egos. They are forced to have more than one life. They become more highly organized. Besides, every experience is of value, and, whatever one may say against marriage, it is certainly an experience. I hope that Dorian Gray will make this girl his wife, passionately adore her for six months, and then suddenly become fascinated by some one else. He would be a wonderful study."[7]

"You don't mean all that, Harry; you know you don't. If Dorian Gray's life were spoiled, no one would be sorrier than yourself. You are much better than you pretend to be."

Lord Henry laughed. "The reason we all like to think so well of others is that we are all afraid for ourselves. The basis of optimism is sheer terror. We think that we are generous because we credit our neighbor with those virtues that are likely to benefit ourselves. We praise the banker that we may overdraw our account, and find good qualities in the highwayman in the hope that he may spare our pockets.[8] I mean everything that I have said. I have the greatest contempt for optimism.[9] And as for a spoiled life, no life is spoiled but one whose growth is arrested. If you want to mar a nature, you have merely to reform it. But here is Dorian himself. He will tell you more than I can."

"My dear Harry, my dear Basil, you must both congratulate me!" said the boy, throwing off his evening cape with its satin-lined wings,

---

6. Wilde added several lines here in 1891.
7. Wilde made several minor changes in this paragraph in 1891.
8. "and find good qualities . . . pockets" added in TS.
9. This sentence and the four immediately following were added in TS.

and shaking each of his friends by the hand in turn. "I have never been so happy. Of course it is sudden: all really delightful things are. And yet it seems to me to be the one thing I have been looking for all my life." He was flushed with excitement and pleasure, and looked extraordinarily handsome.

"I hope you will always be very happy, Dorian," said Hallward, "but I don't quite forgive you for not having let me know of your engagement. You let Harry know."

"And I don't forgive you for being late for dinner," broke in Lord Henry, putting his hand on the lad's shoulder, and smiling as he spoke. "Come, let us sit down and try what the new *chef* here is like, and then you will tell us how it all came about."

"There is really not much to tell," cried Dorian, as they took their seats at the small round table. "What happened was simply this. After I left you yesterday evening, Harry, I had some dinner at that curious little Italian restaurant in Rupert Street,[1] you introduced me to, and went down afterwards to the theatre. Sibyl was playing Rosalind. Of course the scenery was dreadful, and the Orlando absurd. But Sibyl! You should have seen her! When she came on in her boy's dress she was perfectly wonderful. She wore a moss-colored velvet jerkin with cinnamon sleeves, slim brown cross-gartered hose, a dainty little green cap with a hawk's feather caught in a jewel, and a hooded cloak lined with dull red. She had never seemed to me more exquisite. She had all the delicate grace of that Tanagra figurine that you have in your studio, Basil. Her hair clustered round her face like dark leaves round a pale rose. As for her acting—well, you will see her to-night. She is simply a born artist. I sat in the dingy box absolutely enthralled. I forgot that I was in London and in the nineteenth century. I was away with my love in a forest that no man had ever seen. After the performance was over I went behind, and spoke to her. As we were sitting together, suddenly there came a look into her eyes that I had never seen there before. My lips moved towards hers. We kissed each other. I can't describe to you what I felt at that moment. It seemed to me that all my life had been narrowed to one perfect point of rose-colored joy. She trembled all over, and shook like a white narcissus. Then she flung herself on her knees and kissed my hands. I feel that I should not tell you all this, but I can't help it. Of course our engagement is a dead secret. She has not even told her own mother. I don't know what my guardians will say. Lord Radley is sure to be furious. I don't care. I shall be of age in less than a year, and then I can do what I like. I have been right, Basil, haven't I, to take my love out

1. Wilde added this detail in TS.

of poetry, and to find my wife in Shakespeare's plays? Lips that Shakespeare taught to speak have whispered their secret in my ear. I have had the arms of Rosalind around me, and kissed Juliet on the mouth."

"Yes, Dorian, I suppose you were right," said Hallward, slowly.

"Have you seen her to-day?" asked Lord Henry.

"Dorian Gray shook his head. "I left her in the forest of Arden, I shall find her in an orchard in Verona."

Lord Henry sipped his champagne in a meditative manner. "At what particular point did you mention the word marriage, Dorian? and what did she say in answer? Perhaps you forgot all about it."

"My dear Harry, I did not treat it as a business transaction, and I did not make any formal proposal. I told her that I loved her, and she said she was not worthy to be my wife. Not worthy! Why, the whole world is nothing to me compared to her."

"Women are wonderfully practical," murmured Lord Henry,— "much more practical than we are. In situations of that kind we often forget to say anything about marriage, and they always remind us."

Hallward laid his hand upon his arm. "Don't, Harry. You have annoyed Dorian. He is not like other men. He would never bring misery upon any one. His nature is too fine for that."

Lord Henry looked across the table. "Dorian is never annoyed with me," he answered. "I asked the question for the best reason possible, for the only reason, indeed, that excuses one for asking any question,—simple curiosity. I have a theory that it is always the women who propose to us, and not we who propose to the women, except, of course, in middle-class life. But then the middle classes are not modern."

Dorian Gray laughed, and tossed his head. "You are quite incorrigible, Harry; but I don't mind. It is impossible to be angry with you. When you see Sibyl Vane you will feel that the man who could wrong her would be a beast without a heart. I cannot understand how any one can wish to shame what he loves. I love Sibyl Vane. I wish to place her on a pedestal of gold, and to see the world worship the woman who is mine. What is marriage? An irrevocable vow. And it is an irrevocable vow that I want to take.[2] Her trust makes me faithful, her belief makes me good. When I am with her, I regret all that you have taught me. I become different from what you have known me to be. I am changed, and the mere touch of Sibyl Vane's hand makes me forget you and all your wrong, fascinating, poisonous, delightful[3] theories."

2. Wilde crossed out the following in MS: "Why she would loathe me if she thought I merely meant to use her till I grew weary of her and then throw her away."

3. "Delightful" added in TS. Wilde inserted almost two additional pages at this point in 1891.

"You will always like me, Dorian," said Lord Henry. "Will you have some coffee, you fellows?—Waiter, bring coffee, and *fine-champagne*, and some cigarettes. No: don't mind the cigarettes; I have some.— Basil, I can't allow you to smoke cigars. You must have a cigarette. A cigarette is the perfect type of a perfect pleasure. It is exquisite, and it leaves one unsatisfied. What more can you want?—Yes, Dorian, you will always be fond of me. I represent to you all the sins you have never had the courage to commit."

"What nonsense you talk, Harry!" cried Dorian Gray, lighting his cigarette from a fire-breathing silver dragon that the waiter had placed on the table. "Let us go down to the theatre. When you see Sibyl you will have a new ideal of life. She will represent something to you that you have never known."

"I have known everything," said Lord Henry, with a sad[4] look in his eyes, "but I am always ready for a new emotion. I am afraid that there is no such thing, for me at any rate. Still, your wonderful girl may thrill me. Dorian, you will come with me.—I am so sorry, Basil, but there is only room for two in the brougham. You must follow us in a hansom."

They got up and put on their coats, sipping their coffee standing. Hallward was silent and preoccupied. There was a gloom over him. He could not bear this marriage, and yet it seemed to him to be better than many other things that might have happened. After a few moments, they all passed down-stairs. He drove off by himself, as had been arranged, and watched the flashing lights of the little brougham in front of him. A strange sense of loss came over him. He felt that Dorian Gray would never again be to him all that he had been in the past. His eyes darkened,[5] and the crowded flaring streets became blurred to him. When the cab drew up at the doors of the theatre, it seemed to him that he had grown years older.

Chapter V

For some reason or other, the house was crowded that night, and the fat Jew manager who met them at the door was beaming from ear to ear with an oily, tremulous smile. He escorted them to their box with a sort of pompous humility, waving his fat jewelled hands, and talking at the top of his voice. Dorian Gray loathed him more than ever. He felt as if he had come to look for Miranda and had been met by Caliban. Lord Henry, upon the other hand, rather liked him. At least

4. Changed to "tired" in 1891.
5. Wilde substituted "darkened" for "filled with tears" in MS.

he declared he did, and insisted on shaking him by the hand, and assured him that he was proud to meet a man who had discovered a real genius and gone bankrupt over Shakespeare. Hallward amused himself with watching the faces in the pit. The heat was terribly oppressive, and the huge sunlight flamed like a monstrous dahlia with petals of fire. The youths in the gallery had taken off their coats and waistcoats and hung them over the side. They talked to each other across the theatre, and shared their oranges with the tawdry painted girls who sat by them. Some women were laughing in the pit; their voices were horribly shrill and discordant. The sound of the popping of corks came from the bar.

"What a place to find one's divinity in!" said Lord Henry.

"Yes!" answered Dorian Gray. "It was here I found her, and she is divine beyond all living things. When she acts you will forget everything. These common people here, with their coarse faces and brutal gestures, become quite different when she is on the stage. They sit silently and watch her. They weep and laugh as she wills them to do. She makes them as responsive as a violin. She spiritualizes them, and one feels that they are of the same flesh and blood as one's self."

"Oh, I hope not!" murmured Lord Henry, who was scanning the occupants of the gallery through his opera-glass.

"Don't pay any attention to him, Dorian," said Hallward. "I understand what you mean, and I believe in this girl. Any one you love must be marvellous, and any girl that has the effect you describe must be fine and noble. To spiritualize one's age,—that is something worth doing. If this girl can give a soul to those who have lived without one, if she can create the sense of beauty in people whose lives have been sordid and ugly, if she can strip them of their selfishness and lend them tears for sorrows that are not their own, she is worthy of all your adoration, worthy of the adoration of the world. This marriage is quite right. I did not think so at first, but I admit it now. God[1] made Sibyl Vane for you. Without her you would have been incomplete.

"Thanks, Basil," answered Dorian Gray, pressing his hand. "I knew that you would understand me. Harry is so cynical, he terrifies me. But here is the orchestra. It is quite dreadful, but it only lasts for about five minutes. Then the curtain rises, and you will see the girl to whom I am going to give all my life, to whom I have given everything that is good in me."

A quarter of an hour afterwards, amidst an extraordinary turmoil of applause, Sibyl Vane stepped on to the stage. Yes, she was certainly

---

1. Changed to "the gods" in 1891.

lovely to look at—one of the loveliest creatures, Lord Henry thought, that he had ever seen. There was something of the fawn in her shy grace and startled eyes. A faint blush, like the shadow of a rose in a mirror of silver, came to her cheeks as she glanced at the crowded, enthusiastic house. She stepped back a few paces, and her lips seemed to tremble. Basil Hallward leaped to his feet and began to applaud. Dorian Gray sat motionless, gazing on her, like a man in a dream. Lord Henry peered through his opera-glass, murmuring, "Charming! charming!"

The scene was the hall of Capulet's house, and Romeo in his pilgrim's dress had entered with Mercutio and his friends. The band, such as it was, struck up a few bars of music, and the dance began. Through the crowd of ungainly, shabbily-dressed actors, Sibyl Vane moved like a creature from a finer world. Her body swayed, as she danced, as a plant sways in the water. The curves of her throat were like the curves of a white lily. Her hands seemed to be made of cool ivory.

Yet she was curiously listless. She showed no sign of joy when her eyes rested on Romeo. The few lines she had to speak,—

> Good pilgrim, you do wrong your hand too much,
>   Which mannerly devotion shows in this;
> For saints have hands that pilgrims' hands do touch,
>   And palm to palm is holy palmers' kiss,—

with the brief dialogue that follows, were spoken in a thoroughly artificial manner. The voice was exquisite, but from the point of view of tone it was absolutely false. It was wrong in color. It took away all the life from the verse. It made the passion unreal.

Dorian Gray grew pale as he watched her. Neither of his friends dared to say anything to him. She seemed to them to be absolutely incompetent. They were horribly disappointed.

Yet they felt that the true test of any Juliet is the balcony scene of the second act. They waited for that. If she failed there, there was nothing in her.

She looked charming as she came out in the moonlight. That could not be denied. But the staginess of her acting was unbearable, and grew worse as she went on. Her gestures became absurdly artificial. She over-emphasized everything that she had to say. The beautiful passage,—

> Thou knowest the mask of night is on my face,
> Else would a maiden blush bepaint my cheek
> For that which thou hast heard me speak to-night,—

was declaimed with the painful precision of a school-girl who has been taught to recite by some second-rate professor of elocution.

When she leaned over the balcony and came to those wonderful
lines,—

> Although I joy in thee,
> I have no joy of this contract to-night:
> It is too rash, too unadvised, too sudden;
> Too like the lightning, which doth cease to be
> Ere one can say, "It lightens." Sweet, good-night!
> This bud of love by summer's ripening breath
> May prove a beauteous flower when next we meet,—

she spoke the words as if they conveyed no meaning to her. It was not
nervousness. Indeed, so far from being nervous, she seemed
absolutely self-contained. It was simply bad art. She was a complete
failure.

Even the common uneducated audience of the pit and gallery lost
their interest in the play. They got restless, and began to talk loudly
and to whistle. The Jew manager, who was standing at the back of the
dress-circle, stamped and swore with rage. The only person unmoved
was the girl herself.

When the second act was over there came a storm of hisses, and
Lord Henry got up from his chair and put on his coat. "She is quite
beautiful, Dorian," he said, "but she can't act. Let us go."

"I am going to see the play through," answered the lad, in a hard,
bitter voice. "I am awfully sorry that I have made you waste an evening, Harry. I apologize to both of you."

"My dear Dorian, I should think Miss Vane was ill," interrupted
Hallward. "We will come some other night."

"I wish she was ill," he rejoined. "But she seems to me to be simply callous and cold. She has entirely altered. Last night she was a
great artist. To-night she is merely a commonplace, mediocre
actress."

"Don't talk like that about any one you love, Dorian. Love is a more
wonderful thing than art."

"They are both simply forms of imitation," murmured Lord Henry.
"But do let us go. Dorian, you must not stay here any longer. It is not
good for one's morals to see bad acting. Besides, I don't suppose you
will want your wife to act. So what does it matter if she plays Juliet like
a wooden doll? She is very lovely, and if she knows as little about life
as she does about acting, she will be a delightful experience. There are
only two kinds of people who are really fascinating,—people who
know absolutely everything, and people who know absolutely nothing.
Good heavens, my dear boy, don't look so tragic! The secret of remaining young is never to have an emotion that is unbecoming. Come to
the club with Basil and myself. We will smoke cigarettes and drink to
the beauty of Sibyl Vane. She is beautiful. What more can you want?"

"Please go away, Harry," cried the lad. "I really want to be alone.—Basil, you don't mind my asking you to go? Ah! can't you see that my heart is breaking?" The hot tears came to his eyes. His lips trembled, and, rushing to the back of the box, he leaned up against the wall, hiding his face in his hands.

"Let us go, Basil," said Lord Henry, with a strange tenderness in his voice; and the two young men passed out together.

A few moments afterwards the footlights flared up, and the curtain rose on the third act. Dorian Gray went back to his seat. He looked pale, and proud, and indifferent. The play dragged on, and seemed interminable. Half of the audience went out, tramping in heavy boots, and laughing. The whole thing was a *fiasco*. The last act was played to almost empty benches.

As soon as it was over, Dorian Gray rushed behind the scenes into the greenroom. The girl was standing alone there, with a look of triumph on her face. Her eyes were lit with an exquisite fire. There was a radiance about her. Her parted lips were smiling over some secret of their own.

When he entered, she looked at him, and an expression of infinite joy came over her. "How badly I acted to-night, Dorian!" she cried.

"Horribly!" he answered, gazing at her in amazement,—"horribly! It was dreadful. Are you ill? You have no idea what it was. You have no idea what I suffered."

The girl smiled. "Dorian," she answered, lingering over his name with long-drawn music in her voice, as though it were sweeter than honey to the red petals of her lips,—"Dorian, you should have understood. But you understand now, don't you?"

"Understand what?" he asked, angrily.

"Why I was so bad to-night. Why I shall always be bad. Why I shall never act well again."

He shrugged his shoulders. "You are ill, I suppose. When you are ill you shouldn't act. You make yourself ridiculous. My friends were bored. I was bored."

She seemed not to listen to him. She was transfigured with joy. An ecstasy of happiness dominated her.

"Dorian, Dorian," she cried, "before I knew you, acting was the one reality of my life. It was only in the theatre that I lived. I thought that it was all true. I was Rosalind one night, and Portia the other. The joy of Beatrice was my joy, and the sorrows of Cordelia were mine also.[2] I believed in everything. The common people who acted with me seemed to me to be godlike. The painted scenes were my world. I

2. Wilde rewrote this line in TS, changing it from "If I died as Desdemona, I came back as Juliet."

knew nothing but shadows, and I thought them real. You came,—oh, my beautiful love!—and you freed my soul from prison. You taught me what reality really is. To-night, for the first time in my life, I saw through the hollowness, the sham, the silliness, of the empty pageant in which I had always played. To-night, for the first time, I became conscious that the Romeo was hideous, and old, and painted, that the moonlight in the orchard was false, that the scenery was vulgar, and that the words I had to speak were unreal, were not my words, not what I wanted to say. You had brought me something higher, something of which all art is but a reflection. You have made me understand what love really is. My love! my love! I am sick of shadows. You are more to me than all art can ever be. What have I to do with the puppets of a play? When I came on to-night, I could not understand how it was that everything had gone from me. Suddenly it dawned on my soul what it all meant. The knowledge was exquisite to me. I heard them hissing, and I smiled. What should they know of love? Take me away, Dorian—take me away with you, where we can be quite alone. I hate the stage. I might mimic a passion that I do not feel, but I cannot mimic one that burns me like fire. Oh, Dorian, Dorian, you understand now what it all means? Even if I could do it, it would be profanation for me to play at being in love. You have made me see that."

He flung himself down on the sofa, and turned away his face. "You have killed my love," he muttered.

She looked at him in wonder, and laughed. He made no answer. She came across to him, and stroked his hair with her little fingers. She knelt down and pressed his hands to her lips. He drew them away, and a shudder ran through him.

Then he leaped up, and went to the door. "Yes," he cried, "you have killed my love. You used to stir my imagination. Now you don't even stir my curiosity. You simply produce no effect. I loved you because you were wonderful, because you had genius and intellect, because you realized the dreams of great poets and gave shape and substance to the shadows of art. You have thrown it all away. You are shallow and stupid. My God! how mad I was to love you! What a fool I have been! You are nothing to me now. I will never see you again. I will never think of you. I will never mention your name. You don't know what you were to me, once. Why, once . . . Oh, I can't bear to think of it! I wish I had never laid eyes upon you! You have spoiled the romance of my life. How little you can know of love, if you say it mars your art! What are you without your art? Nothing. I would have made you famous, splendid, magnificent. The world would have worshipped you, and you would have belonged to me. What are you now? A third-rate actress with a pretty face."

The girl grew white, and trembled. She clinched her hands together, and her voice seemed to catch in her throat. "You are not serious, Dorian?" she murmured. "You are acting."

"Acting! I leave that to you. You do it so well," he answered, bitterly.

She rose from her knees, and, with a piteous expression of pain in her face, came across the room to him. She put her hand upon his arm, and looked into his eyes. He thrust her back. "Don't touch me!" he cried.

A low moan broke from her, and she flung herself at his feet, and lay there like a trampled flower. "Dorian, Dorian, don't leave me!" she whispered. "I am so sorry I didn't act well. I was thinking of you all the time. But I will try,—indeed, I will try. It came so suddenly across me, my love for you. I think I should never have known it if you had not kissed me,—if we had not kissed each other. Kiss me again, my love. Don't go away from me. I couldn't bear it.[3] Can't you forgive me for to-night? I will work so hard, and try to improve. Don't be cruel to me because I love you better than anything in the world. After all, it is only once that I have not pleased you. But you are quite right, Dorian. I should have shown myself more of an artist. It was foolish of me; and yet I couldn't help it. Oh, don't leave me, don't leave me." A fit of passionate sobbing choked her. She crouched on the floor like a wounded thing, and Dorian Gray, with his beautiful eyes, looked down at her, and his chiselled lips curled in exquisite disdain. There is always something ridiculous about the passions of people whom one has ceased to love. Sibyl Vane seemed to him to be absurdly melodramatic. Her tears and sobs annoyed him.

"I am going," he said at last, in his calm, clear voice. "I don't wish to be unkind, but I can't see you again. You have disappointed me."

She wept silently, and made no answer, but crept nearer to him. Her little hands stretched blindly out, and appeared to be seeking for him.[4] He turned on his heel, and left the room. In a few moments he was out of the theatre.

Where he went to, he hardly knew. He remembered wandering through dimly-lit streets with gaunt black-shadowed archways and evil-looking houses. Women with hoarse voices and harsh laughter had called after him. Drunkards had reeled by cursing, and chattering to themselves like monstrous apes.[5] He had seen grotesque children huddled upon door-steps, and had heard shrieks and oaths from gloomy courts.

3. Wilde added foreshadowing here in 1891.
4. This sentence added in TS.
5. Wilde wrote in TS, then crossed out the following lines: "A man with curious eyes had suddenly peered into his face and then dogged him with stealthy footsteps, passing and repassing him many times." It is likely that Sibyl's avenging brother, James, added in 1891, may have originated in these lines.

When the dawn was just breaking, he found himself at Covent Garden. Huge carts filled with nodding lilies rumbled slowly down the polished empty street. The air was heavy with the perfume of the flowers, and their beauty seemed to bring him an anodyne for his pain. He followed into the market, and watched the men unloading their wagons. A white-smocked carter offered him some cherries. He thanked him, wondered why he refused to accept any money for them, and began to eat them listlessly. They had been plucked at midnight, and the coldness of the moon had entered into them. A long line of boys carrying crates of striped tulips, and of yellow and red roses, defiled in front of him, threading their way through the huge jade-green piles of vegetables. Under the portico, with its gray sunbleached pillars, loitered a troop of draggled bareheaded girls, waiting for the auction to be over.[6] After some time he hailed a hansom and drove home. The sky was pure opal now, and the roofs of the houses glistened like silver against it.[7] As he was passing through the library towards the door of his bedroom, his eye fell upon the portrait Basil Hallward had painted of him. He started back in surprise,[8] and then went over to it and examined it. In the dim arrested light that struggled through the cream-colored silk blinds, the face seemed to him to be a little changed. The expression looked different. One would have said that there was a touch of cruelty in the mouth. It was certainly curious.

He turned round, and, walking to the window, drew the blinds up. The bright dawn flooded the room, and swept the fantastic shadows into dusky corners, where they lay shuddering. But the strange expression that he had noticed in the face of the portrait seemed to linger there, to be more intensified even. The quivering, ardent sunlight showed him the lines of cruelty round the mouth as clearly as if he had been looking into a mirror after he had done some dreadful thing.

He winced, and, taking up from the table an oval glass framed in ivory Cupids, that Lord Henry had given him, he glanced hurriedly into it. No line like that warped his red lips. What did it mean?

He rubbed his eyes, and came close to the picture, and examined it again. There were no signs of change when he looked into the actual painting, and yet there was no doubt that the whole expression had altered. It was not a mere fancy of his own. The thing was horribly apparent.

6. "A long line . . . to be over" added in TS.
7. This sentence also added in TS. Wilde expanded and revised the rest of the paragraph in 1891.
8. In MS, the following lines were canceled at this point: "then he smiled to himself and went on into his bedroom. 'It is merely an effect of light,' he murmured. 'I did not know that the dawn was so unbecoming.'"

He threw himself into a chair, and began to think. Suddenly there flashed across his mind what he had said in Basil Hallward's studio the day the picture had been finished. Yes, he remembered it perfectly. He had uttered a mad wish that he himself might remain young, and the portrait grow old; that his own beauty might be untarnished, and the face on the canvas bear the burden of his passions and his sins; that the painted image might be seared with the lines of suffering and thought, and that he might keep all the delicate bloom and loveliness of his then just conscious boyhood. Surely his prayer had not been answered? Such things were impossible. It seemed monstrous even to think of them. And, yet, there was the picture before him, with the touch of cruelty in the mouth.

Cruelty! Had he been cruel? It was the girl's fault, not his. He had dreamed of her as a great artist, had given his love to her because he had thought her great. Then she had disappointed him. She had been shallow and unworthy. And, yet, a feeling of infinite regret came over him, as he thought of her lying at his feet sobbing like a little child. He remembered with what callousness he had watched her. Why had he been made like that? Why had such a soul been given to him? But he had suffered also. During the three terrible hours that the play had lasted, he had lived centuries of pain, æon upon æon of torture. His life was well worth hers. She had marred him for a moment, if he had wounded her for an age. Besides, women were better suited to bear sorrow than men. They lived on their emotions. They only thought of their emotions. When they took lovers, it was merely to have some one with whom they could have scenes. Lord Henry had told him that, and Lord Henry knew what women were. Why should he trouble about Sibyl Vane? She was nothing to him now.

But the picture? What was he to say of that?[9] It held the secret of his life, and told his story. It had taught him to love his own beauty. Would it teach him to loathe his own soul? Would he ever look at it again?

No; it was merely an illusion wrought on the troubled senses. The horrible night that he had passed had left phantoms behind it. Suddenly there had fallen upon his brain that tiny scarlet speck that makes men mad. The picture had not changed. It was folly to think so.

Yet it was watching him, with its beautiful marred face and its cruel smile. Its bright hair gleamed in the early sunlight. Its blue eyes met his own. A sense of infinite pity, not for himself, but for the painted image of himself, came over him. It had altered already, and would

9. Wilde canceled the following in TS: "Where was he to hide it? It could not be left for common eyes to gaze at."

alter more. Its gold would wither into gray. Its red and white roses would die. For every sin that he committed, a stain would fleck and wreck its fairness. But he would not sin. The picture, changed or unchanged, would be to him the visible emblem of conscience. He would resist temptation. He would not see Lord Henry any more—would not, at any rate, listen to those subtle poisonous theories that in Basil Hallward's garden had first stirred within him the passion for impossible things. He would go back to Sibyl Vane, make her amends, marry her, try to love her again. Yes, it was his duty to do so. She must have suffered more than he had. Poor child! He had been selfish and cruel to her. The fascination that she had exercised over him would return. They would be happy together. His life with her would be beautiful and pure.

He got up from his chair, and drew a large screen right in front of the portrait, shuddering as he glanced at it. "How horrible!" he murmured to himself, and he walked across to the window and opened it. When he stepped out on the grass, he drew a deep breath. The fresh morning air seemed to drive away all his sombre passions. He thought only of Sibyl Vane. A faint echo of his love came back to him. He repeated her name over and over again. The birds that were singing in the dew-drenched garden seemed to be telling the flowers about her.

Chapter VI

It was long past noon when he awoke. His valet had crept several times into the room on tiptoe to see if he was stirring, and had wondered what made his young master sleep so late. Finally his bell sounded, and Victor came in softly with a cup of tea, and a pile of letters, on a small tray of old Sèvres china, and drew back the olive-satin curtains, with their shimmering blue lining, that hung in front of the three tall windows.

"Monsieur has well slept this morning," he said, smiling.

"What o'clock is it, Victor?"[1] asked Dorian Gray, sleepily.

"One hour and a quarter, monsieur."

How late it was! He sat up, and, having sipped some tea, turned over his letters. One of them was from Lord Henry, and had been brought by hand that morning. He hesitated for a moment, and then put it aside. The others he opened listlessly. They contained the usual collection of cards, invitations to dinner, tickets for private

---

1. In MS the valet was named Jacques. The conversation was in French, as it was whenever Dorian and Jacques spoke. Wilde changed this to English in stages: first, Dorian's speech in MS, then the name of the valet and his dialogue.

views, programmes of charity concerts, and the like, that are showered on fashionable young men every morning during the season.
There was a rather heavy bill, for a chased silver Louis-Quinze toilet-
set, that he had not yet had the courage to send on to his guardians,
who were extremely old-fashioned people and did not realize that we
live in an age when only unnecessary things are absolutely necessary
to us; and there were several very courteously worded communications from Jermyn Street money-lenders offering to advance any
sum of money at a moment's notice and at the most reasonable rates
of interest.

After about ten minutes he got up, and, throwing on an elaborate
dressing-gown, passed into the onyx-paved bath-room. The cool
water refreshed him after his long sleep. He seemed to have forgotten all that he had gone through. A dim sense of having taken part in
some strange tragedy came to him once of twice, but there was the
unreality of a dream about it.

As soon as he was dressed, he went into the library and sat down
to a light French breakfast, that had been laid out for him on a small
round table close to an open window. It was an exquisite day. The
warm air seemed laden with spices. A bee flew in, and buzzed round
the blue-dragon bowl, filled with sulphur-yellow roses, that stood in
front of him. He felt perfectly happy.

Suddenly his eye fell on the screen that he had placed in front of
the portrait, and he started.

"Too cold for Monsieur?" asked his valet, putting an omelette on
the table. "I shut the window?"

Dorian shook his head. "I am not cold," he murmured.

Was it all true? Had the portrait really changed? Or had it been
simply his own imagination that had made him see a look of evil
where there had been a look of joy? Surely a painted canvas could not
alter? The thing was absurd. It would serve as a tale to tell Basil some
day. It would make him smile.

And, yet, how vivid was his recollection of the whole thing! First in
the dim twilight, and then in the bright dawn, he had seen the touch
of cruelty in the warped lips. He almost dreaded his valet leaving the
room. He knew that when he was alone he would have to examine the
portrait. He was afraid of certainty. When the coffee and cigarettes
had been brought and the man turned to go, he felt a mad desire to
tell him to remain. As the door closed behind him he called him back.
The man stood waiting for his orders. Dorian looked at him for a
moment. "I am not at home to any one, Victor," he said, with a sigh.
The man bowed and retired.

He rose from the table, lit a cigarette, and flung himself down on
a luxuriously-cushioned couch that stood facing the screen. The
screen was an old one of gilt Spanish leather, stamped and wrought

with a rather florid Louis-Quatorze pattern. He scanned it curiously, wondering if it had ever before concealed the secret of a man's life.

Should he move it aside, after all? Why not let it stay there? What was the use of knowing? If the thing was true, it was terrible. If it was not true, why trouble about it? But what if, by some fate or deadlier chance, other eyes than his spied behind, and saw the horrible change? What should he do if Basil Hallward came and asked to look at his own picture? He would be sure to do that. No; the thing had to be examined, and at once. Anything would be better than this dreadful state of doubt.

He got up, and locked both doors. At least he would be alone when he looked upon the mask of his shame. Then he drew the screen aside, and saw himself face to face. It was perfectly true. The portrait had altered.

As he often remembered afterwards, and always with no small wonder, he found himself at first gazing at the portrait with a feeling of almost scientific interest.[2] That such a change should have taken place was incredible to him. And yet it was a fact. Was there some subtle affinity between the chemical atoms, that shaped themselves into form and color on the canvas, and the soul that was within him? Could it be that what that soul thought, they realized?— that what it dreamed, they made true? Or was there some other, more terrible reason? He shuddered, and felt afraid, and, going back to the couch, lay there, gazing at the picture in sickened horror.[3]

One thing, however, he felt that it had done for him. It had made him conscious how unjust, how cruel, he had been to Sibyl Vane. It was not too late to make reparation for that. She could still be his wife. His unreal and selfish love would yield to some higher influence, would be transformed into some nobler passion, and the portrait that Basil Hallward had painted of him would be a guide to him through life, would be to him what holiness was to some, and conscience to others, and the fear of God to us all. There were opiates for remorse, drugs that could lull the moral sense to sleep. But here was a visible symbol of the degradation of sin. Here was an ever-present sign of the ruin men brought upon their souls.

Three o'clock struck, and four, and half-past four, but he did not stir. He was trying to gather up the scarlet threads of life, and to weave them into a pattern; to find his way through the sanguine labyrinth of passion through which he was wandering. He did not know what to do, or what to think.[4] Finally, he went over to the table

---

2. Originally, the MS read, "He was strangely calm at this moment."
3. Wilde added the last two sentences of this paragraph in TS.
4. Wilde added to TS the first three sentences of this paragraph.

and wrote a passionate letter to the girl he had loved, imploring her forgiveness, and accusing himself of madness. He covered page after page with wild words of sorrow, and wilder words of pain.[5] There is a luxury in self-reproach. When we blame ourselves we feel that no one else has a right to blame us. It is the confession, not the priest, that gives us absolution. When Dorian Gray had finished the letter, he felt that he had been forgiven.

Suddenly there came a knock to the door, and he heard Lord Henry's voice outside. "My dear Dorian, I must see you. Let me in at once. I can't bear your shutting yourself up like this."

He made no answer at first, but remained quite still. The knocking still continued, and grew louder. Yes, it was better to let Lord Henry in, and to[6] explain to him the new life he was going to lead, to quarrel with him if it became necessary to quarrel, to part if parting was inevitable. He jumped up, drew the screen hastily across the picture, and unlocked the door.

"I am so sorry for it all, my dear boy," said Lord Henry, coming in. "But you must not think about it too much."

"Do you mean about Sibyl Vane?" asked Dorian.

"Yes, of course," answered Lord Henry, sinking into a chair, and slowly pulling his gloves off. "It is dreadful, from one point of view, but it was not your fault.[7] Tell me, did you go behind and see her after the play was over?"

"Yes."

"I felt sure you had. Did you make a scene with her?"

"I was brutal, Harry,—perfectly brutal. But it is all right now. I am not sorry for anything that has happened. It has taught me to know myself better."

"Ah, Dorian, I am so glad you take it in that way! I was afraid I would find you plunged in remorse, and tearing your nice hair."

"I have got through all that," said Dorian, shaking his head, and smiling. "I am perfectly happy now. I know what conscience is, to begin with. It is not what you told me it was. It is the divinest thing in us. Don't sneer at it, Harry, any more,—at least not before me. I want to be good. I can't bear the idea of my soul being hideous."

"A very charming artistic basis for ethics, Dorian! I congratulate you on it. But how are you going to begin?"

"By marrying Sibyl Vane."

"Marrying Sibyl Vane!" cried Lord Henry, standing up, and looking at him in perplexed amazement. "But, my dear Dorian—"

---

5. This sentence added in TS.
6. TS originally read "to sever their friendship at once."
7. Wilde canceled in TS the following: "And besides, no one knows that you were at the theatre last night." The *Lippincott's* text misprinted "slowing pulling his gloves off."

"Yes, Harry, I know what you are going to say. Something dreadful about marriage. Don't say it. Don't ever say things of that kind to me again. Two days ago I asked Sibyl to marry me. I am not going to break my word to her. She is to be my wife."

"Your wife! Dorian! . . . Didn't you get my letter? I wrote to you this morning, and sent the note down, by my own man."

"Your letter? Oh, yes, I remember. I have not read it yet, Harry. I was afraid there might be something in it that I wouldn't like."

Lord Henry walked across the room, and, sitting down by Dorian Gray, took both his hands in his, and held them tightly. "Dorian," he said, "my letter—don't be frightened—was to tell you that Sibyl Vane is dead."

A cry of pain rose from the lad's lips, and he leaped to his feet, tearing his hands away from Lord Henry's grasp. "Dead! Sibyl dead! It is not true! It is a horrible lie!"

"It is quite true, Dorian," said Lord Henry, gravely. "It is in all the morning papers. I wrote down to you to ask you not to see any one till I came. There will have to be an inquest, of course, and you must not be mixed up in it. Things like that make a man fashionable in Paris. But in London people are so prejudiced. Here, one should never make one's *début* with a scandal. One should reserve that to give an interest to one's old age. I don't suppose they know your name at the theatre. If they don't, it is all right. Did any one see you going round to her room? That is an important point."

Dorian did not answer for a few moments. He was dazed with horror. Finally he murmured, in a stifled voice, "Harry, did you say an inquest? What did you mean by that? Did Sibyl—? Oh, Harry, I can't bear it! But be quick. Tell me everything at once."

"I have no doubt it was not an accident, Dorian, though it must be put in that way to the public. As she was leaving the theatre with her mother, about half-past twelve or so, she said she had forgotten something up-stairs. They waited some time for her, but she did not come down again. They ultimately found her lying dead on the floor of her dressing-room. She had swallowed something by mistake, some dreadful thing they use at theatres. I don't know what it was, but it had either prussic acid or white lead in it. I should fancy it was prussic acid, as she seems to have died instantaneously. It is very tragic, of course, but you must not get yourself mixed up in it. I see by the *Standard* that she was seventeen. I should have thought she was almost younger than that. She looked such a child, and seemed to know so little about acting. Dorian, you mustn't let this thing get on your nerves. You must come and dine with me, and afterwards we will look in at the Opera. It is a Patti night, and everybody will be there. You can come to my sister's box. She has got some smart women with her."

"So I have murdered Sibyl Vane," said Dorian Gray, half to himself,—"murdered her as certainly as if I had cut her little throat with a knife. And the roses are not less lovely for all that. The birds sing just as happily in my garden. And to-night I am to dine with you, and then go on to the Opera, and sup somewhere I suppose, afterwards. How extraordinarily dramatic life is! If I had read all this in a book, Harry, I think I would have wept over it. Somehow, now that it has happened actually, and to me, it seems far too wonderful for tears. Here is the first passionate love-letter I have ever written in my life. Strange, that my first passionate love-letter should have been addressed to a dead girl. Can they feel, I wonder, those white silent people we call the dead? Sibyl! Can she feel, or know, or listen? Oh, Harry, how I loved her once! It seems years ago to me now. She was everything to me. Then came that dreadful night—was it really only last night?—when she played so badly, and my heart almost broke. She explained it all to me. It was terribly pathetic. But I was not moved a bit. I thought her shallow. Then something happened that made me afraid. I can't tell you what it was, but it was awful. I said I would go back to her. I felt I had done wrong. And now she is dead. My God! my God! Harry, what shall I do? You don't know the danger I am in, and there is nothing to keep me straight. She would have done that for me. She had no right to kill herself. It was selfish of her."

"My dear Dorian, the only way a woman can ever reform a man is by boring him so completely that he loses all possible interest in life. If you had married this girl you would have been wretched. Of course you would have treated her kindly. One can always be kind to people about whom one cares nothing. But she would have soon found out that you were absolutely indifferent to her. And when a woman finds that out about her husband, she either becomes dreadfully dowdy, or wears very smart bonnets that some other woman's husband has to pay for. I say nothing about the social mistake, but I assure you that in any case the whole thing would have been an absolute failure."

"I suppose it would," muttered the lad, walking up and down the room, and looking horribly pale. "But I thought it was my duty. It is not my fault that this terrible tragedy has prevented my doing what was right. I remember your saying once that there is a fatality about good resolutions—that they are always made too late. Mine certainly were."

"Good resolutions are simply a useless attempt to interfere with scientific laws. Their origin is pure vanity. Their result is absolutely *nil*. They give us, now and then, some of those luxurious sterile emotions that have a certain charm for us. That is all that can be said for them."

"Harry," cried Dorian Gray, coming over and sitting down beside

him, "why is it that I cannot feel this tragedy as much as I want to? I
don't think I am heartless. Do you?"

"You have done too many foolish things in your life[8] to be entitled
to give yourself that name, Dorian," answered Lord Henry, with his
sweet, melancholy smile.

The lad frowned. "I don't like that explanation, Harry," he rejoined,
"but I am glad you don't think I am heartless. I am nothing of the
kind. I know I am not. And yet I must admit that this thing that has
happened does not affect me as it should. It seems to me to be simply like a wonderful ending to a wonderful play. It has all the terrible
beauty of a great tragedy, in which I took part, a tragedy, but by which
I have not been wounded."

"It is an interesting question," said Lord Henry, who found an
exquisite pleasure in playing on the lad's unconscious egotism,—"an
extremely interesting question. I fancy that the explanation is this. It
often happens that the real tragedies of life occur in such an inartistic manner that they hurt us by their crude violence, their absolute
incoherence, their absurd want of meaning, their entire lack of style.
They affect us just as vulgarity affects us. They give us an impression
of sheer brute force, and we revolt against that. Sometimes, however,
a tragedy that has artistic elements of beauty crosses our lives. If
these elements of beauty are real, the whole thing simply appeals to
our sense of dramatic effect. Suddenly we find that we are no longer
the actors but the spectators of the play. Or rather we are both. We
watch ourselves, and the mere wonder of the spectacle enthralls us.
In the present case, what is it that has really happened? Some one
has killed herself for love of you. I wish I had ever had such an experience. It would have made me in love with love for the rest of my life.
The people who have adored me—there have not been very many, but
there have been some—have always insisted on living on, long after
I had ceased to care for them, or they to care for me. They have
become stout and tedious, and when I meet them they go in at once
for reminiscences. That awful memory of woman! What a fearful
thing it is! And what an utter intellectual stagnation it reveals! One
should absorb the color of life, but one should never remember its
details. Details are always vulgar.

"Of course, now and then things linger. I once wore nothing but
violets all through one season, as mourning for a romance that
would not die. Ultimately, however, it did die. I forget what killed it.
I think it was her proposing to sacrifice the whole world for me. That
is always a dreadful moment. It fills one with the terror of eternity.
Well,—would you believe it?—a week ago, at Lady Hampshire's, I
found myself seated at dinner next the lady in question, and she

8. Wilde made a change here in 1891.

insisted on going over the whole thing again, and digging up the past, and raking up the future. I had buried my romance in a bed of poppies. She dragged it out again, and assured me that I had spoiled her life. I am bound to state that she ate an enormous dinner, so I did not feel any anxiety. But what a lack of taste she showed! The one charm of the past is that it is the past. But women never know when the curtain has fallen. They always want a sixth act, and as soon as the interest of the play is entirely over they propose to continue it. If they were allowed to have their way, every comedy would have a tragic ending, and every tragedy would culminate in a farce. They are charmingly artificial, but they have no sense of art. You are more fortunate than I am. I assure you, Dorian, that not one of the women I have known would have done for me what Sibyl Vane did for you. Ordinary women always console themselves. Some of them do it by going in for sentimental colors. Never trust a woman who wears mauve, whatever her age may be, or a woman over thirty-five who is fond of pink ribbons. It always means that they have a history. Others find a great consolation in suddenly discovering the good qualities of their husbands. They flaunt their conjugal felicity in one's face, as if it was the most fascinating sins. Religion consoles some. Its mysteries have all the charm of a flirtation, a woman once told me; and I can quite understand it. Besides, nothing makes one so vain as being told that one is a sinner. There is really no end to the consolations that women find in modern life. Indeed, I have not mentioned the most important one of all."

"What is that, Harry?" said Dorian Gray, listlessly.

"Oh, the obvious one. Taking some one else's admirer when one loses one's own. In good society that always whitewashes a woman. But really, Dorian, how different Sibyl Vane must have been from all the women one meets! There is something to me quite beautiful about her death. I am glad I am living in a century when such wonders happen. They make one believe in the reality of the things that shallow, fashionable people play with, such as romance, passion, and love."

"I was terribly cruel to her. You forget that."

"I believe that women appreciate cruelty more than anything else. They have wonderfully primitive instincts. We have emancipated them, but they remain slaves looking for their masters, all the same. They love being dominated. I am sure you were splendid. I have never seen you angry, but I can fancy how delightful you looked. And, after all, you said something to me the day before yesterday that seemed to me at the time to be merely fanciful, but that I see now was absolutely true, and it explains everything."

"What was that, Harry?"

"You said to me that Sibyl Vane represented to you all the heroines of romance—that she was Desdemona one night, and Ophelia the other; that if she died as Juliet, she came to life as Imogen."

"She will never come to life again now," murmured the lad, buying his face in his hands.

"No, she will never come to life. She has played her last part. But you must think of that lonely death in the tawdry dressing-room simply as a strange lurid fragment from some Jacobean tragedy, as a wonderful scene from Webster, or Ford, or Cyril Tourneur. The girl never really lived, and so she has never really died. To you at least she was always a dream, a phantom that flitted through Shakespeare's plays and left them lovelier for its presence, a reed through which Shakespeare's music sounded richer and more full of joy. The moment she touched actual life, she marred it, and it marred her, and so she passed away. Mourn for Ophelia, if you like. Put ashes on your head because Cordelia was strangled. Cry out against Heaven because the daughter of Brabantio died. But don't waste your tears over Sibyl Vane. She was less real than they are."

There was a silence. The evening darkened in the room. Noiselessly, and with silver feet, the shadows crept in from the garden. The colors faded wearily out of things.

After some time Dorian Gray looked up. "You have explained me to myself, Harry," he murmured, with something of a sigh of relief. "I felt all that you have said, but somehow I was afraid of it, and I could not express it to myself. How well you know me! But we will not talk again of what has happened. It has been a marvellous experience. That is all. I wonder if life has still in store for me anything as marvellous."

"Life has everything in store for you, Dorian. There is nothing that you, with your extraordinary good looks, will not be able to do."

"But suppose, Harry, I became haggard, and gray, and wrinkled? What then?"

"Ah, then," said Lord Henry, rising to go,—"then, my dear Dorian, you would have to fight for your victories. As it is, they are brought to you. No, you must keep your good looks. We live in an age that reads too much to be wise, and that thinks too much to be beautiful. We cannot spare you. And now you had better dress, and drive down to the club. We are rather late, as it is."

"I think I shall join you at the Opera, Harry. I feel too tired to eat anything. What is the number of your sister's box?"

"Twenty-seven, I believe. It is on the grand tier. You will see her name on the door. But I am sorry you won't come and dine."

"I don't feel up to it," said Dorian, wearily. "But I am awfully obliged to you for all that you have said to me. You are certainly my best friend. No one has ever understood me as you have."

"We are only at the beginning of our friendship, Dorian," answered

Lord Henry, shaking him by the hand. "Good-by. I shall see you before nine-thirty, I hope. Remember, Patti is singing."

As he closed the door behind him, Dorian Gray touched the bell, and in a few minutes Victor appeared with the lamps and drew the blinds down. He waited impatiently for him to go. The man seemed to take an interminable time about everything.

As soon as he had left, he rushed to the screen, and drew it back. No; there was no further change in the picture. It had received the news of Sibyl Vane's death before he had known of it himself. It was conscious of the events of life as they occurred. The vicious cruelty that marred the fine lines of the mouth had, no doubt, appeared at the very moment that the girl had drunk the poison, whatever it was. Or was it indifferent to results? Did it merely take cognizance of what passed within the soul? he wondered, and hoped that some day he would see the change taking place before his very eyes, shuddering as he hoped it.

Poor Sibyl! what a romance it had all been! She had often mimicked death on the stage, and at last Death himself had touched her, and brought her with him. How had she played that dreadful scene? Had she cursed him, as she died? No; she had died for love of him, and love would always be a sacrament to him now. She had atoned for everything, by the sacrifice she had made of her life. He would not think any more of what she had made him go through, that horrible night at the theatre. When he thought of her, it would be as a wonderful tragic figure to show Love had been a great reality. A wonderful tragic figure? Tears came to his eyes as he remembered her child-like look and winsome fanciful ways and shy tremulous grace. He wiped them away hastily, and looked again at the picture.[9]

He felt that the time had really come for making his choice. Or had his choice already been made? Yes, life had decided that for him,— life, and his own infinite curiosity about life. Eternal youth, infinite passion, pleasures subtle and secret, wild joys and wilder sins,—he was to have all these things. The portrait was to bear the burden of his shame: that was all.

A feeling of pain came over him as he thought of the desecration that was in store for the fair face on the canvas. Once, in boyish mockery of Narcissus, he had kissed, or feigned to kiss, those painted lips that now smiled so cruelly at him. Morning after morning he had sat before the portrait wondering at its beauty, almost enamoured of it, as it seemed to him at times. Was it to alter now with every mood to which he yielded? Was it to become a hideous and loathsome thing, to be hidden away in a locked room, to be shut out from the

9. This paragraph added in TS.

sunlight that had so often touched to brighter gold the waving wonder of the hair? The pity of it! the pity of it!

For a moment he thought of praying that the horrible sympathy
that existed between him and the picture might cease. It had changed
in answer to a prayer; perhaps in answer to a prayer it might remain
unchanged. And, yet, who, that knew anything about Life, would surrender the chance of remaining always young, however fantastic that
chance might be, or with what fateful consequences it might be
fraught? Besides, was it really under his control? Had it indeed been
prayer that had produced the substitution? Might there not be some
curious scientific reason for it all? If thought could exercise its influence upon a living organism, might not thought exercise an influence
upon dead and inorganic things? Nay, without thought or conscious
desire, might not things external to ourselves vibrate in unison with
our moods and passions, atom calling to atom, in secret love or
strange affinity? But the reason was of no importance. He would
never again tempt by a prayer any terrible power. If the picture was
to alter, it was to alter. That was all. Why inquire too closely into it?[1]

For there would be a real pleasure in watching it. He would be able
to follow his mind into its secret places. This portrait would be to him
the most magical of mirrors. As it had revealed to him him own body,
so it would reveal to him his own soul. And when winter came upon
it, he would still be standing where spring trembles on the verge of
summer. When the blood crept from its face, and left behind a pallid mask of chalk with leaden eyes, he would keep the glamour of boyhood. Not one blossom of his loveliness would ever fade. Not one
pulse of his life would ever weaken. Like the gods of the Greeks, he
would be strong, and fleet, and joyous. What did it matter what happened to the colored image on the canvas? He would be safe. That
was everything.

He drew the screen back into its former place in front of the picture, smiling as he did so, and passed into his bedroom, where his
valet was already waiting for him. An hour later he was at the Opera,
and Lord Henry was leaning over his chair.

Chapter VII

As he was sitting at breakfast next morning, Basil Hallward was
shown into the room.

"I am so glad I have found you, Dorian," he said, gravely. "I called
last night, and they told me you were at the Opera. Of course I knew

1. This paragraph added in TS.

that was impossible. But I wish you had left word where you had really gone to. I passed a dreadful evening, half afraid that one tragedy might be followed by another. I think you might have telegraphed for me when you heard of it first. I read of it quite by chance in a late edition of the *Globe,* that I picked up at the club. I came here at once, and was miserable at not finding you. I can't tell you how heartbroken I am about the whole thing. I know what you must suffer. But where were you? Did you go down and see the girl's mother? For a moment I thought of following you there. They gave the address in the paper. Somewhere in the Euston Road, isn't it? But I was afraid of intruding upon a sorrow that I could not lighten. Poor woman! What a state she must be in! And her only child, too![1] What did she say about it all?"

"My dear Basil, how do I know?" murmured Dorian, sipping some pale-yellow wine from a delicate gold-beaded bubble of Venetian glass, and looking dreadfully bored. "I was at the Opera. You should have come on there. I met Lady Gwendolen, Harry's sister, for the first time. We were in her box. She is perfectly charming; and Patti sang divinely. Don't talk about horrid subjects. If one doesn't talk about a thing, it has never happened. It is simply expression, as Harry says, that gives reality to things. Tell me about yourself and what you are painting."

"You went to the Opera?" said Hallward, speaking very slowly, and with a strained touch of pain in his voice. "You went to the Opera while Sibyl Vane was lying dead in some sordid lodging? You can talk to me of other women being charming, and of Patti singing divinely, before the girl you loved has even the quiet of a grave to sleep in? Why, man, there are horrors in store for that little white body of hers!"

"Stop, Basil! I won't hear it!" cried Dorian, leaping to his feet. "You must not tell me about things. What is done is done. What is past is past."

"You call yesterday the past?"

"What has the actual lapse of time got to do with it? It is only shallow people who require years to get rid of an emotion. A man who is master of himself can end a sorrow as easily as he can invent a pleasure. I don't want to be at the mercy of my emotions. I want to use them, to enjoy them, and to dominate them."

"Dorian, this is horrible! Something has changed you completely. You look exactly the same wonderful boy who used to come down to my studio, day after day, to sit for his picture. But you were simple,

---

1. Wilde let this stand in 1891, but added Dorian's reply below that Sibyl had a brother (an invention of the revised edition; see p. 90).

natural, and affectionate then. You were the most unspoiled creature in the whole world. Now, I don't know what has come over you. You talk as if you had no heart, no pity in you. It is all Harry's influence. I see that."

The lad flushed up, and, going to the window, looked out on the green, flickering garden for a few moments. "I owe a great deal to Harry, Basil," he said, at last,—"more than I owe to you. You only taught me to be vain."

"Well, I am punished for that, Dorian,—or shall be some day."

"I don't know what you mean, Basil," he exclaimed, turning round. "I don't know what you want. What do you want?"

"I want the Dorian Gray I used to know."

"Basil," said the lad, going over to him, and putting his hand on his shoulder, "you have come too late. Yesterday when I heard that Sibyl Vane had killed herself—"

"Killed herself! Good heavens! is there no doubt about that?" cried Hallward, looking up at him with an expression of horror.

"My dear Basil! Surely you don't think it was a vulgar accident? Of course she killed herself.[2] It is one of the great romantic tragedies of the age. As a rule, people who act lead the most commonplace lives. They are good husbands, or faithful wives, or something tedious. You know what I mean,—middle-class virtue, and all that kind of thing. How different Sibyl was! She lived her finest tragedy. She was always a heroine. The last night she played—the night you saw her—she acted badly because she had known the reality of love. When she knew its unreality, she died, as Juliet might have died. She passed again into the sphere of art. There is something of the martyr about her. Her death has all the pathetic uselessness of martyrdom, all its wasted beauty. But, as I was saying, you must not think I have not suffered. If you had come in yesterday at a particular moment,—about half-past five, perhaps, or a quarter to six,—you would have found me in tears. Even Harry, who was here, who brought me the news, in fact, had no idea what I was going through. I suffered immensely, then it passed away. I cannot repeat an emotion. No one can, except sentimentalists. And you are awfully unjust, Basil. You come down here to console me. That is charming of you. You find me consoled, and you are furious. How like a sympathetic person! You remind me of a story Harry told me about a certain philanthropist who spent twenty years of his life in trying to get some grievance redressed, or some unjust law altered,—I forget exactly what it was. Finally he succeeded, and nothing could exceed his disappointment. He had absolutely nothing to do, almost died of *ennui*, and became a con-

2. Wilde added lines here in 1891.

firmed misanthrope. And besides, my dear old Basil, if you really want
to console me, teach me rather to forget what has happened, or to see
it from a proper artistic point of view. Was it not Gautier who used to
write about *la consolation des arts*? I remember picking up a little
vellum-covered book in your studio one day and chancing on that
delightful phrase. Well, I am not like that young man you told me of
when we were down at Marlowe together, the young man who used
to say that yellow satin could console one for all the miseries of life.
I love beautiful things that one can touch and handle. Old brocades,
green bronzes, lacquer-work, carved ivories, exquisite surroundings,
luxury, pomp,—there is much to be got from all these. But the artistic temperament that they create, or at any rate reveal, is still more
to me. To become the spectator of one's own life, as Harry says, is to
escape the suffering of life. I know you are surprised at my talking to
you like this. You have not realized how I have developed. I was a
school-boy when you knew me. I am a man now. I have new passions,
new thoughts, new ideas. I am different, but you must not like me
less. I am changed, but you must always be my friend. Of course I am
very fond of Harry. But I know that you are better than he is. You are
not stronger,—you are too much afraid of life,—but you are better.
And how happy we used to be together! Don't leave me, Basil, and
don't quarrel with me. I am what I am. There is nothing more to be
said."

Hallward felt strangely moved. Rugged and straightforward as he
was, there was something in his nature that was purely feminine in
its tenderness.[3] The lad was infinitely dear to him, and his personality had been the great turning-point in his art. He could not bear the
idea of reproaching him any more. After all, his indifference was
probably merely a mood that would pass away. There was so much in
him that was good, so much in him that was noble.

"Well, Dorian," he said, at length, with a sad smile, "I won't speak
to you again about this horrible thing, after to-day. I only trust your
name won't be mentioned in connection with it. The inquest is to
take place this afternoon. Have they summoned you?"

Dorian shook his head, and a look of annoyance passed over his
face at the mention of the word "inquest." There was something so
crude and vulgar about everything of the kind. "They don't know my
name," he answered.

"But surely she did?"

"Only my Christian name, and that I am quite sure she never mentioned to any one. She told me once that they were all rather curious
to learn who I was, and that she invariably told them my name was

3. This sentence deleted in 1891.

Prince Charming. It was pretty of her. You must do me a drawing of her, Basil. I should like to have something more of her than the memory of a few kisses and some broken pathetic words."

"I will try and do something, Dorian, if it would please you. But you must come and sit to me yourself again. I can't get on without you."

"I will never sit to you again, Basil. It is impossible!" he exclaimed, starting back.

Hallward stared at him, "My dear boy, what nonsense!" he cried. "Do you mean to say you don't like what I did of you? Where is it? Why have you pulled the screen in front of it? Let me look at it. It is the best thing I have ever painted. Do take that screen away, Dorian. It is simply horrid of your servant hiding my work like that. I felt the room looked different as I came in."

"My servant has nothing to do with it, Basil. You don't imagine I let him arrange my room for me? He settles my flowers for me sometimes,—that is all. No; I did it myself. The light was too strong on the portrait."

"Too strong! Impossible, my dear fellow! It is an admirable place for it. Let me see it." And Hallward walked towards the corner of the room.

A cry of terror broke from Dorian Gray's lips, and he rushed between Hallward and the screen. "Basil," he said, looking very pale, "you must not look at it. I don't wish you to."

"Not look at my own work! you are not serious. Why shouldn't I look at it?" exclaimed Hallward, laughing.

"If you try to look at it, Basil, on my word of honor I will never speak to you again as long as I live. I am quite serious. I don't offer any explanation, and you are not to ask for any. But, remember, if you touch this screen, everything is over between us."

Hallward was thunderstruck. He looked at Dorian Gray in absolute amazement. He had never seen him like this before. The lad was absolutely pallid with rage. His hands were clinched, and the pupils of his eyes were like disks of blue fire. He was trembling all over.

"Dorian!"

"Don't speak!"

"But what is the matter? Of course I won't look at it if you don't want me to," he said, rather coldly, turning on his heel, and going over towards the window. "But, really, it seems rather absurd that I shouldn't see my own work, especially as I am going to exhibit it in Paris in the autumn. I shall probably have to give it another coat of varnish before that, so I must see it some day, and why not to-day?"

"To exhibit it! You want to exhibit it?" exclaimed Dorian Gray, a strange sense of terror creeping over him. Was the world going to be shown his secret? Were people to gape at the mystery of his life? That was impossible. Something—he did not know what—had to be done at once.

"Yes: I don't suppose you will object to that. Georges Petit is going to collect all my best pictures for a special exhibition in the Rue de Sèze, which will open the first week in October. The portrait will only be away a month. I should think you could easily spare it for that time. In fact, you are sure to be out of town. And if you hide it always behind a screen, you can't care much about it."

Dorian Gray passed his hand over his forehead. There were beads of perspiration there. He felt that he was on the brink of a horrible danger. "You told me a month ago that you would never exhibit it," he said. "Why have you changed your mind? You people who go in for being consistent have just as many moods as others. The only difference is that your moods are rather meaningless. You can't have forgotten that you assured me most solemnly that nothing in the world would induce you to send it to any exhibition. You told Harry exactly the same thing." He stopped suddenly, and a gleam of light came into his eyes. He remembered that Lord Henry had said to him once, half seriously and half in jest, "If you want to have an interesting quarter of an hour, get Basil to tell you why he won't exhibit your picture. He told me why he wouldn't, and it was a revelation to me." Yes, perhaps Basil, too, had his secret. He would ask him and try.

"Basil," he said, coming over quite close, and looking him straight in the face, "we have each of us a secret. Let me know yours, and I will tell you mine. What was your reason for refusing to exhibit my picture?"

Hallward shuddered in spite of himself. "Dorian, if I told you, you might like me less than you do, and you would certainly laugh at me. I could not bear your doing either of those two things. If you wish me never to look at your picture again, I am content. I have always you to look at. If you wish the best work I have ever done to be hidden from the world, I am satisfied. Your friendship is dearer to me than any fame or reputation."

"No, Basil, you must tell me," murmured Dorian Gray. "I think I have a right to know." His feeling of terror had passed away, and curiosity had taken its place. He was determined to find out Basil Hallward's mystery.

"Let us sit down, Dorian," said Hallward, looking pale and pained. "Let us sit down. I will sit in the shadow, and you shall sit in the sunlight. Our lives are like that. Just answer me one question. Have you noticed in the picture something that you did not like?—something that probably at first did not strike you, but that revealed itself to you suddenly?"[4]

4. Wilde deleted the following in MS: "Something that filled you perhaps with a sense of shame?" and made further alterations in 1891.

"Basil!" cried the lad, clutching the arms of his chair with trembling hands, and gazing at him with wild, startled eyes.

"I see you did. Don't speak. Wait till you hear what I have to say. It is quite true that I have worshipped you with far more romance of feeling than a man usually[5] gives to a friend. Somehow, I had never loved a woman. I suppose I never had time. Perhaps, as Harry says, a really 'grande passion' is the privilege of those who have nothing to do, and that is the use of the idle classes in a country. Well, from the moment I met you, your personality had the most extraordinary influence over me. I quite admit that I adored you madly, extravagantly, absurdly. I was jealous of every one to whom you spoke. I wanted to have you all to myself. I was only happy when I was with you. When I was away from you, you were still present in my art. It was all wrong and foolish. It is all wrong and foolish still. Of course I never let you know anything about this. It would have been impossible. You would not have understood it; I did not understand it myself. One day I determined to paint a wonderful portrait of you. It was to have been my masterpiece. It is my masterpiece. But, as I worked at it, every flake and film of color seemed to me to reveal my secret.[6] I grew afraid that the world would know of my idolatry. I felt, Dorian, that I had told too much. Then it was that I resolved never to allow the picture to be exhibited. You were a little annoyed; but then you did not realize all that it meant to me. Harry, to whom I talked about it, laughed at me. But I did not mind that. When the picture was finished, and I sat alone with it, I felt that I was right. Well, after a few days the portrait left my studio, and as soon as I had got rid of the intolerable fascination of its presence it seemed to me that I had been foolish in imagining that I had said anything in it, more than that you were extremely good-looking and that I could paint. Even now I cannot help feeling that it is a mistake to think that the passion one feels in creation is ever really shown in the work one creates. Art is more abstract than we fancy. Form and color tell us of form and color—that is all. It often seems to me that art conceals the artist far more completely than it ever reveals him. And so when I got this offer from Paris I determined to make your portrait the principal thing in my exhibition. It never occurred to me that you would refuse. I see now that you were right. The picture must not be shown. You must not be angry with me, Dorian, for what I have told you. As I said to Harry, once, you are made to be worshipped."[7]

---

5. Stoddart changed Wilde's "should ever give" to this reading in TS.
6. Stoddart canceled the following in TS: "There was love in every line, and in every touch there was passion."
7. Wilde made extensive revisions to this paragraph in 1891, deleting two passages, "It is quite true . . . country" and "I quite admit . . . was with you," and adding as much as he

Dorian Gray drew a long breath. The color came back to his cheeks, and a smile played about his lips. The peril was over. He was safe for the time. Yet he could not help feeling infinite pity for the young man who had just made this strange confession to him. He wondered if he would ever be so dominated by the personality of a friend. Lord Harry had the charm of being very dangerous. But that was all.[8] He was too clever and too cynical to be really fond of. Would there ever be some one who would fill him with a strange idolatry? Was that one of the things that life had in store?

"It is extraordinary to me, Dorian," said Hallward, "that you should have seen this in the picture.[9] Did you really see it?"

"Of course I did."

"Well, you don't mind my looking at it now?"

Dorian shook his head. "You must not ask me that, Basil. I could not possibly let you stand in front of that picture."

"You will some day, surely?"

"Never."

"Well, perhaps you are right. And now good-by, Dorian. You have been the one person in my life of whom I have been really fond.[1] I don't suppose I shall often see you again. You don't know what it cost me to tell you all that I have told you."

"My dear Basil," cried Dorian, "what have you told me? Simply that you felt that you liked me too much. That is not even a compliment."

"It was not intended as a compliment. It was a confession."

"A very disappointing one."

"Why, what did you expect, Dorian? You didn't see anything else in the picture, did you? There was nothing else to see?"

"No: there was nothing else to see. Why do you ask? But you mustn't talk about not meeting me again, or anything of that kind. You and I are friends, Basil, and we must always remain so."

"You have got Harry," said Hallward, sadly.

"Oh, Harry!" cried the lad, with a ripple of laughter. "Harry spends his days in saying what is incredible, and his evenings in doing what is improbable. Just the sort of life I would like to lead. But still I don't think I would go to Harry if I was in trouble. I would sooner go to you, Basil."

"But you won't sit to me again?"

"Impossible!"

---

removed (pp. 95–96). Carson made much of such passages during the first cross-examination of Wilde at the libel trial.
8. Wilde canceled "He felt no romance for him" in TS.
9. A canceled passage in MS reads: "Perhaps you did not see it. But you suspected it. You were conscious of something you did not like."
1. MS originally had "whom I have loved."

"You spoil my life as an artist by refusing, Dorian. No man comes across two ideal things. Few come across one."

"I can't explain it to you, Basil, but I must never sit to you again. I will come and have tea with you. That will be just as pleasant."

"Pleasanter for you, I am afraid," murmured Hallward, regretfully. "And now good-by. I am sorry you won't let me look at the picture once again. But that can't be helped. I quite understand what you feel about it."

As he left the room, Dorian Gray smiled to himself. Poor Basil! how little he knew of the true reason! And how strange it was that, instead of having been forced to reveal his own secret, he had succeeded, almost by chance, in wresting a secret from his friend! How much that strange confession explained to him! Basil's absurd fits of jealousy, his wild devotion, his extravagant panegyrics, his curious reticences,—he understood them all now, and he felt sorry. There was something tragic in a friendship so colored by romance.[2]

He sighed, and touched the bell. The portrait must be hidden away at all costs. He could not run such a risk of discovery again. It had been mad of him to have the thing remain, even for an hour, in a room to which any of his friends had access.

Chapter VIII

When his servant entered, he looked at him steadfastly, and wondered if he had thought of peering behind the screen. The man was quite impassive, and waited for his orders. Dorian lit a cigarette, and walked over to the glass and glanced into it. He could see the reflection of Victor's face perfectly. It was like a placid mask of servility. There was nothing to be afraid of, there. Yet he thought it best to be on his guard.

Speaking very slowly, he told him to tell the housekeeper that he wanted to see her, and then to go to the frame-maker's and ask him to send two of his men round at once. It seemed to him that as the man left the room he peered in the direction of the screen. Or was that only his fancy?[1]

After a few moments, Mrs. Leaf, a dear old lady in a black silk dress, with a photograph of the late Mr. Leaf framed in a large gold brooch at her neck, and old-fashioned thread mittens on her wrinkled hands, bustled into the room.

---

2. Stoddart changed the original reading in TS: "something infinitely tragic in a romance that was at once so passionate and so sterile," to this more circumspect version.
1. Wilde added this effect in TS, which originally read, "the man bowed and retired."

"Well, Master Dorian," she said, "what can I do for you?[2] I beg your pardon, sir,"—here came a courtesy,—"I shouldn't call you Master Dorian any more. But, Lord bless you, sir, I have known you since you were a baby, and many's the trick you've played on poor old Leaf. Not that you were not always a good boy, sir; but boys will be boys, Master Dorian, and jam is a temptation to the young, isn't it, sir?"

He laughed. "You must always call me Master Dorian, Leaf. I will be very angry with you if you don't. And I assure you I am quite as fond of jam now as I used to be. Only when I am asked out to tea I am never offered any. I want you to give me the key of the room at the top of the house."

"The old school-room, Master Dorian? Why, it's full of dust. I must get it arranged and put straight before you go into it. It's not fit for you to see, Master Dorian. It is not, indeed."

"I don't want it put straight, Leaf. I only want the key."

"Well, Master Dorian, you'll be covered with cobwebs if you goes into it. Why, it hasn't been opened for nearly five years—not since his lordship died."

He winced at the mention of his dead uncle's name. He had hateful memories of him. "That does not matter, Leaf," he replied. "All I want is the key."

"And here is the key, Master Dorian," said the old lady, after going over the contents of her bunch with tremulously uncertain hands. "Here is the key. I'll have it off the ring in a moment. But you don't think of living up there, Master Dorian, and you so comfortable here?"

"No, Leaf, I don't. I merely want to see the place, and perhaps store something in it,—that is all. Thank you, Leaf. I hope your rheumatism is better; and mind you send me up jam for breakfast."

Mrs. Leaf shook her head. "Them foreigners doesn't understand jam, Master Dorian. They calls it 'compot.' But I'll bring it to you myself some morning, if you lets me."

"That will be very kind of you, Leaf," he answered, looking at the key; and, having made him an elaborate courtesy, the old lady left the room, her face wreathed in smiles. She had a strong objection to the French valet. It was a poor thing, she felt, for any one to be born a foreigner.

As the door closed, Dorian put the key in his pocket, and looked round the room. His eye fell on a large purple satin coverlet heavily embroidered with gold, a splendid piece of late seventeenth-century Venetian work that his uncle had found in a convent near Bologna.

2. Wilde's 1891 revision all but removed the comic side of Leaf's personality found here. Most of her dialogue and Dorian's replies were changed in both substance and tone. This is the lone instance when Wilde eclipsed a character or diluted a scene in his last revision.

Yes, that would serve to wrap the dreadful thing in. It had perhaps served often as a pall for the dead. Now it was to hide something that had a corruption of its own, worse than the corruption of death itself,—something that would breed horrors and yet would never die. What the worm was to the corpse, his sins would be to the painted image on the canvas. They would mar its beauty, and eat away its grace. They would defile it, and make it shameful. And yet the thing would still live on. It would be always alive.

He shuddered, and for a moment he regretted that he had not told Basil the true reason why he had wished to hide the picture away. Basil would have helped him to resist Lord Henry's influence, and the still more poisonous influences that came from his own temperament. The love that he bore him—for it was really love—had something noble and intellectual in it. It was not that mere physical admiration of beauty that is born of the senses, and that dies when the senses tire. It was such love as Michael Angelo had known, and Montaigne, and Winckelmann, and Shakespeare himself. Yes, Basil could have saved him. But it was too late now. The past could always be annihilated. Regret, denial, or forgetfulness could do that. But the future was inevitable. There were passions in him that would find their terrible outlet, dreams that would make the shadow of their evil real.

He took up from the couch the great purple-and-gold texture that covered it, and, holding it in his hands, passed behind the screen. Was the face on the canvas viler than before? It seemed to him that it was unchanged; and yet his loathing of it was intensified. Gold hair, blue eyes, and rose-red lips,—they all were there. It was simply the expression that had altered. That was horrible in its cruelty. Compared to what he saw in it of censure or rebuke, how shallow Basil's reproaches about Sibyl Vane had been!—how shallow, and of what little account! His own soul was looking out at him from the canvas and calling him to judgment. A look of pain came across him, and he flung the rich pall over the picture. As he did so, a knock came to the door. He passed out as his servant entered.

"The persons are here, monsieur."[3]

He felt that the man must be got rid of at once. He must not be allowed to know where the picture was being taken to. There was something sly about him, and he had thoughtful, treacherous eyes. Sitting down at the writing-table, he scribbled a note to Lord Henry, asking him to send him round something to read, and reminding him that they were to meet at eight-fifteen that evening.

---

3. Victor originally spoke in French in MS. This was followed by Dorian's directions given in French to take a letter round to Lord Henry in Curzon Street and to ask for the "French book of which he had spoken to him."

"Wait for an answer," he said, handing it to him, "and show the men in here."

In two or three minutes there was another knock, and Mr. Ashton himself, the celebrated frame-maker of South Audley Street, came in with a somewhat rough-looking young assistant. Mr. Ashton was a florid, red-whiskered little man, whose admiration for art was considerably tempered by the inveterate impecuniosity of most of the artists who dealt with him. As a rule, he never left his shop. He waited for people to come to him. But he always made an exception in favor of Dorian Gray. There was something about Dorian that charmed everybody. It was a pleasure even to see him.

"What can I do for you, Mr. Gray?" he said, rubbing his fat freckled hands. "I thought I would do myself the honor of coming round in person. I have just got a beauty of a frame, sir. Picked it up at a sale. Old Florentine. Came from Fonthill, I believe. Admirably suited for a religious picture, Mr. Gray."

"I am so sorry you have given yourself the trouble of coming round, Mr. Ashton. I will certainly drop in and look at the frame,—though I don't go in much for religious art,—but to-day I only want a picture carried to the top of the house for me. It is rather heavy, so I thought I would ask you to lend me a couple of your men."

"No trouble at all, Mr. Gray. I am delighted to be of any service to you. Which is the work of art, sir?"

"This," replied Dorian, moving the screen back. "Can you move it, covering and all, just as it is? I don't want it to get scratched going upstairs."

"There will be no difficulty, sir," said the genial frame-maker, beginning, with the aid of his assistant, to unhook the picture from the long brass chains by which it was suspended. "And, now, where shall we carry it to, Mr. Gray?"

"I will show you the way, Mr. Ashton, if you will kindly follow me. Or perhaps you had better go in front. I am afraid it is right at the top of the house. We will go up by the front staircase, as it is wider."

He held the door open for them, and they passed out into the hall and began the ascent. The elaborate character of the frame had made the picture extremely bulky, and now and then, in spite of the obsequious protests of Mr. Ashton, who had a true tradesman's dislike of seeing a gentleman doing anything useful, Dorian put his hand to it so as to help them.

"Something of a load to carry, sir," gasped the little man, when they reached the top landing. And he wiped his shiny forehead.

"A terrible load to carry,"[4] murmured Dorian, as he unlocked the

4. Wilde changed this line three times. In TS there was another sort of pun in Dorian's reply: "There is a good deal of heaviness in modern art." In 1891, Wilde changed it again to the deliberately prosaic "I am afraid it is rather heavy," emphasizing a different mood entirely.

door that opened into the room that was to keep for him the curious secret of his life and hide his soul from the eyes of men.

He had not entered the place for more than four years,—not, indeed, since he had used it first as a play-room when he was a child and then as a study when he grew somewhat older. It was a large, well-proportioned room, which had been specially built by the last Lord Sherard for the use of the little nephew whom, being himself childless, and perhaps for other reasons, he had always hated and desired to keep at a distance. It did not appear to Dorian to have much changed. There was the huge Italian *cassone*, with its fantastically-painted panels and its tarnished gilt mouldings, in which he had so often hidden himself as a boy. There was the satin-wood bookcase filled with his dog-eared school-books. On the wall behind it was hanging the same ragged Flemish tapestry where a faded king and queen were playing chess in a garden, while a company of hawkers rode by, carrying hooded birds on their gauntleted wrists. How well he recalled it all! Every moment of his lonely child-hood came back to him, as he looked round. He remembered the stainless purity of his boyish life, and it seemed horrible to him that it was here that the fatal portrait was to be hidden away. How little he had thought, in those dead days, of all that was in store for him!

But there was no other place in the house to secure from prying eyes as this. He had the key, and no one else could enter it. Beneath its purple pall, the face painted on the canvas could grow bestial, sodden, and unclean. What did it matter? No one could see it. He himself would not see it. Why should he watch the hideous corruption of his soul? He kept his youth,—that was enough. And, besides, might not his nature grow finer, after all? There was no reason that the future should be so full of shame. Some love might come across his life, and purify him, and shield him from those sins that seemed to be already stirring in spirit and in flesh,—those curious unpictured sins whose very mystery lent them their subtlety and their charm. Perhaps, some day, the cruel look would have passed away from the scarlet sensitive mouth, and he might show to the world Basil Hallward's masterpiece.

No; that was impossible. The thing upon the canvas was growing old, hour by hour, and week by week. Even if it escaped the hideousness of sin, the hideousness of age was in store for it. The cheeks would become hollow or flaccid. Yellow crow's-feet would creep round the fading eyes and make them horrible. The hair would lose its brightness, the mouth would gape or droop, would be foolish or gross, as the mouths of old men are. There would be the wrinkled throat, the cold blue-veined hands, the twisted body, that he remembered in the uncle who had been so stern to him in his boyhood. The picture had to be concealed. There was no help for it.

"Bring it in, Mr. Ashton, please," he said, wearily, turning round. "I am sorry I kept you so long. I was thinking of something else."

"Always glad to have a rest, Mr. Gray," answered the frame-maker, who was still gasping for breath. "Where shall we put it, sir?"

"Oh, anywhere, Here, this will do. I don't want to have it hung up. Just lean it against the wall. Thanks."

"Might one look at the work of art, sir?"

Dorian started. "It would not interest you, Mr. Ashton," he said, keeping his eye on the man. He felt ready to leap upon him and fling him to the ground if he dared to lift the gorgeous hanging that concealed the secret of his life. "I won't trouble you any more now. I am much obliged for your kindness in coming round."

"Not at all, not at all, Mr. Gray. Ever ready to do anything for you, sir." And Mr. Ashton tramped down-stairs, followed by the assistant, who glanced back at Dorian with a look of shy wonder in his rough, uncomely face. He had never seen any one so marvellous.

When the sound of their footsteps had died away, Dorian locked the door, and put the key in his pocket. He felt safe now. No one would ever look on the horrible thing. No eye but his would ever see his shame.

On reaching the library he found that it was just after five o'clock, and that the tea had been already brought up. On a little table of dark perfumed wood thickly incrusted with nacre, a present from his guardian's wife, Lady Radley, who had spent the preceding winter in Cairo, was lying a note from Lord Henry, and beside it was a book bound in yellow paper, the cover slightly torn and the edges soiled. A copy of the third edition of the *St. James's Gazette* had been placed on the tea-tray. It was evident that Victor had returned. He wondered if he had met the men in the hall as they were leaving the house and had wormed out of them what they had been doing. He would be sure to miss the picture,—had no doubt missed it already, while he had been laying the tea-things. The screen had not been replaced, and the blank space on the wall was visible. Perhaps some night he might find him creeping up-stairs and trying to force the door of the room. It was a horrible thing to have a spy in one's house. He had heard of rich men who had been blackmailed all their lives by some servant who had read a letter, or overheard a conversation, or picked up a card with an address, or found beneath a pillow a withered flower or a bit of crumpled lace.

He sighed, and, having poured himself out some tea, opened Lord Henry's note. It was simply to say that he sent him round the evening paper, and a book that might interest him, and that he would be at the club at eight-fifteen. He opened the *St. James's* languidly, and looked through it. A red pencil-mark on the fifth page caught his eye. He read the following paragraph:

"INQUEST ON AN ACTRESS.—An inquest was held this morning at the Bell Tavern, Hoxton Road, by Mr. Danby, the District Coroner, on the body of Sibyl Vane, a young actress recently engaged at the Royal Theatre, Holborn. A verdict of death by misadventure was returned. Considerable sympathy was expressed for the mother of the deceased, who was greatly affected during the giving of her own evidence, and that of Dr. Birrell, who had made the post-mortem examination of the deceased."

He frowned slightly, and, tearing the paper in two, went across the room and flung the pieces into a gilt basket.[5] How ugly it all was! And how horribly real ugliness made things! He felt a little annoyed with Lord Henry for having sent him the account. And it was certainly stupid of him to have marked it with red pencil. Victor might have read it. The man knew more than enough English for that.[6]

Perhaps he had read it, and had begun to suspect something. And, yet, what did it matter? What had Dorian Gray to do with Sibyl Vane's death? There was nothing to fear. Dorian Gray had not killed her.

His eye fell on the yellow book that Lord Henry had sent him. What was it, he wondered. He went towards the little pearl-colored octagonal stand, that had always looked to him like the work of some strange Egyptian bees who wrought in silver, and took the volume up.[7] He flung himself into an arm-chair, and began to turn over the leaves. After a few minutes, he became absorbed. It was the strangest book he had ever read. It seemed to him that in exquisite raiment, and to the delicate sound of flutes, the sins of the world were passing in dumb show before him. Things that he had dimly dreamed of were suddenly made real to him. Things of which he had never dreamed were gradually revealed.

It was a novel without a plot, and with only one character, being, indeed, simply a psychological study of a certain young Parisian, who spent his life trying to realize in the nineteenth century all the passions and modes of thought that belonged to every century

---

5. Wilde reduced this to "flung away" in 1891.
6. A vestige of Jacques, the French valet, in MS.
7. Stoddart canceled the following here: "*Le Secret de Raoul* par Catulle Sarrazin. What a curious title." All subsequent references to the title of the notorious yellow book were also removed by Stoddart. The author and title are fictitious, although Wilde knew a Gabriel Sarrazin, a French writer who reviewed for Wilde's *Woman's World* magazine. The title may have suggested to Stoddart the scandalous French novel by Rachilde (Marguerite Vallette), *Monsieur Venus* (1889), in which there is a character, M. Raoule de Vénérande. The fictitious title may have had its origin in a letter Wilde sent to Robert Ross in July 1889, following publication of "The Portrait of Mr. W. H." in *Blackwood's*: "Now that Willie Hughes has been revealed to the world, we must have another secret" (*Letters* 247). That is the kind of inside joke Wilde enjoyed playing in his fiction for the benefit of friends. Willie Hughes is the hypothetical original of the "Mr. W. H." to whom Shakespeare dedicated his sonnets.

except his own, and to sum up, as it were, in himself the various moods through which the world-spirit had ever passed, loving for their mere artificiality those renunciations that men have unwisely called virtue, as much as those natural rebellions that wise men still call sin. The style in which it was written was that curious jewelled style, vivid and obscure at once, full of *argot* and of archaisms, of technical expressions and of elaborate paraphrases, that character-izes the work of some of the finest artists of the French school of *Décadents*.[8] There were in it metaphors as monstrous as orchids, and as evil in color. The life of the senses was described in the terms of mystical philosophy. One hardly knew at times whether one was reading the spiritual ecstasies of some mediæval saint or the mor-bid confessions of a modern sinner. It was a poisonous book. The heavy odor of incense seemed to cling about its pages and to trouble the brain. The mere cadence of the sentences, the subtle monotony of their music, so full as it was of complex refrains and movements elaborately repeated, produced in the mind of the lad, as he passed from chapter to chapter, a form of revery, a malady of dreaming, that made him unconscious of the falling day and the creeping shadows.

Cloudless, and pierced by one solitary star, a copper-green sky gleamed through the windows. He read on by its wan light till he could read no more. Then, after his valet had reminded him several times of the lateness of the hour, he got up, and, going into the next room, placed the book on the little Florentine table that always stood at his bedside, and began to dress for dinner.

It was almost nine o'clock before he reached the club, where he found Lord Henry sitting alone, in the morning-room, looking very bored.

"I am so sorry, Harry," he cried, "but really it is entirely your fault. That book you sent me so fascinated me that I forgot what the time was."

"I thought you would like it," replied his host, rising from his chair.

"I didn't say I liked it, Harry. I said it fascinated me. There is a great difference."

"Ah, if you have discovered that, you have discovered a great deal," murmured Lord Henry, with his curious smile. "Come, let us go in to dinner. It is dreadfully late, and I am afraid the champagne will be too much iced."[9]

8. Wilde added "full of *argot* . . . elaborate paraphrases" and "the work . . . artists of" in TS. *Décadents* was changed to *Symbolistes* in 1891.
9. Wilde shortened and simplified the last paragraph in 1891, changing its focus.

Chapter IX

For years, Dorian Gray could not free himself from the memory of this book. Or perhaps it would be more accurate to say that he never sought to free himself from it. He procured from Paris no less than five large-paper copies of the first edition, and had them bound in different colors, so that they might suit his various moods and the changing fancies of a nature over which he seemed, at times, to have almost entirely lost control. The hero, the wonderful young Parisian, in whom the romantic temperament and the scientific temperament were so strangely blended, became to him a kind of prefiguring type of himself. And, indeed, the whole book seemed to him to contain the story of his own life, written before he had lived it.

In one point he was more fortunate than the book's[1] fantastic hero. He never knew—never, indeed, had any cause to know—that somewhat grotesque dread of mirrors, and polished metal surfaces, and still water, which came upon the young Parisian[2] so early in his life, and was occasioned by the sudden decay of a beauty that had once, apparently, been so remarkable. It was with an almost cruel joy—and perhaps in nearly every joy, as certainly in every pleasure, cruelty has its place—that he used to read the latter part[3] of the book, with its really tragic, if somewhat over-emphasized, account of the sorrow and despair of one who had himself lost what in others, and in the world, he had most valued.

He, at any rate, had no cause to fear that. The boyish beauty that had so fascinated Basil Hallward, and many others besides him, seemed never to leave him. Even those who had heard the most evil things against him (and from time to time strange rumors about his mode of life crept through London and became the chatter of the clubs) could not believe anything to his dishonor when they saw him. He had always the look of one who had kept himself unspotted from the world. Men who talked grossly became silent when Dorian Gray entered the room. There was something in the purity of his face that rebuked them. His mere presence seemed to recall to them the innocence that they had tarnished. They wondered how one so charming and graceful as he was could have escaped the stain of an age that was at once sordid and sensuous.

He himself, on returning home from one of those mysterious and prolonged absences that gave rise to such strange conjecture among

---

1. Stoddart changed from "Catulle Sarrazin's."
2. Stoddart's substitute for Wilde's "Raoul."
3. Canceled in MS: "twelfth and thirteenth chapters." No parallels seem to exist in these and other allusions between the contents of the yellow book and either *A Rebours* or *Monsieur Venus* except for similarities in tone, general subject matter, and angle of treatment.

those who were his friends, or thought that they were so, would creep up-stairs to the locked room, open the door with the key that never left him, and stand, with a mirror, in front of the portrait that Basil Hallward had painted of him, looking now at the evil and aging face on the canvas, and now at the fair young face that laughed back at him from the polished glass. The very sharpness of the contrast used to quicken his sense of pleasure. He grew more and more enamoured of his own beauty, more and more interested in the corruption of his own soul. He would examine with minute care, and often with a monstrous and terrible delight, the hideous lines that seared the wrinkling forehead or crawled around the heavy sensual mouth, wondering sometimes which were the more horrible, the signs of sin or the signs of age. He would place his white hands beside the coarse bloated hands of the picture, and smile. He mocked the misshapen body and the failing limbs.

There were moments, indeed, at night, when, lying sleepless in his own delicately-scented chamber, or in the sordid room of the little ill-famed tavern near the Docks, which, under an assumed name, and in disguise, it was his habit to frequent, he would think of the ruin he had brought upon his soul, with a pity that was all the more poignant because it was purely selfish. But moments such as these were rare. That curiosity about life that, many years before, Lord Henry had first stirred in him, as they sat together in the garden of their friend, seemed to increase with gratification. The more he knew, the more he desired to know. He had mad hungers that grew more ravenous as he fed them.

Yet he was not really reckless, at any rate in his relations to society. Once or twice every month during the winter, and on each Wednesday evening while the season lasted, he would throw open to the world his beautiful house and have the most celebrated musicians of the day to charm his guests with the wonders of their art. His little dinners, in the settling of which Lord Henry always assisted him, were noted as much for the careful selection and placing of those invited, as for the exquisite taste shown in the decoration of the table, with its subtle symphonic arrangements of exotic flowers, and embroidered cloths, and antique plate of gold and silver. Indeed, there were many, especially among the very young men, who saw, or fancied that they saw, in Dorian Gray the true realization of a type of which they had often dreamed in Eton or Oxford days, a type that was to combine something of the real culture of the scholar with all the grace and distinction and perfect manner of a citizen of the world. To them he seemed to belong to those whom Dante describes as having sought to "make themselves perfect by the worship of beauty." Like Gautier, he was one for whom "the visible world existed."

And, certainly, to him life itself was the first, the greatest, of the arts, and for it all the other arts seemed to be but a preparation. Fashion, by which what is really fantastic becomes for a moment universal, and Dandyism, which, in its own way, is an attempt to assert the absolute modernity of beauty, had, of course, their fascination for him. His mode of dressing, and the particular styles that he affected from time to time, had their marked influence on the young exquisites of the Mayfair balls and Pall Mall club windows, who copied him in everything that he did, and tried to reproduce the accidental charm of his graceful, though to him only half-serious, fopperies.

For, while he was but too ready to accept the position that was almost immediately offered to him on his coming of age, and found, indeed, a subtle pleasure in the thought that he might really become to the London of his own day what to imperial Neronian Rome the author of the "Satyricon" had once been, yet in his inmost heart he desired to be something more than a mere *arbiter elegantiarum*, to be consulted on the wearing of a jewel, or the knotting of a necktie, or the conduct of a cane. He sought to elaborate some new scheme of life that would have its reasoned philosophy and its ordered principles and find in the spiritualizing of the senses its highest realization.

The worship of the senses has often, and with much justice, been decried, men feeling a natural instinct of terror about passions and sensations that seem stronger than ourselves, and that we are conscious of sharing with the less highly organized forms of existence. But it appeared to Dorian Gray that the true nature of the senses had never been understood, and that they had remained savage and animal merely because the world had sought to starve them into submission or to kill them by pain, instead of aiming at making them elements of a new spirituality, of which a fine instinct for beauty was to be the dominant characteristic. As he looked back upon man moving through History, he was haunted by a feeling of loss. So much had been surrendered! and to such little purpose! There had been mad wilful rejections, monstrous forms of self-torture and self-denial, whose origin was fear, and whose result was a degradation infinitely more terrible than that fancied degradation from which, in their ignorance, they had sought to escape, Nature in her wonderful irony driving the anchorite out to herd with the wild animals of the desert and giving to the hermit the beasts of the field as his companions.

Yes, there was to be, as Lord Henry had prophesied, a new hedonism that was to re-create life, and to save it from that harsh, uncomely puritanism that is having, in our own day, its curious revival. It was to have its service of the intellect, certainly; yet it was never to accept any theory or system that would involve the sacrifice

of any mode of passionate experience. Its aim, indeed, was to be experience itself, and not the fruits of experience, sweet or bitter as they
might be. Of the asceticism that deadens the senses, as of the vulgar
profligacy that dulls them, it was to know nothing. But it was to teach
man to concentrate himself upon the moments of a life that is itself
but a moment.

There are few of us who have not sometimes wakened before
dawn, either after one of those dreamless nights that make one
almost enamoured of death, or one of those nights of horror and
misshapen joy, when through the chambers of the brain sweep
phantoms more terrible than reality itself, and instinct with that
vivid life that lurks in all grotesques, and that lends to Gothic art its
enduring vitality, this art being, one might fancy, especially the art
of those whose minds have been troubled with the malady of revery.
Gradually white fingers creep through the curtains, and they appear
to tremble. Black fantastic shadows crawl into the corners of the
room, and crouch there. Outside, there is the stirring of birds among
the leaves, or the sound of men going forth to their work, or the sigh
and sob of the wind coming down from the hills, and wandering
round the silent house, as though it feared to wake the sleepers. Veil
after veil of thin dusky gauze is lifted, and by degrees the forms and
colors of things are restored to them, and we watch the dawn remaking the world in its antique pattern. The wan mirrors get back their
mimic life. The flameless tapers stand where we have left them, and
beside them lies the half-read book that we had been studying, or the
wired flower that we had worn at the ball, or the letter that we had
been afraid to read, or that we had read too often. Nothing seems to
us changed. Out of the unreal shadows of the night comes back the
real life that we had known. We have to resume it where we had left
off, and there steals over us a terrible sense of the necessity for the
continuance of energy in the same wearisome round of stereotyped
habits, or a wild longing, it may be, that our eyelids might open some
morning upon a world that had been re-fashioned anew for our pleasure in the darkness, a world in which things would have fresh
shapes and colors, and be changed, or have other secrets, a world in
which the past would have little or no place, or survive, at any rate,
in no conscious form of obligation or regret, the remembrance even
of joy having its bitterness, and the memories of pleasure their pain.

It was the creation of such worlds as these that seemed to Dorian
Gray to be the true object, or among the true objects, of life; and in his
search for sensations that would be at once new and delightful, and
possess that element of strangeness that is so essential to romance, he
would often adopt certain modes of thought that he knew to be really
alien to his nature, abandon himself to their subtle influences, and
then, having, as it were, caught their color and satisfied his intellectual

curiosity, leave them with that curious indifference that is not incompatible with a real ardor of temperament, and that indeed, according to certain modern psychologists, is often a condition of it.

It was rumored of him once that he was about to join the Roman Catholic communion; and certainly the Roman ritual had always a great attraction for him. The daily sacrifice, more awful really than all the sacrifices of the antique world, stirred him as much by its superb rejection of the evidence of the senses as by the primitive simplicity of its elements and the eternal pathos of the human tragedy that it sought to symbolize. He loved to kneel down on the cold marble pavement, and with the priest, in his stiff flowered cope,[4] slowly and with white hands moving aside the veil of the tabernacle, and raising aloft the jewelled lantern-shaped monstrance with that pallid wafer that at times, one would fain think, is indeed the "panis cælestis," the bread of angels, or, robed in the garments of the Passion of Christ, breaking the Host into the chalice, and smiting his breast for his sins. The fuming censers, that the grave boys, in their lace and scarlet, tossed into the air like great gilt flowers, had their subtle fascination for him. As he passed out, he used to look with wonder at the black confessionals, and long to sit in the dim shadow of one of them and listen to men and women whispering through the tarnished grating the true story of their lives.

But he never fell into the error of arresting his intellectual development by any formal acceptance of creed or system, or of mistaking, for a house in which to live, an inn that is but suitable for the sojourn of a night, or for a few hours of a night in which there are no stars and the moon is in travail. Mysticism, with its marvellous power of making common things strange to us, and the subtle antinomianism that always seems to accompany it, moved him for a season; and for a season he inclined to the materialistic doctrines of the *Darwinismus* movement in Germany, and found a curious pleasure in tracing the thoughts and passions of men to some pearly cell in the brain, or some white nerve in the body,[5] delighting in the conception of the absolute dependence of the spirit on certain physical conditions, morbid or healthy, normal or diseased. Yet, as has been said of him before, no theory of life seemed to him to be of any importance compared with life itself. He felt keenly conscious of how barren all intellectual speculation is when separated from action and experiment. He knew that the senses, no less than the soul, have their mysteries to reveal.

4. Changed to "dalmatic" in 1891.
5. Stoddart or another editor at *Lippincott's* knew anatomy better than Wilde and revised the TS from Wilde's "ivory cell . . . or scarlet nerve."

And so he would now study perfumes, and the secrets of their manufacture, distilling heavily-scented oils, and burning odorous gums from the East. He saw that there was no mood of the mind that had not its counterpart in the sensuous life, and set himself to discover their true relations, wondering what there was in frankincense that made one mystical, and in ambergris that stirred one's passions, and in violets that woke the memory of dead romances, and in musk that troubled the brain, and in champak that stained the imagination; and seeking often to elaborate a real psychology of perfumes, and to estimate the several influences of sweet-smelling roots, and scented pollen-laden flowers, of aromatic balms, and of dark and fragrant woods, of spikenard that sickens, of hovenia that makes men mad, and of aloes that are said to be able to expel melancholy from the soul.

At another time he devoted himself entirely to music, and in a long latticed room, with a vermilion-and-gold ceiling and walls of olive-green lacquer, he used to give curious concerts in which mad gypsies tore wild music from little zithers, or grave yellow-shawled Tunisians plucked at the strained strings of monstrous lutes, while grinning negroes beat monotonously upon copper drums, or turbaned Indians, crouching upon scarlet mats, blew through long pipes of reed or brass, and charmed, or feigned to charm, great hooded snakes and horrible horned adders. The harsh intervals and shrill discords of barbaric music stirred him at times when Schubert's grace, and Chopin's beautiful sorrows, and the mighty harmonies of Beethoven himself, fell unheeded on his ear. He collected together from all parts of the world the strangest instruments that could be found, either in the tombs of dead nations or among the few savage tribes that have survived contact with Western civilizations, and loved to touch and try them. He had the mysterious *juruparis* of the Rio Negro Indians, that women are not allowed to look at, and that even youths may not see till they have been subjected to fasting and scourging, and the earthen jars of the Peruvians that have the shrill cries of birds, and flutes of human bones such as Alfonso de Ovalle heard in Chili, and the sonorous green stones that are found near Cuzco and give forth a note of singular sweetness. He had painted gourds filled with pebbles that rattled when they were shaken; the long *clarin* of the Mexicans, into which the performer does not blow, but through which he inhales the air; the harsh *turé* of the Amazon tribes, that is sounded by the sentinels who sit all day long in trees, and that can be heard, it is said, at a distance of three leagues; the *teponaztli*, that has two vibrating tongues of wood, and is beaten with sticks that are smeared with an elastic gum obtained from the milky juice of plants; the *yotl*-bells of the Aztecs, that are hung in clusters like grapes; and a huge cylindrical drum, covered with the skins of great serpents, like the one that Bernal Diaz saw when he went with Cortes into the Mexican temple, and of whose doleful sound he has left us so vivid a description. The fantastic character of these instruments fascinated him, and he felt a curious delight in the thought that Art, like Nature, has her monsters, things of bestial shape and with hideous voices. Yet, after some time, he wearied of them, and would sit in his box at the Opera, either alone or with Lord Henry, listening in rapt pleasure to "Tannhäuser," and seeing in that great work of art a presentation of the tragedy of his own soul.

On another occasion he took up the study of jewels, and appeared at a costume ball as Anne de Joyeuse, Admiral of France, in a dress covered with five hundred and sixty pearls. He would often spend a whole day settling and resettling in their cases the various stones that he had collected, such as the olive-green chrysoberyl that turns red by lamplight, the cymophane with its wire-like line of silver, the pistachio-colored peridot, rose-pink and wine-yellow topazes, carbuncles of fiery scarlet with tremulous four-rayed stars, flame-red cinnamon-stones, orange and violet spinels, and amethysts with their alternate layers of ruby and sapphire. He loved the red gold of the sunstone, and the moonstone's pearly whiteness, and the broken rainbow of the milky opal. He procured from Amsterdam three emeralds of extraordinary size and richness of color, and had a turquoise *de la vieille roche* that was the envy of all the connoisseurs.

He discovered wonderful stories, also, about jewels.[6] In Alphonso's "Clericalis Disciplina" a serpent was mentioned with eyes of real jacinth, and in the romantic history of Alexander he was said to have found snakes in the vale of Jordan "with collars of real emeralds growing on their backs." There was a gem in the brain of the dragon, Philostratus told us, and "by the exhibition of golden letters and a scarlet robe" the monster could be thrown into a magical sleep, and slain. According to the great alchemist Pierre de Boniface, the diamond rendered a man invisible, and the agate of India made him eloquent. The cornelian appeased anger, and the hyacinth provoked sleep, and the amethyst drove away the fumes of wine. The garnet cast out demons, and the hydropicus deprived the moon of her color.

---

6. Wilde added four paragraphs here in three long MS pages to TS beginning "He discovered wonderful stories . . ." and ending "luxury of the dead was wonderful" on the next page. The following lines of the insert never appeared in print. Since there were no instructions from Stoddart or other editorial marks, the omission may have been a typesetting error or a deliberate omission to avoid an ambiguity of reference or syntax: "It was a pearl that Julius Caesar had given to Servilia when he loved her. Their child had been Brutus. [New paragraph] The young priest of the Sun, who while yet a boy had been slain for his sins, used to walk in jewelled shoes on dust of gold and silver."

The selenite waxed and waned with the moon, and the meloceus, that discovers thieves, could be affected only by the blood of kids. Leonardus Camillus had seen a white stone taken from the brain of a newly-killed toad, that was a certain antidote against poison. The bezoar, that was found in the heart of the Arabian deer, was a charm that could cure the plague. In the nests of Arabian birds was the aspilates, that, according to Democritus, kept the wearer from any danger by fire.

The King of Ceilan rode through his city with a large ruby in his hand, as the ceremony of his coronation. The gates of the palace of John the Priest were "made of sardius, with the horn of the horned snake inwrought, so that no man might bring poison within." Over the gable were "two golden apples, in which were two carbuncles," so that the gold might shine by day, and the carbuncles by night. In Lodge's strange romance "A Margarite of America" it was stated that in the chamber of Margarite were seen "all the chaste ladies of the world, inchased out of silver, looking through fair mirrours of chrysolites, carbuncles, sapphires, and greene emeraults." Marco Polo had watched the inhabitants of Zipangu place a rose-colored pearl in the mouth of the dead. A sea-monster had been enamoured of the pearl that the diver brought to King Perozes, and had slain the thief, and mourned for seven moons over his loss. When the Huns lured the king into the great pit, he flung it away,—Procopius tells the story,— nor was it ever found again, though the Emperor Anastasius offered five hundred-weight of gold pieces for it. The King of Malabar had shown a Venetian a rosary of one hundred and four pearls, one for every god that he worshipped.[7]

When the Duke de Valentinois, son of Alexander VI., visited Louis XII. of France, his horse was loaded with gold leaves, according to Brantôme, and his cap had double rows of rubies that threw out a great light. Charles of England had ridden in stirrups hung with three hundred and twenty-one diamonds. Richard II. had a coat, valued at thirty thousand marks, which was covered with balas rubies. Hall described Henry VIII., on his way to the Tower previous to his coronation, as wearing "a jacket of raised gold, the placard embroidered with diamonds and other rich stones, and a great bauderike about his neck of large balasses." The favorites of James I. wore ear-rings of emeralds set in gold filigrane. Edward II. gave to Piers Gaveston a suit of red-gold armor studded with jacinths, and a collar of gold roses set with turquoise-stones, and a skull-cap *parsemé* with pearls. Henry II. wore jewelled gloves reaching to the elbow, and had a hawk-glove set with twelve rubies and fifty-two great pearls. The ducal hat of

7. Wilde changed this to "three hundred and four pearls" in 1891.

Charles the Rash, the last Duke of Burgundy of his race, was studded with sapphires and hung with pear-shaped pearls.

How exquisite life had once been! How gorgeous in its pomp and decoration! Even to read of the luxury of the dead was wonderful.

Then he turned his attention to embroideries, and to the tapestries that performed the office of frescos in the chill rooms of the Northern nations of Europe. As he investigated the subject,—and he always had an extraordinary faculty of becoming absolutely absorbed for the moment in whatever he took up,—he was almost saddened by the reflection of the ruin that time brought on beautiful and wonderful things. He, at any rate, had escaped that. Summer followed summer, and the yellow jonquils bloomed and died many times, and nights of horror repeated the story of their shame, but he was unchanged. No winter marred his face or stained his flower-like bloom. How different it was with material things! Where had they gone to? Where was the great crocus-colored robe, on which the gods fought against the giants, that had been worked for Athena? Where the huge velarium that Nero had stretched across the Colosseum at Rome, on which were represented the starry sky, and Apollo driving a chariot drawn by white gilt-reined steeds? He longed to see the curious table-napkins wrought for Elagabalus,[8] on which were displayed all the dainties and viands that could be wanted for a feast; the mortuary cloth of King Chilperic, with its three hundred golden bees; the fantastic robes that excited the indignation of the Bishop of Pontus, and were figured with "lions, panthers, bears, dogs, forests, rocks, hunters,—all, in fact, that a painter can copy from nature;" and the coat that Charles of Orleans once wore, on the sleeves of which were embroidered the verses of a song beginning *"Madame, je suis tout joyeux,"* the musical accompaniment of the words being wrought in gold thread, and each note, a square shape in those days, formed with four pearls. He read of the room that was prepared at the palace at Rheims for the use of Queen Joan of Burgundy, and was decorated with "thirteen hundred and twenty-one parrots, made in broidery, and blazoned with the king's arms, and five hundred and sixty-one butterflies, whose wings were similarly ornamented with the arms of the queen, the whole worked in gold." Catherine de Médicis had a mourning-bed made for her of black velvet powdered with crescents and suns. Its curtains were of damask, with leafy wreaths and garlands, figured upon a gold and silver ground, and fringed along the edges with broideries of pearls, and it stood in a room hung with rows of the queen's devices in cut black velvet upon cloth of silver. Louis

---

8. Wilde changed this to "Priest of the Sun" in 1891. Elagabalus was priest of the sun god at Emesa and later Roman emperor under the name Marcus Aurelius Antoninus.

XIV. had gold-embroidered caryatides fifteen feet high in his apartment. The state bed of Sobieski, King of Poland, was made of Smyrna gold brocade embroidered in turquoises with verses from the Koran. Its supports were of silver gilt, beautifully chased, and profusely set with enamelled and jewelled medallions. It had been taken from the Turkish camp before Vienna, and the standard of Mohammed had stood under it.

And so, for a whole year, he sought to accumulate the most exquisite specimens that he could find of textile and embroidered work, getting the dainty Delhi muslins, finely wrought, with gold-thread palmates, and stitched over with irridescent beetles' wings; the Dacca gauzes, that from their transparency are known in the East as "woven air," and "running water," and "evening dew;" strange figured cloths from Java; elaborate yellow Chinese hangings; books bound in tawny satins or fair blue silks and wrought with *fleurs de lys,* birds, and images; veils of *lacis* worked in Hungary point; Sicilian brocades, and stiff Spanish velvets; Georgian work with its gilt coins, and Japanese *Foukousas* with their green-toned golds and their marvellously-plumaged birds.

He had a special passion, also, for ecclesiastical vestments, as indeed he had for everything connected with the service of the Church. In the long cedar chests that lined the west gallery of his house he had stored away many rare and beautiful specimens of what is really the raiment of the Bride of Christ, who must wear purple and jewels and fine linen that she may hide the pallid macerated body that is worn by the suffering that she seeks for, and wounded by self-inflicted pain. He had a gorgeous cope of crimson silk and gold-thread damask, figured with a repeating pattern of golden pomegranates set in six-petalled formal blossoms, beyond which on either side was the pine-apple device wrought in seed-pearls. The orphreys were divided into panels representing scenes from the life of the Virgin, and the coronation of the Virgin was figured in colored silks upon the hood. This was Italian work of the fifteenth century. Another cope was of green velvet, embroidered with heart-shaped groups of acanthus-leaves, from which spread long-stemmed white blossoms, the details of which were picked out with silver thread and colored crystals. The morse bore a seraph's head in gold-thread raised work. The orphreys were woven in a diaper of red and gold silk, and were starred with medallions of many saints and martyrs, among whom was St. Sebastian. He had chasubles, also, of amber-colored silk, and blue silk and gold brocade, and yellow silk damask and cloth of gold, figured with representations of the Passion and Crucifixion of Christ, and embroidered with lions and peacocks and other emblems; dalmatics of white satin and pink silk damask, decorated with tulips and dolphins and *fleurs de lys;* altar frontals of crimson velvet and blue linen; and many corporals, chalice-veils, and sudaria. In the mystic offices to which these things were put there was something that quickened his imagination.[9]

For these things, and everything that he collected in his lovely house, were to be to him means of forgetfulness, modes by which he could escape, for a season, from the fear that seemed to him at times to be almost too great to be borne. Upon the walls of the lonely locked room where he had spent so much of his boyhood, he had hung with his own hands the terrible portrait whose changing features showed him the real degradation of his life, and had draped the purple-and-gold pall in front of it as a curtain. For weeks he would not go there, would forget the hideous painted thing, and get back his light heart, his wonderful joyousness, his passionate pleasure in mere existence. Then, suddenly, some night he would creep out of the house, go down to dreadful places near Blue Gate Fields,[1] and stay there, day after day, until he was driven away.[2] On his return he would sit in front of the picture, sometimes loathing it and himself, but filled, at other times, with that pride of rebellion that is half the fascination of sin, and smiling, with secret pleasure, at the misshapen shadow that had to bear the burden that should have been his own.

After a few years he could not endure to be long out of England, and gave up the villa that he had shared at Trouville with Lord Henry, as well as the little white walled-in house at Algiers where he had more than once spent his winter. He hated to be separated from the picture that was such a part of his life, and he was also afraid that during his absence some one might gain access to the room, in spite of the elaborate bolts and bars that he had caused to be placed upon the door.

He was quite conscious that this would tell them nothing. It was true that the portrait still preserved, under all the foulness and ugliness of the face, its marked likeness to himself; but what could they learn from that? He would laugh at any one who tried to taunt him. He had not painted it. What was it to him how vile and full of shame it looked? Even if he told them, would they believe it?

Yet he was afraid. Sometimes when he was down at his great house in Nottinghamshire, entertaining the fashionable young men of his own rank who were his chief companions, and astounding the county by the wanton luxury and gorgeous splendor of his mode of life, he would suddenly leave his guests and rush back to town to see that the door had not been tampered with and that the picture was still there. What if it should be stolen? The mere thought made him cold with

9. Wilde added this paragraph on two handwritten pages inserted into TS.
1. Wilde originally wrote "the Docks."
2. The last phrase is Stoddart's. The original read, "till they almost drove him out in horror and had to be appeased with monstrous bribes."

horror. Surely the world would know his secret then. Perhaps the world already suspected it.

For, while he fascinated many, there were not a few who distrusted him. He was blackballed at a West End club of which his birth and social position fully entitled him to become a member, and on one occasion, when he was brought by a friend into the smoking-room of the Carlton,[3] the Duke of Berwick and another gentleman got up in a marked manner and went out. Curious stories became current about him after he had passed his twenty-fifth year. It was said that he had been seen brawling with foreign sailors in a low den in the distant parts of Whitechapel, and that he consorted with thieves and coiners and knew the mysteries of their trade. His extraordinary absences became notorious, and, when he used to reappear again in society, men[4] would whisper to each other in corners, or pass him with a sneer, or look at him with cold searching eyes, as if they were determined to discover his secret.

Of such insolences and attempted slights he, of course, took no notice, and in the opinion of most people his frank debonair manner, his charming boyish smile, and the infinite grace of that wonderful youth that seemed never to leave him, were in themselves a sufficient answer to the calumnies (for so they called them) that were circulated about him. It was remarked, however, that those who had been most intimate with him appeared, after a time, to shun him. Of all his friends, or so-called friends, Lord Henry Wotton was the only one who remained loyal to him.[5] Women who had wildly adored him, and for his sake had braved all social censure and set convention at defiance, were seen to grow pallid with shame or horror if Dorian Gray entered the room.[6]

Yet these whispered scandals only lent him, in the eyes of many, his strange and dangerous charm. His great wealth was a certain element of security. Society, civilized society at least, is never very ready to believe anything to the detriment of those who are both rich and charming. It feels instinctively that manners are of more importance than morals, and the highest respectability is of less value in its opinion that the possession of a good *chef*. And, after all, it is a very poor consolation to be told that the man who has given one a bad dinner,

---

3. Changed in 1891. The Carlton was a famous conservative political club located in Pall Mall.
4. Stoddart canceled the following here: "who were jealous of the strange love he inspired in women."
5. Stoddart also canceled the following marginal insert that ended the sentence: "and in the eyes of some it was a question whether that was an honor or a disgrace."
6. The conclusion of this paragraph, crossed out by Stoddart in TS, was as follows: "It was said that even the sinful creatures who prowl the streets at night had cursed him as he passed by, seeing in him a corruption greater than their own and knowing but too well the horror of his real life." An additional passage in the same spirit, which Wilde blotted out in MS, described Dorian's appeal in terms of his "strange and dangerous charm."

or poor wine, is irreproachable in his private life. Even the cardinal virtues cannot atone for cold *entrées,* as Lord Henry remarked once, in a discussion on the subject; and there is possibly a good deal to be said for his view. For the canons of good society are, or should be, the same as the canons of art. Form is absolutely essential to it. It should have the dignity of a ceremony, as well as its unreality, and should combine the insincere character of a romantic play with the wit and beauty that make such plays charming. Is insincerity such a terrible thing? I think not. It is merely a method by which we can multiply our personalities.

Such, at any rate, was Dorian Gray's opinion. He used to wonder at the shallow psychology of those who conceive the Ego in man as a thing simple, permanent, reliable, and of one essence. To him, man was a being with myriad lives and myriad sensations, a complex-multi-form creature that bore within itself strange legacies of thought and passion, and whose very flesh was tainted with the monstrous maladies of the dead. He loved to stroll through the gaunt cold picture-gallery of his country-house and look at the various portraits of those whose blood flowed in his veins. Here was Philip Herbert, described by Francis Osborne, in his "Memories on the Reigns of Queen Elizabeth and King James," as one who was "caressed by the court for his handsome face, which kept him not long company." Was it young Herbert's life that he sometimes led? Had some strange poisonous germ crept from body to body till it had reached his own? Was it some dim sense of that ruined grace that had made him so suddenly, and almost without cause, give utterance, in Basil Hallward's studio, to that mad prayer that had so changed his life? Here, in gold-embroidered red doublet, jewelled surcoat, and gilt-edged ruff and wrist-bands, stood Sir Anthony Sherard, with his silver-and-black armor piled at his feet. What had this man's legacy been? Had the lover of Giovanna of Naples bequeathed him some inheritance of sin and shame? Were his own actions merely the dreams that the dead man had not dared to realize? Here, from the fading canvas, smiled Lady Elizabeth Devereux, in her gauze hood, pearl stomacher, and pink slashed sleeves. A flower was in her right hand, and her left clasped an enamelled collar of white and damask roses. On a table by her side lay a mandolin and an apple. There were large green rosettes upon her little pointed shoes. He knew her life, and the strange stories that were told about her lovers.[7] Had he something of her temperament in him? Those oval heavy-lidded eyes seemed to look curiously at him. What of George Willoughby, with his powdered hair and fantastic patches? How evil he looked! The face was saturnine

7. Wilde added and Stoddart canceled the following, thus reinstating the original reading: "the deaths of those whom she had granted her favors."

and swarthy, and the sensual lips seemed to be twisted with disdain. Delicate lace ruffles fell over the lean yellow hands that were so over-laden with rings. He had been a macaroni of the eighteenth century, and the friend, in his youth, of Lord Ferrars. What of the second Lord Sherard, the companion of the Prince Regent in his wildest days, and one of the witnesses at the secret marriage with Mrs. Fitzherbert? How proud and handsome he was, with his chestnut curls and inso-lent pose! What passions had he bequeathed? The world had looked upon him as infamous. He had led the orgies at Carlton House. The star of the Garter glittered upon his breast. Beside him hung the por-trait of his wife, a pallid, thin-lipped woman in black. Her blood, also, stirred within him. How curious it all seemed!

Yet one had ancestors in literature, as well as in one's own race, nearer perhaps in type and temperament, many of them, and cer-tainly with an influence of which one was more absolutely conscious. There were times when it seemed to Dorian Gray that the whole of history was merely the record of his own life, not as he had lived it in act and circumstance, but as his imagination had created it for him, as it had been in his brain and in his passions. He felt that he had known them all, those strange terrible figures that had passed across the stage of the world and made sin so marvellous and evil so full of wonder. It seemed to him that in some mysterious way their lives had been his own.

The hero[8] of the dangerous novel that had so influenced his life had himself had this curious fancy. In a chapter[9] of the book he tells how, crowned with a laurel, lest lightning might strike him, he had sat, as Tiberius, in a garden at Capri, reading the shameful books of Elephantis, while dwarfs and peacocks strutted round him and the flute-player mocked the swinger of the censer; and, as Caligula,[1] had caroused with the green-shirted jockeys in their stables, and supped in an ivory manger with a jewel-frontleted horse; and, as Domitian, had wandered through a corridor lined with marble mirrors, looking round with haggard eyes for the reflection of the dagger that was to end his days, and sick with that ennui, that *tædium vitæ,* that comes on those to whom life denies nothing; and had peered through a clear emerald at the red shambles of the Circus, and then, in a litter of pearl and purple drawn by silver-shod mules, been carried through the Street of Pomegranates to a House of Gold, and heard men cry on Nero Cæsar as he passed by; and, as Elagabalus, had painted his face with colors, and plied the distaff among the women, and brought

---

8. Originally "Raoul" in TS. In 1891 Wilde changed "dangerous" to "wonderful."
9. "Fourth" is canceled in TS and changed by Wilde to "seventh" in 1891.
1. Stoddart deleted "had drank the live philter of Caesonia, and wore the habit of Venus by night, and by day a false gilded beard."

the Moon from Carthage, and given her in mystic marriage to the Sun.

Over and over again Dorian used to read this fantastic chapter,[2] and the chapter immediately following, in which the hero describes the curious tapestries that he had had woven for him from Gustave Moreau's[3] designs, and on which were pictured the awful and beautiful forms of those whom Vice and Blood and Weariness had made monstrous or mad.[4] Filippo, Duke of Milan, who slew his wife, and painted her lips with a scarlet poison; Pietro Barbi, the Venetian, known as Paul the Second, who sought in his vanity to assume the title of Formosus, and whose tiara, valued at two hundred thousand florins, was bought at the price of a terrible sin; Gian Maria Visconti, who used hounds to chase living men, and whose murdered body was covered with roses by a harlot who had loved him; the Borgia on his white horse, with Fratricide[5] riding beside him, and his mantle stained with the blood of Perotto; Pietro Riario, the young Cardinal Archbishop of Florence, child and minion of Sixtus IV., whose beauty was equalled only by his debauchery, and who received Leonora of Aragon in a pavilion of white and crimson silk, filled with nymphs and centaurs, and gilded a boy that he might serve her at the feast as Ganymede or Hylas; Ezzelin, whose melancholy could be cured only by the spectacle of death, and who had a passion for red blood, as other men have for red wine,—the son of the Fiend, as was reported, and one who had cheated his father at dice when gambling with him for his own soul; Giambattista Cibo, who in mockery took the name of Innocent, and into whose torpid veins the blood of three lads was infused by a Jewish doctor; Sigismondo Malatesta, the lover of Isotta, and the lord of Rimini, whose effigy was burned at Rome as the enemy of God and man, who strangled Polyssena with a napkin, and gave poison to Ginerva d'Este in a cup of emerald, and in honor of a shameful passion built a pagan church for Christian worship; Charles VI., who had so wildly adored his brother's wife that a leper had warned him of the insanity that was coming on him, and who could only be soothed by Saracen cards painted with the images of Love and Death and Madness; and, in his trimmed jerkin and jewelled cap and acanthus-like curls, Grifonetto Baglioni, who slew

2. Changed by Wilde from "passage" in TS. In the next line, Stoddart substituted "the hero" for "Raoul."

3. Gustave Moreau (1826–98) was a famous painter of Decadent themes and subjects whose style became synonymous with the movement. Wilde added his name in TS and removed it in 1891.

4. Stoddart changed the original "Lust" to "Vice" in the line above, deleted "here was Manfred, King of Apulia who dressed always in green, and consorted only with cortezans and buffoons," and in the line below, after "scarlet poison," canceled "that her guilty lover might suck swift death from the dead thing he had fondled."

5. Stoddart removed "Incest and" here in TS. Wilde restored "harlot" to the line above after Stoddart had changed it to "one."

Astorre with his bride, and Simonetto with his page, and whose comeliness was such that, as he lay dying in the yellow piazza of Perugia, those who had hated him could not choose but weep, and Atalanta, who had cursed him, blessed him.

There was a horrible fascination in them all. He saw them at night, and they troubled his imagination in the day. The Renaissance knew of strange manners of poisoning,—poisoning by a helmet and a lighted torch, by an embroidered glove and a jewelled fan, by a gilded pomander and by an amber chain. Dorian Gray had been poisoned by a book.[6] There were moments when he looked on evil simply as a mode through which he could realize his conception of the beautiful.

Chapter X

It was on the 7th[1] of November, the eve of his own thirty-second birthday, as he often remembered afterwards.

He was walking home about eleven o'clock from Lord Henry's, where he had been dining, and was wrapped in heavy furs, as the night was cold and foggy. At the corner of Grosvenor Square and South Audley Street a man passed him in the mist, walking very fast, and with the collar of his gray ulster turned up. He had a bag in his hand. He recognized him. It was Basil Hallward. A strange sense of fear, for which he could not account, came over him. He made no sign of recognition, and went on slowly, in the direction of his own house.

But Hallward had seen him. Dorian heard him first stopping, and then hurrying after him. In a few moments his hand was on his arm.

"Dorian! What an extraordinary piece of luck! I have been waiting for you ever since nine o'clock in your library. Finally I took pity on your tired servant, and told him to go to bed, as he let me out. I am off to Paris by the midnight train, and I wanted particularly to see you before I left. I thought it was you, or rather your fur coat, as you passed me. But I wasn't quite sure. Didn't you recognize me?"

"In this fog, my dear Basil? Why, I can't even recognize Grosvenor Square. I believe my house is somewhere about here, but I don't feel at all certain about it. I am sorry you are going away, as I have not seen you for ages. But I suppose you will be back soon?"

"No: I am going to be out of England for six months. I intend to

6. The original ending of the chapter read: "Lord Henry had given him one, and Basil Hallward had painted the other." Wilde then moved the lines beginning "The Renaissance . . ." to their present location on the page.
1. Changed to "9th" in 1891 and the birthday from the "thirty-second" to "thirty-eighth."

take a studio in Paris, and shut myself up till I have finished a great picture I have in my head. However, it wasn't about myself I wanted to talk. Here we are at your door. Let me come in for a moment. I have something to say to you."

"I shall be charmed. But won't you miss your train?" said Dorian Gray, languidly, as he passed up the steps and opened the door with his latch-key.

The lamp-light struggled out through the fog, and Hallward looked at his watch. "I have heaps of time," he answered. "The train doesn't go till twelve-fifteen, and it is only just eleven. In fact, I was on my way to the club to look for you, when I met you. You see, I shan't have any delay about luggage, as I have sent on my heavy things. All I have with me is in this bag, and I can easily get to Victoria in twenty minutes."

Dorian looked at him and smiled. "What a way for a fashionable painter to travel! A Gladstone bag, and an ulster! Come in, or the fog will get into the house. And mind you don't talk about anything serious. Nothing is serious nowadays. At least nothing should be."

Hallward shook his head, as he entered, and followed Dorian into the library. There was a bright wood fire blazing in the large open hearth. The lamps were lit, and an open Dutch silver spirit-case stood, with some siphons of soda-water and large cut-glass tumblers, on a little table.

"You see your servant made me quite at home, Dorian. He gave me everything I wanted, including your best cigarettes. He is a most hospitable creature. I like him much better than the Frenchman you used to have. What has become of the Frenchman, by the bye?"

Dorian shrugged his shoulders. "I believe he married Lady Ashton's maid, and has established her in Paris as an English dressmaker. *Anglomanie* is very fashionable over there now, I hear. It seems silly of the French, doesn't it? But—do you know?—he was not at all a bad servant. I never liked him, but I had nothing to complain about. One often imagines things that are quite absurd. He was really very devoted to me, and seemed quite sorry when he went away. Have another brandy-and-soda? Or would you like hock-and-seltzer? I always take hock-and-seltzer myself. There is sure to be some in the next room."

"Thanks, I won't have anything more," said Hallward, taking his cap and coat off, and throwing them on the bag that he had placed in the corner. "And now, my dear fellow, I want to speak to you seriously. Don't frown like that. You make it so much more difficult for me."

"What is it all about?" cried Dorian, in his petulant way, flinging himself down on the sofa. "I hope it is not about myself. I am tired of myself to-night. I should like to be somebody else."

"It is about yourself," answered Hallward, in his grave, deep voice, "and I must say it to you. I shall only keep you half an hour."

Dorian sighed, and lit a cigarette. "Half an hour!" he murmured.

"It is not much to ask of you, Dorian, and it is entirely for your own sake that I am speaking. I think it right that you should know that the most dreadful things are being said about you in London,—things that I could hardly repeat to you."[2]

"I don't wish to know anything about them. I love scandals about other people, but scandals about myself don't interest me. They have not got the charm of novelty."

"They must interest you, Dorian. Every gentleman is interested in his good name. You don't want people to talk of you as something vile and degraded. Of course you have your position, and your wealth, and all that kind of thing. But position and wealth are not everything. Mind you, I don't believe these rumors at all. At least, I can't believe them when I see you. Sin is a thing that writes itself across a man's face. It cannot be concealed. People talk of secret vices. There are no such things as secret vices. If a wretched man has a vice, it shows itself in the lines of his mouth, the droop of his eyelids, the moulding of his hands, even. Somebody—I won't mention his name, but you know him—came to me last year to have his portrait done. I had never seen him before, and had never heard anything about him at the time, though I have heard a good deal since. He offered an extravagant price. I refused him. There was something in the shape of his fingers that I hated. I know now that I was quite right in what I fancied about him. His life is dreadful. But you, Dorian, with your pure, bright, innocent face, and your marvellous untroubled youth,—I can't believe anything against you. And yet I see you very seldom, and you never come down to the studio now, and when I am away from you, and I hear all these hideous things that people are whispering about you, I don't know what to say. Why is it, Dorian, that a man like the Duke of Berwick leaves the room of a club when you enter it? Why is it that so many gentlemen in London will neither go to your house nor invite you to theirs? You used to be a friend of Lord Cawdor. I met him at dinner last week. Your name happened to come up in conversation, in connection with the miniatures you have lent to the exhibition at the Dudley. Cawdor curled his lip, and said that you might have the most artistic tastes, but that you were a man whom no pure-minded girl should be allowed to know, and whom no chaste woman should sit in the same room with. I reminded him that I was a friend of yours, and asked him what he meant. He told me. He told me right out before everybody.

2. This line was dropped in 1891.

It was horrible! Why is your friendship so fateful to young men?[3] There was that wretched boy in the Guards who committed suicide. You were his great friend. There was Sir Henry Ashton, who had to leave England, with a tarnished name. You and he were inseparable. What about Adrian Singleton, and his dreadful end? What about Lord Kent's only son, and his career? I met his father yesterday in St. James Street. He seemed broken with shame and sorrow. What about the young Duke of Perth? What sort of life has he got now? What gentleman would associate with him?[4] Dorian, Dorian, your reputation is infamous. I know you and Harry are great friends. I say nothing about that now, but surely you need not have made his sister's name a by-word. When you met Lady Gwendolen, not a breath of scandal had ever touched her. Is there a single decent woman in London now who would drive with her in the Park? Why, even her children are not allowed to live with her. Then there are other stories,—stories that you have been seen creeping at dawn out of dreadful houses and slinking in disguise into the foulest dens in London. Are they true? Can they be true? When I first heard them, I laughed. I hear them now, and they make me shudder. What about your country-house, and the life that is led there? Dorian, you don't know what is said about you.[5] I won't tell you that I don't want to preach to you. I remember Harry saying once that every man who turned himself into an amateur curate for the moment always said that, and then broke his word. I do want to preach to you. I want you to lead such a life as will make the world respect you. I want you to have a clean name and a fair record. I want you to get rid of the dreadful people you associate with. Don't shrug your shoulders like that. Don't be so indifferent. You have a wonderful influence. Let it be for good, not evil. They say that you corrupt every one whom you become intimate with, and that it is quite sufficient for you to enter a house, for shame of some kind to follow after you. I don't know whether it is so or not. How should I know? But it is said of you. I am told things that it seems impossible to doubt. Lord Gloucester was one of my greatest friends at Oxford. He showed me a letter that his wife had written to him when she was dying alone in her villa at Mentone. Your name was implicated in[6] the most terrible confession I ever read. I told him that it was absurd,—that I knew you thoroughly, and that you were incapable of anything of the kind. Know

---

3. Stoddart substituted the rest of the sentence after "why is" for the original reading: "why is it that every young man that you take up seems to come to grief, to go to the bad at once?"
4. Wilde added a new paragraph here in 1891.
5. Stoddart canceled the following in TS: "It is quite sufficient to say of a young man that he goes to stay at Selby Royal, for people to sneer and titter."
6. Stoddart changed this from "It was" and then canceled the next sentence, which read: "He said that he suspected you."

you? I wonder do I know you? Before I could answer that, I should
have to see your soul."

"To see my soul!" muttered Dorian Gray, starting up from the sofa
and turning almost white from fear.

"Yes," answered Hallward, gravely, and with infinite sorrow in his
voice,—"to see your soul. But only God can do that."

A bitter laugh of mockery broke from the lips of the younger man.
"You shall see it yourself, to-night!" he cried, seizing a lamp from the
table. "Come: it is your own handiwork. Why shouldn't you look at
it? You can tell the world all about it afterwards, if you choose.
Nobody would believe you. If they did believe you, they'd like me all
the better for it. I know the age better than you do, though you will
prate about it so tediously. Come, I tell you. You have chattered
enough about corruption. Now you shall look on it face to face."[7]

There was the madness of pride in every word he uttered. He
stamped his foot upon the ground in his boyish insolent manner. He
felt a terrible joy at the thought that some one else was to share his
secret, and that the man who had painted the portrait that was the
origin of all his shame was to be burdened for the rest of his life with
the hideous memory of what he had done.

"Yes," he continued, coming closer to him, and looking steadfastly
into his stern eyes, "I will show you my soul. You shall see the thing
that you fancy only God can see."

Hallward started back. "This is blasphemy, Dorian!" he cried. "You
must not say things like that. They are horrible, and they don't mean
anything."

"You think so?" He laughed again.

"I know so. As for what I said to you to-night, I said it for your good.
You know I have been always devoted[8] to you."

"Don't touch me. Finish what you have to say."

A twisted flash of pain shot across Hallward's face. He paused for
a moment, and a wild feeling of pity came over him. After all, what
right had he to pry into the life of Dorian Gray? If he had done a tithe
of what was rumored about him, how much he must have suffered!
Then he straightened himself up, and walked over to the fireplace,
and stood there, looking at the burning logs with their frost-like ashes
and their throbbing cores of flame.

"I am waiting, Basil," said the young man, in a hard, clear voice.

He turned round. "What I have to say is this," he cried. "You must
give me some answer to these horrible charges that are made against
you. If you tell me that they are absolutely untrue from beginning to
end, I will believe you. Deny them, Dorian, deny them! Can't you see

7. Wilde canceled these lines in MS: "Now, I will show you my soul. You shall see the thing
   you fancy only God can see."
8. Changed to "a staunch friend" in 1891.

what I am going through? My God! don't tell me that you are infamous!"[9]

Dorian Gray smiled. There was a curl of contempt in his lips.
"Come up-stairs, Basil," he said, quietly. "I keep a diary of my life
from day to day, and it never leaves the room in which it is written. I
will show it to you if you come with me."

"I will come with you, Dorian, if you wish it. I see I have missed
my train. That makes no matter. I can go to-morrow. But don't ask
me to read anything to-night. All I want is a plain answer to my question."

"That will be given to you up-stairs. I could not give it here. You
won't have to read long. Don't keep me waiting."

Chapter XI

He passed out of the room, and began the ascent, Basil Hallward following close behind. They walked softly, as men instinctively do at
night. The lamp cast fantastic shadows on the wall and staircase. A
rising wind made some of the windows rattle.

When they reached the top landing, Dorian set the lamp down on
the floor, and taking out the key turned it in the lock. "You insist on
knowing, Basil?" he asked, in a low voice.

"Yes."

"I am delighted," he murmured, smiling. Then he added, somewhat bitterly, "You are the one man in the world who is entitled to
know everything about me. You have had more to do with my life than
you think." And, taking up the lamp, he opened the door and went in.
A cold current of air passed them, and the light shot up for a moment
in a flame of murky orange. He shuddered. "Shut the door behind
you," he said, as he placed the lamp on the table.

Hallward glanced round him, with a puzzled expression. The room
looked as if it had not been lived in for years. A faded Flemish tapestry, a curtained picture, an old Italian *cassone,* and an almost empty
bookcase,—that was all that it seemed to contain, besides a chair and
a table. As Dorian Gray was lighting a half-burned candle that was
standing on the mantel-shelf, he saw that the whole place was covered with dust, and that the carpet was in holes. A mouse ran scuffling behind the wainscoting. There was a damp odor of mildew.

"So you think that it is only God who sees the soul, Basil? Draw
that curtain back, and you will see mine."

The voice that spoke was cold and cruel. "You are mad, Dorian, or
playing a part," muttered Hallward, frowning.

9. Wilde made a change here in 1891.

"You won't? Then I must do it myself," said the young man; and he tore the curtain from its rod, and flung it on the ground.

An exclamation of horror broke from Hallward's lips as he saw in the dim light the hideous thing on the canvas leering at him.[1] There was something in its expression that filled him with disgust and loathing. Good heavens! it was Dorian Gray's own face that he was looking at! The horror, whatever it was, had not yet entirely marred that marvellous beauty. There was still some gold in the thinning hair and some scarlet on the sensual lips. The sodden eyes had kept something of the loveliness of their blue, the noble curves had not yet passed entirely away from chiselled nostrils and from plastic throat. Yes, it was Dorian himself. But who had done it? He seemed to recognize his own brush-work, and the frame was his own design. The idea was monstrous, yet he felt afraid. He seized the lighted candle, and held it to the picture. In the left-hand corner was his own name, traced in long letters of bright vermilion.

It was some foul parody, some infamous, ignoble satire. He had never done that. Still, it was his own picture. He knew it, and he felt as if his blood had changed from fire to sluggish ice in a moment. His own picture! What did it mean? Why had it altered? He turned, and looked at Dorian Gray with the eyes of a sick man. His mouth twitched, and his parched tongue seemed unable to articulate. He passed his hand across his forehead. It was dank with clammy sweat.

The young man was leaning against the mantel-shelf, watching him with that strange expression that is on the faces of those who are absorbed in a play when a great artist is acting. There was neither real sorrow in it nor real joy. There was simply the passion of the spectator, with perhaps a flicker of triumph in the eyes. He had taken the flower out of his coat, and was smelling it, or pretending to do so.

"What does this mean?" cried Hallward, at last. His own voice sounded shrill and curious in his ears.

"Years ago, when I was a boy," said Dorian Gray, "you met me, devoted yourself to me, flattered me, and taught me to be vain of my good looks. One day you introduced me to a friend of yours, who explained to me the wonder of youth, and you finished a portrait of me that revealed to me the wonder of beauty. In a mad moment, that I don't know, even now, whether I regret or not, I made a wish. Perhaps you would call it a prayer. . . ."

"I remember it! Oh, how well I remember it! No! the thing is impossible. The room is damp. The mildew has got into the canvas.

1. To compare this and the following paragraphs with the revised, 1891 text (see p. 130) is to appreciate how many little improvements Wilde made in revising the first printed version. The evidence of the texts therefore contradicts the myth that Wilde tossed off his work carelessly and hastily.

The paints I used had some wretched mineral poison in them. I tell you the thing is impossible."[2]

"Ah, what is impossible?" murmured the young man, going over to the window, and leaning his forehead against the cold, mist-stained glass.

"You told me you had destroyed it."

"I was wrong. It has destroyed me."

"I don't believe it is my picture."

"Can't you see your romance in it?" said Dorian, bitterly.[3]

"My romance, as you call it . . ."

"As you called it."

"There was nothing evil in it, nothing shameful. This is the face of a satyr."

"It is the face of my soul."

"God![4] what a thing I must have worshipped! This has the eyes of a devil."

"Each of us has Heaven and Hell in him, Basil," cried Dorian, with a wild gesture of despair.

Hallward turned again to the portrait, and gazed at it. "My God! if it is true," he exclaimed, "and this is what you have done with your life, why, you must be worse even than those who talk against you fancy you to be!" He held the light up again to the canvas, and examined it. The surface seemed to be quite undisturbed, and as he had left it. It was from within, apparently, that the foulness and horror had come. Through some strange quickening of inner life the leprosies of sin were slowly eating the thing away. The rotting of a corpse in a watery grave was not so fearful.

His hand shook, and the candle fell from its socket on the floor, and lay there sputtering. He placed his foot on it and put it out. Then he flung himself into the rickety chair that was standing by the table and buried his face in his hands.

"Good God, Dorian, what a lesson! what an awful lesson!" There was no answer, but he could hear the young man sobbing at the window.

"Pray, Dorian, pray," he murmured. "What is it that one was taught to say in one's boyhood? 'Lead us not into temptation. Forgive us our sins. Wash away our iniquities.' Let us say that together. The prayer of your pride has been answered. The prayer of your repentance will be answered also. I worshipped you too much. I am punished for it. You worshipped yourself too much. We are both punished."

2. Wilde added in TS margin, "The room is damp . . . impossible."
3. Wilde changed "romance" to "ideal" in 1891 and added another line further down (see p. 131).
4. Stoddart changed the original "Christ!" here, but Wilde put it back into the 1891 text.

Dorian Gray turned slowly around, and looked at him with tear-dimmed eyes. "It is too late, Basil," he murmured.

"It is never too late, Dorian. Let us kneel down and try if we can remember a prayer. Isn't there a verse somewhere, 'Though your sins be as scarlet, you I will make them white as snow'?"

"Those words mean nothing to me now."

"Hush! don't say that. You have done enough evil in your life. My God! don't you see that accursed thing leering at us?"

Dorian Gray glanced at the picture, and suddenly an uncontrollable feeling of hatred for Basil Hallward came over him.[5] The mad passions of a hunted animal stirred within him, and he loathed the man who was seated at the table, more than he had ever loathed anything in his whole life. He glanced wildly around. Something glimmered on the top of the painted chest that faced him. His eye fell on it. He knew what it was. It was a knife that he had brought up, some days before, to cut a piece of cord, and had forgotten to take away with him. He moved slowly towards it, passing Hallward as he did so. As soon as he got behind him, he seized it, and turned round. Hallward moved in his chair as if he was going to rise. He rushed at him, and dug the knife into the great vein that is behind the ear, crushing the man's head down on the table, and stabbing again and again.

There was a stifled groan, and the horrible sound of some one choking with blood. The outstretched arms shot up convulsively three times, waving grotesque stiff-fingered hands in the air. He stabbed him once more, but the man did not move. Something began to trickle on the floor. He waited for a moment, still pressing the head down. Then he threw the knife on the table, and listened.

He could hear nothing, but the drip, drip on the threadbare carpet. He opened the door, and went out on the landing. The house was quite quiet. No one was stirring.

He took out the key, and returned to the room, locking himself in as he did so.

The thing was still seated in the chair, straining over the table with bowed head, and humped back, and long fantastic arms. Had it not been for the red jagged tear in the neck, and the clotted black pool that slowly widened on the table, one would have said that the man was simply asleep.

How quickly it had all been done! He felt strangely calm, and, walking over to the window, opened it, and stepped out on the balcony. The wind had blown the fog away, and the sky was like a monstrous peacock's tail, starred with myriads of golden eyes. He looked down, and saw the policeman going his rounds and flashing a

5. Wilde added as "though . . . grinning lips" in 1891.

bull's-eye lantern on the doors of the silent houses. The crimson spot
of a prowling hansom gleamed at the corner, and then vanished. A
woman in a ragged shawl was creeping round by the railings, staggering as she went. Now and then she stopped, and peered back.
Once, she began to sing in a hoarse voice. The policeman strolled
over and said something to her. She stumbled away, laughing. A bitter blast swept across the Square. The gas-lamps flickered, and
became blue, and the leafless trees shook their black iron branches
as if in pain.[6] He shivered, and went back, closing the window
behind him.

He passed to the door, turned the key, and opened it. He did not
even glance at the murdered man. he felt that the secret of the whole
thing was not to realize the situation. The friend who had painted the
fatal portrait, the portrait to which all his misery had been due, had
gone out of his life. That was enough.

Then he remembered the lamp. It was a rather curious one of
Moorish workmanship, made of dull silver inlaid with arabesques of
burnished steel. Perhaps it might be missed by his servant, and questions would be asked. He turned back, and took it from the table.
How still the man was! How horribly white the long hands looked! He
was like a dreadful wax image.

He locked the door behind him, and crept quietly down-stairs. The
wood-work creaked, and seemed to cry out as if in pain. He stopped
several times, and waited. No: everything was still. It was merely the
sound of his own footsteps.

When he reached the library, he saw the bag and coat in the corner. They must be hidden away somewhere. He unlocked a secret
press that was in the wainscoting, and put them into it. He could easily burn them afterwards. Then he pulled out his watch. It was twenty
minutes to two.

He sat down, and began to think. Every year—every month,
almost—men were strangled in England for what he had done. There
had been a madness of murder in the air. Some red star had come too
close to the earth.

Evidence? What evidence was there against him? Basil Hallward
had left the house at eleven. No one had seen him come in again.
Most of the servants were at Selby Royal. His valet had gone to bed.

Paris! Yes. It was to Paris that Basil had gone, by the midnight train,
as he had intended. With his curious reserved habits, it would be
months before any suspicions would be aroused. Months? Everything
could be destroyed long before then.

A sudden thought struck him. He put on his fur coat and hat, and

---

6. Wilde changed this from "in the uncertain gloom" in TS and made another alteration in
the effect in 1891.

went out into the hall. There he paused, hearing the slow heavy tread of the policeman outside on the pavement, and seeing the flash of the lantern reflected in the window. He waited, holding his breath.

After a few moments he opened the front door, and slipped out, shutting it very gently behind him. Then he began ringing the bell. In about ten minutes his valet appeared, half dressed, and looking very drowsy.

"I am sorry to have had to wake you up, Francis," he said, stepping in, "but I had forgotten my latch-key. What time is it?"

"Five minutes past two, sir," answered the man, looking at the clock and yawning.

"Five minutes past two? How horribly late! You must wake me at nine to-morrow. I have some work to do."

"All right, sir."

"Did any one call this evening?"

"Mr. Hallward, sir. He stayed here till eleven, and then he went away to catch his train."

"Oh! I am sorry I didn't see him. Did he leave any message?"

"No, sir, except that he would write to you."[7]

"That will do, Francis. Don't forget to call me at nine tomorrow."

"No, sir."

The man shambled down the passage in his slippers.

Dorian Gray threw his hat and coat upon the yellow marble table, and passed into the library. He walked up and down the room for a quarter of an hour, biting his lip, and thinking.[8] Then he took the Blue Book down from one of the shelves, and began to turn over the leaves. "Alan Campbell, 152, Hertford Street, Mayfair." Yes; that was the man he wanted.

Chapter XII

At nine o'clock the next morning his servant came in with a cup of chocolate on a tray, and opened the shutters. Dorian was sleeping quite peacefully, lying on his right side, with one hand underneath his cheek. He looked like a boy who had been tired out with play, or study.

The man had to touch him twice on the shoulder before he woke, and as he opened his eyes a faint smile passed across his lips, as though he had been having some delightful dream, yet he had not dreamed at all. His night had been untroubled by any images of plea-

---

7. Wilde added "except . . . you" in TS.
8. Wilde added this sentence in TS.

sure or of pain. But youth smiles without any reason. It is one of its chiefest charms.[1]

He turned round, and, leaning on his elbow, began to drink his chocolate. The mellow November sun was streaming into the room. The sky was bright blue, and there was a genial warmth in the air. It was almost like a morning in May.

Gradually the events of the preceding night crept with silent blood-stained feet into his brain, and reconstructed themselves there with terrible distinctness. He winced at the memory of all that he had suffered, and for a moment the same curious feeling of loathing for Basil Hallward, that had made him kill him as he sat in the chair, came back to him, and he grew cold with passion. The dead man was still sitting there, too, and in the sunlight now. How horrible that was! Such hideous things were for the darkness, not for the day.

He felt that if he brooded on what he had gone through he would sicken or grow mad. There were sins whose fascination was more in the memory than in the doing of them, strange triumphs that gratified the pride more than the passions, and gave to the intellect a quickened sense of joy, greater than any joy they brought, or could ever bring, to the senses. But this was not one of them. It was a thing to be driven out of the mind, to be drugged with poppies, to be strangled lest it might strangle one itself.

He passed his hand across his forehead, and then got up hastily,[2] and dressed himself with even more than his usual attention, giving a good deal of care to the selection of his necktie and scarf-pin, and changing his rings more than once.

He spent a long time over breakfast, tasting the various dishes, talking to his valet about some new liveries that he was thinking of getting made for the servants at Selby, and going through his correspondence. Over some of the letters he smiled. Three of them bored him. One he read several times over, and then tore up with a slight look of annoyance in his face. "That awful thing, a woman's memory!" as Lord Henry had once said.

When he had drunk his coffee, he sat down at the table, and wrote two letters. One he put in his pocket, the other he handed to the valet.

"Take this round to 152, Hertford Street, Francis, and if Mr. Campbell is out of town, get his address."

As soon as he was alone, he lit a cigarette, and began sketching upon a piece of paper, drawing flowers, and bits of architecture, first, and then faces. Suddenly he remarked that every face that he drew seemed to have an extraordinary likeness to Basil Hallward. He

---

1. Wilde added the last two sentences in TS.
2. Here Wilde canceled the following in TS: "and having thrown on his heavy white dressing gown, passed into the bathroom. When he came out again, he felt calmer."

frowned, and, getting up, went over to the bookcase and took out a volume at hazard. He was determined that he would not think about what had happened, till it became absolutely necessary to do so.

When he had stretched himself on the sofa, he looked at the title-page of the book. It was Gautier's "Émaux et Camées,"[3] Charpentier's Japanese-paper edition, with the Jacquemart etching. The binding was of citron-green leather with a design of gilt trellis-work and dotted pomegranates. It had been given to him by Adrian Singleton.[4] As he turned over the pages his eye fell on the poem about the hand of Lacenaire, the cold yellow hand *"du supplice encore mal lavée,"* with its downy red hairs and its *"doigts de faune."* He glanced at his own white taper fingers, and passed on, till he came to those lovely verses upon Venice:

> Sur une gamme chromatique,
>   Le sein de perles ruisselant,
> La Vénus de l'Adriatique
>   Sort de l'eau son corps rose et blanc.
>
> Les dômes, sur l'azur des ondes
>   Suivant la phrase au pur contour,
> S'enflent comme des gorges rondes
>   Que soulève un soupir d'amour.
>
> L'esquif aborde et me dépose,
>   Jetant son amarre au pilier,
> Devant une façade rose,
>   Sur le marbre d'un escalier.

How exquisite they were! As one read them, one seemed to be floating down the green water-ways of the pink and pearl city, lying in a black gondola with silver prow and trailing curtains. The mere lines looked to him like those straight lines of turquoise-blue that follow one as one pushes out to the Lido. The sudden flashes of color reminded him of the gleam of the opal-and-iris-throated birds that flutter round the tall honey-combed Campanile, or stalk, with such stately grace, through the dim arcades. Leaning back with half-closed eyes, he kept saying over and over to himself,—

> Devant une façade rose,
>   Sur le marbre d'un escalier.

The whole of Venice was in those two lines. He remembered the autumn that he had passed there, and a wonderful love that had

---

3. Wilde's original choice in MS was a volume of "sonnets by Verlaine."
4. Wilde added "the binding . . . Singleton" in MS.

stirred him to delightful fantastic follies. There was romance in every place. But Venice, like Oxford, had kept the background for romance, and background was everything, or almost everything. Basil had been with him part of the time, and had gone wild over Tintoret. Poor Basil! what a horrible way for a man to die!

He sighed, and took up the book again, and tried to forget. He read of the swallows that fly in and out of the little café at Smyrna where the Hadjis sit counting their amber beads and the turbaned merchants smoke their long tasselled pipes and talk gravely to each other; of the Obelisk in the Place de la Concorde that weeps tears of granite in its lonely sunless exile, and longs to be back by the hot lotus-covered Nile, where there are Sphinxes, and rose-red ibises, and white vultures with gilded claws, and crocodiles, with small beryl eyes, that crawl over the green steaming mud; and of that curious statue that Gautier compares to a contralto voice, the *"monstre charmant"* that couches in the porphyry-room of the Louvre. But after a time the book fell from his hand. He grew nervous, and a horrible fit of terror came over him. What if Alan Campbell should be out of England? Days would elapse before he could come back. Perhaps he might refuse to come. What could he do then? Every moment was of vital importance.

They had been great friends once, five years before,—almost inseparable, indeed. Then the intimacy had come suddenly to an end. When they met in society now, it was only Dorian Gray who smiled: Alan Campbell never did.

He was an extremely clever young man, though he had no real appreciation of the visible arts, and whatever little sense of the beauty of poetry he possessed he had gained entirely from Dorian. His dominant intellectual passion was for science. At Cambridge he had spent a great deal of his time working in the Laboratory, and had taken a good class in the Natural Science tripos of his year. Indeed, he was still devoted to the study of chemistry, and had a laboratory of his own, in which he used to shut himself up all day long, greatly to the annoyance of his mother, who had set her heart on his standing for Parliament and had a vague idea that a chemist was a person who made up prescriptions. He was an excellent musician, however, as well, and played both the violin and the piano better than most amateurs. In fact, it was music that had first brought him and Dorian Gray together,—music and that indefinable attraction that Dorian seemed to be able to exercise whenever he wished, and indeed exercised often without being conscious of it. They had met at Lady Berkshire's the night that Rubinstein played there, and after that used to be always seen together at the Opera, and wherever good music was going on. For eighteen months their intimacy lasted. Campbell was always either at Selby Royal or in Grosvenor

Square. To him, as to many others, Dorian Gray was the type of everything that is wonderful and fascinating in life. Whether or not a quarrel had taken place between them no one ever knew. But suddenly people remarked that they scarcely spoke when they met, and that Campbell seemed always to go away early from any party at which Dorian Gray was present. He had changed, too,—was strangely melancholy at times, appeared almost to dislike hearing music of any passionate character, and would never himself play, giving as his excuse, when he was called upon, that he was so absorbed in science that he had no time left in which to practise. And this was certainly true. Every day he seemed to become more interested in biology, and his name appeared once or twice in some of the scientific reviews, in connection with certain curious experiments.

This was the man that Dorian Gray was waiting for, pacing up and down the room, glancing every moment at the clock, and becoming horribly agitated as the minutes went by. At last the door opened, and his servant entered.[5]

"Mr. Alan Campbell, sir."

A sigh of relief broke from his parched lips, and the color came back to his cheeks.

"Ask him to come in at once, Francis."

The man bowed, and retired. In a few moments, Alan Campbell walked in, looking very stern and rather pale, his pallor being intensified by his coal-black hair and dark eyebrows.

"Alan! this is kind of you. I thank you for coming."

"I had intended never to enter your house again, Gray. But you said it was a matter of life and death." His voice was hard and cold. He spoke with slow deliberation. There was a look of contempt in the steady searching gaze that he turned on Dorian. He kept his hands in the pockets of his Astrakhan coat, and appeared not to have noticed the gesture with which he had been greeted.

"It is a matter of life and death, Alan, and to more than one person. Sit down."

Campbell took a chair by the table, and Dorian sat opposite to him. The two men's eyes met. In Dorian's there was infinite pity. He knew that what he was going to do was dreadful.

After a strained moment of silence, he leaned across and said, very quietly, but watching the effect of each word upon the face of the man he had sent for,[6] "Alan, in a locked room at the top of this house, a room to which nobody but myself has access, a dead man is seated at a table. He has been dead ten hours now. Don't stir, and

5. Wilde made alterations and additions here in 1891.
6. Wilde added "very quietly . . . sent for" in TS.

don't look at me like that. Who the man is, why he died, how he died, are matters that do not concern you. What you have to do is this—"

"Stop, Gray. I don't want to know anything further. Whether what you have told me is true or not true, doesn't concern me. I entirely decline to be mixed up in your life. Keep your horrible secrets to yourself. They don't interest me any more."

"Alan, they will have to interest you. This one will have to interest you. I am awfully sorry for you, Alan. But I can't help myself. You are the one man who is able to save me. I am forced to bring you into the matter. I have no option. Alan, you are a scientist. You know about chemistry, and things of that kind. You have made experiments. What you have got to do is to destroy the thing that is up-stairs,—to destroy it so that not a vestige will be left of it. Nobody saw this person come into the house. Indeed, at the present moment he is supposed to be in Paris. He will not be missed for months. When he is missed, there must be no trace of him found here. You, Alan, you must change him, and everything that belongs to him, into a handful of ashes that I may scatter in the air."

"You are mad, Dorian."

"Ah! I was waiting for you to call me Dorian."

"You are mad, I tell you,—mad to imagine that I would raise a finger to help you, mad to make this monstrous confession. I will have nothing to do with this matter, whatever it is. Do you think I am going to peril my reputation for you? What is it to me what devil's work you are up to?"

"It was a suicide, Alan."

"I am glad of that. But who drove him to it? You, I should fancy."

"Do you still refuse to do this, for me?"

"Of course I refuse. I will have absolutely nothing to do with it. I don't care what shame comes on you. You deserve it all. I should not be sorry to see you disgraced, publicly disgraced. How dare you ask me, of all men in the world, to mix myself up in this horror? I should have thought you knew more about people's characters. Your friend Lord Henry Wotton can't have taught you much about psychology, whatever else he has taught you. Nothing will induce me to stir a step to help you. You have come to the wrong man. Go to some of your friends. Don't come to me."

"Alan, it was murder. I killed him. You don't know what he had made me suffer. Whatever my life is, he had more to do with the making or the marring of it than poor Harry has had. He may not have intended it, the result was the same."

"Murder! Good God, Dorian, is that what you have come to? I shall not inform upon you. It is not my business. Besides, you are certain to be arrested, without my stirring in the matter. Nobody ever com-

mits a murder without doing something stupid. But I will have nothing to do with it."

"All I ask of you is to perform a certain scientific experiment. You
go to hospitals and dead-houses, and the horrors that you do there
don't affect you. If in some hideous dissecting-room or fetid laboratory you found this man lying on a leaden table with red gutters
scooped out in it, you would simply look upon him as an admirable
subject. You would not turn a hair. You would not believe that you
were doing anything wrong. On the contrary, you would probably feel
that you were benefiting the human race, or increasing the sum of
knowledge in the world, or gratifying intellectual curiosity, or something of that kind. What I want you to do is simply what you have
often done before. Indeed, to destroy a body must be less horrible
than what you are accustomed to work at. And, remember, it is the
only piece of evidence against me. If it is discovered, I am lost; and
it is sure to be discovered unless you help me."

"I have no desire to help you. You forget that.[7] I am simply indifferent to the whole thing. It has nothing to do with me."

"Alan, I entreat you. Think of the position I am in. Just before you
came I almost fainted with terror. No! don't think of that. Look at the
matter purely from the scientific point of view. You don't inquire
where the dead things on which you experiment come from. Don't
inquire now. I have told you too much as it is. But I beg of you to do
this. We were friends once, Alan."

"Don't speak about those days, Dorian: they are dead."

"The dead linger sometimes. The man up-stairs will not go away.
He is sitting at the table with bowed head and outstretched arms.
Alan! Alan! if you don't come to my assistance I am ruined. Why, they
will hang me, Alan! Don't you understand? They will hang me for
what I have done."[8]

"There is no good in prolonging this scene. I refuse absolutely to
do anything in the matter. It is insane of you to ask me."

"You refuse absolutely?"

"Yes."

The same look of pity came into Dorian's eyes, then he stretched
out his hand, took a piece of paper, and wrote something on it. He
read it over twice, folded it carefully, and pushed it across the table.
Having done this, he got up, and went over to the window.

Campbell looked at him in surprise, and then took up the paper,
and opened it. As he read it, his face became ghastly pale, and he
fell back in his chair. A horrible sense of sickness came over him.

7. Wilde canceled "Had this happened three years ago, I might have consented to be your
   accomplice" in MS.
8. Wilde added "Why, they . . . have done" in TS.

He felt as if his heart was beating itself to death in some empty hollow.[9]

After two or three minutes of terrible silence, Dorian turned round, and came and stood behind him, putting his hand upon his shoulder.

"I am so sorry, Alan," he murmured, "but you leave me no alternative. I have a letter written already. Here it is. You see the address. If you don't help me, I must send it. You know what the result will be. But you are going to help me. It is impossible for you to refuse now. I tried to spare you. You will do me the justice to admit that. You were stern, harsh, offensive. You treated me as no man has ever dared to treat me,—no living man, at any rate. I bore it all. Now it is for me to dictate terms."

Campbell buried his face in his hands, and a shudder passed through him.

"Yes, it is my turn to dictate terms, Alan. You know what they are. The thing is quite simple. Come, don't work yourself into this fever. The thing has to be done. Face it, and do it."

A groan broke from Campbell's lips, and he shivered all over. The ticking of the clock on the mantel-piece seemed to him to be dividing time into separate atoms of agony, each of which was too terrible to be borne. He felt as if an iron ring was being slowly tightened round his forehead, and as if the disgrace with which he was threatened had already come upon him. The hand upon his shoulder weighed like a hand of lead. It was intolerable. It seemed to crush him.

"Come, Alan, you must decide at once."

He hesitated a moment. "Is there a fire in the room up-stairs?" he murmured.

"Yes, there is a gas-fire with asbestos."

"I will have to go home and get some things from the laboratory."

"No, Alan, you will not leave the house. Write on a sheet of note-paper what you want, and my servant will take a cab and bring the things back to you."

Campbell wrote a few lines, blotted them, and addressed an envelope to his assistant. Dorian took the note up and read it carefully. Then he rang the bell, and gave it to his valet, with orders to return as soon as possible, and to bring the things with him.

When the hall door shut, Campbell started, and, having got up from the chair, went over to the chimney-piece.[1] He was shivering with a sort of ague. For nearly twenty minutes, neither of the men

---

9. Wilde canceled "He tried to speak, but his tongue seemed to be paralyzed" in TS.
1. Wilde canceled "The pain in his forehead was less than it had been but" in TS.

spoke. A fly buzzed noisily about the room, and the ticking of the clock was like the beat of a hammer.

As the chime struck one, Campbell turned around, and, looking at Dorian Gray, saw that his eyes were filled with tears. There was something in the purity and the refinement of that sad face that seemed to enrage him. "You are infamous, absolutely infamous!" he muttered.

"Hush, Alan: you have saved my life," said Dorian.

"*Your* life? Good heavens! what a life that is! You have gone from corruption to corruption, and now you have culminated in crime. In doing what I am going to do, what you force me to do, it is not of *your* life that I am thinking."

"Ah, Alan," murmured Dorian, with a sigh, "I wish you had a thousandth part of the pity for me that I have for you." He turned away, as he spoke, and stood looking out at the garden. Campbell made no answer.

After about ten minutes a knock came to the door, and the servant entered, carrying a mahogany chest of chemicals, with a small electric battery set on top of it. He placed it on the table, and went out again, returning with a long coil of steel and platinum wire and two rather curiously-shaped iron clamps.

"Shall I leave the things here, sir?" he asked Campbell.

"Yes," said Dorian. "And I am afraid, Francis, that I have another errand for you. What is the name of the man at Richmond who supplies Selby with orchids?"

"Harden, sir?"

"Yes,—Harden. You must go down to Richmond at once, see Harden personally, and tell him to send twice as many orchids as I ordered, and to have as few white ones as possible. In fact, I don't want any white ones. It is a lovely day, Francis, and Richmond is a very pretty place, otherwise I wouldn't bother you about it."

"No trouble, sir. At what time shall I be back?"

Dorian looked at Campbell. "How long will your experiment take, Alan?" he said, in a calm, indifferent voice. The presence of a third person in the room seemed to give him extraordinary courage.

Campbell frowned, and bit his lip. "It will take about five hours," he answered.

"It will be time enough, then, if you are back at half-past seven, Francis. Or stay: just leave my things out for dressing. You can have the evening to yourself. I am not dining at home, so I shall not want you."

"Thank you, sir," said the man, leaving the room.

"Now, Alan, there is not a moment to be lost. How heavy this chest is! I'll take it for you. You bring the other things." He spoke rapidly, and in an authoritative manner. Campbell felt dominated by him. They left the room together.

When they reached the top landing, Dorian took out the key and turned it in the lock. Then he stopped, and a troubled look came into his eyes. He shuddered. "I don't think I can go in, Alan," he murmured.

"It is nothing to me. I don't require you," said Campbell, coldly.

Dorian half opened the door. As he did so, he saw the face of the portrait grinning in the sunlight. On the floor in front of it the torn curtain was lying. He remembered that the night before, for the first time in his life, he had forgotten to hide it, when he crept out of the room.[2]

But what was that loathsome red dew that gleamed, wet and glistening, on one of the hands, as though the canvas had sweated blood? How horrible it was!—more horrible, it seemed to him for the moment, than the silent thing that he knew was stretched across the table, the thing whose grotesque misshapen shadow on the spotted carpet showed him that it had not stirred, but was still there, as he had left it.

He opened the door a little wider, and walked quickly in, with half-closed eyes and averted head, determined that he would not look even once upon the dead man. Then, stooping down, and taking up the gold-and-purple hanging, he flung it over the picture.

He stopped, feeling afraid to turn round, and his eyes fixed themselves on the intricacies of the pattern before him. He heard Campbell bringing in the heavy chest, and the irons, and the other things that he had required for his dreadful work. He began to wonder if he and Basil Hallward had ever met, and, if so, what they had thought of each other.

"Leave me now," said Campbell.

He turned and hurried out, just conscious that the dead man had been thrust back into the chair and was sitting up in it, with Campbell gazing into the glistening yellow face. As he was going downstairs he heard the key being turned in the lock.

It was long after seven o'clock when Campbell came back into the library. He was pale, but absolutely calm. "I have done what you asked me to do," he muttered. "And now, good-by. Let us never see each other again."

"You have saved me from ruin, Alan. I cannot forget that," said Dorian, simply.

As soon as Campbell had left, he went up-stairs. There was a horrible smell of chemicals in the room. But the thing that had been sitting at the table was gone.

2. Wilde made some changes here in 1891.

Chapter XIII[1]

"There is no good telling me you are going to be good, Dorian," cried Lord Henry, dipping his white fingers into a red copper bowl filled with rose-water. "You are quite perfect. Pray don't change."

Dorian shook his head. "No, Harry, I have done too many dreadful things in my life. I am not going to do any more. I began my good actions yesterday."

"Where were you yesterday?"

"In the country, Harry. I was staying at a little inn by myself."

"My dear boy," said Lord Henry smiling, "anybody can be good in the country. There are no temptations there. That is the reason why people who live out of town are so uncivilized. There are only two ways, as you know, of becoming civilized. One is by being cultured, the other is by being corrupt. Country-people have no opportunity of being either, so they stagnate."

"Culture and corruption," murmured Dorian. "I have known something of both. It seems to me curious now that they should ever be found together. For I have a new ideal, Harry. I am going to alter. I think I have altered."

"You have not told me yet what your good action was. Or did you say you had done more than one?"

"I can tell you, Harry. It is not a story I could tell to any one else. I spared somebody. It sounds vain, but you understand what I mean. She was quite beautiful, and wonderfully like Sibyl Vane. I think it was that which first attracted me to her. You remember Sibyl, don't you? How long ago that seems! Well, Hetty[2] I was not one of our own class, of course. She was simply a girl in a village. But I really loved her. I am quite sure that I loved her. All during this wonderful May that we have been having, I used to run down and see her two or three times a week.[3] Yesterday she met me in a little orchard. The apple-blossoms kept tumbling down on her hair, and she was laughing. We were to have gone away together this morning at dawn. Suddenly[4] I determined to leave her as flower-like as I had found her."

"I should think the novelty of the emotion must have given you a thrill of real pleasure, Dorian," interrupted Lord Henry. "But I can

---

1. Wilde added chapters 15–18 here in 1891. *Lippincott's* chapter 13 was then divided into 19 and 20 (1891).
2. Wilde reconstructed the first part of this paragraph in TS, adding "to her. . . . Well, Hetty" in TS.
3. Stoddart canceled "Finally, she promised to come with me to town. I had taken a house for her, and arranged everything." Wilde canceled Stoddart's emendation: "She would have come away with me."
4. Stoddart canceled "said to myself, 'I won't ruin this girl. I won't bring her to shame. And I . . . '" in TS.

finish your idyl for you. You gave her good advice, and broke her heart. That was the beginning of your reformation."

"Harry, you are horrible! You mustn't say these dreadful things. Hetty's heart is not broken. Of course she cried, and all that. But[5] there is no disgrace upon her. She can live, like Perdita, in her garden."

"And weep over a faithless Florizel," said Lord Henry, laughing. "My dear Dorian, you have the most curious boyish moods. Do you think this girl will ever be really contented now with any one of her own rank? I suppose she will be married some day to a rough carter or a grinning ploughman. Well, having met you, and loved you, will teach her to despise her husband, and she will be wretched.[6] From a moral point of view I really don't think much of your great renunciation. Even as a beginning, it is poor. Besides, how do you know that Hetty isn't floating at the present moment in some mill-pond, with water-lilies round her, like Ophelia?"

"I can't bear this, Harry! You mock at everything, and then suggest the most serious tragedies. I am sorry I told you now. I don't care what you say to me, I know I was right in acting as I did. Poor Hetty! As I rode past the farm this morning, I saw her white face at the window, like a spray of jasmine. Don't let me talk about it any more, and don't try to persuade me that the first good action I have done for years, the first little bit of self-sacrifice I have ever known, is really a sort of sin. I want to be better. I am going to be better. Tell me something about yourself. What is going on in town? I have not been to the club for days."

"The people are still discussing poor Basil's disappearance."

"I should have thought they had got tired of that by this time," said Dorian, pouring himself out some wine, and frowning slightly.

"My dear boy, they have only been talking about it for six weeks, and the public are really not equal to the mental strain of having more than one topic every three months. They have been very fortunate lately, however. They have had my own divorce-case, and Alan Campbell's suicide. Now they have got the mysterious disappearance of an artist. Scotland Yard still insists that the man in the gray ulster who left Victoria by the midnight train on the 7th of November was poor Basil, and the French police declare that Basil never arrived in Paris at all. I suppose in about a fortnight we will be told that he has been seen in San Francisco. It is an odd thing, but every one who

5. Stoddart canceled "her life is not spoiled" here in TS.
6. Stoddart again canceled a passage, this one a marginal addition by Wilde: "Upon the other hand, had she become your mistress, she would have lived in the society of charming and cultivated men. You would have educated her, taught her how to dress, how to talk, how to move. You would have made her perfect, and she would have been extremely happy. After a time, no doubt, you would have grown tired of her. She would have made a scene. You would have made a settlement. Then a new career would have begun for her."

disappears is said to be seen at San Francisco. It must be a delightful city, and possess all the attractions of the next world."

"What do you think has happened to Basil?" asked Dorian, holding up his Burgundy against the light, and wondering how it was that
he could discuss the matter so calmly.

"I have not the slightest idea. If Basil chooses to hide himself, it is
no business of mine. If he is dead, I don't want to think about him.
Death is the only thing that ever terrifies me. I hate it. One can survive everything nowadays except that. Death and vulgarity are the
only two facts in the nineteenth century that one cannot explain
away. Let us have our coffee in the music-room, Dorian. You must
play Chopin to me. The man with whom my wife ran away played
Chopin exquisitely. Poor Victoria![7] I was very fond of her. The house
is rather lonely without her."

Dorian said nothing, but rose from the table, and, passing into the
next room, sat down to the piano and let his fingers stray across the
keys. After the coffee had been brought in, he stopped, and, looking
over at Lord Henry, said, "Harry, did it ever occur to you that Basil
was murdered?"

Lord Henry yawned. "Basil had no enemies, and always wore a
Waterbury watch. Why should he be murdered?[8] He was not clever
enough to have enemies. Of course he had a wonderful genius for
painting. But a man can paint like Velasquez and yet be as dull as possible. Basil was really rather dull. He only interested me once, and
that was when he told me, years ago, that he had a wild adoration for
you."

"I was very fond of Basil," said Dorian, with a sad look in his eyes.
"But don't people say that he was murdered?"

"Oh, some of the papers do. It does not seem to be probable. I
know there are dreadful places in Paris, but Basil was not the sort of
man to have gone to them. He had no curiosity. It was his chief
defect.[9] Play me a nocturne, Dorian, and, as you play, tell me, in a low
voice, how you have kept your youth. You must have some secret. I
am only ten years older than you are, and I am wrinkled, and bald,
and yellow. You are really wonderful, Dorian. You have never looked
more charming than you do to-night. You remind me of the day I saw
you first. You were rather cheeky, very shy, and absolutely extraordinary. You have changed, of course, but not in appearance. I wish you

---

7. Stoddart canceled the following: "She was desperately in love with you at one time, Dorian.
   It used to amuse me to watch her paying you compliments. You were so charmingly indifferent. Do you know I really miss her? She never bored me. She was so delightfully improbable in everything that she did." Wilde added several lines here in 1891.
8. Wilde added "and always . . . murdered?" in TS.
9. Wilde added about four new pages here in 1891, beginning "What would you say, Harry"
   and ending with "given up our belief in the soul" (see pp. 175–77).

would tell me your secret. To get back my youth I would do anything in the world, except take exercise, get up early, or be respectable. Youth! There is nothing like it. It's absurd to talk of the ignorance of youth. The only people whose opinions I listen to now with any respect are people much younger than myself. They seem in front of me. Life has revealed to them her last wonder. As for the aged, I always contradict the aged. I do it on principle. If you ask them their opinion on something that happened yesterday, they solemnly give you the opinions current in 1820, when people wore high stocks and knew absolutely nothing. How lovely that thing you are playing is! I wonder did Chopin write it at Majorca, with the sea weeping round the villa, and the salt spray dashing against the panes? It is mar-velously romantic. What a blessing it is that there is one art left to us that is not imitative! Don't stop. I want music to-night. It seems to me that you are the young Apollo, and that I am Marsyas listening to you. I have sorrows, Dorian, of my own, that even you know nothing of.[1] The tragedy of old age is not that one is old, but that one is young.[2] I am amazed sometimes at my own sincerity. Ah, Dorian, how happy you are! What an exquisite life you have had![3] You have drunk deeply of everything. You have crushed the grapes against your palate. Noth-ing has been hidden from you. But it has all been to you no more than the sound of music. It has not marred you. You are still the same.

"I wonder what the rest of your life will be. Don't spoil it by renun-ciations. At present you are a perfect type. Don't make yourself incomplete. You are quite flawless now. You need not shake your head: you know you are. Besides, Dorian, don't deceive yourself. Life is not governed by will or intention. Life is a question of nerves, and fibres, and slowly-built-up cells in which thought hides itself and pas-sion has its dreams. You may fancy yourself safe, and think yourself strong. But a chance tone of color in a room or a morning sky, a par-ticular perfume that you had once loved and that brings strange memories with it, a line from a forgotten poem that you had come across again, a cadence from a piece of music that you had ceased to play,—I tell you, Dorian, that it is on things like these that our lives depend. Browning writes about that somewhere; but our own senses will imagine them for us. There are moments when the odor of heliotrope passes suddenly across me, and I have to live the strangest year of my life over again.[4]

"I wish I could change places with you, Dorian. The world has cried out against us both, but it has always worshipped you. It always

1. Wilde canceled in MS "moments of anguish and regret" here.
2. Wilde added this epigram in TS.
3. Wilde canceled the following in TS: "I have always been too much of a critic. I have been afraid of things wounding me, and have looked on."
4. Wilde made alterations here in 1891 (see p. 179).

will worship you. You are the type of what the age is searching for, and
what it is afraid it has found. I am so glad that you have never done
anything, never carved a statue, or painted a picture, or produced
anything outside of yourself! Life has been your art. You have set
yourself to music. Your days have been your sonnets."

Dorian rose up from the piano, and passed his hand through his
hair. "Yes, life has been exquisite," he murmured, "but I am not going
to have the same life, Harry. And you must not say these extravagant
things to me. You don't know everything about me. I think that if you
did, even you would turn from me. You laugh. Don't laugh."

"Why have you stopped playing, Dorian? Go back and play the nocturne over again. Look at that great honey-colored moon that hangs
in the dusky air. She is waiting for you to charm her, and if you play
she will come closer to the earth. You won't? Let us go to the club,
then. It has been a charming evening, and we must end it charmingly.
There is some one at the club who wants immensely to know you,—
young Lord Poole, Bournmouth's eldest son. He has already copied
your neckties, and has begged me to introduce him to you. He is quite
delightful, and rather reminds me of you."

"I hope not," said Dorian, with a touch of pathos in his voice. "But
I am tired to-night, Harry. I won't go to the club. It is nearly eleven,
and I want to go to bed early."

"Do stay. You have never played so well as to-night. There was
something in your touch that was wonderful. It had more expression
than I had ever heard from it before."

"It is because I am going to be good," he answered, smiling. "I am
a little changed already."

"Don't change, Dorian; at any rate, don't change to me. We must
always be friends."

"Yet you poisoned me with a book once. I should not forgive that.
Harry, promise me that you will never lend that book to any one. It
does harm."

"My dear boy, you are really beginning to moralize. You will soon
be going about warning people against all the sins of which you have
grown tired. You are much too delightful to do that. Besides, it is no
use. You and I are what we are, and will be what we will be.[5] Come
round to-morrow. I am going to ride at eleven, and we might go
together. The Park is quite lovely now. I don't think there have been
such lilacs since the year I met you."

"Very well. I will be here at eleven," said Dorian. "Good-night,
Harry." As he reached the door he hesitated for a moment, as if he
had something more to say. Then he sighed and went out.[6]

5. A dozen lines or so were added here in 1891, nearly half of which argue against art influ-
encing human action.
6. Chapter 19 (1891) ends here.

It was a lovely night, so warm that he threw his coat over his arm, and did not even put his silk scarf round his throat. As he strolled home, smoking his cigarette, two young men in evening dress passed him. He heard one of them whisper to the other, "That is Dorian Gray." He remembered how pleased he used to be when he was pointed out, or stared at, or talked about. He was tired of hearing his own name now. Half the charm of the little village where he had been so often lately was that no one knew who he was. He had told the girl whom he had made love him that he was poor, and she had believed him. He had told her once that he was wicked, and she had laughed at him, and told him that wicked people were always very old and very ugly. What a laugh she had!—just like a thrush singing. And how pretty she had been in her cotton dresses and her large hats! She knew nothing, but she had everything that he had lost.

When he reached home, he found his servant waiting up for him. He sent him to bed, and threw himself down on the sofa in the library, and began to think over some of the things that Lord Henry had said to him.

Was it really true that one could never change? He felt a wild longing for the unstained purity of his boyhood,—his rose-white boyhood, as Lord Henry had once called it. He knew that he had tarnished himself, filled his mind with corruption, and given horror to his fancy; that he had been an evil influence to others, and had experienced a terrible joy in being so; and that of the lives that had crossed his own it had been the fairest and the most full of promise that he had brought to shame. But was it all irretrievable? Was there no hope for him?[7]

It was better not to think of the past. Nothing could alter that. It was of himself, and of his own future, that he had to think.[8] Alan Campbell had shot himself one night in his laboratory, but had not revealed the secret that he had been forced to know. The excitement, such as it was, over Basil Hallward's disappearance would soon pass away. It was already waning. He was perfectly safe there. Nor, indeed, was it the death of Basil Hallward that weighed most upon his mind. It was the living death of his own soul that troubled him. Basil had painted the portrait that had marred his life. He could not forgive him that. It was the portrait that had done everything. Basil had said things to him that were unbearable, and that he had yet borne with patience. The murder had been simply the madness of a moment. As for Alan Campbell, his suicide had been his own act. He had chosen to do it. It was nothing to him.

---

7. Wilde added two paragraphs here in 1891.
8. Wilde added a reference to Sibyl's brother here in 1891.

A new life! That was what he wanted. That was what he was waiting for. Surely he had begun it already. He had spared one innocent
thing, at any rate. He would never again tempt innocence. He would
be good.

As he thought of Hetty Merton, he began to wonder if the portrait
in the locked room had changed. Surely it was not still so horrible as
it had been? Perhaps if his life became pure, he would be able to expel
every sign of evil passion from the face. Perhaps the signs of evil had
already gone away. He would go and look.

He took the lamp from the table and crept up-stairs. As he
unlocked the door, a smile of joy flitted across his young face and lingered for a moment about his lips. Yes, he would be good, and the
hideous thing that he had hidden away would no longer be a terror
to him. He felt as if the load had been lifted from him already.

He went in quietly, locking the door behind him, as was his custom, and dragged the purple hanging from the portrait. A cry of pain
and indignation broke from him. He could see no change, unless that
in the eyes there was a look of cunning, and in the mouth the curved
wrinkle of the hypocrite. The thing was still loathsome,—more loathsome, if possible, than before,—and the scarlet dew that spotted the
hand seemed brighter, and more like blood newly spilt.

Had it been merely vanity that had made him do his one good
deed? Or the desire of a new sensation, as Lord Henry had hinted,
with his mocking laugh? Or that passion to act a part that sometimes
makes us do things finer than we are ourselves? Or, perhaps, all
these?

Why was the red stain larger than it had been? It seemed to have
crept like a horrible disease over the wrinkled fingers. There was
blood on the painted feet, as though the thing had dripped,—blood
even on the hand that had not held the knife.

Confess? Did it mean that he was to confess? To give himself up,
and be put to death? He laughed. He felt that the idea was monstrous. Besides, who would believe him, even if he did confess? There
was no trace of the murdered man anywhere. Everything belonging
to him had been destroyed. He himself had burned what had been
below-stairs. The world would simply say he was mad. They would
shut him up if he persisted in his story.

Yet it was his duty to confess, to suffer public shame, and to make
public atonement. There was a God who called upon men to tell their
sins to earth as well as to heaven. Nothing that he could do would
cleanse him till he had told his own sin. His sin? He shrugged his
shoulders. The death of Basil Hallward seemed very little to him. He
was thinking of Hetty Merton.

It was an unjust mirror, this mirror of his soul that he was looking
at. Vanity? Curiosity? Hypocrisy? Had there been nothing more in his

THE PICTURE OF DORIAN GRAY (1890)

renunciation than that? There had been something more. At least he thought so. But who could tell?[9]

And this murder,—was it to dog him all his life? Was he never to get rid of the past? Was he really to confess? No. There was only one bit of evidence left against him. The picture itself,—that was evidence.

He would destroy it. Why had he kept it so long? It had given him pleasure once to watch it changing and growing old. Of late he had felt no such pleasure. It had kept him awake at night. When he had been away, he had been filled with terror lest other eyes should look upon it. It had brought melancholy across his passions. Its mere memory had marred many moments of joy. It had been like conscience to him. Yes, it had been conscience. He would destroy it.

He looked round, and saw the knife that had stabbed Basil Hallward. He had cleaned it many times, till there was no stain left upon it. It was bright, and glistened.[1] As it had killed the painter, so it would kill the painter's work, and all that that meant. It would kill the past, and when that was dead he would be free.[2] He seized it, and stabbed the canvas with it, ripping the thing right up from top to bottom.[3]

There was a cry heard, and a crash. The cry was so horrible in its agony that the frightened servants woke, and crept out of their rooms. Two gentlemen, who were passing in the Square below, stopped, and looked up at the great house. They walked on till they met a policeman, and brought him back. The man rang the bell several times, but there was no answer. The house was all dark, except for a light in one of the top windows. After a time, he went away, and stood in the portico of the next house and watched.

" 'Whose house is that, constable?" asked the elder of the two gentlemen.

"Mr. Dorian Gray's, sir," answered the policeman.

They looked at each other, as they walked away, and sneered. One of them was Sir Henry Ashton's uncle.

Inside, in the servants' part of the house, the half-clad domestics were talking in low whispers to each other. Old Mrs. Leaf was crying, and wringing her hands.[4] Francis was as pale as death.

After about a quarter of an hour, he got the coachman and one of the footmen and crept up-stairs. They knocked, but there was no reply. They called out. Everything was still. Finally, after vainly trying

---

9. Wilde added five lines here in 1891.
1. Wilde canceled in MS "He took it up and darted it into the canvas."
2. Wilde added this sentence in TS and another in 1891.
3. Wilde deleted "ripping . . . bottom," after changing "canvas" to "picture."
4. Wilde changed TS from "One of the maids was crying."

to force the door, they got on the roof, and dropped down on to the balcony. The windows yielded easily: the bolts were old.

When they entered, they found hanging upon the wall a splendid portrait of their master as they had last seen him, in all the wonder of his exquisite youth and beauty. Lying on the floor was a dead man in evening dress, with a knife in his heart. He was withered, wrinkled and loathsome of visage. It was not till they had examined the ring that they recognized who it was.[5]

---

5. Wilde altered the original ending in TS, which read: "When they entered, they found on the wall the portrait of a young man of extraordinary personal beauty, their master as they had last seen him. Lying on the floor was a dead body, withered, wrinkled, and loathsome of visage with a knife in its heart."

BACKGROUNDS

Throughout his creative life, Oscar Wilde proved to be a marvelous fabricator. He could form beautiful and effective prose with workman-like efficiency, and he also had the deft ability to distill defining features of literary antecedents into original and imaginatively engaging works. *The Picture of Dorian Gray* in many ways embodies Wilde's fine sense of literary tradition, highlights the major influences of his literary apprenticeship, and introduces the mature style that will characterize his writings in the 1890s.

In presenting backgrounds to Wilde's writing, this edition attempts a delicate balance. No writers of any merit produce their works absent the influence of powerful imaginations that preceded them. Particular influences will vary from author to author, but the consistent feature of awareness of a literary tradition remains a constant. Wilde, trained as a classicist and deeply aware of contemporary literature and aesthetic theory, doubtless had a range of forces shaping his creative efforts. Limitations of space, however, have forced the editor to offer a selective sampling of both influential writers and Wilde's early creative efforts derived from that engagement.

The following collection of backgrounds to *The Picture of Dorian Gray* attempts to illustrate some specific influences as they appear in the work of other writers and then as they are interpreted in Wilde's own work. Although the expunged details of the "yellow book" in the manuscript and typescript reveal that Joris Karl Huysmans' *A Rebours (Against Nature)* was less definitively influential on the writing of *The Picture of Dorian Gray* than critics had once supposed, there is no denying that its influence was both important and direct. That is why a representative chapter is included here in translation. As Wilde admitted in a letter of April 15, 1892: "The book in *Dorian Gray* is one of the many books I have never written, but it is partly suggested by Huysmans's *A Rebours,* which you will get at any French booksellers" (*Letters,* 1962, p. 313). The chief parallels between *A Rebours* and *The Picture of Dorian Gray* may be summarized briefly: Each develops an interest in curious and even arcane history; each emphasizes the aesthetic and even sensuous dimensions of church ritual and pageantry; each reflects a love of Renaissance demonology and the baroque temper in art and in mores; each shows devotion to the exotic, to sensation, and to decadent taste; each offers the reader extensive if not tedious inventories of jewels, perfumes, and other luxuries of art; and each hints at a spectrum of forbidden practices, especially homoeroticism. But for all these similarities, we should recall that unlike Des Esseintes, the hero of *A Rebours,* Dorian does not cultivate mere vicarious pleasures, even though he certainly does indulge in sensations artificially produced. The approaches to life of the two self-destructive protagonists are quite distinct. Each fails for different reasons in his quest to create a life that is an extension of art, and the fatal miscalculation in both cases was the willful confusion of art with life.

The selections from Walter Pater's *The Renaissance* reveal two kinds of influence. The direct borrowings, paraphrasings, and echoes of *The Renaissance* are many, but perhaps no single chapter served as a more obvious source for some of the most telling effects than "Leonardo Da Vinci," as the notes testify. Almost the entire chapter is reprinted here to give the reader the sense of the whole out of which Wilde selected some of the most famous and also most appropriate passages to express his own intentions. The famous Conclusion of *The Renaissance* was for Wilde what Ruskin's chapter "On the Nature of Gothic" was for William Morris. It contained the outline of a philosophy of art that was quickly taken by Pater's disciples as a philosophy of life. While it may be argued that Morris understood and followed Ruskin more faithfully than Wilde interpreted Pater, the Conclusion was a document that interpreted past culture from a perspective whose assumptions and very language were conspicuously modern. It seemed in a few pages to synthesize classic tenets of hedonism, Renaissance cultural enlightenment, modern science, and liberalism. It was in its way a foreshadowing of modern existentialism, only with art at the center of life rather than ethical idealism. Pater was well enough aware of the possible seductiveness of the philosophy espoused in the Conclusion and so removed what was perhaps the book's most famous chapter from its second edition. It was reinstated by Pater in the third and subsequent editions. Wilde's application of Pater's speculations in the practical sphere is evident enough in the two fictional lives he was creating at the time: Dorian's and his own.

Those selections from Wilde's own essays offer the reader an opportunity to assess the extent to which the ideas and themes of *The Picture of Dorian Gray* occupied Wilde's mind and imagination during the years from 1889 to 1891. The portions of his essays reprinted here emphasize the thematic unity, aesthetic consistency, and stylistic echoings of his poems, short stories, essays, novel, and even plays. Particular comparisons between essays and novel will reveal the ways Wilde expressed and developed his ideas in these different genres.

JORIS-KARL HUYSMANS

From Against Nature†

* * *

Sinking into an armchair, he gave himself up to his thoughts.

For years now he had been an expert in the science of perfumes; he maintained that the sense of smell could procure pleasures equal to those obtained through sight or hearing, each of the senses being capable, by virtue of a natural aptitude supplemented by an erudite education, of perceiving new impressions, magnifying these tenfold, and co-ordinating them to compose the whole that constitutes a work of art. After all, he argued, it was no more abnormal to have an art that consisted of picking out odorous fluids than it was to have other arts based on a selection of sound waves or the impact of variously coloured rays on the retina of the eye; only, just as no one, without a special intuitive faculty developed by study, could distinguish a painting by a great master from a paltry daub, or a Beethoven theme from a tune by Clapisson, so no one, without a preliminary initiation, could help confusing at first a *bouquet* created by a true artist with a potpourri concocted by a manufacturer for sale in grocers' shops and cheap bazaars.

One aspect of this art of perfumery had fascinated him more than any other, and that was the degree of accuracy it was possible to reach in imitating the real thing.

Hardly ever, in fact, are perfumes produced from the flowers whose names they bear; and any artist foolish enough to take his raw materials from Nature alone would get only a hybrid result, lacking both conviction and distinction, for the very good reason that the essence obtained by distillation from the flower itself cannot possibly offer more than a very distant, very vulgar analogy with the real aroma of the living flower, rooted in the ground and spreading its effluvia through the open air.

Consequently, with the solitary exception of the inimitable jasmine, which admits of no counterfeit, no likeness, no approximation even, all the flowers in existence are represented to perfection by combinations of alcoholates and essences, extracting from the model its distinctive personality and adding that little something, that extra tang, that heady savour, that rare touch which makes a work of art.

In short, the artist in perfumery completes the original natural

† From *Against Nature* (À rebours), trans. Robert Baldick (Baltimore: Penguin, 1959), 118–29. This is the tenth chapter. Reprinted by permission of the publisher.

odour, which, so to speak, he cuts and mounts as a jeweller improves
and brings out the water of a precious stone.

Little by little the arcana of this art, the most neglected of them all,
had been revealed to Des Esseintes, who could now decipher its complex language that was as subtle as any human tongue, yet wonderfully concise under its apparent vagueness and ambiguity.

To do this he had first had to master the grammar, to understand
the syntax of smells, to get a firm grasp on the rules that govern them,
and, once he was familiar with this dialect, to compare the works of
the great masters, the Atkinsons and Lubins, the Chardins and Violets, the Legrands and Piesses, to analyse the construction of their
sentences, to weigh the proportion of their words, to measure the
arrangement of their periods.

The next stage in his study of this idiom of essences had been to
let experience come to the aid of theories that were too often incomplete and commonplace.

Classical perfumery was indeed little diversified, practically colourless, invariably cast in a mould fashioned by chemists of olden times;
it was still drivelling away, still clinging to its old alembics, when the
Romantic epoch dawned and, no less than the other arts, modified
it, rejuvenated it, made it more malleable and more supple.

Its history followed that of the French language step by step. The
Louis XIII style in perfumery, composed of the elements dear to that
period—orris-powder, musk, civet, and myrtle-water, already known
by the name of angel-water—was scarcely adequate to express the
cavalierish graces, the rather crude colours of the time which certain
sonnets by Saint-Amand have preserved for us. Later on, with the aid
of myrrh and frankincense, the potent and austere scents of religion,
it became almost possible to render the stately pomp of the age of
Louis XIV, the pleonastic artifices of classical oratory, the ample, sustained, wordy style of Bossuet and the other masters of the pulpit.
Later still, the blasé, sophisticated graces of French society under
Louis XV found their interpreters more easily in frangipane and
maréchale, which offered in a way the very synthesis of the period.
And then, after the indifference and incuriosity of the First Empire,
which used eau-de-Cologne and rosemary to excess, perfumery followed Victor Hugo and Gautier and went for inspiration to the lands
of the sun; it composed its own Oriental verses, its own highly spiced
salaams, discovered new intonations and audacious antitheses,
sorted out and revived forgotten nuances which it complicated, sub-
tilized and paired off, and in short resolutely repudiated the voluntary
decrepitude to which it had been reduced by its Malesherbes, its
Boileaus, its Andrieux, its Baour-Lormians, the vulgar distillers of its
poems.

But the language of scents had not remained stationary since the 1830 epoch. It had continued to develop, had followed the march of the century, had advanced side-by-side with the other arts. Like them, it had adapted itself to the whims of artists and connoisseurs, joining in the cult of things Chinese and Japanese, inventing scented albums, imitating the flower-posies of Takeoka, mingling lavender and clove to produce the perfume of the Rondeletia, marrying patchouli and camphor to obtain the singular aroma of China ink, combining citron, clove, and neroli to arrive at the odour of the Japanese Hovenia.

Des Esseintes studied and analysed the spirit of these compounds and worked on an interpretation of these texts; for his own personal pleasure and satisfaction he took to playing the psychologist, to dismantling the mechanism of a work and reassembling it, to unscrewing the separate pieces forming the structure of a composite odour, and as a result of these operations his sense of smell had acquired an almost infallible flair.

Just as a wine-merchant can recognize a vintage from the taste of a single drop; just as a hop-dealer, the moment he sniffs at a sack, can fix the precise value of the contents; just as a Chinese trader can tell at once the place of origin of the teas he has to examine, can say on what estate in the Bohea hills or in what Buddhist monastery each sample was grown and when the leaves were picked, can state precisely the degree of torrefaction involved and the effect produced on the tea by contact with plum blossom, with the Aglaia, with the Olea fragrans, indeed with any of the perfumes used to modify its flavour, to give it an unexpected piquancy, to improve its somewhat dry smell with a whiff of fresh and foreign flowers; so Des Esseintes, after one brief sniff at scent, could promptly detail the amounts of its constituents, explain the psychology of its composition, perhaps even give the name of the artist who created it and marked it with the personal stamp of his style.

It goes without saying that he possessed a collection of all the products used by perfumers; he even had some of the genuine Balsam of Mecca, a balm so rare that it can be obtained only in certain regions of Arabia Petraea and remains a monopoly of the Grand Turk.

Sitting now at his dressing-room table, he was toying with the idea of creating a new *bouquet* when he was afflicted with that sudden hesitation so familiar to writers who, after months of idleness, make ready to embark on a new work.

Like Balzac, who was haunted by an absolute compulsion to blacken reams of paper in order to get his hand in, Des Esseintes felt that he ought to get back into practice with a few elementary exercises. He thought of making some heliotrope and picked up two bottles of almond and vanilla; then he changed his mind and decided to try sweet pea instead.

The relevant formula and working method escaped his memory, so that he had to proceed by trial and error. He knew, of course, that in the fragrance of this particular flower, orange-blossom was the dominant element; and after trying various combinations he finally hit on the right tone by mixing the orange-blossom with tuberose and rose, binding the three together with a drop of vanilla.

All his uncertainty vanished; a little fever of excitement took hold of him and he felt ready to set to work again. First he made some tea with a compound of cassia and iris; then, completely sure of himself, he resolved to go ahead, to strike a reverberating chord whose majestic thunder would drown the whisper of that artful frangipane which was still stealing stealthily into the room.

He handled, one after the other, amber, Tonquin musk, with its overpowering smell, and patchouli, the most pungent of all vegetable perfumes, whose flower, in its natural state, gives off an odour of mildew and mould. Do what he would, however, visions of the eighteenth century haunted him: gowns with panniers and flounces danced before his eyes; Boucher Venuses, all flesh and no bone, stuffed with pink cotton-wool, looked down at him from every wall; memories of the novel *Thémidore,* and especially of the exquisite Rosette with her skirts hoisted up in blushing despair, pursued him. He sprang to his feet in a fury, and to rid himself of these obsessions he filled his lungs with that unadulterated essence of spikenard which is so dear to Orientals and so abhorrent to Europeans on account of its excessive valerian content. He was stunned by the violence of the shock this gave him. The filigree of the delicate scent which had been troubling him vanished as if it had been pounded with a hammer; and he took advantage of this respite to escape from past epochs and antiquated odours in order to engage, as he had been used to do in other days, in less restricted and more up-to-date operations.

At one time he had enjoyed soothing his spirit with scented harmonies. He would use effects similar to those employed by the poets, following as closely as possible the admirable arrangements of certain poems by Baudelaire such as *L'Irréparable* and *Le Balcon,* in which the last of the five lines in each verse echoes the first, returning like a refrain to drown the soul in infinite depths of melancholy and languor. He used to roam haphazardly through the dreams conjured up for him by these aromatic stanzas, until he was suddenly brought back to his starting point, to the motif of his meditation, by the recurrence of the initial theme, reappearing at fixed intervals in the fragrant orchestration of the poem.

At present his ambition was to wander at will across a landscape full of changes and surprises, and he began with a simple phrase that was ample and sonorous, suddenly opening up an immense vista of countryside.

With his vaporizers he injected into the room an essence composed of ambrosia, Mitcham lavender, sweet pea, and other flowers—an extract which, when it is distilled by a true artist, well merits the name it has been given of 'extract of meadow blossoms'. Then into this meadow he introduced a carefully measured amalgam of tuberose, orange, and almond blossom; and immediately artificial lilacs came into being, while linden-trees swayed in the wind, shedding on the ground about them their pale emanations, counterfeited by the London extract of tilia.

Once he had roughed out this background in its main outlines, so that it stretched away into the distance behind his closed eyelids, he sprayed the room with a light rain of essences that were half-human, half-feline, smacking of the petticoat, indicating the presence of woman in her paint and powder—stephanotis, ayapana, opopanax, chypre, champaka, and schoenanthus—on which he superimposed a dash of syringa, to give the factitious, cosmetic, indoor life they evoked the natural appearance of laughing, sweating, rollicking pleasures out in the sun.

Next he let these fragrant odours, escape through a ventilator, keeping only the country scent, which he renewed, increasing the dose so as to force it to return like a ritornel at the end of each stanza.

The women he had conjured up had gradually disappeared, and the countryside was once more uninhabited. Then, as if by magic, the horizon was filled with factories, whose fearsome chimneys belched fire and flame like so many bowls of punch.

A breath of industry, a whiff of chemical products now floated on the breeze he raised by fanning the air, though Nature still poured her sweet effluvia into this foul-smelling atmosphere.

Des Esseintes was rubbing a pellet of styrax between his fingers, warming it so that it filled the room with a most peculiar smell, an odour at once repugnant and delightful, blending the delicious scent of the jonquil with the filthy stench of gutta-percha and coal tar. He disinfected his hands, shut away his resin in a hermetically-sealed box, and the factories disappeared in their turn.

Now, in the midst of the revivified effluvia of linden-trees and meadow flowers, he sprinkled a few drops of the perfume 'New-mown Hay', and on the magic spot momentarily stripped of its lilacs there rose piles of hay, bringing a new season with them, spreading summer about them in these delicate emanations.

Finally, when he had sufficiently savoured this spectacle, he frantically scattered exotic perfumes around him, emptied his vaporizers, quickened all his concentrated essences and gave free rein to all his balms, with the result that the suffocating room was suddenly filled with an insanely sublimated vegetation, emitting powerful exhalations, impregnating an artificial breeze with raging alcoholates—an unnatural yet charming vegetation, paradoxically uniting tropical spices such as the pungent odours of Chinese sandalwood and Jamaican hediosmia with French scents such as jasmine, hawthorn, and vervain; defying climate and season to put forth trees of different smells and flowers of the most divergent colours and fragrances; creating out of the union or collision of all these tones one common perfume, unnamed, unexpected, unusual, in which there reappeared, like a persistent refrain, the decorative phrase he had started with, the smell of the great meadow and the swaying lilacs and linden-trees.

All of a sudden he felt a sharp stab of pain, as if a drill were boring into his temples. He opened his eyes, to find himself back in the middle of his dressing-room, sitting at his table; he got up and, still in a daze, stumbled across to the window, which he pushed ajar. A gust of air blew in and freshened up the stifling atmosphere that enveloped him. He walked up and down to steady his legs, and as he went to and fro he looked up at the ceiling, on which crabs and salt-encrusted seaweed stood out in relief against a grained background as yellow as the sand on a beach. A similar design adorned the plinths bordering the wall panels, which in their turn were covered with Japanese crape, a water green in colour and slightly crumpled to imitate the surface of a river rippling in the wind, while down the gentle current floated a rose petal round which there twisted and turned a swarm of little fishes sketched in with a couple of strokes of the pen.

But his eyes were still heavy, and so he stopped pacing the short distance between font and bath and leaned his elbows on the window-sill. Soon his head cleared, and after carefully putting the stoppers back in all his scent-bottles, he took the opportunity to tidy up his cosmetic preparations. He had not touched these things since his arrival at Fontenay, and he was almost surprised to see once again this collection to which so many women had had recourse. Phials and jars were piled on top of each other in utter confusion. Here was a box of green porcelain containing schnouda, that marvellous white cream which, once it is spread on the cheeks, changes under the influence of the air to a delicate pink, then to a flesh colour so natural that it produces an entirely convincing illusion of a flushed complexion; there, lacquered jars inlaid with mother-of-pearl held Japanese gold and Athens green the colour of a blister-fly's wing, golds and greens that turn dark crimson as soon as they are moistened. And beside pots of filbert paste, of harem serkis, of Kashmir-lily

emulsions, of strawberry and elder-berry lotions for the skin, next to
little bottles full of China-ink and rose-water solutions for the eyes,
lay an assortment of instruments fashioned out of ivory and mother-
of-pearl, silver and steel, mixed up with lucern brushes for the
gums—pincers, scissors, strigils, stumps, hair-pads, powder-puffs,
back-scratchers, beauty-spots, and files.

He poked around among all this apparatus, bought long ago to
please a mistress of his who used to go into raptures over certain aro-
matics and certain balms—an unbalanced, neurotic woman who
loved to have her nipples macerated in scent, but who only really
experienced complete and utter ecstasy when her scalp was scraped
with a comb or when a lover's caresses were mingled with the smell
of soot, of wet plaster from houses being built in rainy weather, or of
dust thrown up by heavy rain-drops in a summer thunderstorm.

As he mused over these recollections, one memory in particular
haunted him, stirring up a forgotten world of old thoughts and
ancient perfumes—the memory of an afternoon he had spent with
this woman at Pantin, partly for want of anything better to do and
partly out of curiosity, at the house of one of her sisters. While the
two women were chattering away and showing each other their
frocks, he had gone to the window and, through the dusty panes,
had seen the muddy street stretching into the distance and heard it
echo with the incessant beat of galoshes tramping through the puddles.

This scene, though it belonged to a remote past, suddenly presented itself to him in astonishing detail. Pantin was there before
him, bustling and alive in the dead green water of the moon-rimmed
mirror into which his unthinking gaze was directed. An hallucination
carried him away far from Fontenay; the looking-glass conjured up
for him not only the Pantin street but also the thoughts that street
had once evoked; and lost in a dream, he said over to himself the
ingenious, melancholy, yet consoling anthem he had composed that
day on getting back to Paris:

'Yes, the season of the great rains is upon us; hearken to the song
of the gutter-pipes retching under the pavements; behold the horse-
dung floating in the bowls of coffee hollowed out of the macadam;
everywhere the foot-baths of the poor are overflowing.

'Under the lowering sky, in the humid atmosphere, the houses
ooze black sweat and their ventilators breathe foul odours; the horror
of life becomes more apparent and the grip of spleen more oppressive; the seeds of iniquity that lie in every man's heart begin to ger-
minate; a craving for filthy pleasures takes hold of the puritanical,
and the minds of respected citizens are visited by criminal desires.

'And yet, here I am, warming myself in front of a blazing fire, while
a basket of full-blown flowers on the table fills the room with the

scent of benzoin, geranium, and vetiver. In mid-November it is still springtime at Pantin in the Rue de Paris, and I can enjoy a quiet laugh at the expense of those timorous families who, in order to avoid the approach of winter, scuttle away at full speed to Antibes or to Cannes.

'Inclement Nature has nothing to do with this extraordinary phenomenon; let it be said at once that it is to industry, and industry alone, that Pantin owes this factitious spring.

'The truth is that these flowers are made of taffeta and mounted on binding wire, while this vernal fragrance has come filtering in through cracks in the window-frame from the neighbouring factories where the Pinaud and St. James perfumes are made.

'For the artisan worn out by the hard labour of the workshops, for the little clerk blessed with too many offspring, the illusion of enjoying a little fresh air is a practical possibility—thanks to these manufacturers.

'Indeed, out of this fabulous counterfeit of the countryside a sensible form of medical treatment could be developed. At present, gay dogs suffering from consumption who are carted away to the south generally die down there, finished off by the change in their habits, by their nostalgic longing for the Parisian pleasures that have laid them low. Here, in an artificial climate maintained by open stoves, their lecherous memories would come back to them in a mild and harmless form, as they breathed in the languid feminine emanations given off by the scent factories. By means of this innocent deception, the physician could supply his patient platonically with the atmosphere of the boudoirs and brothels of Paris, in place of the deadly boredom of provincial life. More often than not, all that would be needed to complete the cure would be for the sick man to show a little imagination.

'Seeing that nowadays there is nothing wholesome left in this world of ours; seeing that the wine we drink and the freedom we enjoy are equally adulterate and derisory; and finally, seeing that it takes a considerable degree of goodwill to believe that the governing classes are worthy of respect and that the lower classes are worthy of help or pity, it seems to me,' concluded Des Esseintes, 'no more absurd or insane to ask of my fellow men a sum total of illusion barely equivalent to that which they expend every day on idiotic objects, to persuade themselves that the town of Pantin is an artificial Nice, a factitious Menton.'

'All that,' he muttered, interrupted in his reflections by a sudden feeling of faintness, 'doesn't alter the fact that I shall have to beware of these delicious, atrocious experiments, which are just wearing me out.'

He heaved a sigh.

'Ah, well, that means more pleasures to cut down on, more precautions to take!'—and he shut himself up in his study, hoping that there he would find it easier to escape from the obsessive influence of all these perfumes.

He threw the window wide open, delighted to take a bath of fresh air; but suddenly it struck him that the breeze was bringing with it a whiff of bergamot oil, mingled with a smell of jasmine, cassia, and rose-water. He gave a gasp of horror, and began to wonder whether he might not be in the grip of one of those evil spirits they used to exorcize in the Middle Ages. Meanwhile the odour, though just as persistent, underwent a change. A vague scent of tincture of Tolu, Peruvian balsam, and saffron, blended with a few drops of musk and amber, now floated up from the sleeping village at the foot of the hill; then all at once the metamorphosis took place, these scattered whiffs of perfume came together, and the familiar scent of frangipane, the elements of which his sense of smell had detected and recognized, spread from the valley of Fontenay all the way to the Fort, assailing his jaded nostrils, shaking anew his shattered nerves, and throwing him into such a state of prostration that he fell fainting, almost dying, across the window-sill.

WALTER PATER

From Leonardo da Vinci†

*   *   *

* * *But it is still by a certain mystery in his work, and something enigmatical beyond the usual measure of great men, that he fascinates, or perhaps half repels. His life is one of sudden revolts, with intervals in which he works not at all, or apart from the main scope of his work. By a strange fortune the works on which his more popular fame rested disappeared early from the world, as the *Battle of the Standard;* or are mixed obscurely with the work of meaner hands, as the *Last Supper.* His type of beauty is so exotic that it fascinates a larger number than it delights, and seems more than that of any other artist to reflect ideas and views and some scheme of the world within; so that he seemed to his contemporaries to be the possessor of some unsanctified and secret wisdom; as, to Michelet and others, to have anticipated modern ideas. He trifles with his genius, and

---

† Of the ten chapters in the 1888 edition of Pater's *The Renaissance: Studies in Art and Poetry,* this is the sixth, a chapter famous for its description of Leonardo's *Mona Lisa.* It is followed here by the Conclusion.

crowds all his chief work into a few tormented years of later life; yet
he is so possessed by his genius that he passes unmoved through the
most tragic events, overwhelming his country and friends, like one
who comes across them by change on some secret errand.

His *legend,* as the French say, with the anecdotes which everyone
knows, is one of the most brilliant in Vasari. Later writers merely
copied it, until, in 1804, Carlo Amoretti applied to it a criticism
which left hardly a date fixed, and not one of those anecdotes
untouched. The various questions thus raised have since that time
become, one after another, subjects of special study, and mere antiquarianism has in this direction little more to do. For others remain
the editing of the thirteen books of his manuscripts, and the separation by technical criticism of what in his reputed works is really
his, from what is only half his, or the work of his pupils. But a lover
of strange souls may still analyze for himself the impression made
on him by those works, and try to reach through it a definition of
the chief elements of Leonardo's genius. The *legend,* corrected and
enlarged by its critics, may now and then intervene to support the
results of this analysis.

His life has three divisions—thirty years at Florence, nearly twenty
years at Milan, then nineteen years of wandering, till he sinks to rest
under the protection of Francis the First at the Château de Cloux.
The dishonor of illegitimacy hangs over his birth. Piero Antonio, his
father, was of a noble Florentine house, of Vinci in the Val d'Arno,
and Leonardo, brought up delicately among the true children of that
house, was the love child of his youth, with the keen, puissant nature
such children often have. We see him in his youth fascinating all
men by his beauty, improvising music and songs, buying the caged
birds and setting them free, as he walked the streets of Florence,
fond of odd bright dresses and spirited horses.

From his earliest years he designed many objects, and constructed
models in relief, of which Vasari mentions some of women smiling.
His father, pondering over this promise in the child, took him to the
workshop of Andrea del Verrocchio, then the most famous artist in
Florence. Beautiful objects lay about there—reliquaries, pyxes, silver
images for the pope's chapel at Rome, strange fancywork of the Middle Ages, keeping odd company with fragments of antiquity, then but
lately discovered. Another student Leonardo may have seen there—a
boy into whose soul the level light and aerial illusions of Italian sunsets had passed, in after days famous as Perugino, Verrocchio was
an artist of the earlier Florentine type, carver, painter, and worker in
metals, in one; designer, not of pictures only, but of all things for
sacred or household use, drinking vessels, ambries, instruments of
music, making them all fair to look upon, filling the common ways
of life with the reflection of some faroff brightness; and years of

patience had refined his hand till his work was now sought after from distant places.

It happened that Verrocchio was employed by the brethren of Vallombrosa to paint the Baptism of Christ, and Leonardo was allowed to finish the angel in the left-hand corner. It was one of those moments in which the progress of a great thing—here, that of the art of Italy—presses hard and sharp on the happiness of an individual, through whose discouragement and decrease, humanity, in more fortunate persons, comes a step nearer to its final success.

For beneath the cheerful exterior of the mere well-paid craftsman, chasing brooches for the copes of Santa Maria Novella, or twisting metal screens for the tombs of the Medici, lay the ambitious desire of expanding the destiny of Italian art by a larger knowledge and insight into things, a purpose in art not unlike Leonardo's still unconscious purpose; and often, in the modeling of drapery, or of a lifted arm, or of hair cast back from the face there came to him something of the freer manner and richer humanity of a later age. But in this *Baptism* the pupil had surpassed the master; and Verrocchio turned away as one stunned, and as if his sweet earlier work must thereafter be distasteful to him, from the bright animated angel of Leonardo's hand.

The angel may still be seen in Florence, a space of sunlight in the cold, labored old picture; but the legend is true only in sentiment, for painting had always been the art by which Verrocchio set least store. And as in a sense he anticipates Leonardo, so to the last Leonardo recalls the studio of Verrocchio, in the love of beautiful toys, such as the vessel of water for a mirror, and lovely needlework about the implicated hands in the *Modesty and Vanity,* and of reliefs, like those cameos which in the *Virgin of the Balances* hang all round the girdle of Saint Michael, and of bright variegated stones, such as the agates in the *Saint Anne,* and in a hieratic preciseness and grace, as of a sanctuary swept and garnished. Amid all the cunning and intricacy of his Lombard manner this never left him. Much of it there must have been in that lost picture of *Paradise,* which he prepared as a cartoon for tapestry, to be woven in the looms of Flanders. It was the perfection of the older Florentine style of miniature painting, with patient putting of each leaf upon the trees and each flower in the grass, where the first man and woman were standing.

And because it was the perfection of that style, it awoke in Leonardo some seed of discontent which lay in the secret places of his nature. For the way to perfection is through a series of disgusts; and this picture—all that he had done so far in his life at Florence—was after all in the old slight manner. His art, if it was to be something in the world, must be weighted with more of the meaning of nature and purpose of humanity. Nature was "the true mistress of higher intelligences." So he plunged into the study of nature. And in doing this he followed the manner of the older students; he brooded over the hidden virtues of plants and crystals, the lines traced by the stars as they moved in the sky, over the correspondences which exist between the different orders of living things, through which, to eyes opened, they interpret each other; and for years he seemed to those about him as one listening to a voice, silent for other men.

He learned here the art of going deep, of tracking the sources of expression to their subtlest retreats, the power of an intimate presence in the things he handled. He did not at once or entirely desert his art; only he was no longer the cheerful, objective painter, through whose soul, as through clear glass, the bright figures of Florentine life, only made a little mellower and more pensive by the transit, passed onto the white wall. He wasted many days in curious tricks of design, seeming to lose himself in the spinning of intricate devices of lines and colors. He was smitten with a love of the impossible—the perforation of mountains, changing the course of rivers, raising great buildings, such as the church of San Giovanni, in the air; all those feats for the performance of which natural magic professes to have the key. Later writers, indeed, see in these efforts an anticipation of modern mechanics; in him they were rather dreams, thrown off by the overwrought and laboring brain. Two ideas were especially fixed in him, as reflexes of things that had touched his brain in childhood beyond the measure of other impressions—the smiling of women and the motion of great waters.

And in such studies some interfusion of the extremes of beauty and terror shaped itself, as an image that might be seen and touched, in the mind of this gracious youth, so fixed that for the rest of his life it never left him; and as catching glimpses of it in the strange eyes or hair of chance people, he would follow such about the streets of Florence till the sun went down, of whom many sketches of his remain. Some of these are full of a curious beauty, that remote beauty apprehended only by those who have sought it carefully; who, starting with acknowledged types of beauty, have refined as far upon these, as these refine upon the world of common forms. But mingled inextricably with this there is an element of mockery also; so that, whether in sorrow of scorn, he caricatures Dante even. Legions of grotesques sweep under his hand; for has not nature too her grotesques—the rent rock, the distorting light of evening on lonely roads, the unveiled structure of man in the embryo, or the skeleton?

All these swarming fancies unite in the *Medusa* of the Uffizi. Vasari's story of an earlier Medusa, painted on a wooden shield, is perhaps an invention; and yet, properly told, has more of the air of truth about it than anything else in the whole legend. For its real subject is not the serious work of a man, but the experiment of a child. The lizards and glowworms and other strange small creatures which haunt an Italian vineyard bring before one the whole picture of a child's life in a Tuscan dwelling, half castle, half farm; and are as a true to nature as the pretended astonishment of the father for whom the boy has prepared a surprise. It was not in play that he painted that other Medusa, the one great picture which he left behind him in Florence. The subject has been treated in various ways; Leonardo alone cuts to its center; he alone realizes it as the head of a corpse, exercising its power through all the circumstances of death. What may be called the fascination of corruption penetrates in every touch its exquisitely finished beauty. About the dainty lines of the cheek the bat flits unheeded. The delicate snakes seem literally strangling each other in terrified struggle to escape from the Medusa brain. The hue which violent death always brings with it is in the features: features singularly massive and grand, as we catch them inverted, in a dexterous foreshortening, sloping upward, almost sliding down upon us, crown foremost, like a great calm stone against which the wave of serpents breaks. But it is a subject that may well be left to the beautiful verses of Shelley.

The science of that age was all divination, clairvoyance, unsubjected to our exact modern formulas, seeking in an instant of vision to concentrate a thousand experiences. Later writers, thinking only of the well-ordered treatise on painting which a Frenchman, Raffaelle du Fresne, a hundred years afterwards, compiled from Leonardo's bewildered manuscripts, written strangely, as his manner was, from right to left, have imagined a rigid order in his inquiries. But this rigid order was little in accordance with the restlessness of his character; and if we think of him as the mere reasoner who subjects design to anatomy, and composition to mathematical rules, we shall hardly have of him that impression which those about him received from him. Poring over his crucibles, making experiments with color, trying by a strange variation of the alchemist's dream to discover the secret, not of an elixir to make man's natural life immortal, but rather of giving immortality to the subtlest and most delicate effects of painting, he seemed to them rather the sorcerer or the magician, possessed of curious secrets and a hidden knowledge, living in a world of which he alone possessed the key. What his philosophy seems to have been most like is that of Paracelsus or Cardan; and much the spirit of the older alchemy still hangs about it, with its confidence in short cuts and odd byways to knowledge. To him philosophy was to be something giving strange swiftness and double sight, divining the sources of springs beneath the earth or of expression beneath the human countenance, clairvoyant of occult gifts in common or uncommon things, in the reed at the brookside, or the star which draws near to us but once in a century. How, in this way, the clear purpose was overclouded, the fine chaser's hand perplexed, we but dimly see; the mystery which at no point quite lifts from Leonardo's life is deepest here. But it is certain that at one period of his life he had almost ceased to be an artist.

The year 1483—the year of the birth of Raphael and the thirty-first of Leonardo's life—is fixed as the date of his visit to Milan by the letter in which he recommends himself to Lodovico Sforza, and offers to tell him, for a price, strange secrets in the air of war. It was that Sforza who murdered his young nephew by slow poison, yet was so susceptible of religious impressions that he blended mere earthly passions with a sort of religious sentimentalism, and who took for his device the mulberry tree—symbol, in its long delay and sudden yielding of flowers and fruit together, of a wisdom which economizes all forces for an opportunity of sudden and sure effect. The fame of Leonardo had gone before him, and he was to model a colossal statue of Francesco, the first duke of Milan. As for Leonardo himself, he came not as an artist at all, or careful of the fame of one; but as a player on the harp, a strange harp of silver of his own construction, shaped in some curious likeness to a horse's skull. The capricious spirit of Lodovico was susceptible also of the charm of music, and Leonardo's nature had a kind of spell in it. Fascination is always the word descriptive of him. No portrait of his youth remains; but all tends to make us believe that up to this time some charms of voice and aspect, strong enough to balance the disadvantage of his birth, had played about him. His physical strength was great; it was said that he could bend a horseshoe like a coil of lead.

The Duomo, the work of artists from beyond the Alps, so fantastic to the eye of a Florentine, used to the mellow, unbroken surfaces of Giotto and Arnolfo, was then in all its freshness; and below, in the streets of Milan, moved a people as fantastic, changeful, and dreamlike. To Leonardo least of all men could there be anything poisonous in the exotic flowers of sentiment which grew there. It was a life of brilliant sins and exquisite amusements—Leonardo became a celebrated designer of pageants—and it suited the quality of his genius, composed in almost equal parts of curiosity and the desire of beauty, to take things as they came.

Curiosity and the desire of beauty—these are the two elementary forces in Leonardo's genius; curiosity often in conflict with the desire of beauty, but generating, in union with it, a type of subtle and curious grace.

The movement of the fifteenth century was twofold; partly the Renaissance, partly also the coming of what is called the "modern spirit," with its realism, its appeal to experience, it comprehended a return to antiquity, and a return to nature. Raphael represents the return to antiquity, and Leonardo the return to nature. In this return to nature, he was seeking to satisfy a boundless curiosity by her perpetual surprises, a microscopic sense of finish by her finesse, or delicacy of operation, that *subtilitas naturae* which Bacon notices. So we find him often in intimate relations with men of science, with Fra Luca Paccioli the mathematician, and the anatomist Marc Antonio della Torre. His observations and experiments fill thirteen volumes of manuscript; and those who can judge describe him as anticipating long before, by rapid intuition, the later ideas of science. He explained the obscure light of the unilluminated part of the moon, knew that the sea had once covered the mountains which contain shells, and the gathering of the equatorial waters above the polar.

He who thus penetrated into the most secret parts of nature preferred always the more to the less remote, what, seeming exceptional, was an instance of law more refined, the construction about things of a peculiar atmosphere and mixed lights. He paints flowers with such curious felicity that different writers have attributed to him a fondness for particular flowers, as Clement the cyclamen, and Rio the jasmine; while, at Venice, there is a stray leaf from his portfolio dotted all over with studies of violets and the wild rose. In him first, appears the taste for what is bizarre or *recherché* in landscape; hollow places full of the green shadow of bituminous rocks, ridged reefs of trap-rock which cut the water into quaint sheets of light—their exact antitype is in our own western seas; all the solemn effects of moving water; you may follow it springing from its distant source among the rocks on the heath of the *Madonna of the Balances,* passing as a little fall into the treacherous calm of the *Madonna of the Lake,* next, as a goodly river, below the cliffs of the *Madonna of the Rocks,* washing the white walls of its distant villages, stealing out in a network of divided streams in *La Gioconda* to the seashore of the *Saint Anne*—that delicate place, where the wind passes like the hand of some fine etcher over the surface, and the untorn shells are lying thick upon the sand, and the tops of the rocks, to which the waves never rise, are green with grass, grown as fine as hair. It is the landscape, not of dreams or of fancy, but of places far withdrawn, and hours selected from a thousand with a miracle of finesse. Through Leonardo's strange veil of sight things reach him so; in no ordinary night or day, but as in faint light of eclipse, or in some brief interval of falling rain at daybreak, or through deep water.

And not into nature only; but he plunged also into human personality, and became above all a painter of portraits; faces of a modeling more skillful than has been seen before or since, embodied with a reality which almost amounts to illusion, on dark air. To take a character as it was, and delicately sound its stops, suited one so curious in observation, curious in invention. So he painted the portraits of

Lodovico's mistresses, Lucretia Crivelli and Cecilia Galerani the poetess, of Lodovico himself, and the Duchess Beatrice. The portrait of Cecilia Galerani is lost, but that of Lucretia Crivelli has been identified with *La Belle Feronière* of the Louvre, and Lodovico's pale, anxious face still remains in the Ambrosian Library. Opposite is the portrait of Beatrice d'Este, in whom Leonardo seems to have caught some presentiment of early death, painting her precise and grave, full of the refinement of the dead, in sad earth-colored raiment, set with pale stones.

Sometimes this curiosity came in conflict with the desire of beauty; it tended to make him go too far below that outside of things in which art begins and ends. This struggle between the reason and its ideas, and the senses, the desire of beauty, is the key to Leonardo's life at Milan—his restlessness, his endless retouchings, his odd experiments with color. How much must he leave unfinished, how much recommence! His problem was the transmutation of ideas into images. What he had attained so far had been the mastery of that earlier Florentine style, with its naive and limited sensuousness. Now he was to entertain in this narrow medium those divinations of a humanity too wide for it, that larger vision of the opening world, which is only not too much for the great, irregular art of Shakespeare; and everywhere the effort is visible in the work of his hands. This agitation, this perpetual delay, give him an air of weariness and ennui. To others he seems to be aiming at an impossible effect, to do something that art, that painting, can never do. Often the expression of physical beauty at this or that point seems strained and marred in the effort, as in those heavy German foreheads—too heavy and German for perfect beauty.

For there was a touch of Germany in that genius which, as Goethe said, had *müde sich gedacht* ("thought itself weary"). What an anticipation of modern Germany, for instance, in that debate on the question whether sculpture or painting is the nobler art.[1] But there is this difference between him and the German, that, with all that curious science, the German would have thought nothing more was needed; and the name of Goethe himself reminds one how great for the artist may be the danger of overmuch science; how Goethe, who, in the *Elective Affinities* and the first part of *Faust*, does transmute ideas into images, who wrought many such transmutations, did not invariably find the spell-word, and in the second part of *Faust* presents us with a mass of science which has almost no artistic characters at all. But Leonardo will never work till the happy moment comes—that moment of *bien-être*, which to imaginative men is a moment of

---

1. How princely, how characteristic of Leonardo, the answer: *Quanto più, un' arte porta seco fatica di corpo, tanto più è vilel* [To the degree an art bears the strain of the body, the lower it is—*Editor*].

invention. On this moment he waits; other moments are but a preparation, or aftertaste of it. Few men distinguish between them as jeal-
ously as he did. Hence, so many flaws even in the choicest work. But
for Leonardo the distinction is absolute, and in the moment of *bien-
être*, the alchemy complete; the idea is stricken into color and
imagery; a cloudy mysticism is refined to a subdued and graceful
mystery, and painting pleases the eye while it satisfies the soul.

This curious beauty is seen above all in his drawings, and in these
chiefly in the abstract grace of the bounding lines. Let us take some
of these drawings, and pause over them awhile; and, first, one of
those at Florence—the heads of a woman and a little child, set side
by side, but each in its own separate frame. First of all, there is much
pathos in the reappearance in the fuller curves of the face of the
child, of the sharper, more chastened lines of the worn and older
face, which leaves no doubt that the heads are those of a little child
and its mother. A feeling for maternity is indeed always characteristic of Leonardo; and this feeling is further indicated here by the half-
humorous pathos of the diminutive, rounded shoulders of the child.
You may note a like pathetic power in drawings of a young man,
seated in a stooping posture, his face in his hands, as in sorrow; of a
slave sitting in an uneasy inclined posture, in some brief interval of
rest; of a small Madonna and Child, peeping sideways in half-
reassured terror, as a mighty griffin with batlike wings, one of
Leonardo's finest *inventions*, descends suddenly from the air to
snatch up a lion wandering near them. But note in these, as that
which especially belongs to art, the contour of the young man's hair,
the poise of the slave's arm above his head, and the curves of the head
of the child, following the little skull within, thin and fine as some
seashell worn by the wind.

Take again another head, still more full of sentiment, but of a
different kind, a little drawing in red chalk which everyone remembers who has examined at all carefully the drawings by old masters
at the Louvre. It is a face of doubtful sex, set in the shadow of its own
hair, the cheekline in high light against it, with something volup-
tuous and full in the eyelids and the lips. Another drawing might
pass for the same face in childhood, with parched and feverish lips,
but with much sweetness in the loose, short-waisted childish dress,
with necklace and *bulla*, and in the daintily bound hair. We might
take the threat of suggestion which these two drawings offer, when
thus set side by side, following it through the drawings at Florence,
Venice, and Milan, construct a sort of series, illustrating better than
anything else Leonardo's type of womanly beauty. Daughters of
Herodias, with their fantastic headdresses knotted and folded so
strangely, to leave the dainty oval of the face disengaged, they are not
of the Christian family, or of Raphael's. They are the clairvoyants,

through whom, as through delicate instruments, one becomes aware of the subtler forces of nature, and the modes of their action, all that is magnetic in it, all those finer conditions wherein material things rise to that subtlety of operation which constitutes them spiritual, where only the finer nerve and the keener touch can follow; it is as if in certain revealing instances we actually saw them at their work on human flesh. Nervous, electric, faint always with some inexplicable faintness, they seem to be subject to exceptional conditions, to feel powers at work in the common air unfelt by others, to become, as it were, receptables of them, and pass them on to us in a chain of secret influences.

But among the more youthful heads there is one at Florence, which Love chooses for its own—the head of a young man, which may well be the likeness of Andrea Salaino, beloved of Leonardo for his curled and waving hair—*belli capelli ricci e inanellati*—and afterward his favorite pupil and servant. Of all the interests in living men and women which may have filled his life at Milan, this attachment alone is recorded; and in return, Salaino identified himself so entirely with Leonardo, that the picture of *Saint Anne,* in the Louvre, has been attributed to him. It illustrates Leonardo's usual choice of pupils, men of some natural charm of person or intercourse like Salaino, or men of birth, and princely habits of life like Francesco Melzi—men with just enough genius to be capable of initiation into his secret, for the sake of which they were ready to efface their own individuality. Among them, retiring often to the villa of the Melzi at Canonica al Vaprio, he worked at his fugitive manuscripts and sketches, working for the present hour, and for a few only, perhaps chiefly for himself. Other artists have been as careless of present or future applause, in self-forgetfulness, or because they set moral or political ends above the ends of the art; but in him this solitary culture of beauty seems to have hung upon a kind of self-love, and a carelessness in the work of art of all but art itself. Out of the secret places of a unique temperament he brought strange blossoms and fruits hitherto unknown; and for him, the novel impression conveyed, the exquisite effect woven, counted as an end in itself—a perfect end.

And these pupils of his acquired his manner so thoroughly, that though the number of Leonardo's authentic works is very small indeed, there is a multitude of other men's pictures, through which we undoubtedly see him, and come very near to his genius. Sometimes, as in the little picture of the *Madonna of the Balances,* in which, from the bosom of his mother, Christ is weighing the pebbles of the brook against the sins of men, we have a hand, rough enough by contrast, working upon some fine hint or sketch of his. Sometimes, as in the subjects of the *Daughter of Herodias* and the *Head of John the Baptist,* the lost originals have been re-echoed and varied upon again and again by Luini and others. At other times the original remains, but has been a mere theme or motive, a type of which the accessories might be modified or changed; and these variations have but brought out the more the purpose, or expression of the original. It is so with the so-called *Saint John the Baptist* of the Louvre— one of the few naked figures Leonardo painted—whose delicate brown flesh and woman's hair no one would go out into the wilderness to seek, and whose treacherous smile would have us understand something far beyond the outward gesture, or circumstance. But the long, reedlike cross in the hand, which suggests Saint John the Baptist, becomes faint in a copy of the Ambrosian Library, and disappears altogether in another, in the Palazzo Rosso at Genoa. Returning from the last to the original, we are no longer surprised by Saint John's strange likeness to the *Bacchus* which hangs near it, which set Théophile Gautier thinking of Heine's notion of decayed gods, who, to maintain themselves, after the fall of paganism, took employment in the new religion. We recognize one of those symbolical inventions in which the ostensible subject is used, not as matter for definite pictorial realization, but as the starting point of a train of sentiment, as subtle and vague as a piece of music. No one ever ruled over his subject more entirely than Leonardo, or bent it more dexterously to purely artistic ends. And so it comes to pass that though he handles sacred subjects continually, he is the most profane of painters; the given person or subject, Saint John in the Desert, or the Virgin on the knees of Saint Anne, is often merely the pretext for a kind of work which carries one quite out of the range of its conventional associations.

About the *Last Supper,* its decay and restorations, a whole literature has risen up, Goethe's pensive sketch of its sad fortunes being far the best. The death in childbirth of the Duchess Beatrice was followed in Lodovico by one of those paroxysms of religious feeling which in him were constitutional. The low, gloomy Dominican church of Saint Mary of the Graces had been the favorite shrine of Beatrice. She had spent her last days there, full of sinister presentiments; at last it had been almost necessary to remove her from it by force; and now it was here that mass was said a hundred times a day for her repose. On the damp wall of the refectory, oozing with mineral salts, Leonardo painted the *Last Supper.* A hundred anecdotes were told about it, his retouchings and delays. They show him refusing to work except at the moment of invention, scornful of whoever thought that art was a work of mere industry and rule, often coming the whole length of Milan to give a single touch. He painted it, not in fresco, where all must be impromptu, but in oils, the new method which he had been one of the first to welcome, because it

allowed of so many afterthoughts, so refined a working out of perfection. It turned out that on a plastered wall no process could have
been less durable. Within fifty years it had fallen into decay. And now
we have to turn back to Leonardo's own studies, above all, to one
drawing of the central head at the Brera, which in a union of tenderness and severity in the face lines, reminds one of the monumental work of Mino da Fiesole, to trace it as it was.

It was another effort to set a given subject out of the range of its
conventional associations. Strange, after all the misrepresentations
of the Middle Ages, was the effort to see it, not as the pale host of the
altar, but as one taking leave of his friends. Five years afterwards, the
young Raphael, at Florence, painted it with sweet and solemn effect
in the refectory of Saint Onofrio; but still with all the mystical unreality of the school of Perugino. Vasari pretends that the central head
was never finished; but finished or unfinished, or owing part of its
effect to a mellowing decay, this central head does but consummate
the sentiment of the whole company; ghosts through which you see
the wall, faint as the shadows of the leaves upon the wall on autumn
afternoons—this figure is but the faintest, most spectral of them all.
It is the image of what the history it symbolizes has been more and
more ever since, paler and paler as it recedes from us. Criticism came
with its appeal from mystical unrealities to originals, and restored no
lifelike reality but these transparent shadows, spirits which have not
flesh and bones.

The *Last Supper* was finished in 1497; in 1498 the French entered
Milan, and whether or not the Gascon bowman used it as a mark for
their arrows, the model of Francesco Sforza certainly did not survive.
What, in that age, such work was capable of being, of what nobility,
amid what racy truthfulness to fact, we may judge from the bronze
statue of Bartolomeo Colleoni on horseback, modeled by Leonardo's
master, Verrocchio—he died of grief, it was said, because, the mold
accidentally failing, he was unable himself to complete it—still
standing in the piazza of Saint John and Saint Paul at Venice. Some
traces of the thing may remain in certain of Leonardo's drawings, and
also, perhaps, by a singular circumstance, in a faroff town of France.
For Lodovico became a prisoner, and ended his days at Loches in
Touraine; allowed, it is said, at last to breathe fresher air for awhile
in one of the rooms of a high tower there, after many years of cap-
tivity in the dungeons below, where all seems sick with barbarous
feudal memories, and where his prison is still shown, its walls covered with strange painted arabesques, ascribed by tradition to his
hand, amused a little thus through the tedious years—vast helmets
and faces and pieces of armor, among which in great letters the motto
Infelix Sum, is woven in and out, and in which perhaps it is not too
fanciful to see the fruit of a wistful afterdreaming over all those

experiments with Leonardo on the armed figure of the great duke, which had occupied the two so often, during the days of his fortune at Milan.

The remaining years of Leonardo's life are more or less years of wandering. From his brilliant life at court he had saved nothing, and he returned to Florence a poor man. Perhaps necessity kept his spirit excited: the next four years are one prolonged rapture or ecstasy of invention. He painted the pictures of the Louvre, his most authentic works, which came there straight from the cabinet of Francis the First, at Fontainebleau. One picture of his, the *Saint Anne*— not the *Saint Anne* of the Louvre, but a mere cartoon, now in London— revived for a moment a sort of appreciation more common in an earlier time, when good pictures had still seemed miraculous; and for two days a crowd of people of all qualities passed in naive excitement through the chamber where it hung, and gave Leonardo a taste of Cimabue's triumph. But his work was less with the saints than with the living women of Florence; for he lived still in the polished society that he loved, and in the houses of Florence, left perhaps a little subject to light thoughts by the death of Savonarola, (the latest gossip is of an undraped Mona Lisa, found in some out-of-the-way corner of the late Orléans collection) he saw Ginevra di Benci, and Lisa, the young third wife of Francesco del Giocondo. As we have seen him using incidents of the sacred legend, not for their own sake, or as mere subjects for pictorial realization, but as a symbolical language for fancies all his own, so now he found a vent for his thoughts in taking one of these languid women, and raising her, as Leda or Pomona, Modesty or Vanity, to the seventh heaven of symbolical expression.

La Gioconda is, in the truest sense, Leonardo's masterpiece, the revealing instance of his mode of thought and work. In suggestiveness, only the *Melancholia* of Dúrer is comparable to it; and no crude symbolism disturbs the effect of its subdued and graceful mystery. We all know the face and hands of the figure, set in its marble chair, in that cirque of fantastic rocks, as in some faint light under sea. Perhaps of all ancient pictures time has chilled it least.[2] As often happens with works in which invention seems to reach its limit, there is an element in it given to, not invented by, the master. In that inestimable folio of drawings, once in the possession of Vasari, were certain designs by Verrocchio, faces of such impressive beauty that Leonardo in his boyhood copied them many times. It is hard not to connect with these designs of the elder, by-passed master, as with its germinal principle, the unfathomable smile, always with a touch of something sinister in it, which plays over all Leonardo's work.

2. Yet for Vasari there was some further magic of crimson in the lips and cheeks, lost for us.

Besides, the picture is a portrait. From childhood we see this image
defining itself on the fabric of his dreams; and but for express historical testimony, we might fancy that this was but his ideal lady,
embodied and beheld at last. What was the relationship of a living
Florentine to this creature of his thought? By means of what strange
affinities had the person and the dream grown up thus apart, and yet
so closely together? Present from the first, incorporeal in Leonardo's
thought, dimly traced in the designs of Verrocchio, she is found present at last in Il Giocondo's house. That there is much of mere portraiture in the picture is attested by the legend that by artificial
means, the presence of mimes and flute players, that subtle expression was protracted on the face. Again, was it in four years, and by
renewed labor never really completed, or in four months, and as by
stroke of magic, that the image was projected?

The presence that thus rose so strangely beside the waters, is
expressive of what in the ways of a thousand years man had come to
desire. Hers is the head upon which all "the ends of the world are
come," and the eyelids are a little weary. It is a beauty wrought out
from within upon the flesh, the deposit, little cell by cell, of strange
thoughts and fantastic reveries and exquisite passions. Set it for a
moment beside one of those white Greek goddesses or beautiful
women of antiquity, and how would they be troubled by this beauty,
into which the soul with all its maladies has passed? All the thoughts
and experience of the world have etched and molded there, in that
which they have the power to refine and make expressive the outward
form, the animalism of Greece, the lust of Rome, the reverie of the
Middle Ages with its spiritual ambition and imaginative loves, the
return of the pagan world, the sins of the Borgias. She is older than
the rocks among which she sits; like the vampire, she has been dead
many times, and learned the secrets of the grave; and has been a diver
in deep seas, and keeps their fallen day about her; and trafficked for
strange webs with Eastern merchants; and, as Leda, was the mother
of Helen of Troy, and, as Saint Anne, the mother of Mary; and all this
has been to her but as the sound of lyres and flutes, and lives only in
the delicacy with which it has molded the changing lineaments, and
tinged the eyelids and the hands. The fancy of a perpetual life, sweeping together ten thousand experiences, is an old one; and modern
thought has conceived the idea of humanity as wrought upon by, and
summing up in itself, all modes of thought and life. Certainly Lady
Lisa might stand as the embodiment of the old fancy, the symbol of
the modern idea.

During these years at Florence, Leonardo's history is the history
of his art; he himself is lost in the bright cloud of it. The outward
history begins again in 1502, with a wild journey through central
Italy, which he makes as the chief engineer of Cesare Borgia. The

biographer, putting together the stray jottings of his manuscripts, may follow him through every day of it, up the strange tower of Siena, which looks toward Rome, elastic like a bent bow, down to the seashore at Piombino, each place appearing as fitfully as in a fever dream.

One other great work was left for him to do, a work all trace of which soon vanished, *The Battle of the Standard,* in which he had Michelangelo for his rival. The citizens of Florence, desiring to decorate the walls of the great council chamber, had offered the work for competition, and any subject might be chosen from the Florentine wars of the fifteenth century. Michelangelo chose for his cartoon an incident of the war with Pisa, in which the Florentine soldiers, bathing in the Arno, are surprised by the sound of trumpets, and run to arms. His design has reached us only in an old engraving, which perhaps helps us less than what we remember of the background of his *Holy Family* in the Uffizi to imagine in what superhuman form, such as might have beguiled the heart of an earlier world, those figures may have risen from the water. Leonardo chose an incident from the battle of Anghiari, in which two parties of soldiers fight for a standard. Like Michelangelo's, his cartoon is lost, and has come to us only in sketches, and in a fragment of Rubens. Through the accounts given we may discern some lust of terrible things in it, so that even the horses tore each other with their teeth; and yet one fragment of it, in a drawing of his at Florence, is far different—a waving field of lovely armor, the chased edgings running like lines of sunlight from side to side. Michelangelo was twenty-seven years old; Leonardo more than fifty; and Raphael, then nineteen years old, visiting Florence for the first time, came and watched them as they worked.

We catch a glimpse of him again, at Rome in 1514, surrounded by his mirrors and vials and furnaces, making strange toys that seemed alive of wax and quicksilver. The hesitation which had haunted him all through life, and made him like one under a spell, was upon him now with double force. No one had ever carried political indifferentism farther; it had always been his philosophy to "fly before the storm"; he is for the Sforzas, or against them, as the tide of their fortune turns. Yet now in the political society of Rome, he came to be suspected of concealed French sympathies. It paralyzed him to find himself among enemies; and he turned wholly to France, which had long courted him.

France was about to become an Italy more Italian than Italy itself. Francis the First, like Lewis the Twelfth before him, was attracted by the finesse of Leonardo's work; *La Gioconda* was already in his cabinet, and he offered Leonardo the little Château de Cloux, with its vineyards and meadows, in the pleasant valley of the Masse, just

outside the walls of the town of Amboise, where, especially in the
hunting season, the court then frequently resided. *A Monsieur
Lyonard, peinteur du Roy pour Amboyse*—so the letter of Francis the
First is headed. It opens a prospect, one of the most attractive in the
history of art, where, under a strange mixture of lights, Italian art dies
away as a French exotic.

Two questions remain, after much busy antiquarianism, concerning Leonardo's death—the question of the form of his religion, and
the question whether Francis the First was present at the time. They
are of about equally little importance in the estimate of Leonardo's
genius. The directions in his will about the thirty masses and the
great candles for the church of Saint Florentin are things of course,
their real purpose being immediate and practical; and on no theory
of religion could these hurried offices be of much consequence. We
forget them in speculating how one who had been always so desirous
of beauty, but desired it always in such definite and precise forms, as
hands or flowers or hair, looked forward now into the vague land, and
experienced the last curiosity.

Conclusion [The Renaissance]†

Αέγει που'Ηράκλειτος ότι άντα χωρεί καί ούδέν μένει[1]

To regard all things and principles of things as inconstant modes
or fashions has more and more become the tendency of modern
thought. Let us begin with that which is without—our physical life.
Fix upon it in one of its more exquisite intervals, the moment, for
instance, of delicious recoil from the flood of water in summer heat.
What is the whole physical life in that moment but a combination
of natural elements to which science gives their names? But those
elements, phosphorus and lime and delicate fibres, are present not
in the human body alone: we detect them in places most remote
from it. Our physical life is a perpetual motion of them—the passage
of the blood, the waste and repairing of the lenses of the eye, the
modification of the tissues of the brain under every ray of light and
sound—processes which science reduces to simpler and more elementary forces. Like the elements of which we are composed, the

---

† This brief "Conclusion" was omitted in the second edition of this book, as I conceived it
might possibly mislead some of those young men into whose hands it might fall. On the
whole, I have thought it best to reprint it here, with some slight changes which bring it
closer to my original meaning. I have dealt more fully in *Marius the Epicurean* with the
thoughts suggested by it [*Pater's note*].
1. "Heraclitus says, 'All things give way; nothing remains.'"

action of these forces extends beyond us: it rusts iron and ripens corn. Far out on every side of us those elements are broadcast, driven in many currents; and birth and gesture and death and the springing of violets from the grave are but a few out of ten thousand resultant combinations. That clear, perpetual outline of face and limb is but an image of ours, under which we group them—a design in a web, the actual threads of which pass out beyond it. This at least of flame-like our life has, that it is but the concurrence, renewed from moment to moment, of forces parting sooner or later on their ways.

Or if we begin with the inward world of thought and feeling, the whirlpool is still more rapid, the flame more eager and devouring. There it is no longer the gradual darkening of the eye, the gradual fading of colour from the wall—movements of the shore-side, where the water flows down indeed, though in apparent rest—but the race of the mid-stream, a drift of momentary acts of sight and passion and thought. At first sight experience seems to bury us under a flood of external objects, pressing upon us with a sharp and importunate, reality, calling us out of ourselves in a thousand forms of action. But when reflexion begins to play upon those objects they are dissipated under its influence; the cohesive force seems suspended like some trick of magic; each object is loosed into a group of impressions—colour, odour, texture—in the mind of the observer. And if we continue to dwell in thought on this world, not of objects in the solidity with which language invests them, but of impressions, unstable, flickering, inconsistent, which burn and are extinguished with our consciousness of them, it contracts still further: the whole scope of observation is dwarfed into the narrow chamber of the individual mind. Experience, already reduced to a group of impressions, is ringed round for each one of us by that thick wall of personality through which no real voice has ever pierced on its way to us, or from us to that which we can only conjecture to be without. Every one of those impressions is the impression of the individual in his isolation, each mind keeping as a solitary prisoner its own dream of a world. Analysis goes a step farther still, and assures us that those impressions of the individual mind to which, for each one of us, experience dwindles down, are in perpetual flight; that each of them is limited by time, and that as time is infinitely divisible, each of them is infinitely divisible also; all that is actual in it being a single moment, gone while we try to apprehend it, of which it may ever be more truly said that it has ceased to be than that it is. To such a tremulous wisp constantly re-forming itself on the stream, to a single sharp impression, with a sense in it, a relic more or less fleeting, of such moments gone by, what is real in our life fines itself down. It is with this movement, with the passage and dissolution of impressions, images, sensations, that analysis leaves off—that continual vanishing away, that strange, perpetual weaving and unweaving of ourselves.

Philosophiren, says Novalis, *ist dephlegmatisiren vivificiren.*[2] The service of philosophy, of speculative culture, towards the human spirit, is to rouse, to startle it to a life of constant and eager observation. Every moment some form grows perfect in hand or face; some tone on the hills or the sea is choicer than the rest; some mood of passion or insight or intellectual excitement is irresistibly real and attractive to us,—for that moment only. Not the fruit of experience, but experience itself, is the end. A counted number of pulses only is given to us of a variegated, dramatic life. How may we see in them all that is to be seen in them by the finest senses? How shall we pass most swiftly from point to point, and be present always at the focus where the greater number of vital forces unite in their purest energy?

To burn always with this hard, gemlike flame, to maintain this ecstasy, is success in life. In a sense it might even be said that our failure is to form habits: for, after all, habit is relative to a stereotyped world, and meantime it is only the roughness of the eye that makes any two persons, things, situations, seem alike. While all melts under our feet, we may well grasp at any exquisite passion, or any contribution to knowledge that seems by a lifted horizon to set the spirit free for a moment, or any stirring of the senses, strange dyes, strange colours, and curious odours, or work of the artist's hands, or the face of one's friend. Not to discriminate every moment some passionate attitude in those about us, and in the very brilliancy of their gifts some tragic dividing of forces on their ways, is, on this short day of frost and sun, to sleep before evening. With this sense of the splendour of our experience and of its awful brevity, gathering all we are into one desperate effort to see and touch, we shall hardly have time to make theories about the things we see and touch. What we have to do is to be for ever curiously testing new opinions and courting new impressions, never acquiescing in a facile orthodoxy of Comte, or of Hegel, or of our own. Philosophical theories or ideas, as points of view, instruments of criticism, may help us to gather up what might otherwise pass unregarded by us. "Philosophy is the microscope of thought." The theory or idea or system which requires of us the sacrifice of any part of this experience, in consideration of some interest into which we cannot enter, or some abstract theory we have not identified with ourselves, or of what is only conventional, has no real claim upon us.

One of the most beautiful passages of Rousseau is that in the sixth book of the *Confessions,* where he describes the awakening in him of

---

2. "To philosophize is to cast off inertia, to vitalize."

the literary sense. An undefinable taint of death had clung always about him, and now in early manhood he believed himself smitten by mortal disease. He asked himself how he might make as much as possible of the interval that remained; and he was not biassed by anything in his previous life when he decided that it must be by intellectual excitement, which he found just then in the clear, fresh writings of Voltaire. Well! we are all *condamnés,* as Victor Hugo says: we are all under sentence of death but with a sort of indefinite reprieve—*les hommes sont tous condamnés à mort avec des sursis indéfinis:*[3] we have an interval, and then our place knows us no more. Some spend this interval in listlessness, some in high passions, the wisest, at least among "the children of this world,"[4] in art and song. For our one chance lies in expanding that interval, in getting as many pulsations as possible into the given time. Great passions may give us this quickened sense of life, ecstasy and sorrow of love, the various forms of enthusiastic activity, disinterested or otherwise, which come naturally to many of us. Only be sure it is passion—that it does yield you this fruit of a quickened, multiplied consciousness. Of such wisdom, the poetic passion, the desire of beauty, the love of art for its own sake, has most. For art comes to you proposing frankly to give nothing but the highest quality to your moments as they pass, and simply for those moments' sake.

OSCAR WILDE

From The Critic as Artist†

Part Two

* * *

GILBERT: Yes; the critic will be an interpreter, if he chooses. He can pass from his synthetic impression of the work of art as a whole, to an analysis or exposition of the work itself, and in this lower sphere, as I hold it to be, there are many delightful things to be said and done. Yet his object will not always be to explain the work of art. He may seek rather to deepen its mystery, to raise round it, and round its maker, that mist of wonder which is dear to both gods and worshippers alike. Ordinary people are "terribly at ease in Zion." They

---

3. "Men are all condemned to death with indefinite reprieves."
4. Luke 16.8.
† From *The Complete Works of Oscar Wilde,* rev. ed., ed. Vyvyan Holland (London: Collins, 1966), 1032–41.

propose to walk arm in arm with the poets, and have a glib ignorant way of saying, "Why should we read what is written about Shakespeare and Milton? We can read the plays and the poems. That is enough." But an appreciation of Milton is, as the late Rector of Lincoln remarked once, the reward of consummate scholarship. And he who desires to understand Shakespeare truly must understand the relations in which Shakespeare stood to the Renaissance and the Reformation, to the age of Elizabeth and the age of James; he must be familiar with the history of the struggle for supremacy between the old classical forms and the new spirit of romance, between the school of Sidney, and Daniel, and Johnson, and the school of Marlowe and Marlowe's greater son; he must know the materials that were at Shakespeare's disposal, and the method in which he used them, and the conditions of theatric presentation in the sixteenth and seventeenth century, their limitations and their opportunities for freedom, and the literary criticism of Shakespeare's day, its aims and modes and canons; he must study the English language in its progress, and blank or rhymed verse in its various developments; he must study the Greek drama, and the connection between the art of the creator of the Agamemnon and the art of the creator of Macbeth; in a word, he must be able to bind Elizabethan London to the Athens of Pericles, and to learn Shakespeare's true position in the history of European drama and the drama of the world. The critic will certainly be an interpreter, but he will not treat Art as a riddling Sphinx, whose shallow secret may be guessed and revealed by one whose feet are wounded and who knows not his name. Rather, he will look upon Art as a goddess whose mystery it is his province to intensify, and whose majesty his privilege to make more marvellous in the eyes of men.

And here, Ernest, this strange thing happens. The critic will indeed be an interpreter, but he will not be an interpreter in the sense of one who simply repeats in another form a message that has been put into his lips to say. For, just as it is only by contact with the art of foreign nations that the art of a country gains that individual and separate life that we call nationality, so, by curious inversion, it is only by intensifying his own personality that the critic can interpret the personality and work of others, and the more strongly this personality enters into the interpretation, the more real the interpretation becomes, the more satisfying, the more convincing, and the more true.

ERNEST: I would have said that personality would have been a disturbing element.

GILBERT: No; it is an element of revelation. If you wish to understand others you must intensify your own individualism.

ERNEST: What, then, is the result?

GILBERT: I will tell you, and perhaps I can tell you best by definite example. It seems to me that, while the literary critic stands of course first, as having the wider range, and larger vision, and nobler material, each of the arts has a critic, as it were, assigned to it. The actor is a critic of the drama. He shows the poet's work under new conditions, and by a method special to himself. He takes the written word, and action, gesture and voice become the media of revelation. The singer or the player on lute and viol is the critic of music. The etcher of a picture robs the painting of its fair colours, but shows us by the use of a new material its true colour-quality, its tones and values, and the relations of its masses, and so is, in his way, a critic of it, for the critic is he who exhibits to us a work of art in a form different from that of the work itself, and the employment of a new material is a critical as well as a creative element. Sculpture, too, has its critic, who may be either the carver of a gem, as he was in Greek days, or some painter like Mantegna, who sought to reproduce on canvas the beauty of plastic line and the symphonic dignity of processional bas-relief. And in the case of all these creative critics of art it is evident that personality is an absolute essential for any real interpretation. When Rubinstein plays to us the *Sonata Appassionata* of Beethoven he gives us not merely Beethoven, but also himself, and so gives us Beethoven absolutely—Beethoven reinterpreted through a rich artistic nature, and made vivid and wonderful to us by a new and intense personality. When a greater actor plays Shakespeare we have the same experience. His own individuality becomes a vital part of the interpretation. People sometimes say that actors give us their own Hamlets, and not Shakespeare's; and this fallacy—for it is a fallacy—is, I regret to say, repeated by that charming and graceful writer who has lately deserted the turmoil of literature for the peace of the House of Commons; I mean the author of *Obiter Dicta*. In point of fact, there is no such thing as Shakespeare's Hamlet. If Hamlet has something of the definiteness of a work of art, he has also all the obscurity that belongs to life. There are as many Hamlets as there are melancholies.

ERNEST: As many Hamlets as there are melancholies?

GILBERT: Yes; and as art springs from personality, so it is only to personality that it can be revealed, and from the meeting of the two comes right interpretative criticism.

ERNEST: The critic, then, considered as the interpreter, will give no less than he receives, and lend as much as he borrows?

GILBERT: He will be always showing us the work of art in some new relation to our age. He will always be reminding us that great works of art are living things—are, in fact, the only things that live. So much, indeed, will he feel this, that I am certain that, as civilisation progresses and we become more highly organised, the elect

spirits of each age, the critical and cultured spirits, will grow less
and less interested in actual life, and *will seek to gain their impressions almost entirely from what Art has touched.* For life is terribly
deficient in form. Its catastrophes happen in the wrong way and to
the wrong people. There is a grotesque horror about its comedies,
and its tragedies seem to culminate in farce. One is always wounded
when one approaches it. Things last either too long or not long
enough.

ERNEST: Poor life! Poor human life! Are you not even touched by
the tears that the Roman poet tells us are part of its essence.

GILBERT: Too quickly touched by them, I fear. For when one looks
back upon the life that was so vivid in its emotional intensity, and
filled with such fervent moments of ecstasy or of joy, it all seems to
be a dream and an illusion. What are the unreal things, but the passions that once burned one like fire? What are the incredible things,
but the things that one has faithfully believed? What are the
improbable things? The things that one has done oneself. No,
Ernest; life cheats us with shadows, like a puppet-master. We ask it
for pleasure. It gives it to us, with bitterness and disappointment in
its train. We come across some noble grief that we think will lend
the purple dignity of tragedy to our days, but it passes away from us,
and things less noble take its place, and on some grey windy dawn,
or odorous eve of silence and of silver, we find ourselves looking
with callous wonder, or dull heart of stone, at the trees of gold-
flecked hair that we had once so wildly worshipped and so madly
kissed.

ERNEST: Life then is a failure?

GILBERT: From the artistic point of view, certainly And the chief
things that makes life a failure from this artistic point of view is the
thing that lends to life its sordid security, the fact that one can never
repeat exactly the same emotion. How different it is in the world of
Art!* * *

It is a strange thing, this transference of emotion. We sicken with
the same maladies as the poets, and the singer lends us his pain.
Dead lips have their message for us, and hearts that have fallen to
dust can communicate their joy. We run to kiss the bleeding mouth
of Fantine, and we follow Manon Lescaut over the whole world. Ours
is the love-madness of the Tyrian, and the terror of Orestes is ours
also. There is no passion that we cannot feel, no pleasure that we may
not gratify, and we can choose the time of our initiation and the time
of our freedom also. Life! Life! Don't let us go to life for our fulfillment or our experience. It is a thing narrowed by circumstances,
incoherent in its utterance, and without that fine correspondence of
form and spirit which is the only thing that can satisfy the artistic and

critical temperament. It makes us pay too high a price for its wares, and we purchase the meanest of its secret at a cost that is monstrous and infinite.

ERNEST: Must we go, then, to Art for everything?

GILBERT: For everything. Because Art does not hurt us. The tears that we shed at a play are a type of the exquisite sterile emotions that it is the function of Art to awaken. We weep, but we are not wounded. We grieve, but our grief is not bitter. In the actual life of man, sorrow, as Spinoza says somewhere, is a passage to a lesser perfection. But the sorrow with which Art fills us both purifies and initiates, if I may quote once more from the great art critic of the Greeks. It is through Art, and through Art only, that we can realise our perfection; through Art, and through Art only, that we can shield ourselves from the sordid perils of actual existence. This results not merely from the fact that nothing that one can imagine is worth doing, and that one can imagine everything, but from the subtle law that emotional forces, like the forces of the physical sphere, are limited in extent and energy. One can feel so much, and no more. And how can it matter with what pleasure life tries to tempt one, or with what pain it seeks to maim and mar one's soul, if in the spectacle of the lives of those who have never existed one has found the true secret of joy, and wept away one's tears over their deaths who, like Cordelia and the daughter of Brabantio, can never die?

ERNEST: Stop a moment. It seems to me that in everything that you have said there is something radically immoral.

GILBERT: All art is immoral.

ERNEST: All art?

GILBERT: Yes. For emotion for the sake of emotion is the aim of art, and emotion for the sake of action is the aim of life, and of that practical organisation of life that we call society. Society, which is the beginning and basis of morals, exists simply for the concentration of human energy, and in order to ensure its own continuance and healthy stability it demands, and no doubt rightly demands, of each of its citizens that he should contribute some form of productive labour to the common weal, and toil and travail that the day's work may be done. Society often forgives the criminal; it never forgives the dreamer. The beautiful sterile emotions that art excites in us are hateful in its eyes, and so completely are people dominated by the tyranny of this dreadful social ideal that they are always coming shamelessly up to one at Private Views and other places that are open to the general public, and saying in a loud stentorian voice, "What are you doing?" whereas "What are you thinking?" is the only question that any single civilised being should ever be allowed to whisper to another. They mean well, no doubt, these honest

beaming folk. Perhaps that is the reason why they are so excessively
tedious. But some one should teach them what while, in the opinion of society, Contemplation is the gravest sin of which any citizen
can be guilty, in the opinion of the highest culture it is the proper
occupation of man.

ERNEST: Contemplation?

GILBERT: Contemplation. I said to you some time ago that it was far
more difficult to talk about a thing than to do it. Let me say to you
now that to do nothing at all is the most difficult thing in the world,
the most difficult and the most intellectual. To Plato, with his passion for wisdom, this was the noblest form of energy. To Aristotle,
with his passion for knowledge, this was the noblest form of energy
also. It was to this that the passion for holiness led the saint and the
mystic of mediæval days.

ERNEST: We exist, then, to do nothing?

GILBERT: It is to do nothing that the elect exist. Action is limited
and relative. Unlimited and absolute is the vision of him who sits at
ease and watches, who walks in loneliness and dreams. But we who
are born at the close of this wonderful age are at once too cultured
and too critical, too intellectually subtle and too curious of exquisite
pleasures, to accept any speculations about life in exchange for life
itself. To us the *città divina*[1] is colourless, and the *fruitio Dei*[2] without meaning. Metaphysics do not satisfy our temperaments, and religious ecstasy is out of date. The world through which the Academic
philosopher becomes "the spectator of all time and of all existence"
is not really an ideal world, but simply a world of abstract ideas.
When we enter it, we starve amidst the chill mathematics of thought.
The courts of the city of God are not open to us now. Its gates are
guarded by Ignorance, and to pass them we have to surrender all that
in our nature is most divine. It is enough that our fathers believed.
They have exhausted the faith-faculty of the species. Their legacy to
us is the scepticism of which they were afraid. Had they put it into
words, it might not live within us as thought. No, Ernest, no. We cannot go back to the saint. There is far more to be learned from the sinner. We cannot go back to the philosopher, and the mystic leads us
astray. Who, as Mr. Pater suggests somewhere, would exchange the
curve of a single rose-leaf for that formless intangible Being which
Plato rates so high? What to us is the Illumination of Philo, the Abyss
of Eckhart, the vision of Böhme, the monstrous Heaven itself that
was revealed to Swedenborg's blinded eyes? Such things are less than
the yellow trumpet of one daffodil of the field, far less than the meanest of the visible arts; for just as Nature is matter struggling into

1. Heavenly city.
2. Enjoyment of God.

mind, so Art is mind expressing itself under the conditions of matter, and thus, even in the lowliest of her manifestations, she speaks to both sense and soul alike. To the æsthetic temperament the vague is always repellent. The Greeks were a nation of artists, because they were spared the sense of the infinite. Like Aristotle, like Goethe after he had read Kant, we desire the concrete, and nothing but the concrete can satisfy us.

ERNEST: What then do you propose?

GILBERT: It seems to me that with the development of the critical spirit we shall be able to realise, not merely our own lives, but the collective life of the race, and so to make ourselves absolutely modern, in the true meaning of the word modernity. For he to whom the present is the only thing that is present, knows nothing of the age in which he lives. To realise the nineteenth century, one must realise every century that has preceded it and that has contributed to its making. To know anything about oneself one must know all about others. There must be no mood with which one cannot sympathise, no dead mode of life that one cannot make alive. Is this impossible? I think not. By revealing to us the absolute mechanism of all action, and so freeing us from the self-imposed and trammelling burden of moral responsibility, the scientific principle of Heredity has become, as it were, the warrant for the contemplative life. It has shown us that we are never less free than when we try to act. It has hemmed us round with the nets of the hunter, and written upon the wall the prophecy of our doom. We may not watch it, for it is within us. We may not see it, save in a mirror that mirrors the soul. It is Nemesis without her mask. It is the last of the Fates, and the most terrible. It is the only one of the Gods whose real name we know.

And yet, while in the sphere of practical and external life it has robbed energy of its freedom and activity of its choice, in the subjective sphere, where the soul is at work, it comes to us, this terrible shadow, with many gifts in its hands, gifts of strange temperaments and subtle susceptibilities, gifts of wild ardours and chill moods of indifference, complex multiform gifts of thoughts that are at variance with each other, and passions that war against themselves. And so it is not our own life that we live, but the lives of the dead, and the soul that dwells within us is no single spiritual entity, making us personal and individual, created for our service, and entering into us for our joy. It is something that has dwelt in fearful places, and in ancient sepulchres has made its abode. It is sick with many maladies, and has memories of curious sins. It is wiser than we are, and its wisdom is bitter. It fills us with impossible desires, and makes us follow what we know we cannot gain. One thing, however, Ernest, it can do for us. It can lead us away from surroundings whose beauty is dimmed to us by the mist of familiarity, or whose ignoble ugliness and sordid claims are marring the perfection of our development. It can help us to leave the age in which we were born, and to pass into other ages, and find ourselves not exiled from their air. It can teach us how to escape from our experience, and to realise the experiences of those who are greater than we are. The pain of Leopardi crying out against life becomes our pain. Theocritus blows on his pipe, and we laugh with the lips of nymph and shepherd. In the wolfskin of Pierre Vidal we flee before the hounds, and in the armour of Lancelot we ride from the bower of the Queen. We have whispered the secret of our love beneath the cowl of Abelard, and in the stained raiment of Villon have put our shame into song. We can see the dawn through Shelley's eyes, and when we wander with Endymion the Moon grows amorous of our youth. Ours is the anguish of Atys, and ours the weak rage and noble sorrows of the Dane. Do you think that it is the imagination that enables us to live these countless lives? Yes; it is the imagination; and the imagination is the result of heredity. It is simply concentrated race-experience.

ERNEST: But where in this is the function of the critical spirit?

GILBERT: The culture that this transmission of racial experiences makes possible can be made perfect by the critical spirit alone, and indeed may be said to be one with it. For who is the true critic but he who bears within himself the dreams, and ideas, and feelings of myriad generations, and to whom no form of thought is alien, no emotional impulse obscure? And who the true man of culture, if not he who by fine scholarship and fastidious rejection has made instinct self-conscious and intelligent, and can separate the work that has distinction from the work that has it not, and so by contact and comparison makes himself master of the secrets of style and school, and understands their meanings, and listens to their voices, and develop that spirit of disinterested curiosity which is the real root, as it is the real flower, of the intellectual life, and thus attains to intellectual clarity, and, having learned "the best that is known and thought in the world," lives—it is not fanciful to say so—with those who are the Immortals.

*   *   *

From The Decay of Lying†

* * *

VIVIAN: * * * Personal experience is a most vicious and limited circle. All that I desire to point out is the general principle that Life imitates Art far more than Art imitates Life, and I feel sure that if you
think seriously about it you will find that it is true. Life holds the mirror up to Art, and either reproduces some strange type imagined by
painter or sculptor, or realises in fact what has been dreamed in fiction. Scientifically speaking, the basis of life—the energy of life, as
Aristotle would call it—is simply the desire for expression, and Art is
always presenting various forms through which the expression can be
attained. Life seizes on them and uses them, even if they be to her
own hurt. Young men have committed suicide because Rolla did so,
have died by their own hand because by his own hand Werther died.
Think of what we owe to the imitation of Christ, of what we owe to
the imitation of Cæsar.

CYRIL: The theory is certainly a very curious one, but to make it
complete you must show that Nature, no less than Life, is an imitation of Art. Are you prepared to prove that?

VIVIAN: My dear fellow, I am prepared to prove anything.

CYRIL: Nature follows the landscape painter, then, and takes her
effects from him?

VIVIAN: Certainly. Where, if not from the Impressionists, do we get
those wonderful brown fogs that come creeping down our streets,
blurring the gas-lamps and changing the houses into monstrous
shadows? To whom, if not to them and their master, do we owe the
lovely silver mists that brood over our river, and turn to faint forms of
fading grace curved bridge and swaying barge? The extraordinary
change that has taken place in the climate of London during the last
ten years is entirely due to a particular school of Art. You smile. Consider the matter from a scientific or a metaphysical point of view, and
you will find that I am right. For what is Nature? Nature is no great
mother who has borne us. She is our creation. It is in our brain that
she quickens to life. Things are because we see them, and what we
see, and how we see it, depends on the Arts that have influenced us.
To look at a thing is very different from seeing a thing. One does not
see anything until one sees its beauty. Then, and then only, does it
come into existence. At present, people see fogs, not because there
are fogs, but because poets and painters have taught them the mysterious loveliness of such effects. There may have been fogs for

---

† From *The Complete Works of Oscar Wilde*, rev. ed., ed. Vyvyan Holland (London: Collins,
1966), 985–92.

centuries in London. I dare say there were. But no one saw them, and so we do not know anything about them. They did not exist till Art had invented them. Now, it must be admitted, fogs are carried to excess. They have become the mere mannerism of a clique, and the exaggerated realism of their method gives dull people bronchitis. Where the cultured catch an effect, the uncultured catch cold. And so, let us be humane, and invite Art to turn her wonderful eyes elsewhere. She has done so already, indeed. That white quivering sunlight that one sees now in France, with its strange blotches of mauve, and its restless violet shadows, is her latest fancy, and, on the whole, Nature reproduces it quite admirably. Where she used to give us Corots and Daubignys, she gives us now exquisite Monets and entrancing Pissaros. Indeed there are moments, rare, it is true, but still to be observed from time to time, when Nature becomes absolutely modern. Of course she is not always to be relied upon. The fact is that she is in this unfortunate position. Art creates an incomparable and unique effect, and, having done so, passes on to other things. Nature, upon the other hand, forgetting that imitation can be made the sincerest form of insult, keeps on repeating this effect until we all become absolutely wearied of it. Nobody of any real culture, for instance, ever talks nowadays about the beauty of a sunset. Sunsets are quite old-fashioned. They belong to the time when Turner was the last note in art. To admire them is a distinct sign of provincialism of temperament. Upon the other hand they go on. Yesterday evening Mrs. Arundel insisted on my going to the window and looking at the glorious sky, as she called it. Of course I had to look at it. She is one of those absurdly pretty Philistines to whom one can deny nothing. And what was it? It was simply a very second-rate Turner, a Turner of a bad period, with all the painter's worst faults exaggerated and over-emphasised. Of course I am quite ready to admit that Life very often commits the same error. She produces her false Renés and her sham Vautrins, just as Nature gives us, on one day a doubtful Cuyp, and on another a more than questionable Rousseau. Still, Nature irritates one more when she does things of that kind. It seems so stupid, so obvious, so unnecessary. A false Vautrin might be delightful. A doubtful Cuyp is unbearable. However, I don't want to be too hard on Nature. I wish the Channel, especially at Hastings, did not look quite so often like a Henry Moore, grey pearl with yellow lights, but then, when Art is more varied, Nature will, no doubt, be more varied also. That she imitates Art, I don't think even her worst enemy would deny now. It is the one thing that keeps her in touch with civilised man. But have I proved my theory to your satisfaction?

CYRIL: You have proved it to my dissatisfaction, which is better. But even admitting this strange imitative instinct in Life and Nature, surely you would acknowledge that Art expresses the temper of its age, the spirit of its time, the moral and social conditions that surround it, and under whose influence it is produced.

VIVIAN: Certainly not! Art never expresses anything but itself. This is the principle of my new æsthetics; and it is this, more than that vital connection between form and substance, on which Mr. Pater dwells, that makes basic the type of all the arts. Of course, nations and individuals, with that healthy natural vanity which is the secret of existence, are always under the impression that it is of them that the Muses are talking, always trying to find in the calm dignity of imaginative art some mirror of their own turbid passions, always forgetting that the singer of life is not Apollo but Marsyas. Remote from reality and with her eyes turned away from the shadows of the cave, Art reveals her own perfection, and the wondering crowd that watches the opening of the marvellous many-petalled rose fancies that it is its own history that is being told to it, its own spirit that is finding expression in a new form. But it is not so. The highest art rejects the burden of the human spirit, and gains more from a new medium or a fresh material than she does from any enthusiasm for art, or from any lofty passion, or from any great awakening of the human consciousness. She develops purely on her own lines. She is not symbolic of any age. It is the ages that are her symbols.

Even those who hold that Art is representative of time and place and people cannot help admitting that the more imitative an art is the less it represents to us the spirit of its age. The evil faces of the Roman emperors look out at us from the foul porphyry and spotted jasper in which the realistic artists of the day delighted to work and we fancy that in those cruel lips and heavy sensual jaws we can find the secret of the ruin of the Empire. But it was not so. The vices of Tiberius could not destroy that supreme civilisation, any more than the virtues of the Antonines could save it. It fell for other, for less interesting reasons. The sibyls and prophets of the Sistine may indeed serve to interpret for some that new birth of the emancipated spirit that we call the Renaissance; but what do the drunken boors and bawling peasants of Dutch art tell us about the great soul of Holland? The more abstract, the more ideal an art is the more it reveals to us the temper of its age, If we wish to understand a nation by means of its art, let us look at its architecture or its music.

CYRIL: I quite agree with you there. The spirit of an age may be best expressed in the abstract ideal arts, for the spirit itself is abstract and ideal. Upon the other hand, for the visible aspect of an age, for its look, as the phrase goes, we must of course go to the arts of imitation.

VIVIAN: I don't think so. After all, what the imitative arts really give us are merely the various styles of particular artists, or of certain schools of artists. Surely you don't imagine that the people of the Middle Ages bore any resemblance at all to the figures on mediæval stained glass, or in mediæval stone and wood carving, or on mediæval metal-work, or tapestries, or illuminated MSS. They were probably very ordinary-looking people, with nothing grotesque, or remarkable, or fantastic in their appearance. The Middle Ages, as we know them in art, are simply a definite form of style, and there is no reason at all why an artist with this style should not be produced in the nineteenth century. No great artist ever sees things as they really are. If he did he would cease to be an artist. Take an example from our own day. I know that you are fond of Japanese things. Now, do you really imagine that the Japanese people, as they are presented to us in art, have any existence? If you do, you have never understood Japanese art at all. The Japanese people are the deliberate self-conscious creation of certain individual artists. If you set a picture by Hokusai or Hokkei, or any of the great native painters, beside a real Japanese gentleman or lady, you will see that there is not the slightest resemblance between them. The actual people who live in Japan are not unlike the general run of English people; that is to say, they are extremely commonplace, and have nothing curious or extraordinary about them. In fact, the whole of Japan is a pure invention. There is no such country, there are no such people. One of our most charming painters went recently to the Land of the Chrysanthemum in the foolish hope of seeing the Japanese. All he saw, all he had the chance of painting, were a few lanterns and some fans. He was quite unable to discover the inhabitants, as his delightful exhibition at Messrs. Dowdeswell's Gallery showed only too well. He did not know that the Japanese people are, as I have said, simply a mode of style, an exquisite fancy of art. And so, if you desire to see a Japanese effect, you will not behave like a tourist and go to Tokio. On the contrary, you will stay at home and steep yourself in the work of certain Japanese artists and then, when you have absorbed the spirit of their style, and caught their imaginative manner of vision, you will go some afternoon and sit in the Park or stroll down Piccadilly, and if you cannot see an absolutely Japanese effect there, you will not see it anywhere. Or, to return again to the past, take as another instance the ancient Greeks. Do you think that Greek art ever tells us what the Greek people were like? Do you believe that the Athenian women were like the stately dignified figures of the Parthenon frieze, or like those marvellous goddesses who sat in the triangular pediments of the same building? If you judge from the art, they certainly were so. But read an authority like Aristophanes, for instance. You will find that the Athenian ladies laced tightly, wore high-heeled shoes, dyed their hair yellow, painted and rouged their faces and were exactly like any silly fashionable or fallen creature of our own day. The fact is that we look back on the ages entirely through the medium of art, and art, very fortunately, has never once told us the truth.

CYRIL: But modern portraits by English painters, what of them? Surely they are like the people they pretend to represent?

VIVIAN: Quite so. They are so like them that a hundred years from now no one will believe in them. The only portraits in which one believes are portraits where there is very little of the sitter and a very great deal of the artist. Holbein's drawings of the men and women of his time impress us with a sense of their absolute reality. But this is simply because Holbein compelled life to accept his conditions, to restrain itself within his limitations, to reproduce his type and to appear as he wished it to appear. It is style that makes us believe in a thing—nothing but style. Most of our modern portrait painters are doomed to absolute oblivion. They never paint what they see. They paint what the public sees, and the public never sees anything.

CYRIL: Well, after that I think I should like to hear the end of your article.

VIVIAN: With pleasure. Whether it will do any good I really cannot say. Ours is certainly the dullest and most prosaic century possible. Why, even Sleep has played us false, and has closed up the gates of ivory, and opened the gates of horn. The dreams of the great middle classes of this country, as recorded in Mr. Myers's two bulky volumes on the subject, and in the Transactions of the Psychical Society, are the most depressing things I have ever read. There is not even a fine nightmare among them. They are commonplace, sordid and tedious. As for the Church, I cannot conceive anything better for the culture of a country than the presence in it of a body of men whose duty it is to believe in the supernatural, to perform daily miracles, and to keep alive that mythopœic faculty which is so essential for the imagination. But in the English Church a man succeeds, not through his capacity for belief, but through his capacity for disbelief. Ours is the only Church where the sceptic stands at the altar, and where St. Thomas is regarded as the ideal apostle. Many a worthy clergyman, who passes his life in admirable works of kindly charity, lives and dies unnoticed and unknown; but it is sufficient for some shallow uneducated passman out of either University to get up in his pulpit and express his doubts about Noah's ark, or Balaam's ass, or Jonah and the whale, for half of London to flock to hear him, and to sit open-mouthed in rapt admiration at his superb intellect. The growth of common sense in the English Church is a thing very much to be regretted. It is really a degrading concession to a low form of realism. It is silly, too. It springs from an entire ignorance of psychology. Man can believe the impossible, but man can never believe the improbable. However, I must read the end of my article:—

"What we have to do, what at any rate it is our duty to do, is revive

this old art of Lying. Much, of course, may be done in the way of edu-
cating the public, by amateurs in the domestic circle, at literary
lunches, and at afternoon teas. But this is merely the light and graceful side of lying, such as was probably heard at Cretan dinner-parties.
There are many other forms. Lying for the sake of gaining some
immediate personal advantage, for instance—lying with a moral purpose, as it is usually called—though of late it has been rather looked
down upon, was extremely popular with the antique world. Athena
laughs when Odysseus tells her 'his words of sly devising,' as Mr.
William Morris phrases it, and the glory of mendacity illumines the
pale brow of the stainless hero of Euripidean tragedy, and sets among
the noble women of the past the young bride of one of Horace's most
exquisite odes. Later on, what at first had been merely a natural
instinct was elevated into a self-conscious science. Elaborate rules
were laid down for the guidance of mankind, and an important school
of literature grew up round the subject. Indeed, when one remembers
the excellent philosophical treatise of Sanchez on the whole question, one cannot help regretting that no one has ever thought of publishing a cheap and condensed edition of the works of that great
casuist. A short primer, 'When to Lie and How,' if brought out in an
attractive and not too expensive a form, would no doubt command a
large sale, and would prove of real practical service to many earnest
and deep-thinking people. Lying for the sake of the improvement of
the young, which is the basis of home education, still lingers amongst
us, and its advantages are so admirably set forth in the early books of
Plato's *Republic* that it is unnecessary to dwell upon them here. It is
a mode of lying for which all good mothers have peculiar capabilities,
but it is capable of still further development, and has been sadly over-
looked by the School Board. Lying for the sake of a monthly salary is,
of course, well known in Fleet Street, and the profession of a political leader-writer is not without its advantages. But it is said to be a
somewhat dull occupation, and it certainly does not lead to much
beyond a kind of ostentatious obscurity. The only form of lying that
is absolutely beyond reproach is lying for its own sake, and the highest development of this is, as we have already pointed out, Lying in
Art. Just as those who do not love Plato more than Truth cannot pass
beyond the threshold of the Academe, so those who do not love
Beauty more than Truth never know the inmost shrine of Art. The
solid, stolid British intellect lies in the desert sands like the Sphinx
in Flaubert's marvellous tale, and fantasy, *La Chimère*, dances round
it, and calls to it with her false, flute-toned voice. It may not hear her
now, but surely some day, when we are all bored to death with the
commonplace character of modern fiction, it will hearken to her and
try to borrow her wings.

"And when that day dawns, or sunset reddens, how joyous we shall be! Facts will be regarded as discreditable, Truth will be found mourning over her fetters, and Romance, with her temper of wonder, will return to the land. The very aspect of the world will change to our startled eyes. Out of the sea will rise Behemoth and Leviathan, and sail round the high-pooped galleys, as they do on the delightful maps of those ages when books on geography were actually readable. Dragons will wander about the waste places, and the phœnix will soar from her nest of fire into the air. We shall lay our hands upon the basilisk, and see the jewel in the toad's head. Champing his gilded oats, the Hippogriff will stand in our stalls, and over our heads will float the Blue Bird singing of beautiful and impossible things, of things that are lovely and that never happen, of things that are not and that should be. But before this comes to pass we must cultivate the lost art of Lying."

CYRIL: Then we must entirely cultivate it at once. But in order to avoid making any error I want you to tell me briefly the doctrines of the new æsthetics.

VIVIAN: Briefly, then, they are these. Art never expresses anything but itself. It has an independent life, just as Thought has, and develops purely on its own lines. It is not necessarily realistic in an age of realism, nor spiritual in an age of faith. So far from being the creation of its time, it is usually in direct opposition to it, and the only history that it preserves for us is the history of its own progress. Sometimes it returns upon its footsteps, and revives some antique form, as happened in the archaistic movement of late Greek Art, and in the pre-Raphaelite movement of our own day. At other times it entirely anticipates its age, and produces in one century work that it takes another century to understand, to appreciate, and to enjoy. In no case does it reproduce its age. To pass from the art of a time to the time itself is the great mistake that all historians commit.

The second doctrine is this. All bad art comes from returning to Life and Nature, and elevating them into ideals. Life and Nature may sometimes be used as part of Art's rough material, but before they are of any real service to Art they must be translated into artistic conventions. The moment Art surrenders its imaginative medium it surrenders everything. As a method Realism is a complete failure, and the two things that every artist should avoid are modernity of form and modernity of subject-matter. To us, who live in the nineteenth century, any century is a suitable subject for art except our own. The only beautiful things are the things that do not concern us. It is, to have the pleasure of quoting myself, exactly because Hecuba is nothing to us that her sorrows are so suitable a motive for a tragedy. Besides, it is only the modern that ever becomes old-fashioned. M. Zola sits down to give us a picture of the Second Empire. Who cares for the Second Empire now? It is out of date. Life goes faster than Realism, but Romanticism is always in front of Life.

The third doctrine is that Life imitates Art far more than Art imitates Life. This results not merely from Life's imitative instinct, but from the fact that the self-conscious aim of Life is to find expression, and that Art offers it certain beautiful forms through which it may realise that energy. It is a theory that has never been put forward before, but it is extremely fruitful, and throws an entirely new light upon the history of Art.

It follows, as a corollary from this, that external Nature also imitates Art. The only effects that she can show us are effects that we have already seen through poetry, or in paintings. This is the secret of Nature's charm, as well as the explanation of Nature's weakness.

The final revelation is that Lying, the telling of beautiful untrue things, is the proper aim of Art. But of this I think I have spoken at sufficient length. And now let us go out on the terrace, where "droops the milk-white peacock like a ghost," while the evening star "washes the dusk with silver." At twilight nature becomes a wonderfully suggestive effect, and is not without loveliness, though perhaps its chief use is to illustrate quotations from the poets. Come! We have talked long enough.

REVIEWS AND REACTIONS

The Picture of Dorian Gray occupies an important place in the social and legal history of literature. The reviews, responses, and testimony collected in this section are the very raw materials of a chapter in that history, one that seems to possess a dramatic form of its own rarely found in life outside art. It was Wilde who insisted in one of his most celebrated paradoxes from "The Decay of Lying" that "life imitates art," but then in the record of controversy that followed in the wake of *Dorian Gray,* life had more than a little assistance from the artist. Seldom has a work of art reflected its times in more ways than *Dorian Gray.* It is a benchmark of Decadence in English, a key to the psychic and creative life of its author, and a mirror of the prejudices of an era that used it against its author in a court of law as evidence of his moral corruption.

We might well wish to use *Dorian Gray* to measure important cultural and social changes over the intervening years. It is necessary to remind ourselves that the novel was considered scandalous in its day by many. Wilde, eager to press the point with one eye on sales and the other on culture, insisted that his book was "poisonous but perfect," thus inflaming his critics the more. Today's sympathies are almost entirely with the author and against his critics, at least on the matter of art and morality, as chronicled briefly in the following pages.

Readers who have looked into the text of the *Lippincott's* edition of the novel above will be more aware of what the fuss was all about than those who have read only the revised edition, through which the novel has been known since its publication by Ward, Lock and Company. However, even to the alerted reader, the issues and consequences of the controversy will seem disproportionate to the apparent cause unless some of the emotional and cultural feeling of those years can be recaptured. Even American readers of *Lippincott's* gave *Dorian Gray* a far more friendly response than the London critics. In the Sunday *New York Times* for June 29, 1890, the London correspondent filed the following report on the *Dorian Gray* eruption:

> Up to the appearance of "In Darkest Africa" [Stanley's book], Oscar Wilde's novel in *Lippincott's* had monopolized the attention of Londoners who talk about books. It must have excited vastly more interest here than in America simply because since last year's exposure of what are euphemistically styled the West End scandals, Englishmen have been abnormally sensitive to the faintest suggestion of pruriency in the direction of friendships. Very likely this bestial suspicion did not cross the mind of one American reader out of ten thousand, but here the whole town leaped at it with avidity, and one moral journal called for the intervention of the Public Prosecutor. So much has been said

about this phase of the book that Wilde is writing long letters to
the press, not denying the imputation that his work is a study in
puppydom, but insisting that such beings are more picturesque
than good people.[1]

The "West End scandals" mentioned in the report received some
attention in the New York press, chiefly the *Herald,* but had little to
interest American readers except for the suggestion that a member of
the English royal family had been mentioned in connection with
"loathsome and disgusting practices" (one of the dysphemisms of the
times for homosexuality). In the English press, however, the scandals, also referred to as the "Cleveland Street affair," nearly grew to
the proportions of a Victorian Watergate, involving cover-up charges
against the prime minister, Lord Salisbury, and his government; several sensational trials of telegraph boys procured for a gay brothel at
19 Cleveland Street that catered to swells and aristocrats; the scandalous involvement of Lord Arthur Somerset, a member of the Prince
of Wales's household; and the rumored involvement of Prince Albert
Victor ("Eddy"), eldest son of the Prince of Wales and second in line
to the English throne.[2]

The most publicized of the trials arising out of the affair was a libel
suit brought by Henry James Fitzroy, earl of Euston, against Ernest
Parke, editor of the *North London Press.* It was tried at the Old Bailey on January 15, 1890. The guilty verdict of "libel without justification" sent Parke to prison for a year and effectively ended press
coverage of the Cleveland Street affair until Labouchere's dramatic
parliamentary accusations of official cover-up. On the whole, the
affair had provided the press with stories of scandals in high places
and degradations in low ones for about five months, carrying into
March 1890, sixty days before the *Lippincott's Dorian Gray* appeared
on the newsstands.

Several months before the Cleveland Street affair broke in the
press, Wilde published "The Portrait of Mr. W. H." in *Blackwell's,*
which contributed as much as the notoriety of the Cleveland Street
affair to prejudice press critics against Wilde's aesthetic puppets.
The essay offers an elegant and deliberately transparent defense of
an old theory that Shakespeare's sonnets were dedicated to and written for a young actor, Willie Hughes, whose existence has never
been proven. Wilde's essay is in a way a demonstration of the thesis
of "The Critic as Artist" that true criticism should be creative enough
to move beyond the limits of its materials to the region of artistic

1. *New York Times* (Sunday) June 29, 1890: 1.
2. The scandal is fully discussed in H. Montgomery Hyde, *Their Good Names* (London:
Hamilton, 1970); by the same author in *The Cleveland Street Scandal* (New York: Coward,
1976); and in Colin Simpson, et al., *The Cleveland Street Affair* (Boston: Little, Brown,
1976).

invention. Wilde's essay both creates and disposes of the fiction of Willy Hughes as the "Mr. W. H." to whom Shakespeare made his dedication. The Hughes theory almost perfectly explains the problem of the dedication; it is flawed only by the total absence of any evidence that Willy Hughes ever existed. The essay demonstrates in a manner deliberately paradoxical the superiority of art (in this case criticism) to life. But it was not the perverse cleverness of Wilde's argument that put his critics on notice as much as it was Wilde's espousal of a view that implied that England's greatest poet was gay and, what was worse, had plenty of company among the world's geniuses.

The critics had little to say publicly on the matter of their suspicions, perhaps because Shakespeare was beyond the reach of cavil or because of the tone and manner of Wilde's witty, fictionalized scholarship. However, given the provocation of "The Portrait of Mr. W. H." and the intervening Cleveland Street scandal, it is little wonder that *Dorian Gray* produced the nearly hysterical reaction in the press that it did, especially in the *Pall Mall Gazette,* whose editor, William Stead, found muckraking and personal exposé good for circulation. To what extent Wilde expected or even counted on this reaction it is impossible to say, but he proved more than a match for his adversaries. The exchanges in the press, especially in the *St. James's Gazette,* brought out the best of Wilde's polemical talents, as the letters in this section attest.

The criticism leveled at *Dorian Gray* stresses several points. The foremost is, of course, the morality issue, and the objection was that Wilde had published an account of male friendship that stressed inadmissable homosexual attitudes. We may openly wonder at the apparent naïveté of the Victorians and at the emotional impact Wilde's story had on so many press critics. To some extent, at least, the naïveté was an effect of the prevailing code that the way to deal with unpleasant things was to suppress any mention of them. Wilde broke that code at a time when people in the press were especially sensitive on the issue and seems to have compelled some to recognize the existence of behavior with which many of Wilde's press critics were well acquainted through practice but to which they would and could not publicly admit. To be sure, we should give the Victorian establishment its due. Wilde knew that to raise the spectre of homosexualism, however indirectly, would cause a sensation; and he said as much.

Other related charges against the morality of the story mentioned Wilde's treatment of vice and crime, the poisonous atmosphere of sin and corruption that Wilde builds up so suggestively. His defense was that this was necessary for working out Dorian's fate. Again we see in the criticism the suggestion that an author should avoid aspects of life that the Victorian middle class simply did not wish to acknowledge or think about.

The complaint that the characters are mere puppets who strike poses and converse was a criticism that Wilde himself made of the novel, along with an admission that *Dorian Gray* contained too many melodramatic incidents.[3] While he does have more changes of scene in the revised novel, the focus of the action remains London, with a brief excursion to the country estate of Selby Royal.

Two happy and important exceptions to the otherwise predictable and dreary insistence upon critical moralizing from contemporaries are included here, partly as a contrast to the art and morality debate and partly because each marks an important critical statement about the novel. The Hawthorne essay, a review of the *Lippincott's* version published in the following number, raises important issues about the novel's properties as fantasy and romance, issues that have not received the attention they deserve from subsequent critics. The Pater essay was a review of the revised bound novel of 1891 and gives valuable insights into Wilde's intentions and practice in making his last revision of the novel. Pater was especially qualified to do this by virtue of his position as Wilde's mentor and confidant during the writing of *Dorian Gray* and by virtue of his own powers of criticism and analysis. Although more thorough and complete studies of the novel have been produced in the intervening century, Pater's review remains the best analysis of the novel.

The effect of the "art and morality" debate, as it subsequently came to be known, on Wilde's writing and life has yet to be studied in sufficient depth. However, one or two conclusions relevant to this collection may be outlined here. Certainly the debate produced the rejoinders Wilde published separately as "The Preface" to *Dorian Gray,* and its influence is at work both in the revised versions of the essays collected in 1891 under the title *Intentions* and in parts of "The Soul of Man under Socialism," which appeared in the *Fortnightly Review* (February 1891), the number immediately preceding that of "The Preface." The effect on Wilde's life is more difficult to assess, but his victories in the press seem to have encouraged him to live more boldly and more dangerously than he had in the past. To the extent that there is linkage, the art and morality debate and the famous defense of *Dorian Gray* at the first trial may seem to be engagements in the long war over free speech and censorship still being vigorously debated at all levels of society.

3. The term "puppyism," used by a reviewer for the *St. James's Gazette* and by Wilde in a response, meant "affectation or excessive art in costume or posture," according to Eric Partridge, *A Dictionary of Slang and Unconventional English,* 5th ed. (New York: Macmillan, 1961), 669.

A brief account of events surrounding the trials will be useful for the contemporary reader unfamiliar with one of the juicier late Victorian scandals. The trial at which *Dorian Gray* made up the "literary part of the case" was the first of three prosecutions involving Oscar Wilde in the spring of 1895. The first trial was an action for libel brought by Wilde against the Marquess of Queensberry, who had left his card at Wilde's club with the words "For Oscar Wilde posing as a somdomite [*sic*]" scrawled upon it. Not only was the critical word misspelled but also the card itself had been put in an envelope by the porter and seen by no one. No action need have been taken, except that Wilde was convinced by Alfred Douglas, Queensberry's estranged son, that this was an opportunity to send his father to prison. Douglas had made a spectacle of himself both posing as and being Wilde's "boy," and Queensberry had grown more and more publicly outraged by this behavior and had threatened to make a scandal. When Wilde brought his ill-conceived charges, Queensberry pleaded justification. Although Wilde stoutly maintained the pose of one entirely innocent of the alleged libel, he was in fact guilty of a great deal more than Queensberry asserted.

Wilde had to face Edward Carson, an able criminal barrister and a former Trinity College, Dublin, classmate. Perhaps a renewal of their youthful rivalry added even more spirit to a courtroom clash that has become one of the classic duels in trial history. Although the literary phase was by no means the strong point of Carson's case, he pursued a line of questioning that raised once again the art and morality issue. Carson was determined to prove that Wilde was a corrupt person and had exercised a morally bad influence over Alfred Douglas. However, the art and morality issue was one on which Wilde was well-schooled, and he clearly got the better of the exchanges. Had the rest of the trial gone as well as Wilde's celebrated defense of his novel, he would have walked off in triumph. As it was, however, on the second day of the trial, Carson scored heavily in questioning Wilde about a series of associations with newsboys, telegraph boys, and young men identified by the police as homosexual prostitutes. When Carson produced and began questioning these witnesses about their relations with Wilde, the jig was up. Wilde's counsel, Sir Edward Clarke, conceded justification for the libel, thereby hoping to avoid criminal prosecution against his client. That action was not long in coming. However, a decent interval was allowed for Wilde to follow the example of Lord Arthur Somerset of Cleveland Street fame and leave the country. Everyone held his breath; but instead of "levanting," as it was called, Wilde stayed in a room at the Cadogen Hotel and awaited martyrdom in a nearly paralyzed state of indecision and apprehension. Two trials followed, the first ending in a hung jury, the second in conviction, which sent Wilde away for two years at hard labor.

The cost of the Queensbury trial ruined Wilde financially, and the conviction and imprisonment destroyed him socially and as a writer. Wilde's genius flourished in society but withered in prison and died during his continental exile, plagued as he was by poverty and ill health and haunted by the specter of his ruined life. And yet a sympathetic observer cannot help but conclude that Wilde had blindly reached toward a stage of self-development that would raise him above the sordidness of his own life, and he found it in suffering. He died in Paris as the century ended, in November 1900.

ST. JAMES'S GAZETTE

A Study in Puppydom†

(June 24, 1890)

Time was (it was in the '70's) when we talked about Mr Oscar Wilde; time came (it came in the '80's) when he tried to write poetry and, more adventurous, we tried to read it;[1] time is when we had forgotten him, or only remember him as the late editor of *The Woman's World*[2]—a part for which he was singularly unfitted, if we are to judge him by the work which he has been allowed to publish in *Lippincott's Magazine* and which Messrs Ward, Lock & Co. have not been ashamed to circulate in Great Britain. Not being curious in ordure, and not wishing to offend the nostrils of decent persons, we do not propose to analyse "The Picture of Dorian Gray": that would be to advertise the developments of an esoteric prurience. Whether the Treasury or the Vigilance Society will think it worth while to prosecute Mr Oscar Wilde or Messrs Ward, Lock & Co., we do not know; but on the whole we hope they will not.

The puzzle is that a young man of decent parts, who enjoyed (when he was at Oxford)[3] the opportunity of associating with gentlemen, should put his name (such as it is) to so stupid and vulgar a piece of work. Let nobody read it in the hope of finding witty paradox or racy wickedness. The writer airs his cheap research among the garbage of the French *Décadents* like any drivelling pedant, and he bores you unmercifully with his prosy rigmaroles about the beauty of the Body

---

† From Stuart Mason (pseud. Christopher Sclater Millard, 1872–1927), *Oscar Wilde: Art and Morality* (1912; New York: Haskell House, 1971), 27–34. All notes are Mason's.
1. His *Poems*, published by David Bogue in 1881 at 10s. 6d., went through two editions and five printings within a year.
2. Wilde edited this publication for Messrs Cassell from 1887 to 1889.
3. Wilde was a demy (a foundation scholar) of Magdalen College, 1874–78. The term came from the amount of a demy's allowance, which was half that of a fellow.

and the corruption of the Soul. The grammar is better than Ouida's; the erudition equal; but in every other respect we prefer the talented lady who broke off with "pious aposiopesis" when she touched upon "the horrors which are described in the pages of Suetonius and Livy"—not to mention the yet worse infamies believed by many scholars to be accurately portrayed in the lost works of Plutarch, Venus, and Nicodemus, especially Nicodemus.

Let us take one peep at the young men in Mr Oscar Wilde's story. Puppy No. 1 is the painter of the picture of Dorian Gray; Puppy No. 2 is the critic (a courtesy lord, skilled in all the knowledge of the Egyptians and aweary of all the sins and pleasures of London); Puppy No. 3 is the original, cultivated by Puppy No. 1 with a "romantic friendship." The Puppies fall a-talking: Puppy No. 1 about his Art, Puppy No. 2 about his sins and pleasures and the pleasures of sin, and Puppy No. 3 about himself—always about himself, and generally about his face, which is "brainless and beautiful." The Puppies appear to fill up the intervals of talk by plucking daisies and playing with them, and sometimes by drinking "something with strawberry in it." The youngest Puppy is told that he is charming; but he mustn't sit in the sun for fear of spoiling his complexion. When he is rebuked for being a naughty, wilful boy, he makes a pretty *moue*—this man of twenty! This is how he is addressed by the Blasé Puppy at their first meeting:

"Yes, Mr. Gray, the gods have been good to you. But what the gods give they quickly take away. . . . When your youth goes, your beauty will go with it, and then you will suddenly discover that there are no triumphs left for you. . . . Time is jealous of you, and wars against your lilies and roses. You will become sallow, and hollow-cheeked, and dull-eyed. You will suffer horribly."

Why, bless our souls! haven't we read something of this kind somewhere in the classics? Yes, of course we have! But in what recondite author? Ah—yes—no—yes, it *was* in Horace! What an advantage it is to have received a classical education! And how it will astonish the Yankees! But we must not forget our Puppies, who have probably occupied their time in lapping "something with strawberry in it." Puppy No. 1 (the Art Puppy) has been telling Puppy No. 3 (the Doll Puppy) how much he admires him. What is the answer? "I am less to you than your ivory Hermes or your silver Faun. You will like them always. How long will you like me? Till I have my first wrinkle, I suppose. I know now that when one loses one's good looks, whatever they may be, one loses everything. . . . I am jealous of the portrait you have painted of me. Why should it keep what I must lose? . . . Oh, if it was only the other way! If the picture could only change, and I could be always what I am now!"

No sooner said than done! The picture *does* change: the original doesn't. Here's a situation for you! Théophile Gautier could have made it romantic, entrancing, beautiful. Mr Stevenson could have made it convincing, humorous, pathetic. Mr Anstey could have made it screamingly funny. It has been reserved for Mr Oscar Wilde to make it dull and nasty. The promising youth plunges into every kind of mean depravity, and ends in being "cut" by fast women and vicious men. He finishes with murder: the New Voluptuousness always leads up to blood-shedding—that is part of the cant. The gore and gashes wherein Mr Rider Haggard takes a chaste delight are the natural diet for a cultivated palate which is tired of mere licentiousness. And every wickedness or filthiness committed by Dorian Gray is faithfully registered upon his face in the picture; but his living features are undisturbed and unmarred by his inward vileness. This is the story which Mr Oscar Wilde has tried to tell; a very lame story it is, and very lamely it is told.

Why has he told it? There are two explanations; and, so far as we can see, not more than two. Not to give pleasure to his readers: the thing is too clumsy, too tedious, and—alas! that we should say it—too stupid. Perhaps it was to shock his readers, in order that they might cry Fie! upon him and talk about him, much as Mr Grant Allen recently tried in *The Universal Review* to arouse, by a licentious theory of the sexual relations, an attention which is refused to his popular chatter about other men's science. Are we then to suppose that Mr Oscar Wilde has yielded to the craving for a notoriety which he once earned by talking fiddle-faddle about other men's art, and sees his only chance of recalling it by making himself obvious at the cost of being obnoxious, and by attracting the notice which the olfactory sense cannot refuse to the presence of certain self-asserting organisms? That is an uncharitable hypothesis, and we would gladly abandon it. It may be suggested (but is it more charitable?) that he derives pleasure from treating a subject merely because it is disgusting. The phenomenon is not unknown in recent literature; and it takes two forms, in appearance widely separate—in fact, two branches from the same root, a root which draws its life from malodorous putrefaction. One development is found in the Puritan prurience which produced Tolstoy's "Kreutzer Sonata" and Mr Stead's famous outbursts.[4] That is odious enough and mischievous enough, and it is rightly execrated, because it is tainted with an hypocrisy not the less culpable because charitable persons may believe it to be unconscious. But is it more odious or more mischievous than the "frank Paganism" (that is the word, is it not?) which delights in dirtiness and confesses its delight? Still they are both chips from the same block—"The Maiden Tribute

4. In the *Pall Mall Gazette*.

of Modern Babylon"[5] and "The Picture of Dorian Gray"—and both of them ought to be chucked into the fire. Not so much because they are dangerous and corrupt (they are corrupt but not dangerous) as because they are incurably silly, written by simpleton *poseurs* (whether they call themselves Puritan or Pagan) who know nothing about the life which they affect to have explored, and because they are mere catchpenny relevations of the non-existent, which, if they reveal anything at all, are revelations only of the singularly unpleasant minds from which they emerge.

OSCAR WILDE

To the Editor of the *St. James's Gazette*†

25 June [1890]   *16 Tite Street*

Sir, I have read your criticism of my story, *The Picture of Dorian Gray,* and I need hardly say that I do not propose to discuss its merits or demerits, its personalities or its lack of personality. England is a free country, and ordinary English criticism is perfectly free and easy. Besides, I must admit that, either from temperament or from taste, or from both, I am quite incapable of understanding how any work of art can be criticised from a moral standpoint. The sphere of art and the sphere of ethics are absolutely distinct and separate; and it is to the confusion between the two that we owe the appearance of Mrs Grundy, that amusing old lady who represents the only original form of humour that the middle classes of this country have been able to produce. What I do object to most strongly is that you should have placarded the town with posters on which was printed in large letters: MR OSCAR WILDE'S LATEST ADVERTISEMENT; A BAD CASE.

Whether the expression "A Bad Case" refers to my book or to the present position of the Government, I cannot tell. What was silly and unnecessary was the use of the term "advertisement."

5. *Pall Mall Gazette,* July 6–10, 1885.
† [The text of this selection is printed in full from *The Letters of Oscar Wilde,* ed. Rupert Hart-Davis (London: Hart-Davis; New York: Harcourt, 1962), 257.] Sidney James Mark Low (1857–1932, knighted 1918) was editor of the *St James's Gazette* 1888–97. Wilde's only novel, *The Picture of Dorian Gray,* was first published on 20 June 1890, in the July number of *Lippincott's Monthly Magazine,* where it occupied pp. 3–100. It was extensively reviewed. The *St James's Gazette* printed a scurrilous notice on 24 June, under the heading "A Study in Puppydom." Its anonymous author was Samuel Henry Jeyes (1857–1911). The full text of all the important reviews of, and letters about, *Dorian Gray* is given in Stuart Mason's *Art and Morality* (1912). This letter of Wilde's was published on 26 June, under the heading MR OSCAR WILDE'S "BAD CASE."

I think I may say without vanity—though I do not wish to appear to run vanity down—that of all men in England I am the one who requires least advertisement. I am tired to death of being advertised. I feel no thrill when I see my name in a paper. The chronicler does not interest me any more. I wrote this book entirely for my own pleasure, and it gave me very great pleasure to write it. Whether it becomes popular or not is a matter of absolute indifference to me. I am afraid, sir, that the real advertisement is your cleverly written article. The English public, as a mass, takes no interest in a work of art until it is told that the work in question is immoral, and your *réclame* will, I have no doubt, largely increase the sale of the magazine; in which sale, I may mention with some regret, I have no pecuniary interest.

I remain, sir, your obedient servant OSCAR WILDE

ST. JAMES'S GAZETTE

Editorial Note†

(June 25, 1890)

In the preceding column will be found the best reply which Mr Oscar Wilde can make to our recent criticism of his mawkish and nauseous story, "The Picture of Dorian Gray." Mr Wilde tells us that he is constitutionally unable to understand how any work of art can be criticised from a moral standpoint. We were quite aware that ethics and æsthetics are different matters, and that is why the greater part of our criticism was devoted not so much to the nastiness of "The Picture of Dorian Gray," but to its dulness and stupidity. Mr Wilde pretends that we have advertised it. So we have, if any readers are attracted to a book which, we have warned them, will bore them insufferably.

That the story is corrupt cannot be denied; but we added, and assuredly believe, that it is not dangerous, because, as we said, it is tedious and stupid.

Mr Wilde tells us that he wrote the story for his own pleasure, and found great pleasure in writing it. We congratulate him; there is no triumph more precious to your "æsthete" than the discovery of a delight which outsiders cannot share or even understand. The author of "The Picture of Dorian Gray" is the only person likely to find pleasure in it.

† From Stuart Mason, *Oscar Wilde: Art and Morality* (1912; New York: Haskell House, 1971), 37–38.

OSCAR WILDE

To the Editor of the *St. James's Gazette*†

26 June [1890]   16 Tite Street

In your issue of today you state that my brief letter published in your columns is the "best reply" I can make to your article upon *Dorian Gray*. This is not so. I do not propose to fully discuss the matter here, but I feel bound to say that your article contains the most unjustifiable attack that has been made upon any man of letters for many years. The writer of it, who is quite incapable of concealing his personal malice, and so in some measure destroys the effect he wishes to produce, seems not to have the slightest idea of the temper in which a work of art should be approached. To say that such a book as mine should be "chucked into the fire" is silly. That is what one does with newspapers.

Of the value of pseudo-ethical criticism in dealing with artistic work I have spoken already. But as your writer has ventured into the perilous grounds of literacy criticism I ask you to allow me, in fairness not merely to myself but to all men to whom literature is a fine art, to say a few words about his critical method.

He begins by assailing me with much ridiculous virulence because the chief personages in my story are "puppies." They *are* puppies. Does he think that literature went to the dogs when Thackeray wrote about puppydom? I think that puppies are extremely interesting from an artistic as well as from a psychological point of view. They seem to me to be certainly far more interesting than prigs; and I am of opinion that Lord Henry Wotton is an excellent corrective of the tedious ideal shadowed forth in the semi-theological novels of our age.

He then makes vague and fearful insinuations about my grammar and my erudition. Now, as regards grammar, I hold that, in prose at any rate, correctness should always be subordinate to artistic effect and musical cadence; and any pecularities of syntax that may occur in *Dorian Gray* are deliberately intended, and are introduced to show the value of the artistic theory in question. Your writer gives no instance of any such peculiarity. This I regret, because I do not think that any such instances occur.

As regards erudition, it is always difficult, even for the most modest of us, to remember that other people do not know quite as much

† The text of this selection is printed in full from *The Letters of Oscar Wilde*, ed. Rupert Hart-Davis (London: Hart Davis; New York: Harcourt, 1962), 258–59. The editorial note which accompanied Wilde's letter of the 25th was so offensive that it called forth this further letter, which appeared on the 27th, under the heading MR OSCAR WILDE AGAIN.

as one does oneself. I myself frankly admit I cannot imagine how a casual reference to Suetonius and Petronius Arbiter can be construed into evidence of a desire to impress an unoffending and ill-educated public by an assumption of superior knowledge. I should fancy that the most ordinary of scholars is perfectly well acquainted with the *Lives of the Caesars* and with the *Satyricon*. The *Lives of the Caesars*, at any rate, forms part of the curriculum at Oxford for those who take the Honour School of *Literæ Humaniores*; and as for the *Satyricon*, it is popular even among passmen, though I suppose they are obliged to read it in translations.

The writer of the article then suggests that I, in common with that great noble artist Count Tolstoi, take pleasure in a subject because it is dangerous. About such a suggestion there is this to be said. Romantic art deals with the exception and with the individual. Good people, belonging as they do to the normal, and so, commonplace, type, are artistically uninteresting. Bad people are, from the point of view of art, fascinating studies. They represent colour, variety and strangeness. Good people exasperate one's reason; bad people stir one's imagination. Your critic, if I must give him so honourable a title, states that the people in my story have no counterpart in life; that they are, to use his vigorous if somewhat vulgar phrase, "mere catch-penny revelations of the non-existent." Quite so. If they existed they would not be worth writing about. The function of the artist is to invent, not to chronicle. There are no such people. If there were I would not write about them. Life by its realism is always spoiling the subject-matter of art. The supreme pleasure in literature is to realise the non-existent.

And finally, let me say this. You have reproduced, in a journalistic form, the comedy of *Much Ado about Nothing,* and have, of course, spoilt it in your reproduction. The poor public, hearing, from an authority so high as your own, that this is a wicked book that should be coerced and suppressed by a Tory Government, will, no doubt, rush to it and read it. But, alas! they will find that it is a story with a moral. And the moral is this: All excess, as well as all renunciation, brings its own punishment. The painter, Basil Hallward, worshipping physical beauty far too much, as most painters do, dies by the hand of one in whose soul he has created a monstrous and absurd vanity. Dorian Gray, having led a life of mere sensation and pleasure, tries to kill conscience, and at that moment kills himself. Lord Henry Wotton seeks to be merely the spectator of life. He finds that those who reject the battle are more deeply wounded than those who take part in it. Yes; there is a terrible moral in *Dorian Gray*—a moral which the prurient will not be able to find in it, but which will be revealed to all whose minds are healthy. Is this an artistic error? I fear it is. It is the only error in the book. OSCAR WILDE

ST. JAMES'S GAZETTE

Editorial Note†

(June 26, 1890)

Mr Oscar Wilde may perhaps be excused for being angry at the remarks which we allowed ourselves to make concerning his "moral tale" of the Three Puppies and the Magic Picture; but he should not misrepresent us. He says we suggested that his novel was a "wicked book which should be coerced and suppressed by a Tory Government." We did nothing of the kind. The authors of books of much less questionable character have been proceeded against by the Treasury or the Vigilance Society; but we expressly said that we hope Mr Wilde's masterpiece would be left alone.

Then, Mr Wilde (like any young lady who has published her first novel "at the request of numerous friends") falls back on the theory of the critic's "personal malice." This is unworthy of so experienced a literary gentleman. We can assure Mr Wilde that the writer of that article had, and has, no "personal malice" or personal feeling towards him. We can surely censure a work which we believe to be silly, and know to be offensive, without the imputation of malice—especially when that book is written by one who is so clearly capable of better things.

As for the critical question, Mr Wilde is beating the air when he defends idealism and "romantic art" in literature. In the words of Mrs Harris to Mrs Gamp, "Who's a-deniging of it?"

Heaven forbid that we should refuse to an author the "supreme pleasure of realising the nonexistent"; or that we should judge the "æsthetic" from the purely "ethical" standpoint.

No; our criticism starts from lower ground. Mr Wilde says that his story is a moral tale, because the wicked persons in it come to a bad end. We will not be so rude as to quote a certain remark about morality which one Mr Charles Surface made to Mr Joseph Surface. We simply say that every critic has the right to point out that a work of art or literature is dull and incompetent in its treatment—as "The Picture of Dorian Gray" is; and that its dulness and incompetence are not redeemed because it constantly hints, not obscurely, at disgusting sins and abominable crimes—as "The Picture of Dorian Gray" does.

† From Stuart Mason, *Oscar Wilde: Art and Morality* (1912; New York: Haskell House, 1971), 44–46.

OSCAR WILDE

To the Editor of the *St. James's Gazette*†

27 June [*1890*]   *16 Tite Street*

Sir, As you still keep up, though in a somewhat milder form than
before your attacks on me and my book, you not merely confer on me
the right but you impose upon me the duty, of reply.

You state, in your issue of today, that I misrepresented you when I
said that you suggested that a book so wicked as mine should be
"suppressed and coerced by a Tory Government." Now you did not
propose this, but you did suggest it. When you declare that you do not
know whether or not the Government will take action about my book,
and remark that the authors of books much less wicked have been
proceeded against in law, the suggestion is quite obvious. In your
complaint of misrepresentation you seem to me, sir, to have been not
quite candid. However, as far as I am concerned, the suggestion is of
no importance. What is of importance is that the editor of a paper
like yours should appear to countenance the monstrous theory that
the Government of a country should exercise a censorship over imaginative literature. This is a theory against which I, and all men of letters of my acquaintance, protest most strongly; and any critic who
admits the reasonableness of such a theory shows at once that he is
quite incapable of understanding what literature is, and what are the
rights that literature possess[es]. A Government might just as well try
to teach painters how to paint, or sculptors how to model, as attempt
to interfere with the style, treatment and subject-matter of the literary artist; and no writer, however eminent or obscure, should ever
give his sanction to a theory that would degrade literature far more
than any didactic or so-called immoral book could possibly do.

You then express your surprise that "so experienced a literary gentleman" as myself should imagine that your critic was animated by
any feeling of personal malice towards him. The phrase "literary
gentleman" is a vile phrase; but let that pass. I accept quite readily
your assurance that your critic was simply criticising a work of art
in the best way that he could; but I feel that I was fully justified in
forming the opinion of him that I did. He opened his article by a
gross personal attack on myself. This, I need hardly say, was an

---

† The text of this selection is printed in full from *The Letters of Oscar Wilde,* ed. Rupert Hart-
Davis (London: Hart-Davis; New York: Harcourt, 1962), 259–61. Once again the editor of
the *St James's Gazette* had added an abusive note to Wilde's previous letter. This one
appeared on June 28, under the heading MR OSCAR WILDE'S DEFENCE.

TO THE EDITOR OF THE ST. JAMES'S GAZETTE (JUNE 27, 1890) 367

absolutely unpardonable error of critical taste. There is no excuse for it, except personal malice; and you, sir, should not have sanctioned it. A critic should be taught to criticise a work of art without making any reference to the personality of the author. This, in fact, is the beginning of criticism. However, it was not merely his personal attack on me that made me imagine that he was actuated by malice. What really confirmed me in my first impression was his reiterated assertion that my book was tedious and dull. Now, if I were criticising my book, which I have some thoughts of doing, I think I would consider it my duty to point out that it is far too crowded with sensational incident, and far too paradoxical in style, as far, at any rate, as the dialogue goes. I feel that from a standpoint of art these are two defects in the book. But tedious and dull the book is not. Your critic has cleared himself of the charge of personal malice, his denial and yours being quite sufficient in the manner; but he has only done so by a tacit admission that he has really no critical instinct about literature and literary work, which, in one who writes about literature, is, I need hardly say, a much graver fault than malice of any kind.

Finally, sir, allow me to say this. Such an article as you have published really makes one despair of the possibility of any general culture in England. Were I a French author, and my book brought out in Paris, there is not a single literary critic in France, on any paper of higher standing, who would think for a moment of criticising it from an ethical standpoint. If he did so, he would stultify himself, not merely in the eyes of all men of letters, but in the eyes of the majority of the public. You have yourself often spoken against Puritanism. Believe me, sir, Puritanism is never so offensive and destructive as when it deals with art matters. It is there that its influence is radically wrong. It is this Puritanism, to which your critic has given expression, that is always marring the artistic instinct of the English. So far from encouraging it, you should set yourself against it, and should try to teach your critics to recognise the essential difference between art and life. The gentleman who criticised my book is in a perfectly hopeless confusion about it, and your attempt to help him out by proposing that the subject-matter of art should be limited does not mend matters. It is proper that limitations should be placed on action. It is not proper that limitations should be placed on art. To art belong all things that are and all things that are not, and even the editor of a London paper has no right to restrain the freedom of art in the selection of subject-matter.

I now trust, sir, that these attacks on me and on my book will cease. There are forms of advertisement that are unwarranted and unwarrantable.

I am, sir, your obedient servant. OSCAR WILDE

ST. JAMES'S GAZETTE

Editorial Note

(September 24, 1890)†

Mr Oscar Wilde has explained. We know now how "Dorian Gray" came to be written. In 1887, about the genial season of Christmas, a Canadian lady artist[1] yearned to transfer to the glowing canvas the classic features of Mr Oscar Wilde. Mr Wilde gave her a sitting. When the sitting was over and Mr Wilde had looked at the portrait, it occurred to him that a thing of beauty, when it takes the form of a middle-aged gentleman, is unhappily not a joy for ever. "What a tragic thing it is," he exclaimed. "This portrait will never grow older, and I shall. If," he added, "if it was only the other way." Then the passion of his soul sought refuge in prose composition, and the result was "Dorian Gray." No wonder Mr Wilde didn't like it when we hinted that this great work was a study of puppydom, and its hero himself a puppy of an unpleasant kind.

DAILY CHRONICLE

Review

(June 30, 1890)‡

Dulness and dirt are the chief features of *Lippincott's* this month. The element in it that is unclean, though undeniably amusing, is furnished by Mr Oscar Wilde's story of "The Picture of Dorian Gray." It is a tale spawned from the leprous literature of the French *Décadents*—a poisonous book, the atmosphere of which is heavy with the mephitic odours of moral and spiritual putrefaction—a gloating study of the mental and physical corruption of a fresh, fair and golden youth, which might be horrible and fascinating but for its effeminate frivolity, its studied insincerity, its theatrical cyni-

---

† From Stuart Mason, *Oscar Wilde: Art and Morality* (1912; New York: Haskell House, 1971), 63.
1. Miss Frances Richards, a pupil of Carolus Durand.
‡ From Stuart Mason, *Oscar Wilde: Art and Morality* (1912; New York: Haskell House, 1971), 65–69.

cism, its tawdry mysticism, its flippant philosophisings, and the contaminating trail of garish vulgarity which is over all Mr Wilde's elaborate Wardour Street æstheticism and obtrusively cheap scholarship.

Mr Wilde says his book has "a moral." The "moral," so far as we can collect it, is that man's chief end is to develop his nature to the fullest by "always searching for new sensations," that when the soul gets sick the way to cure it is to deny the senses nothing, for "nothing," says one of Mr Wilde's characters, Lord Henry Wotton, "can cure the soul but the senses, just as nothing can cure the senses but the soul." Man is half angel and half ape, and Mr Wilde's book has no real use if it be not to inculcate the "moral" that when you feel yourself becoming too angelic you cannot do better than to rush out and make a beast of yourself. There is not a single good and holy impulse of human nature, scarcely a fine feeling or instinct that civilisation, art, and religion have developed throughout the ages as part of the barriers between Humanity and Animalism that is not held up to ridicule and contempt in "Dorian Gray," if, indeed, such strong words can be fitly applied to the actual effect of Mr Wilde's airy levity and fluent impudence. His desperate effort to vamp up a "moral" for the book at the end is, artistically speaking, coarse and crude, because the whole incident of Dorian Gray's death is, as they say on the stage, "out of the picture." Dorian's only regret is that unbridled indulgence in every form of secret and unspeakable vice, every resource of luxury and art, and sometimes still more piquant to the jaded young man of fashion, whose lives "Dorian Gray" pretends to sketch, by every abomination of vulgarity and squalor is—what? Why, that it will leave traces of premature age and loathsome sensualness on his pretty facy, rosy with the loveliness that endeared youth of his odious type to the paralytic patricians of the Lower Empire.

Dorian Gray prays that a portrait of himself which an artist, who raves about him as young men do about the women they love not wisely but too well, has painted may grow old instead of the original. This is what happens by some supernatural agency, the introduction of which seems purely farcical, so that Dorian goes on enjoying unfading youth year after year, and might go on for ever using his senses with impunity "to cure his soul," defiling English society with the moral pestilence which is incarnate in him, but for one thing. That is his sudden impulse not merely to murder the painter—which might be artistically defended on the plea that it is only a fresh development of his scheme for realising every phase of life-experience— but to rip up the canvas in a rage, merely because, though he had permitted himself to do one good action, it had not made his portrait less hideous. But all this is inconsistent with Dorian Gray's cool, calculating, conscienceless character, evolved logically enough by Mr Wilde's "New Hedonism."

Then Mr Wilde finishes his story by saying that on hearing a heavy fall Dorian Gray's servants rushed in, found the portrait on the wall as youthful looking as ever, its senile ugliness being transferred to the foul profligate himself, who is lying on the floor stabbed to the heart. This is a sham moral, as indeed everything in the book is a sham, except the one element in the book which will taint every young mind that comes in contact with it. That element is shockingly real, and it is the plausibly insinuated defence of the creed that appeals to the senses "to cure the soul" whenever the spiritual nature of man suffers from too much purity and self-denial.

The rest of this number of *Lippincott* consists of articles of harmless padding.

OSCAR WILDE

To the Editor of the *Daily Chronicle*†

30 June [1890]   *16 Tite Street*

Sir, Will you allow me to correct some errors into which your critic has fallen in his review of my story, *The Picture of Dorian Gray*, published in today's issue of your paper?

Your critic states, to begin with, that I make desperate attempts to "vamp up" a moral in my story. Now, I must candidly confess that I do not know what "vamping" is. I see, from time to time, mysterious advertisements in the newspapers about "How to Vamp," but what vamping really means remains a mystery to me—a mystery that, like all other mysteries, I hope some day to explore.

However, I do not propose to discuss the absurd terms used by modern journalism. What I want to say is that, so far from wishing to emphasise any moral in my story, the real trouble I experienced in writing the story was that of keeping the extremely obvious moral subordinate to the artistic and dramatic effect.

When I first conceived the idea of a young man selling his soul in exchange for eternal youth—an idea that is old in the history of literature, but to which I have given new form—I felt that, from an aesthetic point of view, it would be difficult to keep the moral in

---

† The text of this selection is printed in full from *The Letters of Oscar Wilde*, ed. Rupert Hart-Davis (London: Hart-Davis; New York: Harcourt, 1962), 265–67.

its proper secondary place; and even now I do not feel quite sure that I have been able to do so. I think the moral too apparent. When the book is published in a volume I hope to correct this defect.

As for what the moral is, your critic states that it is this—that when a man feels himself becoming "too angelic" he should rush out and make a "beast of himself!" I cannot say that I consider this a moral. The real moral of the story is that all excess, as well as all renunciation, brings its punishment, and this moral is so far artistically and deliberately suppressed that it does not enunciate its law as a general principle, but realises itself purely in the lives of individuals, and so becomes simply a dramatic element in a work of art, and not the object of the work of art itself.

Your critic also falls into error when he says that Dorian Gray, having a "cool, calculating, conscienceless character," was inconsistent when he destroyed the picture of his own soul, on the ground that the picture did not become less hideous after he had done what, in his vanity, he had considered his first good action. Dorian Gray has not got a cool, calculating, conscienceless character at all. On the contrary, he is extremely impulsive, absurdly romantic, and is haunted all through his life by an exaggerated sense of conscience which mars his pleasures for him and warns him that youth and enjoyment are not everything in the world. It is finally to get rid of the conscience that had dogged his steps from year to year that he destroys the picture; and thus in his attempt to kill conscience Dorian Gray kills himself.

Your critic then talks about "obtrusively cheap scholarship." Now, whatever a scholar writes is sure to display scholarship in the distinction of style and the fine use of language; but my story contains no learned or pseudo-learned discussions, and the only literary books that it alludes to are books that any fairly educated reader may be supposed to be acquainted with, such as the *Satyricon* of Petronius Arbiter, or Gautier's *Émaux et Camées*. Such books as Alphonso's *Clericalis Disciplina* belong not to culture, but to curiosity. Anybody may be excused for not knowing them.

Finally, let me say this—the aesthetic movement produced certain colours, subtle in their loveliness and fascinating in their almost mystical tone. They were, and are, our reaction against the crude primaries of a doubtless more respectable but certainly less cultivated age. My story is an essay on decorative art. It reacts against the crude brutality of plain realism. It is poisonous if you like, but you cannot deny that it is also perfect, and perfection is what we artists aim at.

I remain, sir, your obedient servant OSCAR WILDE

SCOTS OBSERVER

From Reviews and Magazines†

(July 5, 1890)

Why go grubbing in muck heaps? The world is fair, and the proportion of healthy-minded men and honest women to those that are foul, fallen, or unnatural is great. Mr Oscar Wilde has again been writing stuff that were better unwritten; and while "The Picture of Dorian Gray," which he contributes to *Lippincott's,* is ingenious, interesting, full of cleverness, and plainly the work of a man of letters, it is false art—for its interest is medico-legal; it is false to human nature—for its hero is a devil; it is false to morality—for it is not made sufficiently clear that the writer does not prefer a course of unnatural iniquity to a life of cleanliness, health, and sanity. The story—which deals with matters only fitted for the Criminal Investigation Department or a hearing in camera—is discreditable alike to author and editor. Mr Wilde has brains, and art, and style; but if he can write for none but outlawed noblemen and perverted telegraph-boys, the sooner he takes to tailoring (or some other decent trade) the better for his own reputation and the public morals.

OSCAR WILDE

To the Editor of the *Scots Observer*‡

9 July 1890   *16 Tite Street, Chelsea*

Sir, You have published a review of my story, *The Picture of Dorian Gray.* As this review is grossly unjust to me as an artist, I ask you to allow me to exercise in your columns my right of reply.

✳   ✳   ✳

Your reviewer, sir, while admitting that the story in question is "plainly the work of a man of letters," the work of one who has

---

† From Stuart Mason, *Oscar Wilde: Art and Morality* (1912; New York: Haskell House, 1971), 75–76.

‡ The text of this selection is printed in full from *The Letters of Oscar Wilde,* ed. Rupert Hart-Davis (London: Hart-Davis); New York: Harcourt, 1962), 265–67. The *Scots Observer's* anonymous notice of *Dorian Gray* on 5 July was for long thought to have been written by W. E. Henley, the paper's editor; the author was in fact his henchman Charles Whibley (1860–1930). The outlawed nobleman and perverted telegraph-boys refer to Lord Arthur Somerset and the Cleveland Street scandal of 1889. This letter of Wilde's appeared on 12 July, under the heading MR WILDE'S REJOINDER. It was reprinted in *Miscellanies.*

"brains, and art, and style," yet suggests, and apparently in all seriousness, that I have written it in order that it should be read by the most depraved members of the criminal and illiterate classes. Now, sir, I do not suppose that the criminal and illiterate classes ever read anything except newspapers. They are certainly not likely to be able to understand anything of mine. So let them pass, and on the broad question of why a man of letters writes at all let me say this. The pleasure that one has in creating a work of art is a purely personal pleasure, and it is for the sake of this pleasure that one creates. The artist works with his eye on the object. Nothing else interests him. What people are likely to say does not even occur to him. He is fascinated by what he has in hand. He is indifferent to others. I write because it gives me the greatest possible artistic pleasure to write. If my work pleases the few, I am gratified. If it does not, it causes me no pain. As for the mob, I have no desire to be a popular novelist. It is far too easy.

Your critic then, sir, commits the absolutely unpardonable crime of trying to confuse the artist with his subject-matter. For this, sir, there is no excuse at all. Of one who is the greatest figure in the world's literature since Greek days Keats remarked that he had as much pleasure in conceiving the evil as he had in conceiving the good.[1] Let your reviewer, sir, consider the bearings of Keats's fine criticism, for it is under these conditions that every artist works. One stands remote from one's subject-matter. One creates it, and one contemplates it. The further away the subject-matter is, the more freely can the artist work. Your reviewer suggests that I do not make it sufficiently clear whether I prefer virtue to wickedness or wickedness to virtue. An artist, sir, has no ethical sympathies at all. Virtue and wickedness are to him simply what the colours on his palette are to the painter. They are no more, and they are no less. He sees that by their means a certain artistic effect can be produced, and he produces it. Iago may be morally horrible and Imogen stainlessly pure. Shakespeare, as Keats said, had as much delight in creating the one as he had in creating the other.

It was necessary, sir, for the dramatic development of this story to surround Dorian Gray with an atmosphere of moral corruption. Otherwise the story would have had no meaning and the plot no issue. To keep this atmosphere vague and indeterminate and wonderful was the aim of the artist who wrote the story. I claim, sir, that he has succeeded. Each man sees his own sin in Dorian Gray. What Dorian Gray's sins are no one knows. He who finds them has brought them.

---

1. "The poetical character . . . has as much delight in conceiving an Iago as an Imogen. What shocks the virtuous philosopher delights the cameleon poet." John Keats to Richard Woodhouse, 27 October 1818.

In conclusion, sir, let me say how really deeply I regret that you
should have permitted such a notice as the one I feel constrained to
write on to have appeared in your paper. That the editor of the *St
James's Gazette* should have employed Caliban as his art-critic was
possibly natural. The editor of the *Scots Observer* should not have
allowed Thersites to make mows in his review. It is unworthy of so
distinguished a man of letters. I am, etc. OSCAR WILDE

JULIAN HAWTHORNE

The Romance of the Impossible†

Fiction, which flies at all game, has latterly taken to the Impossible as its quarry. The pursuit is interesting and edifying, if one goes
properly equipped, and with adequate skill. But if due care is not
exercised, the Impossible turns upon the hunter and grinds him to
powder. It is a very dangerous and treacherous kind of wild-fowl. The
conditions of its existence—if existence can be predicted of that
which does not exist—are so peculiar and abstruse that only genius
is really capable of taming it and leading it captive. But the capture,
when it is made, is so delightful and fascinating that every tyro would
like to try. One is reminded of the princess of the fairy tale, who was
to be won on certain preposterous terms, and if the terms were not
met, the discomfited suitor lost his head. Many misguided or over-
weening youths perished; at last the One succeeded. Failure in a
romance of the Impossible is apt to be a disastrous failure; on the
other hand, success carries great rewards.

Of course, the idea is not a new one. The writings of the alchemists
are stories of the Impossible. The fashion has never been entirely
extinct. Balzac wrote the "Peau de Chagrin," and probably this tale is
as good a one as was ever written of that kind. The possessor of the
Skin may have everything he wishes for; but each wish causes the
Skin to shrink, and when it is all gone the wisher is annihilated with
it. By the art of the writer this impossible thing is made to appear
quite feasible; by touching the chords of coincidence and fatality, the
reader's common sense is soothed to sleep. We feel that all this might
be, and yet no natural law be violated; and yet we know that such a
thing never was and never will be. But the vitality of the story, as of
all good stories of the sort, is due to the fact that it is the symbol of a

† From Stuart Mason, *Oscar Wilde: Art and Morality* (1912; New York: Haskell House, 1971),
175–85. This essay review of *Dorian Gray* by Julian Hawthorne (son of the American novelist Nathaniel Hawthorne) appeared in *Lippincott's Magazine* in September 1890.

spiritual verity: the life of indulgence, the selfish life, destroys the soul. This psychic truth is so deeply felt that its sensible embodiment is rendered plausible. In the case of another famous romance— "Frankenstein"—the technical art is entirely wanting: a worse story, from the literary point of view, has seldom been written. But the soul of it, so to speak, is so potent and obvious that, although no one actually reads the book nowadays, everybody knows the gist of the idea. "Frankenstein" has entered into the language, for it utters a perpetual truth of human nature.

At the present moment, the most conspicuous success in the line we are considering is Stevenson's "Dr Jekyll and Mr Hyde." The author's literary skill, in that awful little parable, is at its best, and makes the most of every point. To my thinking, it is an artistic mistake to describe Hyde's transformation as actually taking place in plain sight of the audience; the sense of spiritual mystery is thereby lost, and a mere brute miracle takes its place. But the tale is strong enough to carry this imperfection, and the moral significance of it is so catholic—it so comes home to every soul that considers it—that it has already made an ineffaceable impression on the public mind. Every man is his own Jekyll and Hyde, only without the magic powder. On the bookshelf of the Impossible, Mr Stevenson's book may take its place beside Balzac's.

Mr Oscar Wilde, the apostle of beauty, has in the July number of *Lippincott's Magazine* a novel or romance (it partakes of the qualities of both), which everybody will want to read. It is a story strange in conception, strong in interest, and fitted with a tragic and ghastly climax. Like many stories of its class, it is open to more than one interpretation; and there are, doubtless, critics who will deny that it has any meaning at all. It is, at all events, a salutary departure from the ordinary English novel, with the hero and heroine of different social stations, the predatory black sheep, the curate, the settlements, and Society. Mr Wilde, as we all know, is a gentleman of an original and audacious turn of mind, and the commonplace is scarcely possible to him. Besides, his advocacy of novel ideas in life, art, dress, and demeanour had led us to expect surprising things from him; and in this literary age it is agreed that a man may best show the best there is in him by writing a book. Those who read Mr Wilde's story in the hope of finding in it some compact and final statement of his theories of life and manners will be satisfied in some respects, and dissatisfied in others; but not many will deny that the book is a remarkable one, and would attract attention even had it appeared without the author's name on the title page.

"The Picture of Dorian Gray" begins to show its quality in the opening pages. Mr Wilde's writing has what is called "colour,"—the quality that forms the mainstay of many of Ouida's works,—and it appears in the sensuous descriptions of nature and of the decorations and environments of the artistic life. The general aspect of the characters and the tenor of their conversation remind one a little of "Vivian Gray" and a little of "Pelham," but the resemblance does not go far: Mr Wilde's objects and philosophy are different from those of either Disraeli or Bulwer. Meanwhile his talent for aphorisms and epigrams may fairly be compared with theirs: some of his clever sayings are more than clever,—they show real insight and a comprehensive grasp. Their wit is generally cynical; but they are put into the mouth of one of the characters, Lord Harry, and Mr Wilde himself refrains from definitely committing himself to them; though one cannot help suspecting that Mr Wilde regards Lord Harry as being an uncommonly able fellow. Be that as it may, Lord Harry plays the part of Old Harry in the story, and lives to witness the destruction of every other person in it. He may be taken as an imaginative type of all that is most evil and most refined in modern civilisation,—a charming, gentle, witty, euphemistic Mephistopheles, who depreciates the vulgarity of goodness, and muses aloud about "those renunciations that men have unwisely called virtue, and those natural rebellions that wise men still call sin." Upon the whole, Lord Harry is the most ably portrayed character in the book, though not the most original in conception. Dorian Gray himself is as nearly a new idea in fiction as one has nowadays a right to expect. If he had been adequately realised and worked out, Mr Wilde's first novel would have been remembered after more meritorious ones were forgotten. But, even as "nemo repente fuit turpissimus," so no one, or hardly any one, creates a thoroughly original figure at a first essay. Dorian never quite solidifies. In fact, his portrait is rather the more real thing of the two. But this needs explanation.

The story consists of a strong and marvelous central idea, illustrated by three characters, all men. There are a few women in the background, but they are only mentioned: they never appear to speak for themselves. There is, too, a valet who brings in his master's breakfasts, and a chemist who, by some scientific miracle, disposes of a human body: but, substantially, the book is taken up with the artist who paints the portrait, with his friend Lord Harry aforesaid, and with Dorian Gray, who might, so far as the story goes, stand alone. He and his portrait are one, and their union points the moral of the tale.

The situation is as follows: Dorian Gray is a youth of extraordinary physical beauty and grace, and pure and innocent of soul. An artist sees him and falls æsthetically in love with him, and finds in him a new inspiration in his art, both direct and general. In the lines of his form and features, and in his colouring and movement, are revealed fresh and profound laws: he paints him in all guises and combinations, and it is seen and admitted on all sides that he has never before painted so well. At length he concentrates all his knowledge and power in a final portrait, which has the vividness and grace of life itself, and, considering how much both of the sitter and of the painter is embodied in it, might almost be said to live. The portrait is declared by Lord Harry to be the greatest work of modern art; and the painter himself thinks so well of it that he resolves never to exhibit it, even as he would shrink from exposing to public gaze the privacies of his own nature.

On the day of the last sitting a singular incident occurs. Lord Harry, meeting on that occasion for the first time with Dorian, is no less impressed than was Hallward, the artist, with the youth's radiant beauty and freshness. But whereas Hallward would keep Dorian unspotted from the world, and would have him resist evil temptations and all the allurements of corruption, Lord Harry, on the contrary, with a truly Satanic ingenuity, discourses to the young man on the matchless delights and privileges of youth. Youth is the golden period of life: youth comes never again: in youth only are the senses endowed with divine potency; only then are joys exquisite and pleasures unalloyed. Let it therefore be indulged without stint. Let no harsh and cowardly restraints be placed upon its glorious impulses. Men are virtuous through fear and selfishness. They are too dull or too timid to take advantage of the godlike gifts that are showered upon them in the morning of existence; and before they can realise the folly of their self-denial, the morning has passed, and weary day is upon them, and the shadows of night are near. But let Dorian, who is matchless in the vigour and resources of his beauty, rise above the base shrinking from life that calls itself goodness. Let him accept and welcome every natural impulse of his nature. The tragedy of old age is not that one is old, but that one is young: let him so live that when old age comes he shall at least have the satisfaction of knowing that no opportunity of pleasure and indulgence has escaped untasted.

This seductive sermon profoundly affects the innocent Dorian, and he looks at life and himself with new eyes. He realises the value as well as the transitoriness of that youth and beauty which hitherto he had accepted as a matter of course and as a permanent possession. Gazing on his portrait, he laments that it possesses the immortality of liveliness and comeliness that is denied to him; and, in a sort of imaginative despair, he utters a wild prayer that to the portrait, and not to himself, may come the feebleness and hideousness of old age; that whatever sins he may commit, to whatever indulgences he may surrender himself, not upon him but upon the portrait may the penalties and disfigurements fall. Such is Dorian's prayer; and, though at first he suspects it not, his prayer is granted. From that

hour the evil of his life is registered upon the face and form of his
pictured presentment, while he himself goes unscathed. Day by day,
each fresh sin that he commits stamps its mark of degradation upon
the painted image. Cruelty, sensuality, treachery, all nameless
crimes, corrupt and render hideous the effigy on the canvas; he sees
in it the gradual pollution and ruin of his soul, while his own fleshy
features preserve unstained all the freshness and virginity of his sin-
less youth. The contrast at first alarms and horrifies him; but at
length he becomes accustomed to it, and finds a sinister delight in
watching the progress of the awful change. He locks up the portrait
in a secret chamber, and constantly retires thither to ponder over the
ghastly miracle. No one but he knows or suspects the incredible
truth; and he guards like a murder-secret this visible revelation of
the difference between what he is and what he seems. This is a powerful situation; and the reader may be left to discover for himself
how Mr Wilde works it out.

WALTER PATER

A Novel by Mr. Oscar Wilde†

There is always something of an excellent talker about the writing of
Mr Oscar Wilde; and in his hands, as happens so rarely with those
who practise it, the form of dialogue is justified by its being really
alive. His genial, laughter-loving sense of life and its enjoyable intercourse, goes far to obviate any crudity there may be in the paradox,
with which, as with the bright and shining truth which often under-
lies it, Mr Wilde, startling his "countrymen," carries on, more perhaps than any other writer, the brilliant critical work of Matthew
Arnold. "The Decay of Lying,"[1] for instance, is all but unique in its
half-humorous, yet wholly convinced, presentment of certain valuable truths of criticism. Conversational ease, the fluidity of life, felicitous expression, are qualities which have a natural alliance to the
successful writing of fiction; and side by side with Mr Wilde's "Intentions" (so he entitles his critical efforts) comes a novel, certainly original, and affording the reader a fair opportunity of comparing his
practice as a creative artist with many a precept he has enounced as
critic concerning it.

---

† From Stuart Mason, *Oscar Wilde: Art and Morality* (1912; New York: Haskell House,
1971), 188–95. This review of the revised edition of *Dorian Gray* appeared in the first number of *The Book-man* (October 1891).
1. Appeared first in *The Nineteenth Century*, January 1889, and was afterward included in
"Intentions" *[Mason's note]*.

A wholesome dislike of the common place, rightly or wrongly identified by him with the *bourgeois,* with our middle-class—its habits
and tastes—leads him to protest emphatically against so-called "realism" in art; life, as he argues, with much plausibility, as a matter of
fact, when it is really awake, following art—the fashion an effective
artist sets; while art, on the other hand, influential and effective art,
has never taken its cue from actual life. In "Dorian Gray" he is true
certainly, on the whole, to the æsthetic philosophy of his "Intentions"; yet not infallibly, even on this point: there is a certain amount
of the intrusion of real life and its sordid aspects—the low theatre,
the pleasures and griefs, the faces of some very unrefined people,
managed, of course, cleverly enough. The interlude of Jim Vane, his
half-sullen but wholly faithful care for his sister's honour, is as good
as perhaps anything of the kind, marked by a homely but real pathos,
sufficiently proving a versatility in the writer's talent, which should
make his books popular. Clever always, this book, however, seems
intended to set forth anything but a homely philosophy of life for the
middle-class—a kind of dainty Epicurean theory, rather—yet fails, to
some degree, in this; and one can see why. A true Epicureanism aims
at a complete though harmonious development of man's entire
organism. To lose the moral sense therefore, for instance, the sense
of sin and righteousness, as Mr Wilde's hero—his heroes are bent on
doing as speedily, as completely as they can, is to lose, or lower,
organisation, to become less complex, to pass from a higher to a lower
degree of development. As a story, however, a partly supernatural
story, it is first-rate in artistic management; those Epicurean niceties
only adding to the decorative colour of its central figure, like so many
exotic flowers, like the charming scenery and the perpetual, epi-
grammatic, surprising, yet so natural, conversations, like an atmosphere all about it. All that pleasant accessory detail, taken straight
from the culture, the intellectual and social interests, the conven-
tionalities, of the moment, have, in fact, after all, the effect of the
better sort of realism, throwing into relief the adroitly-devised supernatural element after the manner of Poe, but with a grace he never
reached, which supersedes that earlier didactic purpose, and makes
the quite sufficing interest of an excellent story.

We like the hero, and, spite of his, somewhat unsociable, devotion
to his art, Hallward, better than Lord Henry Wotton. He has too
much of a not very really refined world in and about him, and his
somewhat cynic opinions, which seem sometimes to be those of the
writer, who may, however, have intended Lord Henry as a satiric
sketch. Mr Wilde can hardly have intended him, with his cynic amity
of mind and temper, any more than the miserable end of Dorian himself, to figure the motive and tendency of a true Cyrenaic or Epicurean doctrine of life. In contrast with Hallward, the artist, whose

sensibilities idealise the world around him, the personality of Dorian Gray, above all, into something magnificent and strange, we might say that Lord Henry, and even more the, from the first, suicidal hero, loses too much in life to be a true Epicurean—loses so much in the way of impressions, of pleasant memories, and subsequent hopes, which Hallward, by a really Epicurean economy, manages to secure. It should be said, however, in fairness, that the writer is impersonal: seems not to have identified himself entirely with any one of his characters: and Wotton's cynicism, or whatever it be, at least makes a very clever story possible. He becomes the spoiler of the fair young man, whose bodily form remains un-aged; while his picture, the *chef d'œuvre* of the artist Hallward, changes miraculously with the gradual corruption of his soul. How true, what a light on the artistic nature, is the following on actual personalities and their revealing influence in art. We quote it as an example of Mr Wilde's more serious style.

> I sometimes think that there are only two eras of any importance in the world's history. The first is the appearance of a new medium for art, and the second is the appearance of a new personality for art also. What the invention of oil-painting was to the Venetians, the face of Antinoüs was to late Greek sculpture, and the face of Dorian Gray will some day be to me. It is not merely that I paint from him, draw from him, sketch from him. Of course I have done all that. But he is much more to me than a model or a sitter. I won't tell you that I am dissatisfied with what I have done of him, or that his beauty is such that Art cannot express it. There is nothing that Art cannot express, and I know that the work I have done, since I met Dorian Gray, is good work, is the best work of my life. But in some curious way . . . his personality has suggested to me an entirely new manner in art, an entirely new mode of style. I see things differently, I think of them differently. I can now recreate life in a way that was hidden from me before.

Dorian himself, though certainly a quite unsuccessful experiment in Epicureanism, in life as a fine art, is (till his inward spoiling takes visible effect suddenly, and in a moment, at the end of his story) a beautiful creation. But his story is also a vivid, though carefully considered, exposure of the corruption of a soul, with a very plain moral pushed home, to the effect that vice and crime make people coarse and ugly. General readers nevertheless, will probably care less for this moral, less for the fine, varied, largely appreciative culture of the writer, in evidence from page to page, than for the story itself, with its adroitly managed supernatural incidents, its almost equally wonderful applications of natural science; impossible, surely, in fact, but plausible enough in fiction. Its interest turns on that very old theme, old because based on some inherent experience or fancy of the human brain, of a double life: of Doppelgänger—not of two *persons,* in this case, but of the man and his portrait; the latter of which, as we hinted above, changes, decays, is spoiled, while the former, through a long course of corruption, remains, to the outward eye, unchanged, still in all the beauty of a seemingly immaculate youth— "the devil's bargain." But it would be a pity to spoil the reader's enjoyment by further detail. We need only emphasise once more, the skill, the real subtlety of art, the ease and fluidity withal of one telling a story by word of mouth, with which the consciousness of the supernatural is introduced into, and maintained amid, the elaborately conventional, sophisticated, disabused world Mr Wilde depicts so cleverly, so mercilessly. The special fascination of the piece is, of course, just there—at that point of contrast. Mr Wilde's work may fairly claim to go with that of Edgar Poe, and with some good French work of the same kind, done, probably, in more or less conscious imitation of it.

ART VERSUS MORALITY:
DORIAN GRAY ON TRIAL

The first trial was an action for libel brought by Wilde at the instigation of Lord Alfred Douglas against the latter's father, John Sholto Douglas, eighth Marquess of Queensberry. The purpose of the suit was to punish and silence "The Scarlet Marquess," who had threatened both Wilde and his own son with scandal. Indeed, he had threatened in a letter to his son to shoot Wilde on sight if rumors of Wilde's homosexual activities should be proved publicly. To that end, perhaps, Queensberry left the now famous calling card with the words "For Oscar Wilde posing as a somdomite [sic]." Those were the fighting words that provoked Wilde to sue for criminal libel. During the trial, Queensberry's defense attorney, Edward Carson, confronted Wilde with *Dorian Gray* as evidence of his corrupting influence on Alfred Douglas.

From Edward Carson's Cross-Examination of Wilde (First Trial)†

* * *

After the criticisms that were passed on *Dorian Gray,* was it modified a good deal?—No. Additions were made. In one case it was pointed out to me—not in a newspaper or anything of that sort, but by the only critic of the century whose opinion I set high, Mr. Walter Pater—that a certain passage was liable to misconstruction, and I made an addition.

This is in your introduction to *Dorian Gray:* "There is no such thing as a moral or an immoral book. Books are well written, or badly written." That expresses your view?—My view on art, yes.

Then, I take it, that no matter how immoral a book may be, if it is well written, it is, in your opinion, a good book?—Yes, if it were well written so as to produce a sense of beauty, which is the highest sense of which a human being can be capable. If it were badly written, it would produce a sense of disgust.

Then a well-written book putting forward perverted moral views may be a good book?—No work of art ever puts forward views. Views belong to people who are not artists.

† From H. M. Hyde, *The Trials of Wilde* (1956; Dover, 1973), 121–33.

A perverted novel might be a good book?—I don't know what you mean by a "perverted" novel.

Then I will suggest *Dorian Gray* as open to the interpretation of being such a novel?—That could only be to brutes and illiterates. The views of Philistines on art are incalculably stupid.

An illiterate person reading *Dorian Gray* might consider it such a novel?—The views of illiterates on art are unaccountable. I am concerned only with my view of art. I don't care twopence what other people think of it.

The majority of persons would come under your definition of Philistines and illiterates?—I have found wonderful exceptions.

Do you think that the majority of people live up to the position you are giving us?—I am afraid they are not cultivated enough.

Not cultivated enough to draw the distinction between a good book and a bad book?—Certainly not.

The affection and love of the artist of *Dorian Gray* might lead an ordinary individual to believe that it might have a certain tendency?—I have no knowledge of the views of ordinary individuals.

You did not prevent the ordinary individual from buying your book?—I have never discouraged him.

[Mr. CARSON then read the following extracts from *The Picture of Dorian Gray,* in which the painter Basil Hallward tells Lord Henry Wooton of his first meetings with Dorian Gray. The quotations were from the original version of the work as it appeared in *Lippincott's Monthly Magazine* for July, 1890.]

> . . . The story is simply this. Two months ago I went to a crush at Lady Brandon's. You know we poor painters have to show ourselves in society from time to time, just to remind the public that we are not savages. With an evening coat and a white tie, as you told me once, anybody, even a stockbroker, can gain a reputation for being civilized. Well, after I had been in the room about ten minutes, talking to huge over-dressed dowagers and tedious Academicians, I suddenly became conscious that some one was looking at me. I turned half-way round, and saw Dorian Gray for the first time. When our eyes met, I felt that I was growing pale. A curious instinct of terror came over me. I knew that I had come face to face with some one whose mere personality was so fascinating that, if I allowed it to do so, it would absorb my whole nature, my whole soul, my very art itself. I did not want any external influence in my life. You know yourself, Harry, how independent I am by nature. My father destined me for the army. I insisted on going to Oxford. Then he made me enter my name at the Middle Temple. Before I had eaten half a dozen dinners I gave up the Bar, and announced my intention of becoming a painter. I have always been my own master; had at least always

been so, till I met Dorian Gray. Then—but I don't know how to explain it to you. Something seemed to tell me that I was on the verge of a terrible crisis in my life. I had a strange feeling that Fate had in store for me exquisite joys and exquisite sorrows. I knew that if I spoke to Dorian I would become absolutely devoted to him, and that I ought not to speak to him. I grew afraid, and turned to quit the room. It was not conscience that made me do so: it was cowardice. I take no credit to myself for trying to escape.

*   *   *

Cross-examination continued—Now I ask you, Mr. Wilde, do you consider that that description of the feeling of one man towards a youth just grown up was a proper or an improper feeling?—I think it is the most perfect description of what an artist would feel on meeting a beautiful personality that was in some way necessary to his art and life.

You think that is a feeling a young man should have towards another?—Yes, as an artist.

[Counsel began to read another extract from the book. Witness asked for a copy and was given one of the original version]

MR. CARSON (in calling witness's attention to the place—*Lippincott's Monthly Magazine*, Vol. XLVI, at p. 56)—I believe it was left out in the purged edition.

WITNESS—I do not call it purged.

MR. CARSON—Yes, I know that; but we will see.

"Let us sit down, Dorian," said Hallward, looking pale and pained. "Let us sit down. I will sit in the shadow, and you shall sit in the sunlight. Our lives are like that. Just answer me one question. Have you noticed in the picture something that you did not like?—something that probably at first did not strike you, but that revealed itself to you suddenly?"

"Basil!" cried the lad, clutching the arms of his chair with trembling hands, and gazing at him with wild, startled eyes.

"I see you did. Don't speak. Wait till you hear what I have to say. It is quite true that I have worshipped you with far more romance of feeling than a man usually gives to a friend. Somehow, I have never loved a woman. I suppose I never had time. Perhaps, as Harry says, a really 'grande passion' is the privilege of those who have nothing to do, and that is the use of the idle classes in a country. Well, from the moment I met you, your personality had the most extraordinary influence over me. I quite admit that I adored you madly, extravagantly, absurdly. I was jealous of every one to whom you spoke. I wanted to have you all to myself. I was only happy when I was with you. When

I was away from you, you were still present in my art. It was all
wrong and foolish. It is all wrong and foolish still. Of course I
never let you know anything about this. It would have been
impossible. You would not have understood it; I did not understand it myself. One day I determined to paint a wonderful portrait of you. It was to have been my masterpiece. It is my
masterpiece. But, as I worked at it, every flake and film of
colour seemed to me to reveal my secret. I grew afraid that the
world would know of my idolatry. I felt, Dorian, that I had told
too much. Then, it was that I resolved never to allow the picture to be exhibited. You were a little annoyed; but then you did
not realize all that it meant to me. Harry, to whom I talked
about it, laughed at me. But I did not mind that. When the picture was finished and I sat alone with it, I felt that I was right.
Well, after a few days the portrait left my studio, and as soon
as I had got rid of the intolerable fascination of its presence it
seemed to me that I had been foolish in imagining that I had
said anything in it, more than that you were extremely good-
looking and that I could paint. Even now I cannot help feeling
that it is a mistake to think that the passion one feels in creation is ever really shown in the work one creates. Art is more
abstract than we fancy. Form and colour tell us of form and
colour—that is all. It often seems to me that art conceals the
artist far more completely than it ever reveals him. And so
when I got this offer from Paris I determined to make your portrait the principal thing in my exhibition. It never occurred to
me that you would refuse. I see now that you were right. The
picture must not be shown. You must not be angry with me,
Dorian, for what I have told you. As I said to Harry, once, you
are made to be worshipped."

Cross-examination continued—Do you mean to say that that passage describes the natural feeling of one man towards another?—It
would be the influence produced by a beautiful personality.

A beautiful person?—I said a "beautiful personality." You can describe
it as you like. Dorian Gray's was a most remarkable personality.

May I take it that you, as an artist, have never known the feeling
described here?—I have never allowed any personality to dominate
my art.

Then you have never known the feeling you described?—No. It is
a work of fiction.

So far as you are concerned you have no experience as to its being
a natural feeling?—I think it is perfectly natural for any artist to
admire intensely and love a young man. It is an incident in the life of
almost every artist.

But let us go over it phrase by phrase. "I quite admit that I
adored you madly." What do you say to that? Have you ever adored

a young man madly?—No, not madly; I prefer love—that is a higher form.

Never mind about that. Let us keep down to the level we are at now?—I have never given adoration to anybody except myself. (Loud laughter.)

I suppose you think that a very smart thing?—Not at all.

Then you have never had that feeling?—No. The whole idea was borrowed from Shakespeare, I regret to say—yes, from Shakespeare's sonnets.

I believe you have written an article to show that Shakespeare's sonnets were suggestive of unnatural vice?—On the contrary I have written an article to show that they are not.[1] I objected to such a perversion being put upon Shakespeare.

"I have adored you extravagantly"?—Do you mean financially?

Oh, yes, financially! Do you think we are talking about finance?—I don't know what you are talking about.

Don't you? Well, I hope I shall make myself very plain before I have done. "I was jealous of every one to whom you spoke." Have you ever been jealous of a young man?—Never in my life.

"I wanted to have you all to myself." Did you ever have that feeling?—No; I should consider it an intense nuisance, an intense bore.

"I grew afraid that the world would know of my idolatry." Why should he grow afraid that the world should know of it?—Because there are people in the world who cannot understand the intense devotion, affection, and admiration that an artist can feel for a wonderful and beautiful personality. These are the conditions under which we live. I regret them.

These unfortunate people, that have not the high understanding that you have, might put it down to something wrong?—Undoubtedly; to any point they chose. I am not concerned with the ignorance of others.

In another passage Dorian Gray receives a book. Was the book to which you refer a moral book?—Not well written, but it gave me an idea.

Was not the book you have in mind of a certain tendency?—I decline to be cross-examined upon the work of another artist. It is an impertinence and a vulgarity.

[Witness admitted that the book in question was a French work, *A Rebours*, by J. K. Huysmans. MR. CARSON persisted in his desire to elicit the witness's view as to the morality of this book, with the result

1. "The Portrait of Mr. W. H.," which appeared in *Blackwood's Edinburgh Magazine*, Vol. cxlvi, No. 885 (July, 1889). A revised and enlarged version of this essay was later announced by Wilde's publishers, but the manuscript which had been returned to Wilde by the publishers on the day of his arrest, mysteriously disappeared, no doubt stolen during the sale of Wilde's effects in his bankruptcy. It turned up many years afterward in New York, where the complete text was published in a limited edition in 1921 by Mr. Mitchell Kennerley, the collector who had acquired the manuscript.

that Sir EDWARD CLARKE appealed to Mr. JUSTICE COLLINS, who ruled against any further reference to it.[2]

MR. CARSON then read a further extract from *The Picture of Dorian Gray*, quoting the following conversation between the painter and Dorian Gray.]

". . . I think it right that you should know that the most dreadful things are being said about you in London—things that I could hardly repeat to you."

"I don't wish to know anything about them. I love scandals about other people, but scandals about myself don't interest me. They have not got the charm of novelty."

"They must interest you, Dorian. Every gentleman is interested in his good name. You don't want people to talk of you as something vile and degraded. Of course you have your position, and your wealth, and all that kind of thing. But position and wealth are not everything. Mind you, I don't believe these rumours at all. At least, I can't believe them when I see you. Sin is a thing that writes itself across a man's face. It cannot be concealed. People talk of secret vices. There are no such things as secret vices. If a wretched man has a vice, it shows itself in the lines of his mouth, the droop of his eyelids, the moulding of his hands even. Somebody—I won't mention his name, but you know him—came to me last year to have his portrait done. I had never seen him before, and had never heard anything about him at the time, though I have heard a good deal since. He offered an extravagant price. I refused him. There was something in the shape of his fingers that I hated. I know now that I was quite right in what I fancied about him. His life is dreadful. But you, Dorian, with your pure, bright, innocent face, and your marvellous untroubled youth—I can't believe anything against you. And yet I see you very seldom, and you never come down to the studio now, and when I am away from you, and I hear all these hideous things that people are whispering about you, I don't know what to say. Why is it, Dorian, that a man like the Duke of Berwick leaves the room of a club when you enter it? Why is it that so many gentlemen in London will neither go to your house nor invite you to theirs? You used to be a friend of Lord Cawdor. I met him at dinner last week. Your name happened to come up in conversation, in connexion with the miniatures you have lent

2. *A Rebours* was first published in 1884. "It was a novel without a plot," wrote Wilde in the passage alluded to by Carson in *The Picture of Dorian Gray*, "and with only one character, being, indeed, simply a psychological study of a certain young Parisian, who spent his life trying to realize in the nineteenth century all the passions and modes of thought that belonged to every century except his own, and to sum up, as it were, in himself the various modes through which the world-spirit had ever passed, loving for their mere artificiality those renunciations that men have unwisely called virtue, as much as those natural rebellions that wise men still call sin."

388   A<small>RT</small> V<small>ERSUS</small> M<small>ORALITY</small>: <small>D</small>ORIAN G<small>RAY ON</small> T<small>RIAL</small>

to the exhibition at the Dudley. Cawdor curled his lip, and said that you might have the most artistic tastes, but that you were a man whom no pure-minded girl should be allowed to know, and whom no chaste woman should sit in the same room with. I reminded him that I was a friend of yours, and asked him what he meant. He told me. He told me right out before everybody. It was horrible! Why is your friendship so fateful to young men? There was that wretched boy in the Guards who committed suicide. You were his great friend. There was Sir Henry Ashton, who had to leave England with a tarnished name. You and he were inseparable. What about Adrian Singleton, and his dreadful end? What about Lord Kent's only son, and his career? I met his father yesterday in St. James Street. He seemed broken with shame and sorrow. What about the young Duke of Perth? What sort of life has he got now? What gentleman would associate with him? Dorian, Dorian, your reputation is infamous . . . ."

Cross-examination continued—Does not this passage suggest a charge of unnatural vice?—It describes Dorian Gray as a man of very corrupt influence, though there is no statement as to the nature of the influence. But as a matter of fact I do not think that one person influences another, nor do I think there is any bad influence in the world.

A man never corrupts a youth?—I think not.

Nothing could corrupt him?—If you are talking of separate ages.

No, sir, I am talking common sense?—I do not think one person influences another.

You don't think that flattering a young man, making love to him, in fact, would be likely to corrupt him?—No.

Where was Lord Alfred Douglas staying when you wrote that letter to him?—At the Savoy; and I was at Babbacombe, near Torquay.

It was a letter in answer to something he had sent you?—Yes, a poem.

Why should a man of your age address a boy nearly twenty years younger as "My own boy"?—I was fond of him. I have always been fond of him.

Do you adore him?—No, but I have always liked him. I think it is a beautiful letter. It is a poem. I was not writing an ordinary letter. You might as well cross-examine me as to whether *King Lear* or a sonnet of Shakespeare was proper.

Apart from art, Mr. Wilde?—I cannot answer apart from art.

Suppose a man who was not an artist had written this letter, would you say it was a proper letter?—A man who was not an artist could not have written that letter.

Why?—Because nobody but an artist could write it. He certainly could not write the language unless he were a man of letters.

I can suggest, for the sake of your reputation, that there is nothing very wonderful in this "red rose-leaf lips of yours"?—A great deal depends on the way it is read.

"Your slim gilt soul walks between passion and poetry." Is that a beautiful phrase?—Not as you read it, Mr. Carson. You read it very badly.

I do not profess to be an artist; and when I hear you give evidence, I am glad I am not—

* * *

From Edward Carson's Opening Speech for the Defense (First Trial)†

* * *

Let us contrast the position which Mr. Wilde took up in cross-examination as to his books, which are for the select and not for the ordinary individual, with the position he assumed as to the young men to whom he was introduced and those he picked up for himself. His books were written by an artist for artists; his words were not for Philistines or illiterates. Contrast that with the way in which Mr. Wilde chose his companions! He took up with Charles Parker, a gentleman's servant, whose brother was a gentleman's servant; with young Alphonse Conway, who sold papers on the pier at Worthing; and with Scarfe, also a gentlemen's servant. Then his excuse was no longer that he was dwelling in regions of art but that he had such a noble, such a democratic soul (Laughter.), that he drew no social distinctions, and that it was quite as much pleasure to have the sweeping boy from the streets to lunch or dine with him as the greatest *litérateur* or artist.

In my judgment, if the case had rested on Mr. Wilde's literature alone, Lord Queensberry would have been absolutely justified in the course he has taken. Lord Queensberry has undertaken to prove that Mr. Wilde has been "posing" as guilty of certain vices. Mr. Wilde never complained of the immorality of the story "The Priest and the Acolyte" which appeared in *The Chameleon*. He knows no distinction, in fact, between a moral and an immoral book. Nor does he care whether the article is in its very terms blasphemous. All that Mr. Wilde says is that he did not approve of the story from a literary point of view. What is that story? It is a story of the love of a priest for the acolyte who attended him at Mass. Exactly the same idea that runs through the two letters to Lord Alfred Douglas runs through that

† From H. M. Hyde, *The Trials of Wilde* (1956; Dover, 1973), 166–67.

story, and also through *The Picture of Dorian Gray*. When the boy was discovered in the priest's bed, the priest made exactly the same defence as Mr. Wilde has made—that the world does not understand the beauty of this love. The same idea runs through these two letters which Mr. Wilde has called beautiful, but which I call an abominable piece of disgusting immorality.

Moreover, there is in this same *Chameleon* a poem which shows some justification for the frightful anticipations which Lord Queensberry entertained for his son. The poem was written by Lord Alfred Douglas and was seen by Mr. Wilde before its publication. Is it not a terrible thing that a young man on the threshold of life, who has for several years been dominated by Oscar Wilde and has been "adored and loved" by Oscar Wilde, as the two letters prove, should thus show the tendency of his mind upon this frightful subject? What would be the horror of any man whose son wrote such a poem?

Passing now to *The Picture of Dorian Gray*, it is the tale of a beautiful young man who, by the conversation of one who has great literary power and ability to speak in epigrams—just as Mr. Wilde has—and who, by reading of exactly the same kind as that in "Phrases and Philosophies for the Use of the Young," has his eyes opened to what they are pleased to call the "delights of the world." If *Dorian Gray* is a book which it can be conclusively proved advocates the vice imputed to Mr. Wilde, what answer, then, is there to Lord Queensberry's plea of justification?

* * *

CRITICISM

MICHAEL PATRICK GILLESPIE

Picturing Dorian Gray: Resistant Readings in Wilde's Novel†

From oblique appearances in the youthful storytelling of his earliest artistic projects through the insistent polyphony of *The Picture of Dorian Gray* and *The Importance of Being Earnest*, an aura of ambivalence and ambiguity increasingly mediates relations among Wilde, his writing, and his readers.[1] As a result, the most satisfying interpretations that one can draw from the canon incorporate into readings this uncertainty as an element that enhances our imaginative pleasure. Specifically, these responses cultivate an ability to balance Wilde's flair for representing with graphic clarity the foibles of late-nineteenth-century English society against his ongoing need for public approval and apparent willingness to shape his creative efforts into forms that would earn that approval.

One begins this process by looking at details from Wilde's life that help understand the way that multiple perspectives came to condition his consciousness. A sense of pluralism always informed his public persona. Beginning with his student days at Portora Royal, continuing at Trinity and Oxford, and throughout his triumphal tours of America and Great Britain, one finds Wilde devoting as much energy to garnering society's approval through his charm as he does to breaking down public complacency through outrageousness.[2] The same dual impulses continued to characterize his behavior during the years that he spent establishing himself as London's most exquisite purveyor of discriminating taste.

Over the course of his public life, in fact, Wilde demonstrated a flair for gaining notoriety through extravagant behavior; and until his very last years he always balanced this ability with a sense of knowing precisely how far such conduct could go.[3] Throughout the 1880s and

---

† From *Oscar Wilde and the Aesthetics of Chaos* (Gainesville: UP of Florida, 1996), 57–74. Reprinted by permission of the University Press of Florida. Bracketed page numbers refer to this Norton Critical Edition.

1. Perhaps the clearest alternative delineations of the ambivalent sensibilities of the Victorian ethos that shaped Wilde's world appear in Regenia Gagnier, *Idylls of the Marketplace: Oscar Wilde and the Victorian Public*; Ellen Moers, *The Dandy: Brummell to Beerbohm*; and Richard D. Altick, *The Presence of the Present: Topics of the Day in the Victorian Novel*.
2. See Richard Ellmann, *Oscar Wilde*, especially 37–52 and 157–210; Lord Alfred Bruce Douglas, *Oscar Wilde: A Summing-Up*; H. Montgomery Hyde, *Oscar Wilde: The Aftermath* and *Oscar Wilde: A Biography*; Philippe Jullian, *Oscar Wilde*; and Frances Winwar, *Oscar Wilde and the Yellow Nineties*.
3. For an example of Wilde's sense of the limits of public tolerance, see Ellmann's account of the feuds with James A. McNeill Whistler and Queensberry in *Oscar Wilde*, 270–74, 456–78.

into the 1890s, Wilde's uninhibited, sardonic self-dramatization, ever suggestive but always comfortably nebulous, delighted many within the British middle class. The indeterminacy that surrounded his life allowed people to sustain a range of possible opinions about him without having to confront any of the implications that would grow out of an indisputable sense of his proclivities. In a complementary fashion, the expectations engendered by the ambiguity of Wilde's public persona disposed Victorian readers and theatergoers to assume the same interpretive freedom in their responses to *The Picture of Dorian Gray* and other writings.

Indeed, never losing sight of the power of multiplicity to invigorate his work, Wilde fostered this inclination in his audiences: Time and again one finds his writing stimulating approaches that support disparate methodologies, acknowledge the presence of multiple levels of reading (an aesthetic metasystem), and bind together disparate meanings into a response accommodating their inherent diversities. In a 12 February 1894 letter to Ralph Payne, for example, Wilde neatly summarized the antinomies of *The Picture of Dorian Gray* and gently mocked simplistic reactions to it through a series of concise analogies between himself and the novel's central characters: "I am so glad you like that strange coloured book of mine: it contains much of me in it. Basil Hallward is what I think I am: Lord Henry what the world thinks me: Dorian what I would like to be—in other ages perhaps" (*Letters*, 352).

The playful ambivalences within these comments point up exactly the disposition for indeterminacy that runs throughout the narrative of *The Picture of Dorian Gray*. Rather than enforcing the hegemony of a single perspective, Wilde deftly undermines support for any concept of narrowly defined intentionality or even for the sense that any particular point of view can have an implicit dominance or an inherent legitimacy. In their place he offers the example of his personality which embodies the range of valid responses that one could possibly make to his work. Further, by presenting each response as equally valid, Wilde eschews any move toward closure. Instead, he conjoins a broad consideration of the structure of the novel with a sportive indulgence of the particular interpretive impulses of the individual reader.

In addition to this anecdotal evidence of the importance of pluralism within Wilde's writing, a range of intra- and extratextual features specifically associated with *The Picture of Dorian Gray* creates clearly identifiable antinomies within the discourse that resist amalgamation into unified linear interpretations. Within the narrative, for example, frequent references to the mores of Victorian society invite one to judge the actions of individual characters according to the values of the world in which they exist. At the same time, as a number of the cultural studies already cited have noted, the contradictory elements that make up fin de siècle English society call for a great deal of flexibility in any reading based upon general assumptions about these other Victorians of whom and for whom Wilde wrote.

This incorporation of simultaneous multiple responses into an overview of the work relies upon an openness to subjective approaches akin to the reception of history outlined by critics as divergent as Carlo Ginzburg and Hayden White.[4] In readings of *The Picture of Dorian Gray*, such a method starts from the dual premises outlined above: The novel emerges as very much a product of the Victorian era, yet no fixed or single image of that period—no Platonic ideal—exists as a unified and consistent vision within the consciousness of either the author or his readers. As a result, any notion of the age projected by the narrative of Wilde's novel will necessarily incite a multitude of different visions.

The diversity inspired by Wilde's discourse goes well beyond the class stratification of late-nineteenth-century English life embodied by the cultural differences among the aristocrats with whom Dorian passes most of his time, the working poor represented by Sibyl Vane and her family, and the denizens of the Limehouse district where Dorian debauches himself. These groups in fact exemplify fairly stable elements of the narrative. The real antinomies within the discourse emerge when one examines the metaphysical assumptions behind the social institutions that define the Victorian world of the novel. In particular, the ability of characters to sustain a multitude of conflicting moral values without any sense of disruption or contradiction within their consciousnesses enforces the idea that to understand these individuals one must come to grips with the concept that a breadth of contending principles guides their behavior without any one holding primacy.

In chapter 14, for instance, Dorian articulates a range of responses during the hours immediately following the death of Basil Hallward, with different—and, in some cases, conflicting—ethical precepts informing each expression. His initial reaction to recollections of the murder shows a mixture of anger, self-pity, and revulsion over the circumstances; but he displays no regret over committing the act itself: "Gradually the events of the preceding night crept with silent blood-stained feet into his brain, and reconstructed themselves there with terrible distinctness. He winced at the memory of all that he had suffered, and for a moment the same curious feeling of loathing for Basil

---

4. For a good example of a sophisticated response to a complex and distant social system, see Carlo Ginzburg, *The Cheese and the Worms: The Cosmos of a Sixteenth-Century Miller.* Ginzburg's study shows how one can write against stereotypical responses to a familiar historical event (in his case, the Inquisition) yet retain the ability to reach conclusions and initiate investigations based upon concepts of the event that the writer and the reader share.

Hallward, that had made him kill him as he sat in the chair, came back to him and he grew cold with passion" [135]. Later, when he must blackmail Alan Campbell into agreeing to dispose of Basil Hallward's body, Dorian feels genuine regret for what he must do: "The same look of pity came into Dorian Gray's eyes. Then he stretched out his hand, took a piece of paper, and wrote something on it. He read it over twice, folded it carefully, and pushed it across the table [to Campbell]" [142]. Finally, as Dorian contemplates the image of Campbell confronting the body of the murdered man, the inane social concerns that come to mind underscore a chilling detachment from all that is happening: "He began to wonder if [Alan Campbell] and Basil Hallward had ever met, and, if so, what they had thought of each other" [145]. No one of these views seems a more valid representation of Dorian's feelings than any of the others, yet each in an important way contributes to the reader's full sense of Dorian's nature.[5]

Because the narrative repeatedly lends equal support to such contrasting points of view in an undifferentiated fashion, *The Picture of Dorian Gray* inevitably blurs the boundaries that define the novel's social repertoire (in the sense that Wolfgang Iser has given to the term). This gesture toward indeterminacy in turn recasts the reader's assumptions about the way that one experiences meaning, underscoring the tenuousness of any premise that we use to form a text. Up to this point, of course, the multiplicity that I have identified in *The Picture of Dorian Gray* seems little more than a range of linear, cause-and-effect options for generating meaning. The hypostatic quality of these perspectives, however, gives the narrative its unique pluralistic character. This ability to create characterizations that sustain multiple perspectives in an imaginative equilibrium stands as the defining feature of Wilde's emergence as a mature artist. (Likewise, the ability to recognize and sustain these variant points of view in an interpretive response becomes the decisive trait of a mature reader.) This characteristic dominates the narrative of *The Picture of Dorian Gray* from the opening pages of the novel, and nowhere does one find it more evident than in the protean representation of the central character.

Over the course of Wilde's novel, the narrative gradually shifts its attention from Dorian Gray's striking physical appearance, made so much of in the opening episodes, to the methodical, horrific metamorphosis of his portrait throughout the middle and final chapters. This is not, however, a simple plot displacement that accommodates Dorian's unfolding story. The ambivalent feelings that sweep across

5. For a more detailed examination of the way that moral values shape our interpretation of the novel, see Michael Patrick Gillespie, "Ethics and Aesthetics in *Dorian Gray*," in Sandulescu, *Rediscovering Wilde*, 137–55.

his consciousness as he experiences the changes in his nature and assesses the alterations in his portrait render a linear perspective inadequate. One instance of Dorian in a moment of reflection, midway through the novel, perfectly conveys this condition of flux. "[H]e would sit in front of the picture, sometimes loathing it and himself, but filled, at other times, with that pride of individualism that is half the fascination of sin, and smiling, with secret pleasure, at the misshapen shadow that had to bear the burden that should have been his own" [117–18]. Once the discourse has foregrounded Dorian's oscillating moral, psychological, and spiritual perspectives, monologic explanations begin to lose their efficacy.

Throughout the narrative, one finds numerous other instances that encourage us to sustain simultaneous, multiple, diverse readings. Lord Henry's exposition on New Hedonism [19–23], for example, seems at first glance to offer clear-cut alternatives for interpretation: One might accept it with the same credulity that Dorian expresses, modify its tenets to compensate for Harry's inclination toward extravagant language, or simply dismiss it as mere cant. At the same time, because each choice enriches our sense of New Hedonism, it becomes difficult to suppress any alternative in favor of just one. Indeed, if one follows the logic that supports New Hedonism, one can hardly justify such an exclusionary gesture.

The manner of Lord Henry's presentation further underscores the efficacy of a pluralistic response. His aura of insouciance compounds one's sense of the appropriateness of ambivalence, and this feeling in turn intensifies one's inclination to defer any sort of interpretive closure. The casualness that surrounds his discourse leaves readers unsure of his attitude toward New Hedonism. Does he see it as a legitimate form of behavior, a transitory inspiration created on the spur of the moment to justify one of his verbal flights of fancy, or a random and meaningless response to a random and meaningless universe?

Each point of view provides the basis for a logical interpretation of Harry's disquisition, and the narrative offers no compelling reason to prefer one over the others. Moreover, as the novel progresses, one finds that each of these points of view contributes to a more detailed illumination of the discourse and in doing so blunts inclinations to privilege any one of these perspectives over the others. New Hedonism in fact defines itself only through the symbiotic support of multiple systems of values, and any effort to view it in isolation would prove reductive.

The narrative also encourages perceptions of multiplicity through numerous representations of characters reforming their values to meet evolving conditions, yet at the same time the discourse still relies upon the counterforce of existing attitudes to define events and disrupt any sense of stability that one might acquire by completely abandoning an old system of belief in favor of a newer one. Later, I will take up in greater detail Dorian's final conversation with Lord Henry [172–80] to illustrate this point, but for now a more general reference to it will support my argument.

Tension runs throughout the scene, which dominates the penultimate chapter of the novel. To a large degree the strain grows out of the reader's need to come to grips with Dorian's ambivalently presented views, which are thrown into relief by the consistently cynical outlook of Lord Henry's commitment to New Hedonism. A full and balanced impression of this exchange cannot emerge unless one accommodates these multiple perspectives. That is, we strive to achieve what I referred to in the introduction as Burke's idea of a "compensation for disunity." In other words, paraphrasing Hugh Kenner's advice on how to approach the *Cantos* of Ezra Pound, one privileges coherence over correctness.

In this fashion, the structure of the novel's discourse reconfigures habits of interpretation with or without our awareness or assent. A reading of *The Picture of Dorian Gray* grows out of individual experiences mingled with the diverse perspectives projected throughout the narrative. The pluralism of the consequent discourse must inevitably resist the prescriptiveness that one associates with a single, dominant perspective.

This privileged position of multiplicity becomes apparent as soon as one calls into question the assumptions that would ordinarily begin to narrow one's perception of the novel. I have already touched upon the different ways that Dorian manifests his character throughout the narrative. One can apply the same considerations to the way that one perceives the painted representation of Dorian. One might, for example, resist the impulse to see the title—*The Picture of Dorian Gray*—as identifying a single representation of a particular character and instead develop concepts of pluralism that contain far richer implications in their suggestion of the range of possibilities inherent in the gesture of portrayal. A definite article (*the*) seems to single out the next word in the title (*picture*) as a specific object. With a sense of multiplicity, however, one can no longer assume that the portrait acts as anything more than an invocation to any one of a number of subjective images of Dorian Gray. To read the title less idiosyncratically would invite a false sense of objectivity that would in turn distort all subsequent contact with the work.

From this assumption, one inevitably moves to embrace the relativity of broader responses to *The Picture of Dorian Gray*. The ambiguity within the title has significance not only in its immediate context but also in terms of the expectations that it introduces into the reader's consciousness. Once one accepts its both/and ambivalence as a guiding attitude, the entire process of interpreting the novel takes on new significance. (Acknowledging a relativity among various readings does not, of course, automatically relegate all interpretation to a program of unrestrained, eccentric free association. For example, the social repertoire alluded to earlier in this chapter takes on great significance as alternative and at times conflicting interpretations that one must consider in any effort at articulating meaning. At the same time, incorporating a sense of relativity into one's horizon of expectations does point up the broad imaginative parameters within which one can operate to determine meaning.)

One finds just as much diversity in the pictures of Dorian's consciousness composed by Basil Hallward, Lord Henry, Dorian himself, and the reader. We can readily see that each character's apprehension of Dorian's nature functions kinetically. Each does not simply see Dorian; each constructs a comprehension of him.

Consciously or not, the impulse to create and thereby interpret dominates responses of characters at every stage of the narrative. This persistent inclination to privilege subjective perspectives stands as an important illustration of the self-reflexive system that I have been describing. Throughout the novel the delineation of Dorian recurs as a central narrative feature. In consequence, this defining and composing an image of Dorian—actions going well beyond the passive reception of impressions—emerge as the real focus of attention for characters and readers.

What differentiates characters from readers, however, is the ability of the latter to go beyond the individualistic gesture of defining and composing to sustain multiple definitions and compositions. Readers have the benefit of a range of diverse constructions, while each character in the novel remains fixed within the parameters of a single response. In the opening scenes, for example, through his descriptions of Dorian and his painting, Basil Hallward creates an arresting manifestation of physical beauty that takes on an emblematic significance throughout the narrative. In addition, Basil's efforts produce an epiphanic animation of Dorian's consciousness, not simply calling attention to his beauty but making him aware of the temporal relation of that beauty to the way that he sees the world around him: "'How sad it is!' murmured Dorian Gray with his eyes still fixed upon his own portrait. 'How sad it is! I shall grow old, and horrible, and dreadful. But this picture will remain always young. It will never be older than this particular day in June'" [25].

For Dorian, Basil's painting operates in conjunction with Lord Henry's doctrine of New Hedonism, which has already disposed the young man's mind to assign paramount importance to sensual pleasure. Readers enjoy a broader perspective. As the narrative unfolds, Dorian's egocentric behavior counterpoints our first perceptions of his nature, reshaping our sense of his consciousness as it evolves during his continual search for new pleasures. At the same time, the initial representations of Dorian as an ingenuous youth, admittedly embellished by Basil's rapture, remain distinct for the remainder of our reading.

This illumination of Dorian's nature illustrates the ways that the narrative affects a reader's interpretive disposition. From the novel's start, the discourse encourages attentiveness to the multiplicity that initially emerges in the response of individual characters to Dorian's physical presence. Thus, while we see that the completion of the painting marks an awakening in the sensibilities of Dorian, we also note that these early impressions have just the opposite effect upon Hallward. They freeze his sense of the young man.

As a result, when, in chapter 13, Dorian confronts Basil with the transmuted portrait and, by extension, with his own radically altered nature, Basil's allegiance to the past remains unshaken.

> "Years ago, when I was a boy," said Dorian Gray, crushing the flower in his hand, "you met me, flattered me, and taught me to be vain of my good looks. One day you introduced me to a friend of yours, who explained to me the wonder of youth, and you finished a portrait of me that revealed to me the wonder of beauty. In a mad moment, that, even now, I don't know whether I regret or not, I made a wish, perhaps you would call it a prayer. . . ."
>
> "I remember it! Oh, how well I remember it! No! [looking at the painting] the thing is impossible. The room is damp. Mildew had got into the canvas. The paints I used had some wretched mineral poison in them. I tell you the thing is impossible." [131]

Even as he comes to acknowledge the horror of the painting before him, Basil disassociates it from his original work and his first impression of Dorian. "There was nothing evil in [the original painting], nothing shameful. You were to me such an ideal as I shall never meet again. This is the face of a satyr."

Although he finally comprehends the behavior that has produced such a change in the portrait, Basil still resists seeing Dorian's condition as anything more than a superficial flaw that one can expunge by supplication to God.

> Dorian Gray turned slowly around, and looked at [Basil] with tear-dimmed eyes. "It is too late, Basil," he faltered.
>
> "It is never too late, Dorian. Let us kneel down and try if we cannot remember a prayer. Isn't there a verse somewhere, 'Though your sins be as scarlet, yet I will make them as white as snow.'" [132]

This loyalty to initial impressions brings the past into collision with the present. Because Basil cannot perceive the condition of duality, he cannot revise his perception of Dorian, even when confronted with the horrors of the painting.

Nonetheless, this narrative hypostasis inhibits inclinations among readers to replace one set of assumptions about Dorian with another. Thus, despite the material evidence that we have of Dorian's degeneration, Basil's stubborn adherence to his own idealized view reminds us of the elements in Dorian's nature that run counter to moral corruption. Further, Basil's either/or view, as it supplements our sense of Dorian, paradoxically enforces the both/and idea that one cannot speak of a single Dorian Gray existing in the novel when so many characters see him from so many different perspectives.

Initial impressions prove to have an equally tenacious hold on the consciousness of Lord Henry. During their first meeting, Harry entrances Dorian by creating a psychological model that the young man seems anxious to adopt: "Ah! realize your youth while you have it. Don't squander the gold of your days, listening to the tedious, trying to improve the hopeless failure, or giving away your life to the ignorant, the common, and the vulgar. These are sickly aims, the false ideals, of our age. Live! Live the wonderful life that is in you" [23]. Nonetheless, Lord Henry proves as susceptible as his listener to the power of his own language; and despite minor adjustments, his felicitous description of the young man that he has met in Basil Hallward's studio remains forever associated with his conception of Dorian Gray: "You have a wonderfully beautiful face, Mr. Gray. Don't frown. You have. And Beauty is a form of Genius—is higher, indeed, than Genius, as it needs no explanation" [22].

Early on, of course, Lord Henry seems to enjoy a precise sense of the elements constituting Dorian's personality. After Dorian falls in love with Sibyl Vane, for example, Harry explains to him the full implications of those emotions. When Dorian expresses regret at revealing his feelings, Lord Henry smugly replies: "You could not have helped telling me, Dorian. All through your life you will tell me everything you do" [47]. At the time, Dorian's slavish devotion affirms, for both Harry and the reader, the accuracy of the statement.

As Dorian becomes more worldly, however, Harry proves to be as unwilling as Basil to acknowledge changes in his friend's nature. Late in the novel, with Dorian again on the point of unburdening his conscience to his friend, one finds the relationship subtly altered. Lord Henry no longer seems to have confidence in his own ability to cope with the vagaries within Dorian's nature, and he retreats from hearing a revelation that would call his own convictions into question.

"What would you say, Harry, if I told you that I had murdered
Basil?" said the younger man. He watched him intently after he
had spoken.
"I would say, my dear fellow, that you were posing for a character that doesn't suit you. All crime is vulgar, just as all vulgarity
is a crime. It is not in you, Dorian, to commit a murder. I am
sorry if I hurt your vanity by saying so, but I assure you it is true.
Crime belongs exclusively to the lower orders. I don't blame
them in the smallest degree. I should fancy that crime was to
them what art is to us, simply a method of procuring sensations."
[175–76]

For a man who has given experience a privileged position over all
else, this relegation of crime to the lower orders has a disingenuous
ring. Ultimately, of course, maintaining the integrity of his initial
impressions means much more to Harry than maintaining a consistent philosophical position or attaining any genuine insight into
Dorian's character. Nonetheless, his attitude raises crucial questions
for us as we try to assess both Lord Henry's and our own perceptions.
I am not, of course, suggesting that one could deny the fact that
Dorian has actually committed murder. Lord Henry himself seems
careful not to make such a statement. On the other hand, Harry con-
ceives of murder as an act completely out of character for Dorian,
an aberrant gesture alien to his true nature. If we accept Harry's
views as even partially valid—that a "true nature" exists to which
Dorian, despite any atypical behavior, will invariably return—then
the picture of Dorian's linear degeneration cannot remain unquali-
fied.

Alternately, if we supplant Lord Henry's opinions with our own—
in the same way that his have supplanted Basil's views in the narrative discourse—then we end up in the same tenuous position that
Lord Henry has occupied, speaking as an authority yet without the
interpretive latitude necessary to have full confidence in the accuracy of our views. From these contradictory viewpoints emerges the
principle that the discourse here—or elsewhere in the work—does
not enforce the validity of one interpretation over another. Rather,
it consistently undermines the notion of certitude that informs any
single view and instead invites incorporation rather than stratification.

As we read through *The Picture of Dorian Gray*, it becomes evident
that an insistent nostalgia continually informs the images of Dorian
created in the minds of both Basil and Harry. Each retains a retrospective view of Dorian's nature remarkably close to the judgments
reached in Basil Hallward's studio on the June day described in chapter 2, counterpointing the sense of change that surrounds the later
stages of the novel. Furthermore, each reflects, in a limited way, the

problem facing anyone who tries to read the novel from a single, exclusionary point of view. Each man thinks he sees a complete individual, yet each sees only the picture that he created from the single perspective that he has adopted and validated.

Of course, the narrative does not represent the points of view and the attitudes of each character quite as neatly as I have indicated. As individuals within the novel seek to trace the nature of Dorian, however, the inescapable consideration emerges that each character places extraordinary emphasis on his perception of the human figure as reflecting a particular aspect of Dorian's personality. Readers adopting the same sort of monocular perspective—Dorian's, Lord Henry's, Basil's, or some other's—will limit themselves to any one of a number of equally valid interpretations ranging from very sympathetic to extremely harsh.

Impressions, in fact, develop according to a number of diverse attitudes, all demanding recognition. Consequently, while readers may acknowledge Dorian's beauty as an essential feature of the environment of the novel, they continually face the question of what value to apportion to it as any sort of prescriptive standard for judgment. While everyone who meets Dorian praises his appearance, what that beauty means as an influence on or reflection of his character changes from chapter to chapter. As a result, the reader sees diverse attitudes within the narrative that fall short of a clear articulation of its significance: Basil Hallward's naïve conjunction of beauty and goodness, Lord Henry's narrow perception of beauty as a sole source of gratification, and Dorian's reductive view of beauty as a source of power. This in turn means that the limitations of pursuing only a direct interpretive approach—of assigning a single or even a primary hermeneutic significance to his beauty—become increasingly apparent.

Dorian himself reinforces the need for readers to embrace multiplicity; for as the narrative unfolds, it shows his increasing resistance to adopting the prescriptive role of a passive archetype. As his appetite for aesthetic pleasure grows more diverse and more sophisticated, he derives his greatest satisfaction not from the recognition of static physical attributes but from a realization of his kinetic power to change the rendition of his nature that appears in Basil Hallward's painting. As a result, a much more complex and critically rewarding exploration of the issue of creativity—the relationship between the figurative ugliness of the portrait and his own power to imbue his nature with a clandestine ugliness—comes to obsess Dorian and shape the discourse.

The changes that the picture undergoes as the novel progresses invite the reader to realign his or her aesthetic sensibilities. In essence, the painting reverts imaginatively to a previous state—

from being to becoming—that reflects evolving creativity rather than immobile achievement. The alterations that Dorian effects present one with the example of a piece of art always open to the diverse creative efforts of its audience. This in turn offers us the opportunity to elaborate upon the pluralistic process of reading the novel itself. The painting's changing image enforces the range of possible responses that one might make to the entire discourse. At the same time, the picture provides multiple possibilities for interpretive protocols without precluding the coexistence of a range of alternative readings.

As I demonstrated in a passage quoted previously (*DG*, 25), when Hallward finishes the painting and gives it to Dorian, he precipitates a crisis. The completion of the portrait disrupts the equilibrium among painter, sitter, and picture. Dorian must now face his own blooming sensuality, and Basil must confront his own arrested emotional development. Neither character clearly addresses these conditions, and the limitations that we perceive in their responses remind us of the larger interpretive need to overcome tendencies toward linear either/or thinking. A reading of the passage must reflect both the homoerotic tensions of the scene and the archetypal echoes of classical mythology; it must also touch upon questions of aesthetic sensibilities, authorship, and the range and the limits of a piece of art. No single consideration stands as more or less important than another, but all demand attention.

Like the Impressionist paintings contemporaneous with Basil's work, his portrait of Dorian serves as a gauge of developing sensibilities rather than a manifestation of passive reception. Early in the narrative, Basil's picture straightforwardly enforces an idea of the painter's talent and sensitivity. Later, as Basil uses recollections of the painting to cling to a nostalgic view of Dorian, the radically changed portrait draws attention to the inherent flaws that limit his ability to see his model from more than one perspective.

For Dorian, too, the painting acquaints us with a range of responses. He develops a far more complex sense of the portrait, but in his own way he also succumbs to a circumscribed point of view. When he slips the restraints of Basil's asceticism, he falls into a state of self-indulgence. As it did with Basil, the picture leaves a marked impression upon Dorian's consciousness; but even though its kinetic features cause him to read the painting pluralistically, it still has an inhibiting rather than liberating effect upon his approach to life: "After a few years he could not endure to be long out of England, and gave up the villa that he had shared at Trouville with Lord Henry, as well as the little white walled-in house at Algiers where they had more than once spent the winter. He hated to be separated from the picture that was such a part of his life" [118].

The irony of the painting's oppressive influence comes to the fore when, near the close of the novel, Lord Henry begins to assess the impact of the painting on Basil: "It was really a masterpiece. I remember I wanted to buy it. I wish I had now. It belonged to Basil's best period. Since then, his work has that curious mixture of bad painting and good intentions that always entitles a man to be called a representative British artist" [176]. Harry then sets this dismissal of Basil's life in contrast with praise for Dorian's mode of living in a manner that emerges as all the more effective for its unconscious irony: "You are the type of what the age is searching for, and what it is afraid it has found. I am so glad that you have never done anything, never carved a statue, or painted a picture, or produced anything outside of yourself! Life has been your art. You have set yourself to music. Your days are your sonnets" [179].

This monologic cynicism assesses the two characters in a manner too reductive to satisfy readers conditioned, by this point in the narrative, to the polyphony of Wilde's discourse. The picture, on the other hand, underscores for us the unvoiced multiplicity inherent in the natures of both of Harry's friends. It emphasizes Basil's combination of naïveté and fidelity and Dorian's mixture of callousness and tenderness.

In different ways, that inability to face all that the portrait comes to represent destroys both Basil and Dorian. Each man succumbs to a monocular self-regard and a compulsion to maintain stasis. Each confronts the degraded picture as a static object and rejects the kinetic ugliness that it manifests in favor of an ideal, flawless image. Even here, of course, a hypostatic ambivalence insinuates itself. In trying to re-form the surface of the painting in the last moments of their lives, both men embrace contradiction: Basil wishes through prayer to reclaim the aura of homoerotic innocence that first attracted him to Dorian [132]. Dorian seeks through violence to brutalize the artifact whose coarseness now betrays his own lack of innocence [183]. More than just a rejection of ugliness, however, the response of each man foregrounds an attitude antipathetic to evolution and committed to stagnation.

Dorian's case in particular cries out for the intervention of the reader to acknowledge the pluralism informing perceptions of his nature. To a degree, his desire to experience existence to the fullest possible measure justifies Lord Henry's equation of Dorian's life with a work of art. At the same time, for all his interest in new experiences and feelings, one sees most of Dorian's energy consumed by retrograde gestures that seek merely to hoard the sensations that he apprehends. Further, he continually contravenes the most creative aspect of his nature—his capacity to live outside the bounds imposed by society—by seeking to suppress all physical evidence of his accomplishments. This tendency moves quickly from a simple concern for his appearance to a compulsive abhorrence of any sign of temporality.

Change and exchange of any sort repel him. As a consequence, he becomes de facto a miser. He stops loving Sibyl, for example, when her acting ability fades because of her love for him. "[Y]ou have killed my love. You used to stir my imagination. Now you don't even stir my curiosity. You simply produce no effect. I loved you because you were marvellous, because you had genius and intellect, because you realized the dreams of great poets and gave shape and substance to the shadows of art. You have thrown it all away. You are shallow and stupid. My God! how mad I was to love you! What a fool I have been! You are nothing to me now" [74]. He cannot interest himself in new aspects of her nature because such a gesture puts at risk the enjoyment of familiar pleasures and involves shared feelings in a reciprocal relationship rather than the exclusive sensations he formerly enjoyed during her performances.

In keeping with the ambiguity that characterizes the entire discourse, the failure of Dorian's experiment with New Hedonism does not affirm the efficacy of the conventional environment that he apparently cannot escape. Indeed, the narrative does everything it can to undermine the impulse toward any form of closure in the novel's putatively moral ending, surrounding Dorian's death with an ambivalence that subverts its apparent finality. *The Picture of Dorian Gray* in fact ends with what appears to be an unfortunate accident, the consequence of recklessness and not of considered action. Dorian willfully lashes out at something that reminds him of the consequences of his behavior.

> But this murder—was it to dog him all his life? Was he always to be burdened by his past? Was he really to confess? Never. There was only one bit of evidence left against him. The picture itself— that was evidence. He would destroy it. Why had he kept it so long? Once it had given him pleasure to watch it changing and growing old. Of late he had felt no such pleasure. It had kept him awake at night. When he had been away, he had been filled with terror lest other eyes should look upon it. It had brought melancholy across his passions. It had been like conscience to him. Yes, it had been conscience. He would destroy it. [183]

When Dorian sees the knife that he had used to kill Basil Hallward, he seizes it and stabs the painting. "There was a cry heard, and a crash. The cry was so horrible in its agony that the frightened servants woke, and crept out of their rooms" [183]. They find the now-grotesque body of Dorian Gray lying before the painting, which is restored to the condition it had been in when Basil completed it.

A simplistic response to the scene would say that Dorian pays the price for his self-indulgence and recklessness because his assault on the painting brings about his own destruction. At the same time, the apparent capriciousness of this gesture makes the result seem, if not ridiculous, certainly rather melodramatic. More complex conditions obtain, for one can hardly interpret it as either confirming or refuting the powerful tenets of New Hedonism that Lord Henry has preached in the garden in chapter 2: "Let nothing be lost upon you. Be always searching for new sensations. Be afraid of nothing. . . . [Wilde's ellipses] A new Hedonism—that is what our century wants" [23]. Throughout his life Dorian has heeded Lord Henry's urging to seek out new sensations, but in his final moments he fails to follow the injunction to have no fear. Thus, even on the brink of death Dorian vacillates between alternative points of view. Choosing a single way of reading the picture leads to self-destruction.

Lord Henry offers a more complex representation of the consequences of failing to accept the full implications of New Hedonism. Throughout much of the novel he embraces pluralism in a particularly uninhibited fashion (for its own sake, not in accordance with a specific ethical disposition), and he seems to behave without reservation no matter what the situation. Indeed, until the penultimate chapter, of all the major characters only Lord Henry seems able to accept change; and his behavior (although not his judgment of others) suggests a model for reading analogous to what I have been advocating. Whether one focuses on his ability to accommodate Dorian's engagement to Sibyl or his equanimity over his wife's elopement with a pianist, this behavior asserts a flexibility that readers find lacking in most of the other figures in the novel: the emergence of an incipient pluralistic sensibility as an alternative to the monocular way of seeing the world.

In essence, an intellectualism based on a receptiveness to numerous systems of values distinguishes Lord Henry from the other characters. In the end, unfortunately, as I have already observed, his ego makes him a prisoner of the same sort of retrograde impulses that have limited the perceptions of others; and his final judgments become as narrow and prescriptive as Basil's or Dorian's. Up to that point, however, his methodology for reaching those choices reminds readers of the aesthetic values that directed the novel's composition.

In the early and middle portions of the narrative Lord Henry combines a range of attitudes found only selectively in others. He refuses to accept received wisdom, yet he keeps in mind the strictures imposed upon behavior by society. As he demonstrates in chapter 3, at lunch at Lady Agatha's, he is fully able to articulate a logic for his New Hedonism; yet, when pressed, he conveniently claims not to remember what he has said (*DG*, 42). As an individual comfortable with both multiplicity and ambiguity, Lord Henry enjoys disturbing the complacent assumptions of those who make up society but has no intention or desire to separate himself from their company. If he is sui generis, his approach evokes pluralistic attributes familiar to contemporary readers.

In the introduction to her edition of *The Picture of Dorian Gray*, Isobel Murray rightly notes the impact of Matthew Arnold's concepts of Hellenism upon the ethos of the work, but I believe that she goes too far in asserting that the death of Dorian in his effort to kill his conscience actually represents a defeat of Lord Henry's propositions (xv–xvi). Murray judges Lord Henry's role reductively by placing too much faith in a moralistic reading of Wilde's remark (quoted in her introduction) that "Lord Henry Wotton seeks to be merely the spectator of life. He finds that those who reject the battle are more deeply wounded than those who take part in it" (xvi). While maintaining the image of Lord Henry as spectator, Murray undermines her own argument by quoting his description of intercourse with Dorian based upon the simile of a musician: "Talking to him [Dorian] was like playing upon an exquisite violin. . . . There was nothing that one could not bring him to do" (xvi). Murray's analogy unconsciously affirms just how active and engaged Lord Henry is. In considering how his detachment from Dorian's dilemma differs from Dorian's detachment from the death of Sibyl and the murder of Basil, one can only conclude that Murray consistently misses the point about the nature of Lord Henry. She brings the narrative down to the level of the morality tale that Wilde's contemporary detractors apparently expected, reverting to the simplistic form of reading that I have been arguing against throughout this essay. Certainly, as I have repeatedly noted, the views of Lord Henry alone do not provide readers with a perspective sufficient to interpret the characters and events of the work. On the other hand, his willingness to take his own ideas seriously and his openness to change in others serve as an excellent guide for the disposition we might undertake for the most complete response to this work.

The discourse uses this oscillation to invite one to return to Lord Henry for some sense of how to read all the characters, but even in this role of paragon he provides ample opportunity for misperception. Ultimately, Lord Henry, like many contemporary critics of the novel, fails in his own efforts at interpretation; yet that, too, seems inevitable. In the end, his refusal to acknowledge the capacity for violence within Dorian's nature shows that he cannot fully appreciate the scope of New Hedonism. His love of proportions (either/or) overbears intellectual playfulness (both/and), stifles the pluralistic impulse, and impels him to impose symmetry on all his views.

The diverse elements within the narrative, however, do not permit the closure that Harry seeks to enforce. In *The Picture of Dorian Gray* the numerous alternatives for reading disrupt easy categorization. As a work derived from a range of Victorian attitudes, it remains nonetheless dependent for its completion upon the imagination of the individual reader, even as the individual reader must depend upon a range of approaches to exploit the hypostatic multiplicity inherent in the text.

SIMON JOYCE

Sexual Politics and the Aesthetics of Crime: Oscar Wilde in the Nineties†

At the center of G. K. Chesterton's *The Man who was Thursday* (1908) is a band of master anarchists, each named for one of the days of the week, all of whom are ultimately revealed in the course of the novel to be undercover detectives. One of them explains what they think they are fighting against:

> This new movement of ours is a very different affair. We deny the snobbish English assumption that the uneducated are the dangerous criminals. We remember the Roman Emperors. We remember the great poisoning princes of the Renaissance. We say that the dangerous criminal is the educated criminal. We say that the most dangerous criminal now is the entirely lawless modern philosopher. Compared to him, burglars and bigamists are essentially moral men; my heart goes out to them. They accept the essential ideal of man; they merely seek it wrongly. Thieves respect property. They merely wish the property to become their property that they may more properly respect it. But philosophers dislike property as property; they wish to destroy the very idea of personal possession.[1]

This passage usefully introduces my essay, because I will be arguing that the idea of the criminal as an intellectual or artistic genius (which had seemed so radical when Thomas De Quincey first offered it in his 1827 essay, "On Murder, Considered as One of the Fine Arts") had become a conservative and reassuring notion by the end of the nineteenth century—quite literally in this case, since there are

† From "Sexual Politics and the Aesthetics of Crime: Oscar Wilde in the Nineties," *ELH* 69.2 (Summer 2002): 501–23. Copyright © The Johns Hopkins University Press. Bracketed page numbers refer to this Norton Critical Edition. Reprinted by permission of The Johns Hopkins University Press.
1. G. K. Chesterton, *The Man who was Thursday* (New York: Dover Publications, 1986), 25.

ultimately no philosopher criminals in Chesterton's book, only philosopher policemen.

The idea of an aesthetic of crime had begun to pick up steam again
about 40 years after De Quincey, in part as a response to falling crime
rates. By 1869, Leslie Stephen (writing under the pseudonym of "A
Cynic") was bemoaning the "perceptible decline" in the style of murder, while *The Spectator* echoed the same theme thirteen years later,
predicting a more prosaic era in the history of crime, "in which evil
is stolid, and careful, and prudent, and obtuse."[2] Late Victorian readers could of course look to popular fiction—to Gothic novels, sensation fiction, and the Sherlock Holmes detective stories—for a more
elevated style of criminality, or to newspaper accounts of Jack the
Ripper: indeed, it became a commonplace of contemporary commentary to highlight how strikingly *literary* these murders appeared,
with noticeable parallels to Poe, Sade, and especially to *Dr. Jekyll and
Mr. Hyde* (1886).[3] Stevenson's earliest critics and reviewers had
mainly praised his formal construction and prose style, while advanc-
ing mild concerns about the text's possible impact on popular audiences. Two years later, though, the five murders ascribed to Jack the
Ripper seemed to correlate closely with the recorded actions of Mr.
Hyde, and thus incited a retroactive rereading. Soon after the second
victim, Annie Chapman, was discovered, the *East London Advertiser*
speculated that "a murderous lunatic [is] concealed in the slums of
Whitechapel, who issues forth at night like another Hyde, to prey
upon the defenceless women of the 'unfortunate' class"; a month
(and two deaths) later, the same paper looked for parallels in Gothic
fables and vampire legends, noting that "the most morbid imagination can conceive nothing worse than this terrible reality; for what
can be more appalling than the thought that there is a being in
human shape stealthily moving about a great city, burning with the
thirst for human blood, and endowed with such diabolical astute-
ness, as to enable him to gratify his fiendish lust with absolute
impunity?"[4]

At its most literal level, the connection between Jekyll and Jack the
Ripper was made in September 1888 after the second murder, when
a sensationalistic dramatization of Stevenson's story was closed
down. Indeed, some newspaper correspondents even suspected the

2. A Cynic [Leslie Stephen], "The Decay of Murder" (1869), and "The Fenayrou Trial"
   (1882), both cited in Martin Wiener, *Reconstructing the Criminal: Culture, Law, and Pol-
   icy in England, 1830–1914* (Cambridge: Cambridge Univ. Press, 1990), 224–25.
3. W. T. Stead's article on "Murder and More to Follow," which appeared in the *Pall Mall
   Gazette* in September 1888, referred to the Ripper as "a Mr. Hyde of Humanity," as well
   as a "plebeian Marquis de Sade at large in Whitechapel." See Judith Walkowitz, *City of
   Dreadful Delight: Narratives of Sexual Danger in Late Victorian London* (London: Virago,
   1992), 196, 206–7.
4. *East London Advertiser*, 8 September, and 6 October 1888.

actor Richard Mansfield of the murders, because he performed the
role of Hyde so well.[5] Other high profile figures were also considered
in the Ripper investigation, once the usual suspects (Leftists, Russian Jews, and other European immigrants) were dismissed: among
them Samuel Barnett of Toynbee Hall, the trade unionist John Burns
who would lead the successful dockers' strike in the following year,
children's campaigner Dr. Barnado, and a director of the Bank of England who entered the area in disguise in an ill-judged attempt to
catch the murderer.[6] Such speculations about the Ripper's identity—
and his presumed resemblance to other literary figures—suggest a
renewed interest in crime as not only imaginative and aesthetic, but
as the province of the privileged classes: by the turn of the century,
for example, we get the first appearance of Raffles, E. W. Hornung's
aristocratic cat burglar, to place alongside Dr. Jekyll, Dorian Gray,
and all those hard-up minor aristocrats who usually turn out to be the
culprits in Conan Doyle.[7] What I take to be distinctly conservative
about this renewed conjunction of crime, class, and aesthetics is the
way that it explicitly sets itself against a causality rooted in socioeco-
nomic conditions, with a consequent refusal to rethink strategies of
policing.[8] Having reluctantly conceded that the Ripper probably
didn't live in Whitechapel, and that he was far more likely a professional man exploiting the increasing exposure of East End life as a
screen for his crimes, the authorities proceeded to tear down the
slums anyway—in a move which was trumpeted by the *Daily Telegraph* under the slogan of "A Safe Four Per Cent" profit margin—and
did little to investigate the more privileged suspects.[9] Hence, of

5. See Donald Rumbelow, *The Complete Jack the Ripper*, with an introduction by Colin Wilson (Harmondsworth: Penguin, 1988), 113.
6. See Christopher Frayling, "The House that Jack Built: Some Stereotypes of the Rapist in
Popular Culture," in *Rape*, ed. Sylvia Tomaselli and Roy Porter (Oxford: Basil Blackwell,
1986), 201. The incident of the Bank director was reported in the *East London Advertiser*,
17 November 1888.
7. In his *Atlas of the European Novel, 1880–1900* (London: Verso, 1998), Franco Moretti
points out the astonishing fact that Holmes only once ventures into the East End, and
even this is presumably in the doppleganger story, "The Man with the Twisted Lip,"
in which the culprit turns out to be a bourgeois journalist disguised as a beggar
(Moretti, 34).
8. Wiener has noted that the professionalization of policing brought with it a corresponding
upgrade in the public image of criminals, who needed to be apprehended: "As crime detection, in both fact and fiction, was being removed to an expert and esoteric real, suspicions
appeared that there existed much hitherto unsuspected expert and esoteric crime. The
increasing sense of conquest of the external criminality of the streets combined with the
blurring of the stark moral certainties of the early nineteenth century to turn middle-class
attention inward . . . from the unruly populace to persons and scenes of apparent
respectability" (244).
9. As Walkowitz notes, "despite the theories about upper-class perverts and maniacal reform-
ers, the police still arrested the same collection of motley East End down-and-outers . . .
They conducted a house-to-house search of Whitechapel, but not of the areas where the
Ripper, if he were a 'toff' (that is, a gentleman) would be lodging. Long-standing patterns
of deference and assumptions of bourgeois respectability ultimately prevailed over speculations about bourgeois criminality circulating in the press" (212)

course, a continuing conspiracy industry surrounding these murders which is second only to that associated with J. F. K.

The privileged offender is, in a sense, a cultural fiction, the product of a wish fulfillment which had the useful effect of diverting attention away from genuine social problems of poverty, unemployment, and labor unrest that had recently begun to reassert themselves. The desire to see crime itself as a fine art is key here, since it concentrates on exceptional and essentially motiveless actions. In this essay, I want to think through some of the implications of this renewed aesthetic interest in crime by focusing on and around Oscar Wilde's *The Picture of Dorian Gray* (1890), a text which is generally thought to embody it through the main character of Dorian, but which in fact offers an exemplary critique of its tendency to shift attention away from lower-class crime. In a sense, Wilde fits the picture almost too perfectly, especially when considered in retrospect after his trial in 1895, when he literally became a criminal aesthete and jokingly insisted that "The Ballad of Reading Gaol" be offered for publication to *Reynolds's Magazine*, which "circulates widely amongst the criminal classes, to which I now belong, so I shall be read by my peers."[1] He also wrote an essay called "Pen Pencil Poison," which is often paired with De Quincey's, in which the poisoner Thomas Wainewright is described as "a poet and a painter, an art-critic, an antiquarian, and a writer of prose, an amateur of beautiful things, and a dilettante of things delightful, but also a forger of no mean or ordinary capabilities, and as a subtle and secret poisoner almost without rival in this or any age."

The essay goes on to detail some of his literary and art criticism, his friendships with Hazlitt, Lamb, and others around the *London Magazine*, in addition to his early successes on the social scene, before stating quite bluntly that "if we set aside his achievements in the sphere of poison, what he has left to us hardly justifies his reputation."[2] As Regenia Gagnier has persuasively argued, though, Wilde's insouciant tone has led most critics to miss the sense of irony, and thus to misinterpret statements like this or to take them at face value; Richard Ellmann, for instance, suggests that "forgery was a crime which perhaps seems closest to Wilde's social presentation of himself," and concludes that this essay demonstrates that "Wainewright's criminal craft revealed a true artist."[3] The key point here is not that he might be more appropriately considered to be an artist in the particular sphere of poisoning, but rather that there is no basis for considering him an artist

1. Oscar Wilde to Leonard Smithers, 19 October 1897, in *The Letters of Oscar Wilde*, ed. Rupert Hart-Davis (New York: Harcourt Brace, 1962), 663.
2. Wilde, "Pen Pencil Poison," in *The Artist as Critic: Critical Writings of Oscar Wilde*, ed. Richard Ellman (Chicago: Univ. of Chicago Press, 1969), 321.
3. Regenia Gagnier, *Idylls of the Marketplace: Oscar Wilde and the Victorian Public* (Stanford: Stanford Univ. Press, 1986), 34; Ellmann, *Oscar Wilde* (London: Hamish Hamilton, 1987), 282–83.

at all; thus, while "[t]he fact of a man being a poisoner is nothing against his prose," it is also not an argument in its favor.[4]

Wilde, moreover, is equally critical of claims concerning Wainewright's status as a master criminal, and of his celebrity among the intelligentsia of the Romantic era. His cell at Newgate, the essay notes, "was for some time a kind of fashionable lounge," yet Wainewright himself felt isolated from those around him. He apparently told visitors that "I have been determined through life to hold the position of a gentleman. I have always done so. I do so still. It is the custom of this place that each of the inmates of a cell shall take his morning's turn of sweeping it out. I occupy a cell with a bricklayer and a sweep, but they never once offer me the broom!" On leaving Newgate, he was transported to Van Diemen's Land and felt a similar sense of superiority over the "country bumpkins" on board, so different from the "poets and artists" with whom he was used to associating when he was still a celebrity criminal. Commenting on this last quote, Wilde repeats his dictum from "The Soul of Man under Socialism" (to which I shall return) in order to explain Wainewright's sense of alienation from his fellow criminals: "The phrase that he applies to his companions need not surprise us," he notes, since "[c]rime in England is rarely the result of sin. It is nearly always the result of starvation."[5] Despite his pretensions to culture and celebrity status, then, the artist/poisoner ultimately emerges from this essay as a rather sad anomaly, whose claim to fame rests on his combination of disparate qualities rather than on his abilities at anything in particular. Wainewright might stand in this respect as a prototype for Dorian Gray, who aims for a similar accommodation of crime and culture. But the conjunction tells us little about either one: crime, Wilde seems to be saying, is best left to those with purpose and motive, while the cultural kudos which come from a criminal reputation cannot finally compensate for a lack of artistic talent.

"All Crime Is Vulgar": The Wildean Critique

Envisaged as the poster boy for a "new Hedonism," Dorian ranges freely between aesthetic pursuits (like the study of perfumes, music, jewels, and embroidery) and criminal ones, beginning in the opium dens of the East End docklands and climaxing in murder. Lord Henry Wotton, who many have wrongly taken to be a disguised portrait of Wilde himself, hopes that his protégé will "live out his life fully and completely . . . give form to every feeling, expression to every thought, reality to every dream" without fear of conscience, the law,

4. Wilde, "Pen Pencil Poison," 339.
5. Wilde, "Pen Pencil Poison," 337–38.

or public censure, and Dorian certainly does his best [19]. He articulates a fashionable contempt for the poor, for example, while
exploiting the landscape of London street-life as his inspiration after
the manner of the Baudelairean *flâneur*, and is quick to disassociate
himself from any philanthropic enterprise which is designed to
improve working-class lives. (We can hardly blame him, though, for
canceling an engagement to play piano duets in Whitechapel with
Lord Henry's Aunt Agatha.)

   Dorian's relationship with the actress Sibyl Vane condenses these
attitudes towards the poor and represents an early—but flawed—
attempt at converting social experience into aesthetic pleasures. He
first discovers Sibyl while on a ramble about town: "One evening
about seven o'clock," he later recalls, "I determined to go out in
search of some adventure. I felt that this grey, monstrous London of
ours, with its myriads of people, its sordid sinners, and its splendid
sins . . . must have something in store for me" [44]. Sibyl (from
Euston Road, we are told, to clarify her lower-class, North London
background) is performing in a shabby theater, whose patrons he
later describes as "common, rough people, with their coarse faces
and brutal gestures" [69]. The audience is humanized only when
Sibyl acts Shakespeare for them, and this performance is also what
enables Dorian to maintain a slummer's fantasy of love between the
classes; as soon as she stops acting, he loses interest and leaves her
to commit suicide over her departed "Prince Charming." Later, he
uses this same alias on nocturnal trips to the opium dens around the
docks, one of which is described in some detail. Dorian hails a cab
late one night in Bond Street and lies back in the seat, "his hat pulled
over his forehead." In imagery which is familiar from the period's
obsessive investigations of East London, including such complex acts
of disguised infiltration as James Greenwood's "A Night in the Work-
house" (1886), C. F. Masterman's *From the Abyss* (1902), or Jack
London's *The People of the Abyss* (1903), the journey takes him
through "streets like the web of some sprawling spider," past monotonous brickfields and along "rough-paven streets" which are home to
"monstrous marionettes," who only remind Dorian in turn of how
much "[h]e hated them" [154].[6]

   From passages like this, it is easy to imagine Dorian—
contemptuous of the people around him, in disguise, and out for
immediate gratification—as another Doctor Jekyll, or even a possible
Ripper suspect; elsewhere, for example, the litany of his sins include

---

6. Masterman's subtitle, *Of the Inhabitants by One of Them*, nicely illustrates the ambivalent
   attitude of these studies, which desire to simultaneously collapse and reassert the distance
   between their respectable authors and the disreputable objects of inquiry.

"brawling with foreign sailors in a low den in the distant parts of Whitechapel," as if to solidify the connection to the recent murders [118].[7] But if Dorian has some success embodying the goals and attitudes of the aesthetic movement, he's a major disappointment as a criminal, and thus, in a sense, the reverse of Thomas Wainewright. Dorian's criminal centerpiece, the murder of the painter Basil Hallward, is particularly poor and undertaken for the most pedestrian of motives. Having confronted Dorian with a list of his rumored (and typically vague) indiscretions, Hallward wonders about the quality of his friend's soul, at which point he is invited to view the picture and see it for himself; but Dorian suddenly feels an intense hatred towards the painter for having set the process in motion and kills him out of resentment, before hastening to cover up his crime. Commenting on this incident, Alan Sinfield concludes that it arises "from sentimental self-indulgence and want of intelligence and self-control, not from aestheticism and amorality. . . . Dorian arrives at disaster not because he abjures conventional moral principles but because he remains under their sway."[8] As we shall see, this is a judgment with which Wilde himself would reluctantly concur.

Dorian's crime doesn't sound very elevated and artistic because—like the portrait itself—it needs to remain hidden from the public. This is presumably Lord Henry Wotton's point, when he tells his protégé that "murder is always a mistake. One should never do anything that one cannot talk about after dinner." Behind the familiar rhetoric of inversion which underpins the epigram, though, Lord Henry has another reason for disbelieving Gray's hypothetical confession: "I would say," he replies,

> that you were posing for a character that doesn't suit you. All crime is vulgar, just as all vulgarity is crime. It is not in you, Dorian, to commit a murder. I am sorry if I hurt your vanity by saying so, but I assure you it is true. Crime belongs exclusively to the lower orders. I don't blame them in the smallest degree. I should fancy that crime was to them what art is to us, simply a method of procuring extraordinary sensations. [175–76]

That last line can mislead us into thinking that Wilde is offering up his usual blend of rhetorical insouciance and imagining a world in which only "extraordinary sensations" count. But there's a more

---

7. Sure enough, Wilson reports on a new theory in his introduction to *The Complete Jack the Ripper* that the Ripper was Wilde's one time friend and housemate Frank Miles, on whom the character of Dorian was supposedly based; and "that Wilde knew Miles to be Jack the Ripper, and dropped clues about it in the novel—for example, Dorian's murder of the painter Basil Hallward with a knife" (13–14).
8. Alan Sinfield, *The Wilde Century: Effeminacy, Oscar Wilde and the Queer Moment* (New York: Columbia Univ. Press, 1994), 100.

serious point here, which he expresses in "The Soul of Man under
Socialism" as well as in the essay on Wainewright: that, given the
harshness of working-class life, and especially the constant search for
the means of subsistence rather than pleasure, Wilde felt that the
poor criminal was entirely exonerated. But for someone like Dorian
to commit murder is ultimately to borrow a form of justification
which is unwarranted in his case, and which cannot be secured by
simply renaming murder as an art form: since he has the wealth,
leisure, and cultural training which are necessary for finding enjoyment in the aesthetic, an aristocrat really has no business committing
crimes which can be supported only as a response to material need
and suffering.

Rather than endorsing the notion of an aesthetics of crime, then,
Wilde seems instead to offer here a powerful critique of the tendency
to flatten out the differences between crime and culture. By acting
out the role of the privileged offender, Dorian is simply taking to
extremes a process of slumming that Wilde consistently attacked in
political terms, since it effectively enabled and justified an ongoing
exploitation of the real miseries of East End life. His critique of charitable philanthropy, which aimed to make the lives of the poor more
bearable instead of abolishing the conditions under which poverty is
allowed to exist, develops along similar lines. Part of the current problem, he notes in "The Soul of Man," lies with those same forms of
fashionable altruism, which "have really prevented the carrying out
of this aim"; like kindly slave-owners in the earlier part of the century,
whose actions and attitudes delayed a recognition of the systematic
basis of slavery, "the people who do most harm are the people who try
to do most good." If this superficially reads like a standard Wildean
paradox, the essay goes on to suggest a more precise target: in recent
years, he noted, "we have had the spectacle of men who have really
studied the problem and know the life—educated men who live in
the East-end—coming forward and imploring the community to
restrain its altruistic impulses of charity, benevolence, and the like.
They do so on the ground that such charity degrades and demoral-
izes. They are perfectly right. Charity creates a multitude of sins."[9]

Instead of placing the onus back on the poor and demanding from
them a more thrifty attitude toward household economics (as many
of the Christian philanthropists and neo-Benthamites of the period
would do), Wilde concludes that labor is as inherently unpleasant as
poverty; that the goal of life is individual fulfillment, especially

9. Wilde, "The Soul of Man under Socialism," in *The Artist as Critic*, 256, emphasis in original. I have discussed this passage in a different context in "Castles in the Air: The People's
Palace, Cultural Reformism, and the East End Working Class," *Victorian Studies* 39
(1996): 513–38.

through a cultivation of art and the aesthetic; and that society must therefore be reconstructed on the basis of socialist cooperation. One important step in this process entails a recognition that crimes are committed as a result of "starvation, and not sin." Punishing criminals is therefore counter-productive, and the mark of a debased society: "*a community is infinitely more brutalised by the habitual employment of punishment, than it is by the occasional occurrence of crime.* . . . The less punishment, the less crime."[1] Echoing an argument which was simultaneously being worked out in response to the Ripper murders by Leftists like H. M. Hyndman of the Social Democratic Federation, William Morris, and George Bernard Shaw, Wilde insisted that since most crimes arise out of economic hardship and are therefore mainly directed against property (which the legal system has been developed in turn to protect), they should largely wither away under socialism: "When there is no punishment, crime will either cease to exist, or if it occurs, will be treated by physicians as a very distressing form of dementia, to be cured by care and kindness."[2] Morris makes an almost identical argument in his Utopian novel *News from Nowhere* (1890), arguing from the other end that the abolition of private property would mean that "all the laws and all the legal 'crimes' which it had manufactured of course came to an end," thereby ending the necessity for the punitive apparatus of criminal justice and the courts.[3]

I realize that I am conjuring up an unfashionably sincere (even *earnest*) Wilde here, which doesn't sit too easily with our dominant image of him as a kind of proto-postmodern jester who was largely uninterested in ethics or politics, or sacrificed both at the altar of aesthetics. As with the character of Lord Henry Wotton, it is easy to misread Wilde's more overt political commentary as articulating a callous indifference to human suffering and a corresponding delight in the trivialities which attended upon a more privileged lifestyle.

1. Wilde, "The Soul of Man," 267, emphasis in original.
2. Wilde, "The Soul of Man," 267. *Justice*, the newspaper of the Social Democratic Federation, commented, for example, that "[w]hoever may be the wretch who committed these sanguinary outrages, the real criminal is the vicious bourgeois system which, based on class injustice, condemns thousands to poverty, vice and crime, manufactures criminals, and then punishes them!" Cited in William Fishman, *East End 1888: Life in a London Borough among the Labouring Poor* (Philadelphia: Temple Univ. Press, 1988), 226. George Bernard Shaw wrote to *The Star* that "if the habits of duchesses only admitted of their being decoyed into Whitechapel back-yards, a single experiment in slaughterhouse anatomy on an aristocratic victim might fetch in round half a million and save the necessity of sacrificing four women of the people. Such is the stark-naked reality of these abominable bastard Utopias of genteel charity, in which the poor are first to be robbed and then pauperized by way of compensation, in order that the rich man may combine the idle luxury of the protected thief with the unctuous self-satisfaction of the pious philanthropist." Shaw, "Blood Money to Whitechapel," reprinted in *Agitations: Letters to the Press, 1875–1950* (New York: Frederick Ungar, 1985), 10–11.
3. William Morris, *News from Nowhere, and Other Writings* (Harmondsworth: Penguin, 1993), 112–13.

Around the same time that he was writing *Dorian Gray* Wilde was also engaged in furnishing a grand home in fashionable Chelsea. Adrian Hope reported after his first visit to the house in Tite Street, with its white high gloss paint, Japanned lacquer work and elaborate furnishings, that one room at the back (Wilde's study) incorporated a Turkish motif, but unfortunately looked out onto a slum, so its windows were "covered with a wooden grating on the inside copied from a Cairo pattern which considerably reduced the little light there was."[4] The gesture would seem to be an impatient one which wanted to abolish poverty in the here and now by simply hiding it from view, although a more generous reading might suggest that Wilde instead wanted the home to serve an exemplary function as a show house for the new aesthetic movement; in this sense Tite Street, the contents of which were ultimately auctioned to pay off Wilde's legal costs, might be seen as embodying the principles of pleasurable self-realization which he outlined as the utopian aim in "The Soul of Man."

In the mid 1880s, Wilde met the novelist Olive Schreiner, one of a loose network of "New Women" who found a liberatory potential in charity work in East London, and asked why she lived in the East End; on hearing her say, "Because the people there don't wear masks," he supposedly replied, "And I live in the West End because the people there do."[5] Again, such a statement might be seen as registering a simple preference for artifice and triviality at the expense of human misery or the sincere effort towards its amelioration; or, as my reading of *Dorian Gray* might conclude, it is instead a powerful critique of Schreiner's assumption that she could know a transparent truth about the East End, either through a transferential identification or the voluntary divestment of social privilege. It is fair to say, of course, that Wilde's critiques do little to offer an alternative to the charitable philanthropy which dominated the liberal agenda of the 1880s and 1890s, besides a rather vague call for revolution and the more fundamental insistence that the poor would need to enact it on their own terms. To his credit, though, there is also considerable evidence that he was committed to basic principles of social justice, both before and after his imprisonment. In his biography, for example, Ellmann reports that Wilde signed a petition circulated by Shaw against the Haymarket massacres and attended a Hyde Park demonstration with his wife in support of the dock strike of 1889, two years prior to "The Soul of Man" essay, and just one year before *Dorian Gray*.[6]

4. Cited in Philippe Jullian, *Oscar Wilde* (London: Constable, 1969), 145–46.
5. Reported by Ellmann, 243.
6. See Ellmann, 273, 268.

By this point, he had also rejected the simplistic calls for "art for art's sake" and was engaged in a self-critical reappraisal of the aesthetic movement, which he parodied in "The Decay of Lying" (1889) through the figure of the Tired Hedonists club. That same essay discusses the influence which crime stories about Jack Sheppard and Dick Turpin have held over the imagination of impressionable youths in order to illustrate the thesis that life can sometimes imitate art, although this is saying something very different from the clichéd sentiment that the aesthetic is entirely divorced from the realm of morality.[7] In defending *Dorian Gray* to the press, moreover, Wilde reluctantly admitted that the novel had a moral, namely that "all excess, as well as all renunciation, brings its own punishment": Basil Hallward, he notes, dies because of his excessive investment in beauty, "by the hand of one in whose soul he has created a monstrous and absurd vanity." Dorian Gray suffers from a flawed attempt to "kill conscience" by living "a life of mere sensation and pleasure"; while even Lord Henry finds it hard to maintain the absolute separation of his actions from their effects, or to remain "merely the spectator of life."[8] This renunciation of all responsibility for events in the story involves much the same kind of mystification which enabled criminals to be read in purely aesthetic terms, but it is finally insupportable, as Wotton ends up suffering collateral damage from events which he helped to set in motion. Far from representing a celebration of crime as one of the fine arts, I think these statements suggest its opposite, and argue convincingly for a systematic critique of aestheticism—with its ideological underpinnings of disinterestedness, an overinvestment in pleasure and beauty, and the denial of material consequences for one's actions—as a basis for living. Like Wainewright, Dorian is here denied the cover of art and culture, which might otherwise have excused him, and is held to account for his crimes by something as uncharacteristic of Wilde as a "conscience."

Sex and Socialism: A Wilde for the (18)90s

As I have tried to suggest, I am suspicious of readings of Wilde that retrospectively position the author as a criminal aesthete and thus *Dorian Gray* as a kind of exercise in self-justification. Beginning with Wilde's own trials, discussions of this text in particular have largely tried to identify a model of pernicious influence that might correlate with his supposed corruption of Lord Alfred Douglas and a network of lower-class rent boys. At the first aborted trial—brought by the author himself for libel against Douglas's father, the Marquis of Queensberry—defense counsel repeatedly cross-examined Wilde

7. See Wilde, "The Decay of Lying," in *The Artist as Critic*, 293, 308.
8. Wilde to the editor of the *St. James's Gazette*, 26 June 1890, in *Dorian Gray*, 339.

about whether a novel might be immoral or perverted, holding the same kind of influence over impressionable readers that an unnamed French novel, modeled after J. K. Huysmans's *A Rebours*, is shown to have had over Dorian. Since that text is given to him by Lord Henry, the alignment of Wotton/Wilde and Dorian/Douglas seems clear enough; and even though Wilde would not meet the latter until the year after the book was published, he so strongly resembled Gray that Neil Bartlett has described the real life Douglas as "a fiction" who "already existed in [Wilde's] books."[9] If we consider, though, that it is Dorian who both engages in (generally unspecified) criminal practices and functions as a public figurehead for the new Hellenism, then biographical criticism points in another direction, to the identification of the author with his protagonist.[1]

Again, the details refuse to fit neatly into place. If Wilde's transgressions were importantly both homosexual and across class lines, the same clearly cannot be said either for Dorian's relationship with Sibyl Vane or the few hints the text offers about his dangerous influence over other aristocratic youth like Sir Henry Ashton, Adrian Singleton, and Lord Kent's only son. There is, however, the possible detection of a homosexual subtext in a contemporary review from the *Scots Observer*, which commented that *Dorian Gray* was fit only for the C. I. D. and had been written for "none but outlawed noblemen and perverted telegraph-boys."[2] Here, though, the reference is not to Wilde himself but the Cleveland Street scandal of 1886, in which the seduction of a young telegraph delivery boy led to the discovery of a gay brothel, frequented by illustrious clients like Lord Arthur Somerset. It seems—again in retrospect—like an uncanny foreshadowing of Wilde's own fate, in which he played the part of the "outlawed nobleman" who engaged in the seduction of working-class boys supplied to him by Alfred Taylor; indeed, even the question of location seems appropriate, since the social significance of Cleveland Street (on the fashionable edge of London's Regent's Park) was picked up in Wilde's trial, with constant references to Taylor's rooms in Little College Street, "near the Houses of Parliament" or "close to Westminster Abbey."[3] One way to explain the

9. Neil Bartlett, *Who Was That Man? A Present for Mr. Oscar Wilde* (London: Serpent's Tail, 1988), 195–96.
1. To complicate matters further, Wilde himself thought that he more closely resembled the painter Basil Hallward, although he acknowledged that the world thought of him as Wotton.
2. *Scots Observer*, 5 July 1890. Wilde's response (on 9 July) was that "[t]o keep this atmosphere [of 'moral corruption'] vague and indeterminate and wonderful was the aim of the artist. . . . What Dorian Gray's sins are no one knows. He who finds them has brought them." Both are reprinted in the Norton edition of *Dorian Gray* which I am using here, 346–47.
3. See H. Montgomery Hyde, *Famous Trials: Oscar Wilde* (Harmondsworth: Penguin, 1962), 203, 250.

connection is Bartlett's—that Wilde is working out first in fictional terms the life he would come to live after the novel was published, and which would emerge into public consciousness in the most dramatic ways after his trial and conviction; alternatively, we could argue that the same drama of revelation has retroactively conditioned anything that we might say about Wilde up to that point, as inevitably signaling the concealment, suggestion, or coded revelation of his central secret.[4]

In essays on *The Importance of Being Earnest* and *The Picture of Dorian Gray*, Eve Kosofsky Sedgwick has cautioned against such singlemindedness, arguing in the case of the latter text that its presumed possession of "a thematically full 'homosexual' meaning" ("*this* insistence on narrative content, which means the insistence on *this* narrative content") sits awkwardly against a counteracting assumption of high modernist "emptiness."[5] The impulse to discover a gay subtext seems almost irresistible, given that Wilde was—probably still is—the most famous homosexual of our century. Even the imposition of discreet silences about his precise transgressions fuels this impulse, as two almost identical anecdotes suggest: in the first, a young Beverley Nichols is discovered by his father with a copy of *Dorian Gray* before World War One and accused of being a "pretty little boy," a remark which the parent can only explain by reference to "*Illum crimen horribile quod non nominandum est*" (a variation on "the love that dare not speak its name"—here, the horrible crime which is not to be named); in the second, a character in Nancy Mitford's *The Pursuit of Love* (1945) is told not to mention Wilde's name by his father and is told by his mother only that whatever he had done "was worse than murder, fearfully bad." Echoing Lord Henry's comments about murder and secrecy, he is further asked, "And darling, don't talk about him at meals, will you?" Name and crime coincide, then, as synonyms which both need to be suppressed, since they so directly conjure each other.[6]

But there are distinct interpretive consequences to the search for

4. This is the sense in which Sinfield has suggested that a text like *Dorian Gray* helped "to constitute just those terms in which we might wish, subsequently, to read it" (103).
5. Eve Kosofsky Sedgwick, *Epistemology of the Closet* (Berkeley: Univ. of California Press, 1990), 166. See also her essay "Tales of the Avunculate: *The Importance of Being Earnest*," in her *Tendencies* (Durham: Duke Univ. Press, 1993), 52–72.
6. These incidents are cited respectively in Phillip Hoare, *Wilde's Last Stand: Decadence, Conspiracy, and the Trial of the Century* (New York: Arcade Publishing, 1997), 25; and Michael Bracewell, *England is Mine: Pop Life from Wilde to Goldie* (London: Harper Collins, 1997), 14. The most famous version of this trope appears in E. M. Forster's *Maurice* (London: Edward Arnold, 1971), where the protagonist's declaration that "I am an unspeakable of the Oscar Wilde sort" nicely highlights the relationship between Wilde, silence, and affirmative identification (145). For the origins of the discreet silence of Wilde's transgressions, in the trial itself but more particularly the reporting of it in the press, see Ed Cohen, *Talk on the Wilde Side: Toward a Genealogy of a Discourse on Male Sexualities* (London: Routledge, 1993), chap. 5 and 6.

subtextual truth. Consider, for example, Bartlett's criticisms of the East End scenes in *Dorian Gray*: its author, he notes,

> was involved in the daily, ordinary realm of "other" (homosexual, criminal) London in 1891, so for him discovering the truth, the secret life of the city, was a pleasure rather than a missionary or journalistic employment. His researches, though, were not made public; he kept his personal account of the lower depths a secret until it was forced out of him in 1895 [at trial]. In print all he did was to repeat the clichés of the descent into London's underworld in one of its most hackneyed locales.[7]

This is precisely the imposition of a continuity between text and trial that I have been discussing, and it rests in this instance on a false premise. As we have seen, Wilde's own subcultural forays took him only to the vicinity of Parliament, which has a resonant political symbolism but is not actually that far from his Chelsea home or the gentleman's clubs of Mayfair; to assume he had any direct knowledge of the opium dens of the East End docklands is not only to enforce an identification with Dorian Gray, but also to leave entirely uninterrogated the slide Bartlett makes here between the homosexual and the criminal. It is one thing to insist, as Wilde's case made tragically clear, that homosexuality was (and still is, in some cases) criminalized, but another entirely to force a self-identity between the two categories.

The impulse is certainly understandable, especially as applied to a figure like Wilde who seems to stand more obviously at the beginning of a peculiarly modern sense of personal identity as a form of political affiliation, rather than at the back end of the Victorian era. Jonathan Dollimore, for example, sees in him the transvaluation of dominant categories of subjective depth (truth, essence, substance, authenticity, sincerity) which a deconstructive postmodernism has also famously subjected to critique; in their place, Wilde offers up fiction, artifice, difference, style, pastiche.[8] It is easy to extend such an approach to more overtly political categories, to forge a "chain of democratic equivalence" (in the terms developed by Ernesto Laclau and Chantal Mouffe) or the "Great Refusal" (in a less-fashionable Marcusean terminology): thus, if the exercise of power is normatively associated with white, middle-class, heterosexual males, with colonial authority, or the rule of law, then resistance might variously be

---

7. Bartlett, 144. He goes on to suggest that Dorian's opium den might be Tiger Bay in Limehouse, which had already been described by James Greenwood in the *Daily Telegraph*, and by Richard Rowe in *Found in the Streets* (1880); the implication, of course, is that Wilde had simply "borrowed the details from another book" (144).
8. Jonathan Dollimore, *Sexual Dissidence: Augustine to Wilde, Freud to Foucault* (Oxford: Clarendon Press, 1991), 15. His categories deliberately echo Fredric Jameson's celebrated definition of postmodernism in *Postmodernism, or the Cultural Logic of Late Capitalism* (Durham: Duke Univ. Press, 1991).

ascribed to racial and ethnic minorities, women, the working class, colonial subjects, the criminal, and so on.[9] Such categories are clearly not mutually exclusive, but neither can they be presumed to share common interests which somehow pre-exist the political practices which might engender them. Contemporary critical theory has sometimes made that presumption, however, which helps to explain the modern fascination for Wilde: as Irishman, homosexual, criminal, and self-professed socialist.

His socialism is of an idiosyncratic kind, however, the weak spot of which is precisely its refusal to consider how alliances among different groups or subject positions might be formed. Its basis is in individualism, which Dollimore suggests maintains a close and often mutually generating relationship with crime to the extent that it emphasizes nonconformism.[1] But it is also consciously solipsistic, because its foundation is personal self-development in isolation from social pressures and obligations: "It is to be noted also," Wilde comments in "The Soul of Man,"

> that Individualism does not come to man with any sickly cant about duty, which merely means doing what other people want because they want it; or any hideous cant about self-sacrifice, which is merely a survival of savage mutilation. *In fact, it does not come to man with any claims upon him at all. It comes naturally and inevitably out of man.* It is the point to which all development tends.

Here, as we shall see, there are echoes of the critique of charitable philanthropy discussed earlier, alongside an evolutionist rhetoric which is used to describe individual rather than species development. The problem is that each individual will develop according to idiosyncratic tastes and desires, which leaves little room for cooperative action, or even sympathetic identification: "a man," the essay continues,

> is called selfish if he lives in the manner that seems to him most suitable for the full realisation of his own personality; if, in fact, the primary aim of his life is self-development. But this is the way in which everyone should live. *Selfishness is not living as one wishes to live, it is asking others to live as one wishes to live.* And unselfishness is letting other people's lives alone, not interfering with them. Selfishness always aims at creating around it an absolute uniformity of type. Unselfishness recognizes infinite

9. See Ernesto Laclau and Chantal Mouffe, *Hegemony and Socialist Strategy: Towards a Radical Democratic Politics* (London: Verso, 1985); and Herbert Marcuse, *An Essay on Liberation* (Boston: Beacon Press, 1969).
1. Dollimore, 8–9.

variety of type as a delightful thing, accepts it, acquiesces in it, enjoys it.[2]

Any attempt at claiming Wilde for a modern collectivist socialist or queer politics would need to come to terms with this theory of individualism, which seems if anything to be a precursor of more extreme forms of contemporary identity politics, in which anyone can ultimately speak only for themselves.

Wilde is not quite so naïve, however, and does allow for one interesting exception: that of political agitation, which ought logically to be animated by the same egoistic condescension for which he criticizes philanthropy. Yet, "Agitators are a set of interfering, meddling people, who come down to some perfectly contented class of the community, and sow the seeds of discontent amongst them. That is the reason why agitators are so absolutely necessary. Without them . . . there would be no advance towards civilization." The explanation of this exceptional case demonstrates Wilde's materialist commitment, even when he is arguing within an apparently idealist framework of abstract categories. It is that poverty and starvation, which are also at the roots of justifiable crime, cause a paralysis on the part of the poor, who are not even conscious of suffering. Self-realization is not for all, then, at least under present conditions, because it requires a freedom from a labor which is "absolutely degrading"; it is private property which places the fortunate few "under no necessity to work for a living," thereby enabling them to lead in its place a life of culture—that which (as *Dorian Gray* insists) is the privileged equivalent of what crime represents to the lower classes.[3] In a version of vanguardist accounts of the Party, then, Wilde rejoins a mainstream Marxist tradition here by defining the difficulties of attaining class consciousness and the need for leadership from outside the class itself: the difference is that those leaders are the possessors of economic and cultural capital, and they agitate for individualism!

Wilde's revolution, then, would seem to be a curiously bourgeois one, even Arnoldian in its ultimate goal. As I have argued, it is not easily assimilable to a modern politics, despite the best efforts of contemporary cultural theorists. But it is fully comprehensible when relocated into the appropriate historical context of a wide-ranging debate about the direction of middle-class liberalism in the last decades of the nineteenth century. Broadly speaking, two responses emerged out of the rediscovery of extreme poverty that was necessitated by the economic downturn of the 1860s and 1870s. On the one hand, an older model of welfare provision continued to insist on the

2. Wilde, "The Soul of Man," 284–85, emphases in original.
3. Wilde, "The Soul of Man," 259, 268.

obligations of wealth and felt that the poor were best served by face-to-face charity on behalf of concerned citizens who could also act as role models for the poor—a tendency that was well represented by the university settlement movement, by umbrella groups like the Charity Organisation Service, the Salvation Army, or by Lord Henry's fictional Aunt Agatha. On the other hand, the inability of such agencies to cope with systemic problems meant the beginnings of a more statist position associated with Fabian Socialists like Beatrice and Sidney Webb, the so-called New Liberalism, and Charles Booth and early British sociologists like L. T. Hobhouse.[4] It is against the backdrop of this larger debate that Wilde's discussions of crime and his critique of philanthropy need to be screened.

His criticisms of the first position should be clear from the foregoing discussion of *Dorian Gray*, and it is echoed in those passages on duty and selfishness in "The Soul of Man under Socialism." It is picked up again in "The Critic as Artist" (1891) in terms of a critical disinterestedness that has traditionally been the hallmark of aesthetic appreciation. But prejudice enters in this instance, in hypothetical cases of the "noisy politician," "brawling social reformer, or poor narrow-minded priest," whenever one tries to act on others' behalf out of an "emotional sympathy" which is always (for Wilde) condescending, misguided, and ineffectual. More systematic efforts, such as those measures of Gladstonian Liberalism which helped form the bedrock of the modern welfare state, are less egotistical in their conception, but still represent futile attempts to "stave off the coming crisis, the coming revolution as my friends the Fabianists call it, by means of doles and alms" because they are grounded in statistical abstractions rather than any real knowledge of social conditions.[5] Wilde's critique of this second tendency is less developed, although it presumably appears in his invocation of an imaginary Authoritarian Socialism, in which "an inspector should call every morning at each house to see that each citizen rose up and did manual labour for eight hours."[6]

With this background in mind, we can better understand a brief discussion of the East End which occurs in chapter 3 of *The Picture of Dorian Gray* (the first that Wilde added for the revised 1891 edition) after Dorian's refusal to perform in piano recitals in Whitechapel. Aunt Agatha is a clear representative of the sentimentalist school of personal philanthropy, which believes that high culture provides a role model for the starving poor. "But they are so unhappy in Whitechapel," she laments, as if that were the only

4. I discuss these rival approaches to the question of welfare in "Victorian Continuities: Early British Sociology and the Welfare of the State," in *Disciplinarity at the Fin de Siecle*, ed. Amanda Anderson and Joseph Valente (Princeton: Princeton Univ. Press, 2002), 261–80.
5. Wilde, "The Artist as Critic," in *The Artist as Critic*, 385–86,
6. Wilde, "The Soul of Man," 260.

measure of human life, and later she seconds the rather cliched sentiment that the wealthy "have such grave responsibilities."[7] Lord Henry's response echoes "The Soul of Man" by insisting that it is "morbid" to sympathize with human suffering rather than "the beauty, the joy of life." At this point, he is engaged by a Radical M. P. Sir Thomas Burdon, who I take to be representative of the statist tendency on account of his support for the "reasonable" Americans with their "practical" outlook on social problems. "Still, the East End is a very important problem," he interjects, only to receive what seems initially like another flippant response from Lord Henry: in fact, his reply—that "[i]t is the problem of slavery, and we try to solve it by amusing the slaves" [37]—speaks directly to Wilde's wider critique of the egoism of self-sacrificing charity and to his invocation of the kindly slave-owners as those that do the most harm. Badgered into staking a counter-proposition, he claims first not to "desire to change anything in England except the weather," and then more seriously that it is to science that we should look to restrain the present "over-expenditure" of emotion and sympathy [37]. All of this looks like an evasive forestalling of discussion, especially when a Duchess compliments Wotton for absolving her guilt at taking "no interest at all in the East End" [38], but Wilde surely had a more serious point in mind when he added this scene for the first English edition: it is, I think, that there is no interest that she can take which could short-circuit self-interest, and nothing to propose (taking literally the parallel of slavery) other than the outright elimination of poverty that he proposes in "The Soul of Man." He is, of course, vague about exactly how science or Socialism might accomplish that, but consistently insistent about the defects of the alternatives on offer.

In the Dock Again

In the ways that I have outlined, Wilde was seriously engaged in the early 1890s with working through questions of personal and social ethics and considering the relative merits of socialism, individualism, and aestheticism. Unlike Ellmann, who concludes his monumental biography with the thought that Wilde "belongs to our world more than Victoria's . . . a towering figure, laughing and weeping, with parables and paradoxes," my reading of the texts of this period argues that his conclusions are reasonably consistent (remarkably so, if we accept that he was an unsystematic thinker, and one who even celebrated insincerity), but that they are obscured if we see him only in

---

7. This emphasis on personal happiness, and its source in the pleasures furnished by high art, is the foundation of Walter Besant's East End novel, *All Sorts and Conditions of Men* (1881), and of the People's Palace, the real life institution which it inspired.

light of current concerns rather than those of the time.[8] The evidence of *Dorian Gray* and "The Soul of Man under Socialism" would particularly question the idea that Wilde adopted the perspective of the outlaw or transgressor at this time, as Dollimore has argued, when he is in fact interrogating the valences of that position and seeking to make fine distinctions about who is entitled to take it up and on what basis. His insistence on the justifiable criminality of the underclass in the face of crushing social conditions speaks to a commendable materialism, especially as the dominant political thinking sought to ameliorate, moralize about, or wish away those same conditions.

In a landmark article, Gareth Stedman Jones has attempted to trace elements of an ideological "remaking" of the working class, which included the origins of a distinctive commercial culture within which the new music halls featured prominently, the more reformist emphasis of the new unionism, the beginnings of a marked working-class conservatism and patriotism (articulated especially in support of the Boer campaign), and the powerful appeal of "respectability" among the working poor.[9] Of course, we should not see this as constituting an epochal shift that entirely eradicated those political and cultural associations which had been attached in particular to the poor in London's East End throughout the nineteenth century. Nonetheless, Stedman Jones's analysis usefully anticipates the very different image of that region which has circulated in this century: as strongly pro-family, traditionalist, hard-working, and loyal to the crown, while still sometimes mildly criminal (most notably in its resentment of state interference in its affairs). This is the general context, I think, in which we need to situate the renewed interest in the idea of the aristocratic criminal with which I began this essay, as an attempt to disarticulate crime from a socio-economic etiology and consider it instead as rooted in discrete pathologies or the topic for mass-market fictions and detective stories. In this sense, Wilde seems almost anachronistic in his insistence on the former approach and more closely aligned with a minority Leftist position.

It is a cruel irony, then, that his own trials and conviction did so much to secure the image of the privileged and pathological offender in the public imagination. As Ed Cohen has argued, the persecution of Wilde "could be perceived, both politically and popularly, as the symbolic reversal" of the Cleveland Street trial, which caused widespread anger that the brothel's wealthy clients like Lord Arthur Somerset were able to escape prosecution amid rumors that Prince Albert

---

8. Ellmann, 553–54.
9. Gareth Stedman Jones, "Working-Class Culture and Working-Class Politics in London, 1870–1900: Notes on the Remaking of a Working Class," in his *Languages of Class: Studies in English Working Class History, 1832–1982* (Cambridge: Cambridge Univ. Press, 1983), 179–238.

Victor had also been implicated in the scandal.[1] Six years later, this popular anger was wholeheartedly directed against Wilde himself, in reports that sought to establish a hostile working class opposed to the decadence of an aristocracy which the accused had come to symbolize. The final day of the trial, coming in the midst of a patriotic fervor that marked the Queen's birthday, saw jubilant celebrations outside the Old Bailey when the verdict was read, with prostitutes dancing in the streets. "'E'll 'ave 'is 'air cut reglar *now!*" was shouted by one, in a remark which almost seems crafted to emphasize the cockney dropped aspirates and thus demonstrate that it was the common Londoner who most actively sought Wilde's conviction. "Further up the social scale," the report reads, "feelings were more decently disguised, except perhaps by Lord Queensberry and his friends."[2]

   There is a very distinct dialectic working itself out here, in which a degenerate upper class is confronted by the image of a respectable working class who can henceforth be appealed to in the name of a post-Victorian bourgeois morality. In a variety of ways, this new alignment works itself out in the early years of this century, for example in Lloyd George's so-called "People versus Peers" election campaign of 1910, and it surfaced most spectacularly in yet another scandal trial in which Wilde made a posthumous appearance: the Pemberton Billing libel trial of 1918, in which a Wildean decadence was once again criminalized, this time as potentially traitorous in a context of wartime paranoia. This case was set in motion by the ravings of a far-right M. P. Noel Pemberton Billing, a Georgian Queensberry who declared in print—under the heading of "The Cult of the Clitoris"— that the subscribers to a private performance of Wilde's *Salome* would closely overlap with an alleged list of 47,000 prominent members of British society whose sexual preferences rendered them open to German blackmail. Among Billing's supporters was an apostate Lord Alfred Douglas, who now declared Wilde to be "the greatest force for evil that has appeared in Europe during the last 350 years."[3] During the libel proceedings, Billings also slandered (among others) the trial judge and prosecuting counsel, former Prime Minister Asquith and his wife, along with his War Minister Lord Haldane, and (by implication, at least) members of the royal family. All were lined up with surviving members of the Wilde circle and cast in a massive establishment conspiracy. Amazingly, Pemberton Billing won the case. He did so in part by appealing to an orchestrated gallery of wounded soldiers, and to a wider xenophobia and *ressentiment* out-

1. Cohen, *Talk on the Wilde Side*, 175, 121–25.
2. See Hyde, 273.
3. Hoare, 152.

side the courtroom: according to Philip Hoare, the class dynamic of the campaign consciously targeted "the upper classes, and sought to exploit the distrust of the middle classes (whom, ironically, Douglas hated) which the war had exacerbated," though it crucially also enlisted the support of "respectable" working-class opinion.[4]

The privileged offender becomes a charged position again in this trial, with Wilde once more figured in the background. Between 1895 and 1918, the collapsing of categories of deviance—homosexuality's supposedly "natural" associations with criminal conduct, avant-gardist art, foreign influences, and pacifism, socialism, or treason—proved once more hard to defend against or disentangle. It is not a new equation by any means, but one which was deployed with a virulence and a sophistication which has since been replicated throughout the twentieth century. Despite what modern queer theorists have sometimes suggested, it was not always an affirmative mark of individual or collective identity or a playful subversion of the dominant discourse; when it was adopted as such by fractions of the English upper class, in the decadent 1890s or the Georgian echo which preceded World War One, there was a heavy price to pay. In a sad irony, it was Wilde himself—prior to his own conviction and exile—who would have been best placed to understand the limitations of such a position, and to anticipate the form of the backlash.

DONALD L. LAWLER

Oscar Wilde's First Manuscript of *The Picture of Dorian Gray*†

There have been omens in the past two decades that the long suzerainty of biography, anecdote, and memoir in Oscar Wilde studies may be threatened by a new emphasis upon textual scholarship, critical bibliography, and analytic literary criticism. These new directions should be seen, perhaps, as a sign of the rehabilitation of Oscar Wilde as an important literary figure. Wilde has certainly become respectable as a writer of prose if not of verse and has emerged as one of the major authors of the 1880's and 1890's. It is to be hoped that in the wake of the present revaluation of Wilde's work, there will follow a better and a more balanced assessment of his writing. If this is

4. Hoare, 188.
† From *Studies in Bibliography: Papers of the Bibliographical Society of the University of Virginia* 25 (1972): 125–35. Reprinted by permission from *Studies in Bibliography*.

to be the case, there must be even more attention given to primary scholarship of a bibliographical and textual nature. Such research can offer the literary critic the necessary facts and the accurate texts with which to work. One well-known instance of such a contribution came in 1964 when the Rupert Hart-Davis edition of the Oscar Wilde *Letters* gave us, at last, an accurate text of "De Profundis."[1] The original four act version of *The Importance of Being Earnest* did not come to light in English until Vyvyan Holland edited a composite text in 1957. Sarah Augusta Dickson's two-volume, 1956 edition of the original four act play manuscript was valuable for reprinting the surviving drafts. The revised and enlarged *Portrait of Mr. W. H.* was not generally available until 1958, and the original, sometimes called the short version of *The Picture of Dorian Gray* was practically inaccessible outside the rare book rooms until Wilfred Edener used it as the basis for a critical edition of the novel in 1964.

The Edener edition was only the first step in providing the literary critic with adequate materials for reinterpretation and revaluation of Oscar Wilde's novel. The limited scope of the Edener edition restricted the study to recording variant readings for the two published versions of the novel. The revisions in the manuscripts have never been printed, and as yet, the problems relating to Wilde's intentions and the effects of the revisions remain to be published.[2] In the case of *Dorian Gray* and indeed many other major works by Wilde, collectors happily have preserved manuscripts and typescripts so that comparative studies of the different states of the text may be made. Such studies may reveal more than memoirs, biographies, and letters about the composition of the work and the realized intentions of the author. With this in mind, I offer the following paper as a preliminary study in textual bibliography to a more ambitious inquiry into the significance of the *Dorian Gray* manuscripts.

The text of *The Picture of Dorian Gray* exists in two published states. The novel first appeared as the featured work of fiction in the July, 1890 number of *Lippincott's Monthly Magazine*. There are

---

1. Oscar Wilde, *The Letters of Oscar Wilde*, ed. Rupert Hart-Davis (1962). Other examples of textual scholarship cited above may be mentioned here: Oscar Wilde, *The Importance of Being Earnest*, ed. Sarah Augusta Dickson, 2 vols (1956); Oscar Wilde, *The Importance of Being Earnest*, Original four act version ed. Vyvyan Holland (1957); Oscar Wilde, *The Portrait of Mr. W. H.* Enlarged Edition, ed. Vyvyan Holland (1958); Oscar Wilde, *The Picture of Dorian Gray*, ed. Wilfried Edener (1964). Other works of interest to Wildean scholarship include Abraham Horodisch, *Oscar Wilde's "Ballad of Reading Gaol." A Bibliocritical Study* (New Preston, Connecticut, 1954); Aatos Ojala, *Aestheticism and Oscar Wilde*, 2 vols. (Helsinki, 1954–55); Stuart Mason [Christopher Sclater Millard], *Bibliography of Oscar Wilde* (1914, 1967); E. San Juan, Jr., *The Art of Oscar Wilde* (1967); L. A. Beaurline, "The Director, The Script, and Author's Revisions: A Critical Problem," *Papers in Dramatic Theory and Criticism*, ed. David M. Knauf (1969), pp. 78–91.
2. The revisions and the author's intentions and their effects on the final form of the novel are studied in my own unpublished doctoral dissertation for the University of Chicago, "An Enquiry into Oscar Wilde's Revisions of *The Picture of Dorian Gray*," 1969.

extant two manuscripts for the *Lippincott's Dorian Gray*. The holo-graph manuscript is at the Pierpont Morgan Library and the cor-rected typescript is now at the William Andrews Clark Library. In June of 1891, Wilde published *Dorian Gray*, in an expanded version. The manuscript of the book version of *Dorian Gray*, published by Ward, Lock and Company, has not been found, if indeed a full man-uscript ever existed. Chapters added to the original *Lippincott's Dorian Gray* have turned up here and there over the years: Chapter III and one leaf from Chapter V are in the William Andrews Clark Library. Chapter XV is in the Berg Collection of the New York Pub-lic Library. Chapters XIV and XVI, sold at auction in the twenties, are, presumably, still in the hands of private collectors.

As far as anyone knows, *The Picture of Dorian Gray* was begun sometime in 1889. The first allusion to the novel appears in the frag-ment of a letter Wilde sent to J. M. Stoddart, the editor of *Lippincott's Magazine*, after Stoddart had found one of Wilde's adult fairy tales unsuitable: "I have invented a new story which is better than 'The Fisherman and his Soul,' and I am quite ready to set to work at once on it."[3] The letter is dated 17 December 1889. Subsequent refer-ences in later correspondence make it clear that Wilde was referring to *Dorian Gray* in the letter cited above. It is possible, even likely, that Wilde had begun working on the novel earlier than December of 1889. Indeed, there is some evidence to suggest that Wilde had begun work on *Dorian Gray* before October of 1889.[4] At this point, the manuscripts themselves provide the best evidence of the novel's development. The holograph manuscript, thought to be the original of the novel, was revised extensively by Wilde. These revisions affect characterization, setting, action and theme as well as commonplace minor changes in spelling, syntax, and idiom. After the revisions in the holograph were completed, Wilde had the manuscript typed and then made further changes. The revisions in the typescript are as extensive and as significant as those made in the manuscript. It was from this corrected copy of the typescript that *The Picture of Dorian Gray* was set up in type and printed by *Lippincott's*. There is an inter-val of eleven months between the appearance of *Dorian Gray* in *Lip-pincott's* and the publication of *Dorian Gray* as a book by Ward, Lock & Co. During that period, Wilde made his final revisions of the novel,

---

3. Oscar Wilde, *The Letters of Oscar Wilde*, ed. Rupert Hart-Davis (1962), p. 251.
4. Horace Wyndham, "Edited by Oscar Wilde," *Twentieth Century*, 163 (May, 1958), p. 400. Wyndham reports that when the decision to drop Wilde as editor of *Woman's World* was made, Wilde remarked, "I shall be able to finish a novel, 'The Picture of Dorian Gray,' I have in the stocks."

Wilde was replaced as editor of *Woman's World* in October of 1889. The fact that he con-tributed nothing further of his own after June of 1889 is an indication that he was given notice before that date. If this inference is correct, and if we may rely on the substantial if not the literal truth of Wyndham's anecdote, we may assume that Wilde had been at work on *Dorian Gray* before June of 1889.

and they are the most extensive of all. He added five new chapters, introducing many new characters and continuing with the alterations he had made earlier in atmosphere, theme, and action. The new chapters Wilde added were first written out in longhand. It is not known what procedures Wilde followed for the changes he made in the already published sections of his book. He did not use the original typescript from which the *Lippincott's The Picture of Dorian Gray* was set. If Wilde followed his customary method of revising, he would have worked from a fresh typescript. However, there is no evidence that, in fact, he did so. The novel, published by Ward, Lock & Co. in June of 1891, represents the final state of the text and, therefore, expresses the author's final intention for his work. Wilde never again made any changes in the text.

In the course of examining the manuscript of *Dorian Gray*, I discovered a number of irregularities in the holograph which indicate the existence of a manuscript version of the novel prior to the earliest one now known. The evidence is, I believe, strong enough to suggest that Wilde, in fact, revised his novel not two but at least three times before its original publication by *Lippincott's*. The evidence I have to present is wholly textual, based on Wilde's handwritten corrections in the manuscript. In classifying the various corrections made by Wilde in the holograph manuscript, I discovered a significant number of cases which could not be explained as arising from simple error, stylistic alteration, or those more substantial changes involving characterization, theme, and action. The corrections I shall investigate fall under the general category of errors emended in the course of writing the manuscript or possibly, in some cases, improvements made during the writing of the holograph. This fact is easily established by the character of the text. Each of the corrections to be discussed is part of the original writing, not added above the line or in the margin during a proofreading. The kind of error and revision to be discussed in this paper has led me to the conclusion that in order to account for them, one is forced to postulate the existence of a still earlier original manuscript for the novel from which Wilde was working more or less closely. In some cases, words, parts of words, or phrases are repeated in a manner suggesting that an error had been made in copying rather than in composition. In other cases there are passages which had been deleted by Wilde from an earlier part of the holograph and moved to a later page or recopied further down on the same page. There is only one instance in which Wilde moved a passage from a later page in the manuscript to an earlier one, an exception which, in this case, does not violate the rule.

It helps us immeasurably to have an example of a text which Wilde is known to have copied so that we may see whether or not errors of the kind found in the holograph manuscript of *Dorian Gray* appear there. We have such a specimen in the very manuscript under discussion. There is one part of *The Picture of Dorian Gray* which is known to have been copied by Wilde from one of his own earlier reviews, written while he was editor of *Woman's World* from June, 1887 until October, 1889. In November of 1888, about six months before the first reports that Wilde was working on a novel, he wrote a review of Earnest Lefebure's book, *Embroidery and Lace: Their Manufacture and History from the Remotest Antiquity to the Present Day*.[5] A significant part of the review reproduces or paraphrases Lefebure's text. More important for our purposes, when Wilde was scavenging for material to include in Dorian Gray's decadent pleasure house, he transcribed a number of paragraphs into the text of *Dorian Gray* from his old review of Lefebure's book. The self-plagiarism amounts to almost three pages of the holograph manuscript.[6] The leaves in question were copied verbatim from the text of the review, as a simple comparison reveals. In these copied leaves of the novel, there are four or five cases in which Wilde later made stylistic changes in the borrowed passages. However, there is one passage with an error of copying which has a relevance for this study.

> He longed to see the curious table napkins wrought for Heliogabalus on which were displayed all the dainties and viands that could be wanted for a feast: the mortuary cloth of King Chilperic with its three hundred golden bees; the fantastic robes that excited the indignation of *King Chilperic* the Bishop of Pontus, and were embroidered. . . . [7]

The repetition of the words "King Chilperic" above (in my italics) is obviously in error. The original passage in the review read, "robes that excited the indignation of the bishop of Pontus."[8] Normally, a slip such as the one above would not be notable or likely to excite curiosity. Indeed, such an error would not be significant at all were it not for the fact that the mistake occurs in a passage known to have been copied by Wilde from his own review published in *Woman's World*, November, 1888.

Instances of similarly repeated phrases or expressions dramatically out of place in the narrative may be cited as evidence that the holograph manuscript is probably a copy of an earlier draft. Such errors, while not frequent, occur throughout the holograph manuscript,

5. Oscar Wilde, *The Complete Works of Oscar Wilde*, ed. Padraic Colum, XII (1923), pp. 1–21.
6. Morgan Library Manuscript, 11. 186–188. I wish to thank the Pierpont Morgan Library for permission to examine this manuscript and special thanks go to Herbert Cahoon, curator of the manuscript collection, for his generous assistance.
7. Morgan Manuscript, 1. 186. Wilde crossed out the repeated phrase in the manuscript.
8. Wilde, *Complete Works*, p. 11.

indicating that any prior ur-manuscript must have been a nearly complete draft of the novel.[9]

> He turned to Hallward, and said, "My dear fellow, I have just remembered."
> —"Remembered what, Harry?"
> —"Where I heard the name of Dorian Gray."
> —"Where *I heard the name of* was it" asked Hallward, with a slight frown.
>
> (1. 26.)

> I don't know what my guardians will say. Lord Radley is sure to be furious. I don't care. I shall be of age in less than a year, and then I can do what I like I *don't k* have been right, Basil, haven't I. . . ."
>
> (1. 86.)

> "Nothing is serious now-a-days, at *Hallward* least, nothing should be."
> Hallward shook his head as he entered. . . .
>
> (1. 205).

In each of the cases cited above, the color tones of the ink in the manuscript indicate that Wilde recognized his mistake at once and lined through the offending words. Wilde wrote the holograph manuscript on blue lined folio paper with a steel tipped pen and an India-

---

9. In the quotations given above and below, each line is reproduced as it appears in the manuscript except that I have italicized the repeated elements. The additional examples of copying error given below will show the reader how these passages are distributed throughout the manuscript.

A. Within the world, as men know it, there was a finer world that only artists know of,—*artists of* artists, or those to whom the temperament of the artist has been given. Creation within—that is what Basil Hallward had named it, that is what he had attained to. (1. 43.)

B. —"Then you shall come. And you will come, too, Basil, won't you"
—*"Then you and I will*
—"I can't really, I would sooner not. I have a lot of work to do."
—"Well, then, you and I will go alone, Mr. Gray." (1. 51.)

C. The elaborate character of the frame made the picture extremely heavy, and now and then *he put his hand to it so as to help them in* spite of Mr. Ashton who had a true tradesman's dislike of seeing a gentleman doing anything useful he put his hand to it so as to help them. (1. 160.)

D. "Though your sins be as scarlet, yet I will make them white as snow!"
Suddenly a wild
—"Those words mean nothing to me, now."
—"Hush! Don't say that. You have done enough evil in your life, My God! don't you see that damned thing leering at us?" Dorian Gray glanced at the picture, and suddenly a wild feeling of hatred for Basil Hallward came over him. (1. 219.)

In passage C above, it appears from the ink tones in the holograph manuscript that Wilde did not line through the expression "he put his hand to it" until later, probably in proofreading. I conclude from the evidence of the lighter color of the ink in the deleted passages and in the contiguous script as compared to the much darker cancel line that the repetition is a result of an anticipation of the phrase rather than merely an improvement in style.

type ink. Close examination of the manuscript will often reveal the intervals at which the pen was dipped into the ink. In each of the passages above we have an example of one kind of error Wilde is known to have made in copying from his own book review originally written for *Woman's World*.

There are other anomolies in the manuscript which also suggest that they are errors of transcription rather than of composition. I refer to words left incomplete by Wilde and then lined through. Once again, the color tones of the ink reveal that Wilde must have crossed out the incomplete words before going on. I have chosen three representative examples of words left unfinished from different areas of the manuscript.[1]

There was something in his face that made one trust him at once. All YOU the candour of *youth* was there.

(1. 30.)

Yes: Basil could have saved him. But it was too late now. REGR The past could always be annihilated. *Regret*, denial of forgetfulness could do that.

(1. 156.)

The harsh intervals and shrill discords of barbaric music stirred him at times when Schubert's grace, and Chopin's MI beautiful sorrows, and the *mighty* harmonies of Beethoven himself fell unheeded on his ear.

(1. 183.)

Slips of the kind listed above are significant only as evidence which supports the hypothesis that some of the errors made by Wilde in the holograph manuscript were the result of a copying lapse made in the course of working from an earlier manuscript. It seems to me that the features of the manuscript cited above are of a kind that one might expect when one text is copied from another.

There is further evidence I should like to consider before concluding my case in support of the claim that there existed a manuscript anterior to the holograph manuscript now in the Morgan Library. In the course of writing the holograph, Wilde transposed a number of passages forward in the text from an earlier leaf to a later one. Some passages were recopied further down on the same page. One passage was removed from a later to an earlier page, but that exception is revealing because of a change in pagination. These transposed

1. In order to demonstrate the relevance of the incomplete word, it has been necessary to abstract a significant part of the text. I have used upper case letters to indicate the unfinished word and italics to identify the word when it reappears in the text.

passages are unlike any of the other cases in which Wilde moved phrases, expressions, or more complex elements around from one place to another because they were not written above the line or in the margin but are integrated in the script. This means that such passages were moved either in the course of copying or of composition. The first lines to be transposed by Wilde were spoken originally by Basil Hallward, the painter of Dorian's portrait, to Lord Henry Wotton, the man who tempts Dorian Gray with his gospel of new Hedonism. Wilde removed the passage from the dialogue of Basil Hallward and replaced it in a meditation by Lord Henry on beauty.

> I tell him that beauty like his is genius, is higher than genius, as it needs no explanation and is one of the great facts of the world, like sunlight or springtime, or the reflection in dark waters of that thin silver shell we call the moon.

Wilde transferred these lines verbatim from leaf 22 of the holograph manuscript to leaf 38. The reason for the change is that the lines are really more appropriate to Lord Henry. Also they represent an early step in reducing the importance of Basil Hallward's role in the novel. This process was continued in the revisions Wilde later made on the completed holograph and carried on in the further revisions through which the novel was put before publication in its final form in 1891. I believe that this particular incidence of transferal may be taken as evidence of a pre-existing manuscript. Had Wilde been composing as he went along, it is doubtful that such a change in the importance and in the role of a character would have been conceived before the first chapter was completed and then forgotten in subsequent chapters, whereas the changes made in later proofreading revisions of the novel reveal a consistent program to expand the characterization of Lord Henry and to reduce the influence of Basil Hallward in the story.

There are three other instances in which Wilde moved material from an earlier to a later position in the manuscript. As was the case above, no alterations were made in the passage and the lines were copied into the text without interruption. In the first of these passages, Dorian is speaking to Basil. It is the scene in which Dorian insists that Basil come with him into his abandoned nursery to see the portrait which Basil had painted many years before. The lines appeared first on manuscript leaf 212, lines 6–9. They were crossed out by Wilde and rewritten as lines 23–25 on the same leaf:

> I will show you my soul. You shall see the thing that you fancy only God can see.

The second repeated passage is a phrase which appeared in the narrator's commentary on leaf 231 of the manuscript, was cancelled by Wilde, and rewritten on the following leaf.

. . . during the eighteen months that their friendship had lasted.

In the manuscript leaf 233, lines 30–31, the following passage is deleted, reappearing again on leaf 234 as lines 8–9. The words are those of Dorian Gray addressed to Alan Campbell, the scientist whose alchemy is enlisted to remove all traces of Basil Hallward's corpse from the upstairs nursery of Dorian's house:

So it is, and to more than one person, Alan.

It is obvious from the character of the manuscript that Wilde transposed the passages in question as he was writing. The question is whether the manuscript in which the passages are rearranged was copied or composed. I think that at this point, we may rely, in part, on the weight of the evidence already presented in favor of the hypothesis that the manuscript is a copy rather than a first draft. Further to support this interpretation of the transposed passages in question, I should like to call the reader's attention to Wilde's own habits of composition. After each revision of a text, Wilde liked to have a clear copy. In the beginning he would make a fair copy of his rough draft himself. Later he would have a typescript made and work from that. I submit that it would have been unusual and uncharacteristic of Wilde to have made the kind of changes shown in the removal of the passages cited above while he was composing. Further, the physical evidence of the ink tones supports the view that the passages were recopied rather than moved during the course of composition. As I have mentioned earlier, since Wilde wrote in India ink with a steel tipped pen, it is often easy to tell at which points the pen was returned to the ink well. The ink in the script becomes lighter just before he refreshed the nib. Now in the instances of the transposed lines, the ink tones indicate that the cancel lines were drawn directly after the lines had been written. What is more, there is no detectable alteration in the ink tones as the passages reappear later in the text. Something of the sort should be expected, unless Wilde's memory were so retentive that he could recall as many as eight lines over sixteen pages of newly composed fiction. Otherwise, there should be some indication that Wilde had paused to relocate his original words in the manuscript.

One final passage deserves consideration. The lines below appear in the manuscript on leaf 27b. Wilde removed one passage from its original position at the top of leaf 28, made some additions and used it as the conclusion for Chapter One. Basil Hallward is speaking to Lord Henry Wotton. He begins by saying, "Don't take away the one person who makes life

absolutely lovely to me, and that gives my art whatever wonder or charm it possesses. Mind, Harry, I trust you." He spoke very

> slowly, and the words seemed wrung out of him almost against
> his will.
> "What nonsense you talk," said Lord Henry smiling, and taking
> Hallward by the arm, he almost led him into the house.

This passage is the only instance I have found in which Wilde moved
lines back to an earlier page. It is possible that Wilde made the
change in proofreading, having forgotten to designate the beginning
of Chapter Two as he composed; or he may have divided up a chapter which proved to be too long. If so, he had to have made the
changes before he reached Chapter Four, which is numbered correctly. Once again, the evidence of the ink tones is helpful. There is
a close match between the color tone of the ink in the first cancelled
lines and the writing at the end of the chapter. Likewise there is a
match up between the color tone of the ink in the last lines stricken
and the first words recopied on 27b. This seems to indicate that
Wilde cancelled the lines on the top of leaf 28 as soon as they were
written, that he recopied them with an additional phrase or two on
leaf 27b immediately afterward, and that, therefore, he was probably
using another text from which he could safely copy his lines.

Of course we have been dealing here with inferences drawn from
the corrections made by Wilde in the holograph manuscript of *Dorian
Gray*. The evidence leads, I believe, to but one conclusion: that Wilde
copied his holograph text now at the Morgan Library from a pre-
existing draft. No other hypothesis accounts for the kind of mistake
made by Wilde in the holograph and examined in this paper. We must
assume that such errors were made in the course of transcription and
that the original draft from which the holograph was copied must have
covered the entire story since the transcription errors are to be found
throughout the manuscript from leaf 22 to leaf 219. Therefore, the
original draft was more than merely a working outline. The fact that
the errors occur in passages of trivial significance suggests not only
that Wilde was more likely to be distracted in copying such material
but it implies that the earlier text was more or less a complete draft of
the novel as it appears now in the Morgan Library holograph. Finally,
we may assume that the original manuscript was probably foul papers,
heavily corrected and reworked by the author. That would account for
the trouble Wilde took to make a fair copy of the original. That fair
copy, in turn, was extensively altered and rewritten by Wilde.

The significance of all this for Wildean criticism and for textual
bibliography is easily seen. At the very least, it means that any future
editor of a critical or a scholarly edition of *The Picture of Dorian Gray*
should not treat the Morgan Library holograph as the original manuscript. Although it is an invaluable text in its own right, it cannot be
taken to reveal all those things about Wilde's original inspiration and

shaping of the novel which a first draft would expose. We must also revise upward from two to three the number of times Wilde rewrote his novel before its first publication in *Lippincott's* Magazine. Four full revisions of *Dorian Gray* before the novel took its final form suggest that the stereotyped view of Wilde as a careless and hasty writer may need reassessment. Perhaps a more thorough knowledge of Wilde's work habits would dispel some of the myths, partly self-created, about Wilde's insouciance toward his craft as a writer.

The chances of the original draft of *Dorian Gray* turning up at this late hour do not appear to be good. It is now eighty-two years since Wilde began work on the novel. Not a trace of foul papers or a working manuscript has appeared in the auction room catalogues or in lists describing the holdings of libraries or private collectors. No mention of the original draft appears in the letters or in any of the biographies and reminiscences. It is likely that Wilde himself disposed of the original manuscript. It is also possible that it was lost or destroyed at the time of the infamous auction of Wilde's property from his house at 16 Tite Street, Chelsea, in April of 1895 when the house was thrown open to curiosity seekers and souvenir hunters. At that time, it is said that many manuscripts were taken, and to this day, some have not been recovered. Another, more optimistic view is that the true original manuscript may be in the hands of a private collector or even may be languishing in someone's attic. In any case, the possible existence of another *Dorian Gray* manuscript has a potential value not only for the collector but also for the textual scholar and the literary critic.

SHELDON W. LIEBMAN

Character Design in *The Picture of Dorian Gray*†

Until the 1980s, *The Picture of Dorian Gray* was generally considered to be a deeply flawed novel. To some critics, it was simply badly written.[1] To others, it was hopelessly confused, reflecting Wilde's

---

† From *Studies in the Novel* 31.3 (Fall 1999). Copyright © 1999 by the University of North Texas. Reprinted by permission of the publisher. Bracketed page numbers refer to this Norton Critical Edition.

1. Richard Ellmann, for example, evidently summarizing long-held views of *The Picture of Dorian Gray*, says that "parts of the novel are wooden, padded, self-indulgent" (*Oscar Wilde* [New York: Alfred A. Knopf, 1988], p. 314). More sweepingly, Edward Roditi criticizes Wilde for interrupting his narrative with "esthetic preaching," "useless displays of esthetic erudition," "unnecessary descriptions of works of art," and "paradoxical table talk" ("Fiction as Allegory: The Picture of Dorian Gray," in *Oscar Wilde: A Collection of Critical Essays*, ed. Richard Ellmann [Englewood Cliffs, NJ: Prentice-Hall, 1969], p. 50). Faulting Wilde for insincerity and shallowness, as well as an outdated style, Ted R. Spivey concludes that "many readers find it difficult to take *The Picture of Dorian Gray* seriously" ("Damnation and Salvation in *The Picture of Dorian Gray*," *Boston University Studies in English* 4 [1960]: 162).

uncertainty and irresolution.[2] To still others, it was negligible or, at best, second-rate because it was merely an expression of the 1890s, in which case it was historically important but otherwise unworthy of critical attention.[3] Within the last two decades, however, many readers have called *Dorian Gray* a great book.[4] Indeed, its most recent critics have treated the novel as if it were neither the product of Wilde's confusion nor merely a period-piece. Its irresolution is taken to be an expression of Wilde's understanding of the human condition. And *Dorian Gray*'s broader philosophical concerns are assumed to be those of a moralist who is fully aware of the failure of Victorian (or, in fact, any conventional) morality and is exploring the consequences of its demise.

Interpreting rather than evaluating the novel, most recent critics have seen *Dorian Gray* as in some sense a running debate between two of its major characters, Henry Wotton and Basil Hallward, and, furthermore, a debate carried out in the mind of Dorian Gray. In the past, many readers concluded that this opposition represented a plain choice between right and wrong: "conscience and temptation," "good and evil," "positive and negative moral influences," or "love" and "egoism."[5] Although this opposition was usually seen as a battle symbolically waged by Henry and Basil, it was sometimes taken to be a conflict between warring psychological faculties ("conscience" vs. "libido" or "intelligence" vs. "sensibility") and, for some critics, as

2. Philip K. Cohen argues that Wilde is morally inconsistent and ambivalent because he is "at moral odds with himself" and that the novel, as a result, is characterized by "narrative schizophrenia" (*The Moral Vision of Oscar Wilde* [Rutherford, NJ: Fairleigh Dickinson Univ. Press, 1978], pp. 117–20). Gerald Weales similarly cites Wilde's ambiguity ("Foreword," *The Picture of Dorian Gray and Selected Stories* [New York: New American Library, 1962], p. ix), and Kerry Powell discusses the author's "unresolved confusion" ("Oscar Wilde 'Acting': The Medium as Message in *The Picture of Dorian Gray*," *Dalhousie Review* 58 [1978]: 106).

3. Weales calls the book "terribly *fin de siecle*" (*The Picture of Dorian Gray*, p. x). Ellmann says it is "the aesthetic novel par excellence," portraying "the tragedy of aestheticism" (*Oscar Wilde*, p. 315). And Christopher S. Nassaar contends that the novel is "about the coming of age of Victorian art and attitudes" (*Into the Demon Universe: A Literary Exploration of Oscar Wilde* [New Haven: Yale Univ. Press, 1974], p. 70). Robert K. Miller claims that Wilde attempted (albeit unsuccessfully) to compose "a proper nineteenth-century tale" with a "Victorian conclusion" (*Oscar Wilde* [New York: Frederick Ungar, 1982], p. 30. See also Cohen, *The Moral Vision of Oscar Wilde*, pp. 123, 137.

4. Donald R. Dickson says that *Dorian Gray* is "more artfully contrived than many critics seem willing to grant" (' "In a mirror that mirrors the soul': Masks and Mirrors in Dorian Gray," *English Literature in Transition* 26 [1983]: 5). Nassaar argues that it is "a deeper and more thoughtful novel than its critics have so far been willing to concede (*Into the Demon Universe*, p. 37). Joyce Carol Oates, in particular, has stated that the novel is both subtle and complex: it is "exceptionally good after all." Indeed, it is "one of the strongest and most haunting of English novels" ("*The Picture of Dorian Gray*: Wilde's Parable of the Fall," *Critical Inquiry* 7 [1980]: 420).

5. See Miller, *Oscar Wilde*, p. 31; Nassaar, *Into the Demon Universe*, p. 54; Epifanio San Juan, *The Art of Oscar Wilde* (Princeton: Princeton Univ. Press, 1967), pp. 52, 71; Cohen, *The Moral Vision of Oscar Wilde*, p. 123; Spivey, "Damnation and Salvation," p. 169; Peter Raby, *Oscar Wilde* (Cambridge: Cambridge Univ. Press, 1988), p. 69; and A. Ballesteros Gonzales, "The Mirror of Narcissus in *The Picture of Dorian Gray*," in *Rediscovering Oscar Wilde*, ed. C. George Sandulescu (Gerrards Cross, Bucks: Colin Smythe, 1994), p. 4.

Regenia Gagnier has noted, a projection of the war in Wilde's own psyche.[6] The consensus among these critics was either that, in Wilde's judgment, Dorian Gray chooses wrongly and pays the ultimate price for his serious moral error, thus confirming the existence of cosmic justice, or that Dorian never really makes up his mind, thus reflecting Wilde's "warring energies"—his "schizophrenia" or, less grandly, his "identity crisis" or, less pathologically, his "immaturity."

Nearly thirty years ago, however, Houston A. Baker made the interesting point that in "The Critic as Artist" Wilde calls not for a choice between "conscience and instinct," but for a "merging" of these two faculties. And Dorian's fate, Baker continued, is a result of his inability to reconcile these two aspects of his personality.[7] This approach to the novel is suggestive because it implies, first, that the conflict between Basil and Henry is not simply a matter of good vs. evil and, second, that Dorian's failure to integrate his opposing "selves" is not a consequence of his own psychological inadequacy, but a condition of modern life.[8] From this perspective—and in my judgment, which

6. *Idylls of the Marketplace: Oscar Wilde and the Victorian Public* (Stanford: Stanford Univ. Press, 1986), p. 216, n. 14. The aforementioned pairs of terms are used, respectively, by Kerry Powell, "Hawthorne, Arlo Bates, and *The Picture of Dorian Gray*," *Papers on Language and Literature* 16 (1980): 415; and San Juan, *The Art of Oscar Wilde*, p. 64. The conflict is, to Miller, "the dialogue of the mind with itself" (*Oscar Wilde*, p. 33) and, to Oates, "the warring of consciousness with itself" ("Wilde's Parable of the Fall," p. 421). Ellmann says that Wilde's characters "represent distortions or narrowing of his personality" (*Oscar Wilde*, p. 320). Powell contends that Basil and Henry are "bipolar personalities" who express Wilde's "divided self" ("Oscar Wilde 'Acting,'" p. 113). For more recent expressions of the same view, see Donald L. Lawler, "Keys to the Upstairs Room: A Centennial Essay on Allegorical Performance in Dorian Gray," in *The Picture of Dorian Gray*, ed. Donald L. Lawler (New York: W. W. Norton, 1988), p. 456; John McGowan, "From Pater to Wilde to Joyce: Modernist Epiphany and the Soulful Self," *Texas Studies in Literature and Language* 32 (1990): 426, 430; and Lawrence Danson, *Wilde's Intentions: The Artist in His Criticism* (Oxford: Oxford Univ. Press, 1997), p. 46.

7. "The Tragedy of the Artist: *The Picture of Dorian Gray*," *Nineteenth-Century Fiction* 24 (1969): 355.

8. San Juan says that "Dorian's character is a condition in which extremes meet; his acts signify the temporary triumph of one extreme over the other." Furthermore, Dorian's goal is to reconcile every polarity in the novel: soul and sense, passion and spirit, feeling and artifice, etc. (*The Art of Oscar Wilde*, pp. 67–68). To Powell, Dorian's objective is to "harmonize" opposites ("Oscar Wilde 'Acting,'" p. 106). As Robert Keefe argues, however, "Wilde calls into question the very possibility of full integration" ("Artist and Model in *The Picture of Dorian Gray*," *Studies in the Novel* 5 [1973]: 68). According to Louis J. Poteet, Dorian suffers from "a doom made necessary by the irreconcilability of opposing forces" operating in the novel ("Dorian Gray and the Gothic Novel," *Modern Fiction Studies* 17 [1971]: 247). Thus, although *The Picture of Dorian Gray* looks at first glance like "a reassuringly old-fashioned morality play," says Oates, the tragedy persists in the questions the novel raises but never answers. Specifically "the novel is an elaborate fantasy locating the Fall within the human psyche alone" ("Wilde's Parable of the Fall," pp. 421, 424). See also Dominic Manganiello, "Ethics and Aesthetics in *The Picture of Dorian Gray*," *Canadian Journal of Irish Studies* 9 (1983): 30–31; Norbert Kohl, *Oscar Wilde: The Works of a Conformist Rebel*, trans. David H. Wilson (Cambridge: Cambridge Univ. Press, 1989), p. 151; Alan Sinfield, *The Wilde Century: Effeminacy, Oscar Wilde and the Queer Moment* (London: Cassell, 1994), p. 99; Michael Patrick Gillespie, "Picturing Dorian Gray: Resistant Readings in Wilde's Novel," *English Literature in Transition* 35 (1992): 21, 22; and Michael Patrick Gillespie, *Oscar Wilde and the Poetics of Ambiguity* (Gainesville: Univ. Press of Florida, 1996), p. 72. It is also worth noting that, to most critics, Dorian's demise

I shall try to substantiate in the following pages—Dorian Gray is torn between two mutually exclusive interpretations of human experience: one, optimistic, religious, and emotional; the other, pessimistic, cynical, and intellectual. In the course of the novel, the reader (if not Dorian) discovers that neither interpretation is adequate and that, from Wilde's perspective, there are no alternatives.

Of course, this is essentially the majority view of the novel today, with which I have no quarrel. My only complaint is simply (but significantly, I believe) that the opposition between Basil and Henry has been seriously oversimplified by most critics, reduced as it usually is to a battle between ethics and aesthetics.[9] (This formula also suggests that the novel is really, after all, a product of its time and, because it fails to deal with more universal issues, is not relevant to readers in the twentieth century.) Thus, my main point is not merely that Wilde's characters stand for opposing values, but that the belief systems they embody are complex as well as internally logical and consistent; that the story in which these characters act on their values is a test of their viability and applicability to *real life*, not just to the exotic worlds of decadent sensuality and drawing-room repartee; and that Dorian, as the protagonist in this drama of universal moral conflict, is a major figure in the development of the modern novel.

Briefly, the views of Basil and Henry can be understood in terms of the relationship between their theory of cosmic justice and their concept of morality. Basil believes that the universe is a moral order in which God (or at least Fate) punishes evil and rewards good; that the self is (or can be) unitary and autonomous; and that art—as well as human conduct in general—can (and should) be guided by a moral code in which sympathy and compassion are primary values. This moral position leads to the gestures of melodrama (the inevitably unsuccessful—and therefore sentimental—pursuit of love, fame, or revenge), the disappointment of unrequited love, and suicide prompted by disillusionment. Henry's beliefs are based on the assumption that there is no moral order (the universe is purposeless and indifferent to human needs); that the self is not only multiple, but at war with itself and driven by forces beyond its control; and that morality is arbitrary and relative. This moral position leads to a withdrawal from human engagement, the pursuit of pleasure (both sensual and intellectual) as a distraction from disillu-

---

is not a consequence of his failure to follow Lord Henry's moral code. See, in particular, Kohl, *Oscar Wilde*, p. 153.

9. For a broader than usual view of the contrasts in *Dorian Gray*, see Kohl, *Oscar Wilde*, pp. 142, 156, 158, 162; Rodney Shewan, *Oscar Wilde: Art and Egotism* (New York: Barnes and Noble, 1977), pp. 114, 116, 120; and John Allen Quintus, "Christ, Christianity, and Oscar Wilde," *Texas Studies in Literature and Language* 33 (1991): 514.

sionment, and the manipulation of others for one's own enjoyment and edification.

Wilde wrote in *De Profundis* that "Doom like a purple thread runs through the gold cloth of *Dorian Gray*." Although Basil Hallward introduces this theme, he merely threads the needle; it is really Lord Henry Wotton who weaves the thread. In fact, despite the general critical picture of Lord Henry as dilettante, intellectual lightweight, and effete hedonist, he is actually one of the most philosophical characters in British fiction. As more than one critic has noted, Henry is, first, a scientist and an intellectual, whose most outstanding trait is his curiosity.[1] Early in the novel he recommends science as an antidote to social reform and insists on seeing things from "the scientific point of view" [19]. Although his scientific curiosity occasionally draws him to the exploration of mere sensation, it has evidently led him to more profound discoveries: "Ordinary people [he says] waited till life disclosed to them its secrets, but to the few, to the elect, the mysteries of life were revealed before the veil was drawn away" [51]. As one of the elect, Henry tells Dorian and Basil, "*I have known everything.*" The "tired look in his eyes" suggests that he is weary of this knowledge, from which he cannot, however, escape. And although he is "always ready for a new emotion," he knows "there is no such thing" [68; my emphasis].

Henry's knowledge is revealed in his discussions of two of his favorite topics: nature and human nature. On both subjects, his comments demonstrate that he is an incurable pessimist. His picture of the universe might well have come from T.H. Huxley:[2] "It often happens [he says to Dorian after Sybil Vane's death] that the real tragedies of life occur in such an inartistic manner that they hurt us by their absolute incoherence, their absurd want of meaning, their entire lack of style. They affect us just as vulgarity affects us. They give us an impression of sheer brute force, and we revolt against that" [85]. Of course, Henry's frivolous manner of speaking—his lament about tragedy's "lack of style" and his equation of tragedy and vulgarity—might divert the reader from Henry's main point, i.e., that most tragic events reflect the "sheer brute force" of nature. It may be surmised, as well, that the exceptions to this general rule—namely tragedies "that possess artistic elements of beauty," of which Sybil's death is supposed to be an example—are

---

1. On this point, see Spivey, "Damnation and Salvation," p. 165; and Kohl, *Oscar Wilde*, p. 156. Oates says that Henry's hedonism is a "quest for meaning" ("Wilde's Parable of the Fall," p. 425).
2. On Wilde's interest in science, see John Wilson Foster, "Against Nature? Science and Oscar Wilde," *University of Toronto Quarterly* 63 (1993–94): 331, 334. On the broader philosophical background of Wilde's ideas on nature and human nature, see Bruce Haley, "Wilde's 'Decadence' and the Positivist Tradition," *Victorian Studies* 28 (1985): 215–29.

really only made exceptional (and unthreatening) by a willful effort of the aesthetic (and anaesthetizing) imagination. Later, in his explanation of Sybil's death, Henry indicates that "actual life" destroys: "She marred it, and it marred her" [87]. When he says to one of the guests at Aunt Agatha's luncheon, "I can stand brute force, but brute reason is quite unbearable" [57], Henry is indicating that he is inured to this fundamental aspect of nature—evidently because he has simply accepted it.[3]

Henry's knowledge of psychology is equally extensive, and his view of human nature is equally grim. Wilde comments: "[Henry] had always been enthralled by the methods of natural science, but the ordinary subject-matter of that science had seemed to him trivial and of no import. And so he had begun by vivisecting himself, as he had ended by vivisecting others. Human life—that appeared to him the one thing worth investigating. Compared to it there was nothing else of any value" [51]. Henry acquires his wisdom about "the passions and the intellect" from literature as well as direct observation of human behavior. Sometimes "a complex personality," like Dorian's, gives him an opportunity to examine the human species in its natural habitat. What Henry has learned is, first, that human beings are irrational. When Dorian tells Henry, after the death of Sybil, that he is resolved to reform his life, Henry comments: "Good resolutions are useless attempts to interfere with scientific laws. Their origin is pure vanity. Their result is absolutely *nil*" [84]. Earlier he had said to Basil that human beings cannot abide by moral imperatives defining their obligations to others. Fidelity, for example, is impossible because people are moved by their emotions rather than their will. Thus love is not a product of free choice, but "a question for physiology" [28]. Virtually all that one can say about human nature is precisely what one can say about nature writ large: it is driven by irrational, impersonal physical-biological forces beyond human control and human understanding.

In a world without purpose, the result of faith is disillusionment, the result of action is disappointment, and the result of love or sympathy or compassion is suffering. That is why "nothing is ever quite true" [68] and *ennui* is the unforgivable sin. All truths collapse against the backdrop of chaos, and indifference is the dead end of all human endeavor. At the end of *his* tether, Henry engages in the only kind of action, other than suicide, that fits his desperate moral and metaphysical dilemma: contemplation. This serves both his curiosity,

---

3. Ellman, to the contrary, claims that Henry "denies suffering" (*Oscar Wilde*, p. 318), and Cohen says that he is otherwise unaware of the facts of life (*The Moral Vision of Oscar Wilde*, pp. 142, 147). It is not that Henry is ignorant, but that he tries to escape from his own profound knowledge.

which he cannot quench, and his fear, which he cannot face. Indeed, all of his activities are double-edged and simultaneously serve two opposed ends: approach and avoidance, or the instincts of Eros and death. Detachment enables Henry to see dispassionately, like a true scientist, but also to refrain from emotional involvement, like a schizoid personality. Spectatorism allows him to analyze nonjudgmentally but also to turn reality into art by transforming everyday human events into aesthetically distanced drama. And cynicism permits him to act on the stage of the real world, displaying the fruits of his scientific research, but also to protect himself from succumbing to the emotional temptations of that world, thereby avoiding the suffering that shadows passion.

Quite logically, then, as I have suggested, Henry's cynicism derives from his dark vision of the external and internal realms of human life. His morality comes from his metaphysics, and those who do not share the latter have trouble believing the former. Basil, who evidently knows Henry well, says to him: "I hate the way you talk about your married life, Harry . . . I believe that you are a very good husband, but that you are thoroughly ashamed of your own virtues. You are an extraordinary fellow. You never say a moral thing, and you never do a wrong thing. Your cynicism is simply a pose" [9]. Henry feeds this impression when he tells his dinner-party companions that "one should never do anything that one cannot talk about after dinner" [176]. Nevertheless, although he no longer actively pursues physical pleasure—at least, the kind that Dorian indulges in—and lives a relatively quiet life of intellectual contemplation, he takes almost nothing seriously. And although, unlike Dorian, he would do nothing strenuous to retain his youth ("To get back my youth I would do anything in the world, except take exercise, get up early, or be respectable" [178]), he is quite willing—and even eager—to manipulate Dorian callously and deliberately, in order to satisfy the only desire that he believes is neither futile nor destructive—intellectual curiosity—and to experience the only real pleasures left to him, those he can have vicariously, living through others. He "would sacrifice anybody . . . for the sake of an epigram" [169], as Dorian claims, and he would sacrifice anybody for the sake of an experiment that might yield an aesthetic thrill or an iota of knowledge.

How does one live in a world in which nothing can be believed and no one can be trusted? Henry's answer is what philosophers call ethical egoism. He encourages Dorian to follow his own example of pursuing his own self-interest, which means seeking pleasure and avoiding pain. Henry's "new Hedonism" is based on the assumption that the quest for pleasure is natural because it is an expression of the quest for life, a response to a basic impulse, which Freud would later call the life instinct, as Henry suggests to Dorian: "Live! Live the wonderful life that is in you!" [23]. This impulse or instinct requires human beings to both live and grow by acting on their "natural thoughts" and "natural passions": "The aim of life is self-development. To realize one's nature perfectly—that is what each of us is here for." This is "the duty that one owes to one's self." Henry goes on: "I believe that if one man were to live out his life fully and completely, were to give form to every feeling, expression to every thought, reality to every dream—I believe that the world would gain such a fresh impulse of joy that we would forget all the maladies of medievalism, and return to the Hellenic ideal—to something finer, richer, than the Hellenic ideal, it may be" [19]. By allowing ourselves to develop through the expression of our innate creative drive, we evolve from simple to more complex organisms, becoming "more highly organized," which is "the object of man's existence" [64]. What Henry means by being "in harmony with one's self" is simply obeying the instinct and pursuing the "higher aim" of "individualism." To do otherwise is to "spoil" one's life, to "stagnate," to "make [one's self] incomplete" [178].

In his theory of self-development, Henry may owe something to Aristotle, whose theory of tragedy influenced Wilde's thinking on that subject. However, the Greek ideal of self-realization, which Henry calls Hellenism, was not, at least in Aristotle's version of it, accompanied by an antisocial individualism. With his ardent elitism, his frequent contrast between the strong and the weak (and even between masters and slaves), and, particularly, his attack on the doctrine of self-sacrifice and self-denial, Henry is much closer to Nietzsche than to Aristotle. Like his more recent predecessor, Henry believes that by encouraging charity and social reform, society promotes sickness rather than health, stifles individualism, and inhibits intellectual growth. He says to Dorian: "Don't squander the gold of your days, listening to the tedious, trying to improve the hopeless failure, or giving away your life to the ignorant, the common, and the vulgar. These are the sickly aims, the false ideals, of our age" [23]. "The nineteenth century," he adds later, "has gone bankrupt through an overexpenditure of sympathy." To worry about "one's neighbors" is to be "a prig or a puritan." The true individual flouts "the standard of [his] age," the acceptance of which "is a form of grossest immorality." The ignorant and the poor can afford nothing more than self-denial because their economic and intellectual condition requires it, but "medieval emotions are out of date" for the rich and the civilized [67].

Society succeeds in its endeavor to direct all human activity toward social, collective ends, Henry says, by making people "afraid of themselves." Their fear is created and sustained by "the terror of society" and "the terror of God"—the bases, respectively, of morals and religion. Ironically, however, these two forces actually "starve" rather than nurture the soul: "The mutilation of the savage has its tragic survival in the self-denial that mars our lives. We are punished for our refusals. Every impulse that we strive to strangle broods in the mind, and poisons us." The activities that one pursues in fulfilling one's needs and satisfying one's desires may be sins, but they are "beautiful sins" that are "made monstrous and unlawful" only by "monstrous laws." In an amoral universe governed by no absolute standards, nothing is inherently evil: "It is in the brain, and the brain only, that the great sins of the world take place" [20]. In other words, "[m]oderation is a fatal thing" [150] because no natural law sanctions it, and no growing organism can flourish under its rule and sway.

Yet the real (or, at least, deeper) purpose of Henry's scientific and artistic approach to human experience is actually escapist. His problem, Henry tells Lady Agatha, is that he cannot stand to witness suffering, perhaps because he, more than any other character in the novel, knows that it is not only real but irremediable: "I can sympathize with everything, except suffering . . . I cannot sympathize with that. It is too ugly, too horrible, too distressing. There is something terribly morbid in the modern sympathy with pain. One should sympathize with the colour, the beauty, the joy of life. The less said about life's sores, the better" [37]. It is not that Henry totally ignores the unpleasant facts of existence. Rather, he "plays" with them and "transforms" them. In the process, philosophy is made to serve the pleasure principle, and "facts fled before her like frightened forest things" [38]. It is no surprise, then, that despite his curiosity—his intellectual quest—Henry prefers Beauty to Thought. And although he tells Dorian that "life has always poppies in her hands" [85], he clearly makes every effort to grow his own so that he will never have to do without the opiate of distraction. Reality cannot be changed, but it can be dressed up if "we have [not] lost the faculty of giving lovely names to things." That is why "[n]ames are everything" [161].

The problem Henry faces is that these diversions, which enable him to evade terror, do not satisfy all of his needs—namely, his intellectual curiosity and his creative impulse, without which he is in danger of stagnating from inaction and even perishing from *ennui*. As we have seen, however, action leads to pain, and the pursuit of pleasure leads to the exhaustion of all emotion. Thus, unable to act but needing to know and to create, Henry turns to Dorian Gray, who offers him both the opportunity to analyze a complex personality and the chance to create a new (and beautiful) self. Furthermore, Dorian also represents a new life of sensation, emotion, and thought that Henry can experience vicariously and therefore safely. In this way, Dorian becomes one of *Henry's* multiple selves, created, as such selves always are, to live a life that one's already pained and wounded selves cannot live—to live, in short, in fiction what one can no longer live in fact: "Good artists simply exist in what they make." Great poets "write the poetry that they dare not"—or cannot—"realize" in their lives [50].

Henry reveals the dynamics of this process of self-aggrandizement even before he decides to make Dorian an extension of himself. The young man asks Henry whether he is actually "a very bad influence," as Basil alleges. Henry replies, "All influence is immoral." In the context of his theory of self-development, he goes on to explain, anyone who is strongly influenced loses his individuality, his self-determination [19]. At the same time, the person who influences someone else gains a medium of self-expression, a new stage on which to perform and an opportunity, therefore, to become a spectator in his own—though borrowed or co-opted—life. In this respect, influence (or "domination," as Henry later calls it) is the consummate creative act, partly because it requires extraordinary skill (the victim must be unaware of the influence and assume that it is coming from himself, as Dorian does and partly because it results in the deepest satisfactions of doing, making, and growing: "To project one's soul into some gracious form, and let it tarry there for a moment; to hear one's own intellectual views echoed back to one with all the added music of passion and youth; to convey one's temperament into another as though it were a subtle fluid or a strange perfume; there was a real joy in that" [34].

In many respects, Henry sounds like a spokesman for Wilde. Most of his ideas—his rejection of altruism, his theory of self-development, his hedonism—are recurrent themes in Wilde's essays, and Henry's wit and wisdom are delivered in the urbane style of Vivian in "The Decay of Lying" and Gilbert in "The Critic as Artist." Furthermore, Wilde as the narrator of *Dorian Gray* often expresses Henry's sentiments—sometimes in Henry's characteristic tone.[4] Nevertheless, it would be a mistake to conclude that Henry speaks for his creator. The effect of Henry's influence on Dorian is, after all, disastrous, and Henry is blissfully unaware of Dorian's gradual degeneration. Early in the novel, he says to Dorian, "People like you . . . don't commit crimes" [47]. Late in the book, he tells Dorian, "There is no one who would not be delighted to change places with you" [168]. And in his last conversation with Dorian (long after the latter has caused Sybil's suicide, murdered Basil, cold-bloodedly

---

4. Examples of the latter are Wilde's descriptions of Lord Fermor (pp. 55–56) and the guests at Lady Agatha's luncheon (pp. 61–62).

disposed of the body, caused the suicide of Alan Chapman, and indirectly brought about the accidental murder of James Vane), Henry restates his belief in Dorian's inability to commit murder. He even tells his disciple, who has also become an opium addict, that he has not been "marred" by his experience. Finally, Henry informs Dorian that he "could change places with [him]" because the world has always worshiped him and will continue to do so. "I am so glad that you have never done anything," he continues. "Life has been your art." To these almost moronic words of praise, Dorian calmly replies: "You don't know everything about me. I think that if you did, you would turn from me" [179].

Basil Hallward is a far less complex character than Henry and requires far less attention. However, he is not less important in the moral scheme of *The Picture of Dorian Gray*, joined as he is by almost everyone else in the novel—except, most notably, Dorian—in representing a moral position that is fundamentally different from Henry's. At their first meeting, Dorian sees Henry and Basil as "a delightful contrast" [18] and hears Henry and Sybil speaking in "different" voices. The ensuing battle between the two antagonists, both of whom are fighting for Dorian's loyalty, is intensely personal (at least on Basil's side) but also moral and ideological. The foundation of Basil's actions is his belief in a moral order, in which men and women are punished for their evil deeds and rewarded for their good: Basil assumes that he either has been or will be "punished" for teaching Dorian "to be vain" and for worshiping him too much. Unlike Henry, who believes that Dorian sins without consequence to himself, Basil thinks that sin "cannot be concealed": "Sin is a thing that writes itself across a man's face" [126]. This implicit view of a universe ruled by a deity who gives human beings their due is shared by Sybil Vane, who expects God (who is "very good") to "watch over" her brother, and James Vane, in turn, who swears to avenge his sister "as there is a God in heaven" [60]. Less merciful than Sybil's and less vengeful than James's, Basil's God is the only being, as Basil tells Dorian, who can see the soul.

As an artist, Basil is an idealist, whose goal is not to provide pleasure—either to himself or to others—but to inspire people with an art that portrays the union of feeling and form, "the harmony of soul and body" [13], for which Dorian is a fitting subject: "He is the visible incarnation of that unseen ideal whose memory haunts us artists like an exquisite dream" [95]. To Basil, Dorian represents the ideal of the body, perfect beauty, as well as the ideal of the soul, selflessness. Responding to the young man's description of Sybil's power to "spiritualize" her audience, to make everyone feel "that they are of the same flesh and blood as one's self" [70]—that is, to achieve a feeling of social unity—Basil argues: "To spiritualize one's age—that is something worth doing. If this girl can give a soul to those who have lived without one, if she can create the sense of beauty in people whose lives have been sordid and ugly, if she can strip them of their selfishness and lend them tears for sorrows that are not their own, she is worthy of all your adoration, worthy of the adoration of the world" [70]. Given the universe as Basil sees it, living by this doctrine of sympathy and uplift, embraced also by Lady Agatha, rewards one with peace of mind, while its contradiction results in sorrow. "But, surely, if one lives for one's self," he says to Henry, in response to the latter's defense of his theory of self-development, "one pays a terrible price for doing so." If one sins, he continues, one pays "in remorse, in suffering, in . . . well, in the consciousness of degradation" [67].

In short, Basil is really a moralist, whose art serves his moral vision and whose actions are not inhibited by Henry's assumptions about nature and human nature. For this reason, Basil allows himself not only to identify with others and sympathize with both their suffering and aspirations, but to feel in general. He idolizes Dorian but initially resists any emotional involvement with him because he knows he is capable of being swept away: "I knew that I had come face to face with someone whose mere personality was so fascinating that, if I allowed it to do so, it would absorb my whole nature, my whole soul, my very art itself" [10]. Sybil is less restrained than Basil only because she is even more innocent than he is. Consequently she immediately allows herself to fall in love with Dorian and thereby descends into the trap of emotion, feeling both joy and freedom but only as "a caged bird" living in a "prison of passion" [54]. Not surprisingly, when Dorian criticizes Sybil for not living up to his artistic standards, Basil responds, "Love is a more wonderful thing than Art" [72]. Thus, although he initially seems to accept Henry's fatalism ("We shall all suffer for what the gods have given us"), Basil subsequently defends all the ideals and institutions that Henry attacks, and his fidelity extends even to the most conventional of middle-class values. He refuses to believe that Dorian would sacrifice his "birth, position, and wealth" to marry Sybil, and he later asks Dorian to consider the damage he is doing to his reputation: "Every gentleman is interested in his good name" [126][5]

As a moralist, Basil gives Dorian what the latter sarcastically refers to as "good advice" tells Dorian to ignore Henry's cynicism, and

---

5. On Basil as representative of conventional morality, see Donald H. Ericksen, *Oscar Wilde* (Boston: Twayne, 1977), p. 100; Ellmann, *Oscar Wilde*, p. 316; Powell, "Oscar Wilde 'Acting,'" p. 110; Poteet, "The Gothic Novel," p. 246; and Spivey, "Salvation and Damnation," p. 167. On Basil as Dorian's conscience, see Baker, "The Tragedy of the Artist," p. 355; Miller, *Oscar Wilde*, p. 31; and San Juan, *The Art of Oscar Wilde*, p. 65.

makes him aware of the rumors about his destructive influence on others: "One has a right to judge of a man by the effect he has over his friends. Yours seem to lose all sense of honour, of goodness, of purity. You have filled them with a madness for pleasure. They have gone down into the depths. You led them there" [127]. Basil wants Dorian "to lead such a life as to make the world respect [him]," "to have a clean name and a clean record," and to use his "wonderful influence . . . for good, not for evil" [128]. After Sybil's death, Basil, who is "heart-broken," finds it impossible to believe that Dorian has gone to the Opera "while Sybil Vane was lying dead in some sordid lodging!" [90]. Shocked by Dorian's indifference, he accuses the young man of abandoning the values that he holds dear: "Dorian, this is horrible! Something has changed you completely. You look exactly the same wonderful boy who, day after day, used to come down to my studio to sit for his picture. But you were simple, natural, and affectionate then. You were the most unspoiled creature in the whole world. Now, I don't know what has come over you. You talk as if you had no heart, no pity in you. It is all Harry's influence. I see that" [90]. Later in the conversation, Basil thinks to himself: "There was so much in him that was good, so much in him that was noble" [92]. Sybil Vane occupies the same moral ground as Basil not only in terms of her aesthetic and moral idealism, but also because she inspires in Dorian the same values that Basil tries to inculcate. While he believes that Dorian's nature is "too fine" to "bring misery on anyone," Sybil's "trust" actually makes him "faithful," and her "belief" makes him "good."

Although some critics have suggested that Basil and Sybil represent the moral norm in the novel, I believe they do not.[6] In *Dorian Gray*, Wilde's universe can sustain no traditional moral system. In other words, Basil and Sybil may be good, but they are not wise. And, from Wilde's point of view—at least from the perspective defined in the novel—these two characters (as well as Lady Agatha and James Vane) stand for a merely conventional morality that is based on unfounded assumptions about the nature of things. The moral order that Basil believes in does not exist. At the end of *Dorian Gray*, the stage is strewn with the bodies of the innocent—Sybil, Basil, Alan Campbell, and James Vane—and populated also by the degraded victims of Dorian's influence: Lady Gwendolyn (Henry's sister), Sir Henry Ashton, Adrian Singleton, Lord Kent's son, the Duke of Perth, and no doubt countless others. Among the major characters,

6. Nassaar calls Basil and Sybil the "voice of goodness" in the novel (*Into the Demon Universe*, p. 54). Miller claims that Wilde's "sympathies are with Sybil Vane" (*Oscar Wilde*, p. 29). See also Dickson, "Masks and Mirrors," pp. 6–7; and Cohen, *The Moral Vision of Oscar Wilde*, p. 138.

only the Mephistophelean Henry survives, showing that good and evil are not the essential determinants of cosmic rewards and punishments. Sybil's merciful God is balanced by James's vengeful God, yet both are undermined by a darker god whose influence does not reflect any principle of justice. Henry "merely shot an arrow into the air" and hits Dorian [20], Sir Geoffrey Clouston fires his gun at a hare and kills James Vane, and Dorian stabs his portrait but only destroys himself.

Basil is similarly wrong in his assumptions about human nature. His worship of Dorian is, like Sybil's love for him, self-consuming. The portrait, representing both Basil's idolatry and Dorian's conscience, communicates its hatred of its creator to Dorian, stirring "the wild passions of a hunted animal" in him [132] and prompting him to commit a murder that is, in effect, a suicide. Similarly, Sybil's eyes are "lit with an exquisite fire," and, although she is "transfigured with joy," she is "dominated" (that is, controlled) by her "ecstasy." Her "passion burns [her] like fire," just as Basil's "idolatry" ultimately destroys him. "A burnt child loves the fire" [164], Henry comments, and "what the fire does not destroy, it hardens" [151]. Only Henry has learned this lesson and thereby outgrown his moral childhood. And only he endures because he no longer allows himself to get burned.

As the "son of love and death" [35], Dorian vascillates between Basil and Henry. However, he is not merely the product of other people's influence. Before Dorian meets Henry, Basil reports that he is not only "simple," trustworthy, candid, and pure, but also sadistic, "horribly thoughtless," "wilful," and selfish. That is, *by nature*, Dorian is drawn in opposite directions.[7] Hearing the voices of Henry and Sybil, he does not "know which [one] to follow" [46]. And he is similarly torn between Basil and Henry. "Of course I am very fond of Harry," he says to Basil, "but I know that you are better than he is." Yet, he continues, Basil is weaker than Henry—and more fearful. After his self-described callous reaction to Sybil, Dorian asks, "Why had he been made like that? Why had such a soul been given to him?" [77]. Hearing of Sybil's death and feeling even more remorseful about his behavior toward her, he believes "that the time [has] really come for making his choice" between Basil and Henry [88]. And after hiding the portrait, Dorian wavers between self-loathing, under Basil's influence, and pride, under Henry's.

Dorian lives his life according to Henry's principles rather than Basil's to the extent that he accepts Henry's world view, which first

---

7. Powell refers to Dorian's "joint-stock personality" ("Oscar Wilde 'Acting,'" p. 112), and Ed Cohen calls Dorian a projection of Henry and Basil ("Writing Gone Wilde: Homoerotic Desire in the Closet of Representation," *PMLA* 102 [1987]: 806).

impresses him like a "revelation": "Then had come Lord Henry Wotton with his strange panegyric on youth, his terrible warning of its brevity. That had stirred him at the time, and now, as he stood gazing at the shadow of his own loveliness, the full reality of the description flashed across him . . . The life that was to make his soul would mar his body. He would become dreadful, hideous, uncouth" [25]. Eventually, too, Dorian comes to believe that there is no moral order of the kind that Sybil, James, and Basil believe in. Haunted by memories of his evil deeds, Dorian first surmises that this is the way one pays for one's sins, as Basil had argued: "Each man lived his own life, and paid his own price for living it. The only pity was one had to pay so often for a single fault. One had to pay over and over again, indeed. In her dealings with man, Destiny never closed her accounts" [158]. On second thought, he concludes that this picture of Destiny or Fate or God is merely a product of his imagination: *"In the common world of fact the wicked were not punished, nor the good rewarded. Success was given to the strong, failure thrust upon the weak"* [165, my emphasis]. Although he is able to articulate it only at this rather late moment in the novel, this realization is hardly new to Dorian. After all, ever since his portrait became the repository of his suffering and guilt, he has assumed that he can act without fear of punishment, as his responses to the deaths of his friends indicate. Henry "disclosed to him life's mystery" [22], and he has lived with that understanding since his first encounter with his mentor.

Subsequent to this event, Dorian echoes Henry's sentiments on every subject; calls life, as Henry does, boring and disappointing; and espouses Henry's Nietzschean views: "Like the gods of the Greeks," he thinks, "he would be strong, and fleet, and joyous" [89]. When Basil questions his apparent indifference to Sybil's death, he replies: "A man who is master of himself can end a sorrow as easily as he can invent a pleasure. I don't want to be at the mercy of my emotions. I want to use them, to enjoy them, and to dominate them" [91]. What Dorian has learned in this instance, thanks largely to Henry's instruction, is that life is best experienced from the point of view of a spectator. He describes Sybil's death as extraordinarily dramatic and too wonderful for tears. And when Henry assures him that his reaction is not "heartless," Dorian gives full expression to Henry's theory of spectatorism: "I must admit that this thing that has happened does not affect me as it should. It seems to me simply like a wonderful ending to a wonderful play. It has all the terrible beauty of a Greek tragedy, a tragedy in which I took a great part, but by which I have not been wounded" [84]. Later, when Dorian shows Basil the portrait, he once again assumes the role of spectator—this time without even a shred of doubt or regret:

"The young man was leaning against the mantelshelf, watching [Basil] with that strange expression that one sees on the faces of those who are absorbed in a play when some great artist is acting. There was neither real sorrow in it nor real joy. There was simply the passion of the spectator, with perhaps a flicker of triumph in his eyes" [134].

Like Henry, Dorian is also motivated by intellectual curiosity. Early in the novel, he tells Henry how he wandered around in the East End of London looking for adventure and discovered Sybil Vane "in a labyrinth of grimy streets and black, grassless squares" [64]. He explains to Henry, "You filled me with a wild desire to know everything about life." After his rejection of Sybil, Dorian gazes "at the portrait with a feeling of almost scientific interest" [80]. He thinks that there might be "some curious scientific reason" for the alteration, yet he is content to examine the portrait for its revelations of his own nature: "For there would be a real pleasure in watching it. He would be able to follow his mind into its secret places. This portrait would be to him the most magical of mirrors. As it had revealed to him his own body, so it would reveal to him his own soul" [89]. He returns to the portrait often because "he grew more and more enamoured of his own beauty, more and more interested in the corruption of his own soul" (p. 159). All of this begins, it should be noted, when Dorian realizes that he has already made the choice to follow Henry rather than Basil: "Yes, life had decided that for him—life, and his own infinite curiosity about life" [88]. Eventually, however, his curiosity becomes obsessive and even insatiable: "The more he knew, the more he desired to know."

Dorian's hedonism grows out of Henry's proposal that Dorian should experience everything: "Let nothing be lost upon you. Be always searching for new sensations" [23]. Thus, along with "a mad curiosity" to know, Dorian develops "a passion for sensations" [44]. He justifies his quest for knowledge and pleasure by adopting Henry's theory of self-development: "But it appeared to Dorian that the true nature of the senses had never been understood, and that they had remained savage and animal merely because the world had sought to starve them into submission or to kill them by pain, instead of making them elements of a new spirituality, of which a fine instinct for beauty was to be the dominant characteristic." Dorian shares Henry's contempt for "puritanism"—self-torture and self-denial—but, unlike the man who espouses physical as well as intellectual exploration but only practices pure contemplation, he quests for sensual experience and adventure: the new Hedonism "was to have its service of the intellect, certainly; yet it was never to accept any theory or system that would involve the sacrifice of any mode of passionate experience. Its aim, indeed, was to be experience

itself, and not the fruits of experience, sweet or bitter as they may
be . . . It was to teach man to concentrate himself upon the
moments of a life that is itself but a moment" [108].

Of course, if Dorian had single-mindedly pursued these mental
and physical pleasures, he would have become just another cynic,
aloof from personal relationships, contemptuous of such emotions as
love and compassion (although intrigued by them), happy to watch
the operations of thought and passion in others, and sublimely indifferent to the consequences of his own ideas and actions. As a divided
man, however—"Each of us has heaven and hell in him," he tells
Basil [131]—Dorian cannot entirely repress the other side of his
nature. The day after he rejects Sybil, he suffers from remorse,
regrets his selfishness and cruelty, and considers it his "duty" to go
back to her. When he finds out about her death, he tells Henry: "You
don't know the danger I am in, and there is nothing to keep me
straight. She would have done that for me." Again, he wants to do his
"duty"—to do "what [is] right" [83–84]—thanks to Sybil's influence.
After he has decided to hide the portrait, Dorian regrets his failure to
explain his motives to Basil: "Basil would have helped him to resist
Lord Henry's influence [he thinks], and the still more poisonous
influences that came from his own temperament. The love that he
bore him—for it was really love—had nothing in it that was not noble
and intellectual . . . Yes, Basil could have saved him" [99]. The portrait itself serves as an even stronger reminder of his sins: "Compared
to what he saw in it of censure or rebuke, how shallow Basil's
reproaches about Sybil Vane had been! How shallow and of what
little account! His own soul was looking out at him from the canvas
and calling him to judgement" [99]. Even when Dorian visits "the
little ill-famed tavern near the Docks . . . under an assumed name,
and in disguise," he thinks "of the ruin he had brought upon his soul"
[106].

In fact, despite his powers of rationalization and the continuing
influence of Henry, Dorian is increasingly disturbed by doubts about
his moral freedom and stung by the pangs of a conscience that will
not die. He knows that his soul is "sick to death," and he hopes for
"atonement" although he also knows—or believes—that "forgiveness
[is] impossible" [154]. As he watches the suffering of the grotesque
creatures at his favorite opium den, he thinks: "They were better off
than he was. He was prisoned in thought. Memory, like a terrible
malady, was eating his soul away. From time to time he seemed to see
the eyes of Basil Hallward looking at him . . . He wanted to escape
from himself" [156]. His meeting with Adrian Singleton in the opium
den makes him consider "how terrible it was to think that conscience
could raise such fearful phantoms" as those that so frequently haunt
him:

What sort of life would his be, if day and night, shadows of his crime were to peer at him from silent corners, to mock him from secret places, to whisper in his ear as he sat at the feast, to wake him with icy fingers as he lay asleep! As the thought crept through his brain, he grew pale with terror, and the air seemed to him to have become suddenly colder. Oh! in what a wild hour of madness had he killed his friend! How ghastly the mere memory of the scene! He saw it all again. Each hideous detail came back to him with added horror. Out of the black cave of Time, terrible and swathed in scarlet, rose the image of his sin. When Lord Henry came in at six o'clock, he found him crying as one whose heart will break. [166]

Dorian concludes that he is "too much concentrated" on himself and that his "personality has become a burden" to him [169]. Threatened by James Vane, whose presence reminds him of his responsibility for Sybil's death, Dorian is again terrified: "Life had suddenly become too hideous a burden for him to bear" [170].

Six months later, under the influence of another young woman like Sybil, Dorian announces to Henry that he is in the process of mending his ways and forswearing his sinful pursuits. "I want to be better," he says. "I am going to be better" [172]. Against Henry's claims to the contrary, Dorian insists that "the soul is a terrible reality. It can be bought, and sold, and bartered away. It can be poisoned, or made perfect. There is a soul in each one of us. I know it" [177]. After his futile attempt to confess his murder of Basil to Henry, he continues to believe that he should be punished for his sins and that it is "his duty to confess." Indeed, he thinks, "There was a God who called upon men to tell their sins to earth as well as to heaven" [183]. In this mood of remorse, combined with the realization that he cannot stop sinning, Dorian decides to kill his conscience by destroying the portrait that, to him, embodies his moral sense. When he acts on this desperate impulse, of course, he kills himself because he has been, all along, a child of both Henry and Basil, and, unlike either of his mentors, both a hearty sinner and a reluctant penitent.

Yet the result of his occasional memory of Sybil and his intermittent recollection of the values of duty, conscience, and self-denial is not that Dorian actually changes. In fact, the long-term consequence of his double loyalty to Basil and Henry is that he turns more and more to sensation not as a means of intellectual discovery or a mode of aesthetic enjoyment, but as an escape from consciousness.[8] Of

---

8. "When he ceases to be a spectator of life and becomes enmeshed in the mundane realities of self-gratification and crime, his life and personality cease to be art, and the suspension of time which is art's great gift finally ends" (Ericksen, *Oscar Wilde*, p.115). See also Spivey, "Salvation and Damnation," pp.164–67.

course, Henry had told him that "to become a spectator of one's own life . . . is to escape from suffering" [92]. But when his suffering from experiences that Henry has never had becomes intolerable, Dorian loses control and breaks through the restraints that make Henry's life comparatively rational and relatively safe. Confronted by a "heart-broken" Basil after Sybil's death, Dorian asks him not to "talk about horrid subjects. If one doesn't talk about a thing, it has never happened. It is simply expression, as Henry says, that gives reality to things" [90]. When Basil is evidently upset by Dorian's cold-hearted response, Dorian says, "If you really want to console me, teach me rather to forget what has happened" [92].

By the time he has read—and reacted to—Henry's little yellow book, Dorian has several things to escape from, including the phantoms of memory that remind him of his sins and the portrait that documents the effect of those sins on his soul. He frequently arises from half-waking nightmares with "a wild longing" for a world of "pleasure," but a world, too, "in which the past would have little or no place, or survive, at any rate, in no conscious form of obligation or regret, the remembrance even of joy having its bitterness, and the memories of pleasure their pain" [109]. His collection of *objets d'art,* which might be taken to be a response to his love of beauty, is rather a "means of forgetfulness," a mode of "escape, for a season, from the fear that seemed to him at times to be almost too great to be borne." With "his passionate absorption in mere existence," Dorian can sometimes "forget" the portrait, "the hideous painted thing" that shows him "the real degradation of his life" [117]. After the murder of Basil, Dorian feels "that the secret of the whole thing is not to realize the situation"—that is, simply prevent it from entering his consciousness: "It was a thing to be driven out of the mind, to be drugged with poppies, to be strangled lest it might strangle one itself" [135].

Eventually, too, even Dorian's journeys into the darkest corners of London serve the same purpose. That is, the sordid world of violence, drugs, and prostitution, which originally appealed to him as a source of knowledge and pleasure, sooner or later becomes yet another means of escape: "There were opium dens where one could buy oblivion, dens of horror where the memory of old sins could be destroyed by the madness of sins that were new." Again, although he cannot atone for his sins or expect forgiveness, "forgetfulness was possible still, and he was determined to forget, to stamp the thing out, to crush it as one would crush the adder that had stung one." In the end, the same insatiability that makes his quest for knowledge obsessive and interminable turns his quest for pleasure into a virtual addiction: "Ugliness that had once been hateful to him because it made things real, became dear to him now for that very reason. Ugliness was the

458   SHELDON W. LIEBMAN

one reality. The coarse brawl, the loathsome den, the crude violence
of disordered life, the very vileness of thief and outcast, were more
vivid, in their intense actuality of impression, than all the gracious
shapes of Art, the dreamy shadows of Song. They were what he needed
for forgetfulness" [155]. Both pursuits take on the self-destructive
quality of his "hideous hunger for opium," and neither provides him
with the sense of fulfillment that he originally expected and that Henry,
in his naiveté, continues to believe Dorian is achieving.[9]

As I have suggested, Dorian is best understood as not just another
personage in *The Picture of Dorian Gray*, but as the central character, whose situation is clarified by the opposition between Basil and
Henry, his guides and confidants. Their principal task is to articulate
mutually exclusive moral positions and, in so doing, to define the
moral options available to Dorian. They are essentially "flat" characters in that they do not change in the course of the novel. In effect,
they have already chosen a way of life. And unlike Dorian, therefore,
they are not confronted by either the challenge of moral choice or
the opportunity for moral growth. They simply demonstrate by their
actions the consequences of thinking and living as they do. In this
way, they show the reader (and Dorian) the limitations of their
respective positions. And insofar as they reflect moral tendencies
latent in Dorian (e.g., self-indulgence and self-denial) and even
aspects of his psyche (e.g., instinct and conscience), they reveal, as
well, the human cost of choosing one position over the other. Thus,
if Dorian had accepted Basil's moralism, he would not have fallen
into a life of sin. And if he had fully adopted Henry's insouciance, he
would not have been burdened by remorse. Either way, however, he
would have sacrificed some dimension of his personality, in which
case, from Wilde's point of view, he would have been either a fool
(albeit a "good" one), ignorant of the natural laws of the universe, or
a parasite (albeit an interesting one), morally isolated and emotion-
ally detached from ordinary human relationships.

In this respect, Dorian is truly the man in the middle, unable to
deny the demands of his superego and equally unable to repress the
yearnings of his passions. As a victim of this psychological double
bind, he is not merely a hedonist paying for his sins, but a kind of
Everyman, whose dilemma is a product of his human endowment. In
short, if Wilde's goal was to unite instinct and conscience, then
Dorian appears to be the *locus* on which this endeavor is carried

9. Wilde comments: "There are moments, psychologists tell us, when the passion for sin, or
for what the world calls sin, so dominates a nature, that every fibre of the body, as every
cell of the brain, seems to be instinct with fearful purposes. Men and women at such times
lose the freedom of their will. They move to their terrible ends as automatons move. Choice
is taken from them, and conscience is either killed, or if it lives at all, lives but to give rebellion its fascination, and disobedience its charm" [168].

out—unsuccessfully and inevitably, as Freud would argue almost forty years later in *Civilization and Its Discontents*. In this regard, *The Picture of Dorian Gray* is a test of at least one of Wilde's basic tenets—his belief in self-harmony and self-development—supported, to be sure, by the logic of his theorizing in "The Soul of Man under Socialism" but disconfirmed by the logic of his narrative (perhaps for him, as for T.S. Eliot, a more valid test of truth than mere philosophical speculation).

It may be difficult for some readers to see Dorian Gray as Wilde's Everyman—that is, as the character who, embodying all the elements of humanity (instinct and conscience, skepticism and faith, appreciation of both life and art), represents humanity's last, best hope. In fact, however, Dorian confronts the great moral issue of the nineteenth century, which is dramatized in the novels of the Brontës, Thackeray, Hawthorne, George Eliot, Meredith, Melville, James, and Hardy. This is the war between competing moral visions: paganism vs. puritanism, Hellenism vs. Hebraism, hedonism vs. stoicism.[1] In these writers' works, Wilde's Henry is anticipated by such self-indulgent aristocrats as Edward Rochester, Arthur Donnithorne, and Gilbert Osmond as well as by such philosophical individualists as Heathcliff, Hester Prynne, and Captain Ahab. Wilde's Basil has his literary antecedents in an equally large array of puritans and conformists. And Dorian is that rarer central figure—like Arthur Dimmesdale, Jane Eyre, Isabel Archer, and Tess Derbyfield—whose task is not to *choose* between, say, Silas Marner and Godfrey Cass or between Arabella Donn and Sue Bridehead, but to find a middle (or higher) ground. Psychologically the goal of these central characters is to become fully human, which means not giving up any aspect of the self, but reconciling body and soul, heart and mind, instinct and conscience. Morally their goal is to resolve the conflict between two mutually exclusive standards of conduct, neither of which is tenable on its own terms.

Returning to this perennial battlefield, Dorian may either resolve these opposing visions through accommodation and compromise (or even transcendence) or fail to resolve them, not because he, uniquely, cannot, but because—as in *The Mill on the Floss*, *Pierre*, and *Tess of the d'Urbervilles*—resolution is impossible.[2] In the typical

1. According to Jan B. Gordon, "Wilde's novel recalls those other nineteenth-century novels that, in one way or another, treat of the education of youth" ("'Parody as Initiation': The Sad Education of *Dorian Gray*," *Criticism* 9 [1967]: 355).
2. In this respect, Gordon concludes, *Dorian Gray* is a "semi-parody" of "nineteenth-century prophetic novels" (p.370). Peter Ackroyd comments: "Wilde represents in plangent form the most abiding preoccupations of his period—at the end of a century, it was a time of sadness and sterility when the most acute talents understood that a world, and a world of values, was coming to an end . . . [T]hey could find nothing to put in its place. That is one reason for the emptiness and despair at the heart of *Dorian Gray*, and on one level we may read this book as an epitaph for Victorian civilization" ("Introduction," p.14).

Victorian novel, cosmic justice is confirmed (the good are rewarded, though chastened, and the evil are punished), moral certainty is attainable (indeed, experience itself, though sometimes cruel and harsh, teaches morality), personal responsibility is assumed, and self-unification is possible. In the universe occupied by Dorian Gray, however, these verities do not hold. The novel culminates in a suicide rather than a marriage. The narrator is an observer, not a moralist. And the central character disintegrates instead of acquiring a credible, coping self. In this respect, *The Picture of Dorian Gray* signals the end of a literary era and looks forward to those other turn-of-the-century and pre-World War I novels of cosmic despair and moral paralysis: Gide's *The Immoralist*, Chopin's *The Awakening*, Hardy's *Jude the Obscure*, Mann's *Death in Venice*, Dreiser's *Sister Carrie*, and Wharton's *Ethan Frome*. In all of them, the self, cut loose from its conventional moral and metaphysical moorings, struggles earnestly and ends tragically—a victim of excess, confusion, or obsession. Not merely a nineties romp, Wilde's novel stands among them, as another important work of the period, addressing the major moral issues of the day (and of *any* day), and a significant contribution not only to aestheticism, but to modernism.

MAUREEN O'CONNOR

The Picture of Dorian Gray as Irish National Tale†

It has become increasingly common to link Oscar Wilde's self-identification as Irish to his radically oppositional stance *vis-à-vis* late-Victorian Britain. For Wilde insisted on his Celtic nature whenever he wished to be perverse about identity, and it is the very fissured and fantastic nature of his idea of Ireland that enables what is in this essay to be called Wilde's national (dis)identification. For Wilde, Ireland was as much an imaginary geography as Japan, which the essay 'The Decay of Lying' asserts 'is a pure invention. There is no such country, there are no such people'; it is 'the deliberate self-conscious creation of certain individual artists. . . . If you want to see a Japanese effect, you will not behave like a tourist and go to Tokio.'[1] In fact, if you could not see an 'absolutely Japanese effect' in Piccadilly, you could not see it anywhere. Ireland, as distant from and foreign to

† From *Writing Irishness in Nineteenth-Century British Culture*, ed. Neil McCraw (Aldershot, Hants: England; Burlington, VT: Ashgate, 2004), 194–209. Reprinted by permission. Bracketed page numbers refer to this Norton Critical Edition.
1. Oscar Wilde, 'The Decay of Lying,' in *The Collected Works of Oscar Wilde* (New York, 1989), p.988.

England as Japan, is also seen as experienced most vividly when outside the island's geographical borders, when it becomes an entirely abstract *elsewhere*. Wilde's Irishness could only be realized when most unreal and distant; he recalled that at home his intellect 'had but learned the pathetic weakness of nationality, but in a strange land realized what indomitable forces nationality possesses.'[2]

Ireland has often figured as an *elsewhere*, unable to achieve a materiality in the British imagination. The multiplicity, contradictions, and discontinuities of post-Union colonial Ireland produced startling literary hybrids. Luke Gibbons is just one of the critics who has remarked on the 'proto-modernist strategies of Irish Romanticism' that developed in a society bearing all the hallmarks of modernity's 'disintegration and fragmentation.'[3] In discussing the unassimilability of nineteenth-century Ireland to British conventions of realist fiction, David Lloyd has noted the 'peculiar intensity' with which 'Irish culture plays out the anomalous states of a population whose most typical experience may be that of occupying multiple locations, literally and figuratively.'[4] One manifestation of this irreducible multiplicity occurred early in the century when, in 1806, Sydney Owenson, more famously known as Lady Morgan, wrote *The Wild Irish Girl*, the first 'national tale,' a uniquely Irish literary form that Ina Ferris has called a 'distinct genre founded in the British peripheries.'[5] The Irish national tale will be seen to be a form that uses the conventions of the travel narrative and the gothic, among other genres, telling the story of colonized Ireland often by recounting the journey of a young member of the Anglo-Irish Ascendancy who leaves London to see, usually for the first time, the exotic, unfamiliar land to which he nominally belongs. Yet he is a stranger, neither alien nor native in a land with which his connection must be kept secret, through which he can only enter under disguise. This traumatic experience of estrangement evacuates notions of identity and often entails physical violence and erotic complications. The simultaneous dislocation of the English protagonist and the English reader blurs the distinctions between *over here* and *over there* and threatens the primacy and integrity of patriarchal, metropolitan reasoning.

It is the central contention of this essay that Oscar Wilde's novel *The Picture of Dorian Gray* not only participated in his native country's

2. Quoted in Declan Kiberd's 'The London Exiles: Wilde and Shaw,' in *The Field Day Anthology of Irish Writing*, volume 2, edited by Seamus Deane (Derry, 1991), p.375.
3. Luke Gibbons, *Transformations in Irish lture* (Notre Dame, 1996), pp.6/7
4. David Lloyd, *Anomalous States: Irish Writing and the Postcolonial Moment* (Durham, 1993), p.53.
5. Ina Ferris, 'Narrating Cultural Encounter: Lady Morgan and the Irish National Tale,' *Nineteenth-Century Fiction*, 15:3 (December 1996), p.288.

literary engagement with the gothic, as has often been noted, but also that it resurrected the Romantic genre of the national tale. Like the hero of the national tale, Wilde travels through this uncanny native territory, undercover, without signalling his intentions. And, just as Terry Eagleton suggests that the formal 'dishevelment' of Lady Morgan's national tales most truthfully represents a past that is 'not identical with itself,'[6] in *The Picture of Dorian Gray* Wilde emphasizes the necessarily fantastic nature of the allegorization of a nation traumatized by its relationship to the past in *his* tale of a journey away from the familiar through an exotic inner landscape made by an individual who is imperfectly reflected in a past that both threatens and sustains. Yet, Wilde's deployment in this novel of the national tale is as disembodied and paradoxical as his deployment of Irishness itself, a politically and historically 'feminized' category also wielded with self-consciousness by Lady Morgan. For his enunciation of Irishness, as has been argued elsewhere, proceeds from a site of impious authority gained through the pollution, hybridizing, and transvaluing of the rigid tenets of Victorian determinism, including notions of sex and gender. This reminds us of colonialism's 'feminization' of Irishness, its representation of Gaelic culture as, in Lloyd's words, 'primitive' and 'fragmented.'[7] In what Jonathan Dollimore calls Wilde's 'anti-essentialist transgressive aesthetic,'[8] his radical decentring of the self, the only identification possible is a necessarily impossible one with the *lost* and *fragmented*.

On its publication, *The Picture of Dorian Gray* was roundly excoriated in the press for its 'effeminate frivolity,' for being 'unmanly, sickly, vicious,' and corrupting of morals.[9] Interestingly, Regenia Gagnier contends that 'the outcry against Wildean decadence on the part of gentlemen journalists was in part an outcry against the male author who won support from Society . . . by writing a book that would appeal to women.'[1] Morgan's *The Wild Irish Girl* was also liable to charges of frivolity, whilst being more popularly received among women readers. Its author was (and continued to be until only very recently) 'dismissed as a purveyor of romantic nonsense,'[2] even charged in one contemporary review with attempting to vitiate mankind, of 'attempting to undermine morality by sophistry.'[3] Yet,

6. Terry Eagleton, *Heathclif and the Great Hunger: Studies in Irish Culture* (London, 1996), p.183.
7. Lloyd, 1993, p.45.
8. Jonathon Dollimore, *Sexual Dissidence: Augustine to Wilde, Freud to Foucault* (Oxford, 1991), p.4.
9. Reginia Gagnier, *Idylls of the Marketplace: Oscar Wilde and the Victorian Public* (Stanford, 1986), pp.58–9.
1. *Ibid.*, p.66.
2. Mary Campbell, *Lady Morgan: The Life and Times of Sydney Owenson* (Surrey, 1988), p.240.
3. From an 1806 review in the *Freeman's Journal* by John Wilson Croker, quoted in Campbell, 1988, p.72.

according to Mary Campbell, Morgan 'was really attacked because the political message beneath the nonsense was a powerful and persuasive one,'[4] and Dublin Castle orchestrated negative reviews out of fear of her influence.[5]

Many biographical parallels can be drawn between Morgan and Wilde. Eagleton makes an explicit comparison to Wilde when commending Morgan's 'affront to a certain species of male rationality.' He goes on to applaud her 'calculatedly histrionic attempt to live a kind of utopia in the present, the admirable narcissism and self-devotion by which she refused female obscurity and converted her domestic life into a public stage.'[6] She did so by adopting a persona from her own fiction, 'Glorvina, the wild Irish girl,' names by which she came to be known both socially and in the popular imagination. The novel created a craze among viceregal women for 'Glorvina' brooches and capes, and for golden bodkins to wear the hair in the native style of Morgan's heroine.[7] As with Wilde, Morgan was 'accused of social climbing, of sycophancy to the English aristocrat,'[8] but as Dollimore points out, 'to be half successful is to lay claim to sharing with the dominant [class] (though never equally) a language, culture, and identity: to participate in it is also to contaminate the dominant's authenticity and to counter its discriminatory function.'[9]

Just as Morgan's 'theatricality functioned in large part parodically and polemically as a form of cover or critique,'[1] so did Wilde's outrageously campy self-parody perform a scathing critique of regulating fictions of not only normative masculinity, but of class and country as well. As McCormack notes, Wilde 'understands that style is a miniature politics.'[2] Of Morgan's The Wild Irish Girl, Anne Fogarty has also observed the text 'uncover[s] and insist[s] upon the connections between politics and aesthetics.'[3] Yet Wilde's politics is much more concentrated in the area of self-identity fashioning. In Alan Sinfield's words, Wilde 'validat[es] the frivolous and knowing stance of the dandified, feminine woman' in his assumption of a persona from his own fictional creations,[4] which always feature at least one char-

4. Ibid., p.240.
5. Ibid., p.71.
6. Eagleton, 1996, p.184.
7. See Campbell, pp.71–2, and Thomas Flanagan, The Irish Novelists, 1800–1850 (New York, 1957), p.125.
8. Campbell, 1988, p.4.
9. Dollimore, 1991, p.51.
1. Ibid., p.51.
2. W. J. McCormack, 'Irish Gothic and After,' in Deane (ed.), 1991, p.846.
3. Anne Fogarty, 'Imperfect Concord: Spectres of History in the Irish Novels of Maria Edgeworth and Lady Morgan,' in Gender Perspectives in Nineteenth-Century Ireland; Public and Private Spheres, edited by Margaret Kelleher and James Murphy (Dublin, 1997), p.118.
4. Alan Sinfield, The Wilde Century: Effeminism, Oscar Wilde, and the Queer Moment (London, 1994), p.55.

acter who seems to invite being read as a Wilde surrogate. This threatening, theatrical, aggressively fictional self-fashioning, which problematizes foundational ideas about identity, social role, position, and even race, was seized upon as evidence of hypocrisy and irrelevance by his enemies. From the time of Wilde's lecture tour in America right through to his trial, the popular media abounded with representations of an exceptionally dandified, outrageously aesthetic Wilde, in clumsy attempts at parody. Likewise the figure of 'Glorvina,' who stands in similar metonymic relation to her creator as does the cultural counter known as *Oscar Wilde* to the author of the same name, was pilloried almost exclusively by men, most famously by William Thackeray in his novel *Vanity Fair*. Both authors 'refashioned an Irishness which is both overperformed and overdetermined,'[5] and, paradoxically, used that stylized Irishness both to highlight their otherness, their peripheral status, and at the same time to become privileged insiders. Therein they gained access to the metropolitan 'centre' where they wielded considerable cultural power.

Wilde's politics of dis-identification with hegemony, orthodoxy, and authority is not simply a rejection of patriarchy, but an active embrace of the maternal, the feminine, the abject. The threat to patriarchy that Julia Kristeva has observed in the mother-child relationship, that earliest and most fundamental relationship, which excludes the father and provides a potential refuge from the reign of the official or symbolic,[6] informs Wilde's aesthetics as well as his politics. Paternity is rarely an issue in his plays, for instance, while secrets of origin and identity in relation to mothers are much more common. Note, for example, Mrs Erlynne in *Lady Windermere's Fan*, Mrs Arbuthnot in *A Woman of No Importance*, and the extratextual Mrs Moncrieff of *The Importance of Being Earnest*. The pattern pervades in *The Picture of Dorian Gray*. Dorian's father, an insignificant subaltern in a foot-regiment who is never named, appears in the narrative briefly only to be immediately dispatched and even dehumanized in the casually related story of a duel that leaves him 'spitted . . . as if he had been a pigeon' [32]. It is to his late mother, from whom he has inherited his 'finely-curved scarlet lips, his fair blue eyes, his crisp gold locks' [17], that Dorian turns when pondering the mystery of himself, that 'complex, multiform creature.' In the 'gaunt cold picture gallery of his country house,' Dorian Gray lingers in front of a painting of his mother, the intemperate and fascinating Lady Devereux (whose family name is that of

5. Neil Sammells, describing Wilde's anti-imperialist deployment of style, in *Wilde Style*, p.12.
6. Julia Kristeva, *The Powers of Horror: an essay in abjection*, translated by Leon Roudiez (New York, 1984), p.3.

the Earl of Essex, Lord Lieutenant of Ireland under Elizabeth I who
was beheaded for treason against the crown). She wears 'vine leaves
in her hair,' and a 'loose Bacchante dress,' laughing at him with 'wine-
dashed lips. . . . Her eyes are still wonderful in their depth and brilliancy of colour. They seemed to follow him everywhere.' Under this
ambiguous maternal gaze Dorian reviews the centuries of portraits of
'those whose blood flowed through his veins,' and contemplates his
'strange legacies of thought and passion.' The narrator observes that
'one had ancestors in literature as well as one's own race, nearer perhaps in type and temperament, many of them, and certainly with an
influence of which one was more absolutely conscious' [121]. And
Lady Devereux's legacy of physical beauty, recalling that of Glorvina,
the 'wild Irish girl' of Morgan's novel with her 'eyes rich blue, her
cheek's crimson blush, . . . her golden tresses,'[7] is not the only 'family resemblance' or 'strange legacy of thought' that haunts Wilde's
novel.

The use of gothic elements within the national tale complements
critical discussions of *Dorian Gray*'s incorporation of gothic tropes
and techniques, offering the basis for correspondences between
Wilde's text and the gothic novel, *Melmoth the Wanderer*, written in
1820 by Charles Maturin. Interestingly, Maturin was Wilde's uncle
by marriage. Certainly the character of Melmoth, frozen in an
unbearable immortality, driven by guilt across time and space in
search of an elusive expiation, figures significantly in the creation of
Dorian Gray. Eagleton sees the embodiment of the paradox of Anglo-
Irish relations in Melmoth, whose story functions 'as an allegory of
this strange condition in which exploiter and victim are both
strangers and comrades, and, indeed, in the person of Melmoth himself, inhabit the same personality.'[8] *Dorian Gray*'s debt to the gothic,
especially in its peculiarly Irish survival to the end of the century in
what W. J. McCormack characterizes as a 'fugitive and discontinuous' fashion,[9] has been widely recognized. But another rarely
acknowledged literary ancestor of Dorian's appears in another of
Maturin's Irish national tales, *The Wild Irish Boy*, a parodic response
to Morgan's novel, written in 1808.

The eponymous Wild Irish Boy, Ormsby Bethel, has a 'form to
make libertinism lovely, with a cheek like the red rose leaf.'[1] He drives
admirers to desperation, even to suicide. One observer says of him,
'I wish he would be either angel or human . . . but this mixture of
loveliness and depravity . . . so confounds my mind—what principles

---

7. Lady Morgan, *The Wild Irish Girl* (Poole, 1995), volume 1, p.174.
8. Eagleton, 1996, p.190.
9. W.J. McCormack, 'Irish Gothic and After,' p.831.
1. *The Wild Irish Boy*, volume 1, p.26.

I have left are so shaken and shattered.'[2] 'Why,' another voice cries, 'is vice suffered to look so lovely?' A similar question, 'with your pure, bright, innocent face . . . why is your friendship so fatal to young men?'[3] will be asked of Dorian Gray who shares Bethel's blond beauty, is also 'made out of ivory and rose-leaves' (as Lord Henry describes him) and is the subject of 'strange conjectures' like those that surround Bethel. *The Wild Irish Boy*, then, with its epicene protagonist, 'almost a boy with the form of a girl and the feelings of a man,'[4] provides the pedigree papers, as it were, for the generic transmission being suggested in this essay, but legitimacy is not of much moment when it comes to Wilde, and paternity, again, seems less insistently important than maternity. Maturin enters into a kind of polemical debate with *The Wild Irish Girl* that seeks to, as Ferris puts it, 'unwrite the hopeful trope'[5] of Morgan's plea for tolerance. Maturin literally *counters* Morgan's novel with characters whose correspondences to Morgan's are established, as signalled by the title, through glib reversals. Not only is Bethel a boy rather than a girl, but also, unlike Glorvina's repeatedly detailed and valorized cultural and national identity, Bethel's Irishness is a fugitive, occluded, faintly unsavoury entity, only confirmed with his mysterious father's death. Morgan's admittedly treacly paragons become debauched sexual intriguers in Maturin. Glorvina's sickly, much-sinned-against, saintly, almost incorporeal father, the Prince of Inismore, who spends his dwindling days in rarefied intellectual and spiritual communion with his trusty confessor (the wise and innocent Father John) is revisited by Maturin. He is transfigured into a wild, dissolute Milesian Chief engaged in heated sexual competition with *his* confessor for the favours of a louche French woman. The naive, chaste, unworldly Glorvina herself appears in the novel as a fancy dress costume worn by one of the novel's most lecherous women.

In his polarized literary treatment, Maturin can only imagine what seem to him the intransigent problems of Ireland as rigid oppositions set in bitter counterpoint, at best painfully yoked together. Though Morgan's Irish fiction is at least as partisan, what Maturin binds in inveterate indissoluble hatred, Morgan imagines blending through love. However, Morgan's vision of a salvific marriage of hereditary enemies requires its own violence and is not so easily reduced to facile sentiment. The ancient breach between cultures can only be healed if that wound is realized on the English body and in the English mind. Horatio Mortimer, the Londoner in *The Wild Irish Girl* who leaves the metropolis for the estate of his absentee-landlord

2. *Ibid.*, p.26.
3. *Ibid.*, p.117.
4. *Ibid.*, volume 2, p.22.
5. Ferris, 'Narrating Cultural Encounter,' p.302.

father whose lands were once the demesne of the Prince of Inismore, falls from a crumbling wall at the sound of Glorvina's voice and is seriously injured.[6] Hidden, feminine Ireland pierces his consciousness, and he is literally thrown off balance. Mortimer's injury grants him entry into the Prince's derelict castle where, as his body heals, his imperial identity undergoes further disintegration as he is not only rendered physically passive and immobile, but must adopt an alias, relating the 'feigned story' that he is a poor, but well-born, artmaster travelling Ireland to study its 'wildly picturesque character.' The wound sustained by Mortimer lets indeterminacy, here a softening, feminizing force, enter.

Similarly, in *Dorian Gray*, a female voice sounded from an unreal country, that of Sybil Vane (a woman as untouched by the 'real' world as Glorvina), also precipitates the protagonist's fall into self-estrangement and signals the end of conventional narrative accommodations. Therein it increases the text's resemblance to the 'disheveled,' mongrel genre of the national tale. Wilde's rewriting of the national tale does not unwrite it as Maturin's does, but moreover deploys parody as an ironic inversion that does not ridicule, is not at the expense of the original text.[7] His incognito Englishman becomes *hardened* to feelings as he becomes feminized; that is, as he grows more acquisitive, more enigmatic and ever more preoccupied with his looks, and as the text makes more frequent recourse to the language of melodrama.

Morgan's gesture of pulling the familiar ground out from under the self-sufficient, self-identical metropolitan figure in order to reach a new ground on the unmapped peripheries, a literal dislocation to a 'neutral ground between positive reception and negative hostility,'[8] has much in common with the receding ground of certainty constantly effaced and refigured by Wilde's discursive strategies of defamiliarization, disorientation, dislocation, and misdirection. Morgan describes her own rhetorical strategy as one in which 'approbation is sought rather by a description of what is not, than a portraiture of what is,'[9] looking away from what she would indicate. This is a paradoxical mode similar to that deployed by Wilde, who, as Neil Sammells notes, 'display[s] difference in order to deny it.'[1] Morgan,

---

6. In *Ennui*, a novel that owes much to Morgan's *The Wild Irish Girl*, Maria Edgeworth recreates this scene when her English hero, in Ireland for the first time, suffers a serious fall from his horse at the sound of an Irish woman's voice. According to Julia Kristeva, 'the ear is receptive to conflicts only if the body loses its footing,' *Strangers to Ourselves*, translated by Leon Roudiez (New York, 1984), p.17.
7. Linda Hutcheon, *A Theory of Parody: The Teaching of Twentieth-Century Art Forms* (Urbana, 2000), pp.4–8.
8. Ferris, 'Narrating Cultural Encounter,' p.294.
9. Lady Morgan, *O'Donnel: A National Tale* (London, 1814), p.viii.
1. 'Rediscovering the Irish Wilde,' in *Rediscovering Oscar Wilde* (Gerards Cross, 1994), p.369.

daughter of an Irish father and English mother, repeatedly returns in her fiction to a salutary miscegenation, an erotic dissolving and intermingling of historic antipodes. Similarly, Wilde, recognizing that binary oppositions inhere in each other, worked to undermine perceived antinomies and reveal unsuspected alliances. The erotic charge implicit in this undoing and violation of the categories of 'native' and 'foreigner' lends what may be an unintended suggestiveness to Declan Kiberd's observation that in Wilde's view 'every good man has an element of the woman in him, just as every secret Irishman must have a secret Englishman within himself—and vice-versa.'[2]

The secret shufflings and exchanges of identity, the doublings and redoublings, in both Morgan and Wilde, points to the inherent instability of the project of representing Ireland to the nineteenth-century English reader that produces haunted, reflexive texts. Seamus Deane diagnoses the Irish writer's 'impossible relationship to his audience' as unavoidable 'when the English audience lives in the everyday world; the Irish writer and the Irish culture belong to a surreal world.'[3] Furthermore, Wilde's volatilized, refractive relationship to his culture extends to his interaction with his literary forbears; like Dorian in his picture gallery, the insistently 'modern' Wilde is always in communion with his predecessors, as evident in his densely allusive texts that quote, reformulate, parody, and borrow from a multitude of sources,[4] practices that can now be appreciated as anticipating postmodernism, but which laid Wilde open to repeated charges of plagiarism in his day. Wilde does not simply copy, however, nor does he effect simple reversals; he 'produces more than the inverse of [the] more familiar original,'[5] according to Lawrence Danson, who also speaks of 'that distinctive, unmistakable quality we call Wildean . . . an originality founded on the already made, a newness that flaunts belatedness.'[6] 'The Critic as Artist' claims that 'for he to whom the present is the only thing that is present, knows nothing of the age in which he lives.'[7] Wilde's work constantly engages with other times, other texts. His art is only possible through appreciation and appropriation: 'the imagination is the result of heredity. It is simply concentrated race experience.'[8]

The most famous works of the peerless conversationalist Wilde, his

2. Kiberd, 'Exile,' p.373.
3. Neil Sammells, 'Irish National Character,' in *The Writer as Witness: Literature as Historical Evidence*, edited by Tom Dunne (Cork, 1987), pp.102, 101.
4. Lawrence Danson, *Wilde's Intentions: The Artist in His Criticism* (Oxford, 1997), citing Patricia Clements's adaptation of a term of Harold Bloom's, characterizes Wilde's relations to other writers as 'anthological,' p.168n.
5. Danson, 1997, p.127.
6. *Ibid.*, p.26.
7. Wilde, 'The Critic as Artist,' in *The Collected Works of Oscar Wilde*, p.1040
8. *Ibid.*, p.1041.

plays and essays, are as such essentially dialogues. Morgan's national tales are similarly dialogic heteroglossias in which the narrative competes with extensive historical, ethnographic, and antiquarian footnotes drawn from a wide range of both modern and ancient texts in several different languages. Joep Leerssen says of *The Wild Irish Girl* that it only 'pretends to be about Ireland,' but 'is in fact about other texts about Ireland.'[9] According to Eagleton, in Morgan 'the present continually threatens to open out into complexly stratified genealogies, where . . . the ancient and the modern are brought into arrestingly immediate encounter . . . The present, then, is a kind of allegory, which properly interpreted lays bare the historical forces at its heart.'[1] This links with Richard Pine's reminder that the 'decadent nature of much of Irish narrative' is 'permeated with a sense of ruin,'[2] and with Ina Ferris's recognition of the national tale as the 'unstable matrix of Irish temporalities . . . the weird recognition, that betrays [a] rational sense of time, place, and identity . . . , a stranger temporality, one that places the present inside the past and the past inside the present.'[3] This unfixing of time places past and present in disconcerting proximity and forces 'weird recognition,' recalling the supernatural plot of *Dorian Gray*. The evocation of modernity within the novel is thus distinguished by a particularly insistent and devastating 'sense of ruin,' with a protagonist who experiences self-estrangement as 'an unstable matrix of temporalities' as he places himself outside of chronology. We are told that Dorian 'was imprisoned in thought. Memory, like a horrible malady, was eating his soul away' [156], a malady that succinctly describes colonial Ireland's traumatic relationship to a history that defies linear models of progress.

In the national tales of Morgan and Maturin, Ireland seems at first to promise a place of refuge from temptation for the voyaging Londoner, but because of the irrational survival of an ancient, fractured, traumatized history, the alien land then confronts the protagonist, often violently. The guilt and desire in which he has been implicated due to accidents of heredity, accidents that have established arbitrary designations of 'self' and 'other,' 'native' and 'alien,' prove difficult to maintain on boggy Irish soil where such distinctions are only entertained ironically. The detail of both Morgan and Maturin as regards

---

9. Joep Leerssen, 'How *The Wild Irish Girl* Made Ireland Romantic,' *Dutch Quarterly Review of Anglo-Irish Letters* 18 (1988), p.217.
1. Eagelton, 1996, p.183.
2. Richard Pine, *The Thief of Reason: Oscar Wilde and Modern Ireland* (New York, 1995), p.57.
3. Ferris, 'Writing on the border: The national tale, feminism, and the public sphere,' *Romanticism, history, and the possibilities of genre*, edited by Tilottama Rajan and Julia M. Wright (Cambridge, 1998), p.99.

the journey from London to Ireland, a place hidden from English
eyes, contributes to a sense of degeneracy into atavism and fractured
temporality (and, paradoxically, a sphere of possible redemption).

Crucially, Dorian Gray retreats to a similarly marked territory, the
savage outreaches of the self, rarely seen on the public stage of the
proper Victorian gentleman. As he journeys into this outland, Dorian
accumulates a lavish, dazzling and carefully catalogued collection of
aesthetic objects. The novel's decorative accretions signal ontologi-
cal instability and do so in an Oriental register. Criticism has treated
Dorian's opium and his superfetation of Eastern art objects as reflecting a burgeoning British consumerism built upon the spoils of
empire, but this does not consider all that Empire would imply to the
Irishman Wilde. For Eve Kosofsky Sedgwick aligns *Dorian Gray's* orientalism with consumerism, addiction, and homosexuality.[4] In doing
so Sedgwick focuses on the exemplary moment of the novel's 'com-
modity-based orientalism,' in which Dorian turns to opium for relief
from his agitation after committing murder:

> It was a small Chinese box of black and gold-dust lacquer, elab-
> orately wrought, the sides patterned with curved waves, and the
> silken cords hung with round crystals and tasselled in plaited
> metal threads [. . .]. Inside was a *green* paste, waxy in lustre,
> the odour curiously heavy and persistent [152–53; emphasis
> added].

What Sedgwick does not note (and, to be fair, it is not central to
her argument) is the *greenness* at the heart of this ornate chinoiserie,
a seductive, powerful, dangerous greenness that opens out into the
depths of degeneracy and deviance. And, Greenness comprises a
complex constellation of associations for Wilde, as Vicki Mahaffey
and others have pointed out.[5] In *Sexual Inversions,* Wilde's widely
read contemporary, sexologist Havelock Ellis, observes that 'inverts
exhibit a preference for green garments.'[6] Wilde himself speaks of a
'curious love of green, which in individuals is always the sign of a
subtle artistic sentiment and in countries is said to denote a laxity, if
not a decadence of morals.'[7] Green is at once natural and unnatural, the colour of the artificially tinted carnation he frequently wore,
the colour of resistance and inversion. Wilde is quoted as saying that
'the colour green and Hell are both made for thieves and artists.'[8]
Green is all of these things simultaneously when it is the colour of

---

4. Eve Kosofsky Sedgwick, *Epistemology of the Closet* (Berkeley, 1990), pp.170–78.
5. See Vicki Mahaffey, *States of Desire: Wilde, Yeats, and the Irish Experiment* (Oxford, 1998),
    p.52.
6. Havelock Ellis, *Sexual Inversion* [1897] (New York, 1975), pp.125/6.
7. Wilde, 'Pen, Pencil and Poison: A Study in Green,' in *The Collected Works of Oscar Wilde*,
    p.996.
8. Quoted in Mahaffey, 1998, p.52.

Ireland, itself a conceptual nexus where vexed notions of nation, race, identity, and sexuality intersect. This is reinforced by the complex system of Celtic imagery that supports the decorative scheme of *Dorian Gray*, which David Upchurch has demonstrated at some length.[9]

The equivalence posited aesthetically in Wilde's novel between Ireland and the Orient is one that also appears in Morgan's *The Wild Irish Girl*, an equivalence of significance when its articulation is directed at readers situated within an empire in which, as Joseph Lew observes, 'peripheries can be interchangeable within the imaginative vision.'[1] The qualities Edward Said attributes to the early-nineteenth-century discourse of Orientalism, its lack of an objective Orient, its contention that accuracy is abhorrent to the Oriental mind, for instance,[2] also serves as an iteration of nineteenth-century British attitudes toward Ireland and the Irish. Both Wilde and Morgan attempt demystification and rehabilitation of these stereotypes through transgressive emphasis. Throughout *The Wild Irish Girl* Ireland becomes, as Lew notes, 'interchangeable with more recently acquired colonies in the East,'[3] from Mortimer's initial despair at being stranded in what he considers an 'Arabia Deserta,'[4] to his later admiration of the Irish language to which he has come to pay 'the same respect a Hindoo would to the Sanscrit of the Bramins.'[5] This continues in Glorvina's elaborate Eastern genealogies of Irish costume, music, and dance. While her characters 'view their oriental ancestors as the creators of civilization,'[6] Morgan recognizes the Orient's association with, in the words of Said, 'not only fecundity but sexual promise (and threat), untiring sensuality, unlimited desire, deep generative energies.'[7] Morgan's novel comically conflates these contradictory valuations of the East when Mortimer, who suspects his father of having hidden away a native Irish mistress in a lodge at the wildest, most remote peripheries of his property, discovers that 'his father's Sultana is no other than the Irish Muse.'[8] 'The fancied harem,' he says, 'I found not only divested of its expected fair inhabitant, but wholly destitute of furniture.' And, deeper within the lodge a locked chamber is revealed to be a study containing 'all books related to language, history and antiquities of Ireland.' Ireland as an

9. David Upchurch, *Wilde's Use of Celtic Irish Elements in 'The Picture of Dorian Gray'* (New York, 1993).
1. Joseph Lew, 'Sydney Owenson and the Fate of Empire,' *Keats-Shelley Journal* (1990), p.48.
2. Edward Said, *Orientalism* (New York, 1979), pp.37/8.
3. Lew, 1990, p.41.
4. *The Wild Irish Girl*, volume 1, p.60.
5. *Ibid.*, volume 2, p.239.
6. Lew, 1990, p.62.
7. Said, 1979, p.188.
8. *The Wild Irish Girl*, volume 1, pp.111/12.

orientalized, elusive yet erotically available female body becomes a
body of knowledge, a secret source of intellectual (re)generation.

Glorvina herself is both erotic female body and source of information about the 'language, history and antiquities of Ireland,' and the
image of the mysterious room marked by female absence will recur
as Glorvina's empty boudoir which offers up to Mortimer
labyrinthine secrets of history and identity. Empty female space, with
its hidden dimensions, illogically overflows with regenerative excess,
just as the interior of Dorian's house also contains secret chambers
and hiding places, including the repositories of the various disguises
necessary in making his exotic/erotic journeys. Dorian's mysterious
refuge in the wildest, most remote peripheries of London (in the
alien, foreboding East End, traditionally known as 'the East'[9]) is an
opium den peopled by enigmatic 'crouching Malays' and the hollowed out ghosts of women Dorian has despoiled. It is an ironic
'harem' where Oriental ciphers are comically and subtly Hiberni-
cized, hidden behind a green curtain in an establishment called
'Daly's.' Wilde's vision of the colonial relationship post-famine and
Parnell is certainly less sanguine than the imagining of a post-Union
Irishness in *The Wild Irish Girl*. However, it is true that Morgan's
own optimism dimmed in her later national tales. Even in the first,
there are moments of doubt in Glorvina's eerily vacant boudoir in
which Mortimer finds his father's 'Sultana' leads him into unknow-
ingly stumbling onto his father's secret plan to marry Glorvina without revealing his identity, in recompense for ancient wrongs. The
inappropriateness of this marriage covertly comments on the novel's
own uncomfortable conclusion, with its accumulated doublings,
father and son bridegrooms, two fathers claimed by Mortimer, and its
series of traumas that must be overcome. This includes the death of
the Prince, which must occur before the happy ending that symbolically unites Ireland to England is possible. The 'absences and cancellations' on which the novel's utopian union depends reveal nearly
crippling ambiguities.[1]

The heroines of Morgan's later national tales become more enigmatic, fall silent, or speak in untranslatable tongues, such as Florence McCarthy in the novel of the same name. Or else they burst into
inappropriate hysterical laughter, as *O'Donne*'s Miss O'Halloran.
Increasingly, Morgan can only represent the trauma of Irish history
in what Evelyn Ender calls the unrepresentable 'space of women's

---

9. Dorian's journey east follows in the tracks of many other texts on that fascinating
   nineteenth-century British chimera, the opium den, including Charles Dickens's *The Mystery of Edwin Drood*, Arthur Conan Doyle's 'The Man with the Twisted Lip,' and Gustave
   Doré & Blanchard Jerrold's *London: A Pilgrimage*. See Timothy L. Carens, 'Restyling the
   Secret of the Opium Den,' in *Reading Wilde: Querying Spaces*, edited by Carolyn Dever &
   Martin J. Taylor (New York, 1995), pp.65–75.
1. Fogarty, 1997, p.126.

exile from language . . . a secret territory that escapes the ready perception of representation.'[2] However, paradoxically, this new silence
grants Morgan's heroines more mobility; they move stealthily athwart
the trajectory imposed by historical, teleological constraints. According to Ferris, such figures hold together 'the unstable concept' of the
nation 'in marginal, clandestine spaces and through incoherent
acts.'[3] Dorian Gray's narrative has similar recourse to a rhetoric of the
inexpressible. With few exceptions the supposedly unspeakable sins
that so traumatically transfigure the canvas on which Dorian's soul
is painted remain unrepresented, creating textual aporia that open
access to alternate meanings, like the salutary wounds Morgan
inflicts on Mortimer's body. As such, as Ed Cohen observes, because
painting itself 'stands outside the text' of Dorian Gray, 'by trans-
gressing the limits of verbal representation, it establishes a gap
whereby unverbalized meanings can enter the text.'[4] Morgan's
national tales, as anti-historical as Dorian Gray, expand and unravel
spatially rather than chronologically, and in this both writers' dilatory
narratives ventilate and fracture what Ferris calls, drawing on Homi
Bhabha's notion of 'nation-time,' as well as Julia Kristeva's theory of
'women's time,' the 'wholeness of natural-historic time.'[5] Ferris notes
the 'repetitive and recursive' temporalities encountered among the
native Irish in Morgan's national tales, temporalities that are not simply counter to, but exterior to, an historical, imperial narrative, and
which thereby accommodate Irish 'mobility and metamorphosis,'
especially for Morgan's heroines.[6]

   This traumatized, flexuous, and enigmatic textuality is at once feminine, Oriental, and Irish. For Wilde, both Ireland's and the Orient's
feminine resistance to representation can yield prismatic, imaginative force. The slipperiness of his own nationalism, a quality always
inherently a matter of aesthetics, is evident when he declares, in
response to the refusal of a British licence to perform Salomé: 'I will
not consent to call myself a citizen of a country that shows such nar-
rowness in its artistic judgement. I am not English—I am Irish—
which is quite another thing.'[7] But Irishness and aesthetics,
coextensive markers of difference here, are only representable negatively. Dorian Gray's most overt borrowing from Celtic imagery is its
reworking of the myth of Tír na nOg, the island of eternal youth, itself

2. Evelyn Ender, Sexing the Mind: Nineteenth-Century Fictions of Hysteria (Ithaca, 1995),
   p.253.
3. Ferris, 'Writing on the Border,' p.102.
4. Ed Cohen, 'Writing Gone Wilde: Homoerotic Desire in the Closet of Representation,' in
   Oscar Wilde: A Collection of Critical Essays, edited by Jonathan Freedman (Upper Saddle
   River, N.J., 1996), p.168.
5. Ferris, 'Writing on the Border,' p.94.
6. Ibid., p.94.
7. Wilde, 'The Censure of Salome,' Oscar Wilde: Interviews and Recollections, Vol. 1, edited
   by E. H. Mikhail (New York, 1979), p.186.

a kind of negative shadow world. In the nineteenth-century British imagination, *Tír na nOg* stands in for Ireland itself, an unreconstructed reservoir of soul, a land ever in its cultural youth, a correlation popularized by contemporary theorists of Celticism like Ernest Renan and Matthew Arnold. The myth of the island of *Tír na nOg* is enthusiastically appropriated by the Anglo-Irish in particular, who see reflected in it their own shadowy, purgatorial in-betweenness, neither quite English nor quite Irish. In *The Wild Irish Girl*, Mortimer participates in this culturally sanctioned displacement when he claims to feel as if he had been 'dropt . . . on the wildest shores of the greatest ocean of the universe . . . I felt like the being of some other sphere newly alighted on a distant orb.'[8]

The atemporality of *Tír na nOg*, like the implied stasis of Oriental culture and art, collaborates with Wilde's consistent advocacy of contemplation over action, imagination over reality, an ironic fulfilment of the stereotype of the lazy Celt so antithetical to manly Victorian ideals of duty and industry. Wilde's enthusiastic adaptation of this stereotype transvalues idleness and activity, always privileging the former. In 'The Critic as Artist' we are told that 'the sure way of knowing nothing about life is to make yourself useful,' that 'when man acts he is a puppet. When he describes he is a poet,' and that 'action is limited and relative.'[9] Indeed, in 'The Decay of Lying' Wilde insists that 'no great artist sees things as they are,'[1] which, significantly, inverts Arnold's famous dictum. In this same essay, Oriental art is admired for its 'frank rejection of imitation, its dislike to the actual representation of any object in nature.'[2]

For Wilde, these aesthetic issues are always political ones. McCormack sees Wilde, along with Bram Stoker, as engaged in 'rival attempts to renegotiate the formula whereby the peculiarly Irish subform of the gothic novel attended to political reality' and maintains that 'Wilde's politics were consistently, if not evidently, radical.'[3] Pine points out that 'for the Irishman, seen both in isolation and in terms of Ireland's experience of England, the social construction of reality is in fact "unreal" because he cannot subscribe to its rules and its canon.'[4] And so the debate on the relative merits of realism in the arts in which Wilde participated so vigorously in *Dorian Gray* as much as in his critical essays is really a political one, and one concerned specifically with colonialism. In the preface to *Dorian Gray* this debate is cast in explicitly racial terms: 'The nineteenth-century

8. *The Wild Irish Girl*, volume 1, pp.157/8.
9. 'The Critic as Artist,' p.1042.
1. 'The Decay of Lying,' p.980.
2. *Ibid.*, p.979.
3. McCormack, 'Irish Gothic and After,' pp.842–6.
4. Pine, 1995, p.3.

dislike of Realism is the rage of Caliban seeing his own face in the glass. The nineteenth-century dislike of Romanticism is the rage of Caliban not seeing his own face in the glass' [3]. Caliban, the racial Other, degenerate savage, and common representation of the prognathous Irish in colonial discourse, here figures the unevolved English public, and this disavowed, estranged self in the glass frustrates the imperial subject's narcissism.

This casts new light on Wilde's aim in art to 'shatter the mirror of "realistic" representations, because such representations seem to justify the status quo.'[5] Wilde repeatedly makes clear his hostility to 'the shackles of verisimilitude,' the 'prison-house of realism,' and concludes in 'The Decay of Lying' that 'as a method, realism is a complete failure.'[6] *Dorian Gray* demonstrates the destructive Othering effected by realism, a splitting of the self that provokes both excessive self-love and excessive self-loathing. Basil makes a fateful decision to leave off his romantic, inventive practice of drawing Dorian as 'Paris in dainty armour, and as Adonis with huntsman's cloak,' or 'crowned with heavy lotus blossoms . . . on the prow of an Adrian barge,' in order to paint a portrait, as he tells Dorian, 'not in the costume of dead ages, but in your own dress and in your own time,' a 'method the painter calls Realism' [95]. Yet, in a statement in 'The Decay of Lying' that attempts to 'devalue and demystify' reality by paradoxically denying its claims to the truth, Wilde insists that 'Truth is entirely and absolutely a matter of style.'[7] Dorian's tragedy is ensured when he grants 'reality' the power to tell the truth about him. The devastation wrought on the realist canvas that divides Dorian from his soul is the result of his own paradoxical conformity, his acceptance of dominant beliefs in the corrosive power of sin, his highly unoriginal, even drearily conventional correlation between degeneracy and disfigurement. Dorian has ironically striven for originality by mimicking another, even if it is the outrageous and subversive Lord Henry who, though clearly several years older than Dorian, appears to experience a scarcely noted aging process. He is unmarked by anything like the leprous mutilation or putrefaction being visited on the shameful canvas where Dorian has fixed and framed the secret truths of his identity.

The text's steady feminization of Dorian through Orientalization (i.e. Hibernicization) may also account for the difference in the representation of Dorian's and Henry's ageing: that is, Dorian ages as a woman for whom the process means the loss of her ambivalent powers of attraction. For a man, in this case Henry, ageing is a gaining

5. Mahaffey, 1998, p.68.
6. 'The Decay of Lying,' p.979.
7. See Dollimore for a detailed analysis of this quote, p.11, and Sammells, *Wilde Style, passim.*

of power, just as for Britain history is an accumulation of self-affirming potency.[8] What is unappreciated by Dorian, however, is the imaginative power that lies in disfiguration, the reason realism is distorted when it looks in Caliban's face. Dorian's retreat from the realm of structured, masculinist, British imperatives into what should be an unlimited realm of feminine, imaginative potential, aesthetically indexed as both Irish and Oriental, is disabled by a problematic relationship to history that hinders and distorts. As in the gothic trope described by Eagleton 'in which the clammy hand of the past stretches out and manipulates the present, reducing it to a hollow repetition of itself,'[9] Dorian succumbs to predetermined moral patterns, inherited prescriptions of guilt, even as he believes himself to be transcending them. Rather than multiply his personalities, as is Wilde's exhortation elsewhere, Dorian reifies rigid bifurcation, becomes Caliban raging in the glass, but his violence rebounds on himself; this violence also releases art from the shackles of conscience and prohibition, restoring its static ideal, reclaiming its beauty and innocence. If the national tale enacts, as Niilo Idman suggests, the 'revenge of a subdued and oppressed country upon her master,'[1] the country avenged in *Dorian Gray* is not simply imagined, but the imagination itself, which by extension, or perhaps more (im)properly, by circumlocution, may be read as Ireland.

ELLIE RAGLAND-SULLIVAN

The Phenomenon of Aging in Oscar Wilde's *Picture of Dorian Gray*: A Lacanian View†

Oscar Wilde's only novel, *The Picture of Dorian Gray* (1891), is so rich in what has been termed "pathogenic" material that it has evoked a large amount of psychoanalytic commentary. I shall argue that the appeal of the novel does not inhere in its pathology, but in its dramatization of the dynamic structure of a superego. In the novel superego effects are metaphorized by extreme sentiments regarding physical beauty and normative aging, as well as by graphic

---

8. The argument aligning ageing, nation, gender, history and agency owes much to David Lloyd's comments on an earlier draft of this essay.
9. Eagleton, 1996, p.194.
1. Quoted in Ferris, 'Narrating Cultural Encounter,' p.287.
† From *Memory and Desire: Aging—Literature—Psychoanalysis*, eds. Kathleen M. Woodward and Murray M. Schwartz (Bloomington: Indiana UP, 1986), 114–33. Reprinted with the permission of the Board of Regents of the University of Wisconsin System. Bracketed page numbers refer to this Norton Critical Edition.

caricatures which mix physical ideals with affective torments. Such an interpretation obviously contradicts Wilde's own contention that art and life were separate domains.

Wilde introduces the theme of art versus life at the start of the novel. Dorian Gray, a handsome young aristocrat, is having his portrait painted by Basil Hallward. At the last sitting he meets Lord Henry Wotton, who sets forth several of the principal themes developed in the novel. "Nothing can cure the soul but the senses" [21], Lord Henry tells the innocent, young Dorian. A bit later Lord Henry admires Dorian's beauty, telling him that "beauty . . . is higher, indeed, than Genius as it needs no explanation. It cannot be questioned" [22]. To this Dorian responds with a *cri de coeur*: "I would give my soul if the picture would age, and I stay young. Youth is the only thing worth having." Later Basil confesses that in the portrait he has revealed "the secret of my own soul" [9], thereby defining art as a union of soul and body. Thus although Wilde proclaims *Dorian Gray* a novel about the transcendence of art over life, its fictional message is that life spills over into art.

That art and life are not separate domains will constitute one of the principal themes of my essay. "The fictional is not to be understood as the opposite of the real," Peter McCormick has argued. "Literary truths are not what *would* be true in the real world, but what in fact *may* be true in the real world."[1] We can apply his characterization of the interface between life and art to *Dorian Gray*. But while McCormick distinguishes the real from the fictional, I will go further, viewing the fictional as one category of what the French psychoanalyst Jacques Lacan calls the Real.

As we know, Dorian gets his wish. It is not to the "magic" of wish-fulfillment that the novel owes its enigmatic power, however, but to the strange transformation of the picture. Dorian's portrait does not simply age, it changes into a picture of a grotesque, hideous, gnarled old man with blood stains on his hands and feet. The picture is said to register the passage of time through a depiction of Dorian's soul: "It held the secret of his life, and told his story. It had taught him to love his own beauty. Would it teach him to loathe his own soul?" (p.184). Despite such obvious moral tones, Wilde wrote in the preface to the novel that there is no such thing as a moral or an immoral book. Years later Wilde admitted in a letter that there was a moral to *Dorian Gray*: "All excess brings its own punishment."[2] Asked if this

1. Peter McCormick, "Moral Knowledge and Fiction," *The Journal of Aesthetics and Art Criticism*, 41, No. 4 (Summer 1983), p.407.
2. Bruce B. Clark, "A Burnt Child Loves the Fire: Oscar Wilde's Search for Ultimate Meanings in Life," *Ultimate Reality and Meaning*, 4, No. 3 (1981), p.236.

were an artistic error in the novel, Wilde replied: "I fear it is. It is the only error in the book."[3]

Ironically, this "error" gives the book its power, making it a classic. For the torture of sin and guilt—the more than art in art—makes it a story about the dynamic interplay of Desire and Law in their capacities for shaping and tormenting the human psyche. By looking to the teachings of Jacques Lacan (1901–1981), I shall claim support for the idea that literary art has universal resonance only insofar as it repeats something already "known" by the artist or reader, something "known" at the level of the Real and the "true" of human life. From this perspective, literary art would be a privileged domain in which unconscious (past) knowledge imposes itself on conscious life within the realm of present time through two powerfully evocative modes: the affective resonance of language and its capacity to call forth visual imagery. But were literature only an imagistic mirror, it would be, as Wilde says of all art in his preface to *Dorian Gray*, "quite useless."[4] More than a static system of signs or a set of encoded messages, literary art uses the materiality of language to permit the *moi* (in Lacanian terms, the *moi* is the fictional voice standing between a social *porte-parole*—the *je*—and the alien Desire of the Other) to reconstitute itself identificatorily (Imaginarily) by means of the text. Unconscious representations would provide each person with the specific references constituting a subjective text of their own. Such text is the means by which humans perceive at all.

I

Although Lacanian principles may illuminate first causes underlying some of the "truths" portrayed by Wilde in *The Picture of Dorian Gray*, Lacan did not invent these truths any more than did Wilde. Wilde's fiction reverberates with the "knowledge" (*connaissance*) gleaned from a dissection of the Real (*savoir*) of the human psyche (soul). In the novel Dorian seeks one kind of knowledge: the pleasure of the senses. His sexual and drug experiments become the underside of a commendable deployment of the senses in his role as art connoisseur. By the novel's end he has attained the kind of knowledge he sought and learns that he cannot escape the deeds of his past, that illicit sensual experiences do not lead to immortality, but to death. As

3. Oscar Wilde, Letter to the Editor of the *St. James's Gazette*, June 26, 1890, in *The Letters of Oscar Wilde*, ed. R. Hart-Davis (London: Rupert Hart-Davis, 1962), p.259.
4. As Bruce Clark has observed, Wilde was greatly influenced by his Oxford professor John Ruskin who taught that all things useful should be beautiful (p.227). In *Dorian Gray* Wilde changes this to the idea that art is beautiful; moreover "all art is quite useless" (p.138).

Bruce B. Clark comments: "Dorian discovered that, although things may seem relative, there are absolutes in the world of ethics and the spirit" (p.243).

Unlike Clark, I would not place the source of such knowledge within the realm of traditional religion. Such absolutes are, rather, the limits on human behavior which derive from unconscious requisites in their interplay with social conventions. From a Lacanian perspective, one can break "knowledge" down into various kinds, and place it on different planes. At the conscious level knowledge is imparted by codes and social conventions, and by theories or systems of thought. "Truth," on the other hand, refers to unconscious knowledge: a *savoir* which directs human Desire and intentionality from an invisible source. In conscious life such knowledge is expressed indirectly within language. Genre, affect, rhetorical device, and innuendo all imply a source of meaning (*sens*) beyond meaning (*signification*). Intentionality becomes a matter of positioning oneself in reference to public authority, or within any context where knowledge becomes linked to narcissism and power. Desire points to the fact that human beings are questing (motivated) creatures who pursue multiple substitutes for the lack which is, in fact, inherent within psychic structure itself. In contrast to factual information or various theories, unconscious knowledge has the effect on conscious life of being a *connaissance* (recognition) of something else. It is, thus, unquantifiable.

How can a Lacanian picture of unconscious knowledge tell us anything about the magic of immortality and the ugliness of aging in Wilde's novel? In Clark's opinion, "Wilde's horror of growing old probably accounts for the theme of the magic preservation of youth in *Dorian Gray*. As he approached forty, he accelerated his activity to a frenzy in order to enjoy life before it was too late" (p.229). This answer demands a further question: why did Wilde seek to destroy his own life and his family's reputation at the pinnacle of fame and success? I believe *Dorian Gray* dramatizes Wilde's own conflicts in bits and pieces. The novel thus tells the personal "truth" of one man's *unconscious* guilt. Five years after he had written the preface to *Dorian Gray*, Wilde expressed his guilt consciously. Learning of his mother's death while he was in prison in 1896, Wilde confessed in a letter, "I feel that I have brought such unhappiness on [my wife Constance] and such ruin on my children that I have no right to go against her wishes in anything." Later he wrote, "[My mother's] death was so terrible to me that I . . . have no words in which to express my anguish and my shame. . . . She and my father bequeathed me a name they had made noble and honoured. . . . I had disgraced that name eternally. I had made it a low byword among low people. I had dragged it through the very mire."[5] While the particular shame of which Wilde speaks—his imprisonment for homosexuality, his experimentation with drugs—would perhaps not be shocking to us today, from a universal perspective Wilde's graphic portrayal of a growing horror finds a resonance in a reader's recognition of having "known" both guilt and anxiety, however unconscious that recognition may remain.

Dorian's wish to stop time removes us from the realm of linear narrative and places us squarely in front of Lacan's theory of the gaze: that which deceives the eye by stopping time.[6] While the eye is an organ which ages, and sees others aging as well, the gaze is separable from the eye. The gaze is first perceived by a newborn baby, and introjected as if it were one more object among others. The gaze is, therefore, an object *a*. In Lacanian terms this means that it has the property of being separable, and is linked to lack. Beyond the four primordial *objects* of Desire—the breast, the gaze, the voice, excrement—Lacan named the four supports which later announce themselves as the cause of Desire: the gaze, the voice, the void, and the Phallus.[7] The gaze exists even prior to its own symbolization as a *perceptum*, then, in an irrecuperable network of perceptual equipment, knowable only by its effects. As one element that makes Desire functional—both as a specific symbol and as essential to the dynamics of recognition—the gaze interacts with the unconscious structures of Desire and Law, thus subjectivizing the Real order of seeing (eye).

Lacan has theorized that at the scopic level, we are no longer at the level of the demand [for love], but of desire, of the desire [shown] to the Other:

> It is even at the level of the vocatory drive [*la pulsion invocante*], which is the closest to the experience of the unconscious. In a general sense, relationship of the gaze to what one wants to see is a relationship of lure. The subject presents himself as other than he is, and what one gives him to see is not what he wants to see. It is in this way that the eye can function as object *a*, that is to say at the level of lack (*Sém.* XI, p.96).

In other words, the eye and the gaze are joined in a function of lure (*méconnaissance*). What we see is seen subjectively, rendered such by the gaze that Lacan called "that underside of consciousness" (*Sém*,

5. Wilde, Letter to Robert Ross, March 10, 1896, in *Letters*, p.399; Letter to Lord Alfred Douglas, Jan.–March 1897, in *Letters*, p.458.
6. Jacques Lacan, *Le Séminaire de Jacques Lacan, Livre XI: Les quatre concepts fondamentaux* (1964), text established by Jacques-Alain Miller (Paris: Editions du Seuil, 1973), p.95.
7. Jacques Lacan, *Le Séminaire de Jacques Lacan, Livre XX: Encore* (1972–73), text established by Jacques-Alain Miller (Paris: Editions du Seuil, 1975), pp.96–97.

XI, p.79). Put another way, both the Imaginary and Symbolic orders are enmeshed in a deception that blocks out the "truth"—the knowledge—of the unconscious. The system of language and a person's sense of identity work in tandem to distance humans from the impersonal truths and desires recorded in the unconscious.

Let me suggest that *The Picture of Dorian Gray* is a metaphorical rendering of the power of the gaze in its relationship to the superego. The picture's gaze distorts time, making it an effect of unconscious "truth" rather than a fact of aging. One manifestation of such truth in the novel lies in Dorian's dying an untimely death. Even though the picture appears aged, he in fact was only thirty-eight years old. The sense of being old comes, then, from a dual linking of his own ideal image of "self" to the gaze of the other/Other (a narcissistic function). It comes, as well, from the link between narcissistic dreams and the sense that thwarted desires are somehow connected to deception of or by a Father (a superego function). "If beyond appearance, there is no thing in itself (*chose en soi*)," Lacan said, "there is the gaze" (*Sém*. XI, p.95).

Beyond the icon lies what Lacan called the Name-of-the-Father. These form a pact beyond any image (*Sém*. XI, p.103). Put another way, the superego gives shape and meaning to any drama of identification. One might say, then, that both Dorian and the portrait of him are masks which serve to hide what lies beyond them: the gaze of the other/Other (*Sém*. XI, p.99). Here it is useful to recall that Freud, in one well-known formulation, defined guilt as the tension between the ideal ego and the superego.[8] The murders of Basil and of his own portrait give tacit witness to the unbearable tension Dorian feels. The novel's climax is attributable, then, to Dorian's final realization that it was impossible to sustain his own narcissistic ideal image in light of the harsh judgments meted out by the social order. The picture becomes the ultimate proof that outer voices find an inner resonance within Dorian himself.

The Picture of Dorian Gray is about aging in reverse, about eternal youth. And it is revealed to be a damning state. Dorian's sad life is not about sensual pleasure, but about emotional sterility. When the body itself becomes the object of Desire—as well as its source—a certain normative sexual evolution is attenuated. To live life by substituting the body for psychic lack requires that aging cease. The sexual pleasure that normally accompanies aging is fleshed out by relationships of intimacy, if not concerns of maternity and paternity. Dorian Gray, much like Tirso de Molina's Don Juan, is driven to flit from body to body. Sexuality is split off from bonding. Desire is separated from

---

8. See Ghyslain Charron, *Freud et le Problème de la Culpabilité* (Ottawa: Editions de l'Université d'Ottawa, 1979), p.111.

Law. And Dorian, like Don Juan before him, must finally give his body over to the ultimate Master.

Lacan has spoken about the process of identification by which a person assumes the Other's Desire in an Imaginary tripod where being the Phallus and having the Phallus take on meaning only in the Symbolic order (or in terms of the law of the signifier). In other words, identity only *means* in reference to the Name-of-the-Father. When a question of lack itself is in play, "being" the Phallus and "having" it can become physically confused as mutually exclusive postures.[9] A confusion between identity (secondary narcissim) and body image (primary narcissim) does indeed reify Lacanian Desire at the level of lack during the time when normative aging renders the body a less desirable object. That is, if the body itself is taken as the measure of Desire, then the body becomes the Phallus (the desired object in the Other). Normative options are excluded. A man usually identifies himself as the Phallus (desirable) because he possesses the male sex organ. A woman generally sees herself (at the level of the gaze) as desirable because she is allied to some phallic principle (a lover or husband) or represents phallic authority herself. But when Desire gets stuck on body beauty, and confused with sexual desirability as the measure of worth, then the ideal ego can no longer value itself once some zenith of physical perfection is passed.

Thus the grotesque portrait of Dorian Gray is a caricatured picture of old age, seen from the slant of a skewed narcissism. The picture Wilde paints of Dorian's early years shows him as identifying with feminine desire against the patriarchal order (as we will see later, this finds a parallel in Wilde's life). Dorian was the child of a worthless father—a man rejected by the mother's family—and an extraordinarily beautiful mother. When his mother left her aristocratic home to marry a penniless soldier, her father decided to end the marriage, hiring an adventurer to insult his son-in-law, who in turn engaged in a duel which killed him within a few months of the marriage. Although the daughter returned home, she never spoke to her father again and died within the year, leaving only a son who bore her exquisite beauty. Dorian grew up longing for the mother with whom he identified, and hating his aloof grandfather.

Without any "father" he can fully trust, Dorian seems an emotional orphan. Basil is too smitten by him to counsel him, and Lord Henry's advice leads him astray. Body narcissism becomes a compensation for a psychic lack: a Father's name to which he can happily entrust his identity. Vacillating between a prayer that his demise will be stopped and a rebellious curse to anyone who dare try, Dorian—despite Wilde's disclaimers—is *not* driven by a pleasure quest. Beyond the pleasure principle Lacan found only repetition. More than mere neurotic compulsion, repetition is, according to Lacan, the principle of identity. He equated repetition with *moi* fixations, and *moi* fixations with the death drive. And in *The Picture of Dorian Gray*, death symbolizes punishment for not bowing to social law (or convention), as well as the necessity for joining Desire to Law in some inner psychic balance.

One of the compelling themes in the novel is Dorian's constant dream of redemption. When Basil finally sees the hideous monster that has replaced the beautiful portrait he had painted, Dorian kills him, not only to protect his secret, but also to maintain his illusion of hope. In a discussion of the intersubjective relation, Lacan theorizes that what counts in the dialectic of the gaze "is not that the other see where I am, it is that he see where I am going, that is to say, that he see very exactly, that he see where I am not. In any analysis of the intersubjective relation, the essential thing is not what is there, what is seen. What structures it is what is not there."[1] Dorian does not murder Basil just because his soul has been "seen." Insofar as Dorian's deeds are discussed by one and all, near and far, the picture itself is not needed to disclose his character. Instead, Basil's death testifies to Dorian's growing fear that the future is closing in on him. To allow Basil to live would attenuate the dream that the picture will revert to its pristine state, that Dorian's nonsexual love of a pretty country girl will save him. Indeed Dorian never accepts the truth that Wilde dramatized: a soul cannot escape its own destiny. When Dorian stabs the portrait instead of himself, he still dreams that such an act will free him.

At the novel's end Dorian says, "it was an unjust mirror, this mirror of his soul . . . Was he always to be burdened by his past? Its [the picture's] mere memory had marred many moments of joy. It had been like conscience to him. Yes, it had been conscience. He would destroy it" (pp. 252–53). Wilde describes what psychoanalysts know: that the guilt and anxiety caused by superego (conscience) dicta can destroy a life leading at the limit to suicide. Dorian's conclusion was that youth had destroyed him. "What was youth at best? A green, an unripe time, a time of shallow moods and sickly thoughts. Why had he worn its livery? Youth had spoiled him" (p.252). But as we know, youthful sexual adventures (with women) would be forgiven any young English aristocrat.

Thus *The Picture of Dorian Gray* portrays the human tragedy of

---

1. Jacques Lacan, *Le Séminaire de Jacques Lacan, Livre I: Les écrits techniques de Freud* (1953–54), text established by Jacques-Alain Miller (Paris: Editions du Seuil, 1975), p.249.

"seeing" one's own truth—at the level of the gaze—(*l'instant terminal de voir*) without really understanding what has been "seen." Lacan used the expression, *l'instant terminal de voir*, to describe the primordial nature of artistic painting, the act of deposing the bits and pieces of one's own imagistic structuration on a piece of canvas. Even though Dorian gradually sees himself from the perspective of others, he feels a victim of the portrait's gaze. Never is he a beneficiary of its "truth." The picture symbolizes the hidden, the repressed. First hidden behind a screen in his bedroom and then in the half light of the attic where he had been exiled to play in an unhappy childhood, the picture is never equatable with "insight" (*l'instant de voir*). That Dorian places the picture in the attic where his grandfather had forced him to play is significant. The attic becomes a kind of metaphor for the Lacanian unconscious. Full of remnants and traces of Dorian's childhood, it is not easily accessible. Not only is it physically distant within the house, it is also dusky, dusty, and eerie just as the Lacanian unconscious, with its archaic accounts of the past, is opaque. Only occasionally does it surface into view—into the light—and just as quickly it shuts back on itself. Dorian is haunted by the knowledge that his picture bears secrets he would rather deny; Dorian nonetheless continually creeps to the attic to look at the picture, thus taking in "truth" in spurts. But these moments of illumination are just as quickly shut out, shut up in the dark of the attic.

Although Dorian cannot analyze the "truth" the portrait speaks, he does realize that it metaphorizes his own anxiety (according to Lacan, the role of anxiety in any person's life trajectory is that *it* does not deceive[2]). But while Wilde's story borders on insight, it never enters the realm of light which characterizes Lacan's *le temps pour comprendre*. That is, the moment in clinical analysis when a person begins to piece together the meanings of various gaps in his own life story. In the time of such understanding, the future is seen to flow necessarily from past history.[3]

Daniel Schneider has discussed what Freud named in *Beyond the Pleasure Principle* as "the protective barrier defending the vital processes."[4] Schneider calls this barrier the "paraconscious monitor," which I would risk equating with the Lacanian *moi*, the source of narcissistic cohesion which blocks unconscious messages. Although psychic freedom—the ability to control one's own Desire—can only occur when the *moi* has come to "see" the sources of its own structuration, the *moi*, nonetheless, protects the subject from the impersonality

2. Lacan, *Sém.* XI, p.40.
3. Jacques Lacan, "The subversion of the subject and the dialectic of desire in the Freudian unconscious" (1960), in *Ecrits: A Selection*, p.303.
4. Daniel E. Schneider, "Myth, Literature, and the Heart," in *Psychoanalysis of Heart Attack* (New York: The Dial Press, Inc., 1967), p.51.

of unconscious truths. Schneider concluded that an "injury neurosis" such as the abrupt forcing of insight can impair vitality and herald death; such a breakdown in vitality was described by Freud as "an inner overplus of pain."[5] Freud listed anxiety and then obsessive compulsive repetition as protective shields against injury neuroris.

Both anxiety and compulsive rituals fail to protect Dorian from his efforts to separate soul from body. As he finally stabs his picture in the heart, he falls dead, becoming the monster in the picture. Reverting to its original state, the picture becomes art: that which represents representations. The moral to the novel, then, is that one cannot cut the past off from the present. Indeed, if Lacan is correct, the past has always already structured the probable shape of the future. Within a Lacanian purview, freedom comes in degrees. It lies in gaining psychic distance from *moi* fictions, in taking responsibility for one's Desires, in squaring Desire with pertinent structures of Law. Lacan has described such a process as a de-being of being. Indeed the Greek word "psychoanalysis" means melting, dissolution, and death.[6]

II

In *The Picture of Dorian Gray* death and age are put in suspension until the final reckoning when art, in fact, uncannily prefigures Wilde's own destiny. Dorian's "moral" disobedience could be taken as a metaphor for Wilde's own disobedience. By pursuing his homosexual loves at the cost of the well-being of his wife and children, Wilde disobeyed implicit social conventions, as well as breaking a law against sodomy instituted in 1885. Four years after the publication of the novel Wilde was put on trial for his homosexuality, and accused of corrupting a circle of young men. Six years after this time, and three years after his release from prison, Wilde died an untimely death at age forty-six (by "untimely" I mean that his death was induced by "self" destruction and grief, instead of by normal aging). We are therefore entitled to conclude that Dorian Gray embodied Wilde's own fixation on what Lacan has called the death signifier.

Many critics have written about Wilde's obsession with death in *Dorian Gray*, but none have suggested that Wilde's destructiveness lay, at least partly, in his inability to bend to the requisites of the Symbolic order. In Lacanian terms, the Symbolic order of language and social conventions is inherently neutral and a-thematic. But through the course of History, any social order evolves certain legal codes and

5. Schneider, pp.48–49; Freud is quoted in Schneider, p.52.
6. See Luigi Zoja, "Working against Dorian Gray: Analysis and the Old," *Journal of Analytical Psychology*, No. 28 (1983), p.55.

Imaginary preferences, punishing (castrating) those who flout such conventions and ideals. Wilde's inability to conform would be attributable, within a Lacanian purview, to the structure of his own unconscious knowledge, put in place long before adult life.

Indeed, it is not surprising to note that Wilde's art and his life were both characterized by his subversion of the Symbolic order. In the artistic domain such "subversion" is called irony and paradox, and it won him the fame and money accorded a great writer. But in his private life, such subversion was only tolerable when kept discreet. When the Marquess of Queensberry accused Wilde of sodomy, Wilde insisted, against advice, on prosecuting the Marquess for criminal libel.[7] After his release from prison Wilde, seeking refuge in a Catholic retreat, was refused this courtesy. He was also shunned by friends, wife, and children. Yet despite his own guilty torments, one senses that Wilde could never comprehend how such dire consequences could follow from his pursuit of sensual pleasures and his practice of a kind of love shared by great artists of the past. In Lacanian terms one might say that he never understood that his real crime was to have elevated Desire above Law. (Lacan's Name-of-the-Father is that which demands submission to the laws of a given social order, however inhumane and arbitrary they might be.)

Here we will do well to recall that frustrated desires are linked to deception of or by a Father. Wilde's first deception by a father must have been painful, for it was *his* father. From the moment of his birth, Wilde was subjected to his father's rejection of him. His father (and his mother), wishing that he had been born a girl, treated him as if he indeed were a girl until his sister was born three years later. We see that the Lacanian identity quest—the who am I in my parent's discourse?—was problematic from the start of life. Wilde's early sense of "self" was confused between masculine and feminine images, while the pain of social disapprobation descended upon him through, as it were, the sins of the father during his adolescent years.

Wilde's father, Sir William Wilde, was a successful eye and ear surgeon in Dublin. Not only did he found a hospital and write a text on aural surgery, he also held the post of Surgeon Oculist in Ordinary to Queen Victoria and was knighted for his work on the medical statistics of the Irish census. He was also known as a compulsive womanizer. When Mary Travers accused Sir William of having chloroformed her in order to rape her, Lady Wilde wrote the girl's father, detailing the daughter's complicity. As a result Miss Travers sued the Wildes for

---

7. In the introduction to *The Annotated Oscar Wilde* (London: Orbis, 1982), H. Montgomery Hyde describes Wilde's three trials. In response to the Marquess of Queensberry's accusation that he was a sodomite, Wilde sued for criminal libel. In three trials lasting over a period of two months in 1895, he was found guilty of homosexuality. Wilde was given the maximum sentence of two years in prison at hard labor (pp. 16–20).

libel, the scandal becoming the sensation of the 1860s in Dublin. Miss Travers won (minimally), but Sir William never recovered his reputation. When he died many years later, his prodigal spending had left his family almost destitute.

Given his own early feminization, in tandem with the effects of his own father's degradation, Wilde's Desire evolved in the identificatory pattern labeled as homosexual. He identified strongly with his sister and indeed, he never really recovered from her death, which occurred when he was ten years old. A childhood history such as Wilde's would have been sufficient to place his Desire on a feminine slope (perhaps Wilde would have never given rein to his homosexuality if his second child had not been a son, thus repeating the disappointment he had brought his parents). Many psychoanalytic critics have regarded Wilde's homosexuality as the fuel behind the narcissism portrayed in *Dorian Gray*. Homosexuals desire youth above all, they say, because they are pathologically narcissistic. They can only love an ageless beauty. But such a theory does not acknowledge that primary narcissism (body narcissism) is taught as the basis of femininity to heterosexual women who presumably love others not cast in their own mold. Nor does it problematize narcissism as Lacan has done by making it the cornerstone of all identity. Primary (corporeal) and secondary narcissism are interwoven, although secondary narcissism is characterized by the projecting of one's ideal image in relations with others (ego ideals). Perhaps we can extrapolate from Lacan the theory that one source of human tragedy lies in the injustice that shapes every person's identity (*moi*) from mirror-stage or Oedipal experiences. Early in life, these effects situate persons within a social masquerade where, as male or female, they are required to adhere to certain roles and fictions. The myths and desires that go together to fabricate a human subject have already begun to define that person's destiny even before his or her birth.

In Lacan's view, the Real object of the homosexual's desire is not simply the pleasure of male beauty or sexuality (a displacement), but the desire to defy the Desire of the fathers.[8] Such subversive Desire, thus, takes knowledge of the unconscious into account, while paradoxically denying the existence of the unconscious. Beyond the prohibitions attributed to the fathers lies the dream of eternal *jouissance*. Such an illusion of mirror-stage bliss—or immortality— requires that Castration (psychic separation from the mother) be denied, and submission to the father rejected. But such a psychic ploy is impossible. Constant psychic perfection is unattainable. We remember Basil's utopian definition of art as "a union of soul and body." When Dorian ceases to pose for him, Basil's art loses soul.

8. See Lacan, *Sém*. XI, p.38.

Lord Henry—the champion of verbal art—by breaking up Basil's
mirror-stage dream, makes himself an agent of Castration. Yet, he is
no more a representative of social norms than is Basil. By introducing Dorian to a lawless universe—one without morals—he also
places himself on the side of ejecting ordinary social limits.

Since the normative is the kernel of social structure—that around
which power and recognition revolves—a person "out of step" with
norms is doomed to suffer. Wilde later drew a parallel between the
characters in this novel and himself: "Basil Hallward is what I think
I am, Lord Henry what the world thinks me, Dorian what I would
like to be."⁹ Basil and Dorian could well represent splits in Wilde's
own ideal ego. At the level of primary narcissism, he would like to be
ever young and beautiful (Dorian). At a secondary narcissistic stage,
he would be morally pure and responsible, and divinely inspired
(Basil). What the world sees—the *je* as social representative of the
subject—is the Master of verbal wit and pithy paradox. Given the
importance of public approval for psychic well-being, in opposition
to the already conflictive nature of the splits within himself, Wilde
could not hope for any oedipal resolution to bring *moi* ideals, *je*
façades, or unconscious Desire into harmony with each other, and
with social dicta.

The mirrors in Dorian Gray exist merely to amplify a lie: to reflect
Dorian's façade. In the conclusion Dorian looks at himself in the mirror Lord Henry had given him: "He loathed his own beauty, and,
flinging the mirror on the floor, crushed it into silver splinters
beneath his heel" (p.252). In this novel, then, fascination does not
point to mirror doubles, nor to a "true" versus "false" self. The picture is not a symmetrical mirror, but an allegorical depiction of an
ethical state. Similarly, Dorian's portrait metaphorizes Wilde's own
self-hatred—he could not forgive himself for his homosexuality—as
reflected in the eyes of the fathers he paradoxically disdained. The
gaze of the Other as depicted in this novel is not the gaze at the
moment of its introjection as a part object, a moment prior even to
its own representability. Instead, the gaze is attached to the eye of the
others in their Imaginary power to catalyze the voice of the superego.
The gaze cast by Dorian's loathsome picture represents Phallic dis-
approval, that which exists in relation to one's ideal ego.¹ If Wilde

9. Wilde, Letter to Ralph Payne, Feb. 12, 1894, in *Letters*, p.352.
1. See Catherine Millot, "Le surmoi féminin," *Ornicar? revue du champ freudien*, No. 29
(April–June 1984). In discussing the relationship of the ideal ego to the superego, Millot
says: "Let us note that it is a demand which is at the origin of the formation of the ideal
ego for everyone: a demand of the subject addressed to the Other, and which has seen
opposed to itself an end point of non-receiving. It is on the basis of this refused demand,
on the basis of a privation, that the subject identifies itself with this Other which has the
power to answer it. . . . The question is that of the relationship between the initial demand,
at the origin of the formation of the ideal ego, and the final demand, that of the superego"
(pp.114–15, my translation).

sought to deny Castration, then it would make sense that he would deify the cessation of aging. For Castration is on the side of Thanatos, bringing with it intimations of mortality. This helps us understand the relationship between Dorian's youth and beauty, and the aging portrait of the evil Dorian in the attic. According to Lacan, the power of beauty lies in its being an antithesis to death, the principle signifier around which all life is organized.[2] In consequence moral virtues are attributed to beauty—in itself neutral—because it suggests life, hope, love (Eros). "But you, Dorian, with your pure, bright, innocent face, and your marvelous untroubled youth—I can't believe anything against you," says Basil, in face of contradictory evidence (p.216). Beauty serves not only as a mask screening out death, but as a denial of Castration.

In *The Picture of Dorian Gray*, Wilde sought to deny Castration. But his own unconscious guilt was so strong that creating an idyllic eternity of Peter Pans not only would not suffice. As the novel's conclusion tells us, it was also impossible. Wilde's own life was at stake. The father's name was too much with him. In Lacanian terms, acute anxiety induced by unconscious guilt can affect the *moi* so as to unravel the *moi* unity which gives the illusion of a "self" cohesion. When guilt and thwarted dreams oppress the *moi* to the point that it can no longer "see" in itself the source of good, can no longer offer itself to the world as a symbol of worthy exchange, then affective "death" is but a short step from the emptiness which takes over, literally stopping life. After his three years of exile, poverty, and alcohol, disappointment finally sapped Wilde's vitality.

As autobiography, then, I view *Dorian Gray* as a narrative sliding toward the author's own unconscious truth. The truth at issue here is recorded by Wilde's metaphoric transformation of a sense of guilt into an externalized image of growing old which represents his inner sense of being old. The outer person is but a *trompe l'oeil* while the soul never ceases to keep its corrective accounting. From a nineteenth-century point of view, Wilde hints at the religious myth of a record in God's heavens. From a Lacanian viewpoint, Wilde's fiction reveals the Real presence of unconscious effects, portraying the intimate and fragile link between a person's ideal image of "self" and the superego. The price of a severe imbalance is death, a falling out of the Symbolic order into a horror-house of unbearable Imaginary lures.

The very forces which Wilde claimed gave him vitality also robbed him of it within a ten-year period. In this sense, Wilde's death becomes a form of tragic suicide. In Wilde's life, as in Dorian's, sen-

2. Jacques Lacan, in *Le Séminaire de Jacques Lacan, Livre II: Le moi dans la théorie de Freud et dans la technique de la psychanalyse* (1954–55), text established by Jacques-Alain Miller (Paris: Editions du Seuil, 1978), p.271.

sual pleasures gradually came to dominate. Finally, he offers his body
to death in a kind of symbolic exchange between Desire and death.
"I do not seek happiness, but pleasure," wrote Wilde, "which is more
tragic."[3] Condemned for his kind of pleasure, Wilde lacked the kind
of philosophical stance from which emotional sustenance can be
drawn (at one point he wrote in a letter: "When I think about Religion at all, I feel as if I would like to found an order for those who
cannot believe"[4]). If the fiction of *Dorian Gray* demonstrates the psychic power of unconscious Desire and Oedipal Law as the organizing principles of each human identity, the course of Wilde's life
reveals that he had no freedom from the tyranny that constituted his
soul, and in this he magnifies the propensity, of all human beings to
suffer. In *Dorian Gray* the unfolding of Dorian's story dramatizes
Lacan's idea that the ideal ego gives timing to a discourse in reference
to the Father's Name as inscribed in the unconscious. Far from a
mere conflict between impersonal "instincts," we are confronted with
the timing which punctuated Wilde's own life trajectory.

Wilde's life, and his art, bear out Lacan's contention that unconscious truth is not buried, but floats at the surface of life—or text—
as an enigma to be deciphered. In the preface to *Dorian Gray* Wilde
wrote that "to reveal art and conceal the artist is art's aim" (p.138).
In fact, Wilde does the reverse. He reveals the artist so poignantly
that the pain of Dorian's shame and guilt as told by the picture completely overshadows the overt theme: that Dorian has sold his soul in
order to stay young forever. Both youth and old age become states of
mind, rather than chronological periods. Time is the subject of the
novel. But the time at issue concerns the judgment meted out by the
social order as it finds a resonance in the place of timelessness:
Wilde's unconscious. Indeed Wilde bears out Lacan's contention that
unconscious knowledge shows up in the order of present time, giving shape and coherence to the unfolding of each person's subjectivity. Diachronic time punctuates synchronic time with meanings that
have nothing to do with adult life. Indeed, childhood history structures adult life in its interaction with the Real of social events. Given
such an interface between Lacanian theory and Wilde's text, I would
go so far as to suggest that the story narrated in *Dorian Gray* is itself
secondary. The source of the novel's power resides at the point where
the reader meets Wilde in a field of Imaginary resonance. All the
dreams that go into longing for a second chance, the fear induced by
anxiety, the ache caused by guilt: these bind reader and author by
Real sentiments which need not attach themselves to any specific
cause.

3. Quoted in H. Person, *Oscar Wilde: His Life d Wit* (New York: Harper and Row, 1946), p.5.
4. Wilde, Letter to Lord Alfred Douglas, Jan.–March 1897, in *Letters*, p.468.

III

Erik Erikson's model of eight developmental stages from birth to old age has been criticized by Lacan insofar as it depicts the ego as a whole entity.[5] As we have seen, for Lacan the ego and the superego are multiform networks of interacting parts, and every human subject is inherently divided between conscious and unconscious levels. Thus simplistic attributions of sickness or health are less easy to sustain in a Lacanian reading, as our reading of *The Picture of Dorian Gray* has shown.[6] Indeed Dorian himself "used to wonder at the shallow psychology of those who conceive the Ego in man as a thing simple and permanent, reliable, and of one essence. To him, man was a being with myriad lives and myriad sensations, a complex multiform creature that bore within itself strange legacies of thought and passion, and whose very flesh was tainted with the monstrous maladies of the dead . . ." (pp.211–12).

Elsewhere I have offered another interpretation of the birth to death cycle based on Lacan's theory that the unconscious can count up to six and not beyond.[7] The six numbers would unfold in the successor logic delineated by Frege in his formula where 0, the number and the successor, function to constitute the series of natural numbers.[8] When applied to a logic of the evolution of human subjectivity, Frege's mathematical logic shows the conscious subject being produced as effect, rather than already there as cause. Like his mathematical formula in which every number implies something before it and something after $(n + 1)$, the functioning of subjectivity means that both anticipation and retroaction are always in play. In terms of

5. See Lacan, *Sém.* II, p.179. Erik H. Erikson, *The Life Cycle Completed: A Review* (New York: Norton, 1982).
6. Many critics understand Dorian as representing innate doubleness in Man, to which they attribute the novel's appeal. Certainly the theory of the double places Wilde in Victorian times. *The Portrait of Dorian Gray* is in the line of nineteenth-century novels of monstrous, fictional doubles beginning with Mary Shelley's *Frankenstein, or the Modern Prometheus* (1818) and followed by Robert Louis Stevenson's *The Strange Case of Dr. Jekyll and Mr. Hyde* (1885) and Abraham Stoker's *Dracula* (1897). Psychoanalytic studies of the double which focus on *Dorian Gray* stress a pathogenic narcissism. Harry Tucker, Jr., proposes that Dorian Gray killed his double because his own self-love makes it impossible to love another; see his "The Importance of Otto Rank's Theory of the Double," *Journal of the Otto Rank Association*, 12, No. 2 (Winter 1977–78), p.61. Otto Rank has suggested that the most prominent symptom of such narcissism is a powerful consciousness of guilt which forces the hero to reject responsibility for certain actions of his ego, placing it instead upon another ego, a double who is created by a diabolical pact; see Otto Rank, *Der Doppelgänger: Eine Psychoanalytische Studie* (Leipzig, Vienna, Zurich, 1925), p.76. Such interpretations consider both the ego and the superego as static whole agencies capable of a neurotic division.
7. Ellie Ragland-Sullivan, "Counting From 0 to 6: The Lacanian Imaginary Order," in *The Annual of Lacanian Studies*, ed. Jacques-Alain Miller and Patrick Hogan (Paris: La Foundation du champ freudien, in preparation). This essay is also available as *Working Paper* No. 7 from the Center for Twentieth Century Studies, Univ. of Wisconsin-Milwaukee. For Lacan's theory that the unconscious can count up to six, see *Sém.* XX, p.122.
8. Jacques-Alain Miller, "Suture (elements of the logic of the signifier)," *Screen*, 18, No. 4 (Winter 1977–78), p.27.

the history of the human subject, "time is discontinuous and reversible."[9] Since everything in the history of a subject ultimately comes out from the Other, the historization of one's life always places the Other in advance of one's own conscious suppositions. In Lacan's words: "What is realized in my history is not the past definite of what was, since it is no more, or even the present perfect of what has been in what I am, but the future anterior of what I shall have been for what I am in the process of becoming."[1]

In my view, the six numbers denote the logic of mirror-stage and Oedipal effects as recorded in the unconscious. These are the referents around which societies organize themselves, moving individuals along a blind signifying chain where they represent themselves to one another as objects of love or Desire. Insofar as human subjects are only *represented* in the Symbolic order, they are not tethered to a totalized identity, but to the object (a/A).[2] Thus, the future anterior ultimately refers to the diachronic aspect of a person's life: what is recorded in the unconscious is the history of childhood. These effects punctuate a life and a discourse, structuring them in a synchronic retroactivity.

I have argued that Lacan's six unconscious numbers mark the structuring of perception in a kind of identificatory evolution which organizes human subjects as objects of their own Desire, and their own *moi* repetitions. At zero a neonate identifies with the images of the surrounding world during the first six months of life, by a kind of perceptual fusion or identificatory merger. From six to eighteen months of age a baby passes from the boundarilessness of 0 to No. 1, gaining a sense of stability by identifying with its species, with a *Gestalt*. Following the assumption of a body image in the mirror stage, a child identifies at No. 2 with its own name. That is, the mirror stage is brought to a close by the perceptual awareness of otherness. Lacan called this the intervention of the Oedipal structure. So powerful is the event that Lacan called the division of an originary sense of Oneness between mother and child a Castration. From about eighteen months of age to five or six years of age, a child is in the process of acquiring language. In this post-mirror phase, a sexual identity is acquired. At No. 3 a child learns whether it is a girl or a boy (this is not necessarily correlated with gender), and takes a stance toward father's name.

These early identificatory effects are put in place during childhood. In adult life, a recursive function sets in. Numbers 0 to 3 have struc-

9. Antoine Vergote, "From Freud's 'Other Scene' to Lacan's 'Other'," in *Interpreting Lacan*, ed. Joseph H. Smith and William Kerrigan (New Haven: Yale Univ. Press, 1983), p.207.
1. Jacques Lacan, "The function and field of peech and language in psychoanalysis" (1953), in *Ecrits: A Selection*, p.86.
2. Jacques-Alain Miller, "Another Lacan," *Lacan Study Notes*, No. 3 (Feb. 1984), p.3.

tured reality perception, thus preparing the stage anticipatorily for a retroactive counting from 4 to 6 (7) as the adult subject seeks to inscribe himself in the Symbolic order. From an Imaginary perspective numbers 4, 5, and 6 would be seen as a logical progression (synchronically speaking), a symmetrical inversion of numbers 3, 2, and 1. From a diachronic viewpoint, numbers 4, 5, and 6 denote a mathematical recursion, or a shadow extension of mirror-stage effects and Oedipal experiences into adult life. But by inversion I do not mean that 4, 5, and 6 repeat 3, 2, and 1 in any one-to-one way. Desire infers lack, the number always points to the number preceding and the one following. All the same, a normative evolution from childhood to adult life means that at numbers 4, 5, and 6 individuals change their Imaginary positions on an Oedipal triangle, in the pursuit of reifying narcissism and realizing Desire. At No. 4 young adults identify with others—outside the family—in an exogamous marital-type bonding relation. At No. 5 identification with one's own children in maternal and paternal relations reverses childhood Oedipal effects. At No. 6 one identifies with family or tribal posterity (lineage) in an effort to mollify death and warm oneself with a sense of communal unity. At No. 7 (the one more inferred number) identification is with the ineffable, the mysterious, the impossible. At No. 7 one finds transcendent principles such as God. At No. 7 one might also situate the unconscious. Insofar as there is no Other of the Other, six would be the channel capacity for one-dimensional—identificatory—perception.

Within the model I have proposed no subject can ever be a total self or an essence. Instead, each subject is a set of mathematical units or unities which dramatize the perceptions and representations that constitute human mentality. There is, however, a kind of normativity. A normative Oedipal development means that a person can carry on Plato's hunt for knowledge without ending in death. For these individuals there would be no beyond the Oedipal complex at the level of "self" knowledge. I would go further and propose that normal aging (another No. 7)—three score years and ten—generally ends in normal death. The effect of the Father's name in such a trajectory—the timing to a given life—is predictable. From this perspective, Oscar Wilde's tragedy is to have become stuck between numbers 2 and 3. Wilde's adult quest became a tedious repetition of the question of sexual identity. Am I this? or that? Dorian, in a literal sense, was neither: was Gray.

If Wilde's psychic unfolding was not normative, Dorian's unnecessary death has impelled us to ask what anxieties Wilde was trying to quell in his writing. For Dorian had, in fact, beaten all odds. He had gotten away with murder. The one man who could have murdered him (James Vane) was killed in a hunting accident. Those who wished him ill died themselves. Why, then, did he confess? Why did he stab his portrait, knowing that it *was* his soul, his vitality? I have been suggesting that Dorian's death portrays Wilde's life in the future anterior. The secret of Wilde's own loathsomeness to others was never, in fact, understood by Wilde. His penultimate crime was not to have tasted forbidden fruit, not his sexual illicitness, not any Oedipal breach of some mythic incest taboo. His crime was that of arrogance, to have dared to flout social and religious mores and to flaunt his flouting in the faces of the Fathers. In another era Albert Camus's Mersault was guilty of the same crime as Oscar Wilde. Mersault, anti-hero of *L'Etranger*, also died an untimely death. And Mersault—like Wilde himself—was puzzled that his differentness could be judged so hateful by others, that it was punishable by death.

The painting in *Dorian Gray* never permits the peace Lacan found in paintings: the invitation to "lay down" the gaze. In real life an inner gaze judges each person intra-subjectively and finds an outer resonance in the gaze linked to the eye of others. But painting offers a respite from judgment, from projection of the *moi* in some ideal ego function. By contrast Dorian's picture quickly situates itself in an intersubjective realm. Following Lacan, I have argued that the picture dramatizes the fact that Wilde himself was never free from psychic tyranny. Lacan said that when demand (*demande*) [for love] disappears without repression, one has a true dissolution of the Oedipus complex. In such a case the superego reduces itself to the identity of Desire with Law. In a sense, after the dissolution of the Oedipus complex, a subject has nothing more to ask of anyone.[3] But despite his verbal wit and his philosophical nihilism, Wilde never stopped asking society for forgiveness/love. As a visual depiction of a tormenting superego, Dorian's picture evokes a sense of moral ugliness. When troubled young people sigh, "I feel so old," they do not really tell us how old people feel. They *do* tell us that Western stereotypes equate old age with sickness and pain, with psychic heaviness. Old age, in this sense, is a metaphor for being psychically burdened.

The repugnance of Dorian's picture might also stand as a reproof against the social ideal that aging and dying should occur with dignity and grace. The picture suggests that a life which steps out of the normative sequences imposed by a given social order also upsets the expectation that aging and dying should occur gradually. The novel is about the attenuation of a normal aging for someone whose inner structures cannot withstand the injustice of the collision between psychic reality (what one *is*) and social expectation. I am not so much referring to Dorian, however, for he is indeed pictured as a monster.

3. See Millot, p.30.

Instead, it is the novel as it eddies up from Wilde's own unconscious gaze which interests me, the novel as a metaphor for unconscious (metonymic) truth.

In a Lacanian context, every person's death is their future project, the signifier around which a life is organized. Such a view is the opposite of Simone de Beauvoir's concept of death: "Time is carrying the old person towards an end—death—which is not *his* and which is not postulated or laid down by any project."[4] Lacan postulated an unconscious project of becoming, a dynamic infusion of repressed representations into conscious life. These play in and on language, as long as they are denied or misrecognized. Conscious "knowledge" (*connaissance*) does not recognize this *savoir*, described thus by Lacan: "The truth is invisibly this slave work."[5] The "timing"—deadline—which structures each psyche as either normative, neurotic, perverse, or psychotic derives from a particular relationship to the Father's Name. Such timing structures the unfolding of a life story as a meaningful *mise en forme* of the Real (*Sém*. XI, p.40). Real has a double resonance here: the Real effects of the outside world in structuring a psyche, and the Real of that knowledge as it resurfaces to shape a person's life project.

The meaning attributed to a Father's Name also determines the fixations characteristic of a *moi* ideal. In Lacan's words: "The point of the ideal ego is the one from which the subject will see himself, *as seen by the other*—which will permit him to maintain himself in a dual situation satisfying for him from the point of view of love" (*Sém*. XI, p.241). From a personal viewpoint, Wilde's novel is a rehearsal of his own pathetic *cri de coeur*, his plea for unconditional love. On a broader scale, it is a portrait of the moral structure of any social context, insofar as its organization prescribes sexual norms and certain attributes for masculinity or femininity. Philosophically speaking, the novel could be seen as a "truth-functional" proposition about the Real bonds between literary art and unconscious life. It serves as a testimonial—by antithesis—to the ideal of a gentle aging where death is earned as a peaceful exit to an ordinary life, lived in submission of Desire to social law.

Oscar Wilde never came to any harmonious balance between the forces of Desire and Law. The tragic "truth" revealed in his novel joins hands with Lacanian theory to teach that an individual's psychic structure is but a microcosm of the social macrocosm. Both are the outcome of the structure of the superego, and not the reverse. Within this purview, aging and dying (barring real accidents) evolve

4. Simone de Beauvoir, *Old Age* (London: André Deutsch and Weidenfeld Nicholson, 1972), p.217.
5. Jacques Lacan, *Le Séminaire de Jacques Lacan*, "Entre parenthèses," June 16, 1969, unpublished.

as particular functions of mental causality, and not as accidents of
nature. Finally, *The Picture of Dorian Gray* appeals to the everyday
reader as well as the psychoanalyst. The novel proves that categories
such as normal or pathogenic lose their judgmental resonance when
seen as structures along which human beings evolve in a more or
less intense grappling with forces beyond their ken.

JOHN PAUL RIQUELME

Oscar Wilde's Aesthetic Gothic: Walter Pater, Dark Enlightenment, and The Picture of Dorian Gray†

> "J'ai soif de ta beauté."
>
> —Oscar Wilde, *Salomé*[1]

> It was from within, apparently, that the foulness and horror had
> come.
>
> —Oscar Wilde, *The Picture of Dorian Gray*

Gothic Chiaroscuro and Realism

The Picture of Dorian Gray proceeds against the background of Walter Pater's aesthetic writings, but also against Pater in a stronger
sense.[2] It provides in narrative form a dark, revealing double for

---

† From *Modern Fiction Studies* 46.3 (2000): 610–631. Copyright © Purdue Research Foundation. Reprinted by permission of The Johns Hopkins University Press. Bracketed page
 numbers refer to this Norton Critical Edition.
1. "I am thirsty for thy beauty" (80; my translation). Salomé speaks these words to the sev-
 ered head of John the Baptist near the end of the play just before Herod orders her to be
 killed. I cite from the French version of the play, originally published in Paris in 1893, as
 the only published version indisputably of Wilde's sole authorship. In *The Writings of Oscar
 Wilde*, Isobel Murray describes briefly the publication history of the play in her statement
 concerning the text that accompanies her reprinting of the English translation published
 in Wilde's lifetime (614).
2. Many critics who write about Wilde or Pater touch on the relation their works bear to each
 other. Critics who deal at some length with Wilde and Pater include Julia Prewitt Brown,
 Denis Donoghue, Richard Ellmann, and Christopher S. Nassaar. Nassaar maintains that
 Pater's "*The Renaissance* casts a long, sinister shadow across *Picture*, and the entire novel
 seems to be structured with Pater's book as its focal point" (39). The conclusion that Nassaar draws, however, that Wilde saw art's exploration of evil as somehow separable from
 life needs more defense than he provides. Brown and Donoghue focus on Wilde's significant swerves from Pater concerning art (Brown) or on the less-than-amicable turn in their
 relations (Donoghue). Brown cites *Oscar Wilde's Oxford Notebooks* (14–17) as providing
 "a succinct summary of the major differences between Wilde and Pater" (115n4). In the
 preface to her study of Wilde, Brown gives the following overview: "Walter Pater's place in
 the particular intellectual history already alluded to here is relatively minor, and [. . .] far
 less is said in the following pages about Pater's influence on Wilde than about Wilde's
 divergence from Pater. With attention to the philosophical significance of Wilde's career,
 this loosening of the long-established tie between Pater and Wilde constitutes the main
 revisionary thrust of this book" (xvii). See also Brown 3–4, 49, 59–60. In his main discussion of Wilde's relations with Pater in his biography of Pater, Donoghue maintains that
 "Pater never really liked Wilde" (81) and that "[t]he friendship [. . .] virtually came to an

Pater's aestheticism that emerges from a potential for dark doubling
and reversal within aestheticism itself. The duplication produces not
a repetition of Pater but a new version of his views that says what he
cannot or will not articulate, including a recognition of the dark
dynamics of doubling and reversal that inhabit those views. That
recognition includes the possibility that the process of doubling and
reversal will continue. In the novel, Wilde responds to Pater by projecting the dark implications of Pater's attitudes and formulations in
a mythic Gothic narrative of destruction and self-destruction. Wilde
simultaneously aestheticizes the Gothic and gothicizes the aesthetic. The merger is possible, and inevitable, because of the tendency of Gothic writing to present a fantastic world of indulgence
and boundary-crossing and the tendency of the aesthetic, in Pater, to
press beyond conventional boundaries and to recognize terror within
beauty. As an avatar of Narcissus, Dorian Gray embodies both tendencies in a poisonous, self-negating confluence signifying madness.
But the madness is not his alone. He shares it with others in the narrative and with the fantastic quality of his story. No one is immune
from the madness and its effects. In this allegory about art, Wilde's
book and its producer are themselves implicated. They cannot stand
apart in a realm of clarity that is somehow insulated from the darkness they portray and embody. Despite the mannered elegance of the
book's characters and its style, it sheds only partial light on its subject, which includes itself.

The novel's narrative concerns a dark and darkening recognition
that transforms Dorian's life by actualizing a potential that was
already there in his family, a potential that is one truth about British
society.[3] This dark enlightenment is rendered in a narrative that provides the equivalent of chiaroscuro, understood with reference to
painting as a combination of light and clarity with enigmatic darkness
and obscurity in a space that undermines the coherence and implied
sanity of a representational geometry. By combining clarity and
obscurity, often in a shallowly rendered space, chiaroscuro provides
an alternative and a challenge to visual representations that rely on
general illumination, the appearance of a coherent Cartesian geometry, and a vanishing point. The impression can be enigmatic or
frightening for the person whose vision is impeded, because terror

---

end in the winter of 1891" (83). I find the argument for significant, defining differences
between Wilde and Pater convincing. I pursue some of the differences as they emerge in
specific texts in the present essay and in my essay on *Salomé*.

3.   Henry investigates Dorian's family background in chapter 3, where we learn that it
includes passion and violence, as well as class antagonism and a disregard of conventional
behavior. Dorian's mother married a subaltern without financial resources, obviously
against her father's will. As a consequence, her father, Lord Kelso, arranged to have the
subaltern killed in a duel. Dorian's decision to store the portrait in the room set up for him
by his grandfather to keep him out of the way after his mother's death suggests that the
portrait's meaning emerges in part from the family's history.

tends to arise when insufficient or uneven light creates a sense of disorientation and confusion. Edmund Burke makes this point in his
treatise on the sublime and the beautiful.[4] Things that go bump in
the night scare us, especially if we cannot see them clearly and
understand them by means of familiar categories.

The alternative and the challenge to realism in Wilde's literary
chiaroscuro concern realism's reliance on positive knowledge and on
believable representations that create for the reader an impression of
sanity, intelligibility, and control. The narrative provides in the painting and the book a look at the dark as well as the light, at something
disturbing that exceeds, as Gothic writing regularly does, the boundaries of realistic representation and the limits of bourgeois values. As
a Gothic revisionary interpretation of Pater's late Romanticism, this
particular instance of excess marks a turning point in literary history
toward literary modernism. The reliance on doubling as a symptom
of a darkness within both culture and the mind follows Robert Louis
Stevenson's *The Strange Case of Dr Jekyll and Mr Hyde* (1886) and
anticipates Bram Stoker's *Dracula* (1897) and Joseph Conrad's writings, especially *Heart of Darkness* (1902) and *The Secret Sharer*
(1910). The conjoining of light and dark occurs as the narrative of a
doubling that becomes visible through acts of aesthetic making and
aesthetic response. The collaborative act of creating the painting
brings into being something apparently new, original, and masterful
that turns out to be not only beautiful but also atavistic and terrifyingly at odds with the public values of the society that applauds its
beautiful appearance. That collaborative act parallels and engages
with our own act of reading. It comes to an end at the same time as
our engagement with the book reaches closure, once Dorian and his
painting are finished.

Pater against Wilde: Poe, the French Connection, and Doubling

In *Oscar Wilde*, an award-winning biography, Richard Ellmann
claims that in his review of *The Picture of Dorian Gray*, Pater objects
only to the portrayal of "Lord Henry Wotton, who speaks so many of
Pater's sentences." "But otherwise he was delighted with the book"
(323). This is one of Ellmann's least convincing readings, since it is
deaf to the irony of Pater's response, which is defensive, prejudicial,
and patronizing. Like many other critics, Ellmann reads Pater's
review as positive.[5] In fact, Wilde and Pater had exchanged compli-

---

4. In section 3 of *A Philosophical Inquiry*, "Obscurity," Burke states: "To make any thing very
terrible, obscurity seems in general to be necessary. When we know the full extent of any
danger, when we can accustom our eyes to it, a great deal of the apprehension vanishes.
Every one will be sensible of this, who considers how greatly night adds to our dread [. . .]"
(54).
5. In the midst of reprinting Wilde's letters to editors responding to the antagonistic reviews

ments about some of their earlier writings. Pater wrote admiringly to Wilde about *The Happy Prince* in June 1888 (Wilde, *Letters* 219). And Wilde's anonymous review of Pater's *Imaginary Portraits* a year earlier refers to the prose as "wonderful," though he comments that it is ascetic and in danger of becoming "somewhat laborious" (qtd. in Ellmann 289). But in his later review of Pater's *Appreciations* in March 1890, Wilde's criticisms are blunter and more frequent. He says that "Style," though the "most interesting" of the essays, is also "the least successful, because the subject is too abstract" (*Artist* 230); that Charles Lamb "perhaps [. . .] himself would have had some difficulty in recognising the portrait given of him"; that the essay on Samuel Taylor Coleridge "is in style and substance a very blameless work" (232); and that the essay on William Wordsworth "requires rereading" (234), though he does not say why. Most damning are his comments on Pater's style: "Occasionally one may be inclined to think that there is, here and there, a sentence which is somewhat long, and possibly, if one may venture to say so, a little heavy and cumbersome in movement" (231). Wilde ends with apparently high praise by saying that Pater's work is "inimitable," but also that "he has escaped disciples" (234), presumably including Wilde himself.

Critics who emphasize the positive character of Walter Pater's review of the novel may do so primarily because many of the other reviews were more pointedly negative, even censorious.[6] Only by contrast with the hostile reviews can Pater's be called favorable. On the one hand, Pater was generously siding with Wilde against his troglodytic detractors. But considering Wilde's review of *Appreciations* and his echoing of Pater's views in the words of Lord Henry Wotton, Pater had reasons to be displeased and to pay Wilde back. Ellmann does trace Wilde's shift from an enthusiastic, admiring response to Pater's writings and to aestheticism at Oxford toward his later, more critical stance, but he does not suggest that Pater would have sensed the rift and responded in kind.[7] The details of the review indicate that he did.

In his review, Pater writes as though he were immune from the book's implications, or as though he wishes he were. Taking into account Lord Henry's repetition of Pater's language, which Ellmann

---

of his novel, Rupert Hart-Davis includes a footnote that quotes the opening sentence of Pater's review as an example of "some of the most welcome praise," which "came later" (Wilde, *Letters* 270n1). Donald H. Eriksen refers to "Walter Pater's favorable review in the *Bookman*" (99). By contrast, Donoghue sees the praise in later portions of the review as Pater's being "generous" (85) after he had taken "the occasion to repudiate not only Lord Henry but his creator" (84).

6. Rupert Hart-Davis identifies and describes some of the negative reviews when he publishes Wilde's lengthy letters to the editors of the journals in *Letters* (257–72).

7. Ellmann points out that Wilde sent Pater a presentation copy of *Salomé* when it was published in French (374). But Denis Donoghue mentions that "[t]here is no evidence that Pater acknowledged the gift" (85).

mentions without detailing, it becomes clear that Pater could not have missed the novel's challenge to his own attitudes. Unlike Lamb, he recognized his own portrait. Pater attempts to turn aside the book's force in various ways. Like Lord Henry Wotton and Basil Hallward in their responses to Dorian and his portrait, Pater does not want to admit the bearing that Wilde's Gothic rendering has on his own ideals. He takes exception to Wilde's portrayal of an aesthetic hedonism but not by strategies that effectively answer the challenge, for Wilde's resistance approaches the absolute in its ironic probing of Paterian views and the British society into which they fit all too comfortably. Wilde anticipates Pater's response to seeing his own portrait in *Picture*. In chapter 13, Dorian murders the artist who has painted him, in effect murdering the man who, like a father or mentor, has contributed in a significant way to making him what he is. Just before he dies, Basil Hallward sees the painting late at night by the light of a "half-burned candle" [130] in the former schoolroom of Dorian's house, in a scene that would require for visual rendering a candlelit chiaroscuro like that of paintings by Georges de La Tour (1593–1652). By the "dim light," Hallward sees "a hideous face on the canvas grinning at him" that combines "horror" with "marvellous beauty" in a portrayal of its subject that includes "his own brush-work" and a frame of "his own design" [130]. When he holds the lighted candle to the picture, he finds "his own name" as signature. Hallward's response anticipates Pater's review of the book, for the painter sees at first only "some foul parody" that he feels cannot be his work: "He had never done that. Still, it was his own picture" [130]. As subjective and objective genitive, the phrase "his own picture" suggests both that the painting is one he has produced and that it portrays him.

Like Hallward in the schoolroom, Pater finds in Wilde's *Picture* "a satiric sketch," especially with regard to Lord Henry, in which the presentation of "Epicurean theory" "fails" because it abandons "the moral sense." While Pater finds Dorian "a beautiful creation," he calls him "a quite unsuccessful experiment in Epicureanism, in life as a fine art" ("Novel" 265). In his closing statement, having already mentioned the "Doppelgänger," or "double life," as central to Wilde's narrative, Pater is right to associate Wilde's work "with that of Edgar Poe, and with some good French work of the same kind, done, probably, in more or less conscious imitation of it" (266). His assertion implies that *Picture* is also an act of imitation, but of American and French sources, not a British original. Wilde, in fact, does not *imitate* a British writer; he *echoes* his writing. He does so for the same reason that the mythological figure Echo repeats already existing language: in order to say something quite different. Pater would rather not admit that his own writings are at least as important as Poe's in the texture of Wilde's novel and that they are the object of the satire. He also faces only indirectly how thoroughly Wilde's transformation of aesthetic theory is fused with anti-British attitudes. Pater makes the non-British character of the book and its author clear at the start and the end of the review. Besides closing by drawing attention to foreign models rather than one that is much closer to home, Pater begins with comments that situate Wilde prejudicially as an Irish writer. The book putatively produced on non-British patterns by an Irish writer is, not surprisingly, filled with anti-British sentiments. Wilde has turned the critical direction of the Gothic inward, toward England and toward art as an English writer presents it.

At the start of the review, by means of irony and implication, Pater comes close to responding directly in kind to the book's national antagonism, closer than he ever comes to articulating openly his individual antagonism about the transforming of his own work. He may well have sensed that Wilde's skepticism about the British and about Pater's aestheticism were not separable. Misrepresenting or misunderstanding Wilde's emphatic differences from Matthew Arnold, which are as strong as his differences from Pater's aestheticism, Pater suggests that Wilde "carries on, more perhaps than any other writer, the brilliant critical work of Matthew Arnold" ("Novel" 263). Because Pater's own critical directions include significant disagreements with Arnold, by aligning Wilde with Arnold, he distances the younger writer from himself. He would have been intent on doing that in order to separate his own version of aestheticism from the dark version Wilde attributes to him by implication in the novel. Pater describes the ostensible carrying forward of Arnold as "startling" Wilde's "'countrymen.'" By putting "countrymen" in quotation marks, Pater implies ambiguously that, by following in the footsteps of an English critic who had written about the inevitable, necessary "fusion of all the inhabitants of these islands into one homogeneous, English-speaking whole" (Arnold, "On" 296), Wilde surprises his adoptive countrymen, the British, whose countryman he is not, and that he surprises his real countrymen, the Irish, from whom he must have estranged himself by his switching of allegiance.[8] Pater's antagonism toward his younger contemporary is clear in the review's first two sentences. He suggests that Wilde is "an excellent talker," presumably like all the other voluble Irish, whose work relies on the paradox that written dialogue presents itself as spoken. That paradox participates, according to Pater, in a "crudity" that is acceptable only

---

8. Arnold expresses these sentiments in "On the Study of Celtic Literature" (291–386). In his use of the word "countrymen," Pater may well have been echoing Arnold's use of that word ("my own countrymen"; "Introduction" 391) to refer unambiguously to the English in his introduction to his study of Celtic literature (387–95).

because of what he terms, drawing on another cliché about the Irish, Wilde's "genial, laughter-loving sense of life and its enjoyable intercourse" ("Novel" 263). Under attack, Pater reacts prejudicially to a work by an Irish author who echoes negatively Pater's own writing as part of its presentation of British society's hypocrisy. Although Pater might be willing to admit some of the ills of British society, he cannot do so in a way that implicates himself. Hallward recognizes when he holds "the light up again to the canvas" that "[i]t was from within, apparently, that the foulness and horror had come" [131]. Although Wilde's character locates the source of the horror inside, the major British proponent of aestheticism turns away from the implication. Pater also writes about something within emerging to the surface when he describes the Mona Lisa in a passage that Wilde takes as his antithetical model: "It is a beauty wrought out from within upon the flesh [. . .]" (*Renaissance* 80).

When Pater comments on the Doppelgänger in the novel as the experience "not of two *persons*, in this case, but of the man and his portrait" ("Novel" 266) he points toward but does not describe the novel's complex antirealistic structure of doublings.[9] Rather than presenting the book's alternative to realism in its combination of antirealistic and realistic detail, Pater praises and blames the realistic elements as an "intrusion of real life" that, because it is "managed, of course, cleverly enough," "should make his books popular" (264). Pater damns by faint praise when he suggests that Wilde's writing is cleverly crude enough to attract a crowd. In fact, the combination of realistic and antirealistic elements is a pervasive stylistic sign of the novel's dual quality. The doubling structure of the narrative and the narration implicates the reader of *Picture*, including the reviewer of the book, as the counterpart of the picture's viewer. Instead of bringing out the book's complexity, relying on the hierarchical presuppositions of evolutionary thinking about culture, Pater criticizes Wilde for moving away from a "true Epicureanism" toward something "less complex," and presumably less valuable (264). The narrative's intricate doublings, which derive not only from Poe but from Pater's comments on the Mona Lisa, include a multitude of parallels that anticipate a related complexity in *Dracula*. Because the parallels are so numerous and sometimes involve apparent reversals of position, as is often the case in the modern Gothic, the clear distinction between victim and perpetrator, innocent and guilty, blurs, especially when they change roles. As with the doublings of *Dracula*, the reader is invited to feel implicated.

9. See Chris Baldick's *In Frankenstein's Shadow* for a sketch of some of the book's significant doublings related to the one I provide but emphasizing monstrosity and the multiform character of identity rather than anti-realism and the implicating of the reader (148–152).

Central to the novel's structure is the doubling not only of person and painting that Pater mentions but also of picture and book, both the book within the narrative that Lord Henry gives Dorian, and the book we read that is also a *Picture*. The doublings include Basil Hallward and Lord Henry Wotton as fraternal collaborators in the production of the painting and as doubles of different kinds for Dorian himself. Hallward and Wotton split up the dual role that Leonardo da Vinci fills as the quintessential artist-scientist. As a detached experimenter with human lives, Wotton is an avatar of Victor Frankenstein, who produces an ugly, destructive double of himself. There is, as well, the parallel between Dorian Gray and Sybil Vane, as attractive young people to whom unpleasant, destructive revelations are made. Complicating that parallel is the fact that Dorian stands in relation to Sybil as Lord Henry does to him as the revealer of something harsh and damaging. Dorian also stands eventually in the same relation to Basil, whom he destroys, as he has already destroyed Sybil. At the end, he stands in that same destructive relation to himself. Although Dorian prevents Basil from ripping up the painting with a knife near the end of chapter 2, he ultimately stabs the painter, who says he has revealed himself in the painting, and he pursues Hallward's intention from chapter 2 by trying to stab the painting in the book's final chapter and thereby stabbing its subject. This is ekphrasis with a vengeance and the revenge of the ekphrastic object, which strikes out at the artist and viewer, who wish also to strike it.[1] The roles in revolution become indistinguishable.

So many doublings and shifts of position undermine the possibility of reading the book as realistic, that is, as containing primarily intelligible patterns and answers rather than enigmas that cannot be readily resolved. There is no ultimately controlling perspective based on a geometry of narrative relations that allows us to find a stable, resolving point of vantage. In this narrative garden of forking paths, there appears to be a virus that replicates itself in double, antithetical forms within a maze that leads us not to an exit but to an impasse. The narrative oscillations and echoes arising from and as multiple parallels, reversals, and blurrings are modernist in character, but important details identify the writings of Pater as one of their origins. The brushstrokes and the frame are his. As Wilde says in his "Preface," "[I]t is the spectator, and not life, that art really mirrors" [4]. And as he suggests in another epigram, the reader as Caliban who sees his face in the mirror of art is likely to be enraged or, like Dorian, driven mad. These epigrams pertain to Pater as an inevitable early reader of the novel and to us.

---

1. For studies of the ekphrastic tradition, see Krieger and Hollander.

Wilde against Pater: Echo against Narcissus

As I have already suggested, Wilde neither imitates nor follows Pater in his aesthetic Gothic narrative. Instead, he echoes him as a way to evoke, refuse, and transform what he finds in the earlier writer. This is the work of Echo, whose story is bound up with that of Narcissus. In *Picture*, Wilde provides an early example of what T.S. Eliot called "the mythical method," a defining element of modernism that Eliot locates in James Joyce's *Ulysses* and earlier in some of William Butler Yeats's poems.[2] In fact, the first examples of the mythical method antedate considerably the examples that Eliot gives. As early as Thomas Hardy's *The Mayor of Casterbridge* (1886), we find a long narrative set in recent times that is constructed around extended mythic and literary parallels. Wilde also constructs his narrative around a myth, that of Echo and Narcissus. At first it might seem that Narcissus is the primary mythic figure in *Picture* and that the resulting narrative is not comparable in its mythic dimension to either *A Portrait of the Artist as a Young Man* or *Ulysses*, because the myths surrounding Daedalus and Odysseus are more various and extended than that of Narcissus. But, in fact, Echo and Narcissus, however different from each other, are counterparts, whose stories constitute a single compound myth. Echo as well as Narcissus plays a continuing role in Wilde's novel because of the style's echoic character. By echoing Pater's writings frequently and strategically, Wilde projects the story of a contemporary Narcissus as one truth about Paterian aestheticism. He echoes Pater not in order to agree with the older British writer's views but to present them darkly, in shades of gray, as at base contradictory in destructive and self-destructive ways.

Wilde begins his novel by evoking Pater's aestheticism through a series of statements about beauty and through allusions to the best-known passages of Pater's writing: the "Conclusion" of *Studies in the History of the Renaissance* (1873)[3] and the description of Mona Lisa from the essay on Leonardo da Vinci in that volume. The first epigram in the "Preface," which asserts that "[t]he artist is the creator of beautiful things" [3], is followed in the remaining epigrams by numerous references to "beauty," "beautiful things," and "beautiful meanings." As the reader soon discovers, the narrative is permeated by the aesthetic, since it concerns throughout the desire to create, experience, possess or destroy beauty. Almost immediately, in the second paragraph of chapter 1, we learn that Lord Henry Wotton sees,

2. Eliot uses the term in his review of Joyce's *Ulysses*, "Ulysses, Order, and Myth," originally published in *The Dial* (November, 1923).
3. The title of Pater's *Studies* later became *The Renaissance: Studies in Art and Poetry*. As is well known, Pater withdrew his "Conclusion" after the first edition but restored it in revised form for the third edition (1888) and subsequent editions. Donoghue describes the uproar over the "Conclusion" and the steps Pater took in response (48–67).

along with "the fantastic shadows of birds in flight," laburnum blossoms "whose tremulous branches seemed hardly able to bear the burden of a beauty so flame-like as theirs" [5]. On the one hand, the branches are personified as undergoing an ecstatic experience in which they can hardly endure the deep impression that the blossoms, which they have yielded, or borne, make on them. But their experience is not unalloyed, for it is also the bearing, or carrying, not of a joy but of a heavy, awkward "burden" that can hardly be sustained. Further, the experience includes the play of light and dark in the "fantastic shadows" of something "in flight," either merely flying or trying to escape.

The passage is of particular note because it contains the first instances of personification (branches that feel; bees "shouldering their way" through grass) in a narrative that includes centrally the terrifying coming-to-life of something inanimate. The crossing of the boundaries between human, animal, and insect in the rhetorical figures of the book's second paragraph anticipates what eventually becomes a matter of animation involving creating and destroying life and a matter of the limits defining the human and civilization. Wilde has merged the aesthetic with issues that regularly arise in Gothic writing, issues that are anthropological, aesthetic, and scientific: the creation of the new and the character of the human. Later in chapter 1, when Hallward tells his friend Lord Henry Wotton about his first encounter with Dorian Gray, he indicates his agreement with something Wotton had told him about the difference between "savages" and "being civilized." The distinction is superficial, since everything depends on appearances: "With an evening coat and a white tie, as you told me once, anybody, even a stock-broker, can gain a reputation for being civilized" [9]. Harry had gone out for the evening in public to help prove that "poor artists [. . .] are not savages." They may not be, but in Basil's case, which asks to be taken as representative, the artist contributes to an ostensibly civilized process of creating art that turns out to unleash a destructive, self-destructive savagery antithetical to the principles of civilization itself. In a typically modern transformation of Gothic narrative, the threat in Wilde's novel comes from within culture and within British society, not from foreigners who can be treated as savages. As an Irish writer, Wilde would have been particularly aware of the distinctions the British tended to draw between themselves and ostensibly less civilized racial and national groups who might in some way pose a crude threat, Calibanlike, to British aspirations and identity.

The passage about laburnum is also notable because it initiates three kinds of echoing within the style of the novel. One occurs as language that literally echoes: "blossoms [. . .] laburnum [. . .] branches [. . .] bear [. . .] burden [. . .] beauty [. . .] birds" and

"flame-like [. . .] fantastic [. . .] flight flitted" [5]. The echoic quality of the prose finds one origin in the stories of Poe, the most echoic
stylist among earlier prominent figures in the Gothic tradition. In
"The Fall of the House of Usher," for example, the opening sentence
begins "*During* the whole of a *dull, dark,* and soundless *day* [. . .]
(95). And the title of the story, "*William Wilson,*" about a man with
a double, which provides one precursor for *Picture,* includes an
echoic doubling. The second form of echo involves repetition of the
passage's language or similar language later in the book. Burdens,
flames, and shadows occur regularly, often in passages that are significant and significantly related. The phrase "fantastic shadows,"
with its evocation of the visual impression of chiaroscuro, returns in
a way that punctuates at times the stages in Dorian's destructive
attempt to hide and to experience who he is. In the opening of chapter 13, when Dorian and Hallward mount the stairs toward the
schoolroom in which Dorian will murder the artist, the "lamp cast
fantastic shadows" [125]. Later, when Dorian visits opium dens in an
attempt to forget, he sees mostly dark windows, "but now and then
fantastic shadows were silhouetted against some lamp-lit blind":
"They moved like monstrous marionettes, and made gestures like live
things" [154]. These shadows are cast neither by birds nor marionettes but by human beings. The implications of personification
have been reversed from the book's opening, since now the human is
marked by the loss of consciousness that is memory in Dorian's will
to forget and by a monstrous loss of agency.

   The word "burden" also occurs at important moments, sometimes
in combination with the word "shadow," which becomes associated
with the painting as Dorian's double. In chapter 2, when Dorian first
looks carefully at the completed painting and appears "with cheeks
flushed," "as if he had recognized himself for the first time," he is
described as "gazing at the shadow of his own loveliness" [25]. The
portrait is a kind of mirror that contains not his image with inflamed
cheeks but a dark version, a shadow. In chapter 7, Lord Henry sees
something similar in Sybil when a "faint blush, like the shadow of a
rose in a mirror of silver, came to her cheeks" [70]. Toward the end
of chapter 8, Dorian thinks that the "portrait was to bear the burden
of his shame" [88]. After having "lost control" "almost entirely" in
chapter 9, Dorian oscillates in a darkly narcissistic way between looking at the portrait with "loathing" and gazing "with secret pleasure, at
the misshapen shadow that had to bear the burden that should have
been his own" [117–18].

   "Burden" also reappears at very nearly the novel's end, when
Dorian castigates Lord Henry for being willing to "sacrifice anybody
[. . .] for the sake of an epigram" [169]. When Lord Henry responds
that "[t]he world goes to the altar of its own accord," his language

suggests most obviously a sacrificial altar, but considering Dorian's immediate confession that he has forgotten how to love and wishes he could recover his passion, the word "altar" resonates with the notion of marriage in addition to and together with that of the pain of a sacrifice. In his brief confession, Dorian says that his "own personality has become a burden" and admits his own narcissism: "I am too much concentrated on myself" [169]. Lord Henry's similar preoccupation with himself results, as we learn in the next chapter, in his "divorce-case" [174], because his wife has left him for another man. When Dorian meets Victoria, Lord Henry's wife, early in the novel, Lord Henry makes cynical fun of marriage and women as he commands Dorian: "Never marry at all." Dorian readily agrees because he is "putting into practice" "one of your aphorisms," "as I do everything that you say" [43]. That latter statement means both that he puts all of Lord Henry's aphorisms into practice and that he obeys Lord Henry's commands, like a slave. The phrasing echoes the marriage ceremony's vows, "I do," but not to signify the union of partners in a marriage. Shortly before this exchange, Victoria Wotton has commented that Dorian has just repeated " 'one of Harry's views' " and that she always hears " 'Harry's views from his friends' " [42]. The details of these various scenes involving marriage and self-concern bear on the relation of Wilde's narrative to the story of Echo and Narcissus and to the Gothic tradition.

Gothic narratives regularly include attitudes and situations that challenge the institution of marriage. In this regard, they provide a dark reflection of the concern with domesticity in the history of the realistic novel. Wilde's Gothic narrative is no exception in its presentation of attitudes that make meaningful marriage impossible. Among Wilde's modern innovations is the fusing of a Gothic emphasis on impediments to marriage with the myth of Narcissus, which includes centrally the refusal of Echo's advances. Narcissus would rather not be distracted from gazing at himself. Wilde merges aesthetic narcissism with the Gothic tradition's representation of marriage's difficulty or even impossibility. Further, Victoria Wotton's comment about Dorian's parroting of Lord Henry's views reveals Dorian to be an empty echo, one without a mind of its own. Instead of repeating in order to transform or even counter meaningfully someone else's words, Dorian is the slave of another's attitudes. Echo as a mythological figure represents the possibility of choice under difficult circumstances. Dorian's behavior and his thinking are, by contrast, chosen for him, just as he chooses and manipulates the actions and thoughts of others.

The third type of echo initiated by the laburnum passage is the repeating of words from Pater's aesthetic writings. Throughout his career, Wilde had a reputation for using other writers' language in ways that drew comments amounting to the charge of plagiarism.[4] In that respect, his writing anticipates Eliot's later sometimes unacknowledged borrowings, which challenge Romantic views of the artist's originality. In the case of both writers, their modernist, anti-Romantic borrowings are intentional, motivated, and, because of the new implications of the repeated language, creative. In the laburnum passage, the compound "flame-like" in association with la*burn*um and with birds who are escaping or departing creates a clear echoic link to the "Conclusion" of *The Renaissance*. There Pater closes his first paragraph with the oddly phrased, memorable statement that "[t]his at least of flame-like our life has, that it is but the concurrence, renewed from moment to moment of forces parting sooner or later on their ways" (150). Fire, so prominent in Pater's "Conclusion" in both "flame-like" and "to burn always with this hard, gem-like flame" (152), appears in Dorian's retrospective insight about his boyhood: "Life suddenly became fiery-coloured to him. It seemed to him that he had been walking in fire. Why had he not known it?" [20]. Later, Lord Henry thinks in an apparently positive way about "his friend's young fiery-coloured life" (206). But Dorian's flame-like experiences as a child and later are painful or even infernal, not ecstatic in the way that Pater's "Conclusion" suggests. Wilde's references to flame evoke Pater, but the implications have been reversed. In *Picture*, it is not the flame of art and passion that we choose as our future. Instead, flames of an unpleasant kind have already made us what we are. The flame and its passionate intensity are destructive in Wilde, rather than being the salvation from destruction or a consolation for it.

Dorian's fiery experience also connects him to Narcissus. Lord Henry has already identified Dorian with Narcissus in chapter 1, when he contrasts Basil with Dorian and intellect with beauty: "'Why my dear Basil, he is a Narcissus, and you—well, of course you have an intellectual expression, and all that. But beauty, real beauty, ends where an intellectual expression begins. Intellect is in itself a mode of exaggeration, and destroys the harmony of any face'" [7]. Like separating creativity from criticism, which Wilde addresses in "The Critic as Artist" (*Artist* 340–408), severing the tie between beauty and thinking is a mistake that Wilde does not let stand. In Ovid, Narcissus is *inflamed* by his own beauty, which leads him to self-destruction.[5] In Wilde, as later in part III of Eliot's *The Waste Land*,

4. In the introduction to his study of Wilde, Peter Raby describes Wilde's habitual borrowings and the charge leveled against them (9).
5. In Book III of Ovid's *Metamorphoses*, we find: "uror amore mei: flammas moveoque feroque" ("I am inflamed with love for myself: the flames I both fan and bear"; 463) and "sic attenuatus amore / liquitur et tecto paulatim carpitur igni" ("thus ravaged by his love, he melts away, and gradually he is devoured by that buried fire"; 489–90). I am grateful to

the modern Narcissus is grotesque: a young man with a physically and morally ugly double in Wilde; a young man with an inflamed, carbuncular face who inhabits an infernal contemporary city in Eliot. When Wilde's Narcissus looks into the mirror of his painting, coproduced by his older friends, Basil and Henry, he becomes fascinated first with his own beauty but then with a growing ugliness that he recognizes as also himself.

Mona Lisa as Dark Narcissus/Narcissus as Medusa

The details of Wilde's narration imply that the intense experience central to Paterian aestheticism evoked in the "Conclusion" of *The Renaissance* is narcissistic in character. Wilde established the connection to Pater primarily, as Ellmann points out, by having Lord Henry speak "many of Pater's sentences," or, at least, many sentences that echo Pater. But Lord Henry speaks many of Wilde's sentences as well, and some of those Wildean sentences mimic Pater in their phrasing. Since at Oxford Wilde "adopted 'flamelike' as one of his favorite adjectives" (Ellmann 48), the sentence about the laburnum echoes ambiguously both Pater and Wilde. Although we may be inclined to judge Lord Henry more harshly than the novelist because of his evident misogyny and his general moral blindness, Lord Henry's wit is often in the mode of Oscar Wilde. There is a critical portrait of the artist in progress, as well as a critical portrayal of someone else. In one of his letters, Wilde himself points to his suffused identification with all the major characters in the novel: "I am so glad you like that strange coloured book of mine: it contains much of me in it. Basil Hallward is what I think I am: Lord Henry what the world thinks me: Dorian what I would like to be—in other ages, perhaps" (*Letters* 352). Though Wilde holds Pater's views up for inspection, even mockingly, he does not do so in a self-congratulatory, distanced, or morally superior way. By blurring the distinction between the observer and the subject being observed, Wilde participates in the book's logic of doubling and reversal. If he did not, he would risk adopting a morally superior stance that occupies a position outside the process he presents. The dynamics of his literary chiaroscuro prevent his becoming merely a spectator of the sort that Lord Henry seems to think he is. The critical observer's uncertainty extends to the observer's perspective. Otherwise, that perspective can be narcissistic and blind to its own tendencies, in the way that Lord Henry's self-delusion is, even late in the novel. In

Melanie Benson of the Boston University Department of English for drawing my attention to the flame imagery in Ovid's presentation of Narcissus and for her translation of the relevant phrases.

the penultimate chapter, despite abundant evidence of Dorian's crimes, Lord Henry refuses to see his dark side, calling him "the young Apollo" [178].

Wilde constructs his narrative around an experience that resembles not only the one Narcissus undergoes but the one that Pater mentions in the final paragraph of the "Conclusion" (153) when he turns to the "awakening" in Jean Jacques Rousseau of "the literary sense" that is described in Rousseau's *Confessions*. Pater devotes part of the paragraph to relating how fear of death inspired Rousseau to "make as much as possible of the interval that remained." He concludes that "our one chance lies in expanding the interval, in getting as many pulsations as possible into the given time." Wilde models Dorian Gray's recognition, as he is sitting for his portrait, and the direction that his life takes on Pater's rendition of Rousseau's life story, but Wilde's version is unremittingly dark by comparison with Pater's. Even the name "Dorian Gray" captures the darkening of what should be a bright beauty, since "Dorian" obviously suggests a Greek form, while "Gray" as a color stands in contrast to Apollonian brightness. In writing about the Renaissance, which involves centrally a revival of classical art and thinking, Pater aligns himself with a cultural heritage that includes the "Dorian," but not with tones of gray, understood as either neutral or dark. As Linda Dowling argues, because of the work of Karl Otfried Müller as transmitted by Benjamin Jowett at Oxford, in the latter part of the nineteenth century, the surname "Dorian" also carried suggestions of pederasty deriving from Greek culture.[6] "Dorian Gray" is oxymoronic in a Paterian context. "Gray" blunts the force and implications of "Dorian," and it does so without suggesting vividly a fruitful merger of opposites of the sort that we find in Joyce's revisionary evocation and extension of Pater at the conclusion of part four of *A Portrait of the Artist as a Young Man*. In that climactic portion of Joyce's narrative, whose title echoes the title and the tale of Wilde's book as "a portrait of the artist" [9], Stephen Dedalus, who like Dorian has a Greek name, sees a rim of the moon on the horizon as if stuck into the earth in a union of heaven and earth that is compared to a "silver hoop embedded in grey sand" (Joyce 173). The grayness of Dorian's story yields no such positive, generative mergers. Joyce's modernist mergings in *A Portrait* combine elements of a Paterian prose style with a myth about a creator and with realistic writing. Wilde's antecedent mergings in *The Picture* combine similar elements, though the myth concerns self-absorption, with the Gothic in a darkly modernist move away from

6. See especially Dowling 124–125, but also 74 and 79, where she comments on the influence of Müller's *Die Dorier: Geschicten hellnischer Stämme und Städte*.

aestheticism and late Romanticism, a move that echoes Pater but also exorcises him.

The echoing as exorcism proceeds through the combining of the light and the dark from Pater in a narrative of recognition and delusion structured around the myth of Narcissus. Rousseau's awakening through literature brings into the narrative an optimistic element from Pater's "Conclusion" that for Dorian is dark. The book that Harry gives him is poisonous. But the narrative is more the story of a painting than a book, though the book is important, as it is in both of Pater's long narratives, *Marius the Epicurean* (1885) and *Gaston de Latour* (1896).[7] When Lord Henry calls the portrait "the finest portrait of modern times" (166), the comparison to the Mona Lisa is inevitable. The work is a new Mona Lisa. The story of the picture's creation, however, fuses details from Pater's description of the Mona Lisa with Rousseau's moment of recognition that has become the experience of Narcissus recognizing his own beauty. Pater suggests that Mona Lisa's sitting for her portrait was possible only through an accompaniment: "by artificial means, the presence of mimes and flute-players, that subtle expression was protracted on the face" (*Renaissance* 79). As Lord Henry talks to Dorian, Hallward realizes that "a look had come into the lad's face that he had never seen there before" [19]. Dorian compares the effect to that of music but realizes that it was created by words, as if a literary text were being performed. The recognition that this male version of Mona Lisa experiences is clearly that of Narcissus: "A look of joy came into his eyes, as if he had recognized himself for the first time. [. . .] The sense of his own beauty came on him like a revelation" [25]. But the recognition is equally of something dark: "There was a look of fear in his eyes, such as people have when they are suddenly awakened" [21]. Although that fear comes from Dorian's recognition of his mortality, for which Rousseau found compensation in words, it comes as well from recognizing something monstrously threatening. When Pater looks at the Mona Lisa, he sees not unalloyed beauty but "the unfathomable smile, always with a touch of something sinister in it, which plays over all Leonardo's work" (*Renaissance* 79). This is a beauty that the Greeks would "be troubled by," a "beauty into which the soul with all its maladies has passed." Finally, this is a beauty inseparable from monstrosity: "like the vampire, she has been dead many times, and learned the secrets of the grave" (80).

Late in the novel, Wilde reiterates the connection to the Mona Lisa as Pater presents the painting. Just after calling Dorian "Apollo,"

---

7. Isobel Murray points out the importance of books to Pater's protagonists in her introduction to Wilde's novel (ix).

Lord Henry says to him that "it has all been to you no more than the sound of music"; he goes on that "[l]ife is a question of nerves, and fibres and slowly built-up cells" [178]. As Pater says of Mona Lisa, her vampiric experience "has been to her but as the sound of lyres and flutes." In the same passage, he claims that "it is a beauty wrought out from within upon the flesh, the deposit, little cell by cell, of strange thoughts and fantastic reveries and exquisite passions" (*Renaissance* 80). The darkness is already there, within the painting, waiting for the sitter, Narcissus-like, to behold, to fear, and to desire. Like Patrick Bateman, who videotapes some of his crimes in *American Psycho*, Dorian imagines that "there would be real pleasure in watching it" [89]. Later, we hear more about Dorian's desires in passages that echo Pater on the Mona Lisa but with reversed valences. The vocabulary of "cell" and "thought" is still there, but ugliness has displaced beauty. We learn that a single "thought" "crept" from "cell to cell of his brain": "Ugliness that had once been hateful to him because it made things real, became dear to him now for that very reason. Ugliness was the one reality" [155]. But Dorian is wrong. There are always two realities, and they are perpetually turning into each other.

The novel is replete with evocations of Narcissus, from Lord Henry's early statement to Basil to Dorian's gazing in the final chapter into the "curiously carved mirror" [181], given to him by Lord Henry, just before he breaks it. In that last chapter, however, the mythic references undergo a metamorphosis when Dorian thinks of the mirror as a "polished shield" immediately prior to discarding it. He has earlier thought of the picture itself as a mirror or has compared himself in a mirror to his deformed image in the undead portrait. At the end of chapter 8, it is "the most magical of mirrors" [89] for observing secrets. Two chapters later, the double image of his laughing face in the mirror and "the evil and aging face" of the portrait pleases him: "The very sharpness of the contrast used to quicken his sense of pleasure" [160]. In the ultimate chapter, Dorian is not pleased with the mirror or the painting. The myth of Echo and Narcissus has now merged with that of Medusa and Perseus, whose protection includes a polished shield. Dorian as Narcissus-become-Perseus is about to look at himself-as-Medusa without benefit of his shield and with a knife rather than a sword in hand. The introduction of Medusa here again takes up a prominent detail from Pater's writing and puts it to new use. In the Leonardo essay, Pater devotes an entire vivid paragraph to Leonardo's painting of *Medusa* rendered "as the head of a corpse" (*Renaissance* 68). The paragraph culminates the part of the essay in which Pater evokes the "interfusion of the extremes of beauty and terror" in "grotesques" (67). He says of the painting that "the fascination of corruption penetrates in every touch

its exquisitely finished beauty" (68). In *Marius the Epicurean*, Pater
uses the image again prominently three times. In the last, most memorable instance, in the closing of chapter 21, he merges Medusa
implicitly with Narcissus: "Might this new vision, like the malignant
beauty of pagan Medusa, be exclusive of any admiring gaze upon anything but itself?" (*Marius* 202).

Dorian is about to experience the effect of Medusa, which is himself, but, in fact, he has already had this experience. The morning
after he murders Basil, while he waits impatiently for Alan Campbell
to arrive, Dorian turns his eyes inward, where his "imagination,
made grotesque by terror" has become merely a "puppet," the inanimate but dancing image of a person. Time dies and drags "a hideous
future from its grave," which it shows to him: "He stared at it. Its
very horror made him stone" [140]. Like Pater's vampiric Mona Lisa,
he has "learned the secrets of the grave" (*Renaissance* 80). Like
Medusa, the terrifyingly attractive recognition of his mortality turns
him to stone; it dehumanizes him by robbing him of his ordinary
human passion. Long before the book's final chapter, Dorian has
become undead, still living but not alive as a human being. When
Dorian looks at the painting a final time after breaking the mirror,
he understands that the Medusa-like truth about the painting is the
truth about him. The enraged self-destruction that follows is the
demise of Medusa were she able to look at her own poisonous self
or, Perseus-like, to use a sharp weapon against herself. On the one
hand, the ending restores order and sanity to the narrative by apparently re-establishing the difference between art and life, between the
inanimate and the living, between the beautiful and the ugly. But
within the seemingly restored realism, a myth darker than the story
of Narcissus that involves a mirror has fused with the tale of Narcissus and taken up residence within the ostensible realism, from
which it cannot be separated.

If the vampire can live within Mona Lisa, the death of Dorian Gray
can be the death of Medusa. In addition to this odd ultimate brush-
stroke in the novel's mythic surface, which resists explanation, other
details of the ending remain enigmatic. We still do not know where
we stand in relation to the darkness and the light. There is no vanishing point and no orienting perspective. The beautiful creature
became a destroyer who eventually destroyed himself. But how are
we to understand and name the avenger's act of revenge against himself, a dark Narcissus's divorce from himself, a suicidal Medusa's look
at herself that is also a suicidal Perseus's gazing at Medusa without a
shield: as a fit of madness? as a mistake? as an action consciously
intended? All we know is that art and life, the beautiful and the ugly,
the light and the dark, those counterparts whose relations have been
unstable throughout the narrative, have changed places once again.

For readers, there is no more consolation, resolution, or explanation in the ending than Basil Hallward experiences when he gazes at "his own picture" and realizes that "It was from within, apparently, that the foulness and the horror had come" [131].

Works Cited

Arnold, Matthew. *Lectures and Essays in Criticism. The Complete Prose Works of Matthew Arnold*. Vol. III. Ed. R.H. Super. Ann Arbor: U of Michigan P, 1962.

Baldick, Chris. *In Frankenstein's Shadow: Myth, Monstrosity, and Nineteenth-century Writing*. Oxford: Clarendon, 1987.

Brown, Julia Prewitt. *Cosmopolitan Criticism: Oscar Wilde's Philosophy of Art*. Charlottesville: UP of Virginia, 1997.

Burke, Edmund. *A Philosophical Inquiry into the Origin of Our Ideas of the Sublime and Beautiful*. 1759. Ed. Adam Phillips. Oxford: Oxford UP, 1990.

Conrad, Joseph. *Heart of Darkness*. 1902. New York: Norton, 1978.

———. *The Secret Sharer*. 1910. Ed. Daniel R. Schwarz. Boston: Bedford, 1997.

Donoghue, Denis. *Walter Pater: Lover of Strange Souls*. New York: Knopf, 1995.

Dowling, Linda. *Hellenism and Homosexuality in Victorian Oxford*. Ithaca: Cornell UP, 1994.

Eliot, T.S. "Ulysses, Order, and Myth." *James Joyce: Two Decades of Criticism*. Ed. Seon Givens. New York: Vanguard, 1963. 198–202.

Ellis, Bret Easton. *American Psycho: A Novel*. New York: Vintage, 1991.

Ellmann, Richard. *Oscar Wilde*. New York: Knopf, 1988.

Ericksen, Donald H. *Oscar Wilde*. Boston: Twayne, 1977.

Hardy, Thomas. *The Mayor of Casterbridge*. 1886. Ed. Dale Kramer. New York: Oxford UP, 1987.

Hollander, John. *The Gazer's Spirit: Poems Speaking to Silent Works of Art*. Chicago: U of Chicago P, 1995.

Joyce, James. *"A Portrait of the Artist as a Young Man"; Text, Criticism, and Notes*. Ed. Chester G. Anderson. New York: Viking, 1968.

Krieger, Murray. *Ekphrasis: The Illusion of the Natural Sign*. Baltimore: Johns Hopkins UP, 1992.

Murray, Isobel. "Introduction." *The Picture of Dorian Gray*. Ed. Isobel Murray. Oxford: Oxford UP, 1981. vii–xvi.

Nassaar, Christopher S. *Into the Demon Universe: A Literary Exploration of Oscar Wilde*. New Haven: Yale UP, 1974.

Ovid. *Metamorphoses. Liber 1–5. Ovid's Metamorphoses. Books 1–5*. Ed. William S. Anderson. Norman: U of Oklahoma P, 1997.

Pater, Walter. *Gaston de Latour: an unfinished romance*. Ed. Charles L. Shadwell. London: Macmillan, 1896.

———. *Marius the Epicurean, His Sensations and Ideas*. 1885. Ed. Ian Small. Oxford: Oxford UP, 1986.

———. "A Novel by Mr. Oscar Wilde." *Selected Writings of Walter Pater*. Ed. Harold Bloom. New York: Columbia UP, 1974.

————. *The Renaissance: Studies in Art and Poetry*. 1893. 4th ed. Ed. Adam Phillips. Oxford: Oxford UP, 1986.

Poe, Edgar Allan. *Selected Writings of Edgar Allan Poe*. Ed. Edward H. Davidson. Boston: Houghton Mifflin, 1956.

Raby, Peter. *Oscar Wilde*. Cambridge: Cambridge UP, 1988.

Riquelme, John Paul. "Shalom/Solomon/Salomé: Modernism and Wilde's Aesthetic Politics." *The Centennial Review* 39 (1995): 575–610.

Stevenson, Robert Louis. *The Strange Case of Dr Jekyll and Mr Hyde*. 1886. New York: Dell, 1966.

Stoker, Bram. *Dracula*. London: Archibald Constable, 1897.

Wilde, Oscar. *The Artist as Critic: Critical Writings of Oscar Wilde*. 1969. Ed. Richard Ellmann. Chicago: U of Chicago P, 1982.

————. *The Letters of Oscar Wilde*. Ed. Rupert Hart-Davis. New York: Harcourt, 1962.

————. *Oscar Wilde's Oxford Notebooks: A Portrait of a Mind in the Making*. Ed. Philip E. Smith and Michael S. Helfand. New York: Oxford UP, 1989.

————. *Salomé. A Florentine Tragedy. Vera. The First Collected Edition of the Works of Oscar Wilde*. 1908. Vol. I. Ed. Robert Ross. London: Dawsons of Pall Mall, 1969.

————. *The Writings of Oscar Wilde*. Ed. Isobel Murray. Oxford: Oxford UP, 1989.

Oscar Wilde: A Chronology

1854   Oscar Fingal O'Flahertie Wills Wilde is born in Dublin
            at 21 Westland Row on October 16. He is the second
            child of Dr. (later Sir) William Wilde, noted oculist,
            aural surgeon, and author of medical texts, travel books,
            and antiquarian studies of Irish folklore and custom,
            and Jane Francesca Elgee Wilde, fervent Irish national-
            ist who publishes under the pen name Speranza.

1857   Wilde's younger sister, Isola Francesca Emily Wilde, is
            born on April 2.

1864   William Wilde is given his knighthood.

1864–71   Wilde attends the Portora Royal School at Enniskillen.
            Upon leaving he is awarded the Portora Gold Medal as
            the best classical scholar.

1867   Wilde's younger sister, Isola, dies. Wilde writes the
            poem "Requiescat" to commemorate her passing.

1871–74   Wilde receives a scholarship to Trinity College, Dublin,
            where he wins the Berkeley Gold Medal for his study of
            Greek.

1874–78   After winning a scholarship to Oxford, Wilde enters
            Magdalen College, Oxford, in October of 1874. He
            studies with both Ruskin and Pater and distinguishes
            himself as a scholar, poet, and character.

1876   Wilde's father dies on April 19, and his mother moves
            to England.

1878   Wilde wins the Newdigate Prize for his poem *Ravenna*.
            It is subsequently published by Thomas Shrimpton &
            Son, Oxford. He also completes his degree earning a
            rare double first in his final examinations.

1879   Wilde's flirtation with an academic career ends when
            his essay "The Rise of Historical Criticism" fails to win
            the Chancellor's Prize, which was not awarded that
            year, and he is not elected a fellow of the college. Wilde
            then settles in London and begins to work to secure a
            place in society, drawing attention to himself by loudly
            championing aesthetic pleasure.

1880	Wilde privately publishes his first play, *Vera, or the Nihilists.*
1881	Wilde privately publishes his first volume of verse, *Poems.* He also becomes the subject of a series of cartoons in *Punch* satirizing the "art for art's sake" movement. The Gilbert and Sullivan light opera *Patience,* produced that year, contains a character, Bunthorne, based on Wilde.
1882	Wilde arrives in New York on January 2 and begins a highly successful lecture tour of the United States and Canada. He departs for England on December 27.
1883	Wilde completes his second play, *The Duchess of Padua,* in Paris and has it privately printed. A production of *Vera* is staged in New York but withdrawn after one week.
1883–84	On September 24, 1883, he begins a successful lecture tour of the United Kingdom that will carry over into the next year.
1884	On May 29 Wilde marries Constance Lloyd, the daughter of a Dublin barrister and a woman with financial resources.
1885	On January 1 Wilde takes a house at 16 Tite Street, in Chelsea, an artistic section of London. His son Cyril is born on June 5. He becomes book review editor of the *Pall Mall Gazette.*
1886	His son Vyvian is born on November 3. He begins a friendship with Robbie Ross that will last for the rest of his life. Ross will subsequently act as Wilde's literary executor.
1887–89	Wilde edits *The Woman's World,* bringing a great deal of fame to the magazine by securing contributions from a number of well-known women.
1888	*The Happy Prince and Other Tales,* a collection of fairy tales that Wilde originally composed for his sons, appears.
1889	Wilde publishes "Pen, Pencil and Poison" in *The Fortnightly Review,* "The Decay of Lying" in *Nineteenth Century,* and "The Portrait of Mr. W. H." in *Blackwood's Edinburgh Magazine.*
1890	*The Picture of Dorian Gray* appears in novella form in the July issue of *Lippincott's Monthly Magazine.* It arouses a storm of controversy in the English press.
1891	Wilde publishes "The Soul of Man under Socialism" in the *Fortnightly Review* and a collection of essays, *Intentions.* Taken together they offer important insights into

Wilde's aesthetic philosophy. He also brings out *Lord Arthur Savile's Crime and Other Stories* and *A House of Pomegranates*, two collections of short stories, and a novel-length version of *The Picture of Dorian Gray* (which produces none of the uproar that the novella caused). Wilde also begins his doomed friendship with Lord Alfred Douglas, "Bosie."

1892   *Lady Windermere's Fan* is staged at the St. James's Theatre to great popular acclaim. Wilde writes (in French) *Salome*. The London production is prohibited because of the invocation of a little known and rarely enforced English law forbidding theatrical depiction of biblical characters.

1893   *A Woman of No Importance* is staged at the Theatre Royal. *Lady Windermere's Fan* and *Salome* (French version) are published.

1894   Wilde publishes *Salome* in English translation with illustrations by Aubrey Beardsley. He also publishes a long poem, *The Sphinx*, and the play *A Woman of No Importance*. He writes *The Importance of Being Earnest*.

1895   *An Ideal Husband* opens on January 3 at the Haymarket Theatre, and *The Importance of Being Earnest* opens on February 14 at the St. James's Theatre. Both plays are popular and critical hits. Wilde's increasingly reckless behavior draws public criticism from the Marquess of Queensberry, Lord Douglas's father. Wilde sues for libel but loses the case. Evidence from this trial leads to Wilde's arrest for homosexual offenses. After a hung jury ends his first trial, Wilde is found guilty in a second. On May 25 he is sentenced to two years at hard labor. He is originally imprisoned in Pentonville. On November 20 he is transferred to H.M. Prison Reading.

1895–97 While in prison, Wilde writes *De Profundis*, a sometimes moving description of his spiritual progress and a sometimes violent castigation of Bosie's behavior during their affair. On his release from prison, Wilde goes to the Continent. For the next three years, he lives primarily in France, often subsisting on the charity of friends.

1898   Wilde anonymously publishes his best-known poem, *The Ballad of Reading Gaol*, on February 13. He also publishes two letters on prison reform. His wife, Constance, dies in Genoa on April 7.

1900   On November 30, after being received into the Roman Catholic Church, he dies of cerebral meningitis at the

Hôtel d'Alsace. He is buried initially at Bagneux cemetery.

1909   At the direction of Robert Ross, Wilde's remains are
removed to Père-Lachaise cemetery, Paris, to a tomb
designed by Jacob Epstein.

Selected Bibliography

• indicates works included or excerpted in this Norton Critical Edition.

WORKS

Poems. London: Bogue; Boston: Roberts, 1881.

"L'Envoi." [Introduction.] *Rose Leaf and Apple Leaf.* By Rennell Rodd. Philadelphia: Stoddart, 1882.

The Happy Prince and Other Tales. London: Nutt; Boston: Roberts, 1888.

"The Portrait of Mr. W.H." *Blackwood's Edinburgh Magazine* 146 (July 1889): 1–21. Enl. ed. New York: Kennerley, 1921. Later ed. London: Methuen, 1958.

"The Soul of Man under Socialism." *The Fortnightly Review* 49 (February 1891). Rpt. Arthur L. Humphreys, 1895, 1907, as *The Soul of Man;* and in 1912 intro. Robert Ross as *The Soul of Man under Socialism.*

The Picture of Dorian Gray. Lippincott's Monthly Magazine 46 (July 1890): 3–100; London: Ward, Lock and Company, 1891.

The Picture of Dorian Gray. Ed. Wilfried Edener. Nurnburg: Carl, 1964.

The Picture of Dorian Gray. Ed. Isobel Murray. London: Oxford UP, 1974.

Intentions. London: Osgood, McIlvaine; New York: Dodd, Mead, 1891.

Lord Arthur Savile's Crime and Other Stories. London: Osgood, McIlvaine; New York: Dodd, Mead, 1891.

A House of Pomegranates. London: Osgood, McIlvaine, 1891; New York: Dodd, Mead, 1892.

Lady Windermere's Fan. London: Mathews and Lane, Bodley Head, 1893. Opened at St. James's Theatre in February 1892.

Salomé: drame en un acte. Paris: Librarie de l'Art Independent, 1893. Trans. Alfred Douglas. London: Mathews and Lane, Bodley Head, 1893. London: Mathews and Lane; Boston: Copeland and Day, 1894. Produced at Thèâtre de L'oeuvre, Paris, in February 1896.

The Sphinx. London: Mathews and Lane, Bodley Head; Boston: Copeland and Day, 1894.

A Woman of No Importance. London: Mathews and Lane, Bodley Head, 1894. Opened at Haymarket Theatre, London, in April 1893.

The Ballad of Reading Gaol [pseud. C.3.3.]. London: Smithers, 1898.

The Importance of Being Earnest. London: Smithers, 1899. Opened at the St. James's Theatre, London, in February 1895.

An Ideal Husband. London: Smithers, 1898. Opened at the Haymarket Theatre, London, in January 1895.

De Profundis. London: Methuen; New York: Putnam, 1905. The first of numerous incomplete texts of Wilde's famous letter from prison. The complete authoritative text appears in *Letters* (1962).

COLLECTED EDITIONS

First Collected Edition of the Works of Oscar Wilde. Ed. Robert Ross. Vols. 1–11, 13–24. London: Methuen, 1908; Boston: Luce, 1910. Vol. 12. Paris: Carrington, 1908. The *Second Collected Edition* appeared in 1909 (vols. 1–12), 1910 (vol. 13), and 1912 (vol. 14).

The Complete Works of Oscar Wilde. Rev. ed. Ed. Vyvyan Holland. London: Collins, 1966.

The Annotated Oscar Wilde. Ed. H. Montgomery Hyde. New York: Potter, 1982.

LETTERS

The Letters of Oscar Wilde. Ed. Rupert Hart-Davis. London: Hart-Davis; New York: Harcourt, 1962.
More Letters of Oscar Wilde. Ed. Rupert Hart-Davis. New York: Vanguard, 1985.

BIBLIOGRAPHIES

Fletcher, Ian, and John Stokes. "Oscar Wilde." *Recent Research on Anglo-Irish Writers*. Ed. Richard Finneran. New York: Modern Language Association, 1983.
Mason, Stuart [pseud. Christopher S. Millard]. *Bibliography of Oscar Wilde*. London: Laurie, 1914; rpt. London: Rota, 1967.
Mikhail, E. H. *Oscar Wilde: An Annotated Bibliography of Criticism*. Totowa, NJ: Roman, 1978.

BIOGRAPHIES

Byrne, Patrick. *The Wildes of Merrion Square*. London: Staples, 1953.
Croft-Cooke, Rupert. *The Unrecorded Life of Oscar Wilde*. London: Allen, 1972.
Douglas, Lord Alfred. *My Friendship with Oscar Wilde*. New York: Coventry, 1932. First pub. as *The Autobiography of Lord Alfred Douglas*. London: Martin Secker, 1929.
———. *Oscar Wilde and Myself*. London: Long; New York: Duffield, 1914.
———. *A Summing Up*. London: Duckworth, 1940.
———. *Without Apology*. London: Richards, 1938.
Ellmann, Richard. *Oscar Wilde*. New York: Knopf, 1988.
Harris, Frank. *The Life and Confessions of Oscar Wilde*. New York: Dell, 1960.
Hyde, H. Montgomery. *Oscar Wilde*. New York: Farrar, 1975.
Pearson, Hesketh. *Oscar Wilde*. New York: Harper, 1946.
Ricketts, Charles. *Recollections of Oscar Wilde*. London: Nonesuch, 1932.
Sherard, Robert H. *The Life of Oscar Wilde*. London: Laurie, 1906; New York: Kennerley, 1907.

CRITICISM

Beckson, Karl. *Oscar Wilde: The Critical Heritage*. New York: Barnes and Noble, 1970.
Bloom, Harold, ed. *Oscar Wilde*. New York: Chelsea, 1985.
Chamberlin, J.E. *Ripe Was the Drowsy Hour: The Age of Oscar Wilde*. New York: Seabury, 1977.
Cohen, Ed. *Talk on the Wilde Side: Toward a Genealogy of a Discourse on Male Sexualities*. New York: Routledge, 1993.
Cohen, Philip. *The Moral Vision of Oscar Wilde*. Rutherford, NJ: Fairleigh Dickinson UP, 1978.
Espey, John. "Resources for Wilde Studies at the Clark Library." In *Oscar Wilde: Two Approaches*. Los Angeles: Clark Library, 1977, pp.25–48.
Gagnier, Regenia. *Idylls of the Marketplace: Oscar Wilde and the Victorian Public*. Stanford: Stanford UP, 1986.
Gillespie, Michael Patrick. *The Picture of Dorian Gray: "What the World Thinks Me."* New York: Twayne, 1995.
• ———. "Picturing Dorian Gray: Resistant Readings in Wilde's Novel." *English Literature in Transition* 35.1 (1992): 7–25.
———. *Oscar Wilde and the Aesthetics of Ambiguity*. Gainesville: UP of Florida, 1996.
Hyde, H. Montgomery. *The Cleveland Street Scandal*. New York: Coward, 1976.
———. *Their Good Names*. London: Hamilton, 1970.
———. *The Trials of Wilde*. London: Hodge, 1948; Enl. ed. pub. as *The Three Trials of Oscar Wilde*. New York: NYU Press, 1956.
Jones, John B. "In Search of Archibald Grosvenor: A New Look at Gilbert's *Patience*." *Victorian Studies* 3 (1965): 45–53.
• Joyce, Simon. "Sexual Politics and the Aesthetics of Crime: Oscar Wilde in the Nineties." *ELH* 12. 1 (Summer 2002): 501–23.
Kernahan, Coulson. *In Good Company*. London: Lane, 1917.
Koestenbaum, Wayne. "Wilde's Hard Labor and the Birth of Gay Reading." In *Engendering*

Men: The Question of Male Feminist Criticism, ed. Joseph A. Boone and Michael Cadden, New York: Routledge, 1990, pp.176–89.

• Lawler, Donald L. "Oscar Wilde's First Manuscript of *The Picture of Dorian Gray.*" *Studies in Bibliography* 25 (1972): 125–35.

———. "Oscar Wilde in the *New Cambridge Bibliography of English Literature.*" *PBSA* 67 (1973): 172–88.

———. "The Revisions of *Dorian Gray.*" *Victorian Institute Journal* 3 (1974): 21–36.

Lawler, Donald L., and Charles E. Knott. "The Context of Invention: Suggested Origins of *Dorian Gray.*" *Modern Philology* 73 (1976): 389–98.

• Liebman, Sheldon W. "Character Design in *The Picture of Dorian Gray.*" *Studies in the Novel*, 31. 3 (Fall 1999): 296–316.

Lloyd, Lewis, and Henry Justin Smith. *Oscar Wilde Discovers America*. New York: Harcourt, 1936.

Nassaar, Christopher S. *Into the Demon Universe: A Literary Exploration of Oscar Wilde*. New Haven: Yale UP, 1974.

• O'Connor, Maureen. "*The Picture of Dorian Gray* as Irish National Tale." In *Writing Irishness in 19th-Century British Culture*. Ed. Neil McCaw. Burlington, VT: Ashgate, 2004, pp.194–209.

• Ragland-Sullivan, Ellie. "The Phenomenon of Aging in Oscar Wilde's *Picture of Dorian Gray*: A Lacanian View." In *Memory and Desire: Aging-Literature-Psychoanalysis*. Woodward, Kathleen, and Schwartz, Murray M. (eds.). Bloomington: Indiana UP; 1986, pp.114–33.

Ransome, Arthur. *Oscar Wilde: A Critical Study*. London: Secker, 1912.

• Riquelme, John Paul "Oscar Wilde's Aesthetic Gothic: Walter Pater, Dark Enlightenment, and *The Picture of Dorian Gray.*" *Modern Fiction Studies* 46.3 (Fall 2000): 610–31.

Sammells, Neil. *Wilde Style: The Plays and Prose of Oscar Wilde*. Harlow, Essex: Pearson Education Ltd., 2000.

San Juan, Epifanio, Jr. *The Art of Oscar Wilde*. Princeton: Princeton UP, 1967.

Sandulescu, C. George, ed. *Rediscovering Oscar Wilde*. Gerrards Cross, Bucks: Smythe, 1994.

Shewan, Rodney. *Oscar Wilde: Art and Egoism*. New York: Barnes and Noble, 1977.

Simpson, Colin, et al. *The Cleveland Street Affair*. Boston: Little, Brown, 1976.

Small, Ian. *Oscar Wilde Revalued: An Essay on New Materials & Methods of Research*. Greensboro, NC: ELT Press, 1993.

Symons, Arthur. *A Study of Oscar Wilde*. London: Sawyer, 1930.

Winwar, Francis. *Oscar Wilde and the Yellow Nineties*. New York: Harper, 1940.